The terrorist attacks of September 11, 2001, and the ensuing "war on terror" have focused attention on issues that have previously lurked in a dark corner at the edge of the legal universe. This book presents the first systematic and comprehensive attempt by legal scholars to conceptualize the theory of emergency powers, combining post-September 11 developments with more general theoretical, historical and comparative perspectives. The authors examine the interface between law and violent crises through history and across jurisdictions, bringing together insights gleaned from the Roman republic and Jewish law through to the initial responses to the July 2005 attacks in London. The book examines three unique models of emergency powers that are used to offer a novel conceptualization of emergency regimes, giving a coherent insight into law's interface with and regulation of crisis and a distinctive means to evaluate the legal options open to states for dealing with crises. Particular attention is given to the interface between international law and regulatory mechanisms and emergency powers, as a key element of the contemporary political response to violent crises.

FIONNUALA NÍ AOLÁIN Professor of Law and Associate Director of the Transitional Justice Institute at the University of Ulster and Dorsey & Whitney Professor of Law at the University of Minnesota Law School.

OREN GROSS Irving Younger Professor of Law and Director, Minnesota Center for Legal Studies, at the University of Minnesota Law School.

CAMBRIDGE STUDIES IN INTERNATIONAL AND COMPARATIVE LAW

Established in 1946, this series produces high quality scholarship in the fields of public and private international law and comparative law. Although these are distinct legal sub-disciplines, developments since 1946 confirm their interrelation.

Comparative law is increasingly used as a tool in the making of law at national, regional and international levels. Private international law is now often affected by international conventions, and the issues faced by classical conflicts rules are frequently dealt with by substantive harmonisation of law under international auspices. Mixed international arbitrations, especially those involving state economic activity, raise mixed questions of public and private international law, while in many fields (such as the protection of human rights and democratic standards, investment guarantees and international criminal law) international and national systems interact. National constitutional arrangements relating to "foreign affairs", and to the implementation of international norms, are a focus of attention.

The Board welcomes works of a theoretical or interdisciplinary character, and those focusing on the new approaches to international or comparative law or conflicts of law. Studies of particular institutions or problems are equally welcome, as are translations of the best work published in other languages.

A list of books in the series can be found at the end of this volume.

Law in Times of Crisis
Emergency Powers in Theory and Practice

Oren Gross

and

Fionnuala Ní Aoláin

CAMBRIDGE
UNIVERSITY PRESS

CAMBRIDGE UNIVERSITY PRESS
Cambridge, New York, Melbourne, Madrid, Cape Town, Singapore, São Paulo

Cambridge University Press
The Edinburgh Building, Cambridge CB2 2RU, UK

Published in the United States of America by Cambridge University Press, New York

www.cambridge.org
Information on this title: www.cambridge.org/9780521541237

First published 2006

Printed in the United Kingdom at the University Press, Cambridge

A catalogue record for this publication is available from the British Library

ISBN-13 978-0-521-83351-6 hardback
ISBN-10 0-521-83351-5 hardback

ISBN-13 978-0-521-54123-7 paperback
ISBN-10 0-521-54123-9 paperback

For Aodhtan, Noa, and Malachi

Contents

ix

Acknowledgments

This book is the culmination of many years of teaching, researching, thinking about, and writing about international law, human rights, national security, and emergency powers. Both authors wish to express their deepest thanks to all those, both individuals and institutions, who made this journey possible and who lent their support, intellectual abilities, and friendship, as well as academic environment, space, and financial assistance, to each of us and to this project. Both of us are especially grateful to Abram Chayes, Richard Fallon, Martha Fineman, Arnon Gutfeld, Louis Henkin, Sanford Levinson, Lance Liebman, Uriel Proccacia, Kent Roach, William Scheuerman, Leon Sheleff, Tom Sullivan, and David Weissbrodt. We also wish to thank Catherine Turner and Adrienne Reilly (University of Ulster) and David Brice (University of Minnesota) for their research assistance.

Fionnuala Ní Aoláin also wishes to acknowledge her thanks to her two friends and colleagues Professors Christine Bell and Colm Campbell at the Transitional Justice Institute at the University of Ulster. Both have fostered the intellectual space that has facilitated this work over a number of years. The work on this book commenced for Professor Ní Aoláin while she was a Visiting Fellow at the Law and Public Affairs program at Princeton University in 2001–02. Her thanks go to her collegial fellows in residence that year, and particularly to Professor Chris Eisgruber, then Director of the LAPA program. She also acknowledges receipt of a Research Fellowship in the fall of 2003 from the Transitional Justice Institute that allowed her to work exclusively on this book. The University of Minnesota Law School and Dean Alex Johnson also supported the research for this book while Professor Ní Aoláin was a Visiting Professor in Fall 2003. Numerous individuals read draft chapters over the years including Professors Bill Schabas, Colm Campbell, David Kretzmer, and

David Wippman. Finally, Professor Ní Aoláin gratefully acknowledges the influence that her teacher, friend, and colleague Stephen Livingstone had on the intellectual development that gave birth to the ideas in this work. He is greatly missed.

Personal thanks are due to Julie Harrison and Claire Archbold, god-mothers to Aodhtan and Noa. Without the assistance of many friends and a support network that bails her out on regular occasions, academic life with its hefty publication and conference schedule would be impossible. This network of friends includes Liz McAleer, Laura Lundy, Heather Ryding, Clodach McGrory, Irene Harrison, Lindsay Phillips, Chivy Sok, Jelena Pajic, Anat Horowitz, Carol Liebman, Susan Wolf, and Fionnuala's wonderful younger sister Neasa and mother Catherine.

Oren Gross wishes to acknowledge, first and foremost, Frederick Schauer who was the best doctoral supervisor anyone could hope and wish for. I thank him for his patience, kindness, good advice, suggestions, and critique, and for his ongoing friendship. I owe Phil Heymann and Morton Horwitz a debt greater than I can express in words (and as a result have probably failed to express my thanks to both as often as I should). I gratefully acknowledge the financial assistance that I have received from the British Academy, the Fesler Summer Research Grant, and the Vance K. Opperman Research Scholarship (the last two at the University of Minnesota Law School), as well as the space and vibrant academic community offered by the LAPA program at Princeton University and the Transitional Justice Institute at the University of Ulster in Northern Ireland. Last but not least, my deepest thanks go, with all my love, to my wonderful family: my parents, Rina and Yehoshua, my brother Dror and his wife, Tal, and my wife (and co-author), Fionnuala and my kids Aodhtan, Noa, and Malachi. None of this would have been possible without them.

Finally, some segments of this book rely to a certain extent on work that we have already published. As the list of relevant publications is (fortunately) not a short one, we simply wish to incorporate here our joint acknowledgment of such publications and the cumulative assistance we have received from law review editors, colleagues, and editors of the collected essays where our work has been published and reference to the relevant works as they appear in the bibliography under our names. We would like to note, however, that even in cases where we relied more heavily on such previously published work, we updated, revised, reworked, and rearranged our arguments.

Table of cases

International cases

International Court of Justice

European Commission Human Rights

European Court of Human Rights

Table of treaties

Table of legislation

Constitutions

Canada

France

India

Kenya

Republic of Ireland

Spain

Turkey

United Kingdom

Table of international materials

Council of Europe

European Union

Inter-American Commission on Human Rights

Inter-American Court of Human Rights

Introduction

The terrorist attacks of September 11, 2001 and the ensuing "war on terror" have focused much attention on issues that have previously lurked in a dark corner at the edge of the legal universe. Politicians and academics alike are now preoccupied with a wide range of questions about the possible responses of democratic regimes to violent challenges. The resort to emergency powers at both the national and international level has been so extensive and penetrating that the exercise of these powers and the complex questions that arise in that connection now play a critical role in discussions about the rule of law, legitimacy, and legality.

Despite repeated statements that the events of September 11 have forever changed the world,[1] much of the discussion around matters dealing with terrorism, the structuring of counter-terrorism measures, extraordinary governmental powers to answer future threats, and fashioning legal responses to terrorist threats is not new. As this book illustrates throughout, the quandaries posed by defining and structuring responsible responses to crises did not begin with the events of September 11. They have faced nations embroiled in wars against external enemies, as well as those responding to violent movements within their own borders. They have haunted countries powerful and weak, rich and poor. How to allow government sufficient discretion, flexibility, and powers to meet crises while maintaining limitations and control over governmental actions so as to prevent or at least minimize the danger that such powers would be abused? How to allow government to act responsibly, i.e., "with sufficient vigor to meet the nation's challenges, but without

---

[1] See, e.g., Anthony Lewis, "A Different World," *New York (NY) Times*, Sept. 12, 2001, p. A27; "President Bush's Address on Terrorism Before a Joint Meeting of Congress," *NY Times*, Sep. 21, 2001, p. B4; W. Michael Reisman, "Editorial Comments: In Defense of World Public Order" (2001) 95 *American Journal of International Law* at 833.

intruding on protected liberties"?[2] How to balance security and liberty? These questions are as ancient as the Roman republic and as new as the realities wrought by the terrorist attacks on London's public transportation system on July 7 and July 21, 2005.

Yet, prior to al Qaeda's attacks in New York, Washington, and Pennsylvania, violent crises and emergencies and their implications for legal systems had not attracted much attention in legal scholarship. Writing in 1972, Ian Brownlie perceptively observed: "Books on constitutional law find little to say about emergency powers."[3] This observation, made in the context of English constitutional law, could also be applied with as much force to other jurisdictions. Prior to the attacks of September 11, discussion of emergency powers in general, and counter-terrorism measures in particular, had been relegated to a mere few pages, at most, in American constitutional law texts. Nor had the situation been much different in other countries. Emergencies have been conceptualized as aberrations, rare and uninteresting exceptions to the otherwise ordinary state of affairs. As Frederick Schauer suggests in another, yet related, context, the exception has been "an invisible topic in legal theory."[4] For those steeped in the liberal legal tradition, principles of generality, publicity, and stability of legal norms form part of the bedrock of the rule of law. Violent emergencies challenge those tenets since they often call for particularity and extremely broad discretionary powers, while the forces they bring to bear on the relevant society are inherently destabilizing. Moreover, in the context of the United States, its particular geopolitical position and unique history have facilitated the externalization of conflict. Violent emergencies have been regarded as falling within the realms of foreign affairs and national security, which, as we discuss in chapter 4, have traditionally been viewed as deserving special treatment and as standing outside the normal realm of constitutional legal principles, rules, and norms.

Be that as it may, in recent years the exception has become as "invisible as a nose on a man's face, or a weathercock on a steeple."[5] Thus, in this book we seek to place historical and theoretical ideas about

[2] Mark Tushnet, "Controlling Executive Power in the War on Terrorism" (2005) 118 *Harvard Law Review* 2673 at 2673.
[3] Ian Brownlie, "Interrogation in Depth: The Compton and Parker Reports" (1972) 35 *Modern Law Review* 501 at 501.
[4] Frederick Schauer, "Exceptions" (1991) 58 *University of Chicago Law Review* 871 at 872.
[5] William Shakespeare, *The Two Gentlemen of Verona*, in Stephen Greenblatt (ed.), *The Norton Shakespeare* (New York: W.W. Norton, 1997), act 2, sc. 1, ll. 120–21.

emergency powers in a contemporary context that has been substantially influenced and shaped by the terrorist attacks of September 11, 2001, and more recently by the attacks in Madrid and London. We pay particular attention to the panoply of counter-terrorism measures that have been activated by international legal obligations and put in place across jurisdictions since September 11. We also suggest that, despite their traditional invisibility, emergency powers across jurisdictions have had pervasive and insidious effects on law and legal institutions, the patterns of which bear remarkable similarity across jurisdictions and time. These similarities have largely gone untracked, mostly because much of the writing on emergency powers has tended to be jurisdiction specific, with emphasis on country or case studies or on particular counter-terrorism measures.

The book focuses on responses by democratic regimes to crises and emergencies. Dealing with such crises is not, of course, limited to democracies. However, authoritarian regimes are not faced with the tragic choices that violent emergencies present to democracies. For the former, the only significant parameters by which to evaluate the state's response to the violence are efficiency, allocation of resources, and the political and perhaps physical survival of the regime. No real tension exists, nor can one exist, between liberty and security, because security is everything and liberty does not count for much, if at all. Such authoritarian regimes are motivated by reason of state arguments that are reminiscent of those put forward by political realists. For democracies, however, the story and calculus are different. Writing during the early days of the Cold War, Carl Friedrich, a Harvard University professor of political science, described the tension between national security and civil rights and liberties as arising "wherever a constitutional order of the libertarian kind has been confronted with the Communist challenge, and with the Fascist response to that challenge."[6] In other words, to what extent, if any, can violations of liberal democratic values be justified in the name of the survival of the democratic, constitutional order itself; and if they can be so justified, to what extent can a democratic, constitutional government defend the state without transforming itself into an authoritarian regime? The tension between self-preservation and defending the "inner-most self" of the democratic regime – those attributes that make the regime worth defending – is what presents democracies

---

[6] Carl J. Friedrich, *Constitutional Reason of State: The Survival of the Constitutional Order* (Providence, RI: Brown University Press, 1957), p. 13.

with tragic choices. This tension, which is at the heart of all discussions of emergency powers, can only be captured by those who share the belief in the viability and desirability of a constitutional and democratic regime while taking cognizance of the fact that emergencies require special treatment that may deviate from the ordinary norms.

We do not examine responses of democracies to all types of crisis. Rather, our focus in this work is on violent crises and emergencies, by which we mean such events as wars and international armed conflicts, rebellions, and terrorist attacks as distinguished from economic crises and natural disasters.[7] We note that emergency powers have been used in times of great economic consternation and in situations of severe natural disasters as frequently as, and perhaps even more than, in the context of violent crises.[8] We also note that the distinction between the various categories of crises and emergencies may not always be so clear cut: violent emergencies may lead to the development of emergency powers that are then extended and used in the context of emergencies of an economic nature as the example of the Defence of the Realm Act and the subsequent Emergency Powers Act in Britain shows (discussed in chapter 4). Economic emergencies may be, and have been, equated with violent crises leading to governmental demands for similar broad powers to fight off the threat to the nation.[9] Conversely, economic crises may lead to the routine use of emergency powers that are then employed

---

[7] "Study of the Implications for Human Rights of Recent Developments Concerning Situations Known as States of Siege or Emergency," UN Commission on Human Rights, 35th Sess., Agenda Item 10, at 8–9, UN Doc. E/CN.4/Sub.2/1982/15 (1982); Subrata Roy Chowdhury, Rule of Law in a State of Emergency: The Paris Minimum Standards of Human Rights Norms in a State of Emergency (London: Pinter, 1989), p. 15; Clinton L. Rossiter, Constitutional Dictatorship: Crisis Government in Modern Democracies (Princeton, NJ: Princeton University Press, 1948), p. 6; Aaron S. Klieman, "Emergency Politics: The Growth of Crisis Government" (1976) 70 Conflict Studies 5.

[8] For discussion of emergency powers in the economic context see, for example, William E. Scheuerman, "The Economic State of Emergency" (2000) 21 Cardozo Law Review 1869; Rebecca M. Kahan, "Constitutional Stretch, Snap-Back, and Sag: Why Blaisdell was a Harsher Blow to Liberty than Korematsu" (2005) 99 Northwestern University Law Review 1279; Michal R. Belknap, "The New Deal and the Emergency Powers Doctrine" (1983) 62 Texas Law Review 67; Daniel J. Hulsebosch, "The New Deal Court: Emergence of a New Reason" (1990) 90 Columbia Law Review 1973; Daniel W. Levy, "A Legal History of Irrational Exuberance" (1998) 48 Case Western Reserve Law Review 799; Aaron Perrine, "The First Amendment Versus the World Trade Organization: Emergency Powers and the Battle in Seattle" (2001) 76 Washington Law Review 635 at 654.

[9] Belknap, "The New Deal," 70–76; William E. Leuchtenburg, "The New Deal and the Analogue of War" in John Braeman, Robert H. Bremner, and Everett Walters (eds.), Change and Continuity in Twentieth-Century America (Columbus, OH: Ohio State University Press, 1964), p. 81 at 81–82.

in the context of violent crises, at times with disastrous consequences as the experience of article 48 of the Weimar Constitution amply shows (chapter 1. We address some of the connections between violent emergencies and emergencies of an economic nature in chapters 1 and 4). Yet, while parts of the arguments that we develop below are also applicable to non-violent types of emergency situations, we believe that such a distinction is warranted in light of the different categorical requirements for action that each situation may raise. A violent conflict often requires the executive branch of government to act immediately without the benefit of consultation with other institutions and other branches of government. Economic crises may, but do not have to, allow for longer response periods, thus enabling a more sustained inter-branch action.[10]

The difficulties of distinguishing between economic and violent emergencies are part of a bigger problem of definitions. Exigencies provoke the use of emergency powers by governmental authorities. The vast scope of such powers and their ability to interfere with fundamental individual rights and civil liberties and to allow governmental regulation of virtually all aspects of human activity – as well as the possibility of their abuse – emphasize the pressing need for clearly defining the situations in which they may be invoked. Yet, defining what constitutes a "state of emergency" is no easy task, as both chapter 1 (discussing the experiences of national constitutions) and chapter 5 (looking at the international and regional human rights law) point out. The term "emergency" is, by its nature, an "elastic concept,"[11] which may defy precise definition.[12] As the International Law Association suggested: "It is neither desirable nor possible to stipulate *in abstracto* what particular type or types of events will automatically constitute a public emergency within the meaning of the term; each case has to be judged on its own merits

---

[10] See, e.g., Rossiter, *Constitutional Dictatorship*, pp. 9–11, 290–94; Carl J. Friedrich, *Constitutional Government and Democracy: Theory and Practice in Europe and America* (4th edn, Waltham, MA: Blaisdell, 1968), pp. 563–66; Frederick M. Watkins, "The Problem of Constitutional Dictatorship" (1940) 1 *Public Policy* 324 at 368–79.

[11] H.P. Lee, *Emergency Powers* (Sydney: Law Book Co., 1984), p. 4.

[12] Bhagat Singh and Others v. The King Emperor, A.I.R. 1931 P.C. 111, 111. See also Ningkan v. Government of Malaysia (1970) A.C. 379 at 390; Alex P. Schmid and Albert J. Jongman, *Political Terrorism: A New Guide to Actors, Authors, Concepts, Data Bases, Theories and Literature* (Amsterdam: North-Holland, 1988), pp. 1–38; Oren Gross, " 'Once More unto the Breach': The Systemic Failure of Applying the European Convention on Human Rights to Entrenched Emergencies" (1998) 23 *Yale Journal of International Law* 437 at 438–39; Keith E. Whittington, "Yet Another Constitutional Crisis?" (2002) 43 *William and Mary Law Review* 2093 at 2096–98.

taking into account the overriding concern for the continuance of a democratic society."[13] Whatever the tools employed to attend to this definitional problem, some of the terms that will eventually be used are inherently open-ended and manipulable. Consider, for example, the understanding of the concept of "public emergency" under article 15 of the European Convention for the Protection of Human Rights and Fundamental Freedoms as "a situation of exceptional and imminent danger or crisis affecting the general public, as distinct from particular groups, and constituting a threat to the organised life of the community which composes the State in question."[14]

The difficulty of defining "emergency" in advance was cogently captured by Alexander Hamilton when he wrote that "it is impossible to foresee or to define the extent and variety of national exigencies, and the correspondent extent and variety of the means which may be necessary to satisfy them. The circumstances that endanger the safety of nations are infinite." It was for this reason, he argued, that "no constitutional shackles can wisely be imposed on the power to which the care of it is committed."[15]

Hamilton was surely right in the sense that the difficulties in determining when a state of emergency exists in fact, coupled with the tendency of acute violent crises to result in the expansion of governmental powers and the concomitant contraction of individual freedoms and liberties, make it all the more important to focus on such questions as who determines that an emergency exists? Who may exercise emergency powers when such circumstances materialize and what might those powers be? What legal, political, and social controls are there on the exercise of such powers? Who determines when and how the emergency is over and what the legal effects of such determination are? As chapters 1 through 3 discuss at greater length, Hamilton's solution to the problem – "no constitutional shackles can wisely be imposed on the power to which the care of it is committed" – is but one possible answer.

---

[13] ILA Paris Report (1984), p. 59, quoted in Jaime Oraá, *Human Rights in States of Emergency in International Law* (Oxford: Clarendon Press, 1992), p. 31.

[14] Convention for the Protection of Human Rights and Fundamental Freedoms, Nov. 4, 1950, 213 U.N.T.S. 221 (entered into force Sep. 3, 1953), art. 15; Lawless v. Ireland, 1 Eur. Ct. HR (ser. B) (1960–1961) (Commission report), p. 56 at 82 (para. 90).

[15] Clinton Rossiter (ed.), *The Federalist Papers* (New York: New American Library, 1961), No. 23, p. 153 (Alexander Hamilton). See also John Hatchard, *Individual Freedoms and State Security in the African Context: The Case of Zimbabwe* (Athens, OH: Ohio University Press, 1993), p. 2; Lee, *Emergency Powers*, p. 5.

Violent crises pose the greatest and most sustained danger to constitutional freedoms and principles.[16] In such times, the temptation to disregard constitutional freedoms is at its zenith, while the effectiveness of traditional checks and balances is at its nadir. In times of crisis, it is often argued, legal niceties may be cast aside as luxuries to be enjoyed only in times of peace and tranquility. Those who argue about civil rights and liberties are often chided as having an "airy-fairy" view of the world.[17] At the same time, a commitment to preserving and maintaining rights, freedoms, and liberties must be reconciled with the caution against turning the constitution into a suicide pact.[18] As Justice Robert Jackson wrote more than fifty years ago:

Temperate and thoughtful people find difficulties in such conflicts which only partisans find no trouble in deciding wholly one way or the other. It is easy, by giving way to the passion, intolerance and suspicions of wartime, to reduce our liberties to a shadow, often in answer to exaggerated claims of security. Also, it is easy, by contemptuously ignoring the reasonable anxieties of wartime as mere "hysteria," to set the stage for by-passing courts which the public thinks have become too naïve, too dilatory and too sympathetic with their enemies and betrayers...if the people come deeply to feel that civil rights are being successfully turned against their institutions by their enemies, they will react by becoming enemies of civil rights.[19]

Thus, there exists a tension of "tragic dimensions" between democratic values and responses to violent emergencies.[20] Democratic nations faced with serious crisis by way of terrorist threats or other fundamental political challenges must "maintain and protect life, the liberties necessary to a vibrant democracy, and the unity of the society, the loss of which can turn a healthy and diverse nation into a seriously divided and violent

---

[16] See, e.g., Vernonia Sch. Dist. 47J v. Acton, 515 US 646 at 686 (1995) (O'Connor, J., dissenting); Skinner v. Ry. Labor Executives' Ass'n, 489 US 602 at 635 (1989) (Marshall, J., dissenting).

[17] See, e.g., Brian Groom, "Detaining Suspects not Abuse of Human Rights, Says Blunkett," *Financial Times* (London), Nov. 12, 2001, p. 3 (quoting the British Home Secretary, David Blunkett).

[18] Haig v. Agee, 453 US 280 at 309–10 (1981); Kennedy v. Mendoza-Martinez, 372 US 144 at 160 (1963) ("[W]hile the Constitution protects against invasions of individual rights, it is not a suicide pact"); Terminiello v. Chicago, 337 US 1 at 37 (1949) (Jackson, J., dissenting).

[19] Robert H. Jackson, "Wartime Security and Liberty under Law" (1951) 1 *Buffalo Law Review* 103 at 116.

[20] Pnina Lahav, "A Barrel without Hoops: The Impact of Counterterrorism on Israel's Legal Culture" (1988) 10 *Cardozo Law Review* 529 at 531.

one."[21] At the same time, exigencies and acute crises directly challenge the most fundamental concepts of constitutional democracy.

Consider the notion that a government must be of limited powers, a government of laws, not of men (or women).[22] Crises tend to result in the expansion of governmental powers, the concentration of powers in the hands of the executive, and the concomitant contraction of individual freedoms and liberties. Enhanced and newly created powers are asserted by, and given to, the government as necessary to meet the challenge to the community. Concepts such as separation of powers and federalism are likely to be among the first casualties when a nation needs to respond to a national emergency.[23] The executive branch assumes a leading role in countering the crisis, with the other two branches pushed aside (whether of their own volition or not). The increase in governmental powers leads, in turn, to a contraction of traditional individual rights, freedoms, and liberties. The government's ability to act swiftly, secretly, and decisively against a threat to the life of the nation becomes superior to the ordinary principles of limitation on governmental powers and individual rights.[24] While such expansions and concentrations of powers are not unique to times of crisis, but rather are part of the modernization of society and the need for governmental involvement in an ever-growing number of areas of human activity, it can hardly be denied that such phenomena have been accelerated tremendously (and, at times, initiated) during emergencies.

---

[21] Philip B. Heymann, *Terrorism and America: A Commonsense Strategy for a Democratic Society* (Cambridge, MA: MIT Press, 1998), p. ix; Ruth Wedgwood, "Al Qaeda, Terrorism, and Military Commissions" (2002) 96 *American Journal of International Law* 328 at 330.

[22] Aristotle, *The Complete Works*, ed. Jonathan Barnes (Princeton, NJ: Princeton University Press, 1984), p. 2051; Marbury v. Madison, 5 US (1 Cranch) 137 at 163 (1803).

[23] Edward S. Corwin, *Total War and the Constitution* (New York: A.A. Knopf, 1947), pp. 35–77; Peter Rosenthal, "The New Emergencies Act: Four Times the War Measures Act" (1991) 20 *Manitoba Law Journal* 563 at 576–80.

[24] See, e.g., Harold Hongju Koh, *The National Security Constitution: Sharing Power after the Iran–Contra Affair* (New Haven, CT: Yale University Press, 1990), pp. 117–49; Rossiter, *Constitutional Dictatorship*, pp. 288–90; Pitirim A. Sorokin, *Man and Society in Calamity: The Effects of War, Revolution, Famine, Pestilence upon Human Mind, Behavior, Social Organization and Cultural Life* (New York: E.P. Dutton, 1942), pp. 122–44, 275–76; Arthur S. Miller, "Constitutional Law: Crisis Government Becomes the Norm" (1978) 39 *Ohio State Law Journal* 736 at 738–41; Michael Linfield, *Freedom under Fire: US Civil Liberties in Times of War* (Boston: South End Press, 1990); Charles de Secondat Montesquieu, *The Spirit of Laws* (1748) (Berkeley: University of California Press, 1977), p. 154; Jules Lobel, "Emergency Power and the Decline of Liberalism" (1989) 98 *Yale Law Journal* 1385 at 1386; Watkins, "Constitutional Dictatorship," 343–44; Itzhak Zamir, "Human Rights and National Security" (1989) 23 *Israel Law Review* 375.

Two seemingly antithetical vectors are in a constant tug-of-war. The existence of restrictions and limitations on governmental powers is a fundamental attribute of democratic regimes. The ideals of democracy, individual rights, legitimacy, accountability, and the rule of law suggest that even in times of acute danger, government is limited, both formally and substantively, in the range of activities that it may pursue and powers that it may exercise to protect the state. However, grave violent emergencies challenge this organizing principle. In extreme cases, the reason of state and what Bruce Ackerman calls "the existential rationale" may call for the exercise of unfettered discretion and practically unlimited powers by the government in order to protect the nation.[25] The question then arises as to what extent, if any, violations of fundamental democratic values can be justified in the name of the survival of the democratic, constitutional order itself, and if they can be justified, to what extent a democratic, constitutional government can defend the state without transforming itself into an authoritarian regime.

Part I of the book (chapters 1–4) introduces and analyzes several distinct models that have dominated both the theory and the practice concerning responses to acute national crises. Each model is explained and analyzed both from a theoretical perspective and through concrete examples that range across time and jurisdictions. Indeed we argue that these theoretical frameworks are applicable across legal systems and provide an equally relevant conceptual framework to assess international legal responses to crisis.

Chapter I focuses on a group of models that we call "models of accommodation," which have dominated the discourse concerning emergency regimes in democratic societies. All those models countenance a certain degree of accommodation for the pressures exerted on the state in times of emergency, while, at the same time, maintaining normal legal principles and rules as much as possible. According to the models of accommodation, when a nation is faced with emergencies, its legal, and even constitutional, structure must be somewhat relaxed (and perhaps even suspended in parts). This compromise, it is suggested, enables continued adherence to the principle of the rule of law and faithfulness to fundamental democratic values, while providing the state with adequate measures to withstand the storm wrought by the crisis.

---

[25] Friedrich, *Constitutional Reason of State*, pp. 4–5; Maurizio Viroli, *From Politics to Reason of State: The Acquisition and Transformation of the Language of Politics, 1250–1600* (Cambridge: Cambridge University Press, 1992), pp. 238–80; Bruce Ackerman, "The Emergency Constitution" (2004) 113 *Yale Law Journal* 1029 at 1037–38.

The chapter analyzes the classical models of accommodation, first and foremost of which is the institution of the dictatorship that was used in the Roman republic, before it goes on to discuss three broad categories of models of accommodation, namely constitutional, legislative, and interpretive accommodations. These categories correspond to somewhat different equilibria between maintenance of the ordinary system of rules and norms and accommodation for emergency, as well as to different mechanisms by which such equilibria are established. The relative strength of the models of accommodation inheres in their flexibility and in their accommodation within the constitutional system of shifting and expanding the powers needed to meet exigencies and crises. Yet, these models may be innately susceptible to manipulation and to the challenge that accommodation of counter-emergency responses within the existing legal system starts us down a slippery slope toward excessive governmental infringement on individual rights and liberties while undermining constitutional structures and institutions in the process.

Such challenges have led to the development of an alternative constitutional model of emergency regimes which we discuss in chapter 2, namely the Business as Usual model. This model is based on notions of constitutional absolutism and perfection. According to this model, ordinary legal rules and norms continue to be followed strictly with no substantive change even in times of emergency and crisis. The law in times of war remains the same as in times of peace. In fact, not only do ordinary constitutional norms remain unchanged in times of emergency, but so too does the nature of the substantive outcomes when applied to specific cases. While its appeal is found in its insistence upon clear rules and upon maintaining the ideal that the constitutional framework is not affected by crises and exigencies, the model's main weakness lies in its rigidity in the face of radical changes in the surrounding context. This model is often criticized as being either naive or hypocritical in the sense that it disregards the reality of governmental exercise of extraordinary measures and powers in responding to emergencies.

Both the Business as Usual model and the models of accommodation are constitutional models in as much as they rely on an assumption of constitutionality that tells us that whatever responses are made to the challenges of a particular exigency, such responses are to be found and limited within the confines of the constitution. This assumption of constitutionality is challenged by the realist school of international relations. An extreme version of the challenge would read as follows: there is no room for any kind of "legalistic-moralistic" approach in dealing with emergencies. Legal rules and norms are too inflexible and rigid to accommodate the security needs of states. Governments should have full and unfettered discretion to determine what course of action ought to be taken to fight any given crisis in the most efficient way. Law may well be irrelevant when dealing with violent crises. Under this brand of political realism, democracies face no real conundrum in dealing with emergencies. The only constraints within which government functions are those emanating from efficiency and limited resources.

While we briefly discuss this approach, we note that the core of the theory does not transfer to the domestic sphere and that it cannot be acceptable to those who believe that law matters and that it matters greatly especially in times of crisis as a check against arbitrary actions and unlimited discretion.

The main focus of chapter 3 is, however, another possible model of response to crisis that presents challenges to the assumption of constitutionality and is willing, instead, to accept some form of extra-legal, and perhaps extra-constitutional, action. The Extra-Legal Measures model suggests that under extreme circumstances, public officials may act extra-legally when they believe that such action is necessary for protecting the nation and the public in the face of calamity, provided that they openly and publicly acknowledge the nature of their actions. In other words, according to the model, there may be circumstances where the appropriate method of tackling grave dangers and threats entails going outside the constitutional order, at times even violating otherwise accepted constitutional principles, rules, and norms. Once an extra-legal action is taken, it is then up to the people to decide, either directly or indirectly (e.g., through their elected representatives in the legislature), how to respond to such actions. The Extra-Legal Measures model seeks to promote, and is promoted by, ethical concepts of political and popular responsibility, political morality, and candor.[26] To be implemented properly, the model calls for candor on the part of government agents, who must disclose the nature of their counter-emergency activities. The model then focuses on the need for a direct or indirect popular ex post ratification of such activities. The process leading up to such ratification (or rejection) of those actions promotes deliberation after the fact, as well as establishing the individual responsibility of each member of the

---

[26] Oren Gross, "Chaos and Rules: Should Responses to Violent Crises Always be Constitutional?" (2003) 112 *Yale Law Journal* 1011; Oren Gross, "Are Torture Warrants Warranted? Pragmatic Absolutism and Official Disobedience" (2004) 88 *Minnesota Law Review* 1481.

relevant community for the actions taken on behalf of the public during the emergency.

As noted above, chapter 3 presents several challenges to the assumption of constitutionality. Another basic assumption on which the traditional models of emergency powers are premised is the *assumption of separation*, which is defined by the belief in our ability to separate emergencies and crises from normalcy, counter-terrorism measures from ordinary legal rules and norms. This assumption, which is the subject of chapter 4, facilitates our acceptance of expansive governmental emergency powers and counter-terrorism measures, for it reassures us that once the emergency is removed and terrorism is no longer a threat, such powers and measures will also be terminated and full return to normalcy ensured. It also assures us that counter-emergency measures will be directed not against us, but only against those who pose a threat to the community.

However, chapter 4 demonstrates that bright-line demarcations between normalcy and emergency are all too frequently untenable, and distinctions between the two are difficult, if not impossible. In fact, the exception is hardly an exception at all. In various meaningful ways, "Emergency government has become the norm."[27] Thus, fashioning legal tools to respond to emergencies on the belief that the assumption of separation will serve as a firewall protecting human rights, civil liberties, and the legal system as a whole may be misguided. Since the assumption of separation is also closely linked to the goals of the different models of emergency powers and in as much as it informs each of these models, we must reassess the strength of the arguments supporting each of them. Blind adherence to the models may result in long-term destabilization of such fundamental principles as the rule of law and the strong protection of rights, freedoms, and liberties. Innovative legal concepts to deal with the problem of emergencies may be needed.

Part II of this book (chapters 5–7) focuses on the interaction of international law and some of its specific legal regimes with situations of emergency.

Chapter 5 begins with an analysis, followed by a critical evaluation, of the theory and practice of the interface of international human rights law oversight and the domestic regulation of crisis. The chapter also

---

[27] Harold Relyea, *A Brief History of Emergency Powers in the United States*, Special US Senate Comm. on Nat'l Emergencies and Delegated Emergency Powers, Working Paper No. 36-612, 1974 (Washington, DC: Government Printing Office, 1974), p. v.

examines human rights norms regulating the experience of emergencies in the context of the various models that are introduced in Part I.

Through the mechanism of mutually enforcing multilateral treaty obligations international human rights norms require states to protect and enforce agreed human rights standards for individuals (and in some specific cases for groups). We look specifically at the workings and limitations of the primary regional and UN enforcement/accommodation bodies – the European Court of Human Rights, the Inter-American Court of Human Rights, and the United Nations Human Rights Committee – which enforce and oversee treaty agreements between contracting states. A driving feature of many of these treaties is that they specifically acknowledge the need to make provision for the experience of crisis and emergency. Such treaty law constitutes a form of international legislation, consensually agreed to by states and (dependent on the domestic legal system to which it is imported) validated by domestic legislative and executive processes. However, some of these treaties may be seen as akin to a supra-national constitutional bill of rights. This is particularly true of the European Convention on Human Rights, which has been explicitly incorporated into the constitutional framework of some states, and is treated as a form of "super" constitution by a number of others.

This chapter also pays close attention to the form and content of the interpretive accommodation that has been offered by international and regional courts and tribunals. We identify a number of themes and structural weaknesses that dominate judicial thinking on these matters. For example, we examine the inability of such courts and tribunals to deal with "problem" emergencies, particularly permanent or enduring emergencies, and their abdication of responsibility to decide whether emergency had, in fact, existed. Our analysis also leads us to suggest that the Inter-American Court of Human Rights has generally taken a more robust approach to determining both substantive and procedural questions about emergencies than its European and United Nations counterparts.

We conclude this chapter by taking a close look at the conceptual notion of emergencies that we judge underpins international legal thinking about emergencies. This conceptual framework is heavily influenced by the notion of an "ideal type" emergency, which in practice rarely exists, but affects the way in which courts and other oversight mechanisms conceive and thus respond to emergencies. We tie this discussion to our critique of the assumption of separation in the previous chapter.

Chapter 6 follows with a study of the relationship between emergencies and international humanitarian law. We are particularly interested in the theoretically underexplored and compacted relationship between war and emergency. We explore this relationship in the classic inter-state war situation and follow by examining ill-defined situations of internal armed conflict. Again, following the example of chapter 4, this chapter demonstrates and closely analyzes the breaking down of separation myths, particularly the attempts to separate "war" and "emergency" as unique and entirely distinct phenomena. Specifically, in dealing with the doctrines of self-preservation and self-defense we seek to highlight some interesting contemporary shifts linked in part to the events of September 11 that illustrate this theme.

Through the analysis of the legal regulation of low-intensity conflict we show how the alleged distinctions between humanitarian law and the derogation regime of international human rights law are in fact more apparent than real. In short, there are multiple situations in which what we term "high-intensity" emergencies are almost indistinguishable from low-intensity armed conflicts. This begs the important question of which law actually applies to these situations, and whether it is appropriate to think about such questions in mutually exclusive terms.

Finally, chapter 7 looks at contemporary legal debates and explores whether terrorism constitutes a conceptual category that activates the material conditions that are sufficient to be considered within the conceptual and regulatory space of "emergency" or whether it is a fundamentally distinct phenomenon. We start off by exploring the multiple features and definitions of terrorism. The analysis then seeks to assess how the regulation of terrorism (in its various guises) fits within the models proposed in Part I. We are particularly interested in the legal regimes that are potentially applicable to terrorism, and explore some contemporary concerns related to the international legal regulation of terrorism through which we strive to gain some insights about the broader relationship between law, crisis, and terrorism. Dissection of the term "the war on terrorism" is particularly relevant to exposing the inconsistencies between contemporary political rhetoric and the applicability of law to situations on the ground. We conclude with an examination of how the events of September 11, 2001 have shaped national and international legal responses to terrorism, and the influence of international legal obligations on domestic legal and political systems.

Part I

1   Models of accommodation

The discourse concerning emergency regimes in democratic societies has almost invariably been governed by models that may be grouped together under a general category that we call "models of accommodation." All those models countenance a certain degree of accommodation for the pressures exerted on the state in times of emergency, while, at the same time, maintaining normal legal principles and rules as much as possible. According to the models of accommodation, when a nation is faced with emergencies its legal, and even constitutional, structure must be somewhat relaxed (and perhaps even suspended in parts).[1] This compromise, it is suggested, enables continued adherence to the principle of the rule of law and faithfulness to fundamental democratic values, while providing the state with adequate measures to withstand the storm wrought by the crisis.

Classical models of accommodation

The Roman dictatorship

The institution of the Roman dictatorship is the prototype for all modern forms of models of accommodation. The Romans introduced a system in which an emergency institution was a recognized and regular instrument of government built into a constitutional framework. This institution was hailed by Niccolò Machiavelli as one that "deserves to be considered and numbered among those that were the cause of the greatness of so great an empire."[2] Similarly, Clinton Rossiter suggested

---

[1] Eric A. Posner and Adrian Vermeule, "Accommodating Emergencies" (2003) 56 *Stanford Law Review* 605 at 606–07.

[2] Niccolò Machiavelli, *Discourses on Livy*, trans. Harvey C. Mansfield and Nathan Tarcov (Chicago, IL: University of Chicago Press, 1996), p. 74.

that "The splendid political genius of the Roman people grasped and solved the difficult problem of emergency powers in a manner quite unparalleled in all history, indeed so uniquely and boldly that a study of modern crisis government could find no more propitious a starting point than a brief survey of the celebrated Roman dictatorship."[3] Indeed, the dictatorship is the model on which Rossiter develops his thesis that a democracy can fight a successful total war and still maintain its democratic character when the war is over by employing the principle of the constitutional dictatorship. Rossiter's eleven criteria for what qualifies a dictatorship as constitutional are clearly structured around the Roman experience and the attributes of the dictatorship.[4] Thus, the Roman solution to the problem of emergency powers was touted as "perhaps the most strikingly successful of all known systems of emergency government."[5] The salient features of the "celebrated Roman dictatorship" – its temporary character, recognition of the exceptional nature of emergencies, appointment of a dictator according to specific constitutional forms that separated, among other things, those who declared an emergency and those who exercised dictatorial powers on such occasions, the appointment of dictators for well-defined and limited purposes, and the ultimate goal of upholding the constitutional order rather than changing or replacing it – are often regarded as setting the basic guidelines for modern-day constitutional emergency regimes. In his argument for a strong and vigorous executive Alexander Hamilton invoked the Roman example:

Every man the least conversant in Roman history knows how often that republic was obliged to take refuge in the absolute power of a single man, under the formidable title of dictator, as well against the intrigues of ambitious individuals who aspired to the tyranny, and the seditions of whole classes of the community whose conduct threatened the existence of all government, as against the invasions of external enemies who menaced the conquest and destruction of Rome.[6]

[3] Clinton L. Rossiter, *Constitutional Dictatorship: Crisis Government in Modern Democracies* (Princeton, NJ: Princeton University Press, 1948), p. 15.

[4] Ibid., pp. 3–5, 298–306.

[5] Frederick M. Watkins, "The Problem of Constitutional Dictatorship" (1940) 1 *Public Policy* 324 at 332.

[6] Clinton Rossiter (ed.), *The Federalist Papers* (New York: New American Library, 1961), No. 70, p. 423 (Alexander Hamilton). See also Bruce Ackerman, "The Emergency Constitution" (2004) 113 *Yale Law Journal* 1029 at 1046 (while rejecting the Roman model as impractical in the modern world, Ackerman recognizes that the Roman republic "represents the first great experiment with states of emergency," and acknowledges it as "an inspiration for my heavy reliance on a political system of checks and balances").

The main thrust of this emergency institution was its constitutional nature. Operating within the republican constitutional framework the dictator was vested with extraordinary yet constitutional powers. Emergency was met with special powers of an authoritarian character, but the employment of such powers and the authority to use them were regulated by law.

With the fall of the monarchy in 509 BC, the Roman republic moved to establish an executive branch of government that was headed by two chief magistrates, the consuls.[7] The two consuls had at their disposal immense power. Significantly, each of them had the full and unlimited power to command the army and to exercise jurisdiction in all matters.[8] However, in order to prevent reversion to a monarchical structure of government, the newly established executive offices of the republic were based on two principles:[9] the principle of collegiality and equal power, and the principle of limited, non-renewable, term of office. The two consuls enjoyed equal authority and had the same range of functions, powers, and responsibilities. Each also enjoyed an unlimited veto power over the decisions and actions of his colleague. Each consul was elected for a period of one year without a possibility of consecutive re-election.

At the same time the Romans were aware that a coequal partnership at the helm might not be adequate in times of extreme peril. In such precarious times there might be a need for swift and decisive actions. The possibility of a deadlocked leadership unable to agree on what those actions ought to be posed a real challenge. Thus, another institution – the dictatorship – was created as "a temporary revival of the monarchy used in times of emergency when it was necessary to concentrate the whole power of the state in a single person."[10] The severity of the situation was captured by the fact that when a dictator was appointed – the origin of the term, "*dictus*" (named, appointed), points to the fact that

---

[7] The exact timing of the move is a matter of some controversy. Max Cary and Howard H. Scullard, *A History of Rome down to the Reign of Constantine* (3rd edn, New York: St. Martin's Press, 1975), p. 56.

[8] William E. Heitland, *The Roman Republic* (3 vols., Holmes Beach, FL: Gaunt, 1969), vol. I, para. 70; Herbert F. Jolowicz and Barry Nicholas, *Historical Introduction to the Study of Roman Law* (3rd edn, New York: Greenwood Press, 1972), p. 45.

[9] Cary and Scullard, *A History of Rome*, pp. 62–63.

[10] Jolowicz and Nicholas, *Roman Law*, p. 11; Theodor E. Mommsen, *The History of Rome* (1864) (5 vols., London: Macmillan, 1908), p. 326; Heitland, *The Roman Republic*, vol. I, para. 150; Rossiter, *Constitutional Dictatorship*, p. 19.

the dictator was the only non-elected magistrate of the republic[11] – an axe, symbolizing the power to administer capital punishment, appeared in his *fasces* (a bundle of wooden rods that represented authority) even within Rome's city boundaries, whereas the *fasces* of the consuls included an axe only when presented outside the city.[12] In such grave times any one of the consuls – in case the two could not agree or otherwise act together, the decision regarding which one of them was to act on the matter was decided by lot – could appoint a dictator who, upon entering office, became the highest magistrate of the republic, superior also to the consuls who appointed him. Machiavelli suggests that, since the appointment of a dictator relegated the status and authority of the consuls, it was wise to leave such an appointment in the consuls' hands, because "wounds and other ills which are inflicted of one's own accord and choice, grieve you much less than those that are inflicted on you by others."[13] However, while the dictator combined the powers of the two consuls, he neither replaced them nor took away their powers.[14] The decisions of the dictator, unlike those of all other magistrates (including the consuls), were not subject to appeal to the centuriate assembly. The dictator alone was free from any intercession by the tribunes and from senatorial intervention and direction. He was not restricted in the size of army he could raise, and had full discretion in setting out the strategic as well as tactical goals and means of the force under his command.[15] In addition, he was the only magistrate who did not have to fear a possible punishment and accountability after the termination of his office.[16]

The institution of the dictatorship was alien to the basic governmental structure of the republic. The system of officers coequal in their powers and able fully to veto each other's decisions and actions could not comfortably coexist with the vesting of absolute power in a single person. The notion of sharing the burdens of governance was clearly at

---

[11] Heitland, *The Roman Republic*, vol. I, para. 148.

[12] Jolowicz and Nicholas, *Roman Law*, p. 55.

[13] Machiavelli, *Discourses*, p. 196.

[14] Andrew Lintott, *The Constitution of the Roman Republic* (Oxford: Clarendon Press, 1999), p. 111; Jolowicz and Nicholas, *Roman Law*, p. 55; Olga E. Tellegen-Couperus, *A Short History of Roman Law* (London: Routledge, 1993), p. 40.

[15] Rossiter, *Constitutional Dictatorship*, p. 25.

[16] Ibid., p. 19. However, it was rare for officials to be punished after the completion of their term in office for acts that they had taken in their official capacity. Heitland, *The Roman Republic*, vol. I, para. 70.

odds with the dictatorship.[17] Hence, although giving the dictator all the powers needed to defend the republic against its enemies, well-defined constitutional restrictions were laid out in order to prevent unwarranted aggrandizement and abuse of the powers of the dictator and a return to the monarchical system.[18]

Perhaps the most significant limitations pertained to the exceptional nature of the circumstances that would warrant the appointment of a dictator and to the temporal duration of that extraordinary appointment. Traditionally, the dictator was supposed to carry out military functions that would be necessary to defend the republic against external threats, and would then be considered a dictator *rei gerundae causa* ("for getting things done").[19] The military origin of the institution is apparent from the dictator's original title of *magister populi* (master of the citizen army) and the fact that to assist him in his important task the dictator had the power to appoint a delegate, known as the *magister equitum* ("master of the horse," who was supposed to be the commander of the cavalry), and give him the full power of *imperium*.[20] The dictator's term of office was limited to six months or to the end of the term of the consuls who appointed him, whichever came first, and could not be renewed. Explaining that the short term of office of the dictator was one of the factors that accounted for the ultimate success of the institution, Machiavelli contrasts the dictatorship with the rule of the *Decemviri*, arguing that a major flaw in the latter regime was the fact that these ten men were granted absolute authority for a long period of time (Machiavelli considers a year to be a long time in this context).[21] Similarly, Jean-Jacques Rousseau suggests that the nomination of a dictator, the "supreme ruler," be for a short period, limited in advance and not subject to extension (especially not by the supreme ruler himself):

---

[17] Cary and Scullard, *A History of Rome*, p. 97.

[18] Ibid., p. 63; Carl J. Friedrich, *Constitutional Government and Democracy: Theory and Practice in Europe and America* (4th edn, Waltham, MA: Blaisdell, 1968), p. 559; Wilfried Nippel, "Emergency Powers in the Roman Republic" in Pasquale Pasquino and Bernard Manin (eds.), *La théorie politico-constitutionelle du gouvernement d'exception* (Paris: Les Cahiers du CREA, 2000), p. 5.

[19] Heitland, *The Roman Republic*, vol. I, para. 149; Mommsen, *The History of Rome*, p. 326; Rossiter, *Constitutional Dictatorship*, p. 21; Barthold G. Niebuhr, *The History of Rome*, trans. Julius C. Hare and Connop Thirlwall (3 vols., London: Taylor, Walton, and Maberly, 1851), vol. I, p. 564.

[20] Mommsen, *The History of Rome*, pp. 325–26; Jolowicz and Nicholas, *Roman Law*, p. 55. But see Niebuhr, *History of Rome*, pp. 569–70.

[21] Machiavelli, *Discourses*, pp. 76–77.

However this important trust be conferred, it is important that its duration should be fixed at a very brief period, incapable of being ever prolonged. In the crises which lead to its adoption, the State is either soon lost, or soon saved; and, the present need passed, the dictatorship becomes either tyrannical or idle. At Rome, where dictators held office for six months only, most of them abdicated before their time was up. If their term had been longer, they might well have tried to prolong it still further, as the decemvirs did when chosen for a year. The dictator had only time to provide against the need that had caused him to be chosen; he had none to think of further projects.[22]

The period of six months was chosen to comport with the army's "working year" and thus with the maximum duration of a military campaign.[23] This limitation reflected the military origins of the dictatorship and the fact that dictators were to be appointed to deal with acute military crises. Moreover, according to constitutional custom the dictator was expected to step down and relinquish his powers once he overcame the particular crisis that led to his appointment in the first place. Indeed, in the one case in which a dictator attempted to stay in office after completing the task for which he had been originally appointed, he was quickly forced by the tribunes to resign his position.[24]

Another important restriction on the powers of the dictator resulted from the fact that he was expected to restore order and safety to the republic in the face of a particular (military) threat.[25] With all his immense powers the dictator could not embark, of his own initiative, on an aggressive war against an external enemy. His was a defensive role.[26] Moreover, the dictator was called to maintain and protect the existing constitutional order. As a result he "could not do anything that might diminish the state, as taking away authority from the Senate or from the people, undoing the old orders of the city and making new ones,

---

[22] Jean-Jacques Rousseau, *The Social Contract and Discourses*, trans. G.D.H. Cole (New York: Everyman, 1993), p. 296.

[23] Heitland, *The Roman Republic*, vol. I, para. 150; Rossiter, *Constitutional Dictatorship*, p. 23; Mommsen, *The History of Rome*, pp. 325–26. Another explanation is given by Niebuhr arguing that the six months cap on the term of any appointed dictator reflected the early confederacy between Rome and Latium, having the office of the highest magistrate alternate between the two constitutive elements of the confederacy. Niebuhr, *History of Rome*, p. 564.

[24] Heitland, *The Roman Republic*, vol. I, paras. 148, 150.

[25] Friedrich, *Constitutional Government*, p. 559; Rossiter, *Constitutional Dictatorship*, p. 24.

[26] Rossiter, *Constitutional Dictatorship*, p. 24.

would have been."[27] The dictator could not use his powers in order to change the basic character of the state or its institutional framework. Significantly, his authority did not extend to the promulgation of new legislation, an authority that was reserved to the Senate. In *The Social Contract*, Rousseau similarly emphasizes this significant distinction between the "legislator" and the "supreme ruler." The legislative authority and the dictatorial powers are not to be confused or merged. The "supreme ruler," tailored around the outline of the Roman dictatorship, may enjoy absolute powers as necessary for the preservation of society and its members, and may "silence all the laws and suspend for a moment the sovereign authority,"[28] but he does not possess the power to alter arbitrarily the basic legal framework of that society as put in place by the legislator. The ordinary laws and the constitutional order, in all or in part, may be suspended under the reign of the supreme ruler but they cannot be modified, amended, or repealed during that time. In short, "He can do anything, except make laws."[29]

Although the appointment of a dictator was a radical constitutional move undertaken in exceptional times of crisis, an appearance of normality was maintained as much as possible. During the operation of a dictatorship, the regular institutions of the state – the consulship, the tribunes, the Senate, and all other office holders – continued to fulfill their normal functions and retained their full authority. The result was that "the Senate, the consuls, the tribunes, remaining in their authority, came to be like a guard on [the dictator] to make him not depart from the right way." Machiavelli contrasts this feature of the dictatorship with the rule of the *Decemviri*, "for they annulled the consuls and the tribunes; they gave them[selves] authority to make laws and do any other thing, like the Roman people. So finding themselves alone ... and because of this not having anyone to observe them, they were able to become insolent ... "[30]

Another set of critical checks related to the process and procedures for the appointment of a dictator. Most significantly, the appointment of a dictator by the consuls, coupled with the provision that no consul might appoint himself as dictator, ensured that the dictatorship would be invoked by officers other than the dictator himself. The republican structures ensured a separation between those who decided

---

[27] Machiavelli, *Discourses*, p. 74.
[28] Rousseau, *Social Contract*, p. 294.   [29] Ibid.   [30] Machiavelli, *Discourses*, p. 76.

that an emergency existed and those who exercised the most awesome emergency measures. Thus, the dictator's powers were conferred upon him "according to public orders, and not by his own authority."[31]

Although the appointment of the dictator was a matter for the full discretion of the consuls, the practice that developed was that it could not be made without the Senate's recommendation, and the *imperium* of the dictator had to be confirmed by a law passed by the curiate assembly.[32] This reflected the increase in the political clout of the Senate, but not less importantly it was also the result of a basic fear of tyranny. Once a dictator had been appointed it was extremely difficult (although not impossible) to turn back the wheel.[33] Hence, it was critical that the appointment of a dictator would not be undertaken hastily without due consideration of the circumstances. Involvement in the appointment of a dictator became of special importance for the Senate once the office of the dictator was opened to Plebs and was no longer the sole estate of the Patrician nobility. Internal socio-political considerations, coupled with constitutional consciousness rejecting excessive concentration of power in the hands of any one leader, led to a constitutional practice of "legislative" partial control over the emergency mechanisms of the government and to the rejection of any notion that emergency measures were an exclusive domain of the "executive branch" of government. With the increase in the Senate's power within the structure of government, the Senate not only recommended the appointment of a dictator, but also moved to identify the individual person to be nominated. Such recommendations of the Senate were invariably followed.

Finally, another important check on the exercise of dictatorial powers derived from the political and ethical ethos of Rome and its citizens. Machiavelli alludes to that point when he contends that the citizens of Rome were not corrupt (in an implicit contradiction to the Florentines of his own time). He emphasizes the point that in a republic of law-abiding, non-corrupt citizenry, regulating emergency government under the regular laws of the republic, specifying exact procedures for the exercise of emergency powers, and identifying those who would be vested with such powers make it extremely hard, if not outright impossible, to

---

[31] Ibid., p. 74.
[32] Jolowicz and Nicholas, *Roman Law*, pp. 35, 55; Cary and Scullard, *A History of Rome*, p. 98; Heitland, *The Roman Republic*, vol. I, para. 150; Niebuhr, *History of Rome*, p. 568.
[33] Heitland, *The Roman Republic*, vol. I, para. 150.

deviate from constitutional forms and procedures, and to use the legal emergency mechanisms for the institution of a tyrannical regime. For,

[I]f a citizen wishes to be able to offend and to seize extraordinary authority for himself, he must have many qualities that in a noncorrupt republic he can never have. For he needs to be very rich and to have very many adherents and partisans, which he cannot have where the laws are observed; and even if he had them, men like these are so formidable that free votes do not concur in them.[34]

Machiavelli is clearly aware of the significance of this for he cautions that where people are willing to confer unlimited powers on the government for an unspecified duration, they would not be saved the fate of tyranny merely because they themselves were not corrupt in character, for "absolute authority corrupts the matter in a very short time and makes friends and partisans for itself."[35] Interestingly, whereas Lord Acton's famous parable regarding power and absolute power focuses on the wielders of power, i.e., the rulers, Machiavelli refers in this context to the people rather than the government.

In the annals of Rome no one came closer to the ideal working of the dictatorship than Lucius Quinctius Cincinnatus. According to tradition, Cincinnatus was made dictator in 458 BC in order to save a Roman army, headed by one of the consuls, that was besieged by enemy forces. Heitland recounts the story:

The deputation of senators come on their serious errand: the sturdy farmer is requested to put on his gown and hear it. Washed and gowned...he is saluted Dictator, and steps from the spade or plough straight to the head of the state, apparently without the least exultation or nervousness or even surprise. Coolly he gets together a relieving army, every man bearing twelve stakes, three or four times the usual number, beside his food and arms. The dictator marches off and reaches the seat of war about nightfall, and during the night surrounds the surrounding Aequi with a palisade.[36]

Most significantly and famously, immediately upon his victory over the enemy – merely fifteen days after his appointment – Cincinnatus stepped

---

[34] Machiavelli, *Discourses*, p. 74.   [35] Ibid., p. 77.

[36] Heitland, *The Roman Republic*, vol. I. para. 106; Livy, *The Early History of Rome*, trans. Aubrey de Sélincourt (Harmondsworth: Penguin, 1971), pp. 212–16. Machiavelli invokes the story of Cincinnatus in order to argue that the citizens of the ideal republic ought to be poor for that republic to be successful. He emphasizes the fact that Cincinnatus's poverty did not stand as an obstacle on his way to the supreme office of the republic. The same is true of Cincinnatus's master of the horse who was so poor that he had to fight on foot. Machiavelli, *Discourses*, pp. 475–77.

down, relinquished all his special powers, and returned to work his land.[37] Cincinnatus's unwavering commitment to serve the republic and his willingness to give up the awesome powers that had been entrusted to him came to represent the prime example of the dictatorship and the qualities that were expected of a dictator and a leader. As Machiavelli puts it: "when there came to be a dictator, he acquired the more fame the sooner he resigned."[38] Cincinnatus's willingness to give up his powers has been quoted often as a sign of virtue, leadership, and trustworthiness by whose measure other leaders were considered. Some, most notably George Washington – who, upon the successful conclusion of the American Revolution, voluntarily laid down his weapons, surrendered his powers, and returned to private station, an action on which King George III is reported to have said that "If he indeed does that, he will be the greatest man in the world" – were compared to Cincinnatus.[39]

The French "state of siege": origins

A second classical model of accommodation is the "state of siege," which is the civil law mechanism for dealing with extreme crisis situations. Originating in France, the basic model of the state of siege has been employed most frequently throughout Latin America (where it is mostly known as *estado de sitio*).[40] After a careful study of the French experience with invoking the state of siege during World War I, Clinton Rossiter concluded that, on the whole, "No instrument of crisis government conform[ed] so closely to the theory of constitutional dictatorship as the famed and widely-imitated state of siege."[41]

---

[37] Rossiter, *Constitutional Dictatorship*, p. 16.   [38] Machiavelli, *Discourses*, p. 186.

[39] Garry Wills, *Cincinnatus: George Washington and the Enlightenment* (Garden City, NY: Doubleday, 1984), p. 23. Washington himself served as the first President General of the Society of the Cincinnati – the oldest military hereditary society in the United States – which, in turn, gave its name to the city of Cincinnati, Ohio.

[40] Narciso J. Lugones, *Leyes de emergencia: decretos de necesidad y urgencia* (Buenos Aires: LaLey, 1992); Diego Valadés, *La dictadura constitucional en América Latina* (Mexico: UNAM, Instituto de Investigaciones Jurídicas, 1974); Pedro Cruz Villalón, *El estado de sitio y la constitución: la constitucionalización de la protección extraordinaria del Estado (1789–1878)* (Madrid: Centro de Estudios Constitucionales, 1980); Eduardo L. Gregorini Clusellas, *Estado de sitio y la armonía en la relación individuo-Estado* (Buenos Aires: Depalma, 1987); Héctor R. Baudón, *Estado de sitio* (Buenos Aires: M. Gleizer, 1939); Brian Loveman, *The Constitution of Tyranny: Regimes of Exception in Spanish America* (Pittsburgh, PA: University of Pittsburgh Press, 1993).

[41] Rossiter, *Constitutional Dictatorship*, p. 129. For a somewhat different opinion see Joseph B. Kelly and George A. Pelletier, Jr., "Theories of Emergency Government" (1966) 11 *South Dakota Law Review* 42 at 46.

The state of siege is a legal crisis institution. As Max Radin notes:

[T]he vital point is that the state of siege is not a condition in which law is temporarily abrogated, and the arbitrary fiat of a "commander" takes its place. It is emphatically a legal institution, expressly authorized by the constitutions and the various bills of rights that succeeded each other in France, and organized under this authority by a specific statute.[42]

The basic idea underlying this institution is that emergencies can be anticipated and counter-measures can be put in place by promulgating comprehensive legal rules ex ante. An elaborate legal framework sets forth and prescribes the measures to be taken in order to control or bring to an end any given emergency.

As originally conceived, the state of siege was thought of in terms of full powers of government conferred upon the military commander of a besieged fortress.[43] However, with the French Revolution the character of this concept shifted from a purely military to a political one. State of siege came to be applicable not only to an area actually besieged by foreign invaders, but also to areas endangered by internal rebellion and disquiet. This expansion of the notion of state of siege created the dichotomy between *état de siege réel* (state of siege in its original sense) and *état de siege fictif* ("constructive" state of siege).

Following the imposition of a state of siege on Paris between June 24 and October 12, 1848 and the introduction of article 106 of the Constitution of the Second Republic – providing that a law would be promulgated for the regulation of the institution of state of siege – a law was passed on August 9, 1849, which sought to regulate such issues as the declaration, termination, and the effects of a state of siege. However, the law of 1849 was thereafter used to impose indiscriminately and arbitrarily a state of siege regime for extended periods of time and on a wide scale. This was especially the case after the Constitution of 1852 conferred on the president the power to declare a state of siege. These practices, combined with Marshal MacMahon's failed attempt to overthrow the government in 1877 and to use the measure of state of siege for that purpose, led to a revision of the legal system.

On April 4, 1878, a new law on state of siege came into effect. While the old law of 1849 continued to regulate the effects of the introduction

---

[42] Max Radin, "Martial Law and the State of Siege" (1942) 30 *California Law Review* 634 at 637.

[43] The following brief overview of the history of that concept in France relies, for the most part, on Rossiter, *Constitutional Dictatorship*, pp. 79–129.

of a state of siege, the new law regulated its organizational and procedural aspects. Under the law of 1878, a state of siege could only be
declared by law and only "in the event of imminent danger resulting
from a foreign war or an armed insurrection." It was reserved for the
most exceptional circumstances. The authority to declare a state of siege
was vested in parliament. Furthermore, only the legislature was competent, at its own discretion, to terminate the state of siege, in whole or
in part, by passing a subsequent law to that effect before the end of
the period for which state of siege had been originally imposed. The
law declaring the state of siege must also set out its own period of
duration after which the state of siege would automatically terminate,
unless prolonged by a subsequent law. The prevailing sense at the time
was that the "period of duration" must be relatively short and clearly
limited. In addition, the law declaring a state of siege was to specify
particular areas of the country to which the state of siege would apply.
When a state of siege has been properly declared all powers concerning the "maintenance of order" are transferred, in their entirety, to the
military. The civilian authorities retain all other functions and powers. Military courts can assume jurisdiction over any offense pertaining
to "the safety of the Republic, against the Constitution, against public
peace and order" whether committed by military personnel or civilians.
In addition, the law of 1849 specified particular powers that the military
enjoyed after a state of siege had been declared, such as powers to conduct searches in private premises, to deport certain persons from areas
put under a state of siege regime, and to prohibit publications and assemblies "which it judges to be of a nature to incite or sustain disorder."
However, it was also specifically stated that citizens continued to enjoy
the full panoply of their constitutional rights to the extent that such
rights were not legitimately suspended under the state of siege. The special powers granted to the military were to be strictly construed with
the aim of preserving and maintaining the constitutionally guaranteed
individual rights.

It is also important to note two elements that were not included in this
system. First, the regime of state of siege did not confer any law-making
powers on the executive. Second, the state of siege did not bring about
any fundamental change in the relationship between the legislature and
the executive, or between the civilian government and the military, the
latter continuing to be subject to the directives and instructions of the
ministers. Even when a state of siege had been declared, the national

legislature continued to maintain all of its ordinary powers of control and supervision over the executive.

The first test of the new system came with the advent of World War I. On August 2, 1914, a presidential decree imposed a state of siege on all of France at a time when parliament was in recess in order to maintain public order as a general mobilization was underway. This presidential order was followed three days later by a law declaring that the state of siege would be in effect "for the duration of the war" and that it might be lifted, in whole or in part, by a decree of the president and reintroduced, where previously lifted by a presidential decree, by another decree. Both the decree and the law of August 1914 deviated substantially from both the language and the spirit of the law of 1878. Applying the state of siege to the whole nation and for the duration of the war, while allowing termination and reintroduction of a state of siege by means of presidential decrees, did not comport with the limitations expressed in the law. In its very first test the legal system concerning the state of siege was substantially modified.

Although the main legal effect of a declaration of a state of siege was to be the complete transfer of police and other powers relevant to the maintenance of peace and order from the civilian to the military authorities, the military and civilian authorities worked side by side during the war. Generally, while the military remained the final arbiter on issues of police and security, it attempted to minimize its intervention with the normal functions otherwise performed by the civilian authorities.

Unlike the case with article 48 of the Weimar Constitution, which is discussed below, state of siege was considered an emergency institution to be applied only in a crisis of a violent nature. The economic exigency of the 1920s did, however, spur an increasing use of executive law-making. This executive legislative power was considered necessary in light of the rapid changes of economic realities and political unwillingness of the parliament to assume responsibility for unpopular economic measures. The executive's legislative power was based, at first, on specific (albeit broad) delegations by the legislature. However, on August 3, 1926, an enabling act was passed upon request of the Poincaré government, granting the government the powers to initiate broad administrative reforms. Although most of the executive decrees issued under that act were later repealed by the French parliament, this signaled the turn to enabling acts as the major emergency mechanism of postwar France. By the end of this period the government substituted the parliament as the major legislative branch. The mechanism of the enabling act, used extensively especially in the period after 1934, was employed to regulate by means of executive decrees an increasing array of issues, not all of great importance, as parliament continued to abdicate its responsibilities. The epitome of that situation came with the administration of Daladier who, from April 1938 until the final days of the Third Republic, governed France through executive decrees in accordance with four enabling acts. The break with the classical concept of the state of siege was manifestly demonstrated by the enabling act of March 19, 1939, which authorized the government to issue decrees with respect to "all measures necessary for the defense of the country," and the act of December 8, 1939, which made executive decree a permanent emergency institution for the duration of hostilities – making the existence of hostilities a sufficient condition for executive law-making without further legislative authorization.

Despite the fact that the various enabling acts promulgated in the inter-war period included explicitly certain limitations on the powers of government, the actual significance of such qualifications was minimal. Decrees issued under an enabling act were deemed, in practice if not in theory, to acquire a status equivalent to statutes. The negative effects of the extensive use of the enabling act were recognized after World War II with the insertion of article 13 to the French Constitution of 1946, stating that "The National Assembly alone may vote the laws. It may not delegate this right."

Martial law in the United Kingdom: origins

Much as the state of siege has been the dominant model of accommodating emergencies in civil law countries, martial law has served as the basic emergency instrument of common law systems. The concept of martial law has always been rather vague, as were its operative and implementation guidelines, leading one scholar to observe that, "At the very outset of a study of martial law one is bewildered by the haze of uncertainty which envelops it. The literature of the subject...is replete with dicta and aphorisms often quoted glibly as universal truths, whereas they are properly limited to some particular significance of the term 'martial law.'"[44]

---

[44] Charles Fairman, *The Law of Martial Rule* (2nd edn, Chicago: Callaghan, 1943), p. 19.

Originally, the term "martial law" was often identified with what is known today as military law, i.e., a system of military justice that is designed to guarantee discipline and order in the army and the governance of the military. One response to the abuses by the Stuart kings, who resorted to the "justice of martial law" as a means to punish civilians, even with death, using irregular procedures,[45] was the adoption by parliament in 1628 of the Petition of Right, under which martial law was to apply only to soldiers. In fact, even with respect to soldiers martial law was only to be applied in wartime.[46] Another context in which "martial law" was invoked early on was that of military rule established and operated during a belligerent occupation by an army over an occupied territory. The Duke of Wellington's statement that military law and martial law were "nothing more nor less than the will of the general" referred, in fact, to such a regime of military government outside England proper.[47]

With time "martial law" came to stand for a vast array of non-statutory, extraordinary powers that are aimed at dealing with special violent crises. The scope of such powers remained a matter of much debate with views on the matter informed by disparate positions regarding the legal source of martial law. Two strands concerning that legal source can be identified: martial law as a matter of the common law right to repel force by force and martial law as an expression of the royal prerogative.

Albert Venn Dicey distinguishes between two meanings of "martial law." First, martial law, "in the proper sense of that term," means the suspension of ordinary law and the temporary government of a country or parts thereof by military tribunals. Ordinary law is suspended and replaced by martial law and every person may be arrested, imprisoned, or executed at the will of a military tribunal without regard to regular legal

---

[45] F.K.M.A. Munim, *Legal Aspects of Martial Law* (Dhaka, Bangladesh: Bangladesh Institute of Law and International Affairs, 1989), p. 12.

[46] Fairman, *Martial Rule*, pp. 9–18; Matthew Hale, *The History of the Common Law of England* (1713) (Littleton, CO: F.B. Rothman, 1987), p. 34; Blackstone, *Commentaries on the Laws of England* (1765) (Chicago: University of Chicago Press, 1979), p. 400; George M. Dennison, "Martial Law: The Development of a Theory of Emergency Powers, 1776–1861" (1974) 18 *American Journal of Legal History* 52.

[47] Charles Fairman, "The Law of Martial Rule and the National Emergency" (1942) 55 *Harvard Law Review* 1253 at 1258–59.

process. This type of martial law "is unknown to the law of England."[48] Its absence "is an unmistakable proof of the permanent supremacy of the law under our constitution."[49] A second meaning of "martial law" connotes the power of the government or of citizens "to maintain public order, at whatever cost of blood or property may be necessary." It is in this latter sense that martial law constitutes part of the law of the land.[50] This "English" martial law has the following characteristics.[51] First, its legal source is the common law right to meet force by force. This right is shared by the government and the citizens. Second, the necessity of the circumstances is the only criterion by which to determine the need for the use of the common law right in any given instance and the extent to which emergency measures may be employed. Any excesses and abuses of power, not necessitated by the exigency, are unlawful and give rise to individual liability of the actors. Since the application of the right to meet force by force is based on the necessities of the particular case, its operation is not dependent on the prior proclamation or declaration of martial law by the government. Third, martial law permits the use of all means necessary for the suppression of an internal rebellion or riot as well as the repelling of an invasion. Yet, it does not allow any punitive measures against the invaders or rioters outside the ordinary legal process. Military tribunals and commanders are not authorized to try such persons or otherwise punish them for their participation in the riot or the invasion. Martial law is of a preventive, rather than a punitive, nature.[52] Finally, the ultimate determination of whether the force employed in a particular case was necessary in the circumstances is in the hands of the courts with the burden of proof on the person who invokes the defense of necessity.

Dicey identifies the legal source of martial law with "the common law right of the Crown and its servants to repel force by force in the case of invasion, insurrection, riot, or generally of any violent resistance to the law. This right, or power, is essential to the very existence of orderly government, and is most assuredly recognised in the most ample manner by the law of England."[53] In Dicey's view martial law does not

---

[48] Albert Venn Dicey, *Introduction to the Study of the Law of the Constitution* (8th edn, Indianapolis, IN: Liberty Classics, 1982), p. 182. Throughout this book we refer to the 8th edition of Dicey's work since that was the last edition that he himself prepared.

[49] Ibid., p. 183.   [50] Ibid., p. 185.   [51] Ibid., pp. 398–409.

[52] Ibid., p. 187. But see Frederick Pollock, "What is Martial Law?" (1902) 70 *Law Quarterly Review* 152 at 156 (martial law can be as much punitive as it is preventive in nature); H. Erle Richards, "Martial Law" (1902) 70 *Law Quarterly Review* 133 at 139.

[53] Dicey, *Law of the Constitution*, p. 183.

confer on the government or its officers any extraordinary powers that they do not possess in ordinary times. Rather it invokes powers that public officials, as well as any citizens, possess, but that are regularly dormant. As Corwin notes,

"Martial law," in other words, is little more than a general term for the operation in situations of public emergency of certain well known principles of the common law – the right of self-defense of the individual, his right – attended by the correlative liability – to abate a nuisance, his right and duty to arrest one whom he knows to have committed a felony or whom he observes in the act of committing a breach of the peace...[54]

Dicey's opinion is shared by other prominent jurists. In *History of the Criminal Law in England*, Sir James Stephen identifies martial law with "the common law right of the Crown and its representatives to repel force by force in the case of invasion or insurrection, and to act against rebels as it might against invaders."[55] Similarly, Frederick Pollock states that the "So-called 'martial law,' as distinct from military law, is an unlucky name for the justification by the common law of acts done by necessity for the defence of the Commonwealth when there is war within the realm."[56] In his opinion, "acts done by necessity for the defence of the Commonwealth" can be analogized to the general right of citizens to defend their own persons and property, and the right to preserve the peace against rioters. As the latter rights are part of the common law and do not require any special prerogative, so it is the case with regard to the former acts.[57] Where Dicey and Pollock disagreed on this matter was the important question of what limitations there were on the exercise of martial law. Whereas Dicey sought to put certain actions, such as the use of military tribunals to punish invaders or rioters outside the ordinary criminal legal system, outside the permissible scope of martial law and to leave the final decision on whether necessity existed and to what extent in the hands of the courts, Pollock's view of martial law was significantly more expansive. Necessity, as determined by government, would make practically all actions taken under martial law legal and immune from subsequent challenges. We come back to that important distinction in chapter 3.

---

[54] Edward S. Corwin, "Martial Law, Yesterday and Today" (1932) 47 *Political Science Quarterly* 95 at 97.

[55] James F.-J. Stephen, *History of the Criminal Law in England* (3 vols., London: Macmillan, 1883), pp. 207–08; Lord MacDermott, "Law and Order in Times of Emergency" (1972) 17 *Juridical Review* 1 at 21.

[56] Pollock, "Martial Law?", 156.   [57] Ibid., p. 153.

This "common law right" approach is challenged by a different theory that focuses on the royal prerogative as the legal source for martial law.[58] The origin of that theory is traced back to the Court of the Constable and Marshal, which operated on the basis of the prerogative.[59] It has been argued that the Crown's prerogative to govern ordinary citizens by martial law in times of war has never been abolished. Several pieces of legislation enacted by parliament, which dealt with disturbances and riots in Ireland, stipulated explicitly that "nothing in this act contained shall be construed to take away, abridge or diminish, the acknowledged prerogative of his Majesty, for the public safety, to resort to the exercise of martial law against open enemies or traitors."[60]

Some have sought to underplay the theoretical debate by pointing out that the two theories are similar in their practical effects.[61] The differences between them do not make a great deal of practical significance. One such difference pertains to the question of liability of persons acting under the authority of martial law.[62] Under Dicey's common law theory such persons are accountable if they use excessive force or other measures that are unnecessary in order to defend peace and order. Under the prerogative theory such persons cannot be made liable unless they acted with malice. Another distinction between the two theories is that under the prerogative theory, the exercise of martial law powers is possible only at the command of the government since the prerogative powers are vested solely in the Crown. Contrary to that, most proponents of the common law theory believe that there is a right of each citizen to meet force by force, regardless of the government's actions and decisions.[63]

---

[58] Egan v. Macready (1921) 1 I.R. 265. For further discussion of the two theories see also W.S. Holdsworth, "Martial Law Historically Considered" (1902) 70 *Law Quarterly Review* 117; Colm Campbell, *Emergency Law in Ireland, 1918–1925* (Oxford: Clarendon Press, 1994), pp. 125–48; David L. Keir and Frederick H. Lawson, *Cases in Constitutional Law* (6th edn, Oxford: Clarendon Press, 1979), pp. 216–30.

[59] For a fuller discussion of the Court of the Constable and the Marshal, see Fairman, *Martial Rule*, pp. 1–6; Munim, *Martial Law*, pp. 7–9; J.V. Capua, "Early History of Martial Law in England from the 14th Century to the Petition of Right" (1977) 36 *Cambridge Law Journal* 152.

[60] 39 Geo. III., c. 11 (1799); 43 Geo. III., c. 117 (1803); 3 Will. IV., c. 4 (1833); Campbell, *Emergency Law in Ireland*, pp. 127–28.

[61] Holdsworth, "Martial Law"; Harold M. Bowman, "Martial Law and the English Constitution" (1916) 15 *Michigan Law Review* 93 at 108.

[62] Holdsworth, "Martial Law," 128–29.

[63] Campbell, *Emergency Law in Ireland*, pp. 145–46.

However, there is a deeper distinction between the two theories. Fundamentally, the common law theory rejects any notion of extraordinary powers that can be implemented in times of war or dire internal strife. The source for powers to be used in such times is a common law right – a right that is part of the ordinary, normal, regular laws of the land – to repel force by force. Emergency powers form an integral part of the ordinary law, although the "user's manual" for their operation specifies a prerequisite factual condition that ought to exist before such powers may be exercised in a specific case. Emergencies are met by utilizing powers that exist within the ordinary legal system without need for new or additional governmental powers. According to the prerogative powers theory the powers that may be used in times of war, rebellion, or riot are truly exceptional. They are not part of the regular laws of the realm. Albeit lawful, such powers are unusual and reside outside the ordinary legal system.[64] Emergency powers operate in a legal sphere different and distinct from that occupied by the ordinary legal system. We come back to evaluate this significant distinction between the competing accounts of the legal sources of martial law in the next chapter.

Constitutional accommodation

Emergency provisions in constitutional documents

Niccolò Machiavelli regards the institution of the Roman dictatorship as one of the major contributors to Rome's greatness. He argues that "One sees that while the dictator was appointed according to public orders, and not by his own authority, he always did good to the city."[65] He rejects the contention that the existence of the dictatorship facilitated the demise of the republic, and enabled rulers such as Julius Caesar to wield tyrannical powers over Rome and its citizens. According to Machiavelli, the fault was not in the dictatorship as such, but rather lay in its uses by rulers who deviated from the real meaning of the institution.

His analysis of the Roman dictatorship led Machiavelli to conclude that the ideal republic ought to provide for emergency institutions ex ante and to structure those around the contours of the Roman dictatorship. In times of extraordinary threats and dangers normal decision-making processes may prove to be too slow to deal effectively with the

---

[64] Bowman, "Martial Law," 106–07.
[65] Machiavelli, *Discourses*, p. 74.

impending crisis: "their remedies are very dangerous when they have to remedy a thing that time does not wait for."[66] Therefore,

[R]epublics should have a like mode [to the dictatorship] among their orders...For when a like mode is lacking in a republic, it is necessary either that it be ruined by observing the orders or that it break them so as not to be ruined. In a republic, one would not wish anything ever to happen that has to be governed with extraordinary modes. For although the extraordinary mode may do good then, nonetheless the example does ill; for if one sets up a habit of breaking the orders for the sake of good, then later, under that coloring, they are broken for ill. *So a republic will never be perfect unless it has provided for everything with its laws and has established a remedy for every accident and given the mode to govern it.* So, concluding, I say that those republics that in urgent dangers do not take refuge either in the dictator or in similar authorities will always come to ruin in grave accidents.[67]

The ordinary constitutional system of the republic ought to accommodate and incorporate emergency powers fashioned after the model of the Roman dictatorship. It must supply legal answers to every conceivable contingency. Hence, "that republic can be called happy whose lot is to get one man so prudent that he gives it laws ordered so that it can live securely under them without needing to correct them."[68] If such a comprehensive array of emergency powers is not made available to the government under the regular system of laws then either the republic will be unable to defend itself against its enemies, or, more likely, government will resort to extraordinary means that violate the law in order to do whatever it deems necessary for the survival of the republic.

In *Constitutional Dictatorship*, Clinton Rossiter adopts a similar approach. He concludes the discussion of the Roman dictatorship by pointing to the most important lesson, in his opinion, that the Roman experience teaches us: "in a free state blessed by a high constitutional morality and led by men of good sense and good will, the forms of despotism can be successfully used in time of crisis to preserve and advance the cause of liberty."[69] In his view, the Roman dictatorship, despite its deficiencies, demonstrates that a temporary dictatorship, formed within the boundaries of certain constitutional limitations and directed at maintaining the existing constitutional order, is a feasible means by which a free and democratic society may preserve itself and its constitutional order in extreme exigencies.

---

[66] Ibid., p. 74.   [67] Ibid., pp. 74–75 (emphasis added).
[68] Ibid., p. 10.   [69] Rossiter, *Constitutional Dictatorship*, p. 28.

Today, different constitutional systems differ greatly in their treatment of the subject matter of emergency powers. Following the example of the Roman dictatorship, many modern constitutions contain explicit, frequently detailed, emergency provisions.[70] Such constitutional arrangements tend to follow the general contours of the dictatorship, if not its specific mechanisms. This section examines the emergency arrangements in national constitutions. We leave the discussion of the international regime of emergencies to chapter 5.

While explicit constitutional reference to emergencies is common, it is by no means universal. The constitutions of the United States, Japan,[71] and Belgium,[72] for example, are almost entirely devoid of references to states of emergency and to emergency powers. The American Constitution only refers indirectly to emergencies in article I, section 8, clause 15 which vests the power in Congress "To provide for calling forth the Militia to execute the Laws of the Union, suppress Insurrections and repel Invasions," and article I, section 9, clause 2 which provides that "The Privilege of the Writ of Habeas Corpus shall not be suspended, unless when in Cases of Rebellion or Invasion the public Safety may require it." Although certain other clauses mention terms such as "war," or "time of war," none attaches special powers to any branch of government in the event of such exigencies.[73] However, this omission of

---

[70] See, e.g., European Commission for Democracy through Law, *Emergency Powers* (Strasburg: Council of Europe Pub., 1995), pp. 4–5; John Ferejohn and Pasquale Pasquino, "The Law of the Exception: A Typology of Emergency Powers" (2004) 2 *International Journal of Constitutional Law* 210 at 213.

[71] The Democratic Constitution of Japan (May 3, 1947), which is based on the American constitutional model and the Charter of the United Nations, does not contain emergency provisions or any provisions dealing with acts of war or martial law. However, article 71 of the Japanese Police Law authorizes the prime minister to declare a state of "national emergency" and assume direct control over Japan's police. See L.W. Beer, "Peace in Theory and Practice under Article 9 of Japan's Constitution" (1998) 81 *Marquette Law Review* 815 at 826.

[72] While the Coordinated Constitution of Belgium is silent on the issue of emergency, it does provide that "The constitution may not be wholly or partially suspended" (article 187) as well as state that no constitutional revision may be undertaken or pursued "during times of war or when the Houses are prevented from meeting freely on federal territory" (article 196).

[73] United States Constitution, art. I, sec. 8, cl. 11 (Congress's power to declare war); art. III. sec. 3, cl. 1 (the crime of treason); Third Amendment (prohibition on the quartering of soldiers in private premises); Fifth Amendment (exemption from the requirement of Grand Jury). Other provisions of the constitution concern the armed forces (including Congress's power to raise and support armies, and the president's commander in chief power). Others yet may bear an indirect influence on the issue at hand. Henry P. Monaghan, "The Protective Power of the Presidency" (1993) 93 *Columbia Law Review* 1 at

emergency provisions is limited to the federal level. Unlike the federal constitution, many state constitutions contain explicit emergency provisions.[74]

After examining the measures that had been taken by different European countries against the tide of Fascism and Nazism in the 1930s, Karl Loewenstein suggested a mix of specific and general measures for liberal democracies against such challenges.[75] His basic premise was that the enemies of democracy would abuse the democratic guarantees of the rule of law and hide behind the protection of basic individual rights to promote their cause.[76] Thus, the normal mechanisms of liberal democracy serve as a Trojan horse that is used to destroy the democratic order from within. One of the general mechanisms that Loewenstein proposed was that of "militant democracy." He advocated the abandonment of the "exaggerated formalism of the rule of law," and argued that liberal-democratic order was designed for normal times.[77] In circumstances such as those facing the countries of Europe in the 1930s it was imperative to cast restrictions over democratic fundamentals in order to preserve these very fundamentals from the Fascist onslaught. In times of crisis of that type rigid democratic fundamentalism ought to give way to democratic militancy. The most important attitude of the militant democracy is "the will and the spirit of both the government and the people in democracies to survive."[78] In that respect, "The statute-book is only a subsidiary expedient of the militant will for self-preservation."[79] Democracy must assume autocratic methods to survive and to ensure its preservation. As Loewenstein suggests:

Where fundamental rights are institutionalized, their temporary suspension is justified. When the ordinary channels of legislation are blocked by obstruction and sabotage, the democratic state uses the emergency powers of enabling legislation which implicitly, if not explicitly, are involved in the very notion of

---

32–38; George Winterton. "The Concept of Extra-Constitutional Executive Power in Domestic Affairs" (1979) 7 *Hastings Constitutional Law Quarterly* 1 at 24–35.

[74] Oren Gross, "Providing for the Unexpected: Constitutional Emergency Provisions" (2003) 33 *Israel Yearbook on Human Rights* 13 at 20–21, n. 28.

[75] Karl Loewenstein, "Militant Democracy and Fundamental Rights" (1937) 31 *American Political Science Review* 417 and 638 at 424, 426–31, 638–56; Karl Loewenstein, "Legislative Control of Political Extremism in European Democracies" (1938) 38 *Columbia Law Review* 591 and 725.

[76] Loewenstein, "Militant Democracy," 423–28.

[77] Ibid., p. 432.   [78] Loewenstein, "Legislative Control," 774.

[79] Loewenstein, "Militant Democracy," 657.

government. Government is intended for governing...If democracy believes in the superiority of its absolute values over the opportunistic platitudes of fascism...every possible effort must be made to rescue it, even at the risk and cost of violating fundamental principles.[80]

Loewenstein contrasts the crucial question of whether a democracy could curtail fundamental individual rights and notions of equality in order to fight its attackers from right and left without, in the process, destroying the very basis of the democratic order with "legalistic self-complacency and suicidal lethargy."[81] For him the process of fighting Fascism is one in which democracy looks for its own vulnerable points and seeks to cover them with armor. Loewenstein accepts, at least implicitly, the claim that by doing so democracy is fundamentally changing its face and character. Indeed, in the long run democracy needs to be redefined as "disciplined" or even "authoritarian" and become "the application of disciplined authority, by liberal-minded men, for the ultimate ends of liberal government: human dignity and freedom."[82]

After the end of World War II, the concept of "militant democracy" became one of the cornerstones of the postwar constitutional order of the Federal Republic of Germany. The principle of militant democracy (*Streitbare Demokratie*) came to stand for the defense of the core values of the German polity and of its "free democratic basic order."[83] As one student of the German constitutional system put it, "the Basic Law joins the protection of the *Rechtsstaat* to the principle that the [sic] democracy is not helpless in defending itself against parties or political movements bent on using the Constitution to undermine or destroy it."[84] Thus, article 18 of the German Basic Law provides for the forfeiture of rights from persons who abuse them to combat the free democratic basic order, and article 21(2) of the Basic Law complements it by allowing the declaration as unconstitutional of any political party that has similar goals. Under article 21(2), the German Federal Constitutional Court declared unconstitutional two parties, the Socialist Reich Party and the Communist

---

[80] Ibid., p. 432.   [81] Ibid., p. 431.

[82] Ibid., p. 658; Loewenstein, "Legislative Control," 774.

[83] Donald P. Kommers, *The Constitutional Jurisprudence of the Federal Republic of Germany* (2nd edn, Durham, NC: Duke University Press, 1997), pp. 37–38; David P. Currie, *The Constitution of the Federal Republic of Germany* (Chicago: The University of Chicago Press, 1994), p. 213.

[84] Kommers, *Constitutional Jurisprudence*, p. 38.

Party.[85] Similar concepts appeared also in the jurisprudence of other national[86] and regional courts.[87]

As noted in the introduction, the concept of "emergency" is not amenable to easy a priori definition (if at all). How, then, do drafters

[85] The Socialist Reich Party Case, 2 BVerGE 1 (1952), excerpts reprinted in Kommers, *Constitutional Jurisprudence*, p. 218; The Communist Party Case, 5 BVerGE 85 (1956), excerpts reprinted in Kommers, *Constitutional Jurisprudence*, p. 222. See also The Radical Groups Case, excerpts reprinted in Kommers, *Constitutional Jurisprudence*, p. 224; Ronald J. Krotoszynski, Jr., "A Comparative Perspective on the First Amendment: Free Speech, Militant Democracy, and the Primacy of Dignity as a Preferred Constitutional Value in Germany" (2004) 78 *Tulane Law Review* 1549.

[86] E.A. 1/65, Yardor v. Chairman of Cent. Elections Comm. for Sixth Knesset, 19(3) P.D. 365 addressed the question of whether a party that denied the existence of the State of Israel could be proscribed from participating in the elections for the Israeli Knesset. At the time, the relevant law did not include any express provision on the matter. Writing for the majority, Justice Joel Sussman stated: "The said basic supra-legal rules are merely, in this matter, the right of the organized society in the State to protect itself. Whether we call these rules 'natural law' to indicate that they are the law of the State by virtue of its nature ... or whether we call them by another name, I agree with the opinion that the experience of life requires us not to repeat the same mistake to which we were all witness. The German Constitutional Court, dealing with the legality of a political party, spoke of 'militant democracy' which does not open its gates to subversive activities disguised as legitimate parliamentary activity. For my part, concerning the State of Israel, I am willing to be content with a 'defensive democracy,' and we have tools to protect the existence of the State, even if we do not find them set out in the Elections Law." Ibid., p. 390. See also E.A. 2/84, Neiman v. Chairman of Cent. Elections Comm. for Eleventh Knesset, 39(2) P.D. 225; Claude Klein, "The Defence of the State and the Democratic Regime in the Supreme Court" (1985) 20 *Israel Law Review* 397; Ariel Bendor, "The Right of Parties to Participate in Elections to the Knesset" (1988) 18 *Mishpatim* 269; Ruth Gavison, "Twenty Years to the Yeredor Ruling – The Right to be Elected and the Lessons of History" in Ruth Gavison and Mordechai Kremnitzer (eds.), *Essays in Honour of Shimon Agranat* (Jerusalem: Graf Press, 1986), p. 145; Shlomo Guberman, "Israel's Supra-Constitution" (1967) 2 *Israel Law Review* 455.
      See also Gregory H. Fox and Georg Nolte, "Intolerant Democracies" (1995) 36 *Harvard International Law Journal* 1; Martti Koskenniemi, " 'Intolerant Democracies': A Reaction" (1996) 37 *Harvard International Law Journal* 231; Brad R. Roth, "Democratic Intolerance: Observations on Fox and Nolte" (1996) 37 *Harvard International Law Journal* 235; Gregory H. Fox and Georg Nolte, "Fox and Nolte Response" (1996) 37 *Harvard International Law Journal* 238; Dan Gordon, "Limits on Extremist Political Parties: A Comparison of Israeli Jurisprudence with that of the United States and West Germany" (1987) 10 *Hastings International and Comparative Law Review* 347.

[87] Article 17 of the European Convention for the Protection of Human Rights and Fundamental Freedoms, Nov. 4, 1950, 312 U.N.T.S. 221, provides that "Nothing in this Convention may be interpreted as implying for any State, group or person any right to engage in any activity or perform any act aimed at the destruction of any of the rights and freedoms set forth herein or at their limitation to a greater extent than is provided for in the Convention." See, for example, Refah Partisi v. Turkey (2003) 37 E.H.R.R. 1; Paul Harvey, "Militant Democracy and the European Convention on Human Rights" (2004) 29 *European Law Review* 407.

of national constitutions respond to this difficulty? Many national constitutions differentiate between several types of emergencies, basing the distinctions between the various categories of emergencies on the factual circumstances under which a declaration of a particular type of emergency regime may be constitutionally permissible. Such classifications affect not only the methods by which a particular emergency may be declared and the duration for which such proclamation may hold valid, but also matters such as the nature, extent, and scope of governmental emergency powers, and the possibility of derogating from constitutional rights and safeguards (as discussed below).

Some constitutions establish a dual structure of emergency regimes. Under the constitutions of the Netherlands and Portugal, for example, there are two possible types of emergencies. The Dutch Constitution authorizes the declaration of a "state of war" and a "state of emergency."[88] The Constitution of Portugal distinguishes between a "state of emergency" and a "state of siege." Thus, a state of siege or a state of emergency may be declared "in cases of actual or imminent aggression by foreign forces, serious threat to or disturbance of the democratic constitutional order or public calamity" (article 19(2)), but a "state of emergency is declared where the circumstances mentioned in the preceding paragraph are less serious" (article 19(3)).[89] Similar dual structures can also be found in the constitutions of many former Communist countries such as Belarus, Estonia, Lithuania, Romania, Hungary, Slovakia, Slovenia, and Russia.[90] Thus, for example, article 100(1)(18) of the Constitution of the Republic of Belarus provides that a "state of emergency" may be introduced "in the event of a natural disaster, a catastrophe, or

---

[88] A "state of war" may be declared in accordance with article 96 of the constitution; a "state of emergency" may be declared under the provisions of article 103. While the constitution includes no definition of the former type of emergency, it provides that the latter will be defined by an act of parliament.

[89] Articles 19 and 138 of the Portuguese Constitution.

[90] Articles 87(8), 129 (state of emergency) and 128 (state of war) of the Constitution of Estonia; articles 142, 84(16) (martial law), and 144 (state of emergency) of the Lithuanian Constitution; article 93 (state of siege or state of emergency) of the Constitution of Romania; article 19(3)(h) (state of national crisis) and 19(3)(i) (state of emergency) of the Constitution of the Republic of Hungary; article 102(k) (martial law) and 102(l) (state of emergency) of the Slovak Constitution; article 92 (war and state of emergency) of the Constitution of Slovenia; articles 56(2), 87, and 88 (state of emergency and martial law) of the Russian Constitution. See also Venelin I. Ganev, "Emergency Powers and the New East European Constitutions" (1997) 45 *American Journal of Comparative Law* 585.

unrest involving violence or the threat of violence on the part of a group of persons or organizations that endangers people's lives and health or jeopardizes the territorial integrity and existence of the State." Article 100(1)(25) provides that a "state of martial law" may be imposed "in the event of a military threat or attack."

Many of the constitutions of Latin and South America draw distinctions between a multiplicity of states of exception (*estado de excepción*), allocating different emergency powers to government according to the particular type of exigency at hand. No fewer than nine different states of exception can be identified in those constitutions. These include, among others, the state of siege (*estado de sitio*), state of emergency (*estado de emergencia*), state of alarm (*estado de alarma*), state of prevention (*estado de prevención*), state of defense (*estado de defensa*), and state of war (*estado de guerra*).[91] It is usual to find several distinct states of exception in the same constitutional document. Thus, for example, article 139 of the Constitution of Guatemala lists five distinct situations of emergency: state of prevention; state of alarm; state of public catastrophe (*estado de calamidad publica*); state of siege; and state of war.[92] The mechanism used to distinguish between the various situations is based on general descriptions of factual circumstances that may lead to invoking each particular state of exception. Such factual circumstances include, inter alia, external war, breach of the peace and the public order, economic exigencies, natural disasters, and threats of disturbances.[93] In addition, each constitution explicitly details the legal results that arise out of the declaration of each state of exception by way of suspension of individual rights (*suspensión de garantias*) and the vesting of extraordinary powers in the executive branch of government.

[91] See, e.g., article 111 of the Constitution of Bolivia; article 137 of the Constitution of Peru; article 23 of the Argentine Constitution; article 37(8) of the Constitution of the Dominican Republic; articles 47 and 51 of the Constitution of Panama; article 139 of the Constitution of Guatemala; article 238(7) of the Constitution of Paraguay; article 136 of the Constitution of Brazil. See also Valadés, *La dictadura constitucional en América Latina*.

[92] See also articles 21(v), 84(ix) and (x), and 136–39 of the Brazilian Constitution; articles 40 and 41 of the Constitution of Chile; articles 212, 213, and 215 of the Constitution of Colombia.

[93] See, e.g., article 40(1) of the Constitution of Chile; article 138 of the Constitution of Guatemala; article 185 of the Constitution of Nicaragua; articles 37(7) and 55(7) of the Constitution of the Dominican Republic; articles 136 and 137 of the Brazilian Constitution; article 202(13) of the Constitution of Paraguay.

Multilevel constitutional arrangements can also be found in Germany as well as some former Communist countries.[94] Multilevel arrangements can also be found in countries such as Canada and Spain. Following the May 1968 constitutional amendments that ushered in the "emergency constitution,"[95] the German Basic Law now distinguishes between "internal emergency" (*Innerer Notstand*), a "state of tension" (*Spannungsfall*), and a "state of defense" (*Verteidigungsfall*).[96] An internal emergency occurs in situations when it is necessary "to avert an imminent danger to the existence or free democratic basic order of the Federation or of a Land". A state of defense may be declared when "the federal territory is under attack by armed force or imminently threatened by such an attack." On the other hand, the circumstances that may give rise to a state of tension are not defined in the Basic Law itself.[97] In addition, the Basic Law also deals with situations of "natural disaster or a particularly serious accident" under which police units from several Länder as well as the Federal Border Guard and the armed forces may be called in to assist in combating the threat.[98]

In Canada, emergency doctrine finds its constitutional anchor in the preamble to section 91 of the Constitution Act of 1867, which permits the making of laws "for the Peace, Order and Good Government."[99] The Emergencies Act of 1988 authorizes the federal government to declare four different types of emergencies: "public welfare emergency" may be declared in circumstances of natural disasters; "public order emergency" may be invoked when serious threats to the security of Canada emerge; "international emergency" deals with situations involving acts of intimidation toward Canada or other countries; finally, "war emergency" may be proclaimed in case of real or imminent armed conflict

---

[94] See, e.g., chapter XI of the Polish Constitution of 1997, which authorizes the declaration of three types of states of exception: martial law, state of emergency, and state of natural disaster.

[95] John E. Finn, *Constitutions in Crisis: Political Violence and the Rule of Law* (New York: Oxford University Press, 1991), pp. 196–200.

[96] Articles 91 and 87a(4) of the German Basic Law tackle the issue of internal emergency, articles 12a(5)–(6) and 80a refer to the state of tension, and articles 115a–115l deal with the state of defense. Note, "Recent Emergency Legislation in West Germany" (1969) 82 *Harvard Law Review* 1704.

[97] Note, "Recent Emergency Legislation," 1714.

[98] Article 35(2) and (3) of the German Basic Law.

[99] Peter W. Hogg, *Constitutional Law of Canada* (4th edn, 2 vols., Scarborough, Ontario: Carswell, 1997), vol. I, ch. 17.

involving Canada or any of its allies.[100] Under the act the initial duration of each proclaimed emergency varies (from 30 days in the case of
"public order" up to 120 days when "war emergency" is concerned) and
so do the nature and scope of permissible emergency powers granted to
the federal government.

The Spanish Constitution identifies three distinct scenarios involving a "state of alarm" (*estado de alarma*), "state of emergency" (*estado
de excepción*), and "state of siege" (*estado de sitio*).[101] Article 116 of the
constitution deals with the authority to declare each of the three types
of emergency regimes, outlines general procedures for such declaration,
and prescribes the initial duration for which a declaration may apply.
In addition, article 86 provides for governmental "provisional legislative decisions" in the form of decree-laws in case of "extraordinary and
urgent necessity." The constitution does not define the three classes of
emergencies but rather leaves it for an organic law to regulate them
as well as the corresponding powers and limitations thereon. Organic
Law 4/1981 defines the different circumstances under which each type of
emergency regime may be exercised. Thus, the "state of alarm" arises in
the context of natural disasters and calamities or in periods of scarcity
of basic commodities and essential services. A "state of emergency" may
be declared when "the free exercise of the citizen's rights and liberties
or the normal functions of democratic institutions, public services essential for the community or any other aspect of public order are altered
to the extent that the ordinary powers prove insufficient to reestablish
or maintain them." Finally, a "state of siege" may be proclaimed "in
the event of an insurrection or threat of insurrection or an act of force
against the sovereignty or independence, territorial integrity and constitutional order of Spain which cannot otherwise be resolved."[102]

This pattern of separating several types of emergency regimes is not
universally followed. The Constitution of South Africa, for example, recognizes only one type of emergency regime, following a declaration of
a state of emergency. However, such a state of emergency may be invoked in a range of cases when "the life of the nation is threatened by

[100] Emergencies Act 1988, S.C. 1988, c. 29, s. 80. See also Peter Rosenthal, "The New
Emergencies Act: Four Times the War Measures Act" (1991) 20 *Manitoba Law Journal*
563 at 565–73; Eliot Tenofsky, "The War Measures and Emergency Acts" (1989) 19
American Review of Canadian Studies 293.

[101] Pedro Cruz Villalón, *Estados excepcionales y suspensión de garantías* (Madrid: Tecnos,
1984).

[102] European Commission for Democracy through Law, *Emergency Powers*, pp. 7–8.

war, invasion, general insurrection, disorder, natural disaster or other public emergency."[103] Similarly, the Israeli Basic Law: The government recognizes only the possibility of declaring a state of emergency. However, unlike the South African Constitution, this Basic Law neither defines "state of emergency" nor purports to describe the circumstances that may legitimately give rise to such a declaration. All it does is recognize the possibility of declaring a state of emergency without setting out substantive guidelines as to when such a declaration may be appropriate.[104]

Dual-level and multilevel classifications of emergencies seem to be generally aimed at tailoring and, at the same time, limiting the powers made available to government in connection with a particular type of emergency. Different types of exigencies call for different government powers. It may also be that the constitutional classification may establish a hierarchical order of possible proclamations of emergencies. While each proclamation can be made in the context of a broad panoply of dangers and threats, the powers made available to the executive increase, and the protection of individual rights and civil liberties decrease, as we step up the emergency ladder.[105]

However, we should note that classifying and categorizing emergencies is not without its problems (even assuming that such classification and categorization are viable projects). Review of the existing classifications of states of emergency reveals a substantial degree of vagueness, ambiguity, and overlap between the different categories as may be expected in light of the definitional difficulties which inhere in the term "emergency." Some of the key terms used in this context, such as "danger" and "imminent threat," are broad enough to make the choice between the possible categories mostly a political issue. Creating a sliding scale of emergency regimes may encourage a government to resort to some type of emergency regime. Some emergency regimes may be perceived as "not so serious" as, for example, a state of war. A declaration of such "low-level" state of emergency may be more readily accepted by

---

[103] Article 37(1)(a) of the Constitution of South Africa. See also articles 180–82 of the Constitution of Ecuador; article 29 of the Constitution of Mexico.

[104] Articles 38 and 39 of Basic Law: The Government, 1780 S.H. 158 (2001). See also Baruch Bracha, "Checks and Balances in a Protracted State of Emergency – The Case of Israel" (2003) 33 *Israel Yearbook on Human Rights* 123; Gross, "Providing for the Unexpected," 13–16.

[105] See, e.g., article 139 of the Constitution of Guatemala; article 19 of the Constitution of Portugal.

legislatures, courts, and the general public.[106] Considering certain types
of emergencies to be "not so serious" may undermine the basic notion
that emergencies correspond to exceptional situations, relating especially to the exceptional nature of the threat to the community. This
can also act to condition people to live with some type of emergency.
Once some kind of emergency regime becomes accepted as part of the
normal way of life, it will be easier for government to "upgrade" to a
higher-level emergency regime. On the other hand, when any state of
emergency potentially makes available to government the full panoply
of permissible emergency powers, including the most draconian ones,
the public may be more cautious in accepting as valid a declaration of
emergency in suspect circumstances. In a similar vein, it has been argued
that the existence of legislative provisions that authorize the exercise
of special or extraordinary powers by the executive during a national
emergency weighs in favor of Congress's issuing official declarations of
war as this may shed light on the domestic costs of war resulting from
the expansive executive powers available on the domestic front in times
of war or national emergency.[107] This pronounced effect of "crossing
the threshold" may be absent when a scale of emergencies is offered.[108]
Crossing the threshold in the first place may be made easier. And once
the government crosses that threshold it becomes easier to continue and
resort to claims of emergency.

Constitutional necessity

The previous section discussed the incorporation into constitutional documents of explicit provisions that deal with emergencies. But what if
such explicit provisions are lacking (as in the case of the Constitution
of the United States) or seem to be inadequate in the face of particular
exigencies? One move that attempts to augment the emergency powers that are available to government while doing so within the general

[106] Rosenthal, "The New Emergencies Act," 590–92; Youngstown Sheet & Tube Co. v.
Sawyer, 343 US 579 at 650 (1952) (Jackson J., concurring).
[107] J. Gregory Sidak, "To Declare War" (1991) 41 *Duke Law Journal* 27; J. Gregory Sidak,
"War, Liberty, and Enemy Aliens" (1992) 67 *New York University Law Review* 1402 at
1424–31; Harold H. Koh, "The Coase Theorem and the War Power: A Response" (1991)
41 *Duke Law Journal* 122; J. Gregory Sidak, "The Inverse Coase Theorem and
Declarations of War" (1991) 41 *Duke Law Journal* 325.
[108] Oren Gross, "Cutting Down Trees: Law Making under the Shadow of Great
Calamities" in Ronald J. Daniels, Patrick Macklem, and Kent Roach (eds.), *The Security
of Freedom: Essays on Canada's Antiterrorism Bill* (Toronto: University of Toronto Press,
2001), p. 39.

constitutional structure is to turn to the principle of necessity either as an autonomous source of law or as a meta-rule of constitutional construction. Under both views necessity operates as a constitutional principle that can make legal that which otherwise would have been unlawful and, perhaps, unconstitutional. Necessity either creates new constitutional law including by way of deviating from, and conflicting with, existing constitutional norms, or it shapes constitutional construction in novel ways.

Before looking further at the two approaches noted above, it is important to distinguish them both from a range of alternative views that regard necessity as operating mostly on a political level and somewhat further removed from, or even operating outside, the constitutional sphere. One such alternative approach is to regard necessity in accordance with the maxim *necessitas non habet legem* (necessity knows no law) in the sense that in times of great peril the question as to whether certain actions that are deemed necessary for the safety and existence of the nation are legal and constitutional is, bluntly put, immaterial. Another approach would view necessity not as an autonomous source of law, but rather as a mechanism for temporal suspension of normal legal rules without, at the same time, replacing those suspended norms with new ones. Yet another alternative is to consider necessity as neither supplying an independent source of law nor allowing suspension of legal provisions and rules, but rather as offering the possibility of ex post excuse or justification of particular actions without, by that fact alone, changing the legal (or indeed extra-legal) character of such actions. These three alternative views treat necessity, to varying degrees, as extra-legal and perhaps even extra-constitutional. We come back to look at these issues in chapter 3. For now we focus on the first two approaches.

President Lincoln's actions during the American Civil War, especially in the first twelve weeks between the bombardment of Fort Sumter, on April 12, 1861, and the convening of Congress on July 4, 1861, have been the subject of much study and debate. During this period Lincoln demonstrated perhaps the most awesome display of executive power in American history. Acting as the protector of the Union, Lincoln called forth the militia, imposed a blockade on the ports of the Southern states, paid out unappropriated funds to private persons unauthorized to receive such payments, authorized the commander of the army to suspend the writ of habeas corpus in the area between the cities of Philadelphia and Washington (and, later on, also in the area between Washington and New York), and enlarged the army and navy beyond the limits set by

Congress.[109] By the time Congress did convene, it was faced with extensive *faits accomplis*, leaving it no real choice but to ratify them and give its blessing to the president. Whereas some of these measures could be construed as falling within the constitutional or statutorily delegated presidential powers, others were more questionable. For example, the president's unilateral enlargement of the armed forces violated an express constitutional provision vesting in Congress the power to "raise and support Armies" and to "provide and maintain a Navy."[110] Similarly, the power to suspend the writ of habeas corpus was generally thought at the time to belong exclusively to Congress. The Emancipation Proclamation, which as Dan Farber notes, "With the stroke of a pen (backed, admittedly, by Union guns)...wiped out property rights worth many millions of dollars," was also deemed unconstitutional when made.[111] One possible legal explanation of Lincoln's actions considers such actions to be within the boundaries of the US Constitution under the doctrine of the "war powers" of the federal government. As Lincoln himself argued:

> It became necessary for me to choose whether, using only the existing means, agencies, and processes which Congress had provided, I should let the Government fall at once into ruin or whether, availing myself of *the broader powers conferred by the Constitution in cases of insurrection*, I would make an effort to save it, with all its blessings, for the present age and for posterity.[112]

Lincoln's wartime presidency ushered in a theory of crisis government based on the concept of inherent presidential powers.[113] Since Lincoln's

---

[109] Mark E. Neely, Jr., *The Fate of Liberty: Abraham Lincoln and Civil Liberties* (New York: Oxford University Press, 1991), pp. 3–31; Rossiter, *Constitutional Dictatorship*, pp. 224–27.

[110] US Const. art. I, sec. 8, cls. 12–13.

[111] Daniel A. Farber, *Lincoln's Constitution: The Nation, the President, and the Courts in a Time of Crisis* (Chicago: University of Chicago Press, 2003), p. 171. Farber argues that the proclamation was justified as a war measure under the laws of war because it fell within the president's role as a military leader, ibid., pp. 171–76, and was "relatively unproblematic in terms of the separation of powers," ibid., p. 176; see also Sanford Levinson, "The David C. Baum Memorial Lecture: Was the Emancipation Proclamation Constitutional? Do We/Should We Care What the Answer Is?" (2001) *University of Illinois Law Review* 1135.

[112] James D. Richardson (ed.), *A Compilation of the Messages and Papers of the Presidents* (New York: Bureau of National Literature, 1897), vol. VI, p. 78 (emphasis added).

[113] See, e.g., William C. Banks and Alejandro D. Carrió, "Presidential Systems in Stress: Emergency Powers in Argentina and the United States" (1993) 15 *Michigan Journal of International Law* 1 at 42–46: Monaghan, "The Protective Power," 1; David Gray Adler, "The Steel Seizure Case and Inherent Presidential Power" (2002) 19 *Constitutional Commentary* 155.

presidency, arguments put forward in support of an executive's resort to emergency powers have invariably revolved around the claim that the president enjoys a wide range of constitutionally inherent powers, including emergency powers, and therefore acts legally and constitutionally, rather than outside the constitutional and legal framework.[114] Arguments invoking presidential inherent powers have been heard mostly, albeit not exclusively, in the context of foreign affairs and national security, separating those from ordinary, domestic matters. We come back to examine those distinctions in chapter 4.

During World War I, the French cabinet enjoyed increased powers. Although not formally enjoying any legislative powers under the state of siege regime, instructions issued by the various ministries gained a status similar to that of parliamentary legislation. In addition, the cabinet acquired substantial powers of emergency legislation delegated to it by parliament, either explicitly or tacitly, for specific purposes. Finally, certain decrees promulgated by the cabinet purported to derogate from previously enacted parliamentary laws or to introduce certain measures that otherwise would need to be introduced by way of a statute, without any constitutional or statutory provisions legitimating such sweeping suspensions. This type of emergency executive legislation was claimed to be based on the concept of "war powers" (*pouvoirs de guerre*) or the doctrine of necessity.[115] Protests against this type of cabinet action led to a governmental demand for enabling acts delegating to the government sweeping powers to promulgate emergency legislation. Such demands were stubbornly rejected by the legislature until 1918 when broad powers were granted to the Clemenceau government. In the same year, the *Conseil d'État* recognized the inherent powers of the executive branch of government to make such decisions and take such actions as were considered by it necessary to fight successfully a pending emergency situation. According to this ruling, such executive powers extended to actions derogating from statutory provisions.[116]

The related view that necessity may serve as a principle of constitutional interpretation was recently put forward by Michael Paulsen.

---

[114] See, e.g., Comm. on Gov't Operations, 85th Cong., *Executive Orders and Proclamations: A Study of a Use of Presidential Powers* (Comm. Print, 1957), p. 28; Harold Hongju Koh, *The National Security Constitution: Sharing Power after the Iran–Contra Affair* (New Haven, CT: Yale University Press, 1990); Youngstown, 343 US 579 at 646–54 (Jackson J., concurring).

[115] Rossiter, *Constitutional Dictatorship*, pp. 112–13.

[116] John Bell, *French Constitutional Law* (New York: Oxford University Press, 1992), p. 84.

He argues that, as a matter of US constitutional law, necessity serves as a meta-rule of constitutional construction and, in fact, as a principle of constitutional priority.[117] "The Constitution itself," he suggests, "embraces an overriding principle of constitutional and national self-preservation that operates as a meta-rule of construction for the document's specific provisions and that may even, in cases of extraordinary necessity, trump specific constitutional requirements."[118] In his opinion, the constitution vests the primary duty for making decisions about constitutional interpretation, priority, and necessity in the president via the presidential Oath Clause, according to which the president swears to "preserve, protect and defend the Constitution of the United States."[119] This duty entails the obligation to preserve the nation whose constitution it is, which, in turn, not only informs all constitutional arrangements, but in fact, is superior to them.[120] In that respect necessity is not only part of the constitutional order. It is "the first and originary source of law."[121] No specific constitutional provision may be interpreted in a way that would undermine the preservation of the nation.

Under this principle of construction measures that may have been deemed unconstitutional in ordinary times will become constitutional if they are indispensable for the preservation of the nation. In those circumstances, therefore, necessity operates as an independent source of constitutional law, making legal and constitutional that which otherwise would not have been so. As Lincoln himself wrote on one occasion:

[M]y oath to preserve the constitution to the best of my ability, imposed upon me the duty of preserving, by every indispensable means, that government – that nation – of which that constitution was the organic law. Was it possible to lose the nation, and yet preserve the constitution?...I felt that measures, otherwise unconstitutional, might become lawful, by becoming indispensable to the preservation of the constitution, through the preservation of the nation.[122]

---

[117] Michael Stokes Paulsen, "The Constitution of Necessity" (2004) 79 *Notre Dame Law Review* 1257; Michael Stokes Paulsen, "The Civil War as Constitutional Interpretation" (2004) 71 *University of Chicago Law Review* 691 at 721–26.

[118] Paulsen, "Constitution of Necessity," 1257.

[119] US Constitution, art. II, para. 1, cl. 8; Paulsen, "Constitution of Necessity," 1260–67.

[120] Paulsen, "Constitution of Necessity," 1282–89.

[121] Giorgio Agamben, *State of Exception*, trans. Kevin Attell (Chicago: University of Chicago Press, 2005), p. 27.

[122] Letter from Abraham Lincoln to Albert Hodges (Apr. 4, 1864), in Roy Prentice Basler (ed.), *The Collected Works of Abraham Lincoln* (New Brunswick, NJ: Rutgers University Press, 1953), vol. VII, p. 281. See also Sotirios A. Barber, *On What the Constitution Means* (Baltimore: The Johns Hopkins University Press, 1984), pp. 191–92.

Aside from the important question of whether a particular constitutional design allows for executive inherent powers or recognizes constitutional necessity (with which we do not deal here),[123] there still remains the question of whether, as a normative matter, such powers ought to be made available to government. The general argument for inherent powers and for what may be called constitutional necessity is quite simple, namely the benefits of flexibility in the face of unpredictability. If, as we have already indicated, it is impossible to cover all contingencies by a priori, general, fixed legal norms and rules, there is a need for discretion and flexibility. Since the executive branch of government may be suited best to deal with emergencies, it follows that it should be the one to exercise such flexibility. However, inherent powers invoke the specter of abuse and the concern about the ability to limit governmental powers in times of emergency. If it is the president, for example, who decides when the need arises for the use of such powers and the extent to which such powers ought to be used in any given case, then she enjoys truly unlimited powers. She may decide, at her unfettered discretion, to apply those awesome powers to any situation and be accountable to none.[124] Thus, for example, the Truman administration famously argued in court that the executive had unlimited power in time of emergency and that the executive determined the emergencies without the courts having the authority to review whether such emergencies in fact existed.[125] Justice Jackson rejected these assertions of power in no uncertain terms:

[E]mergency powers are consistent with free government only when their control is lodged elsewhere than in the Executive who exercises them. That is the safeguard that would be nullified by our adoption of the "inherent powers" formula...Such power either has no beginning or it has no end. If it exists, it need submit to no legal restraint. I am not alarmed that it would plunge us straightway into dictatorship, but it is at least a step in that wrong direction.[126]

Justice Jackson then continued to argue that the constitution did not reflect the scope of the president's real power: "That instrument must

---

[123] See, e.g., Adler, "Steel Seizure Case," 163–73.

[124] See, e.g., Lucius Wilmerding, Jr., "The President and the Law" (1952) 67 *Political Science Quarterly* 321 at 330; William Howard Taft, *Our Chief Magistrate and his Powers* (New York: Columbia University Press, 1916), pp. 141–47.

[125] Alan F. Westin, *The Anatomy of a Constitutional Law Case: Youngstown Sheet and Tube Co. v. Sawyer; The Steel Seizure Decision* (New York: Macmillan, 1958), pp. 59–65; Maeva Marcus, *Truman and the Steel Seizure Case: The Limits of Presidential Power* (New York: Columbia University Press, 1977), p. 121.

[126] Youngstown, 343 US 579 at 652–53 (1952) (Jackson, J., concurring).

be understood as an Eighteenth-Century sketch of a government hoped for, not as a blueprint of the Government that is...Subtle shifts take place in the centers of real power that do not show on the face of the Constitution."[127] He identified "vast accretions" of federal power and concentration of such powers in the executive, leading him to conclude that "I cannot be brought to believe that this country will suffer if the Court refuses further to aggrandize the presidential office, already so potent and so relatively immune from judicial review..."[128] One may attempt to counter these difficulties by suggesting three related arguments: (1) that any executive inherent powers and appeals to necessity are subject to substantive and procedural limitations that are provided for in the constitution; (2) that the ultimate question as to the necessity to invoke inherent powers, and the content and scope of such powers once deemed to have been legally and constitutionally invoked, is left in the hands of the other branches of government; and (3) that necessity may operate as a meta-rule of construction only in limited circumstances. These arguments seem, however, flawed.

The test for inherent executive emergency powers must be that of factual necessity. If they do exist they may only be invoked when necessary and to the extent necessary. But if that is the case, and if the necessity is extreme and grave, it may well be that what is necessary is for the executive to disregard constitutional obligations and act against explicit constitutional dictates and statutory norms if, again, that is what must be done to save the nation. But if that is so why should any constitutional provision (setting limitations on inherent powers and their use) be able to withstand such actions? At the end of the day, if necessity is so grave, should not the executive be able to disregard all constitutional and statutory provisions whatever they are? And if so, what is left then of such constitutional limitations? The logical outcome of this is President Nixon's claim of unbridled authority under the constitution. In a 1977 interview with David Frost the former president had this to say:

FROST: So what, in a sense, you're saying is that there are certain situations...where the President can decide that it's in the best interests of the nation or something, and do something illegal.
NIXON: Well, when the President does it, that means that it is not illegal.
FROST: By definition.
NIXON: Exactly, exactly. If the President, for example, approves something because of the national security, or in this case because of a threat to internal

[127] Ibid., p. 653.   [128] Ibid., p. 654.

peace and order of significant magnitude, then the President's decision in that instance is one that enables those who carry it out, to carry it out without violating a law...[129]

Under this reading, inherent powers must amount to, as Justice Jackson suggested, an unlimited power, constrained neither by any legal norms nor by principles and rules of the constitutional order.[130] The second argument highlights the role that courts and the legislature play in checking and balancing the executive's assertions of emergency powers. In the words of Justice O'Connor in *Hamdi v. Rumsfeld*: "[A] state of war is not a blank check for the President when it comes to the rights of the Nation's citizens...in times of conflict [the constitution] most assuredly envisions a role for all three branches when individual liberties are at stake."[131] Justice Souter echoed this when he wrote that, "For reasons of inescapable human nature, the branch of the Government asked to counter a serious threat is not the branch on which to rest the Nation's entire reliance in striking the balance between the will to win and the cost in liberty on the way to victory."[132] Yet this argument runs into difficulties, which we discuss at greater length below, arising from the fact that as a matter of practice neither domestic courts nor any legislature perform their checking and monitoring task particularly well when claims of necessity are made by the executive branch of government during a period of crisis and emergency.

Finally, while Paulsen develops the argument about necessity as a meta-rule of constitutional construction he also seems, at times, to confine the permissible application of such a rule to cases where there exists "legitimate interpretive ambiguity" about, for example, the relative scope of presidential and congressional constitutional powers.[133] But what if no such ambiguity exists, i.e., what if specific constitutional dictates are crystal clear but, in the opinion of the president, they hamper successful action in the face of the extreme emergency that faces

---

[129] "Excerpts from Interview with Nixon about Domestic Effects of Indochina War," *NY Times*, May 20, 1977, p. A16, quoted in Monaghan, "The Protective Power," 7.

[130] Barber, *On What the Constitution Means*, pp. 188–90; Joseph M. Bessette and Jeffrey Tulis, "The Constitution, Politics, and the Presidency" in Joseph M. Bessette and Jeffrey Tulis (eds.), *The Presidency in the Constitutional Order* (Baton Rouge, LA: Louisiana State University Press, 1981), p. 3 at 24–25; Francis D. Wormuth and Edwin B. Firmage, *To Chain the Dog of War: The War Power of Congress in History and Law* (2nd edn, Urbana, IL: University of Illinois Press, 1989), p. 163.

[131] Hamdi v. Rumsfeld, 542 US 507 at 536 (O'Connor, J.).

[132] Ibid., at 545 (Souter, J.).

[133] Paulsen, "Constitution of Necessity," 1273–76.

the nation at a given moment? And who precisely will determine that an interpretive "ambiguity" exists and that it, and the different proposals put forward to resolve that ambiguity, are "legitimate"? Indeed, even the fact that a controversy exists between the branches of government may be argued to prove the existence of such legitimate interpretive ambiguity, and once that exists, the president enjoys priority over both the courts and Congress. Once the president decided that necessity existed there is no escaping the conclusion of ambiguity. For either specific constitutional provisions support the president's actions, or, if they do not then, assuming such actions and powers are deemed necessary by the president for the preservation of the nation and because the constitution may not be interpreted in a way that would undermine the president's duty to preserve the nation, a legitimate controversy about such specific constitutional arrangement arises automatically. In fact, we can take this a step further and argue that the real thrust of the principle of constitutional necessity is that whatever the president considers to be necessary for the preservation of the nation is made, by that very fact, constitutional. There can be no legitimate interpretive ambiguity because the only legitimate interpretation in the face of emergency is the president's. Thus, even while recognizing the significant role of Congress and the courts in checking the executive, Paulsen concludes by accepting that, "If a President concludes that the survival of the nation or its people depends on a course of action that is indispensably necessary to avert such a disaster, his duty as President – his duty *to the Constitution* – requires that he not let a judicial decision to the contrary prevent him from performing what his duty requires."[134]

The authority to declare an emergency

As we saw above, the Roman dictatorship had several important hallmarks: temporary character, recognition of the exceptional nature of emergencies, appointment of a dictator according to specific constitutional forms that separated, among other things, those who declared an emergency and those who exercised dictatorial powers on such occasions, the appointment of dictators for well-defined and limited purposes, and the ultimate goal of upholding the constitutional order rather than changing or replacing it. To varying degrees, modern constitutions attempt to emulate these features of the dictatorship in structuring their own emergency regimes.

---

[134] Ibid., p. 1296 (emphasis in the original).

One important lesson from the Roman example, emphasized by Clinton Rossiter in his seminal study of the constitutional dictatorship, is that such dictatorships must follow certain criteria that govern the initiation, operation, and termination of the constitutional dictatorship.[135] An important criterion is that the initial decision to declare a state of emergency or that circumstances justifying the use of emergency powers exist should not rest with the dictator, i.e., that branch of government to whom emergency powers are entrusted.[136] Thus, as we have already seen, in the Roman republic the appointment of a dictator by the consuls, coupled with the provision that no consul may appoint himself as dictator, ensured that the dictatorship would be invoked by officers other than the dictator himself.

In many of the modern constitutions that provide explicitly for emergency powers, the primary authority for declaring a state of emergency is vested in parliament. At times such power to declare an emergency is coupled with the provision that parliament will act upon the request or proposal of the government.[137] However, it is also common to find provisions allowing the government or the president (where relevant) to declare a state of emergency when circumstances are such that parliament cannot convene or act in time against the exigency. Such circumstances may also pave the way for the exercise of provisional legislative emergency powers by the executive. Such executive declarations of emergency and acts of legislative nature are then subject to a subsequent prompt ratification by parliament if they are to remain in force.[138]

Other constitutional provisions vest the primary responsibility and authority to declare a state of emergency in the executive. Thus, for example, constitutions of Latin and South American countries tend to vest in the president the authority to declare a state of exception as this reflects the strong position traditionally enjoyed by the executive in those countries. A similar pattern is also discernible in the constitutions

---

[135] Rossiter, *Constitutional Dictatorship*, pp. 297–306.

[136] Ibid., pp. 299–300.

[137] See, e.g., article 48(1) of the Greek Constitution; articles 78 and 87 of the Italian Constitution; article 115a of the German Basic Law; article 34(1) of the Constitution of South Africa; article 37(7) and (8) of the Constitution of the Dominican Republic; article 92 of the Slovenian Constitution; article 38(a) of Israel's Basic Law: The Government; article 19(3)(i) of the Constitution of Hungary. See also Ganev, "New East European Constitutions," 587–89.

[138] See, e.g., article 38(c) of the Israeli Basic Law: The Government; article 48(2) of the Greek Constitution; article 18(3) of the Austrian Constitution; article 23 of the Constitution of Denmark. Ganev, "New East European Constitutions," 591–93.

of several of the former Communist countries.[139] Of the constitutions that focus on the executive for declaring a state of emergency, some require prior authorization or subsequent ratification to be given by the legislative branch.[140] Where it is the president who has the constitutional power to declare an emergency it is often the case that a counter-signature by certain ministers or an approval by the government is required for the declaration to be valid.[141] However, where the constitutional system involves a strong presidency, it is often the case that no such counter-signature or further formal approval is required, although consultation with the government prior to declaring a state of emergency may be required.[142] Several constitutional arrangements merely require the government to notify the parliament of the proclamation of a state of emergency without giving an additional role to parliament.[143] Finally, under some constitutional schemes certain types of emergency regimes are declared by the executive while others are declared by the legislature. Thus, for example, article 116(2) of the Spanish Constitution vests the power to declare a state of alarm in the government, while requiring notification to the House of Representatives. Article 116(3) gives the power to declare the next level – state of emergency – to the government, but conditions the exercise of such power on obtaining the prior approval of the House. Article 116(4), dealing with a state of siege – the most wide-ranging of the three emergency regimes – grants the power to declare such a state of exception in the hands of the House, based on governmental proposal.[144]

Various constitutional arrangements can also be found concerning the required majority in parliament that must approve or ratify an executive declaration of emergency or proclaim an emergency when the

---

[139] Banks and Carrió, "Presidential Systems in Stress," 7–9; Ganev, "New East European Constitutions," 589–92.

[140] See, e.g., articles 137(d) and 141 of the Constitution of Portugal; article 111 of the Constitution of Bolivia; articles 2(II) and (V), 49(II) and (IV), 84 (IX) and (X), 136, and 137 of the Brazilian Constitution; article 121(6) of the Constitution of Costa Rica; article 51 of the Constitution of Panama; article 238(7) of the Constitution of Paraguay.

[141] See, e.g., article 143 of the Constitution of Portugal; article 111 of the Constitution of Bolivia; article 190(11) of the Constitution of Venezuela; article 99 of the Constitution of Romania; article 352 of the Constitution of India.

[142] See, e.g., articles 16(1) and 19 of the French Constitution.

[143] See, e.g., article 137 of the Constitution of Peru; article 190(6) of the Constitution of Venezuela; article 16 of the French Constitution; article 78(n) of the Constitution of Ecuador; article 150(9) of the Constitution of Nicaragua.

[144] See also articles 16 and 36 of the French Constitution; article 288 of the Constitution of Paraguay.

power to do so is vested in the legislature. Existing arrangements on this point range from demanding a simple majority to requiring a qualified majority.[145] In addition, some constitutional arrangements require what Bruce Ackerman calls "an escalating cascade of supermajorities." Thus, article 37(2)(b) of the Constitution of South Africa provides that the first renewal of a declaration of a state of emergency requires the supporting vote of a majority of members of the Assembly, whereas further renewals require support of at least 60 percent of those members.[146]

Different arrangements exist also with respect to the duration for which an initial declaration of a state of emergency may be in force and with respect to the possibility of further renewals of that declaration. The principle of temporal duration, so intrinsically linked to the fundamental understanding of the concept of emergency and to the notion of constitutional dictatorship, requires that states of emergency be short lived. This principle is reflected in using one or both of the following techniques: (1) setting temporal limitations on a declared state of emergency; and, (2) setting strict procedures concerning the extension of a declared state of emergency.[147] Some constitutions set limits on the number of permissible extensions to the initial declaration of emergency or on the number of emergencies that may be declared in any given period (usually one calendar year).[148]

Thus, different constitutional arrangements exist with respect to the organ or organs that are authorized to declare an emergency. Under most constitutional schemes the authority to invoke an emergency regime is shared by the executive and legislative branches of government. However, the exact point of equilibrium varies with the specific type of emergency involved and with the general constitutional culture of any given jurisdiction.[149] The constitutional mechanism of institutional power sharing is designed to prevent a situation in which the

---

[145] See, e.g., article 48(1) ("a three-fifths majority of the total number of deputies"), (2), and (3) ("majority of the total number of deputies") of the Greek Constitution; articles 80a (a majority of two-thirds of the votes cast) and 115a (a two-thirds majority of the votes cast and at least a majority of the members of the Bundestag) of the German Basic Law; article 352(6) (a "majority of the total membership of [a] House and by a majority of not less than two-thirds of the members of that House present and voting") of the Constitution of India.

[146] Ackerman, "The Emergency Constitution," 1047–49.

[147] See, e.g., article 38(b) of Israel's Basic Law: The Government; article 352(5) of the Indian Constitution; article 37 of the Constitution of South Africa.

[148] See, e.g., article 111 of the Constitution of Bolivia.

[149] European Commission for Democracy through Law, *Emergency Powers*, p. 9.

organ that is to exercise emergency powers under a declared emergency is also the one authorized to declare that emergency in the first place and activate its own powers. At the same time, it is aimed at ensuring that the branch of government most capable of acting rapidly and effectively to counter a crisis is not rendered unable to take the measures that are deemed necessary to overcome the particular exigency.

Legal results of a declaration of a state of emergency

To what extent may a constitution be suspended, in whole or in part, in times of emergency? May individual rights, otherwise protected by the constitution, be suspended or derogated from under such circumstances? To what extent may emergency measures change the institutional features of the constitutional order? And to what extent may the constitution be modified, amended, changed, or even repealed in such conditions? These are some of the most important questions that ought to be answered in thinking about emergency regimes.

Some constitutions provide that a declaration of emergency may lead to the suspension of certain individual rights and freedoms. For the most part, those constitutions follow one of two approaches on this matter: (1) enlisting those rights and freedoms that *may* be suspended during a declared state of emergency (a positive list approach),[150] or (2) enumerating those rights and freedoms that *may not* be restricted or in any way violated even in times of acute exigency (a negative list approach).[151] Some constitutions take a mixed approach, using a negative list in the context of, for example, a declared state of emergency, while invoking a positive list with respect to a state of natural disaster.[152] Some constitutional arrangements make explicit reference to international instruments such

---

[150] See, e.g., article 121(7) of the Constitution of Costa Rica; article 55 of the Spanish Constitution; article 48 of the Greek Constitution; article 139 of the Brazilian Constitution; article 138 of the Constitution of Guatemala; article 51 of the Constitution of Panama; article 288 of the Paraguayan Constitution; article 187(3) of the Constitution of Fiji; article 29 of the Constitution of El Salvador; article 103(2) of the Dutch Constitution; article 183(2) of the Constitution of Cyprus.

[151] See, e.g., article 186 of the Constitution of Nicaragua; article 19(6) of the Portuguese Constitution; article 37 of the South African Constitution; article 56(3) of the Constitution of Russia; article 200 of the Constitution of Peru; article 241 of the Constitution of Venezuela; article 45 of the Armenian Constitution; article 63(2) of the Constitution of Belarus; article 57(3) of the Constitution of Bulgaria; article 17(3) of the Croatian Constitution; article 130 of the Constitution of Estonia; article 8(4) of the Hungarian Constitution; article 115(8) of the Constitution of Nepal.

[152] See, e.g., article 175 of the Constitution of Albania; article 233 of the Polish Constitution; article 16 of the Slovenian Constitution.

as the major human rights conventions, adopting by reference the limitations prescribed therein on the possibilities of derogation from otherwise protected rights and freedoms.[153] Of course, states that are parties to any of these conventions are legally constrained by the demands of these international agreements and run the risk of violating their own international obligations if they choose to disregard the rules set forth by these agreements.

Another constitutional outcome of a declaration of a state of emergency may be the conferring upon the executive branch of extraordinary powers. Emergencies also lead to expansion of (national) government powers and concentration of such powers in the hands of the executive branch of government: "Crisis government is primarily and often exclusively the business of presidents and prime ministers."[154]

One important aspect of such expansion and concentration of powers concerns the ability of the executive to engage in the process of law-making. Such law-making powers may be granted to the government by an explicit constitutional provision or by way of delegation of some legislative power from the legislature by means of specific and temporary legislation, broad delegation of powers from the legislature, an enabling act, or permanent legislation with an "emergency-flavor."[155] The force of such emergency executive decrees may depend on a subsequent ratification by the legislative organ. Alternatively such executive legislation may be valid so long as not repealed by either the executive or the legislature.[156] Legislative-type emergency powers can take the form of authorizing the executive to issue decree-laws and regulations that may have the power to amend or even suspend parliamentary legislation, or even derogate from constitutional provisions.[157] The power to

---

[153] See, e.g., article 23 of the Constitution of Finland.

[154] Rossiter, *Constitutional Dictatorship*, pp. 12, 288–90. See also Arthur S. Miller, "Constitutional Law: Crisis Government becomes the Norm" (1978) 39 *Ohio State Law Journal* 736 at 738–41; Koh, *The National Security Constitution*, pp. 117–49; Edward S. Corwin, *Total War and the Constitution* (New York: A.A. Knopf, 1947), pp. 172–79.

[155] Rossiter, *Constitutional Dictatorship*, pp. 292–93; Friedrich, *Constitutional Government*, pp. 563–66; Watkins, "Constitutional Dictatorship," 368–79.

[156] See, e.g., article 112 of the Constitution of Bolivia; article 62 of the Brazilian Constitution; article 23 of the Constitution of Denmark; article 24 of the Irish Constitution; article 18(3) of the Austrian Constitution; article 86 of the Spanish Constitution; article 118(19) of the Constitution of Peru; article 153(16) of the Constitution of Panama; article 357 of the Constitution of India. See also Marguerite A. Sieghart, *Government by Decree* (London: Stevens, 1950).

[157] See, e.g., article 39(c) of the Israeli Basic Law: The Government; article 115k of the German Basic Law; article 48(5) of the Greek Constitution. See also Amnon

issue provisional legislation may also be conferred upon the executive in situations such as the German "legislative emergency" (*Gesetzgebungsnotstand*) when the president may, if the Bundestag was to be dissolved following a successful no-confidence vote but has not yet been so dissolved, at the request of the federal government and with the authorization of the Bundesrat, "declare a state of legislative emergency with respect to a bill which is rejected by the Bundestag although declared urgent by the federal government."[158] Similar arrangements conferring law-making power upon the executive are included in many constitutional documents. Where the legislative body is not bicameral, such emergency legislation may be issued by the government (or the president, as the case may be) without the need for a prior authorization of any other governmental branch. In any event, such emergency legislation needs to be approved by parliament once the causes for the legislative emergency have expired.

Several other broad categories of legal effects of a declared state of emergency should be noted. First, in federal states one of the first "victims" of exigencies and crises is the principle of federalism.[159] This is explicit not only in various constitutional provisions found in the constitutions of, for example, Germany, India, and Russia,[160] but also in the constitutional practice in the United States[161] and Canada.[162] Second, in order to prevent repetition of the mistakes that led to the destruction of the Weimar constitutional experiment (see discussion below), modern

---

Rubinstein, *Ha-Mishpat Ha-Konstitutsyoni shel Medinat Israel* (2 vols., 5th rev. edn, Jerusalem: Shoken, 1996), vol. II, pp. 823–24; Itzhak Hans Klinghoffer, "On Emergency Regulations in Israel" in Haim Cohen (ed.), *Sefer yovel le-Pinhas Rozen* (Jerusalem: Hebrew University, 1962), p. 86; European Commission for Democracy through Law, *Emergency Powers*, p. 5.

[158] Article 81(1) of the German Basic Law.

[159] European Commission for Democracy through Law, *Emergency Powers*, p. 13.

[160] Article 53(a)(2) of the German Basic Law; articles 353, 356, and 360 of the Constitution of India; article 88 of the Russian Constitution. See also Durga Das Basu, *Introduction to the Constitution of India* (9th edn, New Delhi: Prentice-Hall of India, 1982), pp. 302–16.

[161] Corwin, *Total War*, pp. 35–77.

[162] Herbert Marx, "The Emergency Power and Civil Liberties in Canada" (1970) 16 *McGill Law Journal* 39 at 57–61; Christopher D. Gilbert, " 'There Will be Wars and Rumours of Wars': A Comparison of the Treatment of Defence and Emergency Powers in the Federal Constitutions of Australia and Canada" (1980) 18 *Osgoode Hall Law Journal* 307 at 319–20; Donald G. Creighton, *Dominion of the North: A History of Canada* (Boston: Houghton Mifflin, 1944), p. 439; Patricia Peppin, "Emergency Legislation and Rights in Canada: The War Measures Act and Civil Liberties" (1993) 18 *Queen's Law Journal* 129 at 131; Rosenthal, "The New Emergencies Act," 576–80.

constitutional provisions often proscribe any change or modification of the constitution itself during an emergency, or at least any change to, or modification of, the nature of the regime and its core constitutional norms.[163] Similarly, it is frequently provided that the legislature may not be dissolved during an emergency.[164] In fact, some constitutions provide that during a state of emergency the term of office of the legislature is automatically extended.[165]

However, certain constitutional doctrines seem to leave the door open for quite broad suspension of constitutional provisions in time of exigency.[166] Thus, for example, under the doctrine of the "*régime des pleins pouvoirs*" (regime of full powers) the Swiss federal government may act in a way that would otherwise be considered unconstitutional, if deemed necessary to safeguard the state's security, its independence, and neutrality as well as its economic interests. This emergency regime may be invoked by the federal government when parliament cannot meet or when the legislative process can no longer function. This emergency regime, which has so far been invoked only during the two world wars, offers practically no constitutional limitations on its employment.[167] The only limitation is derived from Switzerland's accession to the European Convention of Human Rights.

The Irish Constitution goes even further. Article 28.3.2° provides that "In the case of actual invasion...the Government may take *whatever steps they may consider necessary* for the protection of the State..." Article 28.3.3° continues in the same line:

---

[163] See, e.g., articles 187 and 196 of the Constitution of Belgium; articles 170(5) and 177(2) of the Constitution of Albania; article 60(1) of the Constitution of Brazil; article 133 of the Constitution of Cambodia; article 89(4) of the French Constitution; article 113 of the Constitution of Luxembourg; article 148 of the Romanian Constitution; chapter 13, article 5(2) of the Swedish Constitution; article 18(5) of the Austrian Constitution.

[164] See, e.g., articles 16 and 89 of the French Constitution; article 289 of the Constitution of Portugal; articles 169 and 116(5) of the Spanish Constitution; article 101 of the Constitution of Croatia; article 28A of the Constitution of Hungary; article 128 of the Constitution of Macedonia; article 288(9) of the Constitution of Paraguay.

[165] See, e.g., article 115h of the German Basic Law; article 53 of the Constitution of Greece; article 228 of the Polish Constitution. See also Rossiter, *Constitutional Dictatorship*, p. 192.

[166] Article 96(1) of the Algerian Constitution provides that "during a period of state of war, the Constitution is suspended [and] the President of the Republic assumes all the powers."

[167] European Commission for Democracy through Law, *Emergency Powers*, p. 5 and Summary Table of Replies; Jacques Bühler, *Le droit d'exception de l'état: étude des droits publics allemand et suisse de 1871 à nos jours* (Geneva: Droz, 1995).

Nothing in this Constitution shall be invoked to invalidate any law enacted by the Oireachtas [National Parliament] which is expressed to be for the purpose of securing the public safety and the preservation of the State in time of war or armed rebellion, or to nullify any act done or purporting to be done in time of war or armed rebellion in pursuance of any such law.[168]

Thus, Article 28.3.3° immunizes not only legislation but also acts done, "or purporting to be done" in time of violent crises in pursuance of such legislation, from any constitutional challenge. As one of the judges of the Irish Supreme Court suggested, "The Constitution here envisages a crisis during which the normal rule of law is, at least to a considerable extent, superseded by the Rule of the Executive in the domain of emergency law...subject only to the control of the Legislature."[169] The result is "to provide a means of freeing the Oireachtas from the limits imposed upon it by the Constitution...So long as the statute is expressed to be for the purpose specified, nothing whatever in the Constitution may be invoked to invalidate it...In theory [the Oireachtas] could, by invoking the Article 28.3.3° formula and keeping the emergency in being, re-write the Constitution..."[170] It is worth noting that the Irish Constitution puts certain fundamental rights outside the reach of any legislative act. However, the effect of article 28.3.3° is that even such rights may be derogated from, or in fact suspended and revoked, in times of emergency.[171] In an apparent attempt to contain the effects of article 28.3.3°, the Irish Supreme Court ruled in 1977 that, "when a law is saved from invalidity by Art. 28.3.3°, the prohibition against invoking the Constitution in reference to it is only if the invocation is for the purpose of invalidating it. For every other purpose the Constitution may be invoked."[172]

Checks and balances

The main problem facing drafters of constitutional documents results from the need to strike an appropriate balance between granting

---

[168] See generally, James P. Casey, *Constitutional Law in Ireland* (3rd edn, Dublin: Round Hall Sweet & Maxwell, 2000), pp. 149–56; Brian Doolan, *Constitutional Law and Constitutional Rights in Ireland* (3rd edn, Dublin: Gill & Macmillan, 1994), pp. 54–58; John M. Kelly, *The Irish Constitution*, ed., Gerard Hogan and Gerry Whyte (4th edn, Dublin: Butterworths, 2003), pp. 438–55.

[169] State (Walsh) v. Lennon [1941] I.R. 112, 120 (per G. Duffy J.). See also Re McGrath and Harte [1941] I.R. 68.

[170] Casey, *Constitutional Law in Ireland*, p. 150.

[171] D.M. Clark, "Emergency Legislation, Fundamental Rights, and Article 28.3.3 of the Irish Constitution" (1977) 12 *The Irish Jurist* 283.

[172] In re Art. 26 and the Emergency Powers Bill, 1976 [1977] I.R. 159.

sweeping powers to the government to allow it to fight crises successfully, and the need to prevent, or at least minimize, abuses of power by
the government and its agents. There are two general mechanisms of
constitutional control over the exercise of power in response to threats
to national security that are designed to achieve an appropriate balance,
namely judicial review and separation of powers.[173]

Some constitutional provisions provide explicitly for judicial review,
not only of particular emergency measures employed by the government,
but also of the declaration of emergency.[174] Few others limit explicitly,
or outright prevent, judicial review over the declaration of a state of
emergency or of legislative emergency measures.[175] Most constitutions
are silent on this matter. However, as discussed below, practice shows
that domestic courts tend to support the government's position either
by invoking such judicial mechanisms as the political question doctrine
and standing to prevent themselves from having to decide the matter
brought before them on the merits, or, when deciding a case on its merits, accepting the government's position. That tendency of the courts
becomes even more pronounced when they deal with cases *durante bello*
as opposed to deciding them when the crisis is over. This constitutional
experience, which is shared by nations worldwide, may suggest that judicial review of emergency powers ought to be welcomed by governments
as it confers a certain degree of legitimacy on the government's actions
without exposing the executive to substantial risk that its actions may
be curbed by the judiciary.[176]

No less problematic are the checks by the legislative branch of the
executive in times of emergency. Most constitutional arrangements provide for such checks through the required involvement of parliament
in the processes of declaring and terminating an emergency and the
necessity of obtaining parliamentary approval of executive emergency
legislative acts for those to remain in force. This is added to the ordinary methods by which parliament exercises control and supervision
over the government, such as approving appropriations, parliamentary

---

[173] Mark Tushnet, "Controlling Executive Power in the War on Terrorism" (2005) 118
Harvard Law Review 2673.

[174] See, e.g., article VII(18) of the Constitution of the Philippines; article 37(3) of the
Constitution of South Africa.

[175] See, e.g., article 150(8) of the Malaysian Constitution; article 219 of the Constitution
of Thailand; articles 26 and 28.3.3 of the Irish Constitution.

[176] Charles L. Black, Jr., *The People and the Court: Judicial Review in a Democracy* (New York:
Macmillan, 1960), pp. 56–86; Ronen Shamir, " 'Landmark Cases' and the Reproduction
of Legitimacy: The Case of Israel's High Court of Justice" (1990) 24 *Law and Society
Review* 781.

inquiries, hearings and questioning, special parliamentary committees, and no-confidence votes.[177]

Once again, experience demonstrates that legislatures tend to abdicate responsibility in times of emergency. Several reasons may account for that. There is what Bruce Russett calls the "rally 'round the flag" effect, namely the phenomenon by which "a short, low-cost military measure to repel an attack... is almost invariably popular at least at its inception. So too are many other kinds of assertive action or speech in foreign policy."[178] A government's emergency measures are thus likely to draw significant support, at least initially, and generate consensus. Periods of emergency are characterized by an absence of conflict as it is considered dysfunctional for the maintenance or survival of the relevant social system. Indeed, the more acute the particular emergency, the less likely it is that any one will attempt to control the actions of the executive. James Madison already noted that constitutions originated in the midst of great danger that led, among other things, to "an enthusiastic confidence of the people in their patriotic leaders, which stifled the ordinary diversity of opinions on great national questions."[179] This consensus-generating effect of emergencies is particularly significant as it undercuts, at least temporarily, the "ambition to counteract ambition" rationale of the American system of checks and balances, namely the notion that to resist gradual concentration of power in one branch of government a system must be devised so as to give "those who administer each department the necessary constitutional means and personal motives to resist encroachments of the others."[180] Moreover, it

---

[177] Samuel Issacharoff and Richard H. Pildes, "Between Civil Libertarianism and Executive Unilateralism: An Institutional Process Approach to Rights during Wartime" in Mark Tushnet (ed.), *The Constitution in Wartime: Beyond Alarmism and Complacency* (Durham: Duke University Press, 2005), p. 161.

[178] Bruce Russett, *Controlling the Sword: The Democratic Governance of National Security* (Cambridge, MA: Harvard University Press, 1990), pp. 34, 34–38; Gad Barzilai, *Demokratyah be-milhamot: mahloket ve-konsenzus be-Israel* (*A Democracy in Wartime: Conflict and Consensus in Israel*) (Tel Aviv: Sifriyat Poalim, 1992), pp. 247–60.

[179] Rossiter, *The Federalist Papers*, No. 49, p. 315 (James Madison); Karl R. Popper, *The Open Society and its Enemies* (5th edn, 2 vols., Princeton, NJ: Princeton University Press, 1971), vol. I, pp. 43, 198; E.L. Quarantelli and Russell R. Dynes, "Community Conflict: Its Absence and Its Presence in Natural Disasters" (1976) 1 *Mass Emergencies* 139 at 140, 145; Eugene V. Rostow, "The Japanese American Cases – A Disaster" (1945) 54 *Yale Law Journal* 489 at 490–91; John Harwood, "By Big Margin, Americans Support Bush on Fight against Terrorism," *Wall Street Journal*, Sept. 17, 2001, p. A24 (reporting that 80 percent of Americans expressed support for President Bush's response to the World Trade Center and Pentagon attacks).

[180] Rossiter, *The Federalist Papers*, No. 51, p. 319 (James Madison); Tushnet, "Controlling Executive Power," 2674.

is likely that the emotional effects of emergencies (such as fear or rage) and the desire to appear patriotic to voters will lead legislators to support vesting in the government broad and expansive authorizations and powers and to do so without delay.

The executive branch of government has traditionally been considered to be in the best position with respect to the conduct of foreign and national security policies. Perceived advantages such as secrecy, dispatch, and access to broad sources of information are often mentioned in this regard.[181] One result of this structural advantage is that the executive is often the first to act in the face of emergency and, in any event, its actions are most visible since "In drama, magnitude and finality his decisions so far overshadow any others that almost alone he fills the public eye and ear."[182] When added to the consensus-generating quality of emergencies that means that the other branches of government will have to catch up with the executive (should they at all wish to) and react to its actions. The agenda, including the legislative agenda, will be dictated and dominated by the executive.[183] Such domination is facilitated further by the realities of party politics. In parliamentary systems the government is supported by a majority in parliament. In fact, times of acute crises may also lead the opposition to mute its criticisms of the government or even join the government itself as part of a coalition of national unity. While in presidential systems such control of the legislature is not guaranteed, in countries such as the United States the realities of the modern political party system have benefited the executive. Once again, it was Justice Jackson who noted perceptively that, "Party loyalties and interests, sometimes more binding than law, extend [the president's] effective control into branches of government other than his own and he often may win, as a political leader, what he cannot command under the Constitution."[184] Such considerations aside, the fact that in periods of emergency conflicts that seem to be mere partisan politics are set aside (leading, almost inevitably, to the adoption of policies advocated by the executive) ensure that presidents need not be overly envious of prime ministers. All this leads Mark Tushnet to conclude that,

---

[181] See, e.g., Rossiter, *The Federalist Papers*, No. 64, pp. 392–93 (John Jay), No. 75, pp. 451–52 (Alexander Hamilton).

[182] Youngstown, 343 US 579 at 653 (1952) (Jackson, J., concurring).

[183] Rossiter, *Constitutional Dictatorship*, pp. 240–55; Koh, *The National Security Constitution*, pp. 117–23; Tushnet, "Controlling Executive Power," 2677.

[184] Youngstown, 343 US 579 at 654 (1952) (Jackson, J., concurring); Tushnet, "Controlling Executive Power," 2678–79.

When government is unified, in the sense that the President and Congress are in the hands of the same party, and that party is itself more unified than ever, Congress will probably authorize anything for which the President asks. When government is divided, with at least one house of Congress not controlled by the President's party, the story is more complicated, but broad authorizations still seem likely...[185]

Legislative accommodation

One significant problem with constitutional accommodation is, as noted by Alexander Hamilton, the impossibility "to foresee or to define the extent and variety of national exigencies, and the correspondent extent and variety of the means which may be necessary to satisfy them. The circumstances that endanger the safety of nations are infinite."[186] Drafters of constitutions cannot possibly anticipate all future exigencies, nor can they provide detailed and explicit arrangements for all such occasions. Thus, constitutional emergency provisions, to the extent they exist, must use broad and flexible language that sets general frameworks for emergency rule. The adaptation of the constitutional language to concrete circumstances is often done by way of further legislation or (as the next section suggests) by way of creative and novel interpretation, mostly by courts, of the constitutional (and relevant statutory) provisions.

Perhaps the most common method of accommodating security needs in times of crisis is through introducing legislative amendments and modifications into the existing ordinary legal terrain.[187] While it is acknowledged that existing legal rules do not supply a fully adequate answer to the acute problems facing the community, the belief is that such answers exist within some legal framework that does not require a complete overhaul of the existing system. The existing system is kept intact while some special adjustments are introduced through legislative measures. Legislative accommodation may be further divided into two distinct models.

Modifying ordinary laws

Here the normal legal system is maintained intact as much as possible during the period of emergency. However, in order to facilitate the needs of security and the state's safety, certain modifications are introduced

---

[185] Ibid., p. 2679.
[186] Rossiter, *The Federalist Papers*, No. 23, p. 153 (Alexander Hamilton).
[187] Ferejohn and Pasquino, "Typology of Emergency Powers," 215–21.

into that ordinary system. Legislative provisions that are born out of the need to respond to an emergency situation find their way into ordinary legislation and become part and parcel of the ordinary legal system.[188] Under this model – which we label the "Emergency/Ordinary" model because of its focus on inserting emergency-driven legal provisions into existing ordinary rules and structures – the legal framework used for applying emergency measures is the ordinary one as so modified. However, the origin of certain new provisions reveals their close link to the phenomenon of emergency. They are "ordinary" in name only; in substance, they are emergency-driven.

Special emergency legislation

This model also adheres to the notion that emergency must be met under the umbrella of the law. Yet, at the same time, it regards ordinary legal norms to be inadequate for dealing with the pressing needs emanating from specific emergencies. Rather than attempt to modify existing legal norms (as is done under the previous model), the effort is directed at creating replacement or supplementary *emergency* norms that pertain to the particular exigency (or to potential future exigencies).[189] The term "emergency legislation" is thus most at home under this model. Such emergency legislation may, but need not, take the format of stand-alone legislation as when emergency provisions are included in specific "emergency" legislation. Such provisions may also be incorporated into an ordinary piece of legislation while retaining their specific emergency features. Thus, for example, a Special Senate Committee found:

The United States thus [had] on the books at least 470 significant emergency powers statutes without time limitations delegating to the Executive extensive discretionary powers, ordinarily exercised by the Legislature, which affect the lives of American citizens in a host of all-encompassing ways. This vast range of powers, taken together, confer enough authority to rule this country without reference to normal constitutional processes.[190]

---

[188] William J. Stuntz, "Local Policing after the Terror" (2002) 111 *Yale Law Journal* 2137 at 2139, 2162.

[189] Adrian A.S. Zuckerman, "Coercion and the Judicial Ascertainment of Truth" (1989) 23 *Israel Law Review* 357 at 372–73.

[190] Harold Relyea, *A Brief History of Emergency Powers in the United States*, Special US Senate Committee on National Emergencies and Delegated Emergency Powers, Working Paper No. 36–612 (Washington, DC: Government Printing Office, 1974), p. v.

Most of these quasi-emergency[191] provisions would become operative upon a declaration of war by Congress or in the event of a presidential proclamation or an executive order in accordance with the National Emergencies Act.[192] Such a system of "separate statutory grants by Congress of emergency or war-time executive powers...retain[s] Government by law – special, temporary law, perhaps, but law nonetheless."[193]

In addition to the problems with legislative supervision and control over the executive in times of emergency that we have already identified above, we should note another problem that presents a critical challenge to the model of legislative accommodation. Violent emergencies such as shocking terrorist attacks tend to bring about a rush to legislate reminding one of the observation by the Athenian of Plato's *The Laws* that, "no man ever legislates at all. Accidents and calamities occur in a thousand different ways, and it is they that are the universal legislators of the world."[194] The prevailing belief may be that if new offenses are added to the criminal code and the scope of existing offenses broadened, and if the arsenal of law enforcement agencies is enhanced by putting at their disposal more sweeping powers to search and seize, to eavesdrop, to interrogate, to detain without trial, and to deport, the country will be more secure and better able to face the emergency.[195] This is exacerbated further by the problem of legislative myopia. Legislatures tend to provide legislative tools necessary (or deemed necessary) to fight or stop the last war or the most recent threat.[196] The unpredictability of threats and their changing nature, coupled with the need for rapid counter-response, are almost guaranteed to ensure that the legislative branch will suffer from the "red queen effect," i.e., it would take all the legislative running it can do in order to keep in the same

---

[191] The term is taken from John Hatchard, *Individual Freedoms and State Security in the African Context: The Case of Zimbabwe* (Athens, OH: Ohio University Press, 1993), p. 5, which notes that quasi-emergency laws "give the government the sort of powers normally associated with a state of emergency," but are passed "using the ordinary legislative process."

[192] 50 U.S.C. para. 1621 (1994). The same may also apply, of course, to full-fledged emergency legislation.

[193] Youngstown, 343 US 579 at 652–53 (1952) (Jackson, J., concurring).

[194] Plato, *The Laws*, trans. Trevor J. Saunders (London: Penguin Books, 1970), p. 164.

[195] Kent Roach, "The Dangers of a Charter-Proof and Crime-Based Response to Terrorism" in Ronald J. Daniels, Patrick Macklem, and Kent Roach (eds.), *The Security of Freedom: Essays on Canada's Antiterrorism Bill* (Toronto: University of Toronto Press, 2001), p. 131 at 138–42; Conor Gearty, "Airy Fairy," *London Review of Books*, Nov. 29, 2001, p. 9.

[196] Koh, *The National Security Constitution*, pp. 123–26.

place.[197] In that regard, the traditional (at least pre-September 11) lack of interest in the problem of dealing with emergencies and terrorism during peaceful times has also led to the fashioning of emergency and counter-terrorism legislation without much thought and deliberation. It is often easier to pass new legislation than to examine why existing legislation, and the powers granted under it to government and its agencies, was insufficient. By permitting the government to claim that the preexisting legal infrastructure was somehow deficient and forestalled efficient actions against, and responses to, the threats, adding new legislation may result in the piling up of legislative measures into a complex state of emergency.[198] The passage of new legislation allows government, in turn, to demonstrate that it is doing something against the dangers facing the nation rather than sitting idly. As Justice Robert Jackson noted: "fear and anxiety create public demands for greater assurance which may not be justified by necessity but which any popular government finds irresistible."[199] An article in the *Guardian*, referring to the passage of the Prevention of Terrorism Act of 1974, recounts a telling story in this regard:

Clare Short attended the 1974 debate in her capacity as a Home Office civil servant, sitting on the bench reserved for senior Whitehall officials. After listening to a couple of speeches she whispered to her neighbour – the man who had drafted the bill – that it would do nothing to prevent terrorism. "You know very well that is not what it is about," he replied. The point, he said, was to appease the Tories and the tabloids.[200]

Assuring the public that its government is acting forcefully against terrorists is not all bad. A successful terrorist campaign met by a hesitant governmental counteraction may eliminate inhibitions against using force and violence to accomplish political, social, and economic goals by other committed groups and individuals within the community.[201]

---

[197] Lewis Carroll, *Through the Looking Glass and What Alice Found There*, in *The Annotated Alice: Alice's Adventures in Wonderland and Through the Looking Glass* (New York: Bramhall House, 1960), p. 145 at 196–97.

[198] "Study of the Implications for Human Rights of Recent Developments Concerning Situations Known as States of Siege or Emergency", UN Commission on Human Rights, 35th Sess., Agenda Item 10, UN Doc. E/CN.4/Sub.2/1982/15 (1982), p. 29.

[199] Robert H. Jackson, "Wartime Security and Liberty under Law" (1951) 1 *Buffalo Law Review* 103 at 107.

[200] Francis Wheen, "Bill that Costs Too Much," *Guardian* (London), Sept. 2, 2002, p. 5.

[201] Philip B. Heymann, *Terrorism and America: A Commonsense Strategy for a Democratic Society* (Cambridge, MA: MIT Press, 1998), p. 16.

A sense that the government is not doing enough to protect the nation and the life of its citizens may lead to disintegration of political, social, and institutional structures and to their replacement by other, perhaps less democratic, alternatives. It may also lead to loss of popular confidence in existing constitutional institutions and mechanisms and, perhaps, to a general disrespect of the law. If the state is expected to guarantee the "liberty" of its citizens, surely it is supposed to protect and guarantee their "life."[202] Bruce Ackerman has recently emphasized the "reassurance function" of governmental responses to terrorist threats. In his words, "When a terrorist attack places the state's effective sovereignty in doubt, government must act visibly and decisively to demonstrate to its terrorized citizens that the breach was only temporary, and that it is taking aggressive action to contain the crisis and to deal with the prospect of its recurrence."[203] It is in light of this "distinctive interest" that Ackerman sets out to design "a constitutional framework for a temporary state of emergency that enables government to discharge the reassurance function without doing long-term damage to individual rights." It is significant that Ackerman's proposal focuses on a novel constitutional framework, i.e., ex ante, general, constitutional emergency scheme. He does not put his trust in ad hoc, particularistic, legislative measures that are enacted in the face of specific crises. Among other things this feature is supposed to alleviate the problem of rushed legislation that is pushed through without much debate and at times forgoing normal legislative procedures.

Examples of rushed emergency legislation abound. On March 9, 1933, with all the banks in the United States closed for four consecutive days, Congress passed – within an hour of receiving the White House proposal – the Emergency Banking Act, which granted expansive powers to the president.[204] Given the time constraints, the votes of some members of Congress "were not recognized and there was no roll call vote allowed in the House."[205] More recently, Congress overwhelmingly supported the passage of the Uniting and Strengthening America by Providing Appropriate Tools Required to Intercept and Obstruct Terrorism (USA PATRIOT) Act merely a month and a half after the terrorist attacks

---

[202] Irwin Cotler, "Thinking Outside the Box: Foundational Principles for a Counter-Terrorism Law and Policy" in Daniels et al., *The Security of Freedom*, p. 111.

[203] Ackerman, "The Emergency Constitution," 1037.

[204] Pub. L. No. 73–1, 48 Stat. 1 (1933).

[205] Roger I. Roots, "Government by Permanent Emergency: The Forgotten History of the New Deal Constitution" (2000) 33 *Suffolk University Law Review* 259 at 266.

of September 11.[206] Congress moved to act despite strong claims that it was interfering unnecessarily and excessively with individual rights and liberties. Established legislative procedures – such as the committee process and floor debate – were abandoned in the name of speedy process.

A similar story can be told of the British parliament's enactment of the first Prevention of Terrorism (Temporary Provisions) Act of 1974 ("PTA") immediately after the Birmingham pub bombings that killed twenty-one people.[207] The PTA marked a watershed in legal responses to terrorism related to Northern Ireland in that it deviated from the previous pattern of enacting special emergency legislation for Northern Ireland that did not apply to the rest of the United Kingdom.[208] Yet, despite the significant transformation of the British legal landscape wrought by the PTA, little debate took place prior to the passage of the act which was passed through the House of Commons in less than twenty-four hours.[209]

The Terrorism Act of 2000 came into force in the United Kingdom in February 2001. Merely nine months later, as a response to the events of September 11, the British government put the 118-page Anti-Terrorism, Crime and Security Bill before parliament. Despite its complexity, and despite the fact that questions had been raised as to the necessity of passing yet another piece of anti-terrorism legislation, the bill passed in the House of Commons in sixteen hours.[210] Similarly, within days after the terrorist attacks of July 7, 2005 on London's public transportation system – in which more than fifty people lost their lives and scores more were injured after four suicide bombers hit three Tube lines and a double-decker bus – the British Home Secretary, Charles Clarke, announced that the government had cross-party support for its new

[206] Pub. L. No. 107–56, 115 Stat. 272 (2001). See, e.g., Beryl A. Howell, "Seven Weeks: The Making of the USA PATRIOT Act" (2004) 72 *George Washington Law Review* 1145.

[207] Fionnuala Ní Aoláin, "The Fortification of an Emergency Regime" (1996) 59 *Albany Law Review* 1353 at 1357.

[208] Finn, *Constitutions in Crisis*, p. 118; Clive Walker, *The Prevention of Terrorism in British Law* (2nd edn, Manchester: Manchester University Press, 1992), pp. 31–33; Oren Gross and Fionnuala Ní Aoláin, "To Know Where We Are Going, We Need To Know Where We Are: Revisiting States of Emergency" in Angela Hegarty and Siobhan Leonard (eds.), *Human Rights: An Agenda for the 21st Century* (London: Cavendish, 1999), p. 79 at 97.

[209] Paddy Hillyard, *Suspect Community: People's Experience of the Prevention of Terrorism Acts in Britain* (London: Pluto Press, 1993), p. 1.

[210] Philip A. Thomas, "September 11th and Good Governance" (2002) 53 *Northern Ireland Legal Quarterly* 366; Clive Walker, *Blackstone's Guide to the Anti-Terrorism Legislation* (Oxford: Oxford University Press, 2002); Geoffrey Bennett, "Legislative Responses to Terrorism: A View from Britain" (2005) 109 *Penn State Law Review* 947 at 959–66.

Counter-Terrorism Bill and that there were "no main outstanding issues of difference." He said that the government expected to have a range of new powers signed into law in December.[211]

The rush to legislate means that it is not unusual that when emergency legislation is initially adopted, no meaningful debates over it take place. However, as we discuss further in chapter 4, once introduced, emergency provisions may then pass into the ordinary legal system without invoking further debate and discussion.[212]

Interpretive accommodation

Here the focus is on interpretation of existing constitutional and legal rules in a way that is emergency-sensitive. Existing constitutional provisions, as well as laws and regulations, are given new understanding and clothing by way of context-based interpretation without any explicit modification or replacement. The need for additional powers to fend off a dangerous threat is accommodated by judges exercising "the elastic power of interpretation"[213] to give an expansive, emergency-minded interpretive spin to existing norms, transforming various components of the ordinary legal system into counter-emergency facilitating norms. It is certainly an area where legal interpretation (and specifically judicial interpretation) takes place "in a field of pain and death."[214] While the

---

[211] Sam Knight and Simon Freeman, "New Terror Laws by December after Cross-Party Deal," *Times Online*, July 18, 2005, available online at http://www.timesonline.co.uk/article/0,,22989-1698781,00.html (last visited on Aug. 3, 2005); Alan Travis, "Secret Courts for Terror Cases", *Guardian*, Aug. 9, 2005, p. 1.

[212] See, e.g., Dermot P.J. Walsh, "The Impact of the Antisubversive Laws on Police Powers and Practices in Ireland: The Silent Erosion of Individual Freedom" (1989) 62 *Temple Law Review* 1099 at 1129.

[213] Richard A. Posner, *Law, Pragmatism, and Democracy* (Cambridge, MA: Harvard University Press, 2003), p. 295.

[214] Robert M. Cover, "Violence and the Word" (1985) 95 *Yale Law Journal* 1601. While most would look to the courts to carry out such an interpretive task, others would argue that the task of constitutional and legal interpretation is not the monopoly of the judicial branch of government. On the role of other branches of government in interpreting the constitution and the law, see for example, Laurence H. Tribe, *American Constitutional Law* (3rd edn, New York: Foundation Press, 2000), pp. 722–30; Larry Alexander and Frederick Schauer, "On Extrajudicial Constitutional Interpretation" (1997) 110 *Harvard Law Review* 1359 at 1375; Christopher L. Eisgruber, "The Most Competent Branches: A Response to Professor Paulsen" (1994) 83 *Georgetown Law Journal* 347; Michael Stokes Paulsen, "The Most Dangerous Branch: Executive Power to Say What the Law is" (1994) 83 *Georgetown Law Journal* 217; Keith E. Whittington, "Extrajudicial Constitutional Interpretation: Three Objections and Responses" (2002) 80 *North Carolina Law Review* 773.

law on the books does not change in times of crisis, the law in action reveals substantial changes that are introduced into the legal system by way of revised interpretations of existing legal rules. Richard Posner argues, for example, that "If the Constitution is not to be treated as a suicide pact, why should military exigencies not influence the scope of the constitutional rights that the Supreme Court has manufactured from the Constitution's vague provisions?"[215] In other words, "The point is not that law is suspended in times of emergency...The point rather is that law is usually flexible enough to allow judges to give controlling weight to the immediate consequences of decision if those consequences are sufficiently grave."[216] Constitutional provisions leave judges enough wiggle room to accommodate an emergency within the framework of the existing legal system.

If modification of ordinary laws to accommodate for security needs in the context of exigencies focuses on inserting emergency-driven legal provisions into existing ordinary rules and structures and thus is an "Emergency/Ordinary" model, the model of interpretive accommodation applies ordinary rules in times of crisis, but changes the scope of such rules by way of emergency-minded interpretation. It may thus be described in a shorthand form as "Ordinary/Emergency." One obvious tool for such recalibration is the balancing process. It is generally accepted that a certain trade-off exists between liberty and security. Neither interest is absolute. A proper balance must be struck between these conflicting values and principles. But such balance is, in and of itself, flexible and floating. The relative importance of the competing values and interests shifts and changes from time to time and with it so does the point of balancing. As Aharon Barak, the president of the Israeli Supreme Court, notes: "The balancing point between the conflicting values and principles is not fixed. It differs from case to case and from issue to issue. The damage to national security caused by a given terrorist and the nation's response to the act affects the way in which the freedom and dignity of the individual are protected."[217] Of course, one major problem with conducting such an act of balancing in times of great upheaval is that under such extreme circumstances, when panic,

---

[215] Posner, *Law, Pragmatism, and Democracy*, p. 294.

[216] Ibid., p. 295.

[217] Aharon Barak, "The Role of a Supreme Court in a Democracy, and the Fight against Terrorism" (2003) 58 *University of Miami Law Review* 125 at 135; Aharon Barak, "The Supreme Court 2001 Term – Foreword: A Judge on Judging: The Role of a Supreme Court in a Democracy" (2002) 116 *Harvard Law Review* 16 at 93–97.

fear, hatred, and similar emotions prevail, rational discourse and analysis are likely to be pushed aside in formulating the nation's response. When faced with serious terrorist threats or with extreme emergencies, the general public and its leaders are unlikely to be able to assess accurately the risks facing the nation. Balancing – taking into consideration the threats, dangers, and risks that need to be met, the probability of their occurrence, and the costs for society and its members of meeting those risks in different ways – may thus be heavily biased, even when applied with the best of intentions.

William Stuntz suggests that the scope of protection guaranteed by the Fourth and Fifth Amendments to the Constitution of the United States has shifted in response to changes in crime rates. Higher crime rates lead to cutbacks in restrictions imposed on law-enforcement agencies while lower crime rates lead to the strengthening of such restrictions and to their expansion.[218] This ebb-and-flow model of criminal procedure parallels in important parts the interpretive model of accommodation.[219] Constitutional limitations on governmental powers are seen not as fixed and immutable, but rather as designed to minimize the sum of the costs of crime and the costs of crime prevention. There exists a trade-off between police power – with its potential for abuse – and crime.[220] Imposing restrictions on law-enforcement agencies, while having the benefits of stronger protections of individual rights, incurs costs in the form of higher crime rates. As crime rates fluctuate, so does the need to change the point of balance between the various risks. Such changes are often introduced into the legal system by way of judicial interpretation of existing constitutional provisions and legal rules.[221] In times of crisis we can expect expansive judicial interpretations of the scope of police powers, with a concomitant contraction of individual rights.[222] As Harold Lasswell, referring to the constitutional protection against unreasonable searches and seizures, observed: "what seems unreasonable in reasonable times may look reasonable in unreasonable times."[223]

This vision of constitutional fluidity and adjustment to changing circumstances was offered by Chief Justice Chase in his opinion in *Ex parte*

---

[218] Stuntz, "Local Policing," 2138–39.

[219] Paulsen, "Constitution of Necessity," 1276–82.

[220] Stuntz, "Local Policing," 2144–47   [221] Ibid., pp. 2150–56.

[222] Ibid., pp. 2155–59; Kent Roach, "Charter-Proof and Crime-Based Response to Terrorism," 133.

[223] Harold D. Lasswell, *National Security and Individual Freedom* (New York: McGraw-Hill, 1950), p. 141.

Milligan. Speaking for four Justices, the Chief Justice accepted the view that any construction of emergency powers must be constrained within the existing constitutional framework.[224] All the powers that might be used by government in times of both peace and war were to be found, directly or indirectly, in the constitution. However, the Chief Justice believed that when appropriately exercised the war powers of Congress may constitutionally curtail fundamental rights of the individual in a manner that would be impermissible in normal times.[225] While the constitution is the exclusive source of governmental powers, the scope of those powers (and, as a result, the scope of the rights guaranteed under the constitution) is contingent upon the circumstances in which the nation finds itself. The scope of constitutional rights depends on the shifting scope of the powers given to government.[226] Powers expand and rights contract (but are not necessarily suspended) in times of crisis. For Chief Justice Chase, this was the price to be paid by society if it were to survive the crisis and retain its identity and independence.

World War I gave the Supreme Court an opportunity to revisit the matter. In 1917, faced with the prospect of a national general railroad strike as a result of a labor dispute, Congress passed the Adamson Act at the request of President Wilson. The act imposed an eight-hour workday on the railroad industry. In doing so, it accepted, in essence, the employees' position in the dispute. The railroad companies challenged the constitutionality of the legislation, arguing that it fell outside the boundaries of the Commerce Clause power. The Supreme Court, in a five-to-four decision in *Wilson v. New*, upheld the statute.[227]

While conceding that a state of emergency could not create new governmental powers that did not exist previously, Chief Justice White, speaking for the majority, asserted that a crisis could alter the scope

---

[224] Ex parte Milligan, 71 US (4 Wall.) 2, 141 (1866) (Chase, C.J., dissenting).

[225] Ibid, pp. 139–41.

[226] Richard H. Fallon, Jr., "Individual Rights and the Powers of Government" (1993) 27 *Georgia Law Review* 343 at 362; Frederick Schauer, "A Comment on the Structure of Rights" (1993) 27 *Georgia Law Review* 415 at 430–31.

[227] 243 US 332 (1917). The scholarly commentary on this and related World War I "emergency" cases is extensive. See, e.g., Michael R. Belknap, "The New Deal and the Emergency Powers Doctrine" (1983) 62 *Texas Law Review* 67 at 79–84. Other "emergency" cases of that period are Highland v. Russell Car & Snow Plow Co., 279 US 253 (1929) (upholding the Lever Act and subsequent regulations that allowed the president to fix coal prices on the grounds that they were a proper exercise of the government's war powers); Edgar A. Levy Leasing Co. v. Siegel, 258 US 242 (1922) (upholding rent-control statutes enacted to counter the effects of housing shortages owing to World War I mobilization); Marcus Brown Holding Co. v. Feldman, 256 US 170 (1921) (same); Block v. Hirsh, 256 US 135 (1921) (same).

of existing governmental powers: "although an emergency may not call into life a power which has never lived, nevertheless emergency may afford a reason for the exertion of a living power already enjoyed."[228] Chief Justice White's opinion depicted an expansion of governmental powers in times of emergency and a concurrent contraction of the scope of constitutionally protected individual rights. These phenomena would, in turn, enable the government to exercise its emergency powers under the aegis of the constitution in a way that under normal circumstances might brand its action with a mark of unconstitutionality.[229] Thus, the majority in *Wilson v. New* embraced the constitutional emergency powers model originally introduced by the *Milligan* dissent. Courts are able to apply an emergency-sensitive interpretation to constitutional arrangements, structures, powers, and rights. Governmental powers may expand, and the scope of rights protection may contract, so that the crisis can be met effectively. Importantly, when the crisis is over, a return to normalcy should take place, as powers contract to their "normal" extent, and rights concomitantly expand. This emergency powers doctrine, developed and adopted by the majority in *Wilson v. New*, came to serve as the legal peg for much of the early New Deal legislation. With the economic crisis equated to war against a foreign invader, the Roosevelt administration sought to justify such measures as emergency legislation that was constitutional in light of expanded governmental powers in the face of the emergency.[230]

Seventeen years after *Wilson v. New*, the United States Supreme Court, in its first New Deal case – *Home Building & Loan Ass'n v. Blaisdell* – strengthened the doctrinal foundations laid down in *Wilson v. New* and applied the emergency powers doctrine, which was initially developed in wartime, to an emergency situation outside the context of war or violent crisis.[231] This time, the court handed down its decision against the backdrop of the Great Depression. The issue before the court concerned the Minnesota Mortgage Moratorium Law that was challenged as violative of

[228] New, 243 US at 348.   [229] Belknap, "The New Deal," 81.

[230] Franklin D. Roosevelt, *The Public Papers and Addresses of Franklin D. Roosevelt*, ed. Samuel I. Rosenman (13 vols., New York: Random House, 1938), vol. II, p. 15; Belknap, "The New Deal," 84–89.

[231] 290 US 398 (1934). See also Edward S. Corwin, "Moratorium over Minnesota" (1934) 82 *University of Pennsylvania Law Review* 311; Note, "Constitutionality of Mortgage Relief Legislation: Home Building & Loan Ass'n v. Blaisdell" (1934) 47 *Harvard Law Review* 660; Philip Bobbitt, *Constitutional Interpretation* (Oxford: Basil Blackwell, 1991), p. 17; Rebecca M. Kahan, "Constitutional Stretch, Snap-Back, and Sag: Why Blaisdell was a Harsher Blow to Liberty than Korematsu" (2005) 99 *Northwestern University Law Review* 1279.

the constitution's Contract Clause, as well as its Due Process and Equal Protection Clauses. The Minnesota Supreme Court held that the impairment of obligations under mortgage contracts was within the state's police power, which had been invoked to respond to the great economic emergency facing the state and the nation. The Supreme Court affirmed the ruling. Writing for the majority, Chief Justice Hughes, drawing upon Chief Justice White's opinion in *Wilson v. New*, stated:

> Emergency does not create power. Emergency does not increase granted power or remove or diminish the restrictions imposed upon power granted or reserved. The Constitution was adopted in a period of grave emergency. Its grants of power to the Federal Government and its limitations of the power of the States were determined in the light of emergency...*While emergency does not create power, emergency may furnish the occasion for the exercise of power.*[232]

The war power of the US federal government "permits the harnessing of the entire energies of the people in a supreme coöperative effort to preserve the nation."[233] The majority was cautious to pay rhetorical homage to the *Milligan* decision by citing it as precedent for the assertion that "even the war power does not remove constitutional limitations safeguarding essential liberties."[234] It presented the issue at hand as merely a question of proper interpretation of constitutional provisions, thus avoiding any notion of suspension of the constitution under circumstances of emergency. The rights guaranteed by the constitution and the freedoms enshrined therein were not abrogated. The limitations on governmental powers were not swept aside. But the scope of those rights, freedoms, limitations, and powers was redefined in times of grave economic crisis so as to ensure that the emergency would be overcome as soon as possible.[235]

The model of interpretive accommodation focuses on judicial interpretation and on the delicate act of balancing competing interests by the courts. However, it is not clear to what extent the judiciary is able to perform this task well. Experience across jurisdictions shows that when faced with national crises the judiciary tends to "go to war."[236] Judges,

---

[232] Blaisdell, 290 US 398 at 425–26 (emphasis added).
[233] Ibid., p. 426.   [234] Ibid.
[235] Perhaps the most celebrated demonstration of the interpretive model of accommodation came about in the context of interpreting the Commerce Clause against the backdrop of the Great Depression and the New Deal. See, e.g., Peter H. Irons, *The New Deal Lawyers* (Princeton: Princeton University Press, 1982), pp. 52–54.
[236] Michael R. Belknap, "The Supreme Court Goes to War: The Meaning and Implications of the Nazi Saboteur Case" (1980) 89 *Military Law Review* 59.

like the general public and its political leaders, "like to win wars"[237] and are sensitive to the criticism that they impede the war effort. In states of emergency, national courts assume a highly deferential attitude when called upon to review governmental actions and decisions. The courts' abdication of responsibility follows two major alternative judicial attitudes: courts may invoke judicial mechanisms such as the political question doctrine and proclaim issues pertaining to emergency powers to be non-justiciable, or, when deciding cases on their merits, they are likely to uphold the national government's position.[238] As Justice Brennan notes: "With prolonged exposure to the claimed threat, it is all too easy for a nation and judiciary...to accept gullibly assertions that, in times of repose, would be subjected to the critical examination they deserve."[239] In the context of the United States he notes: "There is...a good deal to be embarrassed about, when one reflects on the shabby treatment civil liberties have received in the United States during times of perceived threats to its national security."[240] Another justice of the US Supreme Court observed similarly that, "the judicial handling of wartime cases and controversies still present [sic] disappointing departures, not only from the ideal, but from the ordinary...Judges, too, sometimes give way to passion and partisanship. The judicial process works best in an atmosphere of calmness, patience and deliberation. In

---

[237] Clinton Rossiter and Richard P. Longaker, The Supreme Court and the Commander in Chief (expanded edn, Ithaca: Cornell University Press, 1976), p. 91.

[238] See, e.g., Christina E. Wells, "Questioning Deference" (2004) 69 Missouri Law Review 903; Thomas M. Franck, Political Questions/Judicial Answers: Does the Rule of Law Apply to Foreign Affairs? (Princeton: Princeton University Press, 1992), pp. 10–30, 116–25; Christopher N. May, In the Name of War: Judicial Review and the War Powers since 1918 (Cambridge, MA: Harvard University Press, 1989), pp. 261–64; William H. Rehnquist, All the Laws but One: Civil Liberties in Wartime (New York: Knopf, 1998), pp. 221–22; Michael R. Belknap, "The Warren Court and the Vietnam War: The Limits of Legal Liberalism" (1998) 33 Georgia Law Review 65 at 66–67; Anne-Marie Slaughter Burley, "Are Foreign Affairs Different?" (1993) 106 Harvard Law Review 1980 at 1991–98; Lee Epstein, Daniel E. Ho, Gary King, and Jeffrey A. Segal, "The Supreme Court during Crisis: How War Affects only Non-War Cases" (2005) 80 New York University Law Review 1; Koh, The National Security Constitution, pp. 134–49; John Hart Ely, War and Responsibility: Constitutional Lessons of Vietnam and its Aftermath (Princeton: Princeton University Press, 1993), pp. 54–60; Laurence Lustgarten and Ian Leigh, In from the Cold: National Security and Parliamentary Democracy (Oxford: Clarendon Press, 1994), pp. 320–59; George J. Alexander, "The Illusory Protection of Human Rights by National Courts during Periods of Emergency" (1984) 5 Human Rights Law Journal 1 at 15–27. But see John C. Yoo, "Judicial Review and the War on Terrorism" (2003) 72 George Washington Law Review 427.

[239] William J. Brennan, Jr., "The Quest to Develop a Jurisprudence of Civil Liberties in Times of Security Crises" (1988) 18 Israel Yearbook on Human Rights 11 at 20.

[240] Ibid., p. 11.

times of anxiety, the public demands haste and a show of zeal on the part of judges, whose real duty is neutrality and detachment."[241] Nor is this phenomenon unique to any one country or to any particular period in a nation's history. Evaluating the performance of domestic courts during World War I, George Bernard Shaw was paraphrased as saying that, "during the war the courts in France, bleeding under German guns, were very severe; the courts in England, hearing but the echoes of those guns, were grossly unjust; but the courts in the United States, knowing naught save censored news of those guns, were stark, staring, raving mad."[242]

Indeed, the criticism leveled against domestic courts has led some scholars to argue that international or regional courts, which enjoy detachment and independence from the immediate effects of national emergencies, are better situated to monitor and supervise the exercise of emergency powers by national governments. As one commentator points out, "It is entirely possible that superior courts whose relevant executive authority is not threatened may in fact effectively place limits on subordinate executives."[243] Yet, this conjecture is not borne out in practice. As demonstrated by the experiences of regional and international judicial and quasi-judicial bodies – which are further explored in chapter 5 – governments have fared well when their decisions concerning the existence of a particular situation of emergency are reviewed by such regional and international bodies.[244]

"Each crisis brings its word and deed"[245]

The various models of accommodation offer the benefit of constitutional and legal flexibility in the face of crisis and emergency. Legal principles and rules, as well as legal structures and institutions, may be adjusted,

---

[241] Jackson, "Wartime Security," 112.

[242] Ex parte Starr, 263 F. 145, 147 (D. Mont. 1920). See also Arnon Gutfeld, " 'Stark, Staring, Raving Mad': An Analysis of a World War I Impeachment Trial" (1995) 30 *Yearbook of German-American Studies* 57 at 69.

[243] Alexander, "Illusory Protection," 3; L.C. Green, "Derogation of Human Rights in Emergency Situations" (1978) 16 *Canadian Yearbook of International Law* 92 at 112–13.

[244] See, e.g., Fionnuala Ní Aoláin, "The Emergence of Diversity: Differences in Human Rights Jurisprudence" (1995) 19 *Fordham International Law Journal* 101; Oren Gross, " 'Once More unto the Breach': The Systemic Failure of Applying the European Convention on Human Rights to Entrenched Emergencies" (1998) 23 *Yale Journal of International Law* 437 at 490–500.

[245] John Greenleaf Whittier, "The Lost Occasion," *Atlantic Monthly*, April 1880, 448, 449.

relaxed, or perhaps even suspended in part, in order to meet the needs of answering violent threats successfully. The models are grounded in a strategy of accommodation and flexibility according to which one confronts the inevitable by allowing it rather than by futilely resisting it. Frederick Schauer explains:

This strategy runs the risk that the message of allowance will be taken as saying substantially more than it actually says, or allowing more than it actually allows. In exchange for this risk, however, this strategy maintains the authority or legitimacy of the norm structure at issue because, by allowing the inevitable, the inevitable need not violate the norm structure in order to exist.[246]

Recognizing that extraordinary powers are, in fact, going to be used in times of great peril, the legal system ought to retain enough flexibility to allow such use within legal confines rather than outside them. Over the long term, adherence to the rule of law requires responding to crises from within the system rather than breaking free of it, since a break may be difficult, if not impossible, to repair later. This approach was suggested, for example, by the Landau Commission in Israel as the best available method to balance the needs of state security with the protection of human rights and civil liberties in the context of interrogations of suspected terrorists by the Israeli General Security Service (GSS). Describing its proposed solution as "the truthful road of the rule of law," the commission envisioned a state of affairs in which the GSS and its members operate within the boundaries of the law, while the legal system accommodates the needs of the security services as they arise in the fight against terrorism.[247]

Indeed, it may be argued that resort to the models of accommodation may actually lead to less draconian emergency measures being put in place and implemented. In the absence of legal permission to employ special emergency powers (or in the event that the legally available powers are insufficient), the executive may be reluctant to take emergency measures that are considered illegal. This hesitation may force the government to respond to the emergency only at a later stage, when the crisis has further developed and the danger escalated, and when more

---

[246] Frederick Schauer, "May Officials Think Religiously?" (1986) 27 *William and Mary Law Review* 1075 at 1084. See also Raymond Aron, *France, the New Republic* (New York: Oceana Publications, 1960), pp. 23–24.

[247] Israeli Government Press Office, *Commission of Inquiry into the Methods of Investigation of the General Security Service Regarding Hostile Terrorist Activity* (1987), reprinted in (1989) 23 *Israel Law Review* 146 at 184.

extreme actions are required to overcome it. If emergency powers are part of the government's legal arsenal, it may be able to use them to nip the emergency in the bud.

In short, the argument is made that the benefits of accommodation exceed the potential costs of invoking such models of emergency rule. The models avoid constitutional and legal rigidity in the face of crisis, allowing government to act responsibly, within a legal framework, against threats and dangers. Operating within the confines of a legal system also means that mechanisms of control and supervision against abuse and misuse of powers – such as judicial review and parliamentary oversight over the actions of the executive branch of government – are available and functioning.[248]

However, it is precisely the fear of such abuse and misuse of powers that presents the major challenge to the models. The models, it may be argued, are unprincipled, apologetic, and open to abuse.[249] These models enable the authorities to mold and shape the legal system, including the constitutional edifice, under the pretense of fighting off an emergency. This may also lead to popular disillusionment about the legal system. For if government can provide itself with whatever powers it wishes while acting within the framework of the legal system, there seems to be little sense in maintaining that our government is, indeed, government of laws not of men.

In addition, experience informs us that neither the judicial nor the legislative branches function as meaningful guardians of individual rights and liberties in times of great peril. Thus, it seems extremely dangerous to allow any modifications to the constitutional and legal terrain to take place at such times, regardless of whether such changes are introduced by way of judicial interpretation of existing legal and constitutional provisions, or by way of new legislative initiatives. As Carl Friedrich notes:

[T]here are no ultimate institutional safeguards available for insuring that emergency powers be used for the purpose of preserving the constitution...All in all the quasi-dictatorial provisions of modern constitutional systems, be they martial rule, state of siege, or constitutional emergency powers, fail to conform to any exacting standard of effective limitations upon a temporary concentration

---

[248] Posner and Vermeule, "Accommodating Emergencies," 607.

[249] Martti Koskenniemi, *From Apology to Utopia: The Structure of International Legal Argument* (Helsinki: Finnish Lawyers' Publishing Co., 1989), pp. 40–50; Martti Koskenniemi, "The Politics of International Law" (1990) 1 *European Journal of International Law* 4 at 31–32.

of powers. Consequently, all these systems are liable to be transformed into dictatorial schemes if conditions become at all favorable to it.[250]

Constitutional or legal modifications may tempt the authorities to test their limits and expand their powers.[251] The very existence of such a system of emergency rules and regulations may result in greater and more frequent use of emergency powers by officials, making extraordinary powers part of the ordinary discourse of government. "[E]mergency powers would tend to kindle emergencies."[252] Once created and put into place, such constitutional and legal emergency modifications will be similar to Justice Jackson's famous "loaded weapon ready for the hand of any authority that can bring forward a plausible claim of an urgent need."[253] This is a lesson that students of the Roman dictatorship, the prototype for modern emergency regimes, cannot ignore.

As we discuss further in chapter 4, the end of the fourth century and the third century BC signaled the beginning of a rapid process of decline of the dictatorship. Yet, despite its decline, the dictatorship remained "on the books" in Rome as an available republican emergency institution. During his reign of terror from 83 to 79 BC, L. Cornelius Sulla maintained the semblance of legality by invoking empty constitutional shells that were revived in name only to confer legitimacy and legality upon otherwise unlawful acts. Sulla held the titles of dictator – appointed primarily for the purpose of redrafting the republican constitution – and consul.[254] So great was his desire to coat his actions with a cover of legality that he made sure that a special law approved in advance all his subsequent actions.[255] An elected office, without term limits, put in place with a goal other than the protection of the existing constitutional order (indeed undermining that very order), Sulla's was a republican dictatorship in name only.[256] The same can be said of the

---

[250] Friedrich, *Constitutional Government*, p. 570.

[251] Posner, *Law, Pragmatism, and Democracy*, p. 305.

[252] Youngstown, 343 US 579, 650 (1952) (Jackson, J., concurring). See also Christoph Schreuer, "Derogation of Human Rights in Situations of Public Emergency: The Experience of the European Convention on Human Rights" (1982) 9 *Yale Journal of World Public Order* 113; Mark Tushnet, "Defending *Korematsu?*: Reflections on Civil Liberties in Wartime" (2003) *Wisconsin Law Review* 273 at 303–04.

[253] Korematsu v. United States, 323 US 214, 246 (1944) (Jackson, J., dissenting); Ackerman, "The Emergency Constitution," 1041.

[254] Heitland, *The Roman Republic*, vol. II, paras. 905–07; Cary and Scullard, *A History of Rome*, pp. 230–35; Arthur Keaveney, *Sulla, the Last Republican* (London: Croom Helm, 1982).

[255] Heitland, *The Roman Republic*, vol. II, para. 905; Michael H. Crawford, *The Roman Republic* (Cambridge, MA: Harvard University Press, 1993), p. 151.

[256] Heitland, *The Roman Republic*, vol. II, para. 906. But see Machiavelli, *Discourses*, p. 74.

dictatorship of Gaius Julius Caesar.[257] He was initially appointed dictator in 49 BC and held that position for merely eleven days. He was then reappointed in 48 BC, and this time held on to the office until the end of 46 BC. As of 45 BC, Caesar changed the form of his dictatorship but not its substance. As of that year Caesar was to be appointed dictator on an annual basis, but the office was voted in advance as his to hold for the next ten years. After a little more than a year the form of his dictatorship changed yet again, this time to become indefinite and perpetual (*dictator perpetuo*). Like Sulla before him, Caesar's dictatorship did not comport with any of the constitutional limitations and requirements under the constitution of the republic.[258]

The most infamous example of this theme of abuse and misuse is the role played by article 48 of the Weimar Constitution in bringing down the Weimar republic.[259] With the inclusion of article 48, the Weimar Constitution became the cornerstone of a constitutional order that provided explicitly for emergency powers. Article 48 instituted a modern version of the ancient Roman dictatorship. It integrated into the constitutional system of the republic radical powers that could be traced back to the German empire's institution of the "state of war"[260] and sought to add them to the menu of protective mechanisms available to the republic. Describing the circumstances that led to the incorporation of article 48 in the Weimar Constitution, Rossiter notes that,

The stress of the times had forced men to whom arbitrary government had been lifelong anathema, to put into their model charter a device of emergency

---

[257] Cary and Scullard, *A History of Rome*, pp. 274–80; Ernle D.S. Bradford, *Julius Caesar: The Pursuit of Power* (New York: Morrow, 1984); Matthias Gelzer, *Caesar: Politician and Statesman*, trans. Peter Needham (Cambridge, MA: Harvard University Press, 1968); T. Rice Holmes, *The Roman Republic and the Founder of the Empire* (New York: Russell & Russell, 1967); John F.C. Fuller, *Julius Caesar: Man, Soldier, and Tyrant* (New York: Da Capo Press, 1991); John Dickinson, *Death of a Republic: Politics and Political Thought at Rome 59–44 BC* (New York: Macmillan, 1963); Tom Holland, *Rubicon: The Triumph and Tragedy of the Roman Republic* (London: Abacus, 2003), pp. 337–40. For an example of Machiavelli's critical treatment of Julius Caesar, see Machiavelli, *Discourses*, pp. 31–33.

[258] Tellegen-Couperus, *Roman Law*, p. 41; Jolowicz and Nicholas, *Roman Law*, p. 56.

[259] Frederick M. Watkins, *The Failure of Constitutional Emergency Powers under the German Republic* (Cambridge, MA: Harvard University Press, 1939); Rossiter, *Constitutional Dictatorship*, pp. 33–73; Finn, *Constitutions in Crisis*, pp. 139–80; Hans Mommsen, *The Rise and Fall of Weimar Democracy* (Chapel Hill, NC: University of North Carolina Press, 1996); Peter L. Lindseth, "The Paradox of Parliamentary Supremacy: Delegation, Democracy, and Dictatorship in Germany and France, 1920s–1950s" (2004) 113 *Yale Law Journal* 1341 at 1361–71.

[260] Rossiter, *Constitutional Dictatorship*, pp. 33–37; Finn, *Constitutions in Crisis*, p. 146; Bühler, *Le droit d'exception*.

government that was a relic of the past and a possible platform for despotism. It was their hope and somewhat over-confident expectation that only good democrats devoted to the cause of the Republic would ever be in a position to resort to this unusual fund of power.[261]

Under article 48, the president could use the armed forces to compel a state to fulfill its constitutional obligations. He was authorized, when in his opinion public safety and order were seriously disturbed or endangered, to take measures necessary for the restoration of public safety and order and could use the armed forces for that purpose.[262] Moreover, the president could temporarily suspend seven of the fundamental rights guaranteed by the constitution. The use of article 48 was subject, theoretically, to certain limitations that were either explicitly prescribed in the constitution or implicit in the nature of the constitutional order. Thus, for example, presidential actions under article 48 required ministerial counter-signature. They were to be notified to the Reichstag, and to be revoked upon the demand of the legislature. The constitution also made available various mechanisms for presidential accountability, such as impeachment or removal of the president from office and even making him the subject of criminal prosecution. Other limitations on the presidential powers under article 48 were implicit in the nature of the constitutional order, e.g., they could only be employed for the purpose of restoring normal conditions, and thus were supposed to be of brief temporal duration to be revoked as soon as the goal of restoring public safety and order had been achieved. The presidential oath to observe and defend the constitutional provisions was similarly considered to impose limitations on the president's powers in this regard.[263] However, in practice none of these limitations proved a meaningful obstacle to the exercise of unfettered dictatorial powers.

Between 1919 and 1932, article 48 was invoked more than 250 times.[264] It became a constitutional source for the promulgation of an extensive array of executive decrees, most frequently in the context of economic disturbances.[265] The extensive use of article 48 during the Weimar years led to a broad construction of the range of circumstances in which

---

[261] Rossiter, *Constitutional Dictatorship*, p. 35.

[262] As a matter of constitutional law, the president alone was authorized to judge whether such serious disturbance or danger to the public safety and order had in fact existed. Finn, *Constitutions in Crisis*, p. 148.

[263] Rossiter, *Constitutional Dictatorship*, pp. 65–68; Finn, *Constitutions in Crisis*, pp. 149–51.

[264] Finn, *Constitutions in Crisis*, pp. 151–70; Rossiter, *Constitutional Dictatorship*, pp. 37–60.

[265] Rossiter, *Constitutional Dictatorship*, pp. 51–53.

article 48 powers could be employed so as to encompass crises that did not fall within the traditional understanding of threats "endangering the public safety and order." For example, the German Reichsgericht announced that article 48 allowed the president to "take any measure necessary to the restoration of the public safety and order...Absolutely everything that the circumstances demand is to be allowed him in warding off the dangers that imperil the Reich."[266] The scope and intensity of emergency powers exercised by the Weimar government under that article grew much larger than had ever been anticipated by the framers of the constitution. In fact, toward the end of the life of the Weimar republic, article 48 had been used as practically the exclusive legal source for governmental action, with the ordinary legislative and administrative processes virtually suspended.[267] In addition, the Reichstag – assigned the crucial role of a check on the powers of the president – proved to be no more than a rubber stamp to presidential emergency measures. With its collapse and the combined use of the power to dissolve the Reichstag and article 48 emergency powers,[268] even that mechanism of control and supervision became a dead letter. For their part, the German courts were not, at any time, a real factor in circumscribing presidential authoritarian powers. As Rossiter notes, the courts would, from time to time, "put the stamp of judicial approval upon the latitudinarian conception of the scope of these emergency powers."[269] Finally, and perhaps most importantly, the German people lacked any real sense of constitutionalism and deep appreciation of democracy, being accustomed to, and supportive of, an authoritarian regime.[270] And so it came to be that when Hitler became the chancellor in 1933, article 48 was ready to be used by the Nazis in order to finish off the republic.[271]

---

[266] 55 RGStr. 115, quoted in Rossiter, *Constitutional Dictatorship*, p. 64.

[267] Finn, *Constitutions in Crisis*, pp. 165–68; Rossiter, *Constitutional Dictatorship*, pp. 51–60.

[268] Rossiter, *Constitutional Dictatorship*, pp. 55–57; Finn, *Constitutions in Crisis*, pp. 162–63.

[269] Rossiter, *Constitutional Dictatorship*, pp. 70–71; Finn, *Constitutions in Crisis*, p. 151.

[270] Rossiter, *Constitutional Dictatorship*, p. 71.

[271] Youngstown, 343 US 579, 650–51 (1952) (Jackson, J., concurring).

2   Law for all seasons

The models of accommodation are models of constitutional emergency regimes. They are based on the premise that constitutional norms and legal rules control governmental responses to emergencies and terrorist threats. The fundamental assumption that underlies these models is what we call the assumption of constitutionality: whatever responses are made to the challenges of a particular exigency, such responses are to be found and limited within the confines of the constitution.

The Business as Usual model, which is the subject of this chapter, starts from the same premise. However, this model rejects the attempt to accommodate the fight against crises and emergencies by introducing changes – constitutional, legislative, or (at least in one version of the model) by way of judicial interpretation – to the existing constitutional and legal system. Under the Business as Usual model of emergency powers, a state of emergency does not justify a deviation from the "normal" legal system. No special "emergency" powers are introduced either on an ad hoc or a permanent basis. The ordinary legal system already provides the necessary answers to any crisis without the legislative or executive assertion of new or additional governmental powers. "Extraordinary conditions do not create or enlarge constitutional power."[1] The occurrence of any particular emergency cannot excuse or justify a suspension, in whole or in part, of any existing piece of the ordinary legal system. Thus, Justice Davis could state in *Ex parte Milligan* that the constitution applied equally in times of war and in times of peace.[2] His

---

[1] A.L.A. Schechter Poultry Corporation v. US, 295 US 495 at 528 (1935) (Hughes, C.J.).
[2] Ex parte Milligan, 71 US (4 Wall.) 2 at 120–21 (1866) (Davis, J.). Edward S. Corwin, *Total War and the Constitution* (New York: A.A. Knopf, 1947), pp. 39–80; Jules Lobel, "Emergency Power and the Decline of Liberalism" (1989) 98 *Yale Law Journal* 1385 at 1386–87; Molly Ivins, "Trampling all over the Constitution," *Chicago Tribune*, November 22, 2001, p. N19.

position reflects a theory of constitutional absolutism: whatever powers the government may lawfully wield under the constitution to meet an emergency, such powers cannot diminish the scope of, let alone suspend, constitutional guarantees. In addition, constitutional absolutism means that government may not lawfully wield any special powers to deal with emergencies unless such powers are explicitly provided for by the constitution.[3] Taken together, these propositions focus on the constitution as a constitution of rights.[4] As Justice Davis reasoned:

It is insisted that the safety of the country in time of war demands that this broad claim for martial law shall be sustained. If this were true, it could be well said that a country, preserved at the sacrifice of all the cardinal principles of liberty, is not worth the cost of preservation. Happily, it is not so.[5]

Benjamin Constant, reflecting on the experience of France following the Revolution, suggested similarly that:

All the mediocre minds, ephemeral conquerors of a fragment of authority, were full of all these maxims [public safety and supreme law], the more agreeable to stupidity in that they enable it to cut those knots it cannot untie. They dreamt of nothing else but measures of public safety, great measures, masterstrokes of state; they thought themselves extraordinary geniuses because at every step they departed from ordinary means. They proclaimed themselves great minds because justice seemed to them a narrow preoccupation. With each political crime which they committed, you could hear them proclaiming: "Once again we have saved the country!" Certainly, we should have been adequately convinced by this, that a country saved every day in this manner must be a country that will soon be ruined.[6]

The argument from constitutional absolutism is often joined by an argument about constitutional perfection, namely that the constitution anticipates any future emergency and incorporates, within its framework, all the powers that may be necessary to respond to such a crisis,

---

[3] Charles A. Reich, "Mr. Justice Black and the Living Constitution" (1963) 76 *Harvard Law Review* 673 at 737; Lobel, "Decline of Liberalism", 1386–87.

[4] Louis Henkin, "Constitutionalism and Human Rights" in Louis Henkin and Albert J. Rosenthal (eds.), *Constitutionalism and Rights: The Influence of the United States Constitution Abroad* (New York: Columbia University Press, 1990), p. 383. But see Corwin, *Total War*, pp. 168–80 (noting the transformation of the "Constitution of Rights" into the "Constitution of Powers"); Arthur S. Miller, *Democratic Dictatorship: The Emergent Constitution of Control* (Westport, CT: Greenwood Press, 1981).

[5] Milligan, 71 US (4 Wall.) 2 at 126 (1866).

[6] Benjamin Constant, "The Spirit of Conquest and Usurpation and their Relation to European Civilization" (1814) in Biancamaria Fontana (ed.), *Political Writings* (New York: Cambridge University Press, 1988), p. 43 at 138.

whatever its nature.[7] Statements claiming that the constitutional framework is the same in times of war as in times of peace project a belief in the fortitude, completeness, and perfection of the existing legal system, and in the government's ability to fend off any crisis without deviating from ordinary norms. According to this view, the constitution includes within its purview all the powers that government might need to exercise in order to carry out its functions and duties. The powers given to government under the constitution encompass not only powers that are required in order to deal with the normal functions of government in times of peace, but also those powers that might be necessary in times of war. There is no situation that is not covered by constitutional arrangement or that might necessitate looking outside the basic law of the land for additional powers and authority.[8] Since the constitutional text does not provide for special emergency powers to be vested in government when faced with an emergency, we must conclude that there is no place under the constitution for such exceptional governmental powers.[9]

The Business as Usual model rejects the possibility that a tension exists between protecting the security of the nation and maintaining its basic democratic values, including the rule of law. In times of danger and peril, as in normal times of quiet and calm, the laws (and the powers vested in the government) remain the same. Ordinary legal rules and norms continue to be followed strictly and adhered to with no substantive change or modification. This approach offers a unitary vision of the constitutional order. While the occurrence of emergencies and acute crises is acknowledged, such events are of no constitutional significance because no distinct legal emergency regime is recognized under the constitution. We may think of this model as "Ordinary/Ordinary": Ordinary rules apply not only in times of peace but also in times of emergency.

---

[7] Clinton L. Rossiter, *Constitutional Dictatorship: Crisis Government in Modern Democracies* (Princeton: Princeton University Press, 1948), pp. 212–15. The idea of constitutional perfection has also been extensively discussed in the context of constitutional amending clauses. See, e.g., Sanford Levinson (ed.), *Responding to Imperfection: The Theory and Practice of Constitutional Amendment* (Princeton: Princeton University Press, 1995); Sanford Levinson, "'Veneration' and Constitutional Change: James Madison Confronts the Possibility of Constitutional Amendment" (1990) 21 *Texas Tech Law Review* 2443 at 2451–52. See also Nicholas N. Kittrie, "Patriots and Terrorists: Reconciling Human Rights with World Order" (1981) 13 *Case Western Reserve Journal of International Law* 291 at 295.

[8] Rossiter, *Constitutional Dictatorship*, p. 212.

[9] 71 US (4 Wall.) 2 at 126 (1866) (Davis, J.).

Before going further we should note that there may be two versions of the Business as Usual model. The "soft" version of the model argues that constitutional rules and norms must not be relaxed during an emergency although their outcomes may change. According to this soft version, if a constitutional rule imposes a test of reasonableness when evaluating the constitutionality of governmental powers and measures, this test will be applicable during emergencies as in normal times. However, the substantive content of what "reasonable" is may change, leading to different outcomes about the constitutionality of a law or a certain measure in times of crisis. We suggest that this version of the Business as Usual model, which Eric Posner and Adrian Vermeule call "the strict enforcement view," falls into the category of what we call the model of interpretive accommodation with which we dealt in the previous chapter.[10] The "hard" version of the Business as Usual model contends that not only the ordinary constitutional rules ought not to change in times of emergency, but so too the nature of the substantive outcomes of their application to specific cases.

Ex parte Milligan

Perhaps nowhere has the Business as Usual model been more forcefully debated than in the United States Supreme Court's decision in *Ex parte Milligan*.[11] The accolades and scathing criticisms that the decision has provoked are a testament to the passions invoked by the issues discussed

---

[10] Eric A. Posner and Adrian Vermeule, "Accommodating Emergencies" (2003) 56 *Stanford Law Review* 605 at 608.

[11] 71 US (4 Wall.) 2 (1866). See also Charles Fairman, *History of the Supreme Court of the United States: Reconstruction and Reunion, 1864–88* (New York: Macmillan, 1971), vol. VI, pp. 214–29; Daniel A. Farber, *Lincoln's Constitution: The Nation, the President, and the Courts in a Time of Crisis* (Chicago: University of Chicago Press, 2003), pp. 164–69; J.G. Randall, *Constitutional Problems under Lincoln* (rev. edn, Urbana, IL: University of Illinois Press, 1951), pp. 179–83; William H. Rehnquist, *All the Laws but One: Civil Liberties in Wartime* (New York: Knopf, 1998), pp. 89–137: Philip B. Heymann, "Civil Liberties and Human Rights in the Aftermath of September 11" (2002) 25 *Harvard Journal of Law and Public Policy* 441 at 452; Neal K. Katyal and Laurence H. Tribe, "Waging War, Deciding Guilt: Trying the Military Tribunals" (2002) 111 *Yale Law Journal* 1259 at 1260; Ruth Wedgwood, "Al Qaeda, Terrorism, and Military Commissions" (2002) 96 *American Journal of International Law* 328 at 330, 332; Jordan J. Paust, "Antiterrorism Military Commissions: Courting Illegality" (2001) 23 *Michigan Journal of International Law* 1 at 10–17; Jordan J. Paust, "Antiterrorism Military Commissions: The Ad Hoc DOD Rules of Procedure" (2002) 23 *Michigan Journal of International Law* 677; Michael R. Belknap, "A Putrid Pedigree: The Bush Administration's Military Tribunals in Historical Perspective" (2002) 38 *California Western Law Review* 433 at 440.

in that case. Justice Davis's strong statement that the constitution was "law for rulers and people, equally in war and in peace, and covers with the shield of its protection all classes of men, at all times, and under all circumstances"[12] came to be praised by some as "courageous,"[13] "one of the great doctrines of the Supreme Court,"[14] and "one of the bulwarks of American civil liberty,"[15] while others declared it to be "irrelevant,"[16] "sheer fustian,"[17] and an "evident piece of arrant hypocrisy."[18]

On October 5, 1864, acting under orders from General Alvin P. Hovey, the commander of the military district of Indiana, United States army officials arrested Lambdin P. Milligan in his home in Huntington, Indiana. Milligan, a prominent figure in the Order of the Sons of Liberty (also known as the Order of American Knights), was held in a military prison. On October 21, 1864, he was charged, together with several other antiwar Democrats, with inciting an insurrection, affording aid and comfort to rebels, conspiring against the government of the United States, disloyal practices, and violation of the laws of war. At the time of his arrest the state of Indiana was not subject to military hostilities. Despite the fact that the regular courts were open and functioning, the military authorities decided to bring Milligan and his alleged co-conspirators to trial before a military commission. Although not openly admitted, one of the reasons for that decision was the military's mistrust of a trial by jury in circumstances where jurors might have been hostile to the Union and its goals and supportive of the political agenda of the defendants. Indeed, in the summer of 1864, the subversive movement in Ohio, Indiana, and Illinois was quite substantial.[19] Milligan was convicted by the military commission and sentenced to be hanged. The sentence was approved by President Johnson who directed that it should "be carried into execution without delay." Apparently, when the case was eventually

---

[12] Milligan, 71 US (4 Wall.) 2 at 120–21 (1866).

[13] Ruppert v. Caffey, 251 US 264 at 306 (1919) (McReynolds, J., dissenting).

[14] Randall, Constitutional Problems, p. 513.

[15] J.G. Randall and David Herbert Donald, The Civil War and Reconstruction (Lexington, MA: Heath 1969), p. 304.

[16] Mark E. Neely, Jr., The Fate of Liberty: Abraham Lincoln and Civil Liberties (New York: Oxford University Press, 1991), pp. 179–84.

[17] Corwin, Total War, p. 142.

[18] Neely, The Fate of Liberty, p. 184 (quoting Edward S. Corwin).

[19] Chief Justice Chase hints to that when he writes: "In Indiana, the judges and officers of the courts were loyal to the government. But it might have been otherwise. In times of rebellion and civil war it may often happen, indeed, that judges and marshals will be in active sympathy with the rebels, and courts their most efficient allies." Milligan, 71 US (4 Wall.) 2 at 141 (1866).

argued before the Supreme Court (and maybe even at a later stage, when the opinions of the Justices were written), it was not clear to the court whether Milligan had already been executed.[20] On May 10, 1865, nine days before he was to hang, Milligan filed a petition for discharge from an unlawful imprisonment with the federal circuit court in Indianapolis. The two judges on the court were divided on various issues presented by the petition and the petition was certified to the Supreme Court.

In its decision of April 3, 1866 – the opinions of the Justices were actually released more than eight months later, on December 17, 1866 – the Supreme Court reversed Milligan's conviction by a military commission. The court held that the military commission lacked jurisdiction over Milligan, who was a civilian and a resident of Indiana, which had not joined the Confederacy. Subsequently, the Supreme Court ordered Milligan's release from custody. The Justices based their decision on their interpretation of the Habeas Corpus Act of March 3, 1863,[21] which authorized the president to suspend the privilege of the writ of habeas corpus whenever he deemed it necessary. The court held that the act did not contemplate, and as a result did not authorize, the trial of persons arrested and denied the privilege of habeas corpus in military tribunals.[22]

This element of the court's decision provided a sufficient basis to issue a writ of habeas corpus discharging Milligan from custody. However, from this agreed-upon holding, the Justices parted ways. The two main doctrinal issues at stake were: first, the nature of martial law, the criteria for its lawful imposition under the American legal system, and the scope and range of powers available under such a regime;[23] and second, the sources for emergency powers under the constitution. It is the latter issue that is of interest to us here.

Justice Davis's majority opinion embraces the Business as Usual model. He declares that it is the protection of the law that secures human rights against "wicked rulers, or the clamor of an excited people."[24] He then goes on to identify several constitutional provisions that were violated by the trial of Milligan before a military tribunal and which Justice Davis singles out as fundamental for the protection of criminal defendants.

[20] Ibid., p. 118.
[21] An Act Relating to Habeas Corpus, and Regulating Judicial Proceedings in Certain Cases, ch. 81, 12 Stat. 755 (1863).
[22] Milligan, 71 US (4 Wall.) 2 (1866) at 115–16 (Davis, J.), 134–36 (Chase, C.J., dissenting).
[23] Compare Justice Davis's position in Milligan, 71 US (4 Wall.) 2 at 127 (1866) with the dissenting opinion of Chief Justice Chase, ibid., pp. 137–40.
[24] Ibid., p. 119.

The Founding Fathers and the American people recognized the fundamental nature of those constitutional guarantees and realized that such protections of human liberty might be withered away under the pressures and stress of exigencies. In order to prevent such a dangerous occurrence, which would make naught the safeguards of liberty at a time when they were most needed, those constitutional safeguards are guaranteed immunity against any change or tempering. The laws of the land were applicable to their fullest extent at all times, whatever the circumstances and the exigencies:

Time has proven the discernment of our ancestors ... Those great and good men foresaw that troublous times would arise, when rulers and people would become restive under restraint, and seek by sharp and decisive measures to accomplish ends deemed just and proper; and that the principles of constitutional liberty would be in peril, *unless established by irrepealable law*. The history of the world had taught them that what was done in the past might be attempted in the future.[25]

Justice Davis continues to state the doctrinal conclusion in these famous words:

The Constitution of the United States is a law for rulers and people, equally in war and in peace, and covers with the shield of its protection all classes of men, at all times, and under all circumstances. No doctrine, involving more pernicious consequences, was ever invented by the wit of man than that any of its provisions can be suspended during any of the great exigencies of government. Such a doctrine leads directly to anarchy or despotism, but the theory of necessity on which it is based is false; for the government, within the Constitution, has all the powers granted to it, which are necessary to preserve its existence; as has been happily proved by the result of the great effort to throw off its just authority.[26]

Justice Davis rejects the contention that in a time of war, military commanders have the power to suspend constitutional civil rights. Constitutional guarantees and safeguards cannot be ignored, suspended, or removed in times of war and calamity any more than they can be so ignored, suspended, or removed in times of peace:

This nation, as experience has proved, cannot always remain at peace, and has no right to expect that it will always have wise and humane rulers, sincerely attached to the principles of the Constitution. Wicked men, ambitious of power, with hatred of liberty and contempt of law, may fill the place once occupied

[25] Ibid., p. 120 (emphasis added).   [26] Ibid., pp. 120–21.

by Washington and Lincoln; and if this right is conceded, and the calamities of war again befall us, the dangers to human liberty are frightful to contemplate. If our fathers had failed to provide for just such a contingency, they would have been false to the trust reposed in them. They knew – the history of the world told them – the nation they were founding, be its existence short or long, would be involved in war; how often or how long continued, human foresight could not tell; and that unlimited power, wherever lodged at such a time, was especially hazardous to freemen. For this, and other equally weighty reasons, they secured the inheritance they had fought to maintain, by incorporating in a written constitution the safeguards which *time* had proved were essential to its preservation. Not one of these safeguards can the President, or Congress, or the Judiciary disturb, except the one concerning the writ of *habeas corpus*.[27]

The constitution embodies a fixed and unchanging balance between individual freedom and liberty and governmental powers. This equilibrium is to be maintained at all times. Government does not acquire any new powers in times of acute crisis nor do the powers that government wields in ordinary times expand in times of emergency. When faced with an exigency, the government may employ its regular powers *and those alone*.

The Business as Usual model as explicated by Justice Davis is not to be understood as barring or prohibiting any use of measures to fight an emergency. All it prohibits is the use of extraordinary measures that do not constitute an integral part of the ordinary legal system. The constitution includes within its purview all the powers that the government might need in order to carry out its functions and duties. At the same time, constitutional restrictions and limitations on power and the protections accorded to individual rights are fully applicable not only in times of peace but also in times of war. This means that whatever powers the government may lawfully use under the constitution to meet an emergency cannot diminish the scope of, or suspend, constitutional guarantees. Take the protection of individual rights away – by suspending constitutional safeguards or by contracting the scope of rights protection under the constitution – and you have destroyed the basic justification for the preservation of the constitutional order.

For the *Milligan* majority, the mere concept of "emergency" powers was, therefore, anathema. The government had only one set of powers available to it. Emergency was, from a legal perspective, non-existent. The vision offered by Justice Davis was that of a monistic, unitary view of the constitution.

[27] Ibid., p. 125.

Holding the line

Justice Davis's *Milligan* opinion has often been hailed as a "landmark decision in the protection of individual rights" in the American legal system.[28] It has also faced its share of legal and political criticisms, chastised by some of its harshest critics, who feared that it would obstruct the implementation of the Reconstruction program, as "a second Dred Scott opinion."[29] The constitutional doctrine expounded by Justice Davis is, it has been argued, plainly unrealistic. To the extent that it is designed to set out guidelines for future actions by Congress and the executive it is unworkable in the face of great calamities, as it ignores both the needs of the moment and the realities that push governments to do whatever they can in order to safeguard the nation. For opponents of the majority position, the context in which the decision was rendered, as well as internal inconsistencies within the majority's position, demonstrate the weaknesses of its doctrinal position and of the Business as Usual model.

Several important critiques are offered in this context. It is argued that the non-workability of Justice Davis's constitutional doctrine should have been obvious in light of the experience of the Civil War itself and in light of future developments that were apparent to judges who reiterated the words of Justice Davis. In his opinion, Justice Davis wrote, "for the government, within the Constitution, has all the powers granted to it, which are necessary to preserve its existence; *as has been happily proved by the result of the great effort to throw off its just authority.*"[30] However, the narrative of the use of war powers by President Lincoln casts much doubt on the factual foundation for this assertion.[31] Thus, it is contended that support for the Business as Usual model, as elaborated by Justice Davis, can only be given by those who are either naive or hypocritical. When faced with serious threats to the life of the nation, government will take whatever measures it deems necessary to abate the crisis. Regardless of whether government *ought* to do so, history demonstrates that it *does*. As F.D.R.'s Attorney General, Francis Biddle, wrote in

[28] Robert Fridlington, *The Supreme Court in American Life: The Reconstruction Court, 1864–1888* (Millwood, NY: Associated Faculty Press, 1987), vol. IV, p. 74.

[29] Fairman, *History of the Supreme Court*, pp. 214–33; Bernard Schwartz, *A History of the Supreme Court* (New York: Oxford University Press, 1993), p. 140; John P. Roche, "Executive Power and Domestic Emergency: The Quest for Prerogative" (1952) 5 *Western Political Quarterly* 592 at 600–01.

[30] Milligan, 71 US (4 Wall.) at 121 (emphasis added).

[31] Farber, *Lincoln's Constitution*, pp. 155–57.

1962, in reference specifically to President Roosevelt's Executive Order 9066, which authorized the evacuation of persons of Japanese ancestry from the West Coast, "the Constitution has not greatly bothered any wartime President. That was a question of law, which ultimately the Supreme Court must decide. And meanwhile – probably a long meanwhile – we must get on with the war."[32] Justice Miriam Ben-Porat of the Israeli Supreme Court wrote in a similar vein:

> The smaller the deviation from the legal norm, the easier it would be to reach the optimal degree of harmony between the law and the protection of the State's security. But we, as judges who "dwell among our people," should not harbor any illusions... There simply are cases in which those who are at the helm of the State, and bear responsibility for its survival and security, regard certain deviations from the law for the sake of protecting the security of the State, as an unavoidable necessity.[33]

Adopting the Business as Usual model means either being unaware of the reality of emergency management, or ignoring it and knowingly maintaining an illusory facade of normalcy. That indeed happened in Israel with respect to the use of illegal interrogation techniques by the General Security Service (GSS), which led in 1987 to the establishment of the Landau Commission of Inquiry.[34] When GSS interrogators were faced with an acute need to respond effectively to Palestinian terrorism, legal restrictions limited their ability to conduct the interrogations of terrorist suspects in ways that the GSS deemed necessary. The officers opted to use force in interrogations. In its report, the Landau Commission declared that a legal system that is aware of such a pattern of conduct, but is unwilling to acknowledge it normatively, can be charged with hypocrisy in that it "declares that [it] abide[s] by the rule of law, but turn[s] a blind eye to what goes on beneath the surface."[35]

---

[32] Francis Biddle, *In Brief Authority* (Garden City, NY: Doubleday, 1962), p. 219.

[33] H.C. 428/86, Barzilai v. Gov't of Israel, 40(3) P.D. 505 (1986), reprinted in (1988) *Selected Judgments of the Supreme Court of Israel*, vol. VI, p. 63. Mordechai Kremnitzer, "The Case of the Security Services Pardon" (1987) 12 *Iyunei Mishpat* 595; Pnina Lahav, "A Barrel without Hoops: The Impact of Counterterrorism on Israel's Legal Culture" (1988) 10 *Cardozo Law Review* 529 at 547–56; Alan M. Dershowitz, "Is it Necessary to Apply 'Physical Pressure' to Terrorists – and to Lie about it?" (1989) 23 *Israeli Law Review* 192.

[34] Israeli Government Press Office, *Commission of Inquiry into the Methods of Investigation of the General Security Service Regarding Hostile Terrorist Activity* (1987), reprinted in (1989) 23 *Israel Law Review* 146.

[35] Ibid., p. 183. See also Sanford Levinson, "'Precommitment' and 'Postcommitment': The Ban on Torture in the Wake of September 11" (2003) 81 *Texas Law Review* 2013 at 2042–43.

The United States Supreme Court's own conduct during and after the Civil War demonstrates the idealistic nature of Justice Davis's position. Throughout that bloody period, the court refrained from interfering with military arrests and trials carried out by the Union army, demonstrating a substantial deference to the executive.[36] *Milligan* was a bold decision, but it was handed down more than a year after the end of the Civil War, when the guns were silent and Lincoln dead.[37] The court's decision was no theoretical exercise; it had a very tangible impact on the life of Lambdin Milligan, it set a clear legal rule regarding martial law powers, and it attempted to fortify the protection of individual rights. Yet much of its fiery rhetoric seems ironic in light of the court's judicial role during the war. The relevant facts in *Milligan* were not substantially different from those in previous cases – such as *Vallandigham* – that had been decided during the war.[38] Yet the outcomes were diametrically different. Of course, while *Milligan* was handed down more than a year after the end of the war, the *Vallandigham* ruling was rendered during the very early stages of the war. The *Milligan* majority was aware of this, noting that:

During the late wicked Rebellion, the temper of the times did not allow that calmness in deliberation and discussion so necessary to a correct conclusion of a purely judicial question. *Then*, considerations of safety were mingled with the exercise of power; and feelings and interests prevailed which are happily terminated. *Now* that the public safety is assured, this question, as well as all others, can be discussed and decided without passion or the admixture of any element not required to form a legal judgment.[39]

The sense that the court decided *Milligan* knowing all too well that its decision would not jeopardize the war effort, while it refused to act when most needed, *durante bello*, brought harsh criticism upon *Milligan* as a "mere rhetorical jousting at accomplished wartime deeds," arguing that "It is one thing for a Court to lecture a President when the emergency has passed, quite another to stand up in the middle of the battle

---

[36] See Ex parte Vallandigham, 68 US (1 Wall.) 243 (1863). But see Ex parte Merryman, 17 F. Cas. 144 (C.C.D. Md. 1861) (No. 9487). Merryman was the only wartime case in which a judicial attempt was made to restrain the executive. However, in defiance of a court order to the contrary, Merryman was not released. See also The Prize Cases, 67 US (2 Black) 635 (1862).

[37] Schwartz, *A History of the Supreme Court*, p. 139.

[38] 68 US (1 Wall.) 243; Clinton Rossiter and Richard P. Longaker, *The Supreme Court and the Commander in Chief* (expanded edn, Ithaca, NY: Cornell University Press, 1976), p. 37.

[39] Milligan, 71 US (4 Wall.) at 109.

and inform him that he is behaving unconstitutionally."[40] Indeed, as we saw in the previous chapter, in the first test for the *Milligan* decision, the Supreme Court declined to follow its lead and opted instead to adopt a prudential, pragmatic view, balancing the costs and benefits of expanding governmental power and curtailing individual rights in the context of the impending war.[41] If *Milligan* was decided after the end of the war, *Wilson v. New* was decided on March 19, 1917, at a time when the United States was on the brink of war: Germany had recently announced that it would resume unrestricted submarine warfare against any vessel sailing in European waters, and the United States had severed its diplomatic relations with Germany; on March 9, President Wilson announced that guns would be placed, and naval crews stationed, on American merchant vessels, and, on March 18, after three American vessels had been sunk by German submarines, the railroad companies in fact agreed to the eight-hour workday demand of the workers.[42]

Opponents of the Business as Usual model also assail the internal logic and consistency of the *Milligan* doctrine. A conflict seems to exist between the court's rhetorical assertions of constitutional perfection and absolutism and its willingness to recognize certain circumstances in which application of martial law may be lawful and proper.[43] In those latter situations, constitutional rights would not bar a full-fledged martial law regime. Surely this cannot be reconciled with a constitution that applies "equally in war and in peace."[44]

Linked to the charge of hypocrisy is the related argument that application of the Business as Usual model may result in public realization that law and actual governmental practice diverge systematically when emergencies arise. That may lead, in turn, to portrayal of the legal system as unrealistic because it fails to adjust to the needs of fighting national crises. As a result, particular norms, and perhaps the legal system in general, may break down, as the ethos of obedience to law is seriously shaken and challenges emerge with respect to the reasonableness of following these norms. The risk, as Justice Jackson noted, is that "it is easy, by contemptuously ignoring the reasonable anxieties of wartime as mere 'hysteria,' to set the stage for by-passing courts which the public

---

[40] Rossiter and Longaker, *Supreme Court and Commander in Chief*, pp. xi, 38.

[41] Philip Bobbitt, *Constitutional Interpretation* (Oxford: Basil Blackwell, 1991), p. 17.

[42] Michael R. Belknap, "The New Deal and the Emergency Powers Doctrine' (1983) 62 *Texas Law Review* 67 at 79–80 and n. 91.

[43] Milligan, 71 US (4 Wall.) 2 at 127 (1866).

[44] Lobel, "Decline of Liberalism," 1387 and note 13.

thinks have become too naive, too dilatory and too sympathetic with their enemies and betrayers."[45] Thus, legal rigidity in the face of severe crises is not merely hypocritical, it is, in fact, detrimental to long-term notions of the rule of law. It may, in fact, lead to more, rather than less, radical interference with individual rights and liberties. As Bruce Ackerman suggests, "If respect for civil liberties requires governmental paralysis, serious politicians will not hesitate before sacrificing rights to the war against terrorism. They will only gain popular applause by brushing civil libertarian objections aside as quixotic."[46]

Justice Davis's view that the constitution is the same in times of war as in times of peace is also in danger of being reversed, so that the constitution will be the same in times of peace as in times of war. Government may be tempted to retain its expansive emergency powers in order to have them available even when the emergency has passed and normalcy restored. Emergency norms, measures, and institutions are thus likely to find their way into the ordinary legal system.[47]

Thus, Justice Davis's Business as Usual model came to be regarded as a rhetorical exercise that ought to be, and inevitably will be, disregarded when "subjected to the strain of actual war."[48] As noted above, the first major postbellum crisis that the United States had to face resulted in a shift of the court's majority toward the doctrine proposed by the *Milligan* minority, i.e., a doctrine of accommodation.

Yet, even if one does not subscribe to notions of constitutional absolutism and perfection, there are some weighty arguments that can be marshaled in support of the Business as Usual model and Justice Davis's position.

A strategy of resistance

The models of accommodation are based on a strategy of accommodation. The Business as Usual model is based, in turn, on a strategy of resistance. According to that strategy, "one says 'no' even to the

---

[45] Robert H. Jackson, "Wartime Security and Liberty under Law" (1951) 1 *Buffalo Law Review* 103 at 116. See also Frederick Schauer, "May Officials Think Religiously?" (1986) 27 *William and Mary Law Review* 1075 at 1084.

[46] Bruce Ackerman, "The Emergency Constitution" (2004) 113 *Yale Law Journal* 1029 at 1030.

[47] A. Kenneth Pye and Cym H. Lowell, "The Criminal Process during Civil Disorders" (1975) *Duke Law Journal* 581 at 600–01.

[48] Neely, *The Fate of Liberty*, p. 181 (quoting nineteenth-century political scientist John W. Burgess).

inevitable."[49] The argument from the strategy of resistance is that maintaining the ordinary system of laws unchanged, and not succumbing to pressure to stretch, bend, modify, or replace it, has a significant value in and of itself. Frederick Schauer writes:

> Although disturbing, perhaps reactions similar to those that prompted the internment of the Japanese-Americans never can be expected to disappear, and during time of war or national hysteria the courts will behave the way they did in *Korematsu*. The mere fact that courts will fold under pressure, however, does not dictate that they should be *told* that they may fold under pressure, because the effect of the message may be to increase the likelihood of folding even when the pressure is less.[50]

Such a strategy does not purport to bar governments from resorting to exceptional measures. "Resisting the inevitable is not to be desired because it will prevent the inevitable, but because it may be the best strategy for preventing what is less inevitable but more dangerous."[51] The strategy of resistance may not be able to stop the inevitable – the use of extraordinary powers by government in times of crisis. Rather, it is designed to minimize the likelihood of the use by government of emergency powers in non-emergency situations or of the government's use of excessive powers. Thus, for example, the use of categorical prohibitions on certain governmental actions, or the recognition of categorical rights, may make it harder for governmental actors to exercise extraordinary powers in deviation and violation of such absolutes. Similarly, a firm insistence on the applicability of ordinary legal norms in times of emergency, and on governmental operation only within the limits of the law, and insistence that times of crisis do not give rise to new powers may slow down the rush to use such powers. As Judge Guido Calabresi suggests, there exists a desire "in situations of uncertainty to slow down change until we are sure we want it." Hence, "The use of absolute or categorical language, even when it is inaccurate and leads to inaccurate results, may have substantial merit for this...reason."[52]

Vincent Blasi puts forward a similar argument for adopting a "pathological perspective" – the equivalent of the Business as Usual model – in adjudicating First Amendment disputes and fashioning First Amendment doctrines. "Pathology," says Blasi, "is a social phenomenon,

---

[49] Schauer, "May Officials Think Religiously?" 1084.
[50] Ibid., pp. 1084–85, n. 11.   [51] Ibid., p. 1085.
[52] Guido Calabresi, *A Common Law for the Age of Statutes* (Cambridge, MA: Harvard University Press, 1982), pp. 178–79.

characterized by a notable shift in attitudes regarding the tolerance of unorthodox ideas. What makes a period pathological is the existence of certain dynamics that radically increase the likelihood that people who hold unorthodox views will be punished for what they say or believe."[53] He argues that such an approach is necessary in light of governmental proclivity to violate the rights protected by the First Amendment to the United States Constitution in times of crisis. Courts are called upon to make "a conscious effort ... to strengthen the central norms of the first amendment against the advent of pathology."[54] Emphasis ought to be put "in adjudication during normal times on the development of procedures and institutional structures that are relatively immune from the pressure of urgency by virtue of their formality, rigidity, built-in delays, or strong internal dynamics."[55] Thus, Blasi advocates a "keep it simple" guideline: judges should use simple First Amendment principles in order to strengthen the restraining power of the First Amendment in times of crisis. He suggests that the First Amendment ought to be viewed as concentrating on core values that are more easily defensible in repressive times.[56] Even if one believes that times of crisis justify redefining the scope of protection of the First Amendment and lowering the walls of protection surrounding the expression that falls within its ambit, Blasi points out the danger that the rush to dilute First Amendment protections in times of great peril will not merely end there, but rather will spill over to "normal" First Amendment jurisprudence and doctrine.[57] The long-term dangers of such an act of convenience outweigh the benefits of short-term dilution in order to respond to a given emergency.

The strategy of resistance calls for a rules-based approach. Clear, bright-line rules may make it more likely that decision-makers (including judges) will make unpopular decisions in times of stress, e.g., decisions that are more favorable to individual rights and liberties than those deemed desirable by the general public and its political leaders.[58] Even

---

[53] Vincent Blasi, "The Pathological Perspective and the First Amendment" (1985) 85 *Columbia Law Review* 449 at 450.

[54] Ibid., p. 459.   [55] Ibid., p. 468.   [56] Ibid., pp. 466–80.

[57] Ibid., pp. 456–58; Frederick Schauer, *Free Speech: A Philosophical Enquiry* (New York: Cambridge University Press, 1982); Lillian R. BeVier, "The First Amendment and Political Speech: An Inquiry into the Substance and Limits of Principle" (1978) 30 *Stanford Law Review* 299; Frederick Schauer, "Commercial Speech and the Architecture of the First Amendment" (1988) 56 *University of Cincinnati Law Review* 1181.

[58] Laurence H. Tribe, *American Constitutional Law* (3rd edn, New York: Foundation Press, 2000), p. 794; Antonin Scalia, "The Rule of Law as a Law of Rules" (1989) 56 *University of Chicago Law Review* 1175 at 1180.

if one does not completely disregard doctrinal standards, it is arguable that "mechanistic measures" which confine the range of discretion that is left to future decision-makers may be preferred to standards, such as the "clear and present danger" test, that require in their application an assessment of social conditions and are more likely to bend and be distorted in a way that is less protective of expression under intense pressure.[59] In a famous letter to Zechariah Chafee, Judge Learned Hand criticized the "clear and present danger" test, stating: "Besides even their Ineffabilities, the Nine Elder Statesmen, have not shown themselves wholly immune from the 'herd instinct' and what seems 'immediate and direct' to-day may seem very remote next year even though the circumstances surrounding the utterance be unchanged."[60]

Myths, symbolism, and ideals

An argument related to that made from the strategy of resistance invokes the symbolic value of attachment to ordinary legal principles, rules, and norms even in times of crisis.[61] One may acknowledge the unrealistic attributes of the model and still contend that upholding the myth of regularity and control by normal constitutional principles, even under circumstances of emergency, is socially beneficial.[62] Similarly, Larry Alexander and Frederick Schauer argue that, "there are good arguments for requiring people, and particularly legal officials, on pain of penalty, to follow the law even when they believe they have good reason to disobey and even if they in fact do have good reason to disobey."[63] Laurence Tribe suggests that establishing and maintaining "popular and institutional respect for constitutional structures and liberties," as well as for the constitutional document itself, "may be an even greater bulwark

---

[59] Blasi, "The Pathological Perspective," 474–80; John Hart Ely, *Democracy and Distrust: A Theory of Judicial Review* (Cambridge, MA: Harvard University Press, 1980), pp. 109–16.

[60] Letter from Learned Hand to Zechariah Chafee, Jr. (Jan. 2, 1921), quoted in Gerald Gunther, *Learned Hand: The Man and the Judge* (New York: Knopf, 1994), p. 169. In a similar vein, Chafee himself wrote that "The nine Justices in the Supreme Court can only lock the doors after the Liberty Bell is stolen." Zechariah Chafee, Jr., *Free Speech in the United States* (Cambridge, MA: Harvard University Press, 1941), p. 80.

[61] See, e.g., Sanford Levinson, *Constitutional Faith* (Princeton: Princeton University Press, 1988), p. 11; Levinson, "Veneration," 2452–55; Bruce G. Peabody, "Nonjudicial Constitutional Interpretation, Authoritative Settlement, and a New Agenda for Research" (1999) 16 *Constitutional Commentary* 63 at 67.

[62] Frederick Schauer, "Easy Cases" (1985) 58 *Southern California Law Review* 399 at 439.

[63] Larry Alexander and Frederick Schauer, "On Extrajudicial Constitutional Interpretation" (1997) 110 *Harvard Law Review* 1359 at 1375.

against tyranny than the textual provisions themselves."[64] The model serves as a constant reminder that emergency neither justifies nor excuses forsaking fundamental constitutional values and doctrines.[65]

Thus, the Business as Usual model assumes important symbolic and educational functions. Maintaining an unbending commitment to existing legal norms, the constitution, and the ideal of the rule of law – maintaining a "mood of veneration"[66] toward them – helps us answer the question of what are and what are not "necessary" measures in a particular state of emergency.

Even if one concedes that the Business as Usual model is an aspiration rather than an accurate description of reality, that does not mean that we should discard that ideal just because it may not always work perfectly in practice. Perhaps the Business as Usual model does not purport at all to be an accurate depiction of reality, but is rather a Weberian "ideal type."[67] As such, the model may be regarded as a "theoretical construct... that model[s] certain aspects of social reality and help[s] us to explain particular historical conditions... under explicit assumptions that actually hold true in no historical society."[68] The degree of similarity between the ideal type and the actual reality can be taken as a measure of the level of usefulness and utility of that ideal type as a descriptive and explanatory tool. However, usefulness in that sense is the only criterion by which an ideal type model ought to be evaluated. The

---

[64] Laurence H. Tribe, "The American Constitutional Experience with Emergency Powers," Memorandum to the authors of the Constitution for the Czech and Slovak Federated Republic (January 8, 1991), at 3 (on file with authors).

[65] Calabresi, *Common Law*, pp. 172–73; Schauer, "Easy Cases," 439.

[66] Levinson, "Veneration," 2451–52. On the role of the constitution in American civil religion, see, for example, Max Lerner, "Constitution and Court as Symbols" (1937) 46 *Yale Law Journal* 1290 at 1294–95; Sanford Levinson, "The Constitution in American Civil Religion" (1979) *Supreme Court Review* 123.

[67] Susan J. Hekman, *Weber, the Ideal Type, and Contemporary Social Theory* (South Bend, IN: University of Notre Dame Press, 1983), pp. 18–60; Max Weber, *Economy and Society*, eds. Guenther Roth and Claus Wittich (New York: Bedminster Press, 1968); Max Weber, "'Objectivity' in Social Science and Social Policy" in Edward A. Shils and Henry A. Finch (eds.), *Max Weber on the Methodology of the Social Sciences* (Glencoe, IL: Free Press, 1949), pp. 89–104.

[68] Dhananjai Shivakumar, "The Pure Theory as Ideal Type: Defending Kelsen on the Basis of Weberian Methodology" (1996) 105 *Yale Law Journal* 1383 at 1399; Weber, "Objectivity," 90; Immanuel Kant, "On the Common Saying: 'This May Be True in Theory, but it Does Not Apply in Practice'" in *Political Writings*, ed. Hans Reiss (2nd edn, Cambridge, UK: Cambridge University Press, 1991), p. 61. But see Charles L. Black, Jr., "Mr. Justice Black, the Supreme Court, and the Bill of Rights," *Harper's Magazine*, February 1961, p. 63.

question as to whether such a model is correct or incorrect is irrelevant since the model does not purport to comport with any specific number of empirically observable phenomena.[69]

Slippery slopes

Accommodation of exigency considerations within the body of the legal system may induce the government to use its emergency powers expansively even when such use is uncalled for under the prevailing circumstances. If the power "is there," it is more likely to be used than when it has first to be put in place.[70] Moreover, the existence of such constitutional dictates could encourage unscrupulous political leaders to foment an atmosphere of fear so as to be able to invoke these extraordinary constitutional powers. Choices are frequently shaped more by the framing of outcomes than by the substance of the issues at stake. This is of great importance as it opens the door for manipulation especially when issues are framed in terms of "our" security versus "their" rights. Thus, for example, in order to increase its public support, a government may seek to manipulate information pertaining both to the potential risks to the public and to the costs and benefits of pursuing different measures in response to such risks.[71] Another type of framing takes place when events are characterized in different ways, invoking a potentially different set of parameters of response. Thus, for example, it may well be that framing the events of September 11 using the language and rhetoric of "war" led to different responses to the threats than would have been the case had the events and the threat from al Qaeda been captured through the language of crimes and criminal law.[72] Amos Tversky and Daniel Kahneman demonstrated the significance of "anchoring": the first number with which a decision-maker is presented has a demonstrable effect on that person's ultimate choice. That first number becomes the anchor to which all future assessments are then

---

[69] Shivakumar, "The Pure Theory," 1400–02; Weber, "Objectivity," 91.

[70] Calabresi, *Common Law*, pp. 167–68; Christoph Schreuer, "Derogation of Human Rights in Situations of Public Emergency: The Experience of the European Convention on Human Rights" (1982) 9 *Yale Journal of World Public Order* 113 at 123.

[71] See, e.g., Richard L. Hasen, "Efficiency under Informational Asymmetry: The Effect of Framing on Legal Rules" (1990) 38 *UCLA Law Review* 391; Michael Stohl, *War and Domestic Political Violence: The American Capacity for Repression and Reaction* (Beverly Hills, CA: Sage, 1976), pp. 82–95.

[72] See, e.g., Elaine Tyler May, "Echoes of the Cold War: The Aftermath of September 11 at Home" in Mary L. Dudziak (ed.), *September 11 in History: A Watershed Moment?* (Durham, NC: Duke University Press, 2003), p. 35.

tied. It strongly influences the ultimate decision in so far as it would be taken as the starting point from which certain adjustments can be made.[73] In our context it may be said then that anchoring the events of September 11 in the context of "war" has greatly shaped and influenced the responses to such events. The significance of framing is magnified further in the context of wars, emergencies, and terrorist threats owing to the particular role that "availability entrepreneurs" are likely to play in this context. Such availability entrepreneurs, who have a particular stake in the outcomes of the policy-making process, seek to shape and influence public discourse so as to control the policy selection process.[74] In the context of national security issues the military-industrial complex may well act as such an availability entrepreneur.[75] This interest group, seeking to influence national policy toward increased spending on defense and national security and according greater weight to national security concerns in setting national priorities, enjoys the benefits of being highly organized and of controlling and possessing specialized information and expertise about potential national security risks. Not only may this lead to other organizations and bodies, such as the courts, stepping aside and giving great deference to the judgments of national security experts, but it may also mold, through "information cascades," the general public's perception of the risks that terrorists, wars, or emergencies present to the nation.[76] Thus, if availability entrepreneurs acting in the area of national security present certain risks as highly likely to occur (or of special magnitude) their position is likely to influence greatly decision-makers and the public at large. Moreover, in times of crisis (real or perceived) the consensus-generating nature of emergencies and crises (to which we come back in chapter 4) facilitates further the ability of such availability entrepreneurs to shape and influence public opinion and policy-making. The danger that government will exercise permissible, special emergency powers "and wield [them] oppressively or selfishly, to the detriment of liberty, equality, or enduring national

---

[73] Amos Tversky and Daniel Kahneman, "Framing of Decisions and the Psychology of Choice" (1974) 211 *Science* 453 at 457–58: Scott Plous, *The Psychology of Judgment and Decision Making* (New York: McGraw-Hill, 1993), p. 146.

[74] Timur Kuran and Cass R. Sunstein, "Availability Cascades and Risk Regulation" (1999) 51 *Stanford Law Review* 683 at 727.

[75] Dwight D. Eisenhower, Farewell Address (January 17, 1961), available at http://www.eisenhower.utexas.edu/farewell.htm (last visited August 8, 2005).

[76] Cass R. Sunstein, *Why Societies Need Dissent* (Cambridge, MA: Harvard University Press, 2003), pp. 54–95.

progress,"[77] may be "less inevitable but more dangerous."[78] By the mere incorporation of a set of extraordinary governmental powers into the legal system, a weakening of that legal system will have already taken place and a dangerous threshold will have been crossed. The system will have embarked on its descent along a slippery slope as government will resort to special emergency powers in situations that are further and further away from a real exigency.[79]

Perceptions and misperceptions

It is too trivial to say that in times of crisis, when panic, fear, hatred, and similar emotions prevail, rational discourse and analysis are pushed aside in formulating the nation's response. What is crucial, however, is that when faced with serious terrorist threats or with extreme emergencies, the general public and its leaders are unlikely to be able to assess accurately the risks facing the nation. Balancing – taking into consideration the threats, dangers, and risks that need to be met, and the costs for society and its members of meeting those risks in different ways – is likely to be heavily biased, even when applied with the best of intentions. To the extent that models of accommodation are based on such acts of balancing in the face of crisis they are likely to provide misguided responses to the challenges facing the nation. The Business of Usual model, which seeks to minimize reliance on such balancing, may offer better chances of acting responsibly – "with sufficient vigor to meet the nation's challenges, but without intruding on protected liberties"[80] – in such times.

People operate under a set of cognitive limitations and biases that may prevent them from capturing the real probabilities of the occurrence of certain types of risks and uncertainties. Because accurate risk assessment requires information pertaining to both the magnitude of the risk and the probability of that risk materializing, such cognitive limits color our risk assessment in times of crisis and create a strong tilt toward putting undue emphasis on certain potential risks. While similar observations hold true in a wide variety of areas, the risks involved in acute national crises, in general, and in threats of terrorist activity, in particular, have a special tendency to trigger such cognitive limitations and biases as a

---

[77] Tribe, "Memorandum."
[78] Schauer, "May Officials Think Religiously?," 1085.
[79] Ibid., p. 1084; Frederick Schauer, "Slippery Slopes" (1985) 99 Harvard Law Review 361.
[80] Mark Tushnet, "Controlling Executive Power in the War on Terrorism" (2005) 118 Harvard Law Review 2673 at 2673.

result of not only their potential magnitude, but mostly the manner in which they are perceived.

The concept of "bounded rationality" relates to our limited knowledge and computational imperfections and explains our failure to process information perfectly. As Herbert Simon explains it: "The capacity of the human mind for formulating and solving complex problems is very small compared with the size of the problems whose solution is required for objectively rational behavior in the real world – or even for a reasonable approximation to such objective rationality."[81] An important element of information processing and analysis is the time that is needed to investigate consequences and alternatives. Emergencies, characterized by sudden, urgent, and usually unforeseen events or situations that require immediate action, often without time for prior reflection and consideration, accentuate the problems that are related to our ability to process information and evaluate complex situations. Such crises tend to lead to an increased reliance on cognitive heuristics – short-cuts that people use when making decisions – as a means of countering the lack of sufficient time to evaluate the situation properly. However, while the use of such mechanisms saves time and costs (e.g., information-processing and decision costs), over-reliance on such short-cuts is dangerous. The most common heuristics tend to create patterns of mistaken assessments. Those patterns are reinforced when such heuristics are applied in times of crisis. We note briefly some examples below.

The availability heuristic means that individuals tend to link the probability of a particular event taking place with their ability to imagine similar events taking place.[82] The easier it is to recall an event, i.e., the more "available" it is, the more one is likely to overestimate its occurrence. Past emergencies and terrorist attacks make it easier for us to imagine such events taking place in the future. Terrorism and emergency do not remain abstract notions, but rather are transformed into tangible, real, and probable events.[83] The stronger and the more vivid and salient the images of past terrorist attacks – e.g., the closer they

---

[81] Herbert A. Simon, *Models of Man: Social and Rational* (New York: John Wiley & Sons, 1957), p. 198.

[82] Amos Tversky and Daniel Kahneman, "Availability: A Heuristic for Judging Frequency and Probability" (1973) 5 *Cognitive Psychology* 207; Amos Tversky and Daniel Kahneman, 'Judgment under Uncertainty: Heuristics and Biases" in Daniel Kahneman, Paul Slovic, and Amos Tversky (eds.), *Judgment under Uncertainty: Heuristics and Biases* (New York: Cambridge University Press, 1982), p. 11.

[83] Note, "Responding to Terrorism: Crime, Punishment, and War" (2002) 115 *Harvard Law Review* 1217 at 1230.

are in space or time, or the more emotionally exciting they are – the more such attacks are going to be perceived as likely to occur in the future. As Amos Tversky and Daniel Kahneman suggest, "the impact of seeing a house burning on the subjective probability of such accidents is probably greater than the impact of reading about a fire in the local paper."[84] In the context of September 11, images of the planes hitting the Twin Towers, the towers crumbling down, firefighters and police officers battling against time, and people jumping to their death are extremely powerful. The obsessive public discussion of possible future attacks, regardless of the low probability of many of the specific scenarios ever materializing, coupled with repeated official warnings of pending attacks on bridges, apartment buildings, or attacks carried out on days of particular significance, and periodic changes in the official terror alert level, further feed the terrorism frenzy, increasing the imaginability of various potential hazards and hence their perceived riskiness.[85] Furthermore, once opinions about the risk of future terrorist attacks have been formed (even if somewhat tentatively at first) decision-makers, and the public at large, are likely to seek evidence that confirms their assessments and to reject and exclude relevant evidence that may contradict such assessments leading to further entrenchment of mistakes.

Prospect theory suggests that individuals tend to give excessive weight to low-probability results when the stakes are high enough and the outcomes are particularly bad.[86] Terrorist threats such as those imagined post-September 11 are perceived to raise the stakes to a sufficiently high level.[87] According to Paul Slovic, a risk is "dreaded" if people perceive it to be involuntary and potentially catastrophic, and one over which they lack control. Terrorist attacks are "dreaded" risks and as such are

---

[84] Tversky and Kahneman, "Judgment under Uncertainty," 11. See also Plous, *The Psychology of Judgment and Decision Making*, pp. 125–26; Richard Nisbett and Lee Ross, *Human Inference: Strategies and Shortcomings of Social Judgment* (Englewood Cliffs, NJ: Prentice-Hall, 1980), p. 45; Paul Slovic, Baruch Fischhoff, and Sarah Lichtenstein, "Facts Versus Fears: Understanding Perceived Risk" in Daniel Kahneman et al., *Judgment under Uncertainty*, p. 463 at 465.

[85] Patricia Leigh Brown, "Preparing for a Potential Emergency," *NY Times*, Oct. 4, 2001, at F12.

[86] Daniel Kahneman and Amos Tversky, "Prospect Theory: An Analysis of Decision under Risk" in Daniel Kahneman and Amos Tversky (eds.), *Choices, Values, and Frames* (New York: Cambridge University Press, 2001), p. 17.

[87] See, e.g., David S. Cloud, "Cold War Echo: Soviet Germ Program is a Worry Once Again amid Anthrax Scare," *Wall St. Journal*, Oct. 15, 2001, p. A1; James Dao, "Defense Secretary Warns of Unconventional Attacks," *NY Times*, Oct. 1, 2001, p. B5.

considered by people to be of an especially serious nature.[88] The problem is that "as risks become increasingly dreaded and unknown, people demand that something be done about them regardless of the probability of their occurrence, the costs of avoiding the risk, or the benefits of declining to avoid the risk."[89] Cass Sunstein suggests that the predictions of prospect theory are especially valid where the bad outcome is "affect rich," namely when it involves not merely a serious loss, but one that produces particularly strong emotions such as fear. In such cases, people are likely to overestimate the likelihood of an event's occurrence or suffer from "probability neglect," i.e., fail to assess at all the probability that a certain scenario will materialize, but instead focus exclusively on the worst possible outcome, which, in turn, invokes strong, if not extreme, emotions.[90]

It has also been noted that people entertain myopic perspectives about the future in that they tend to undervalue future benefits and costs when comparing them with present benefits and costs. While a strong governmental response against terrorism is perceived by the public as socially beneficial, the longer-term costs for the rule of law and to individual rights and liberties tend to be overly discounted. The fact that such future costs seem mostly intangible and abstract, especially in comparison with the very tangible sense of fear for one's person and loved ones, coupled with a feeling of increased security as a result of governmental action, only exacerbates this defect in our risk assessment. It should be noted, however, that the problem of myopia may cut both ways as it also indicates that people (and decision-makers) would underestimate the costs of future emergencies and thus be less willing to take preventive measures that would otherwise be appropriate. Indeed, if one adds to the mix what has been identified as the overconfidence bias, i.e., the belief that "good things are more likely than average to happen to us and bad things are less likely than average to happen to us," then it may be argued that decision-makers are likely to use a sub-optimal level of preventive measures to forestall future crises.[91]

---

[88] Paul Slovic, *The Perception of Risk* (London: Earthscan, 2000), pp. 220–31.

[89] Christina E. Wells, "Questioning Deference" (2004) 69 *Missouri Law Review* 903 at 925.

[90] Cass R. Sunstein, "Probability Neglect: Emotions, Worst Cases, and Law" (2002) 112 *Yale Law Journal* 61 at 66, 69; Cass R. Sunstein, "The Laws of Fear" (2002) 115 *Harvard Law Review* 1119 at 1137–44; Cass R. Sunstein, *Laws of Fear: Beyond the Precautionary Principle* (New York: Cambridge University Press, 2005).

[91] Russell B. Korobokin and Thomas S. Ulen, "Law and Behavioral Science: Removing the Rationality Assumption from Law and Economics" (2000) 88 *California Law Review* 1051 at 1091, 1091–93.

All the biases mentioned above suggest that under extreme circumstances governmental overreaction against terrorist and other violent threats is a likely outcome. This overreaction may be the result of the breaking down of traditional checks and balances in times of emergency, as well as of bona fide (but potentially cognitively biased) assessments of the risks facing the nation.

3 Models of extra-legality

In this chapter we introduce a third model of response to crisis that challenges the assumption of constitutionality on which both the models of accommodation and the Business as Usual models are premised. Before going on to discuss what we call the Extra-Legal Measures model in greater detail, we must distinguish it from another model of extra-legality, which comes out of political realism.

One response to the conundrum that terrorism and violent emergencies present to democratic societies may derive from the realist school of international relations. In international relations the tradition of analysis that is identified with realism focuses on the twin images of power and anarchy.[1] Legal and ethical considerations (and other "non-realist" concerns) are mostly irrelevant and do not apply to the affairs of states. Even for those who are willing to allow for such concerns they are always controlled by, and secondary to, considerations of *raison d'état*. Dean Acheson's remarks in the context of the Cuban missile crisis are instructive:

[T]he propriety of the Cuban quarantine is not a legal issue. The power, position and prestige of the United States had been challenged by another state; and law simply does not deal with such questions of ultimate power – power that comes close to the sources of sovereignty. I cannot believe that there are principles of

---

[1] See, e.g., Jack Donnelly, *Realism and International Relations* (Cambridge: Cambridge University Press, 2000); Hans J. Morgenthau, *Politics among Nations: The Struggle for Power and Peace* (6th edn, New York: Knopf, 1985); Hans Morgenthau, "Diplomacy" (1946) 55 *Yale Law Journal* 1067; Edward H. Carr, *Twenty Years' Crisis, 1919–1939: An Introduction to the Study of International Relations* (New York: Palgrave, 2001); George F. Kennan, *American Diplomacy, 1900–1950* (London: Secker & Walburg, 1951); Dean Acheson, "Foreign Policy of the United States" (1964) 18 *Arkansas Law Review* 225; Robert Kagan, *Paradise and Power: America and Europe in the New World Order* (rev. edn, London: Atlantic Books, 2004).

law that say we must accept destruction of our way of life . . . Such a principle would be as harmful to the development of restraining procedures as it would be futile. No law can destroy the state creating the law. The survival of states is not a matter of law.[2]

A political realist argument may be that there exists no room for any kind of "legalistic-moralistic" approach in dealing with emergencies. Where the survival or fundamental interests of the state are concerned, there ought to be no holding back on governmental action to save the nation. Governments ought to forgo legal and constitutional niceties. Law is an irrelevant luxury when dealing with violent crises.[3] Adages such as "necessity knows no law," "*salus populi suprema lex est*," and "*inter arma silent leges*" reflect this approach. In this context one also frequently encounters the argument that since terrorists do not obey any legal principles, victim states need not impose on themselves legal shackles in their struggle against the terrorists. Under this brand of political realism, democracies face no real conundrum in dealing with emergencies. The only constraints within which government functions are those emanating from efficiency and limited resources.

Regardless of the merits of political realism – it has been criticized heavily by both international lawyers and international relations scholars – the core of the theory does not transfer to the domestic sphere. Domestically, states do offer hierarchical political rule and monopoly over the use of force that is, allegedly, lacking on the international sphere. Nor can the political realist approach be acceptable to those who believe that law matters and that it matters greatly especially in times of crisis as a check against arbitrary actions and unlimited discretion. We will come back to the realist school in chapter 7.

The remainder of this chapter focuses on another extra-legal model of emergency regime, which we call the Extra-Legal Measures model of emergency powers.[4] The model introduces the possibility that public officials may act extra-legally when they believe that such action is necessary for protecting the nation and the public in the face of calamity,

[2] Dean Acheson, "The Cuban Quarantine: Remarks" (1963) 57 *American Society of International Law Proceedings* 13 at 14.

[3] Carl J. Friedrich, *Constitutional Reason of State: The Survival of the Constitutional Order* (Providence, RI: Brown University Press, 1957), p. 14; Max Radin, "Martial Law and the State of Siege" (1942) 30 *California Law Review* 634 at 645. See also Gregory S. Kavka, *Hobbesian Moral and Political Theory* (Princeton: Princeton University Press, 1986).

[4] Oren Gross, "Chaos and Rules: Should Responses to Violent Crises Always Be Constitutional?" (2003) 112 *Yale Law Journal* 1011 at 1096–133.

provided that they openly and publicly acknowledge the nature of their actions. In other words, there may be circumstances where the appropriate method of tackling extremely grave national dangers and threats may entail going outside the legal order, at times even violating otherwise accepted constitutional principles. However, for such an action to be appropriate it must be aimed at the advancement of the public good and must be openly, candidly, and fully disclosed to the public. Once disclosed, it is then up to the people to decide, either directly or indirectly (e.g., through their representatives), how to respond to such extra-legal actions. The people may decide to hold the actor to the wrongfulness of her actions, demonstrating commitment to the violated principles and values. In such a case, the acting official may be called to answer, and make legal and political reparations, for her actions. She may need to resign her position, face criminal charges or civil suits, or be subjected to impeachment proceedings. Politically speaking, she may jeopardize her chances for re-election. She may be socially castigated as someone who is willing to act illegally. Alternatively, the people may approve the actions and ratify them ex post.

The two models of extra-legality are not to be confused. As noted above, (international) political realists make the argument that there is no room for "legalistic-moralistic" considerations in deciding the nation's course of action on the international level. The Extra-Legal Measures model reflects a diametrically opposite approach. Apart from being aimed at the domestic sphere, the model seeks to preserve the long-term relevance of, and obedience to, legal principles, rules, and norms. Arguably, going outside the law in appropriate cases may preserve, rather than undermine, the rule of law in a way that constantly bending the law to accommodate emergencies will not. While going outside the legal order may be a "little wrong," it facilitates the attainment of a "great right," namely the preservation not only of the constitutional order, but also of its most fundamental principles and tenets.[5] The Extra-Legal Measures model seeks to promote, and is promoted by, ethical concepts of political and popular responsibility, political morality, and candor. To be implemented properly, the model calls for candor on the part of government agents, who must disclose the nature of their counter-emergency activities. The model then focuses on the need for a direct or indirect

---

[5] "To do a great right, do a little wrong" is the advice given by Bassanio to Portia. William Shakespeare, *The Merchant of Venice*, ed. Stephen Greenblatt (New York: W.W. Norton, 1997), act 4, sc. 1, l. 211. See also Ward Farnsworth, "To Do a Great Right, Do a Little Wrong: A User's Guide to Judicial Lawlessness" (2001) 86 *Minnesota Law Review* 227.

popular ex post ratification of such activities. The process leading up to such ratification (or rejection) of those actions promotes deliberation after the fact, as well as establishing the individual moral and political responsibility of each member of the relevant community for the actions taken on behalf of the public during the emergency.

Ethic of political responsibility

Emergency jurisdiction and temporary measures in Jewish law

For the greater part of the second millennium, the glue holding Jewish communities together was defined not by factors such as territory, citizenship, or subservience to an identifiable secular authority, but rather by adherence to the *Halakhah*, Jewish law comprising written and oral law. Not occupying a land of its own and placed at the mercy of secular rulers of the different countries in which it was located, the strength of the Jewish community depended on the observance of the Jewish law and tradition and on a sense of internal cohesiveness. As Robert Cover notes: "In a situation in which there is no centralized power and little in the way of coercive violence, it is critical that the mythic center of the Law reinforce the bonds of solidarity. Common, mutual, reciprocal obligation is necessary. The myth of divine commandment creates that web."[6] Yet, despite the centrality of law in the life of individual Jews as well as of the Jewish community as a whole, and despite the divine source of that law, it was recognized that halakhic authorities possessed special emergency jurisdiction to deal with exceptional circumstances when application of the ordinary law would produce unacceptable results.[7] Most significantly, such emergency jurisdiction allowed the halakhic authorities of the age to set aside parts of the God-given Torah law (that part of Jewish law which is contained in the five books of Moses), and included the power to suspend ordinary laws, promulgate emergency measures, and resort to extra-legal sanctions that had not been authorized under ordinary law. When crisis was perceived to be severe enough and adherence to the ordinary set of Torah laws was deemed injurious to the overall effort to ensure that the laws are generally obeyed,

---

[6] Robert M. Cover, "Obligation: A Jewish Jurisprudence of the Social Order" (1987) 5 *Journal of Law and Religion* 65.

[7] Neil S. Hecht and Emanuel B. Quint, "Exigency Jurisdiction under Jewish Law" (1978–80) 9 *Dine Israel* 27; Aaron M. Schreiber, *Jewish Law and Decision-Making: A Study through Time* (Philadelphia, PA: Temple University Press, 1979), pp. 342–75; Eliezer Berkovits, *Not in Heaven: The Nature and Function of Halakha* (New York: Ktav Publishing House, 1983).

the appropriate Jewish authorities could act in a manner that amounted to violation of the fundamental law of the Torah. As the Talmud suggests, in such circumstances setting aside the dictates of the Torah was done not to violate the Torah law, but rather to preserve it.[8]

Once the halakhic authorities identified a situation as amounting to such exceptional circumstances, they could exercise emergency jurisdiction. Thus, for example, there were instances in which it was recognized that strict adherence to the stringent rules of criminal procedure and evidence prescribed by the Torah might lead to unacceptable results.[9] Rabbi Shlomo ben Aderet (Rashba), the leading Jewish sage in thirteenth-century Spain, resolved the problem, ruling that: "if you establish everything on the laws prescribed in the Torah...the world would be desolate."[10] Rashba reasoned that following the strict letter of the law in such matters would undermine deterrence and would result in much violation of the law. Thus, the Jewish court might impose punishment not prescribed in the Torah and deviate from the regular rules of evidence applying to criminal proceedings, when it came to the conclusion that "the time requires it" (*Ha-sha'ah zerikhah le-khakh*) as when the court considered such actions to be necessary in order to strengthen the overall observance of the law.[11] Rambam (Maimonides), the great Jewish sage and codificator, clarifies the state of the law on this matter:

> The court may impose flogging on one who is not liable [according to the Torah law] for lashes and execute one who is not liable for the death penalty, [and it may so act] not to transgress the law of the Torah but in order to make a fence around the Torah. When the court sees that the people are dissolute with respect to a certain matter, they [the judges] may safeguard and strengthen that matter as they deem proper, and all this as a temporary measure, and not to establish a precedent for generations to come.[12]

---

[8] Talmud Bavli (the Babylonian Talmud, known as the Bavli): Menahot 99a/b.

[9] See, e.g., Aaron M. Schreiber, "The Jurisprudence of Dealing with Unsatisfactory Fundamental Law: A Comparative Glance at the Different Approaches in Medieval Criminal Law, Jewish Law and the United States Supreme Court" (1991) 11 *Pace Law Review* 535 at 545–51.

[10] Shlomo ben Avraham ben Aderet, *She'elot u-teshuvot ha-Rashba (Responsa)* (Jerusalem: Makhon Masoret Israel, 2000), No. 393.

[11] Nahum Rakover, *Shilton ha-hok be-Israel (The Rule of Law in Israel)* (Jerusalem: Sifriyat ha-mishpat ha-Ivri, 1989), pp. 148–50.

[12] Rambam, *Mishne Torah, Sefer Shoftim, Hilkhot Sanhedrin* 24:4–5. See also *Talmud Bavli: Sanhedrin* 46a; *Talmud Bavli: Yevamot* 90b; Joseph ben Efraim Karo, *Shulkhan Arukh, Khoshen Mishpat, Siman* 2.

During the thirteenth and fourteenth centuries, many Jewish communities found themselves in circumstances when strict observance of
existing rules and norms of criminal procedure was deemed to put
the safety and security, indeed the very existence, of the community at
risk. *Malshinim* (informers) or *Mosrim* (literally meaning "handing over,"
i.e., handing over to the authorities) were members of the Jewish community who would divulge information (often false) to the non-Jewish
authorities, who would then use that information against the Jewish
community as a whole, or against individuals (often the community's
leaders). The informers posed grave physical danger to many and constituted an imminent threat to the integrity of Jewish communal life.[13]
Yet, they could not have been dealt with in accordance with the strict
rules of criminal procedure and law of evidence. For example, while the
Torah law requires that testimonial evidence be given in the presence
of the defendant, many *Malshinim*, who were closely connected to the
non-Jewish authorities, used their contacts to ensure that they would
not be forced to appear before the Jewish court. Insistence on strict adherence to such rules could have undermined the effectiveness of the
criminal process and put the whole community in danger. Rabbi Asher
ben Yechiel (known as the Rosh) put the matter:

[I]t is well known that he who is known to be a *Malshin*, the heathens [the
authorities] befriend him for their own benefit, and if it were necessary to hear
the testimony in his presence...justice would never be made, as he would be
saved by the heathens, for when he is not in danger he hands over [to the
authorities] individuals and groups, let alone when he perceives himself to be in
danger he would hand over by [using] false pretense and endanger the whole of
Israel.[14]

As a result, many of these rules were suspended in order to deal effectively with the crisis.

Another important emergency mechanism that was designed to deal
with exigencies such as the danger that observance of the faith would become lax was that of *hora'at sha'ah* (temporary measure). Recognizing the
danger that abuse of such special measures might lead to a general disrespect for the law, it was accepted that only extreme circumstances involving situations of widespread breakdown in observance of the law, or
fear that such widespread disobedience might follow unless exceptional

---

[13] Abraham A. Neuman, *The Jews in Spain: Their Social, Political and Cultural Life in the Middle
Ages* (2 vols., New York: Octagon, 1980), vol. I, pp. 130–32.
[14] *Responsa Rosh*, rule 17, s. (a); Rakover, *The Rule of Law in Israel*, p. 131.

measures were taken, or those involving habitual offenders, might potentially justify the use of exceptional jurisdiction and extraordinary measures.[15] Thus it is written in the Talmud that, "It is better [that] one letter of the Torah should be uprooted so that the [entire] Torah will not be forgotten by Israel."[16] Rambam summarizes the matter as follows: "If they [the court] should deem it necessary temporarily to set aside a positive commandment or to nullify a negative commandment in order to restore the people to the faith or to save many Jews from becoming lax in other matters, they may act as the needs of the time dictate." And in words similar to Abraham Lincoln's famous rhetorical question some eight hundred years later – "are all the laws *but one* to go unexecuted, and the Government itself go to pieces, lest that one be violated?"[17] – Rambam continues: "Just as a physician amputates a hand or foot to save a life, so a court in appropriate circumstances may decree a temporary violation of some of the commandments to preserve all of them, in line with the approach of the early Sages who said: 'One should violate . . . one Sabbath in order to enable the observance of many Sabbaths.'"[18]

It is worth noting that the notion of emergencies that justify deviating from the law was not confined to the realm of criminal law, but extended to other issues as well. For example, similar notions can be found in such matters as appointments of converts who happened to be the greatest sages of their time as the heads of the Sanhedrin (the chief Jewish court), in contravention of a rule that barred converts from assuming the positions of the president and chief judge of the Sanhedrin.[19]

Cognizant of the problematic nature of this extraordinary jurisdiction, halakhic sages imposed restrictions on the exercise of this

---

[15] Hecht and Quint, "Exigency Jurisdiction," 61–66.

[16] *Talmud Bavli*: Temurah 14b; *Talmud Bavli*: Yevamot 79a.

[17] Abraham Lincoln, Message to Congress in Special Session (July 4, 1861), in Roy Prentice Basler (ed.), *The Collected Works of Abraham Lincoln* (New Brunswick, NJ: Rutgers University Press, 1953), vol. IV, p. 421 at 429–30.

[18] Rambam, *Mishne Torah, Sefer Shoftim, Hilkhot Mamrim* 2:4. See also *Talmud Bavli*: Yoma 85b; *Talmud Bavli*: Eruvin 32b; *Talmud Bavli*: Yevamot 90b (discussing the prophet Elijah's offering of a sacrifice on Mt. Carmel in violation of explicit prohibitions of the Torah permitting such offering only in the Temple); *Talmud Yerushalmi* (the Jerusalem Talmud): Hagiga 2:2, 11b; Menachem Elon, *Jewish Law: History, Sources, Principles*, trans. Bernard Auerbach and Melvin J. Sykes (Philadelphia: Jewish Publication Society, 1994), p. 517.

[19] Alter Hilvitz, "More on the Actions of Yehudah ben Tavai and Shimon ben Shetah because the Hour Required it" (1983) 92 *Sinai* 193.

extraordinary power.[20] First, the court could impose a punishment that was not prescribed by the Torah law or deviate from the evidentiary rules specified therein, only after it had been convinced that the necessities of the times required it. The Talmud mentions two examples in this context:

Once a man rode a horse on the Sabbath in the time of the Greeks, and he was brought to the court and stoned, not because this was the legally prescribed punishment but because the exigencies of the time so required. On another occasion, a man thrust his wife under a fig tree [had sexual intercourse with her in a public place] and he was brought to the court and flogged, not because this was the legally prescribed punishment but because the exigencies of the time so required.[21]

In these two cases, the court is imposing punishments not prescribed by the Torah. In the first case the court is aware of the danger of assimilation under Greek rule. In the second it struggles to maintain a proper level of morality among the people. In order to achieve these purposes, which eventually will lead to more observance of the Torah law, the court is ready to act in a manner not prescribed by that very law. Another example is that of Rabbi Simeon ben Shetah who hanged eighty women in one day without having a conclusive testimony in this matter and without complying with the requirements of interrogation and inquiry. Rabbi ben Shetah's action also violated the law that no two capital cases may be tried on one day.[22] In this a full trial was not given to the women, charged with witchcraft, because of the need to act quickly on the matter and ensure that the people fully understood that undermining belief in God would be severely punished.

Second, in exercising this exceptional jurisdiction the court had to be constantly mindful of the fact that it did so for the sole purpose of fostering the observance of the law and the adherence to the Jewish faith in God. Meting an unusual punishment was to be done neither lightly nor for any other purpose.[23] Third, the court was warned not to disregard human dignity. As Rambam holds:

---

[20] Rambam, *Mishne Torah, Sefer Shoftim, Hilkhot Sanhedrin* 24:10; ben Aderet, *She'elot u-teshuvot*, No. 238; Elon, *Jewish Law*, p. 519.

[21] *Talmud Bavli*: Sanhedrin 46a.

[22] *Talmud Yerushalmi*: Hagigah 2:2; Alter Hilvitz, "Yehudah ben Tavai and Shimon ben Shetah and their Actions" (1980) 89 *Sinai* 266.

[23] *Talmud Bavli*: Yevamot 90b; *Talmud Bavli*: Sanhedrin 46a; Rambam, *Mishne Torah, Sefer Shoftim, Hilkhot Sanhedrin* 24:4 and *Hilkhot Mamrim* 2:4; Karo, *Shulkhan Arukh, Khoshen Mishpat* 2:1.

All these matters apply to the extent that the judge deems appropriate and necessary for the needs of the time. In all matters, he shall act for the sake of Heaven and not regard human dignity lightly, for consideration for human dignity may warrant setting aside rabbinic injunctions...He must be careful not to destroy their dignity; rather he must act solely to increase the honor of God.[24]

Fourth, the jurisdiction of the court and its decision in the specific case heard by it were limited to the particular exigency giving rise to such a unique jurisdiction. They were not permanent or long-standing. They were for that case and that day only. With the exigency over, the special jurisdiction of the court was terminated. Because of its special character, confined as it were to the particular facts of the case at hand, a decision by the court in any concrete case could not serve as a precedent for future cases arising either in ordinary times or under future exigencies.[25] The exceptional nature of those measures is clearly evidenced by the terminology used: *hora'at sha'ah* ("temporary measure"), *ha-sha'ah zerikhah le-khakh* ("the hour requires it"), *lemigdar milta* ("to safeguard the matter"), and *lefi sha'ah* ("temporarily").[26] Significantly, while exigency could excuse the exercise of measures that did not conform to existing law, it could not make legal that which in other, normal, circumstances would have been illegal. Finally, certain restrictions were imposed so as to limit the identity of persons and authorities who might exercise the extraordinary jurisdiction, i.e., "the greatest of his generation" – a person who was known to have attained a unique mastery of the Torah and the *Halakhah* – and the leaders of the community.[27]

Undoubtedly, violating the Torah law even under extreme emergency circumstances, was a bold step to take both intellectually and mentally. That this was so can be appreciated when one considers the fact that according to the convictions and religious beliefs of the persons involved in this process they were deviating from, and acting against, divine law. Deviating from the normative commandments of that law was truly momentous. Yet, rather than engage in interpretive moves designed to reconcile their actions with the dictates of the law – Jewish law

---

[24] Rambam, *Mishne Torah, Sefer Shoftim, Hilkhot Sanhedrin* 24:10.

[25] Ibid., 24:4.   [26] Elon, *Jewish Law*, pp. 533–36.

[27] Debates can be found as to whether being considered among the greatest in the generation was sufficient or whether there existed an additional condition that such a person be appointed by the community, and vice versa – whether appointment as a judge, without being great in the Torah, would be sufficient. Hecht and Quint, "Exigency Jurisdiction," 71–92.

is replete with examples of sophisticated exegesis and hermeneutics of that type[28] – the sages preferred to recognize openly the dilemma and its extraordinary, extra-legal solution. They did not attempt to argue that the necessity of the times somehow transformed their extra-legal actions and made those legal. They chose to perpetrate the lesser harm rather than let the community as a whole suffer the consequences of a much more substantial and sizable injury. Acting in possible contravention of a particular normative dictate was seen as a means, regrettable but necessary, to ensure the long-term maintenance of the legal system as a whole.

Locke's theory of the prerogative power

John Locke's experience was shaped by the abuses of power during the reign of the Stuarts, the controversy between King James I and Sir Edward Coke regarding the Crown's prerogative, the 1628 Petition of Right and, possibly, the Glorious Revolution.[29] Throughout *Two Treatises of Government*, John Locke emphasizes the significance of the rule of law, of having standing rules and established and promulgated laws, in ensuring peace, quiet, and property.[30] Yet, Locke also develops the theory of the prerogative power, which he sees as vested in the executive branch of government,[31] and which is "nothing but the power of doing public good without a rule."[32] Locke's theory of the prerogative power is significant not only because of its intellectual potency, but also because it greatly influenced many of the Founding Fathers of the United States and their contemporaries.[33] According to Locke, the prerogative is the

---

[28] The *Halakhah* is explicit in vesting exclusive competence in the halakhic authorities to determine the meaning of the Torah by way of interpretation and exegesis. See, for example, the famous talmudic story of *tanuro shel Akhnai* in *Talmud Bavli*: Baba Mezia 59b; Itzhak Englard, "Majority Decision vs. Individual Truth: The Interpretations of the 'Oven of Achnai' Aggadah" (1975) 15 *Tradition* 137; David Luban, "The Coiled Serpent of Argument: Reason, Authority, and Law in a Talmudic Tale" (2004) 79 *Chicago-Kent Law Review* 1253.

[29] It is unclear whether the *Two Treatises of Government* was written before or after the Glorious Revolution of 1688. Mark Goldie, "Introduction to Two Treatises of Government" in John Locke, *Two Treatises of Government*, ed. Mark Goldie (London: Tuttle Publishing, 1994), pp. xv, xix–xxi.

[30] See, for example, Locke, *Two Treatises*, paras. 136–37 (all references are to the Second Treatise).

[31] Ibid., para. 159.   [32] Ibid., para. 166.

[33] See, e.g., Quincy Wright, *The Control of American Foreign Relations* (New York: Macmillan Press, 1922), p. 147; William Howard Taft, *Our Chief Magistrate and his Powers* (New York: Columbia University Press, 1916), pp. 139–40; Henry P. Monaghan, "The Protective Power of the Presidency" (1993) 93 *Columbia Law Review* 1 at 12–24.

power "to act according to discretion, for the public good, *without the prescription of the law, and sometimes even against it.*"[34] Put somewhat differently, "prerogative can be nothing, but the people's permitting their rulers, to do several things of their own free choice, where the law was silent, and sometimes too *against the direct letter of the law*, for the public good; and their acquiescing in it when so done."[35] Locke considers such power as necessary in order to deal with situations when strict and rigid observation of the laws may lead to grave social harm.[36] Explaining his reasons for vesting the prerogative power with the executive, Locke argues that the legislature cannot anticipate in advance and regulate by statute all that may be, at any point in the future, beneficial to society, and that law-making power may be too slow to adapt adequately to exigencies and necessities of the times.

According to Locke, the power of prerogative encompasses executive discretion, the power of pardon, and the power to act without the prescription of positive law, and in appropriate cases, even against it. It shares some basic attributes with what Locke calls the "federative power,"[37] namely the broad foreign affairs power that "contains the power of war and peace, leagues and alliances, and all the transactions with all persons and communities without the commonwealth."[38] The federative power "is much less capable to be directed by antecedent, standing, positive laws than the executive [power]; and so must necessarily be left to the prudence and wisdom of those whose hands it is in to be managed for the public good."[39] Thus, Locke identifies the area of foreign affairs as one especially prone to be administered by executive discretion for the public good, i.e., by exercise of the prerogative power.[40] We revisit this idea in the next chapter.

Locke offers a functional litmus test for evaluating whether the prerogative power has been appropriately used in any given case. He focuses on the purpose behind the exercise of the prerogative, i.e., whether it was directed at promoting the public good: "if there comes to be a question between the executive power and the people, about a thing claimed as a prerogative; the tendency of the exercise of such prerogative to the good or hurt of the people, will easily decide that question."[41] Government

---

[34] Locke, *Two Treatises*, para. 160 (emphasis added).

[35] Ibid., para. 164 (emphasis added).   [36] Ibid., paras. 159–60.

[37] Ibid., paras. 146–47.   [38] Ibid., para. 146.   [39] Ibid., para. 147.

[40] See also Franz Neumann, *The Rule of Law: Political Theory and the Legal System in Modern Society* (Dover, NH: Berg, 1986), p. 122.

[41] Locke, *Two Treatises*, para. 161. See also ibid., paras. 163, 164, 168.

cannot have any legitimate ends apart from promoting the good of the community. Governmental power used for any purpose other than the public good is properly regarded as tyrannical[42] and may justify, under certain circumstances, an uprising to restore the people's rights and to limit the government's resort to such arbitrary power.[43]

Locke puts much faith in human reason and rationality as mitigating and limiting factors on the exercise of prerogative power.[44] His theory of the prerogative reveals a substantial degree of trust in government and particularly in times of emergency. He gives the executive the benefit of the doubt: if there are allegations that the ruler's use of the prerogative power has not been for the purpose of promoting the public good, but rather was in the service of the ruler's own interests and purposes, the people have no remedy available from any "judge on earth." Their sole recourse is "to appeal to heaven" or, when the majority of the people feels wronged, to revolt against the oppressive ruler.[45] This is a tall order indeed as Locke recognizes that the right of the people to revolt against a ruler who abuses her powers will likely be exercised on rare occasions.[46] On the other hand, if it appears that the ruler used her prerogative power in an appropriate manner the evaluation of her actions is straightforward: "*prerogative* can be nothing, but *the people's permitting their rulers*, to do several things of their own free choice, where the law was silent, and sometimes too against the direct letter of the law, for the public good; *and their acquiescing in it when so done.*"[47] When the ruler applies her prerogative power for the public good, such action is considered appropriate, right, just, and legitimate. An appropriate exercise of the prerogative power is legitimate per se and ex ante owing to the implicit acquiescence of the public to any such exercise (albeit not necessarily to the specific use of the prerogative power in the circumstances of any particular crisis). There is no need for any further public involvement.

One possible reading of Locke draws distinctions between "extra-legality" and "extra-constitutionality." According to this reading, while Locke may be willing to recognize governmental actions that run contrary to positive law, i.e., extra-legal actions, he does not consider the prerogative to be an extra-constitutional power. Rather, he sees it as an integral part of the broader constitutional scheme.[48] That constitutional order, which enjoys a higher normative value than any particular set of

---

[42] Ibid., paras. 190, 202.   [43] Ibid., paras. 203–09.   [44] Ibid., paras. 163–64.
[45] Ibid., para. 168.   [46] Ibid., paras. 223, 225, 230.
[47] Ibid., para. 164 (emphasis added).
[48] Friedrich, *Reason of State*, pp. 110–12.

positive laws, acknowledges the possibility of extra-legal governmental action in times of emergency and necessity. Thus, the prerogative power ought to be considered as a concrete (extreme to be sure) example of the "political power" – that power "which every man, having in the state of nature, has given up into the hands of the society, and therein to the governors, whom the society hath set over itself, with this express or tacit trust, that it shall be employed for their good, and the preservation of their property"[49] – as distinguished from "despotical power."[50] Locke's warning that exercise of the prerogative power by the good, even "godlike," prince will serve as a precedent for the application of similar powers by a lesser ruler "managing the government with different thoughts,"[51] may also suggest that he considers the prerogative power to be functioning within the boundaries of the constitutional system rather than outside these boundaries. For the implementation of extra-constitutional powers cannot establish a legal precedent for the future and coat with legality the actions of a less worthy prince.

This reading of Locke brings the theory of the prerogative closer to that model of accommodation, discussed in chapter 1, which regards the principle of necessity as an independent source of constitutional law. However, it seems that a more consistent reading of Locke suggests that the prerogative power ought to be recognized for what it is, namely an extra-constitutional and extra-legal power. Locke is generally skeptical about the ability of legal rules and institutions to deal with unforeseen exigencies. Hence, he retains the prerogative as purely a political power that does not emerge out of legal and constitutional structures.[52]

The theory of the prerogative power may seem, at first blush, to be inconsistent with Locke's otherwise staunch support for the rule of law and with notions of constitutionalism.[53] But that apparent contradiction further suggests that he viewed the power as extra-constitutional. To view the prerogative as constitutional power would have meant an expansion of the government's powers under the constitution and the

---

[49] Locke, *Two Treatises*, para. 171.   [50] Ibid., para. 172.

[51] Ibid., para. 166. Locke warns that so perilous may such consequences be that "Upon this is founded that saying, that 'the reigns of good princes have been always most dangerous to the liberties of their people.'"

[52] Clement Fatovic, "Constitutionalism and Contingency: Locke's Theory of Prerogative" (2004) 25 *History of Political Thought* 276.

[53] See, e.g., Edward S. Corwin, *The "Higher Law" Background of American Constitutional Law* (Ithaca, NY: Cornell University Press, 1955), p. 71; Daniel Farber, *Lincoln's Constitution: The Nation, the President, and the Courts in a Time of Crisis* (Chicago: University of Chicago Press, 2003), p. 128.

vesting in the executive of a highly discretionary, in fact arbitrary, power within the constitutional framework. Treating the prerogative as a pragmatically necessary, yet extra-constitutional, power, still allows for a government that is exercised by "established and promulgated laws" while giving government the flexibility that may be required in the face of crisis and exigency. It is, in other words, precisely because of Locke's attachment to the rule of law that he is willing to recognize the possibility of going outside the law in extreme cases and acting, in such circumstances, extra-constitutionally. As we shall see in the next section, Thomas Jefferson came to a similar conclusion.

Locke's theory of the prerogative power was accepted by many of the American Founding Fathers and their contemporaries as a foundation for a theory of extra-legal powers. Yet, as we explain further below, while the prerogative power may be seen as a prototype of the Extra-Legal Measures model, it is lacking a crucial accountability concept identified here: it merges the two issues that the Extra-Legal Measures model seeks to separate, namely doing the pragmatic right thing, and deciding what is legally, politically, and morally the right thing. Locke, as we have seen, focuses on implicit, general, ex ante public acquiescence in the exercise of the prerogative power. An appropriate exercise of the prerogative power is legitimate per se and ex ante owing to the implicit acquiescence of the public to any such exercise, and does not require any further public involvement. In conflating the two issues, the Lockean model fails to impose the ethic of responsibility that is central to the Extra-Legal Measures model. It also fails to create strong enough barriers against the easy use of extra-legal powers by public officials. This becomes clearer when we contrast Locke's theory of the prerogative with Thomas Jefferson's exercise of extra-legal measures.

"Casting behind metaphysical subtleties"

Thomas Jefferson opposed granting broad powers to the executive branch and, indeed, to the federal government as a whole. As suggested above with respect to Locke's prerogative power, it is this general opposition to a strong executive that explains Jefferson's support for a doctrine of extra-legal powers, which was "accepted by every single one of our early statesman."[54] Without such a doctrine of emergency powers, the only way to enable the government to protect the nation in times of

---

[54] Lucius Wilmerding, Jr., "The President and the Law" (1952) 67 *Political Science Quarterly* 321 at 324.

crisis would have been the concession of sweeping constitutional powers to the federal government and the president, allowing them to meet
each and every emergency that might arise. Similar to those who support the theory of inherent powers or similar versions of what we called
in chapter 1 constitutional necessity, Jefferson argued that,

> A strict observance of the written laws is doubtless *one* of the high duties of a
> good citizen, but it is not *the highest*. The laws of necessity, of self-preservation,
> of saving our country when in danger, are of a higher obligation. To lose our
> country by a scrupulous adherence to written law, would be to lose the law
> itself, with life, liberty, property and all those who are enjoying them with us;
> thus absurdly sacrificing the end to the means.[55]

However, he did not seek to anchor emergency powers in the constitution. Rather, his liberal theory of emergency powers facilitated a vision
of more limited powers vested in the national government, for truly exceptional crises could be met by the use of extra-legal powers that go
beyond the strict lines of law while not forming part of the constitutional framework.

His presidency gave Jefferson a number of occasions to put his theory
of emergency powers to the test. One example was the 1803 Louisiana
Purchase.[56] Although the president was actively supported in this matter by Congress and did not act solely on the basis of the constitutional
powers of his office, Jefferson himself believed the purchase and annexa-
tion of a new territory to be utterly outside the constitutional powers of
the federal government.[57] Yet, believing that the situation constituted a
national emergency, Jefferson was of the opinion that it called for extra-
legal powers and acknowledged – albeit in a private letter rather than
publicly – the extra-legal nature of his actions:

---

[55] Letter from Thomas Jefferson to John B. Colvin (Sept. 20, 1810) in Paul Leicester Ford
(ed.), *The Writings of Thomas Jefferson* (New York: G.P. Putnam's Sons, 1986), p. 1231. See
also Jules Lobel, "Emergency Power and the Decline of Liberalism" (1989) 98 *Yale Law
Journal* 1385 at 1392; Abraham D. Sofaer, *War, Foreign Affairs, and Constitutional Power:
The Origins* (Cambridge, MA: Ballinger, 1976), p. 226.

[56] James MacGregor Burns, *The Vineyard of Liberty* (New York: Knopf, 1982), pp. 172–78;
Everett Somerville Brown, *The Constitutional History of the Louisiana Purchase, 1803–1812*
(Berkeley: University of California Press, 1920); Sanford Levinson and Bartholomew
Sparrow (eds.), *The Louisiana Purchase and American Expansion, 1803–1898* (Lanham, MD:
Rowman & Littlefield, 2005).

[57] Marc Karnis Landy and Sidney M. Milkis, *Presidential Greatness* (Lawrence, KS: University
Press of Kansas, 2000), p. 79; Arthur M. Schlesinger, Jr., *The Imperial Presidency* (Boston:
Houghton Mifflin, 1989), pp. 23–25.

The Executive in seizing the fugitive occurrence which so much advances the good of their country, *have done an act beyond the Constitution*. The Legislature in casting behind them metaphysical subtleties, and risking themselves like faithful servants, must ratify and pay for it, and throw themselves on their country for doing for [the people] unauthorized what we know they would have done for themselves had they been in a situation to act.[58]

Similarly, following an attack (during a congressional recess) by a British frigate, the *Leopard*, on an American ship, the *Chesapeake*, President Jefferson spent unappropriated funds for munitions to strengthen certain strongholds in the face of a possible war with England. He later asked Congress for a retroactive approval of this expenditure, explaining:

To have awaited a previous and special sanction by law would have lost occasions which might not be retrieved...I trust that the Legislature, feeling the same anxiety for the safety of our country, so materially advanced by this precaution, will approve, when done, what they would have seen so important to be done if then assembled.[59]

In the congressional debates that ensued, a general agreement with Jefferson's position prevailed across political parties.[60]

Thus, suggested Jefferson, "There are extreme cases where the laws become inadequate even to their own preservation, and where the universal recourse is a dictator, or martial law,"[61] and that "on great occasions every good officer must be ready to risk himself in going beyond the strict lines of law, when the public preservation requires it; his motives will be a justification."[62] Jefferson sought to limit the incidents in which such illegal actions might be taken by claiming that they would be justified if, and only if, three conditions were met:

(1)   The occurrence of certain objective circumstances that amount to "extreme cases" and "great occasions." That such "great occasions" were to be rare is demonstrated by President Madison's refusal to ratify the controversial actions of General Jackson in New Orleans in early 1815. Jackson was fined $1,000 for contempt of court for

---

[58] Letter from Thomas Jefferson to John Breckenridge (Aug. 12, 1803), quoted in Daniel P. Franklin, *Extraordinary Measures: The Exercise of Prerogative Powers in the United States* (Pittsburgh: University of Pittsburgh Press, 1991), p. 45 (emphasis added).

[59] Wilmerding, "The President and the Law," 323–24.

[60] Ibid., pp. 327–28; see also Schlesinger, *The Imperial Presidency*, p. 24.

[61] Letter from Thomas Jefferson to James Brown (Oct. 27, 1808), at http://memory.loc.gov/ammem/mtjhtml/mtjser1.html (last visited on August 8, 2005).

[62] Letter from Thomas Jefferson to William C.C. Claiborne, Governor of Orleans Territory (Feb. 3, 1807), at http://memory.loc.gov/ammem/mtjhtml/mtjser1.html (last visited on August 8, 2005).

ignoring a writ of habeas corpus issued by Judge Dominick Hall and for imprisoning the judge himself. Jackson paid the fine out of his own pocket. It took Congress twenty-nine years before it repaid the fine (with interest) to Jackson. As Justice Field of the United States Supreme Court wrote:

> I confess I have always been taught to believe that Judge Hall was right in imposing the fine, and that General Jackson earned the brightest page in his history by paying it, and gracefully submitting to the judicial power. Such I believe is the judgment of history and of thoughtful judicial inquirers; though a grateful country very properly refunded to her favorite general the sum he had paid for a *necessary but unauthorized* exercise of military power.[63]

(2) Actions by public officials that advance the good of the country.
(3) An ex post approval of these actions by the American people (directly or through their representatives in Congress). Such measures were taken for the sake of preserving the life, liberty, and property of the people, and the people ought to determine whether the actions should be ratified. Similarly, discussing the charge that the Philadelphia Convention exceeded its powers, James Madison rejected the allegation, but added that even

> if they had exceeded their powers, they were not only warranted, but required as the confidential servants of their country, by the circumstances in which they were placed to exercise the liberty which they assumed; and ... if they had violated both their powers and their obligations in proposing a Constitution, this ought nevertheless to be embraced, if it be calculated to accomplish the views and happiness of the people of America.[64]

For this final and most crucial condition – the need for ex post approval – to apply there ought to be open and public acknowledgment of the unlawful nature of such actions and of the necessity that called for committing them in the first place.

[63] Dow v. Johnson, 100 US 158 (1879), pp. 194–95 (Justice Field) (emphasis added); Sofaer, *War, Foreign Affairs*, pp. 333–36; George M. Dennison, "Martial Law: The Development of a Theory of Emergency Powers, 1776–1861" (1974) 18 *American Journal of Legal History* 52 at 61–65; Jonathan Lurie, "Andrew Jackson, Martial Law, Civilian Control of the Military, and American Politics: An Intriguing Amalgam" (1989) 126 *Military Law Review* 133; Abraham D. Sofaer, "Emergency Power and the Hero of New Orleans" (1981) 2 *Cardozo Law Review* 233. See also Wilmerding, "The President and the Law," 326–27 (discussing a heated debate in 1807 in the House of Representatives and noting that all parties were united in agreement that certain circumstances may arise in which an *illegal* suspension of the writ of habeas corpus would be proper).

[64] Clinton Rossiter (ed.), *The Federalist Papers* (New York: New American Library, 1961), No. 40, pp. 254–55 (James Madison).

Whereas Locke puts his trust in an implicit, general, ex ante public acquiescence in the exercise of an executive power to act outside the law, Jefferson's approach insists that an explicit, particular, ex post legislative ratification of the same must be awarded. Extra-legal actions cannot be justified merely by reference to the motives of the actors, laudable as these may be. Rather, a separate and independent ex post ratification process must take place in order for the extra-legal action to be justified or excused. In the absence of ex post ratification the actor may be subject to legal sanctions for violating the dictates of the law, albeit for what are arguably the noblest of reasons. Public officials who act in violation of the law in order to fend off great threats assume the risk of being found criminally and civilly liable for their illegal actions. They must openly and boldly disclose the nature of their actions and the reasons for taking them and "throw [themselves] on the justice of [their] country."[65] This is the ethic of responsibility at its zenith.

The circumstances surrounding *Little v. Barreme*[66] illustrate the distinctions between action and ratification. During a period of hostilities between the United States and France, a merchant vessel, the *Flying Fish*, sailing under the Danish flag, was captured by two American vessels on suspicion of violating an act of Congress prohibiting commerce with France. Under the relevant provision, the president had been authorized to instruct naval commanders to seize any vessel on the high seas bound or sailing *to* any French port. The order issued by President Adams instructed the commanders to seize vessels bound *to* or sailing *from* France. When captured, the *Flying Fish* was sailing *from* France to Denmark, a neutral state in the conflict. The United States Supreme Court affirmed the circuit court's decision to grant damages against Captain George Little, the commanding officer of the *USS Boston*, for the seizure and detention of the Danish vessel. Speaking for a unanimous court, Chief Justice Marshall held that the president could not give lawful instructions that ran contrary to express congressional legislation. The commander's actions could not be legalized by such a presidential order. The instructions of the executive order could not "change the nature of the transaction, nor legalize an act which, without those instructions, would have been a plain trespass."[67] The court did not doubt Captain

---

[65] Wilmerding, "The President and the Law," 322–24, 329; Lobel, "Decline of Liberalism," 1396.

[66] 6 US (2 Cranch) 170 (1804).

[67] Ibid., p. 178. See also United States v. Smith, 27 F. Cas. 1192 at 1230 (C.C.D.N.Y. 1806) (No. 16,342).

Little's motives. Yet, despite the fact that his actions were undertaken for the good of the country (as not only he but also the president saw it), the Supreme Court held such actions illegal and imposed penalties on him.

This judicial decision was not, however, the end of the story. After the Supreme Court had ruled on the matter and after damages had been recovered from Captain Little, Congress reimbursed him for his damages, interest, and charges, with money from the United States Treasury.[68] The action taken by Captain Little was ruled illegal, but the "justice of his country" dictated that he should not bear the brunt for that action. While recognizing that Captain Little's actions were the right thing to do in the circumstances, the Supreme Court found them to be illegal. It was only with the ex post ratification of Little's actions by Congress that the gap between illegality and "the right thing to do" was, for practical purposes, closed. This was by no means a foregone conclusion. Captain Little took a double risk: first, that his actions would, as they indeed were, be found illegal and that he might need to make reparations, both civil and penal, for such actions, and second, that ex post ratification would not materialize. The potential absence of such ratification would have meant that no reimbursement would have been made, and, perhaps more significantly, that the moral and public vindication of Captain Little would not have been forthcoming. Such substantial risks are not lightly taken and their existence militates against acting in a way that falls outside the legal order, although it does not completely bar the possibility of such actions taking place.

Jefferson's approach to emergency powers may be compared with the constitutional vision presented by President Lincoln during the Civil War. As noted in chapter 1 above, one possible reading of Lincoln's assertions of special powers during the war sees the president as having appealed to special emergency powers that are inherent in the constitutional framework and that are available to the executive in times of great peril and risk. There are, however, other possible readings of Lincoln's claims to such powers that bring his actions closer to the Extra-Legal Measures model. Thus, when explaining to Congress the extraordinary measures that he had taken prior to July 4, 1861, Lincoln said that those measures, "whether strictly legal *or not*, were ventured upon, under what appeared to be a popular demand, and a public necessity; *trusting, then as now, that Congress would readily ratify them*. It is believed that nothing

[68] Wilmerding, "The President and the Law," 324, n. 6.

has been done beyond the constitutional competency of Congress."[69] On other occasions, however (as noted in chapter 1), Lincoln seems to consider the necessity and exigency of the times to have made constitutional that which in other circumstances might not have been so, without need for any further form of ex post ratification. Since Lincoln's presidency, arguments about emergency powers have invariably revolved around the claim that the president enjoys a wide range of constitutionally inherent powers, including emergency powers, and therefore acts legally and constitutionally rather than outside the constitutional and legal framework. For presidents, the possibility of arguing that their actions are constitutional is obviously desirable. For the public, the notion that a valiant public official out to save the nation may be forced to employ illegal means and "throw himself on the electorate's judgment" is difficult to accept. Frederick Pollock, commenting on the view that the necessity that leads to the use of martial law may not make, of its own accord, measures taken to protect the nation legal even if otherwise such measures would have been illegal, suggested that such a theory,

[I]mputes gratuitous folly to the common law, which cannot be so perverse as to require a man in an office of trust to choose between breaking the law and being an incompetent officer and a bad citizen...It seems, therefore, that the acts which every courageous and prudent magistrate would certainly do in the circumstances supposed are not a kind of splendid offence, but are..."justifiable and lawful for the maintenance of the Commonwealth."[70]

The obvious discomfort that Chief Justice Marshall felt in deciding against Captain Little reflected similar sentiments: "I confess the first bias of my mind was very strong in favor of the opinion that though the instructions of the executive could not give a right, they might yet excuse from damages."[71] Be that as it may, the subsequent ratification and affirmation of Lincoln's emergency actions by Congress[72] and the

---

[69] Abraham Lincoln, "Message to Congress in Special Session (July 4, 1861)," in Basler, *The Collected Works of Abraham Lincoln*, vol. IV, pp. 421, 429 (emphasis added). See also Farber, *Lincoln's Constitution*, p. 194.

[70] Frederick Pollock, "What is Martial Law?" (1902) 70 *Law Quarterly Review* 152 at 156.

[71] Little v. Barreme, 6 US (2 Cranch) 170 at 179 (1804).

[72] On August 6, 1861, Congress ratified all of the president's actions related to the armed forces and the militia. In 1863, Congress passed a general immunity legislation: An Act Relating to Habeas Corpus, and Regulating Judicial Proceedings in Certain Cases, ch. 81, paras. 4, 7, 12 Stat. 755, 756–58 (1863).

Supreme Court[73] made the question of the legality of those actions practically a moot one.[74]

Dicey's "spirit of legality"

Introduction to the Study of the Law of the Constitution reflects Dicey's suspicion of executive discretion, treating it as leading to use of arbitrary powers. Dicey reminds us that "the supremacy of the law of the land both calls forth the exertion of Parliamentary sovereignty, and leads to its being exercised in a spirit of legality."[75] At the same time, he acknowledges that "The rigidity of the law constantly hampers (and sometimes with great injury to the public) the action of the executive."[76] Specifically, he concedes that "Under the complex conditions of modern life no government can in times of disorder, or of war, keep the peace at home, or perform its duties towards foreign powers, without occasional use of arbitrary authority."[77] How are we supposed to meet the challenge of the need to authorize occasional use of arbitrary (i.e., discretionary) authority while maintaining limitations and checks on the use of such power? Dicey offers us two complementary solutions. First is for the executive to obtain from parliament "the discretionary authority which is denied to the Crown by the law of the land," i.e., by recourse to "exceptional legislation."[78] While exigencies call for the exercise by the executive of discretionary power such power must be governed by statute. The executive must obtain "aid from Parliament" in fashioning the discretionary powers with which to meet, and successfully repel, crises and emergencies.[79] The fact that executive emergency powers are derived from, and based on, statutes reaffirms parliamentary supremacy even in times of grave threats to the nation, while at the same time, it acts to limit and confine the scope of such powers. They may be discretionary. They may be extraordinary. But they are never unlimited and are always open to review by the courts.[80]

What form should "aid from Parliament" take? The obvious response suggested by Dicey is the passage of "exceptional legislation" that would

---

[73] Mitchell v. Clark, 110 US 633 (1884); The Prize Cases, 67 US (2 Black) 635, 668–70 (1862).

[74] But see Sanford Levinson, "The David C. Baum Memorial Lecture: Was the Emancipation Proclamation Constitutional? Do We/Should We Care What the Answer Is?" (2001) *University of Illinois Law Review* 1135.

[75] Albert Venn Dicey, *Introduction to the Study of the Law of the Constitution* (8th edn, Indianapolis, IN: Liberty Classics, 1982), p. 273. As noted above, we refer to the 8th edition of Dicey's work since that was the last edition that he himself prepared.

[76] Ibid., p. 271.   [77] Ibid.   [78] Ibid.   [79] Ibid., p. 272.   [80] Ibid., p. 273.

enable the executive to exercise discretionary powers. Such exceptional legislation, falling squarely within the ambit of the model of legislative accommodation which we discussed in chapter 1, will be enacted ex ante, i.e., prior to the exercise of the relevant powers by the executive. It may be introduced either on an ad hoc (to meet a concrete exigency) or on a permanent basis. Once put in place it serves as the legal background against which executive emergency powers will be exercised, and against which their legality and eventual legitimacy will be measured and evaluated.

Yet, Dicey also recognizes that ex ante special legislation does not "exhaust...the instances in which the rigidity of the law necessitates the intervention of Parliament." Rather, "There are times of tumult or invasion when for the sake of legality itself the rules of law must be broken. The course which the government must then take is clear. *The Ministry must break the law and trust for protection to an Act of Indemnity.*"[81] By enacting such an Act of Indemnity parliament "legalises illegality" and asserts its sovereignty and supremacy.[82] Here, again, the government must obtain aid from parliament. But whereas the exceptional legislation discussed above calls for such legislative aid to be accorded ex ante, legislative Acts of Indemnity furnish the government with an after the fact, retrospective, ex post aid.

Under both special legislation and ex post Act of Indemnity, government must obtain aid from parliament. For Dicey, claims of inherent executive powers to deal with emergencies are inconceivable as they are certain to undermine parliamentary sovereignty and supremacy by leading to practically unfettered discretion and authority in the hands of the government. Dicey also rejects what he calls "the doctrine of political expediency," namely the view that "during an invasion, a general, a mayor, a magistrate, or indeed any loyal citizen, is *legally* justified in doing any act, even though *prima facie* a tort or a crime, as to which he can prove to the satisfaction of a jury that he did it for the public service in good faith, and for reasonable and probable cause."[83] Necessity does not, in and of itself, make legal that which in other circumstances would have been illegal. An Act of Indemnity, Dicey suggests, "legalises illegality." Acts of Indemnity may do one of two things: they may shelter the acting public official from civil or criminal responsibility for her

[81] Ibid., p. 272 (emphasis added).
[82] Ibid., pp. 10–11, 142; A.W. Bradley and K.D. Ewing, *Constitutional and Administrative Law* (13th edn, New York: Longman, 2003), p. 56.
[83] Dicey, *Law of the Constitution*, p. 412 (emphasis added).

violations of the law while holding that her actions were, and remain, illegal. Alternatively they may seek to exculpate the actor from any legal responsibility for her actions by making such actions, retrospectively, lawful. Dicey takes the latter approach: "Acts of Indemnity...are retrospective statutes which free persons who have broken the law from responsibility for its breach, and *thus make lawful acts which when they were committed were unlawful*."[84] An Act of Indemnity is, in this sense, constitutive for it transforms prior illegality into legality. Diecy rejects Frederick Pollock's suggestion that an Act of Indemnity is merely "a measure of prudence and grace. Its office is not to justify unlawful acts ex post facto, but to quiet doubts, to provide compensation for innocent persons in respect of damage inevitably caused by justifiable acts which would not have supported a legal claim."[85] calling it a "very inadequate description of an Act of Indemnity."[86] This fits with Dicey's overall argument for the supremacy of law in general, and with his position about martial law (and the limitations on the exercise of governmental power under it) in particular, since an "Act of Indemnity, again, though it is the legalisation of illegality, is also...itself a law...It is no doubt an exercise of arbitrary sovereign power; but where the legal sovereign is a Parliamentary assembly, even acts of state assume the form of regular legislation."[87] Thus, by "making lawful acts which when they were committed were unlawful," the Act of Indemnity ensures that all actions by public officials are done under a legislative framework and do not exist outside the law. However, it is not the mere fact of necessity that legalizes illegality. Rather, it is a subsequent legislative act of ratification – an ex post approval by the people's representatives in parliament – that may do so. Until and unless such an Act of Indemnity is passed the fact of illegality remains.

Searching for "moral politicians"

In his essay "Politics as a vocation," Max Weber promotes what he calls the "ethic of responsibility" over the "ethic of ultimate ends."[88] Political leaders – those who choose politics as a vocation – must stand ready to violate even fundamental principles and values if such violation is

---

[84] Ibid., p. 142 (emphasis added). See also ibid, p. 10.

[85] Pollock, "Martial Law," 157.

[86] Dicey, *Law of the Constitution*, p. 414.   [87] Ibid., p. 145.

[88] Max Weber, "Politics as a Vocation" in H.H. Gerth and C. Wright Mills (eds. and trans.), *From Max Weber: Essays in Sociology* (New York: Oxford University Press, 1946), p. 77 at 120–21.

genuinely for the good of the community at large: "[I]t is *not* true that good can follow only from good and evil only from evil, but that often the opposite is true. Anyone who fails to see this is, indeed, a political infant."[89] Thus, "Whoever wants to engage in politics at all, and especially in politics as a vocation...lets himself in for the diabolic forces lurking in all violence."[90] However, even if their actions have been genuinely for the public good, political leaders may still be required to pay the price of acting in violation of such principles and values. It is not enough to argue, as Locke suggests, that the public permitted such actions ex ante as part of its implicit acquiescence in the application of the prerogative power in appropriate circumstances. More is needed if the official is not to be held liable for her actions and to be relieved from making reparations for her wrongful acts. Even when she breaks a rule for good reasons, she may still have a duty to make reparations.[91]

Michael Walzer takes a similar position with respect to what is known as "the problem of the dirty hands," namely the notion that no one can hold political power without getting her hands dirty at some point.[92] Walzer points to a distinction between doing the right thing in utilitarian terms and the moral value of such actions: "[A] particular act of government...may be exactly the right thing to do in utilitarian terms and yet leave the man who does it guilty of a moral wrong."[93] Thus, there is no need to choose between upholding an important moral principle and avoiding national catastrophe. Both continue to be applicable at the same time. Government ought to avoid disasters and to overcome them as soon as possible once they occur. This is the right thing to do. But "right" in this context must not be confused with moral rightness. We must not attach moral praise to such actions if they contravene moral principles. They are morally wrong but practically necessary. In this light we can understand Walzer's question of how one recognizes a "moral

---

[89] Ibid., p. 123.   [90] Ibid., p. 125.

[91] Robert Nozick, "Moral Complications and Moral Structures" (1968) 13 *Natural Law Forum* 1 at 35 n. 46.

[92] Michael Walzer, "Political Action: The Problem of Dirty Hands" in Marshall Cohen, Thomas Nagel, and Thomas Scanlon (eds.), *War and Moral Responsibility* (Princeton: Princeton University Press, 1974), p. 62; Thomas Nagel, *Mortal Questions* (New York: Cambridge University Press, 1979), p. 75; Bernard Williams, "Politics and Moral Character" in Bernard Williams, *Moral Luck: Philosophical Papers, 1973-1980* (New York: Cambridge University Press, 1981), p. 54; Jean Bethke Elshtain, "Reflections on the Problem of 'Dirty Hands'" in Sanford Levinson (ed.), *Torture: A Collection* (New York: Oxford University Press, 2004), p. 77; Gross, "Chaos and Rules," 1105.

[93] Walzer, "Dirty Hands," 63.

politician" and his answer: "by his dirty hands."[94] A moral person who is not a political leader will (and can) refuse to act in an immoral way. She keeps her hands clean. A politician who is immoral will merely pretend that her hands were clean, for example, by denying any wrongdoing. Alternatively she may argue that whatever is the pragmatic right thing to do becomes, for that reason only, also moral and legitimate. A moral politician will do the right (pragmatic) thing to save the nation, while openly acknowledging and recognizing that such actions are (morally) wrong – that is, openly admitting that her hands are indeed dirty. The question then becomes not whether a political leader will act in this way in the face of a moral principle to the contrary (for it is clear that she will act), but rather what moral judgment should be attached to such action.

Under both Weber's ethic of responsibility and Walzer's moral politician paradigms, saying that extra-legal action was appropriate under the circumstances does not, in and of itself, absolve the politician from her moral culpability. The Extra-Legal Measures model takes this a step further by exploring the circumstances in which politicians who have done the right thing may actually be absolved from legal liability for their extra-legal actions. For that to happen it is not enough under the model that there be a general agreement that the actions taken were the right thing to do at the relevant time. Something more is needed. That something more is, it is argued, the public's explicit, particular, and ex post ratification.

Disobedience and ratification

Official disobedience

Public officials, like everybody else, ought to obey the law, even when they disagree with specific legal commands. However, there may be extreme exigencies where officials may regard strict obedience to legal authority as irrational or immoral.[95] Those who insist on an unqualified rule of obedience to the law (at least where public officials are concerned), no matter what the circumstances may be, would resolve the official's dilemma in such cases by finding that her obligation to obey legal authority is undiminished by the exigency. Others may

---

[94] Ibid., p. 70.

[95] Frederick Schauer, "The Questions of Authority" (1992) 81 *Georgetown Law Journal* 95 at 110–15.

argue that the decision whether to obey ought to be made on a case-by-case basis, carefully comparing the relative costs and benefits of each alternative. A particularistic calculus may lead to the conclusion that, at least in some cases, the benefits of disobedience exceed its social costs.

One possible pragmatic middle position is to regard the rule of obedience as establishing a strong presumption in favor of obedience that is rebuttable in exceptional cases where the wrong of disobedience is outweighed by the greater wrong that would follow from obeying the rules. Thus, the rule of obedience may require public officials to obey a constitution as it is interpreted by the courts, regardless of whether or not they agree with the courts' particular interpretations. Yet, even if one accepts the case for an unqualified rule of judicial supremacy, there may be circumstances – such as President Lincoln's challenge to the Supreme Court's ruling in the *Dred Scott* case – when disobedience may be justified.[96] Such a "presumptive" approach is not without difficulties. The harder the presumption is to overcome, the more rule-based-like it becomes with all the attendant problems of rule-based decision-making; the easier it is to override the rule of obedience, the less meaningful it becomes with the risk of collapsing the presumption into a mere exercise in particularistic, contextual decision-making.[97]

Under the presumptive approach, the possibility of a lawful override of the rule – the idea that in appropriate circumstances deviating from the rule may be not only morally permissible, but legally acceptable as well – compounds the problem further. The presumptive approach may fail to present adequate safeguards where we have reasons to believe that errors by public officials that result in misuse, abuse, and overuse of emergency powers are going to be more socially costly than errors related to underuse of such powers. Even more significantly, the presumptive approach fails to provide strong enough incentives for officials to play by the rule of obedience rather than justify overriding that rule in a particular case. In the absence of a strong, even absolute, rule of obedience, public officials are left with a "weighted presumption" that may not be amenable to enforcement through sanctions.[98]

---

[96] Larry Alexander and Frederick Schauer, "On Extrajudicial Constitutional Interpretation" (1997) 110 *Harvard Law Review* 1359 at 1382–83.

[97] Oren Gross, "Are Torture Warrants Warranted? Pragmatic Absolutism and Official Disobedience" (2004) 88 *Minnesota Law Review* 1481 at 1496–500.

[98] Emily Sherwin, "Ducking Dred Scott: A Response to Alexander and Schauer" (1998) 15 *Constitutional Commentary* 65 at 70.

The Extra-Legal Measures model and its component of official disobedience offer another middle ground between the diametrically opposed poles. The model potentially alleviates some of the concerns associated with the presumptive model. Most significantly, it may raise the costs of rule deviation for public officials while, at the same time, maintaining a strong commitment to law abidingness.

The Extra-Legal Measures model offers the possibility that public officials having to deal with extreme cases may consider acting outside the legal order while openly acknowledging their actions and the extra-legal nature of such actions. The model rejects the possibility of an ex ante lawful override of concrete legal rules and principles or, indeed, of the rule of obedience itself, as suggested by the presumptive approach, while accepting the possibility that an official who violates the law may escape sanctions in exceptional circumstances.

Under extreme circumstances public officials may regard strict obedience to legal authority as irrational or immoral because of a contextual rebalancing of values that takes place at a level that is antecedent to the relevant legal rule itself, i.e., the level of the rule's underlying reasons or similar first-order, content-dependent, reasons that relate to obedience to the rule.[99] According to the Extra-Legal Measures model, if an official determines that a particular case necessitates her deviation from the rule, she may choose to depart from that rule. But at the time she acts extra-legally and will not know what the personal consequences of violating the rule are going to be. Not only does the basic rule continue to apply to other situations (that is, it is not canceled or terminated), it is not even overridden in the concrete case at hand.[100] Rule departure constitutes, under all circumstances and all conditions, a violation of the relevant legal rule. Yet, whether the actor would be punished for her violation remains a separate question.[101] Society retains the role of making the final determination of whether the actor ought to be punished and rebuked, or rewarded and commended for her actions. As Frederick Schauer notes, in the context of the United States: "[S]ociety presently strikes this balance pursuant to a procedure under which ex

---

[99] Frederick Schauer, *Playing by the Rules: A Philosophical Examination of Rule-Based Decision-Making in Law and in Life* (New York: Oxford University Press, 1991), p. 128; Heidi M. Hurd, "Challenging Authority" (1991) 100 *Yale Law Journal* 1611 at 1625–28; Schauer, "The Questions of Authority," 110–15.

[100] Schauer, "The Questions of Authority," 103 (suggesting "the idea of overridable obligations that survive the override despite being overridden in a particular case").

[101] But see Sherwin, "Ducking Dred Scott," 70–71.

post justified acts of disobedience to the law on the part of officials are punished quite mildly, if at all, while ex post unjustified acts of disobedience to the law are punished somewhat more heavily than those same acts would have been punished merely for being bad policy."[102] It is up to society as a whole, "the people," to decide how to respond ex post to extra-legal actions taken by government officials in response to extreme exigencies. The people may decide to hold the actor accountable for the wrongfulness of her actions, or may approve them retrospectively. Even when acting to advance the public good under circumstances of great necessity, officials remain answerable to the public for their extra-legal actions.

Ex post ratification

Society may determine that certain extra-legal actions, even when couched in terms of preventing future catastrophes, are abhorrent, unjustified, and inexcusable. In such a case, the acting official may be called to answer for her actions and make legal and political amends. She may, for example, need to resign her position, face criminal charges or civil suits, or be subject to impeachment proceedings. Alternatively, the people may approve the actions and ratify them. Such ratification may be formal or informal, legal as well as social or political.

Legal modes of ratification include, for example, the exercise of prosecutorial discretion not to bring criminal charges against officials accused of violating the law,[103] jury nullification where criminal charges are brought, and executive pardoning or clemency where criminal proceedings result in conviction. On at least one occasion, presidential clemency was granted to eleven agents of the Israeli General Security Service, including the head of the service, *prior* to trial, blocking any future possibility of criminal proceedings being brought against them.[104] Governmental indemnification of state agents who are found liable for damages in civil proceedings may also operate as ex post

---

[102] Schauer, "The Questions of Authority," 114.

[103] See, e.g., H.C. 5100/94, Pub. Comm. against Torture in Israel v. The State of Israel, 53(4) P.D. 817, at para. 40 (Barak, P.).

[104] H.C. 428/86, Barzilai v. Gov't of Israel, 40(3) P.D. 505. See also Mordechai Kremnitzer, "The Case of the Security Services Pardon" (1987) 12 *Iyunei Mishpat* 595; Pnina Lahav, "A Barrel without Hoops: The Impact of Counterterrorism on Israel's Legal Culture" (1988) 10 *Cardozo Law Review* 529 at 547–56; Yechiel Gutman, *Taltelah ba-Shabak: ha-yoets ha-mishpati neged ha-memshalah mi-parashat Tovyanski ad parashat Kav 300 (A Storm in the GSS)* (Tel Aviv: Yediot Aharonot, 1995), pp. 15–133; Gross, "Torture Warrants," 1523–24.

ratification of the extra-legal actions of those agents. In the United States, because of the principle of sovereign immunity, existing doctrine bars bringing tort claims for constitutional violations against the federal government, unless Congress has specifically made such a claim available. In *Bivens v. Six Unknown Named Agents of Federal Bureau of Narcotics*, the Supreme Court held that such constitutional violations might be remedied by way of money damages recovered in suits brought against government officials in their individual capacities. Individual responsibility of government officials was thus established as a mechanism to enforce constitutional rights.[105] A public official who acts extra-legally may be exposed to having a *Bivens* claim brought against her and to being found liable for damages to persons whose constitutional rights were violated by her actions. Such threats, even if practically remote, play a role in providing added deterrence against acting extra-legally.[106] While the fact that governmental indemnification has become practically automatic may be the subject of criticism, this does not detract from its characterization as a ratification of extra-legal actions previously taken by public officials. The *Bivens* claims system may not be working optimally,[107] but its basic logic still holds – using individual liability as a mechanism to deter constitutional violations by public officials.

Acts of Indemnity offer another route to ex post ratification. As noted above, A.V. Dicey suggests that, "There are times of tumult or invasion when for the sake of legality itself the rules of law must be broken. The course which the government must then take is clear. *The Ministry must break the law and trust for protection to an Act of Indemnity.*"[108] By enacting such Acts of Indemnity, parliament "legalises illegality," and "free[s]

---

[105] 403 US 388 (1971). See also 42 U.S.C. para. 1983 (1994) (permitting actions against state officials for violation of the constitution and federal statutes, but providing no similar legislative mechanism against federal officials); Akhil Reed Amar, *The Constitution and Criminal Procedure: First Principles* (New Haven: Yale University Press, 1997), p. 40; Richard H. Fallon, Jr. and Daniel J. Meltzer, "New Law, Non-Retroactivity, and Constitutional Remedies" (1991) 104 *Harvard Law Review* 1733 at 1822.

[106] Cornelia T. L. Pillard, "Taking Fiction Seriously: The Strange Results of Public Officials' Individual Liability under *Bivens*" (1999) 88 *Georgetown Law Journal* 65 at 66, 76–77; Carlson v. Green, 446 US 14, 21 (1980); Janell M. Byrd, "Rejecting Absolute Immunity for Federal Officials" (1983) 71 *California Law Review* 1707 at 1718–21; John C. Jeffries, Jr., "In Praise of the Eleventh Amendment and Section 1983" (1998) 84 *Virginia Law Review* 47 at 51.

[107] Pillard, "Taking Fiction Seriously," 77, 79–90; Amar, *The Constitution and Criminal Procedure*, p. 40.

[108] Dicey, *Law of the Constitution*, p. 272 (emphasis added).

persons who have broken the law from responsibility for its breach, and *thus make lawful acts which when they were committed were unlawful.*"[109]

Political and social ratification is also possible. Charles Black suggested, in a different, yet related, context, that once a public official violates the law, "he should at once resign to await trial, pardon, and/or a decoration, as the case might be."[110] Honorific awards can establish ex post ratification in appropriate circumstances. Withholding a decoration may also send a strong message of rejection and condemnation. Michael Walzer notes the remarkable "national dissociation" by the British from the RAF Bomber Command. He argues (although this is contested by others) that the colorful director of the strategic "saturation bombing" of Germany from February 1942 until the end of the war, Air Marshal Arthur Harris – whose nickname, not at all coincidentally, was "Bomber" – was not, unlike other commanders, rewarded with a peerage. Even more tellingly, although bomber pilots suffered heavy casualties, they are not recorded by name in Westminster Abbey, unlike all other pilots of Fighter Command who died during the war. Walzer describes Harris as having "done what his government thought necessary, but what he had done was ugly, and there seems to have been a conscious decision not to celebrate the exploits of Bomber Command or to honor its leader."[111] Withholding of decoration, as well as other forms of social ostracism, is one specific example of informal sanctions that society may apply against officials for acting in violation of a recognized rule. Other forms of informal sanctions may involve the discreditation of the actor in the eyes of others, which may also put in risk past accomplishments of the rule violator, and loss of valued relationships.[112]

---

[109] Ibid., pp. 10–11, 142.

[110] A. Michael Froomkin, "The Metaphor is the Key: Cryptography, the Clipper Chip, and the Constitution" (1995) 143 *University of Pennsylvania Law Review* 709 at 746 n. 153; Richard A. Posner, *Catastrophe: Risk and Response* (New York: Oxford University Press, 2004), p. 241.

[111] Michael Walzer, *Just and Unjust Wars: A Moral Argument with Historical Illustrations* (3rd edn, New York: Basic Books, 2000), p. 324. But see Robin Neillands, *The Bomber War: The Allied Air Offensive against Germany* (Woodstock, NY: Overlook Press, 2001), pp. 401–04 (arguing that there is "no truth in the popular allegations that Harris and Bomber Command were denied any personal or official recognition").

[112] Paul H. Robinson, "Should the Victims' Rights Movement have Influence over Criminal Law Formulation and Adjudication?" (2002) 33 *McGeorge Law Review* 749 at 749; David Cole, "Judging the Next Emergency: Judicial Review and Individual Rights in Times of Crisis" (2003) 101 *Michigan Law Review* 2565 at 2577.

By requiring a process of ex post ratification (or rejection), the Extra-Legal Measures model as outlined here emphasizes an ethic of responsibility on the part not only of public officials, but also of the general public. Officials will need to acknowledge openly the nature of their actions and attempt to justify both their actions and their undertaking of those actions.[113] This open acknowledgment and engagement in public justificatory exercise is a critical component in the moral and legal choices made by the officials. The public then must decide whether to ratify the relevant extra-legal actions retrospectively. Thomas Jefferson analogized extra-legal actions taken by public officials on great occasions to acts of a guardian who is making an advantageous, albeit unauthorized, transaction on behalf of her minor ward. When the minor comes of age, the guardian must explain her actions thus: "I did this for your good; I pretend to no right to bind you: you may disavow me, and I must get out of the scrape as I can: I thought it my duty to risk myself for you."[114] During the process of ratification, each member of the public becomes morally and politically responsible for the decision. "[D]ecent men and women, hard-pressed in war, must sometimes do terrible things," writes Walzer, "and then they *themselves* have to look for some way to reaffirm the values they have overthrown."[115] Yet, according to the Extra-Legal Measures model, it is not only the actors who must attempt to find a way to reaffirm fundamental values they have violated in times of great exigency. Society too must undertake a project of reaffirmation. While Walzer suggests that members of the public may "have a right to avoid, if [they] possibly can, those [political or other] positions in which [they] might be forced to do terrible things,"[116] the model seeks to compel each member of society, in whose name terrible things have been done, to become morally responsible through the process of ratification or rejection.[117] Government agents must decide whether or not to act extra-legally in times of crisis. They must face that question as moral agents. But their grappling with the question is then followed by a public assessment of

---

[113] Mortimer R. Kadish and Sanford H. Kadish, *Discretion to Disobey: A Study of Lawful Departures from Legal Rules* (Stanford: Stanford University Press, 1973), pp. 5–12.

[114] Letter from Thomas Jefferson to John C. Breckinridge (Aug. 12, 1803) in Ford, *Thomas Jefferson*, pp. 1136, 1138–39.

[115] Walzer, *Just and Unjust Wars*, p. 325 (emphasis added).

[116] Walzer, "Dirty Hands," 67; A. John Simmons, *Moral Principles and Political Obligations* (Princeton: Princeton University Press, 1979), pp. 57–100.

[117] Eugene V. Rostow, "The Japanese American Cases – a Disaster" (1945) 54 *Yale Law Journal* 489 at 533.

that same question. In this instance, however, the answer carries not only moral significance, but the potential for very real and tangible legal effects in the form of sanctions that would be imposed on the actor when the public fails to ratify her illegal actions. What if the public does ratify ex post the extra-legal actions taken by public officials in times of emergency? How are we to understand the legal status of those actions once ratified? Much would depend on the nature of the ratification. The answer to such questions would be made on a case-by-case basis. For example, we have already seen Dicey's claim that an Act of Indemnity "legalises illegality."[118] Acts of Indemnity, according to Dicey, exculpate the actor from any legal responsibility for her actions by making such actions – which when taken were unlawful – lawful retrospectively. On the other hand, it is clear that Congress's decision to indemnify Captain Little did not reflect an intention to make his otherwise unlawful actions legal.

An act of ratification may also bear the characteristics of informal (and possibly even formal) constitutional and legal amendment.[119] The combination of a grave crisis, the illegal response to it by the government, the open acknowledgment of the nature of the actions taken to counter the exigency, and the subsequent popular ratification may form a constitutional moment that will lead to a constitutional shift on the issue at hand. Ratification can also be made in the form of an explicit constitutional or statutory change that seeks to legalize and bring within the ambit of the legal system actions that were previously considered outside its boundaries.

In any event, it is worth noting again that even where the illegal actions performed by public officials are taken to preserve and protect the nation, that alone does not, in and of itself, make those actions legal. Necessity does not make legal that which otherwise would have been illegal. It may excuse the actor from subsequent legal liability, but only subsequent ratification *may* (but does not have to) justify such extra-legal conduct.[120] Extra-legal actions and constitutionally permissible acts are not equal in obligation and force under the constitutional scheme.[121] The former are not made legal or constitutional as a result of

[118] Dicey, *Law of the Constitution*, pp. 10–11, 142.
[119] Bruce Ackerman, *We the People: Foundations* (Cambridge, MA: Belknap Press, 1991), pp. 320–21
[120] Lobel, "Decline of Liberalism," 1390–97.
[121] Marbury v. Madison, 5 US (1 Cranch) 137, 176–77 (1803); Schauer, "The Questions of Authority," 102–03.

the necessity of the situation. Indeed, as we discuss below, the very fact that an action is branded "extra-legal" raises the costs of undertaking it.

No security without law

Challenges to the Extra-Legal Measures model are substantial. Perhaps most significant is the argument that the protection of a nation is legitimate only so long as that nation itself is worth saving. A despotic, authoritarian, and oppressive regime is not worth the effort. A democracy may lose the battle against its enemies either by physically crumbling before them or by collapsing inward when it abandons its fundamental principles in the heat of battle. A weak, hesitant action against an impending threat may cause irreparable damage to the state's body. But the instinct of self-preservation may lead to transformation of the very nature of that society and to the loss of its soul. As Paul Wilkinson puts it:

> It is a dangerous illusion to believe one can "protect" liberal democracy by suspending liberal rights and forms of government. Contemporary history abounds in examples of "emergency" or "military" rule carrying countries from democracy to dictatorship with irrevocable ease. What shall it profit a liberal democracy to be delivered from the stress of factional strife only to be cast under the iron heel of despotism?[122]

Similarly, Carl Friedrich observes: "For any community built upon such a faith, the task of survival and of security becomes one of defending the *inner-most self* as well as that of defending the *outer-most boundary*, when confronted with an enemy ... "[123] "To make [man's] innermost self secure," he continues, "is more vital to the security and survival of a constitutional order than any boundary or any secret. It is the very core of constitutional reason of state. It is the reason why a constitutional state is founded and is maintained."[124] "If we do not preserve the rule of law zealously in this area as well," commented the Landau Commission, "the danger is great that the work of those who assail the existence of the State from without will be done through acts of self-destruction from within, with 'men devouring each other.'"[125] Adherence to the rule of law is a necessary element in a nation's security and safety. As

[122] Paul Wilkinson, *Terrorism and the Liberal State* (2nd edn, New York: New York University Press, 1986), pp. 122–23.

[123] Friedrich, *Reason of State*, p. 13.   [124] Ibid., p. 119.

[125] Israeli Government Press Office, *Commission of Inquiry into the Methods of Investigation of the General Security Service Regarding Hostile Terrorist Activity* (1987), reprinted in (1989) 23 *Israel Law Review* 146 at 183.

Aharon Barak, president of the Israeli Supreme Court, wrote in one of his opinions: "[T]here is no security without law, and the rule of law is a component of national security."[126]

Opposition to the Extra-Legal Measures model is rooted in the fear of totalitarianism and authoritarianism that the model seems to enable. If we accept the possibility, in extreme cases, of governmental actions that are extra-legal so long as they are taken to advance the public good, there can be no constitutional or legal limitations on such governmental exercise of power. If we accept that the executive may act outside the law in order to avert or overcome catastrophes, there is nothing to prevent the wielder of such awesome powers from exercising them in violation of any constitutional and legal limitations on the use of such powers. Extra-legal power can only mean an unlimited power, constrained neither by any legal norms nor by principles and rules of the constitutional order.[127]

Another significant concern about the Extra-Legal Measures model takes a swipe at the argument that, in appropriate circumstances, violating the law may better serve the long-term interests of the rule of law than any of the alternatives. The force of the law as regulating behavior is, to a significant extent, a function of a cultivated habit of obedience to its dictates and an established ethos of its supremacy. Violating the law deviates from that pattern of obedience. When such violation is perpetrated by the authorities, it is all the more pernicious. As Justice Brandeis wrote in *Olmstead v. United States*:

Decency, security and liberty alike demand that government officials shall be subjected to the same rules of conduct that are commands to the citizen...Our Government is the potent, the omnipresent teacher. For good or for ill, it teaches the whole people by its example. Crime is contagious. If the Government becomes a law-breaker, it breeds contempt for law; it invites every man to become a law unto himself; it invites anarchy. To declare that in the administration of the criminal law the end justifies the means – to declare that the Government may commit crimes in order to secure the conviction of a private criminal – would bring terrible retribution.[128]

---

[126] H.C. 428/86, Barzilai v. Gov't of Israel, 40(3) P.D. 505 at 622 (Barak, P.).

[127] Sotirios A. Barber, *On What the Constitution Means* (Baltimore: The Johns Hopkins University Press, 1984), pp. 188–90; Joseph M. Bessette and Jeffrey Tulis, "The Constitution, Politics, and the Presidency" in Joseph M. Bessette and Jeffrey Tulis (eds.), *The Presidency in the Constitutional Order* (Baton Rouge, LA: Louisiana State University Press, 1981), p. 3 at 24–25; Cole, "Judging the Next Emergency," 2585.

[128] Olmstead v. United States, 277 US 438 at 485 (1928) (Brandeis, J., dissenting).

If government may deviate from the principle of the rule of law in some cases, would it not be able to do so in others? And why should the public hold the rule of law in any higher regard than its government? Once the rule of law ceases to be thought of as an absolute immovable rule, further incursions are likely to take place into its domain.[129] Violations of the law by public officials may lead to similar conduct by private individuals taking their cue from the government. It may also breed further lawlessness among public officials. Government officials, seeing that they can get away with violating the law and being intoxicated by the immense powers that such conduct confers upon them, may seek to reproduce similar patterns of behavior even after normalcy has been restored. In order to justify the retention of such powers, they may claim that the emergency has not yet terminated, or that new dangers gather over the horizon, thus perpetuating a crisis mentality among the members of the community.

Similar criticism is made by none other than Niccolò Machiavelli. In his discussion of the regime for the ideal republic in *Discourses on Livy*, Machiavelli argues that observance of the laws of the republic by the people and even more so by their government is crucial to the success of the republican enterprise. "I do not believe," he writes, "there is a thing that sets a more wicked example in a republic than to make a law and not observe it, and so much the more as it is not observed by him who made it." He makes this comment in the context of discussing the imprisonment of Appius, the head of the Decemviri, after the Decemviri had been removed from office. Machiavelli notes that the right of appeal against the judgment, recognized under the laws of the Roman republic, was denied Appius. He then comments that, "Although the criminal life of Appius merited every punishment, nonetheless it was hardly a civil thing to violate the laws, and so much the more one that had been made then."[130] Violation of the laws, for whatever reason, creates a harmful precedent for the future. As we saw in chapter 1, Machiavelli's analysis of the Roman dictatorship led him to conclude that the ideal republic ought to provide for emergency institutions ex ante. Emergency powers ought to be incorporated into, and provided for by, the ordinary legal system. Government must not be left to choose between destruction of

---

[129] See, e.g., Liat Collins, "GSS Agent Involved in Death of Harizat Transferred from Post," *Jerusalem Post*, May 1, 1995, p. 1; Bruce Ackerman, "The Emergency Constitution" (2004) 113 *Yale Law Journal* 1029 at 1044.

[130] Niccolò Machiavelli, *Discourses on Livy*, trans. Harvey C. Mansfield and Nathan Tarcov (Chicago: University of Chicago Press, 1996), p. 93.

the republic in the face of an extreme crisis and the use of extra-legal measures to fight off that crisis. Emergency legislation and expansionist interpretation of existing laws can be, in due course, uprooted and replaced by norms approximating the pre-emergency legal system. But once a habit of lawlessness and disobedience has developed, the point of no return may have been crossed.

The fear of establishing a habit of lawlessness also led Machiavelli to criticize the demand for transparency and open acknowledgment by public officials of their extra-legal actions (should such actions be taken). Even in the context of the ideal republic Machiavelli is willing to recognize the possibility of acting extra-legally in the face of emergency as long as the laws *appear* to have been sustained and complied with. If the laws must be broken in a given situation it is still better to disguise the fact of non-compliance and maintain an appearance of observance, rather than expose the extra-legal nature of the relevant actions.[131] The Romans used to conduct various religious rites before taking important public decisions – such as whether to commence or refrain from a military action – and would follow the signs given them by the gods. High-level Roman officials looked for divine signs – such as through the attitude of chicken to food or examination of the entrails of sacrificed animals – of future success or failure. The interpretation of these signs, the *auspicia* ("the watching of birds") was entrusted to special experts, the *augures*. A positive sign was considered a necessary condition for authorizing magistrates to embark on the mission.[132] "Nonetheless," notes Machiavelli, "when reason showed them a thing they ought to do – notwithstanding that the auspices had been adverse – they did it in any mode. But they turned it around with means and modes so aptly that it did not appear that they had done it with disdain for religion."[133] When necessity or prudence dictated a course of action not in accordance with the auspices, necessity prevailed over a strict adherence to the dictates of religion. Yet, even in such cases, every effort was made to maintain the appearance that no violation of these dictates had taken place. Machiavelli compares the actions of two military commanders who embarked on battles despite negative signs. While Papirius knew "how to accommodate his plans to the auspices" and won his battle

---

[131] See also Slavoj Žižek, *Welcome to the Desert of the Real!: Five Essays on September 11 and Related Dates* (London: Verso, 2002), p. 103.

[132] Andrew Lintott, *The Constitution of the Roman Republic* (Oxford: Clarendon Press, 1999), pp. 103–04; Machiavelli, *Discourses*, p. 41.

[133] Machiavelli, *Discourses*, p. 41.

against the Samnites, Appius Pulcher openly ignored the religious signs given him by the *augures* and lost his battle against the Carthaginians. "For this he was condemned at Rome and Papirius honored." However, Machiavelli emphasizes, such respective condemnation and honor were "not so much because one had won and the other lost as because one had acted against the auspices prudently and the other rashly."[134]

The Extra-Legal Measures model is also challenged over its reliance on what we call the assumption of separation. That assumption, which is the subject of the next chapter, is defined by the belief in our ability to separate emergencies and crises from normalcy, counter-terrorism measures from ordinary legal rules and norms. Yet, as discussed in the next chapter, this important assumption has been undermined in significant ways. Models of emergency regimes that are based on it ought to be treated with some suspicion. Yet, so the argument goes, the Extra-Legal Measures model relies on that false assumption to a greater extent than any of the alternative models. The notion of total separation between normalcy and emergency, of impermeable boundaries between the two realities, enables proponents of the model to claim that the ordinary legal system will not be tarnished by the taking of extra-legal measures in times of emergency and crisis as the ordinary legal system will be insulated against adverse long-term effects of such violations. But, if we accept that such clear separation between the two realities is unattainable, then the model may result in more damage than any of the constitutional models.[135]

The case for rule departures

The closing parts of each of the previous two chapters discussed the various challenges to the models of accommodation and the Business as Usual model and the possible responses to those challenges. The structure of this chapter is no different. The previous section examined the major criticisms against the Extra-Legal Measures model. This section concludes by offering possible responses. Before going any further we note that the relative length of this section is mostly a result of the fact that the Extra-Legal Measures model seems, at first blush, more troubling than the constitutional models of emergency powers. It recognizes the possibility of extra-legal actions on the part of public officials. As such,

---

[134] Ibid., p. 42.
[135] Cole, "Judging the Next Emergency," 2587–88.

the model is exposed to weighty critiques and the case for it, i.e., the case for rule departures, may be more complex than it is in the context of the constitutional models of emergency powers.

Prospective and uncertain relief

As noted in the previous section, the most critical challenge to the Extra-Legal Measures model is that it does not offer any meaningful method to maintain constitutional and legal constraints over public officials. If a time of crisis permits stepping outside the legal system, no limits – and certainly no legal limits – can be set on how far such deviations would go and how wide in scope they would be. Even some who expressed certain sympathy with the possibility of exercising powers extra-legally and extra-constitutionally are quick to concede the point.[136] Yet, to acknowledge the possibility of extra-legal action may be different from accepting willy-nilly limitless powers and authority in the hands of state agents. Similarly, as explained below, the fact that under the Extra-Legal Measures model legal norms and rules are neither suspended nor, indeed, overridden, means that legal (as well as political and social) accountability is still possible.

Dicey clearly recognizes this point when he suggests that "there are one or two considerations which limit the practical importance that can fairly be given to an expected Act of Indemnity. The relief to be obtained from it is *prospective and uncertain*.[137] Uncertainty and the prospective nature of the required ex post ratification may not only slow down the rush to act extra-legally in the first place. They may also facilitate meaningful limitations on such actions once they are taken. By separating the extra-legal actions of public officials in extreme cases and subsequent public ratification, and by ordering them so that ratification follows, rather than precedes, action, the Extra-Legal Measures model seeks to add uncertainty to the decision-making calculus of state agents. Such "prudent obfuscation"[138] raises both the individual and national costs of pursuing an extra-legal course of action and, at the same time, reinforces the rule of obedience.

With the need to obtain ex post ratification from the public, officials who decide to act extra-legally undertake a significant risk because of

[136] Mark Tushnet, "Defending *Korematsu*?: Reflections on Civil Liberties in Wartime" (2003) *Wisconsin Law Review* 273 at 306, n. 122.

[137] Dicey, *Law of the Constitution*, pp. 144–45 (emphasis added).

[138] Dan M. Kahan, "Ignorance of Law is an Excuse – But Only for the Virtuous" (1997) 96 *Michigan Law Review* 127 at 139–41.

the uncertain prospects for subsequent ratification. The public may, for example, disagree after the fact with the acting officials' assessment of the situation and the need to act extra-legally. Ratification would be sought ex post, when calm and rationality, rather than heightened emotions, might govern public discourse and when more information about the particular case at hand may be available to the public and possibly after the particular danger has been eliminated or averted.[139] Indeed, if the officials are successful and the harm to the nation is averted, the assessment of the legitimacy of acting extra-legally is likely to be more heavily weighted against them. Success of extra-legal actions may actually strengthen the case against the granting of ex post ratification to the acting officials, deterring them further from acting extra-legally.

The conspiracy of L. Sergius Catilina to take over the control of Rome by invading it with an army from Etruria was one of Marcus Tullius Cicero's greatest moments.[140] Acting as consul, Cicero foiled the conspiracy by mobilizing troops to defend the city and capturing Catiline's accomplices. On December 5, 63 BC, Cicero assembled the Roman Senate in order to obtain its consent for the summary execution of five of Catiline's accomplices. Cicero evidently believed that such action was necessary in order to safeguard Rome. In his fourth Catilinarian Oration before the Senate, Cicero conveyed the following description of what would have befallen Rome had the conspirators been successful:

I seem to myself to see this city, the light of the world and the citadel of all nations, falling on a sudden by one conflagration. I see in my mind's eye miserable and unburied heaps of cities in my buried country; the sight of Cethegus and his madness raging amid your slaughter is ever present to my sight. But when I have set before myself Lentulus reigning, as he himself confesses that he had hoped was his destiny, and this Gabinius arrayed in the purple and Catiline arrived with his army, then I shudder at the lamentation of matrons, and the flight of virgins and of boys and the insults of the vestal virgins.[141]

---

[139] Dicey, *Law of the Constitution*, p. 145; Pollock, "Martial Law?" 153–54.

[140] Ernest George Hardy, *The Catilinarian Conspiracy in its Context: A Re-Study of the Evidence* (Oxford: Basil Blackwell, 1924); Sallust, *The Jugurthine War and the Conspiracy of Catiline*, trans. S.A. Handford (Baltimore: Penguin, 1963); Max Cary and Howard H. Scullard, *A History of Rome down to the Reign of Constantine* (3rd edn, New York: St. Martin's Press, 1975), pp. 246–47.

[141] Marcus Tullius Cicero, *The Orations of Marcus Tullius Cicero*, trans. C. D. Yonge (London: H.G. Bohn, 1856) Part 4, sections 11–12, available online at http://www.perseus.tufts.edu/cgi-bin/ptext?doc=Perseus%3Atext%3A1999.02.0019; query=toc;layout=;loc=Tul.%204 (last visited on August 8, 2005).

It is in light of this existential threat to Rome, and because "these things appear to me exceedingly miserable and pitiable," that Cicero decided to "show myself severe and rigorous to those who have wished to bring about this state of things."[142] Yet, the execution without a proper trial of Roman citizens who were not declared as public enemies and who, at the relevant time, did not present an immediate threat to Rome, was outside the legal authority of the consul or, for that matter, of the Senate.[143] Thus, although the Senate had previously declared a state of emergency (*tumultus*) and passed a resolution of last resort, such proclamation could not legally confer new powers to the consul.[144] Nevertheless Cicero did go ahead and execute the conspirators without trial.

Although Cicero was generally hailed as having saved the republic, the risk to himself of acting extra-legally was significant. Not long after the conspiracy was crushed, an attempt was made by new tribunes, led by one of Cicero's bitterest enemies, Publius Clodius, to impeach Cicero for the unlawful executions by passing a bill that any citizen guilty of putting another to death without trial would be sent into exile. With the political odds stacked high against him Cicero went into exile. Condemned by yet another bill as a criminal for his violation of the law, Cicero's house was demolished and his property confiscated.[145] A year later, when Clodius's term as tribune ended and new forces, backed by Pompey, assumed power in Rome, Cicero was recalled back after a vote of 416 to 1 in the Senate and a subsequent positive public vote.[146] Jean-Jacques Rousseau explains those events:

[I]f, in the first transports of joy, [Cicero's] conduct was approved, he was justly called, later on, to account for the blood of citizens spilt in violation of the laws...He was therefore justly honoured as the liberator of Rome, and also justly punished as a law-breaker. However brilliant his recall may have been, it was undoubtedly an act of pardon.[147]

In a democratic society, where values such as constitutionalism, accountability, and individual rights are firmly entrenched and traditionally respected, we can expect that the public would be circumspect about

---

[142] Ibid.; Hardy, *The Catilinarian Conspiracy*, p. 85.

[143] Cary and Scullard, *History of Rome*, p. 247; Hardy, *The Catilinarian Conspiracy*, pp. 86–87.

[144] Hardy, *The Catilinarian Conspiracy*, pp. 55–57, 98–99.

[145] Tom Holland, *Rubicon: The Triumph and Tragedy of the Roman Republic* (London: Abacus, 2003), pp. 238–40.

[146] Ibid., pp. 253–54.

[147] Jean-Jacques Rousseau, *The Social Contract and Discourses*, trans. G.D.H. Cole (New York: Everyman, 1993), pp. 295–96. See also Walzer, "Dirty Hands," 81.

governmental attempts to justify or excuse illegal actions. That being the case, "Any suspicion on the part of the public, that officials had grossly abused their powers, might make it difficult to obtain a Parliamentary indemnity for things done."[148] The public may also determine that the extra-legal actions violated values and principles that are too important to be encroached upon, as a matter of principle or in the circumstances of the particular case. The greater the moral and legal interests and values infringed upon, the less certain the actor can be of securing ratification.

Uncertainty is also important because it reduces the potential risk of underdeterrence that is involved in the possibility of ex post ratification. Underdeterrence may be a significant concern if public officials have good reasons to believe that ratification will be forthcoming in future cases when they act extra-legally.[149] As Dicey openly acknowledges in the context of Acts of Indemnity, the expectation of the executive that such acts will be passed by parliament "has not been disappointed" as a matter of history and experience.[150] Acts of Indemnity have, in fact, been "passed by all governments when the occasion requires it."[151] This would seem to eliminate, or at least significantly minimize, any uncertainty on the part of public officials about the prospects of ex post ratification. As David Dyzenhaus argues:

If the Extra-Legal Measures model were public, as it must be if it is to promote deliberation, the expectation would be generated of after-the-fact validation of illegal official acts. In an atmosphere of fear that expectation would likely be met rather easily, especially when the threat is, or is claimed to be, a constant one and the government successfully manipulates public opinion.[152]

Underdeterrence may result from what Meir Dan-Cohen calls conditions of low "acoustic separation" between conduct rules and decision rules.[153]

---

[148] Dicey, *Law of the Constitution*, p. 145.

[149] John T. Parry and Welsh S. White, "Interrogating Suspected Terrorists: Should Torture Be an Option?" (2002) 63 *University of Pittsburgh Law Review* 743 at 764–65; Sanford Levinson, " 'Precommitment' and 'Postcommitment': The Ban on Torture in the Wake of September 11" (2003) 81 *Texas Law Review* 2013 at 2045–48.

[150] Dicey, *Law of the Constitution*, p. 144.

[151] Mitchell v. Clark, 110 US 633 at 640 (1884).

[152] David Dyzenhaus, "The State of Emergency in Legal Theory" in Victor V. Ramraj, Michael Hor and Kent Roach (eds.), *Global Anti-Terrorism Law and Policy* (New York: Cambridge University Press, 2005), p. 65 at 72–73. See also Monaghan, "The Protective Power," 26.

[153] Meir Dan-Cohen, "Decision Rules and Conduct Rules: On Acoustic Separation in Criminal Law" (1984) 97 *Harvard Law Review* 625 at 636–41.

Low acoustic separation increases the likelihood that officials will be familiar with both sets of normative messages and will be able to act strategically. This creates substantial risks of undesirable behavioral side-effects on the part of officials, e.g., by allowing decision rules – which recognize the possibility that agents who resort to extra-legal actions in extreme cases may be let off the hook – to affect the conduct of the officials in specific cases (i.e., state agents resorting to such extra-legal actions knowing, or at least having good reason to believe, that they will enjoy immunity against criminal charges and civil claims).[154] However, the element of uncertainty that is so critical to the Extra-Legal Measures model acts to minimize the risks of behavioral side-effects. The more uncertain are the substance and the operation of the decision rules – which are, in the context of the model, directed at the general public as the ex post decision-maker – and the greater is the personal risk involved in wrongly interpreting either of those, the greater the incentive for individual actors to conform their action to the conduct rules – primarily the rule of obedience – and eschew the urge to act extra-legally.

Moreover, even if one accepts that there exists a good chance that ex post ratification will be forthcoming, there are still significant costs to acting extra-legally. For starters, there is still a certain degree of anxiety that ratification will not, in fact, follow. A good chance is not equal to certainty. More significantly, ratification may not be comprehensive or fully corrective. As Dicey notes: "As regards...the protection to be derived from the Act [of Indemnity] by men who have been guilty of irregular, illegal, oppressive, or cruel conduct, *everything depends on the terms of the Act of Indemnity*."[155] Subsequent ratification may, for example, shield the actor against criminal charges, but not bar the possibility of civil proceedings. It may also not shield the actor from liability for all of her actions. Similarly, when ratification assumes the guise of an executive pardon or clemency, it eliminates the criminal penalty that was imposed on the individual actor, but it removes neither the ordeal of criminal prosecution nor the condemnation associated with criminal conviction.[156] Indeed, if we wish to increase the costs of extra-legal

---

[154] Ibid., pp. 631–32.

[155] Dicey, *Law of the Constitution*, p. 145 (emphasis added).

[156] Leon Sheleff, "On Criminal Homicide and Legal Self Defense" (1997) 6 *Plilim* 89 at 111–12; Yale Kamisar, "Physician Assisted Suicide: The Problems Presented by the Compelling, Heartwrenching Case" (1998) 88 *Journal of Criminal Law and Criminology* 1121 at 1143–44.

actions even further we can introduce a duty of compensation and reparations – which can be imposed on the individual public officials or on
the state – to those who were the victims of such actions, whether or
not the actions have enjoyed ex post ratification.[157]

When we consider international legal rules and norms, the costs and
uncertainties that are involved in acting extra-legally are increased further. Even if a particular extra-legal act is domestically ratified it may be
subject to a different judgment on the international level. This may have
significant consequences both for the individual public official and her
government. Acting officials may still be subject to criminal and civil proceedings in jurisdictions other than their own. Moreover, to the extent
that the relevant extra-legal action violates the nation's international
legal obligations, especially its obligations and undertakings under the
major international human rights conventions, and is not covered by
an appropriate derogation (or it is in violation of a non-derogable right),
state agents who engage in such acts expose their government to a range
of possible remedies under the relevant international legal instruments.
Indeed by recognizing what has occurred, a domestic ex post ratification
may facilitate international remedies.

Thus, the Extra-Legal Measures model imposes significant burdens on
public officials. They must act in the face of great uncertainty. If they
believe that the stakes are high enough to merit an extra-legal action,
they may still decide to act extra-legally "for the public good" and expect
to be protected subsequently by some form of ex post ratification. At the
same time, the model makes it extremely costly to resort to such drastic
measures, limiting their use to exceptional exigencies. As Sanford Kadish
notes, "Would not the burden on the official be so great that it would
require circumstances of a perfectly extraordinary character to induce
the individual to take the risk of acting? The answer is of course yes,
that's the point."[158]

The more uncertain it is that ratification will be forthcoming, the
more uncertain its potential scope, and the greater the personal risk
involved in wrongly interpreting either of those is, the greater the incentive for individual actors to conform their action to the existing
legal rules and norms and not risk acting outside them. The burden lies

---

[157] See, e.g., Levinson, "Precommitment," 2049–50; Tushnet, "Defending *Korematsu*?," 307;
Civil Liberties Act of 1988, Pub. L. No. 100-383, 102 Stat. 903 (Congressional formal
apology and restitution to victims of the Japanese internment of World War II).

[158] Sanford H. Kadish, "Torture, the State and the Individual" (1989) 23 *Israel Law Review*
345 at 355.

squarely on the shoulders of the public officials who must act, sometimes extra-legally, without the benefit of legal pre-approval of their actions by the courts or the legislature. Public officials have no one to hide behind. They must put themselves on the front line and act at their own peril. Thomas Jefferson observed:

The officer who is called to act on this superior ground, does indeed risk himself on the justice of the controlling powers of the constitution, and his station makes it his duty to incur that risk... The line of discrimination between cases [where such action is necessary and where it is not] may be difficult; but the good officer is bound to draw it at his own peril, and throw himself on the justice of his country and the rectitude of his motives.[159]

The argument that this puts public officials in a "zone uncontrolled by law"[160] underestimates the significance of such disincentives to step outside the legal framework and of the possibilities for external supervision, both by the public and by other branches of government.

Courts and legislatures

Speaking of the possibilities of external review in the context of Acts of Indemnity, Dicey notes that,

The fact that the most arbitrary powers of the English executive must always be exercised under Act of Parliament places the government, even when armed with the widest authority, under the supervision, so to speak, of the courts. Powers, however extraordinary... are never really unlimited, for they are confined by the words of the Act itself, and, what is more, by the interpretation put upon the statute by the judges.[161]

The fact that the courts will be called to deal with an ex post ratification in the form of an Act of Indemnity may make judicial supervision over the exercise of emergency powers by government officials more meaningful and robust. As we noted in chapter 1, in times of emergency courts assume a highly deferential attitude when called upon to review governmental actions and decisions. The courts' apparent inability to protect individual rights while extreme violence is raging around them, compared with their greater willingness to resume their role as

---

[159] Letter from Thomas Jefferson to John B. Colvin (Sept. 20, 1810), in Ford, *Thomas Jefferson*, p. 1231 at 1233. See also Amnon Reichman, "'When We Sit to Judge We are Being Judged': The Israeli GSS Case, Ex Parte Pinochet and Domestic/Global Deliberation" (2001) 9 *Cardozo Journal of International and Comparative Law* 41 at 67–68.

[160] Dyzenhaus, "Emergency in Legal Theory," 65.

[161] Dicey, *Law of the Constitution*, p. 273.

guardians of rights and liberties once the crisis is over, may suggest a more meaningful judicial review in the context of ex post ratification. In a similar vein, Chief Justice Rehnquist writes that

If, in fact, courts are more prone to uphold wartime claims of civil liberties after the war is over, may it not actually be desirable to avoid decision on such claims during the war?...While the body of case law might benefit from such abstention, those who are actually deprived of their civil liberties would not. But a decision in favor of civil liberty will stand as a precedent to regulate future actions of Congress and the Executive branch in future wars.[162]

A similar rationale may apply to the legislature. As noted above, the use of extra-legal measures by public officials during an emergency involves significant risks to the actors. Thus, it is likely that upon the termination of the crisis the legislature will be called upon to ratify governmental actions by, for example, passing Acts of Indemnity. This process presents the legislative branch of government with an opportunity to review the actions of the executive and assess them ex post, relieved from the pressures of the crisis, before deciding whether to ratify them.[163] The appeal to the legislature to ratify the actions of the government may further invoke public deliberation and force the legislature to take an affirmative stand on issues connected with the emergency. This is of special significance in light of the general reluctance of legislatures to assume responsibility in times of emergency, satisfying themselves with acquiescence in actions taken by the executive.[164]

Open acknowledgment of extra-legal measures taken by government agents will contribute to reasoned discourse and dialogue between the government and its domestic constituency, between the government and other governments, and between the government and non-governmental or international organizations. The benefits of the ex post justificatory exercise are not confined to the domestic sphere; it has international implications, both political and legal. The reasons put forward by a state to justify its actions may be subject to scrutiny by other governments and non-governmental organizations as well as by judicial and quasi-judicial bodies such as the European Court of Human Rights, the

---

[162] William H. Rehnquist, *All the Laws but One: Civil Liberties in Wartime* (New York: Knopf, 1998), p. 222. See also Christopher N. May, *In the Name of War: Judicial Review and the War Powers since 1918* (Cambridge, MA: Harvard University Press, 1989), p. 268; Cole, "Judging the Next Emergency," 2571–77.

[163] Lobel, "Decline of Liberalism," 1396.

[164] Harold H. Koh, *The National Security Constitution: Sharing Power after the Iran–Contra Affair* (New Haven, CT: Yale University Press, 1990), pp. 117–33.

Inter-American Court of Human Rights, and the United Nations Human Rights Commission.[165]

Giving reasons

The limitations on the resort to extra-legal actions that the model offers are further strengthened by the fact that we can and should expect public officials to feel quite uneasy about possible resort to extra-legal measures.[166] This feeling of uneasiness ought to be especially pronounced in nations where the "constitution is old, observed for a long time, known, respected, and cherished."[167] The knowledge that acting in a certain way means acting unlawfully is thus likely, in and of itself, to have some restraining effect on government agents. But, of course, such uneasiness is a matter of subjective feeling and individual conscience and only the agent decides how troubled his conscience will be and how uneasy he would feel about acting extra-legally. When we add the specter of having to give reasons to the public for one's illegal actions after the crisis is over, it seems likely that the mere need to cross the threshold of illegality would serve as a further limiting factor against a governmental rush to assume unnecessary powers.

The need to give reasons ex post, i.e., the need publicly to justify or to excuse (not merely explain) one's actions after the fact, emphasizes accountability of government agents. The fact that specific emergency powers used by the government are extra-legal, and perhaps extra-constitutional, preserves the need not only to give reasons for such actions, but also to give reasons that go beyond pure pragmatic excuses or justifications for the specific conduct in question.[168] The task of giving reasons requires the actor to present publicly various types of arguments – prudential, pragmatic, and moral. This, again, serves to check a possible rush to use extra-legal powers. "Giving reasons" may

---

[165] For the idea of two-level games in international relations, see Robert D. Putnam, "Diplomacy and Domestic Politics: The Logic of Two-Level Games" (1988) 42 *International Organizations* 427.

[166] Weber, "Politics as Vocation," 121.

[167] Guy Howard Dodge, *Benjamin Constant's Philosophy of Liberalism: A Study in Politics and Religion* (Chapel Hill, NC: University of North Carolina Press, 1980), p. 101 (quoting Benjamin Constant); Gabriel L. Negretto and José Antonio Aguilar Rivera, "Liberalism and Emergency Powers in Latin America: Reflections on Carl Schmitt and the Theory of Constitutional Dictatorship" (2000) 21 *Cardozo Law Review* 1797 at 1800–03.

[168] Kadish and Kadish, *Discretion to Disobey*, pp. 5–12. But see Christopher L. Eisgruber, "The Most Competent Branches: A Response to Professor Paulsen" (1994) 83 *Georgetown Law Journal* 347 at 360 (arguing that Justice Jackson's dissent in *Korematsu* suggests that the executive branch does not have to offer reasons beyond the pragmatic).

also limit the government's choice of measures ex ante, adding another layer of restraint on governmental action. Faced with the need to give reasons for her actions, a public official may well decline to engage in extra-legal measures and actions unless she is confident that the people and their representatives will come to see things her way and regard her action as necessary and legitimate. Even then she may still hesitate to act unless she is confident that she will not suffer personally for taking such actions.[169]

Ratifying egregious actions?

Taken to its logical extreme, the Extra-Legal Measures model does not seem to incorporate substantive limitations on the range of possible extra-legal actions taken in the face of emergency that may later be ratified. There is nothing to prevent such ratification from being given to egregious actions.

One attempt to meet this critical challenge is to argue that it is essential to delimit and define clearly the situations that may invoke the use of extra-legal emergency measures since otherwise the risk of subverting the constitutional order by frequent resort to extra-constitutional mechanisms runs very high. However, as noted in the introduction, no clear definition of "emergencies" is readily available. Arthur Schlesinger tries to resolve this difficulty by emphasizing that the acting official (he focuses on the president of the United States) may only use extra-legal emergency measures if, and only if, the specific crisis is "genuinely imperious" not only in the eyes of the president, but also as perceived by Congress and the general public. Double criteria are thus offered: objective – the crisis must be real and exceptional – and subjective – the president must perceive the crisis to be of such qualities and her perception of the emergency as extreme and exceptional must be widely shared.[170] This latter requirement is deemed crucial to distinguishing "real crises threatening the life of the republic from nightmares troubling the minds of paranoid Presidents."[171]

---

[169] Frederick Schauer, "Giving Reasons" (1995) 47 *Stanford Law Review* 633 at 656–57; Bessette and Tulis, "Constitution, Politics, and Presidency," 10; John E. Finn, *Constitutions in Crisis: Political Violence and the Rule of Law* (New York: Oxford University Press, 1991), pp. 30–36; David L. Shapiro, "In Defense of Judicial Candor" (1987) 100 *Harvard Law Review* 731 at 737; David Gray Adler, "The Steel Seizure Case and Inherent Presidential Power" (2002) 19 *Constitutional Commentary* 155 at 174–75.

[170] Schlesinger, *The Imperial Presidency*, pp. 263–66.

[171] Ibid., p. 458.

How are we to evaluate whether the president's perception of the nature of the crisis is "widely shared"? Schlesinger offers an amorphous conception of public consensus as to the existence and the nature of extreme emergency. He does not provide satisfactory means by which to evaluate the formation of such broad consensus. Nor does he explain who may be competent to decide the existence of such a consensus or, indeed, what ought to be considered as "consensus" to start with.[172] Moreover, if emergencies tend to be consensus-generating, creating a wide public consensus, support for the government, and "rallying round the flag,"[173] can the requirement of public consensus amount to a real and meaningful limitation and check on the president's actions in times of grave crises? Schlesinger does not answer explicitly any of these questions, although he seems to focus on congressional support and judicial approval of presidential actions when looking at specific historical examples. Recognizing the practical difficulties with the requirement of public consensus, Schlesinger provides a list of eight "stringent and persuasive conditions" that must exist for recourse to the emergency prerogative to be considered legitimate:

(1) There must be a clear, present and broadly perceived danger to the life of the nation;
(2) The president must define and explain to Congress and the people the nature and urgency of the threat;
(3) The president's view that the life of the nation is truly at stake must be broadly shared by Congress and the American people;
(4) Time must be of the essence. Existing statutory authorizations must be inadequate while waiting for normal legislative action to run its course must constitute an unacceptable risk;
(5) The danger must be one that can be met in no other way than by presidential initiative beyond the laws and the constitution;
(6) Secrecy must be strictly confined to the tactical requirements of the emergency. Every question of basic policy must be opened to national, public debate;
(7) The president must report what he has done to Congress. Congress, along with the courts, and ultimately the people, will serve as the judge of the president's actions.

---

[172] Bessette and Tulis, "Constitution, Politics, and Presidency," 24; Gad Barzilai, *Demokratyah be-milhamot: mahloket ve-konsenzus be-Israel (A Democracy in Wartime: Conflict and Consensus in Israel)* (Tel Aviv: Sifriyat Poalim, 1992), pp. 247–50.

[173] Bruce Russett, *Controlling the Sword: The Democratic Governance of National Security* (Cambridge, MA: Harvard University Press, 1990), pp. 34–38.

(8)   None of the presidential actions can be directed against the domestic
political process and rights.[174]

Another possible way around the challenge of approval of egregious
actions is to incorporate into the model substantive elements, such as
Bruce Ackerman's entrenchment of fundamental rights against constitutional revision and amendment, or John Hart Ely's protection of certain
minority groups.[175] Yet, in addition to the problem of internal inconsis-
tency of such proposals with the process-based theory within which they
are to operate, there is the problem of putting particular constitutional
arrangements beyond the ratification power of the people.[176] But, if no
substantive restraint on the ability to obtain ex post public ratification
for extra-legal actions exists or, indeed, can exist, are we not left with a
totalitarian, lawless police state?

In 1944, Judge Learned Hand, speaking in Central Park at a swearing-in
ceremony of naturalized citizens, told his audience:

I often wonder whether we do not rest our hopes too much upon constitutions,
upon laws and upon courts. These are false hopes...Liberty lies in the hearts of
men and women; when it dies there, no constitution, no law, no court can save
it; no constitution, no law, no court can even do much to help it. While it lies
there it needs no constitution, no law, no court to save it.[177]

Eventually, ideas such as liberty, freedom, democracy, and rule of law
must exist in the hearts of the people if they are to survive the whirl-
wind of crisis and emergency. If they are not there to begin with, neither
model of emergency powers is likely to help much. As Carl Friedrich
notes: "there are no ultimate institutional safeguards available for insuring that emergency powers be used for the purpose of preserving the
Constitution. Only the people's own determination to see them so used
can make sure of that."[178] Whether such determination exists is to be

---

[174] Schlesinger, *The Imperial Presidency*, p. 459.

[175] Ackerman, *We the People*, pp. 320–21; John Hart Ely, *Democracy and Distrust: A Theory of Judicial Review* (Cambridge, MA: Harvard University Press, 1980), pp. 135–79.

[176] See, e.g., Daniel R. Ortiz, "Pursuing a Perfect Politics: The Allure and Failure of Process Theory" (1991) 77 *Virginia Law Review* 721 at 735–41; Laurence H. Tribe, "The Puzzling Persistence of Process-Based Constitutional Theories" (1980) 89 *Yale Law Journal* 1063 at 1076–77.

[177] Learned Hand, *The Spirit of Liberty: Papers and Addresses of Learned Hand*, ed. Irving Dillard (New York: Legal Classics Library, 1989), pp. 189–90. See also Gerald Gunther, *Learned Hand: The Man and the Judge* (New York: Knopf, 1994), pp. 547–52, 639–43.

[178] Carl J. Friedrich, *Constitutional Government and Democracy: Theory and Practice in Europe and America* (4th edn, Waltham, MA: Blaisdell, 1968), p. 570.

reflected, among other things, through the process of ex post ratification (or rejection) of extra-legal measures taken by public officials. The ethics of popular responsibility that is advocated by the Extra-Legal Measures model seeks to avoid that which Justice Brandeis identified as the greatest menace to freedom – an inert public: "Those who won our independence believed ... that the greatest menace to freedom is an inert people; that public discussion is a political duty; and that this should be a fundamental principle of the American government."[179]

Precedents

The unlawfulness of extra-legal measures and powers puts such actions in the context of the exceptional nature of the threat forced on the nation. By refraining from introducing changes to the existing pre-emergency legal system, either by way of direct modification or by way of interpretation, the Extra-Legal Measures model strives to avoid the creation of legal precedents that would be integrated into the normal system of laws and permeate into times of peace and normalcy. As Lucius Wilmerding explains:

A breach of the law, even a necessary one, *that ought to be justified*, can never destroy the law. It stands upon the records of Congress as an exception out of the law to be transmitted to posterity "as a safeguard of the constitution, that in future times no evil might come of it, from a precedent of the highest necessity, and most important service to the country." But an act legally done can always be drawn into precedent ... [and] since "men by habit make irregular stretches of power without discerning the consequence and extent of them," one small wrong must lead to a greater one, and in the end force must become the measure of law, discretion must degenerate into despotism.[180]

Although the sequence of extra-legal action and subsequent public ratification may bring about an eventual change in the law, turning a political precedent into a legal one,[181] such a shift cannot happen under the proposed model without informed public participation in the process.

In his celebrated dissenting opinion in *Korematsu v. United States*, Justice Robert Jackson follows a similar line of argument. Recognizing that "It would be impracticable and dangerous idealism to expect or insist that each specific military command in an area of probable operations

---

[179] Whitney v. California, 274 US 357 at 375 (1927) (Brandeis, J., concurring).

[180] Wilmerding, "The President and the Law," 329–30 (emphasis added).

[181] See, e.g., Cole, "Judging the Next Emergency," 2589; Peter Margulies, "Judging Terror in the 'Zone of Twilight': Exigency, Institutional Equity, and Procedure after September 11" (2004) 84 *Boston University Law Review* 383 at 402, n. 95.

will conform to conventional tests of constitutionality." he rejects the Business as Usual model, stating:

> When an area is so beset that it must be put under military control at all, the paramount consideration is that its measures be successful, rather than legal. The armed services must protect a society, not merely its Constitution...Defense measures will not, and often should not, be held within the limits that bind civil authority in peace.[182]

He goes on to reject the possibility of accommodation:

> But if we cannot confine military expedients by the Constitution, neither would I distort the Constitution to approve all that the military may deem expedient...a judicial construction of the due process clause that will sustain this order is a far more subtle blow to liberty than the promulgation of the order itself. A military order, however unconstitutional, is not apt to last longer than the military emergency...But once a judicial opinion rationalizes such an order to show that it conforms to the Constitution, or rather rationalizes the Constitution to show that the Constitution sanctions such an order, the Court for all time has validated the principle of racial discrimination in criminal procedure and of transplanting American citizens. The principle then lies about like a loaded weapon ready for the hand of any authority that can bring forward a plausible claim of an urgent need.[183]

One method by which the needs for expanded powers (and contracted rights) in times of emergency may be accommodated is by limiting the scope of applicability of individual rights and liberties by way of reading exceptions into their scopes of protection. The "clear and present danger" doctrine[184] and the doctrine developed in *Brandenburg v. Ohio*[185] are examples of such limitations on the scope of First Amendment protection in the United States. Yet, under the Extra-Legal Measures model courts need not be concerned with the prospect of taking an expansive view of constitutional rights coming back to haunt the nation when faced with critical threats and dangers that call for limitations on the exercise of such rights. If the situation is serious enough, there is always the possibility of government officials acting extra-legally to protect the nation and its citizens. Thus, the model enables judges to protect individual rights without having to fear that by doing so they compromise

---

[182] Korematsu v. United States, 323 US 214 at 244 (1944) (Jackson, J., dissenting).
[183] Ibid., pp. 244–46 (Jackson, J., dissenting).
[184] Schenck v. United States, 249 US 47 at 52 (1919).
[185] 395 US 444 at 448–49 (1969).

the security of the state. The possibility of extra-legal action may reduce the pressures for incorporating built-in exceptions to protected rights.[186]

Indeed, the United States Supreme Court recognized the possibility of Congress's acting on the political level to "correct" decisions made by the judicial branch. In *The Apollon*, Justice Joseph Story stated:

> It may be fit and proper for the government, in the exercise of the high discretion confided to the executive, for great public purposes, to act on a sudden emergency, or to prevent an irreparable mischief, by summary measures, which are not found in the text of the laws. Such measures are properly matters of state, and if the responsibility is taken, under justifiable circumstances, the Legislature will doubtless apply a proper indemnity. *But this Court can only look to the questions, whether the laws have been violated; and if they were, justice demands, that the injured party should receive a suitable redress.*[187]

Similarly, in *Public Committee against Torture in Israel v. The State of Israel*, the president of the Israeli Supreme Court stated:

> Deciding these applications has been difficult for us. True, from the legal perspective, the road before us is smooth. We are, however, part of Israeli society. We know its problems and we live its history. We are not in an ivory tower. We live the life of this country. We are aware of the harsh reality of terrorism in which we are, at times, immersed. The fear that our ruling will prevent us from properly dealing with terrorists troubles us. But we are judges. We demand that others act according to the law. This is also the demand that we make of ourselves. When we sit at trial, we stand on trial.[188]

Hard cases make bad laws. Times of emergency make some of the hardest of cases. What the Extra-Legal Measures model attempts to do is keep the ordinary legal system clean and distinct from the dirty and messy reality of emergency so as to prevent, or at least minimize, the perversion of that system in search for answers to hard, exceptional cases. Ordinary rules need not be modified or adapted so as to facilitate governmental crisis measures. In so far as exceptional measures are required to deal with the crisis, these measures are viewed precisely as such, "exceptional." They are not allowed to penetrate the ordinary legal system and "contaminate" it. Once an emergency has terminated,

---

[186] Eisgruber, "The Most Competent Branches," 361–62.

[187] The Apollon, 22 US (9 Wheat.) 362 at 366–67 (1824) (emphasis added).

[188] H.C. 5100/94, Pub. Comm. against Torture in Israel v. The State of Israel, 53(4) P.D. 817 at 845; Aharon Barak, "The Supreme Court 2001 Term – Foreword: A Judge on Judging: The Role of a Supreme Court in a Democracy" (2002) 116 *Harvard Law Review* 16 at 162; Aharon Barak, *Shofet be-hevrah demokratit* (*The Judge in a Democracy*) (Jerusalem: Nevo, 2004), pp. 410–11.

a return to normalcy may be possible without the ordinary legal system being marred by scars of emergency legislation or by interpretive stretch marks.

But can normalcy and emergency be so cleanly separated so as to avoid contamination of the former by actions taken during the emergency? We look at this question and its implications in the next chapter.

Carl Schmitt's dark shadow

Some have argued that the Extra-Legal Measures model resembles, and follows in the footsteps of, another seemingly extra-legal model of emergency powers, namely Carl Schmitt's theory of the exception.[189] As we explain below these models are clearly distinct both conceptually and in their practical implications.[190] We suggest that, if anything, Schmitt's theory of the exception is akin to models of constitutional necessity with which we dealt in chapter 1.

Carl Schmitt's theory of the exception

Schmitt – the most prominent legal scholar and political thinker to lend his active support to the Nazi regime – attacks liberalism for being negligent, if not outright deceitful, in disregarding the state of exception, and in pretending that the legal universe is governed by a complete, comprehensive, and exceptionless normative order.[191] The first of the four chapters on the concept of sovereignty, which together comprise Schmitt's most controversial work, *Political Theology*, revolves around the concept of "the exception" (*Ausnahmezustand*) and its relationship to the idea of sovereignty.[192] The link between the two concepts is made clear by Schmitt from the very first sentence of the book, where he famously declares that the "Sovereign is he who decides on the exception."[193] He emphasizes: "It is precisely the exception that makes relevant the subject

---

[189] Ackerman, "The Emergency Constitution," 1044; Dyzenhaus, "Emergency in Legal Theory," 69.

[190] Oren Gross, "The Normless and Exceptionless Exception: Carl Schmitt's Theory of Emergency Powers and the 'Norm–Exception' Dichotomy" (2000) 21 *Cardozo Law Review* 1825.

[191] John P. McCormick, *Carl Schmitt's Critique of Liberalism: Against Politics as Technology* (New York: Cambridge University Press, 1997), pp. 124–29, 148–52.

[192] Carlo Galli, "Carl Schmitt's Antiliberalism: Its Theoretical and Historical Sources and its Philosophical and Political Meaning" (2000) 21 *Cardozo Law Review* 1597 at 1605.

[193] Carl Schmitt, *Political Theology: Four Chapters on the Concept of Sovereignty*, trans. George Schwab (Cambridge, MA: MIT Press, 1985), p. 5.

of sovereignty, that is, the whole question of sovereignty."[194] According to Schmitt, the existence of exceptional situations refutes the formal face of legal liberalism, which argues that pre-established general norms cover all possible situations.[195] The need to decide the exceptional, concrete situation emphasizes the central role of political decision-makers who have to decide how to deal with the exception on a case-by-case basis. The exception requires concrete decisions that are not, and cannot be, constrained or guided by any sort of a priori rules.

Schmitt considers the exception to be the purest expression and reflection of the political. "The specific political distinction to which political actions and motives can be reduced," he writes, "is that between friend and enemy."[196] It is the ever-present possibility of combat and armed conflict that gives the friend–enemy dichotomy its real meaning: "[T]he exceptional case has an especially decisive meaning which exposes the core of the matter. For only in real combat is revealed the most extreme consequence of the political grouping of friend and enemy. From this most extreme possibility human life derives its specifically political tension."[197] Yet, since every sphere of human conduct could potentially rise to the level of the political – "if it is sufficiently strong to group human beings effectively according to friend and enemy"[198] – the exception inevitably permeates all aspects of human existence, and deciding on it becomes the single most important moment in every respect of human activity.[199]

In *Political Theology*, Schmitt adopts a revolutionary model of emergency regimes that embraces a sovereign dictatorship.[200] According to

---

[194] Ibid., p. 6.
[195] See, e.g., John P. McCormick, "Schmittian Positions on Law and Politics?: CLS and Derrida" (2000) 21 *Cardozo Law Review* 1693; David Dyzenhaus, "'Now the Machine Runs itself': Carl Schmitt on Hobbes and Kelsen" (1994) 16 *Cardozo Law Review* 1 at 10–14.
[196] Carl Schmitt, *The Concept of the Political*, trans. George Schwab (New Brunswick, NJ: Rutgers University Press, 1976), p. 26. See also Judith N. Shklar, *Legalism: Law, Morals and Political Trials* (Cambridge, MA: Harvard University Press, 1986), p. 125; William E. Scheuerman, *Between the Norm and the Exception: The Frankfurt School and the Rule of Law* (Cambridge, MA: MIT Press, 1994), p. 67.
[197] Schmitt, *The Concept of the Political*, p. 35.
[198] Ibid., pp. 37, 38.
[199] George Schwab, *The Challenge of the Exception: An Introduction to the Political Ideas of Carl Schmitt between 1921 and 1936* (2nd edn, New York: Greenwood Press, 1989), pp. 73–75.
[200] McCormick, *Critique of Liberalism*, pp. 133–41; John P. McCormick, "From Constitutional Technique to Caesarist Ploy: Carl Schmitt on Dictatorship, Liberalism, and Emergency Powers" in Peter R. Baehr and Melvin Richter (eds.), *Dictatorship in*

this model of dictatorship, an exception is characterized by a suspension of the entire existing order.[201] Even more significant is the sovereign dictator's power actively to change the existing legal order and transform it, in whole or in part, into something else. The norm becomes subservient to the exception, thereby reversing the relationship between the two. In fact, Schmitt eliminates altogether the notion of the normal and replaces it with the exception. It is not only that the exception confirms the rule and that the rule's very existence "derives only from the exception," but rather that the exception gobbles up the normal case and becomes, in and of itself, the ordinary, general rule. There is no place to continue talking about rule and exception. "The rule proves nothing; the exception proves everything: It confirms not only the rule but also its existence, which derives only from the exception."[202] The exception is no longer merely *normless*; it is also *exceptionless*.

Schmitt argues that every legal norm presupposes the existence of a certain normal and ordinary state of affairs, and can be applied only as long as this state of affairs continues to exist. Schmitt explains that "This effective normal situation is not a mere 'superficial presupposition' that a jurist can ignore; that situation belongs precisely to [the norm's] immanent validity." In exceptional circumstances, when this normal state of affairs is interrupted, the legal norm is no longer applicable and cannot fulfill its ordinary regulatory function. "For a legal order to make sense, a normal situation must exist." General norms are limited in their scope of application to those circumstances in which the normal state of affairs prevails. Crises undermine this factual basis and thus pull the rug out from under the feet of ordinary norms. Law is not omnipresent and omnipotent; general a priori rules cannot regulate the exception. "There exists no norm that is applicable to chaos." The exception resides in those areas where the norm breaks down and loses its "immanent validity."[203] This, together with the idea that the exception "cannot be circumscribed factually and made to conform to a preformed law,"[204] makes it *normless*. The sovereign dictator enjoys unlimited powers: "What characterizes an exception is principally unlimited authority, which means the suspension of the entire existing order."[205] Such unlimited powers pertain both to his unfettered discretion as to whether an

History and Theory: Bonapartism, Caesarism, and Totalitarianism (Washington, DC: German Historical Institute, 2004).

[201] Schmitt, *Political Theology*, p. 12.   [202] Ibid., p. 15.   [203] Ibid., p. 13.
[204] Ibid., p. 6.   [205] Ibid., p. 12.

exception does, in fact, exist, and to what measures ought to be taken in order to counter the concrete threat. In taking such counter-measures, the sovereign dictator is not limited by the existing legal order. He may disregard existing norms, but he may also put in place substitute norms. The powers of the sovereign dictator are not confined to the power to suspend, but also encompass the power to amend, revoke, and replace.

The dictator's unlimited powers are exercisable in the context of the extreme case – i.e., the exception. However, the only logical outcome of Schmitt's collapsing together the power to decide the existence of the exception and the breadth of counter-emergency powers to be used in order to bring the exception to a conclusion, and depositing them both in the hands of one person – the sovereign dictator – is that the dictator's unlimited powers are never turned off. The dictator is the person who needs to decide that the normal state of affairs has been replaced by an extreme case, and then decide what powers to use to counter the particular danger. However, the exception is a possibility that may never be discounted or disregarded since modern politics, according to Schmitt, is nothing short of permanent crisis.[206] It may occur at any given time, without prior warning, and create a "danger to the existence of the state."[207] What ought to count is not the actual occurrence of an exception, but rather the *possibility* of its taking place.[208] In a world governed by the exception, such a possibility is inevitable. The existence of an exception, or a possibility thereof, means that the sovereign must always be vigilant and, in fact, paranoid.[209] The result is that the sovereign is not only the one who decides on the exception, but also the one who definitely decides whether the normal situation actually exists.[210] It is only the sovereign dictator who can authoritatively distinguish the exception from the normal and decide to take state action. At the same time, Schmitt considers sovereignty and the powers attached to it as indivisible.[211] Thus, one cannot say that only some of the sovereign's powers are operational at any given moment. Subject to the personal decision of the sovereign dictator, the sovereign's unlimited powers may be put to use at any time. No external, objective limitations may be

---

[206] Galli, "Schmitt's Antiliberalism," 1615.

[207] Schmitt, *Political Theology*, p. 6.

[208] See, e.g., Schmitt, *The Concept of the Political*, p. 35.

[209] Anthony Carty, "Interwar German Theories of International Law: The Psychoanalytical and Phenomenological Perspectives of Hans Kelsen and Carl Schmitt" (1995) 16 *Cardozo Law Review* 1235 at 1237.

[210] Schmitt, *Political Theology*, p. 13.   [211] Ibid., p. 8.

imposed on the exercise of these powers. Should the dictator so desire, his unlimited powers – originally designed to apply to the exceptional case – may come to control the norm, indeed, *be* the norm. These powers may legitimately be exercised not only in the extreme case, but also under normal, ordinary conditions. The merger of the normal with the exception is virtually complete; it comes about when the exception takes over the normal and replaces it entirely.

Thus, while Schmitt's rhetoric speaks of the normal case and of the exception as two separate and distinct phenomena, his theory virtually advocates the complete destruction of the normal and its substitution by the exception. Schmitt attacks liberalism for its identification of the lawfulness of nature and normative lawfulness. "This pattern of thinking," submits Schmitt, "is characteristic of the natural sciences. It is based on the rejection of all 'arbitrariness,' and attempts to banish from the realm of the human mind every exception."[212] Schmitt's own position attempts to banish from the realm of the human mind every normal case.

There is little wonder why Schmitt's contemporary rivals – first and foremost, Hans Kelsen – have challenged his exceptionalism as practically making any constitutional provisions (save those pertaining to emergencies and emergency powers) wholly redundant and irrelevant. In the context of the Weimar Constitution, Kelsen argued that Schmitt's theory reduced the constitution to nothing more than article 48.[213] However, Schmitt's exceptionalism does not attach much practical significance to *any* constitutional arrangement. The sovereign dictator's unlimited powers include the power to suspend, revoke, amend, and replace. They are by no means confined by the substantive norms – or, indeed, the constitutional procedures – laid out in those provisions related to emergency powers. One should not even expect the constitutional document to be able to give a meaningful indication of the institutional identity of who will assume legal authority during a state of exception. No constitutional provision can withstand the sovereign dictator's unstoppable force.

David Dyzenhaus argues that, "Schmitt could not bring his vision of law completely into line with Nazi ideology. Simply put, he still maintained a shred of hope for law as an autonomous element in politics, one which could stand in the way of an all powerful state."[214] But in

---

[212] Ibid., p. 41.   [213] McCormick, *Critique of Liberalism*, p. 144.

[214] David Dyzenhaus, "Holmes and Carl Schmitt: An Unlikely Pair?" (1997) 63 *Brooklyn Law Review* 165 at 186.

fact Schmitt does not seek any defense mechanisms against the "strong total state" for his vision is precisely that of the "all powerful state."[215] Again, Schmitt argues that, "What characterizes an exception is principally unlimited authority, which means the suspension of the entire existing order. In such a situation it is clear that the state remains, whereas law recedes. Because the exception is different from anarchy and chaos, order in the juristic sense still prevails even if it is not of the ordinary kind."[216] However, to argue that an order that is characterized by an "unlimited authority" of the sovereign dictator is an "order in the juristic sense" means nothing. Since the normal case and the exception collapse into one exceptionless exception, this disorderly order is the "ordinary kind" of order in the Schmittian state.

Schmitt is obsessed with the problem of legal indeterminacy. He claims that liberalism "reduces the legal order to a situation of 'chaos' and 'anarchy,' unable to provide a minimal measure of legal predictability."[217] Yet, the ever existing exception leaves nothing standing but the "decisionistic and personalistic element in the concept of sovereignty."[218] Schmitt's alternative model, which he offers as a replacement to the liberal model, introduces as much predictability as the sovereign's whim. If liberalism's fault inheres in the normative and utopian nature of its structures, Schmitt's fault lies with the apologetic overtones of his proposals. Against liberalism's rigidity, Schmitt puts forward an all-too-flexible alternative. Whatever the sovereign decides is legitimate. There is no substantive content against which legitimacy of such actions can be measured – not even Hobbes's minimalist principle of self-preservation.[219] Despite Schmitt's attacks against the content-neutrality of liberalism and positivism, his theory, in the last account, is nihilistic.[220] A decision emerges out of nothing. It does not presuppose

[215] Peter C. Caldwell, *Popular Sovereignty and the Crisis of German Constitutional Law: The Theory and Practice of Weimar Constitutionalism* (Durham, NC: Duke University Press, 1997), pp. 112–14.

[216] Schmitt, *Political Theology*, p. 12.

[217] William E. Scheuerman, "After Legal Indeterminacy: Carl Schmitt and the National Socialist Legal Order, 1933–1936" (1998) 19 *Cardozo Law Review* 1743 at 1748.

[218] Schmitt, *Political Theology*, p. 48.

[219] Leo Strauss, "Comments on Carl Schmitt's *Der Begriff des Politischen*," reprinted and translated in Schmitt, *The Concept of the Political*, pp. 81, 88–89; Dyzenhaus, "Now the Machine Runs itself," 16.

[220] David Ohana, "The Leviathan Opens Wide its Jaws: Karl Schmidt [sic] and the Origins of Legal Fascism" in Daniel Gutwein and Menachem Mautner (eds.), *Mishpat ve-Historya (Law and History)* (Jerusalem: Merkaz Zalman Shazar le-toldot Israel, 1999), pp. 273–74; Carty, "German Theories of International Law," 1270–71.

any given set of norms, and it does not owe its validity or its legitimacy to any preexisting normative structure. No such structure, therefore, can attempt to limit the decision's scope in any meaningful way. As John McCormick notes: "If the constitution's primary purpose is to establish an institution, such as a presidency, to exclusively embody the preconstitutional sovereign will in a time of crisis, then the constitution is inviting its own disposability."[221] Similarly, since the decision is not the product of any abstract rationality, but is rather reflective of an irrational element, it cannot – by definition – be bound by any element found in the rational dimension.[222] As William Scheuerman pointedly notes: "A rigorous decisionist legal theory reduces law to an altogether arbitrary, and potentially inconsistent, series of power decisions, and thus proves unable to secure even a modicum of legal determinacy. It represents a theoretical recipe for a legal system characterized by a kind of permanent revolutionary dictatorship."[223] Schmitt himself recognized the defects and flaws in his position, and sought to modify it during the 1930s.[224] In the preface to the second edition of *Political Theology*, written in November 1933, Schmitt concedes that "the decisionist, focusing on the moment, always runs the risk of missing the stable content inherent in every great political movement."[225] Personal decisionism cannot, after all, guarantee legal determinacy and predictability, nor political stability. Yet, even now his rhetoric tries to hide the defenselessness of his original position, for he describes the decision-maker as implementing "the good law of the correctly recognized political situation."[226] Even with Hitler already occupying the office of the chancellor for ten months, Schmitt's retreat from radical decisionism was not instigated by any acknowledgment of its potentially catastrophic consequences. On the contrary, it is an attempt to present a position that is even more supportive of the National Socialist cause than the decisionist model by formulating the case for "purifying" the ranks of the legal profession of "alien" – first and foremost Jewish – elements and ensuring their ethnic, racial, cultural, spiritual, and ideological homogeneity.[227]

---

[221] McCormick, *Critique of Liberalism*, p. 153.
[222] Izhak Englard, "Nazi Criticism against the Normativist Theory of Hans Kelsen – Its Intellectual Basis and Post-Modern Tendencies," in Dan Diner and Michael Stolleis (eds.), *Hans Kelsen and Carl Schmitt: A Juxtaposition* (Gerlingen: Bleicher, 1999), p. 133 at 142–47.
[223] Scheuerman, "After Legal Indeterminacy," 1755–56.
[224] Ibid., pp. 1752–64.   [225] Schmitt, *Political Theology*, p. 3.   [226] Ibid., p. 3.
[227] Scheuerman, "After Legal Indeterminacy," 1756–64.

Decisionism and the Extra-Legal Measures model

Schmitt's theory of the exception is not, indeed cannot, be construed as a constitutional or legal theory. For reasons explained above, his theory advocates not only a normless exception, but also an exceptionless exception. The only norm that is available is that of the will of the sovereign, which, for Schmitt, is the president who determines the exception, embodies the nation and the people, and is their protector. Yet what is so dangerous about Schmitt's position is its recognition of a sovereign extra-constitutional authority that stands outside, indeed above, the constitution and the legal order. Such authority, the authority of the sovereign, allows him to ignore and suspend any existing constitutional norms as well as change, modify, amend, and replace it altogether. In that sense, such extra-constitutional authority is the norm. For whatever is done and whatever decreed under it is, by definition, legal and legitimate. There can be no discussion of extra-legality in this context because the sovereign, who decides on the exception, can never act extra-legally. All his actions and decisions are part of the norm, unless and until he decides to change them or their effects. In other words, to say that the sovereign may act extra-constitutionally under Schmitt is to miss the point. His actions and decisions are, ipso facto, constitutional (if that means anything under Schmitt's theory). Indeed, the decision on the exception is an independent source of "law." It is originary and in fact supreme to all other possible sources of legal norms.

It is in this respect that it appears that Schmitt's position comes closer to arguments about constitutional necessity than to the Extra-Legal Measures model. As is the case with constitutional necessity, so too under Schmitt's theory of the exception necessity (i.e., the exception) makes legal and constitutional that which otherwise would not be so. Moreover, the decisionist power is very much in the hands of the president whose decisions enjoy constitutional priority (according to Paulsen's benign argument from constitutional necessity) or supremacy and independence (according to Richard Nixon's more extreme version). Again, as is the case with Schmitt, the president's notion of necessity would be immune from review by any other branch of government, either as a practical matter or, as we suggest in chapter 1, as a matter of principle. Both theories introduce the exception into the constitutional system. And, we would argue, once this is done, the exception can no longer be contained by any constitutional or legal measures.

While Schmitt's theory of the exception presents us with a lawless, authoritarian state where the sovereign is not, in fact, bound by any limitations that constrain his actions, the Extra-Legal Measures model offers a variety of mechanisms for control of such actions. What is important to note here is that the Extra-Legal Measures model does maintain constitutional limitations and constraints on the extra-legal actions that may be taken in times of crisis and retains sovereignty (if one is to use Schmitt here) with the people.

As noted above, under the Extra-Legal Measures model, legal and constitutional norms are not suspended during a crisis. In fact, they are not even overridden. If an official determines that a particular case necessitates her deviation from an existing rule, she may choose to depart from that rule. But even as she does so the rule continues to apply: it applies to other situations (that is, it is not canceled or terminated), and, more significantly, it continues to apply to her actions (i.e., is not even overridden in the concrete case at hand). Rule departure constitutes, under all circumstances and all conditions, a violation of the relevant legal rule. Thus, the Extra-Legal Measures model retains a legal benchmark against which to assess the actions of the public official. Actions taken in the state of exception cannot, in and of themselves, change and modify the legal terrain. They remain, truly, extra-legal.

That extra-legality also opens the door for subsequent legal accountability, which is entirely absent from Schmitt's theory. It is precisely because the actions taken are extra-legal, and not made legal merely because of the decision of the president, that the question of implications for the actor is still relevant. And unlike Schmitt, under the Extra-Legal Measures model the final decision in such matters is given to the people. Perhaps, using Schmitt's most celebrated sentence, we can say that it is the people who are the sovereign because, at the end of the day, it is they who decide on the exception through the process of ex post ratification or rejection. Thus, while Schmitt conflates authority with power and vests them both with the president, the Extra-Legal Measures model seeks to separate the two, acknowledging the possibility of the power to act extra-legally while retaining the final authority with the people.[228]

---

[228] Giorgio Agamben, *State of Exception*, trans. Kevin Attell (Chicago: University of Chicago Press, 2005), pp. 74–85.

4 Five degrees of separation

The first three chapters examined (chapters 1 and 2) and challenged (chapter 3) the assumption of constitutionality that underlies the traditional, constitutional models of emergency regime. This chapter focuses on another fundamental assumption around which models of emergency regimes are structured, namely the *assumption* of *separation*, which is defined by the belief in our ability to separate emergencies and crises from normalcy, counter-terrorism measures from ordinary legal rules and norms. This assumption is closely linked to the different models of emergency powers as their long-term success depends on it. Success here is measured not only in the ability to overcome grave threats and dangers, but also in the ability to confine the application of extraordinary measures to extraordinary times, insulating periods of normalcy from the encroachment of vast emergency powers.

However, as we demonstrate below, bright-line distinctions between normalcy and emergency are frequently untenable. In various meaningful ways, the exception has merged with the rule, and "[e]mergency government has become the norm."[1]

Fashioning legal tools to respond to emergencies in the belief that the assumption of separation will serve as a firewall that protects human rights, civil liberties, and the normal legal system as a whole may be misguided. The belief in our ability to separate emergency from normalcy focuses our attention on the immediate effects of emergency measures

---

[1] Harold Relyea, *A Brief History of Emergency Powers in the United States* (Washington, DC: Government Printing Office, 1974), p. v; Walter Benjamin, "On the Concept of History" in Howard Eiland and Michael W. Jennings (eds.), *Selected Writings* (4 vols., Cambridge, MA: Harvard University Press, 2003), vol. IV, p. 392; Kanishka Jayasuriya, "The Exception Becomes the Norm: Law and Regimes of Exception in East Asia" (2001) 2 *Asian-Pacific Law and Policy Journal* 108 at 110.

and powers while hiding from view their long-term costs. When added to the inherent problems that times of crisis pose in striking an appropriate balance between individual rights and national security needs, as discussed in chapters 1 and 2, this casts grave doubts on our ability to make accurate calculations of the relevant costs and benefits with respect to governmental emergency powers.

Normalcy and emergency: rule and exception

Emergencies are conceptualized in terms of a dichotomized dialectic. The term "emergency" connotes a sudden, urgent, usually unforeseen event or situation that requires immediate action, often without time for reflection and consideration. The notion of "emergency" is inherently linked to the concept of "normalcy" in the sense that the former is considered to be outside the ordinary course of events or anticipated actions. To recognize an emergency we must, therefore, have the background of normalcy. Furthermore, as our discussion of the Roman dictatorship shows, in order to be able to talk about normalcy and emergency in any meaningful way, the concept of emergency is informed by notions of temporal duration and exceptional danger. Although there are many competing definitions of "emergency," temporal duration and exceptional nature of the threat are common starting points for all of them. Thus, a comprehensive study on the implications for human rights of states of emergency, which was prepared for the UN Commission on Human Rights, noted that "above and beyond the rules [of emergency regimes]...one principle, namely, the principle of provisional status, dominates all the others. The right of derogation can be justified solely by the concern to return to normality."[2] For normalcy to be "normal," it has to be the general rule, the ordinary state of affairs. Emergency must constitute no more than an exception to that rule – it must last only a relatively short time and yield no substantial permanent effects. As Cecil Carr notes: "Free peoples, when they temporarily surrender freedom, will expect to see their inheritance restored to them when the storm is over. There will be two anxious questions – how large must

---

[2] "Study of the Implications for Human Rights of Recent Developments Concerning Situations Known as States of Siege or Emergency," UN Commission on Human Rights, 35th Sess., Agenda Item 10, at 20, UN Doc. E/CN.4/Sub.2/1982/15 (1982). See also Subrata Roy Chowdhury, *Rule of Law in a State of Emergency: The Paris Minimum Standards of Human Rights Norms in a State of Emergency* (London: Pinter, 1989), p. 45; Ronald St. J. Macdonald, "Derogations under Article 15 of the European Convention on Human Rights" (1997) 36 *Columbia Journal of Transnational Law* 225 at 241–42.

that surrender be and how soon will the restoration come?"[3] Traditional discourse on emergency powers posits normalcy and crisis as two separate phenomena and assumes that emergency is the exception. Its basic paradigm is that of "normalcy-rule, emergency-exception," which is based on a clear separation of the normal and exceptional cases.[4] The belief that a clear line can be drawn between normal times and times of exceptional threats to the nation underlies all of the models of emergency powers. As Frederick Watkins puts it, "it is in connection with the problem of temporary emergencies, and in this connection only, that the possibility of constitutional dictatorship can ever be said to arise."[5]

Each of the constitutional models of emergency powers takes the assumption of separation as its starting point. This may seem counterintuitive at first in the context of the hard version of the Business as Usual model since it holds a unitary vision of the legal order: if regular legal norms are not subject to modification in times of exigency, one cannot speak of a distinct emergency legal regime. Yet, even for that model the assumption of separation has significant implications. The main challenge facing the model is its perceived detachment from reality. The stronger that perception is, the stronger the challenges to the model become. For example, when faced with situations of entrenched or prolonged emergencies, the Business as Usual model will come under strong pressures to allow the legal system to fight off the threat to the nation. The longer people live under the shadow of emergency, the more likely they are to demand that the legal system accommodate the necessities of the situation. Continued adherence to the Business as Usual model in those circumstances may lead to adjustments to the system that are made in ways that are less transparent. Eventually the system will reach a position where significant portions of the "ordinary" legal system have been formulated and reformulated in response to crises. As emergencies become more prolonged and less exceptional it becomes harder to argue for a business as usual approach since it is clear that much is not "as usual."

---

[3] Cecil T. Carr, "Crisis Legislation in Britain" (1940) 40 *Columbia Law Review* 1309 at 1324–25.

[4] Oren Gross, " 'Once More unto the Breach': The Systematic Failure of Applying the European Convention on Human Rights to Entrenched Emergencies" (1998) 23 *Yale Journal of International Law* 437 at 440; Fionnuala Ní Aoláin, "The Emergence of Diversity: Differences in Human Rights Jurisprudence" (1995) 19 *Fordham International Law Journal* 101.

[5] Frederick M. Watkins, "The Problem of Constitutional Dictatorship" (1940) 1 *Public Policy* 324 at 327.

For the models of accommodation the danger is that emergency-specific accommodation will become an integral part of the regular legal system. In order to ensure that special norms that find their *raison d'être* in a state of emergency do not become confused with ordinary legal rules in times of normalcy, it is essential to keep the two sets of norms and powers apart as much as possible. Without separation, it is but a short step to conflate emergency powers and norms with the "ordinary" and the "normal."

Similarly, any model that recognizes the possibility of extra-legal action in times of emergency is, arguably, premised on a notion of impermeable boundaries between normalcy and emergency. It is that separation which enables proponents of such models to claim that the ordinary legal system will not be tarnished by the necessities of emergency and the extra-legality that they bring about, and will remain intact and ready to resume its fullest extent when the emergency is over.

Common to all the models of emergency regimes is their aim of overcoming specific crises and restoring normalcy. Their ultimate goal is a return to the status quo ante, the normal state of affairs that preceded the emergency.[6] Under each model, application of emergency powers is designed to be of a temporary nature, to serve as a bridge between pre-crisis and post-crisis normalcy. With the termination of the conflict, normalcy ought to be reestablished and the emergency regime withdrawn.

The distinction between the spheres of normalcy and emergency is facilitated and sustained by resorting to several mechanisms of separation. The remainder of this chapter discusses these mechanisms and suggests that each of them is problematic.

Sequencing and temporal distinctions: separating the best and the worst of times

Normalcy and emergency are often seen to occupy alternate, mutually exclusive, time-frames. Normalcy exists prior to crisis and is reinstituted

---

[6] H.P. Lee, *Emergency Powers* (Sydney: Law Book, 1984), p. 1; Carl J. Friedrich, *Constitutional Government and Democracy: Theory and Practice in Europe and America* (4th edn, Waltham, MA: Blaisdell, 1968), pp. 568–70; Clinton L. Rossiter, *Constitutional Dictatorship: Crisis Government in Modern Democracies* (Princeton: Princeton University Press, 1948), p. 306; John Ferejohn and Pasquale Pasquino, "The Law of the Exception: A Typology of Emergency Powers" (2004) 2 *International Journal of Constitutional Law* 210 at 210. But see John E. Finn, *Constitutions in Crisis: Political Violence and the Rule of Law* (New York: Oxford University Press, 1991), pp. 40–43.

after the emergency is over. Crises constitute brief intervals in the otherwise uninterrupted flow of normalcy. Emergency powers are supposed to apply only while the exigency persists. They are not to extend beyond that time-frame into ordinary times.

However, this view of the temporal relationship between normalcy and emergency does not account adequately for the possibility that emergencies will become entrenched and prolonged.[7] Rather than the exception, crises have become the norm leading to a "tendency to slide into a new conception of normality that takes vastly extended controls for granted, and thinks of freedom in smaller and smaller dimensions."[8]

Emergency regimes tend to perpetuate themselves, regardless of the intentions of those who originally invoked them. Once brought to life, they are not so easily terminable. As chapter 5 demonstrates, this holds true across jurisdictions and legal systems. Thus, for example, the State of Israel has been under an unremitting emergency regime since its establishment in May 1948. As originally authorized, however, the declaration of a state of emergency was considered a temporary and necessary evil, a transition mechanism to be operative only for the duration of the War of Independence.[9] However, this temporary regime became a permanent feature in the life of the state, outliving the war that gave it life. It is still an integral part of the Israeli legal terrain today. Similarly, until August 2005, Northern Ireland was subject to emergency rule for a combined period of more than thirty years.[10] A state of emergency had become the norm, the ordinary state of affairs, leading one scholar to suggest that, "The concept of an emergency gives rise to the expectation that such a state of affairs is temporary and that normal conditions will be restored. In Northern Ireland, however, there can be no such expectation."[11] By the mid-1970s, there were four declared states of

---

[7] Oren Gross and Fionnuala Ní Aoláin, "From Discretion to Scrutiny: Revisiting the Application of the Margin of Appreciation Doctrine in the Context of Article 15 of the European Convention on Human Rights" (2001) 23 *Human Rights Quarterly* 625 at 644–47; Oren Gross and Fionnuala Ní Aoláin, "To Know Where We Are Going, We Need To Know Where We Are: Revisiting States of Emergency" in Angela Hegarty and Siobhan Leonard (eds.), *Human Rights: An Agenda for the 21st Century* (London: Cavendish, 1999), p. 79 at 95–98.

[8] Harold D. Lasswell, *National Security and Individual Freedom* (New York: McGraw-Hill, 1950), p. 29.

[9] Menachem Hofnung, *Democracy, Law and National Security in Israel* (Brookfield, VT: Dartmouth, 1996), p. 52.

[10] Fionnuala Ní Aoláin, *The Politics of Force: Conflict Management and State Violence in Northern Ireland* (Belfast: Blackstaff Press, 2000), pp. 17–71.

[11] Kevin Boyle, "Human Rights and Political Resolution in Northern Ireland" (1982) 9 *Yale Journal of World and Public Order* 156 at 175.

emergency in force in the United States spanning a period of more than forty years.[12] As a direct result, more than 470 pieces of legislation, meant to apply only when a state of emergency had been declared, could have been used by the government.[13]

Similarly, time-bound emergency legislation is often the subject of future extensions and renewals, despite Lord Devlin's caution that "It would be very unfortunate if the public were to receive the impression that the continuance of the state of emergency had become a sort of statutory fiction which was used as a means of prolonging legislation initiated under different circumstances and for different purposes."[14] It is commonplace to find on the statute books legislative acts that had originally been enacted as temporary emergency or counter-terrorism measures, but that were subsequently transformed into permanent legislation. Indeed, the longer that emergency legislation, broadly understood, remains on the statute books, the greater the likelihood that extraordinary powers made available to government under this legislation will become part of the ordinary, normal legal system. Moreover, the maintenance of emergency powers may be accompanied by expansion over time of the scope of such powers. At the same time, built-in limitations on the exercise of emergency authority and powers tend to wither away. Thus, for example, Harold Koh and John Yoo have identified a trend of US presidents sidestepping congressional statutory restrictions incorporated into legislation such as the International Emergency Economic Powers Act of 1977[15] and thus gaining access to broad statutory grants of authority without the built-in limitations on the use of that authority.[16]

---

[12] Between 1933 and 1972, four national emergencies were declared. See Proclamation No. 2039, reprinted in *The Public Papers and Addresses of Franklin D. Roosevelt* (New York: Russell & Russell, 1938), p. 24 at 24–26, and in 48 Stat. 1689 (1933) (ordering all banks to close from March 6, 1933, through March 9, 1933); Proclamation No. 2914, 3 C.F.R. 99 (1949–1953) (declaring a national emergency in response to the Korean conflict); Proclamation No. 3972, 3 C.F.R. 473 (1970) (declaring a national emergency in response to the Post Office strike); Proclamation No. 4074, 3 C.F.R. 80 (1971) (declaring a national emergency so that currency and foreign trade restrictions could be implemented).

[13] Glenn E. Fuller, "The National Emergency Dilemma: Balancing the Executive's Crisis Powers with the Need for Accountability" (1979) 52 *Southern California Law Review* 1453 at 1453.

[14] Willcock v. Muckle, 2 K.B. 844 at 853–54 (1951) (Devlin, J.).

[15] 50 U.S.C. paras. 1701–06 (1977).

[16] Harold H. Koh and John C. Yoo, "Dollar Diplomacy/Dollar Defense: The Fabric of Economics and National Security Law" (1992) 26 *International Lawyer* 715 at 742–46; Dames and Moore v. Regan, 453 US 654 (1981).

When originally enacted by the British parliament, the Civil Authorities (Special Powers) Act (Northern Ireland) of 1922 – leading to the
creation of an emergency regime under which "the Government enjoyed powers similar to those current in time of martial law"[17] – was
meant to last for no more than one year. Its radical nature was best
reflected in section 2(4), which provided that "If any person does any
act of such nature as to be calculated to be prejudicial to the preservation of the peace or maintenance of order in Northern Ireland and
not specifically provided for in the regulations, he shall be guilty of an
offence against those regulations." Indeed, the South African minister
of justice was quoted at the time to say, referring to section 2(4), that he
"would be willing to exchange all the [South African] legislation of that
sort for one clause in the Northern Ireland Special Powers Act."[18] The
act was renewed annually until 1928, when it was extended for a five-
year period. Subsequently, the act was made permanent. The story of the
series of Prevention of Terrorism (Temporary Provisions) Acts (PTA) was
much the same. Originally introduced in parliament in 1974, the PTA
was amended in 1975 and 1983, and reenacted in 1984. In 1989, the PTA
became a permanent part of the statute books of the United Kingdom.[19]

The Uniting and Strengthening America by Providing Appropriate
Tools Required to Intercept and Obstruct Terrorism Act of 2001 (USA
PATRIOT), passed merely a month and a half after the traumatic events
of September 11, 2001, greatly expanded the surveillance and investiga-
tive powers of law enforcement agencies in the United States both in the
context of collection of "foreign intelligence" information when there
is probable cause that the target of surveillance is a foreign power or
an agent of a foreign power, and access to communications in ordinary
criminal investigations.[20] To alleviate concerns, a sunset provision was

---

[17] Claire Palley, "The Evolution, Disintegration and Possible Reconstruction of the
Northern Ireland Constitution" (1972) 1 *Anglo-American Law Review* 368 at 400.

[18] Committee on the Administration of Justice, *No Emergency, No Emergency Law:
Emergency Legislation Related to Northern Ireland: The Case for Repeal* (Belfast: CAJ, 1993),
p. 6.

[19] The PTA of 1989 and the Northern Ireland (Emergency Provisions) Act of 1996 have
since been replaced by the Terrorism Act of 2000. A.W. Bradley and K.D. Ewing,
Constitutional and Administrative Law (13th edn, New York: Longman, 2003), p. 615; Clive
Walker, *The Prevention of Terrorism in British Law* (2nd edn, Manchester: Manchester
University Press, 1992), pp. 33–39; Joe Sim and Philip A. Thomas, "The Prevention of
Terrorism Act: Normalising the Politics of Repression" (1983) 10 *Journal of Law and
Society* 71.

[20] Uniting and Strengthening America by Providing Appropriate Tools Required to
Intercept and Obstruct Terrorism (USA PATRIOT) Act, Pub. L. No. 107–56, 115 Stat. 272
(2001).

incorporated into the act. This provision was scheduled to terminate on December 31, 2005 several of the act's sections that enhanced search and electronic surveillance powers of law enforcement agencies. The idea was that such a provision would enable legislators to review carefully, removed from the pressures of the moment, whether the expanded powers were needed and how well they had been used (or abused) as well as to assess their effectiveness, and will give incentives to the administration to cooperate with legislative oversight efforts.[21]

In its final report, the 9/11 Commission recommended that the burden of proof for showing that Congress should renew USA PATRIOT Act powers subject to sunset should be on the president, who must show that each power actually materially enhances security and that there is adequate supervision of the use of such powers to ensure that civil liberties are protected.[22] If the power is granted, the commission emphasized, there must be adequate guidelines and oversight to confine its use properly. The commission further stated: "Because of concerns regarding the shifting balance of power to the government, we think that a full and informed debate on the Patriot Act would be healthy."[23]

Once again, the familiar pattern of a temporary act (or, in this case, provisions thereof) becoming permanent was repeated. On July 21, 2005, the same day as the second round of terrorist attacks on London's transportation system, the United States House of Representatives voted by a wide margin to extend indefinitely and make permanent practically all the provisions of the USA PATRIOT Act which have been subject to the sunset provision.[24] On July 29, 2005, the Senate voted unanimously to make permanent virtually all the main provisions of the act. This was made possible after several proposed changes to the act – which would have expanded further the FBI powers under it to include the authority to demand records in terror investigations through administrative subpoenas, without a judge's order, and to have sole discretion in deciding whether to monitor the mail of terror suspects – had been withdrawn.

---

[21] Section 224 of the USA PATRIOT Act; Robert O'Harrow, Jr., "Six Weeks in Autumn," *Washington Post*, October 27, 2002, p. W06.

[22] "Final Report of the National Commission on Terrorist Attacks upon the United States (The 9/11 Commission Report)" (Washington: US GPO, 2004), available at http://www.gpoaccess.gov/911/index.html (last visited August 8, 2005), pp. 394–95.

[23] Ibid., p. 394.

[24] Glen Johnson, "House Votes to Extend Patriot Act, Democrats Voice Civil Liberties Concerns," *AP DataStream*, July 22, 2005.

While the renewed legislation includes certain new restrictions on the government's powers, it should also be noted that there are already indications that the USA PATRIOT Act is becoming the new normality and benchmark for further legislation with the intelligence community taking its expanded powers and authorities under the act as the new norm and seeking to expand them further.[25]

The advent of the "war on terrorism" led to further questions about the relationship between normalcy and exception in the face of a "war" that may well be endless. In a statement made on September 20, 2001, President Bush declared:

Our enemy is a radical network of terrorists, and every government that supports them. Our war on terror begins with al Qaeda, but it does not end there. It will not end until every terrorist group of global reach has been found, stopped and defeated...From this day forward, any nation that continues to harbor or support terrorism will be regarded by the US as a hostile regime.[26]

The main traditional feature of the international legal system is its dichotomized division between times of peace and wartime, with the former constituting the norm and the latter the exception to that norm. Surrender, armistice agreements, and peace agreements serve formally to separate war from peace and define clearly the end of one (war) and the resumption of the other (peace).[27] Similarly, formal declarations of war, although not required as a matter of international law, may assist in setting the boundaries between war and peace. Such clear distinctions are important from the legal perspective since different laws apply in the two periods: the laws of peace apply in times of peace; the laws of war apply in times of war between belligerent states and regulate certain aspects of the relationship between these states and between them

---

[25] Eric Lichtblau, "Senate Makes Permanent Nearly All Provisions of Patriot Act, with a Few Restrictions," NY Times, July 29, 2005, p. A11.

[26] President George W. Bush, Address to a Joint Session of Congress and the American People (Sept. 20, 2001), available at http://www.whitehouse.gov/news/releases/2001/09/20010920-8.html (last visited on August 8, 2005). See also Bob Woodward, "CIA Told to Do 'Whatever Necessary' to Kill Bin Laden; Agency and Military Collaborating at 'Unprecedented' Level; Cheney Says War Against Terror 'May Never End,'" Washington Post, October 21, 2001, p. A01; Bruce Ackerman, "The Emergency Constitution" (2004) 113 Yale Law Journal 1029 at 1043; Lauren Berlant, "The Epistemology of State Emotion," in Austin Sarat (ed.), Dissent in Dangerous Times (Ann Arbor, MI: University of Michigan Press, 2005), p. 46.

[27] Wolff Heintschel von Heinegg, "Factors in War to Peace Transitions" (2004) 27 Harvard Journal of Law and Public Policy 843 at 848–57.

and other states not party to the conflict. While the distinction between war and peace had been eroding even before the attacks of September 11, 2001,[28] the specter of an endless war on terror is highly problematic on many levels. Consider the issue of the detention of enemy combatants.

The laws of war permit the detention of combatants until the end of hostilities in order to prevent them from returning to the battlefield. Such detainees must be released and repatriated without delay after the cessation of active hostilities, unless they are being lawfully prosecuted or have been lawfully convicted of crimes and are serving sentences.[29] However, as noted in *Hamdi v. Rumsfeld*:

> We recognize that the national security underpinnings of the "war on terror," although crucially important, are broad and malleable. As the Government concedes, "given its unconventional nature, the current conflict is unlikely to end with a formal cease-fire agreement"...If the Government does not consider this unconventional war won for two generations, and if it maintains during that time that Hamdi might, if released, rejoin forces fighting against the United States, then the position it has taken...suggests that Hamdi's detention could last for the rest of his life.[30]

The notion of an endless war, with the attendant disappearance of a clear separation between war and peace, makes a decision that active hostilities have ceased impossible to make or at least subject to an arbitrary decision. Concerned with such implications, the *Hamdi* plurality went on to find that active hostilities were still going on – citing active operations against Taliban fighters in Afghanistan. This supported further the understanding, "based on longstanding law-of-war principles," that Congress intended to authorize the detention of enemy combatants to the end of active hostilities. However, the Justices also acknowledged that, "If the practical circumstances of a given conflict are entirely unlike those of the conflicts that informed the development of the law of war, that understanding may unravel."[31]

---

[28] Oren Gross and Fionnuala Ní Aoláin, "Emergency, War and International Law: Another Perspective" (2001) 70 *Nordic Journal of International Law* 29.

[29] Geneva Convention (III) Relative to the Treatment of Prisoners of War, Aug. 12, 1949 (1955) 6 U.S.T. 3316, T.I.A.S. No. 3364, art. 118. See also ibid., arts. 85, 99, 119, 129.

[30] Hamdi v. Rumsfeld, 124 S. Ct. 2633 at 2641 (2004) (O'Connor, J.).

[31] Hamdi, 124 S. Ct. 2633 at 2641 (2004). See also Curtis A. Bradley and Jack Goldsmith, "Congressional Authorization and the War on Terrorism" (2005) 118 *Harvard Law Review* 2047 at 2123–27; Randolph N. Jonakait, "Rasul v. Bush: Unanswered Questions" (2005) 13 *William and Mary Bill of Rights Journal* 1103 at 1131–32.

It's a bad world out there (I): spatial distinctions

Another line of separation between emergency and normalcy is drawn around geographic distinctions. Different legal principles, rules, and norms may be applied, for example, in distinct geographical areas that belong to the same "control system,"[32] such as Great Britain and North- ern Ireland, Israel and the occupied territories, or France and Algeria. One part of such a "control system" – the controlling territory – ap- plies an emergency regime to the dependent territory. At the same time a putative normal legal regime is maintained in the controlling terri- tory itself. The two legal regimes apply contemporaneously. The depen- dent territory becomes an anomalous zone in which certain legal rules, otherwise regarded as embodying fundamental policies and values of the larger legal system, are locally suspended.[33] However, the claim is that the two realities and the two concomitant legal regimes – that of emergency applicable to the dependent territory and that of normalcy applicable to the controlling territory – are maintained separately and do not affect each other. Maintaining a regime of legal exception in the dependent territory does not adversely affect the form and content of the normal legal order that governs the controlling territory. There is no spillover from one legal regime to the other across geographic boundaries.

However, experience shows that geographic boundaries are permeable, rather than integral, when emergency powers are concerned.[34] Gerald Neuman has already demonstrated that "anomalous zones" threaten to subvert fundamental values in the larger legal system.[35] The belief in our ability to use the politically, legally, socially, and geographically con- structed anomaly in order to contain the exercise of emergency powers and confine their use to that territory may, therefore, be misguided.

Colonies and empire: the origins of DORA

After the defeat of the French fleet at Trafalgar and prior to World War I no war came close to England's shores. Domestically, socio-economic,

---

[32] Baruch Kimmerling, "Boundaries and Frontiers of the Israeli Control System: Analytical Conclusions" in Baruch Kimmerling (ed.), *The Israeli State and Society* (Albany, NY: State University of New York Press, 1989), pp. 265–67.

[33] Gerald L. Neuman, "Anomalous Zones" (1996) 48 *Stanford Law Review* 1197 at 1201.

[34] A.R. Luckham, "A Comparative Typology of Civil–Military Relations" (Winter 1971) 6 *Government and Opposition* 5; Marcus G. Raskin, "Democracy Versus the National Security State" (Summer 1976) 40(3) *Law and Contemporary Problems* 189 at 200.

[35] Neuman, "Anomalous Zones," 1227–28, 1231–33.

political, and legal developments had been marked by smooth evolution without much friction and discontent. An entrenched distrust of the executive added further incentive against the institutionalization of emergency powers. When combined with the common law's distaste for elaborate legislation it comes as little surprise that the common law's main emergency powers mechanism – martial law – was not codified.[36] While martial law had been unused in Britain since 1800, the practice of exercising martial law powers to ensure law and order was a familiar part of the British colonial experience.[37] The two legal regimes were applied contemporaneously by the British government. However, once emergency powers had been used routinely and "normally" in one part of the British empire, the distinction between center and periphery could not contain such use. Within days of the outbreak of World War I a sharp break from the centuries-old tradition of martial law took place. Lulled by extended periods of relative security and peace the British were rudely awakened to an entirely different reality. This led them to move from one extreme – the absence of any statutory structure dealing with emergency powers – to the other extreme of promulgating draconian legislative measures allowing broad discretion and almost unlimited powers to the government. This transformation was accomplished by the passage into law on August 8, 1914 of the Defence of the Realm Act (DORA). DORA was a general statutory scheme of wartime government.[38] It institutionalized emergency powers in Britain. In fact, it was

[36] Oren Gross, " 'Control Systems' and the Migration of Anomalies" in Sujit Choudhry (ed.), *The Migration of Constitutional Ideas* (Cambridge, UK: Cambridge University Press, forthcoming).

[37] Bradley and Ewing, *Constitutional and Administrative Law*, p. 608; Charles Townshend, "Martial Law: Legal and Administrative Problems of Civil Emergency in Britain and the Empire, 1800–1940" (1982) 25 *History Journal* 167; Denys C. Holland, "Emergency Legislation in the Commonwealth" (1960) *Current Legal Problems* 148; A.W. Brian Simpson, "Round Up the Usual Suspects: The Legacy of British Colonialism and the European Convention on Human Rights" (1996) 41 *Loyola Law Review* 629; D.T. Konig, " 'Dale's Laws' and the Non-Common Law Origins of Criminal Justice in Virginia" (1982) 26 *American Journal of Legal History* 354 at 363; A.W. Brian Simpson, "The Devlin Commission (1959): Colonialism, Emergencies, and the Rule of Law" (2002) 22 *Oxford Journal of Legal Studies* 17; Nasser Hussain, *The Jurisprudence of Emergency: Colonialism and the Rule of Law* (Ann Arbor, MI: University of Michigan Press, 2003); Bernard Semmel, *Jamaican Blood and the Victorian Conscience: The Governor Eyre Controversy* (Boston: Houghton Mifflin, 1962); Geoffrey Dutton, *Edward John Eyre: The Hero as Murderer* (New York: Penguin, 1977); Phillips v. Eyre [1870] 6 Q.B. 1.

[38] A.W. Brian Simpson, *In the Highest Degree Odious: Detention without Trial in Wartime Britain* (New York: Clarendon Press, 1992), p. 5; 4 and 5 Geo. V, c. 29 (Aug. 8, 1914). Rossiter, *Constitutional Dictatorship*, pp. 153–70; Cornelius P. Cotter, "Constitutional Democracy and Emergency: Emergency Powers Legislation in Great Britain since 1914" (PhD Dissertation, Harvard University, 1953).

nothing short of "a form of statutory martial law."[39] Preparing for the war, the British army demanded explicit statutory powers rather than contenting itself with the amorphous, uncodified, concept of martial law. If the army were to take extreme measures to save the nation, it wanted to be certain that its officers would not have to face the uncertain legal consequences of their actions and depend on a postwar legislative act of indemnity.

DORA may well have been a new feature of English law, but it was based on a well-established precedent. The source for imitation and adoption was the sweeping legislative scheme of governmental powers then existing in Ireland.[40] Emergency measures applied by the British army overseas found their way into the English legal system. As we discuss further below, once such measures appeared on the English statute books they were there to stay.

The curtailment of the right to silence in the United Kingdom

On August 25, 1988, in response to escalating terrorist attacks – including the August 20 bombing in County Tyrone of a military bus that left eight British soldiers dead and twenty-eight injured[41] – the British government decided to adopt a series of security measures. The package included a measure to limit the right to silence of suspects and defendants – a well-established right – both with respect to their interrogation by the police and with respect to their silence in court during trial.[42] The government's argument for the proposed measure was that the wide and systematic lack of cooperation with the police by those

---

[39] Charles Townshend, *Political Violence in Ireland: Government and Resistance since 1848* (Oxford: Clarendon Press, 1983), p. 183 (quoting a memorandum of July 19, 1920, CAB 21/109).

[40] Simpson, *Odious*, p. 6.

[41] Steve Lohr, "IRA Claims Killing of 8 Soldiers as it Steps up Attacks on British," *NY Times*, August 21, 1988, p. A1.

[42] Charles Hodgson and Raymond Hughes, "King Curbs Right to Remain Silent," *Financial Times* (London), October 21, 1988, p. 28. See generally Fiona McElree and Keir Starmer, "The Right to Silence" in Clive Walker and Keir Starmer (eds.), *Justice in Error* (London: Blackstone Press, 1993), p. 58 at 60; Leonard W. Levy, *Origins of the Fifth Amendment: The Right against Self-Incrimination* (2nd edn, New York: Macmillan, 1986), pp. 13–24; James Wood and Adam Crawford, *Right of Silence: The Case for Retention* (London: Civil Liberties Trust, 1989); Susan M. Easton, *The Case for the Right to Silence* (2nd edn, Aldershot: Ashgate, 1998), pp. 1–3; M.R.T. Macnair, "The Early Development of the Privilege against Self-Incrimination" (1990) 10 *Oxford Journal of Legal Studies* 66: Richard Maloney, "The Criminal Evidence (NI) 1988: A Radical Departure from the Common Law Right to Silence in the UK?" (1993) 16 *Boston College International and Comparative Law Review* 425 at 427–28; Glanville Williams, *The Proof of Guilt: A Study of the English Criminal Trial* (3rd edn, London: Stevens & Sons, 1963), pp. 37–57.

suspected of involvement in terrorist activities in Northern Ireland was critically hampering interrogations.[43] The factual background against which the new limitations on the right to silence were introduced, as well as specific declarations made by senior public officials, created a clear impression that the measures were designed to bolster the state's powers needed to wage a comprehensive war on terrorism in Northern Ireland. Explaining the reasoning behind the government's decision, the Northern Ireland Secretary of State, Tom King, emphasized: "[I]t will help in convicting guilty men. I don't think it will undermine standards of justice. In Northern Ireland, *the whole system of justice is under sustained attack by terrorists* and their aim is to destroy the whole system. They intimidate and murder witnesses and judges and they train people not to answer any questions at all."[44] In the past, debates about the right to silence and its scope have focused on the claims that the right was abused by criminals – and attempts to curtail the right or limit it have failed whenever made; the shift in focus to the struggle against professional terrorists – specifically targeting the Irish Republican Army and other paramilitary groups in Northern Ireland – paved the way to such curtailment.[45] The measures were supported on the assumption that they were going to target an easily definable group and be limited in their geographic application to Northern Ireland. Claims that similar measures might eventually find their way into the criminal law and procedural rules of the rest of the United Kingdom received little attention.[46]

Despite repeated declarations and assurances to the effect that the new limitations were meant to strengthen law-enforcement authorities in their fight against terrorism, once the Criminal Evidence Order

---

[43] 140 Parl. Deb., H.C. (6th ser.) (1988) 184 (comments of Tom King, Secretary of State for Northern Ireland).

[44] Ed Maloney, "Britain Seeks to Abolish Key Civil Liberty in Ulster: London's Move Aimed at Thwarting IRA," *Washington Post*, October 21, 1988, p. Al (emphasis added). See also Charles Hodgson, "Plan to Curb Right to Silence Approved," *Financial Times* (London), November 9, 1988, p. 15; Francis Cornish, "Keeping Terrorism's Advocates off British Air," *NY Times*, November 13, 1988 (Letters to the editor); Viscount Colville of Culross, *Review of the Operation of the Prevention of Terrorism (Temporary Provisions) Act 1984* (London: HMSO, 1987), Cmnd. 264, p. 51.

[45] Oren Gross, "On Terrorists and Other Criminals: States of Emergency and the Criminal Legal System" in Eli Lederman (ed.), *Directions in Criminal Law: Inquiries in the Theory of Criminal Law* (Tel Aviv: Tel Aviv University, 2001), p. 409.

[46] Steven Greer, "The Right to Silence: A Review of the Current Debate" (1990) 53 *Modern Law Review* 709 at 716–17; Edward Rees, "Guilty by Inference," *Guardian*, April 11, 1995, p. 11.

(Northern Ireland) of 1988 was approved – it was approved as an Order in Council, forsaking traditional legislative procedures – its language was not confined to acts of terrorism. As Susan Easton notes, the use of the Order in Council procedure "could not be justified on emergency grounds and its use would seem to rest on either the low significance attached to the change or the desire to circumvent public debate. The right to silence, which symbolised the assertion of the common law and Parliamentary sovereignty against the use of prerogative power...was effectively extinguished by this procedure."[47] Moreover, the Order was enacted not within the framework of emergency legislation that already existed in Northern Ireland, but rather as ordinary criminal legislation.[48] Any mention or indication of the Order's relation to terrorist acts disappeared. The Order's jurisdiction and the restrictions it set on the right to silence were not limited to those suspected of serious crimes related to terrorism, but were expanded and interpreted as relating to every criminal suspect or defendant in Northern Ireland.[49] The Order was "a clear extension of the emergency regime into the ordinary criminal law.[50]

Denouncing the Thatcher government's decision to ban radio and television broadcasting of interviews with persons connected to certain organizations[51] the Labour Party's spokesman on Northern Ireland, Kevin McNamara, blamed the government for using Northern Ireland as "an experimental laboratory for draconian measures."[52] Six years after

---

[47] Easton, *Right to Silence*, pp. 68–69; John D. Jackson, "Recent Developments in Criminal Evidence" (1989) 40 *Northern Ireland Legal Quarterly* 105; Michael Mansfield, "Reform that Pays Lip Service to Justice," *Guardian*, October 6, 1993, p. 22; Andrew Ashworth and Peter Creighton, "The Right of Silence in Northern Ireland" in Jon Hayes and Paul O'Higgins (eds.), *Lessons from Northern Ireland* (Belfast: SLS, 1990), p. 117 at 122–25; Gross, "Terrorists and Other Criminals," 434.

[48] Easton, *Right to Silence*, p. 69.

[49] Antonio Vercher, *Terrorism in Europe: An International Comparative Legal Analysis* (Oxford: Clarendon Press, 1992), pp. 121–25; Gregory W. O'Reilly, "England Limits the Right to Silence and Moves towards an Inquisitorial System of Justice" (1994) 85 *Journal of Criminal Law and Criminology* 402 at 425.

[50] Fionnuala Ní Aoláin, "The Fortification of an Emergency Regime" (1996) 59 *Albany Law Review* 1353 at 1384.

[51] These measures were introduced as part of the anti-terrorism package in 1988. Graham Zellick, "Spies, Subversives, Terrorists and the British Government: Free Speech and Other Casualties" (1990) 31 *William and Mary Law Review* 773 at 775–82; Craig R. Whitney, "Civil Liberties in Britain: Are They under Siege?" *NY Times*, November 1, 1988, p. A18.

[52] Andrew Phillips, "Gagging the IRA: Thatcher Imposes a Controversial Crackdown," *Maclean's*, October 31, 1988, p. 34.

beginning its "experiment" regarding the right to silence in Northern Ireland, the British government decided that the time was ripe to extend the experiment to the rest of the United Kingdom.

In November 1994, parliament passed the Criminal Justice and Public Order Act (CJPOA).[53] Articles 34 through 37 of the act reproduced, almost verbatim, the relevant provisions of the 1988 Northern Ireland Order.[54] In fact, when proposing and explaining the new act, the British Home Secretary relied specifically on the Northern Irish example. Once again, the government claimed that the new legislation was necessary because terrorists were abusing the right to silence. Thus, in a speech to the annual convention of the Conservative Party on October 6, 1993, Home Secretary Michael Howard announced: "The so-called right to silence is ruthlessly exploited by *terrorists*. What fools they must think we are. It's time to call a halt to this charade. The so-called right to silence will be abolished. The innocent have nothing to hide and that is exactly the point the prosecution will be able to make."[55] As with its Northern Ireland prototype, the CJPOA was presented as part of a more comprehensive plan against terrorism and organized crime. As with the Northern Ireland Order, these new limitations on the right to silence were incorporated into criminal legislation and were expanded to apply to every suspected offender, not just those accused of terrorist activities. Gareth Peirce explained the shift from terrorism-focused legislation to ordinary criminal law:

[B]etween this announcement to the Tory Party Conference last autumn [by Michael Howard], and the announcement of the new Criminal Justice Bill some weeks later, came Hume–Adams and revelations of government contacts with the IRA. Suddenly "terrorism" might not be in existence for very much longer. The Criminal Justice Bill ... switched its terminology to "professional criminals",

---

[53] Paul Tain, *Criminal Justice and Public Order Act 1994: A Practical Guide* (London: Longman, 1994).

[54] John D. Jackson, "Curtailing the Right of Silence: Lessons from Northern Ireland" (1991) *Criminal Law Review* 404 at 405–06; Peter Mirfield, *Silence, Confessions and Improperly Obtained Evidence* (Oxford: Clarendon Press, 1997), pp 247–70; Chris Blair, "Miranda and the Right to Silence in England" (2003) 11 *Tulsa Journal of Comparative and International Law* 1 at 12–18.

[55] Alan Travis, "Right to Silence Abolished in Crackdown on Crime," *Guardian*, October 7, 1993, p. 6 (emphasis added); see also Heather Mills, "Tougher Policies Aimed at Helping Victims of Crime," *Independent*, November 19, 1993, p. 6; Colin Brown and Patricia Wynn Davies, "Ministers Want Silent Suspects to Be Filmed," *Independent*, February 18, 1992, p. 2; Alan Travis, "Labour Attacks Justice Bill over End of Right to Silence," *Guardian*, January 12, 1994, p. 6.

invoking them instead of terrorists as the excuse, and proposed the end of the right to silence for us all.[56]

The significant change, in comparison to 1988, was the intensity of objections expressed in 1994 against the CJPOA.[57] However, the opponents of the proposed legislation found themselves fighting an uphill battle, opposing the provisions that they had not previously contested in the case of Northern Ireland.[58] Those who did not object when the 1988 Order curtailed the right to silence in one part of the United Kingdom could not oppose successfully setting the same limitations on their own rights at home. The right to silence, which in the past had been considered one of the basic tenets of the English criminal justice system, no longer enjoyed such status in 1994. The damage that this right had suffered in Northern Ireland six years earlier undermined it in other parts of the country.[59] The British public had been hearing debates on curtailment of the right to silence for over half a decade. It came to accept that this right might be limited without causing grave harm to the nation's democratic character, and it could no longer be convinced that one of the most important individual rights was at stake.

The influence of the struggle against Northern Irish terrorism on the ordinary criminal system was not confined to legislation in the context of the right to silence. A similar trend can be identified in judicial decisions.[60] Initially, judges in Northern Ireland gave narrow construction to the provisions of the Order of 1988. This was the case even in the context of defendants who were charged with criminal involvement in terrorist activity.[61] Soon enough, however, the courts adopted a more prosecution-friendly approach.[62] The shift in judicial

---

[56] Gareth Peirce, "Now for Some Civil Rights," *Guardian*, October 19, 1994, p. 22. See also Michael Howard, "Protection for the Silent Majority," *Independent*, October 19, 1994, p. 19.

[57] Easton, *Right to Silence*, p. 69.

[58] Editorial, "The Judges' Fourth Front," *Guardian*, January 20, 1994, p. 21.

[59] Peirce, "Civil Rights," 22.

[60] For analysis see Gross, "Terrorists and Other Criminals," 447–61; K.A. Cavanaugh, "Emergency Rule, Normalcy Exception: The Erosion of the Right to Silence in the United Kingdom" (2003) 35 *Cornell International Law Journal* 491 at 500–05.

[61] Easton, *Right to Silence*, p. 86; Jackson, "Curtailing the Right to Silence," 410–11; Justice, *Right of Silence Debate: The Northern Ireland Experience* (London: Justice, 1994), pp. 23–25.

[62] See, e.g., R. v. McLernon (1990) 10 NIJB 91; R. v. Kane, Timmons & Kelly (Cr. Ct., N. Ir., Mar. 30, 1990); R. v. Murray (Cr. Ct., N. Ir., Jan. 18, 1991); R. v. Martin & Others (Cr. Ct., N. Ir., May. 8, 1991); Murray v. DPP (1994) 1 WLR 1 (H.L.); Justice, *Right of Silence Debate*, pp. 25–35; John D. Jackson, "Inferences from Silence: From Common Law to Common Sense" (1993) 44 *Northern Ireland Legal Quarterly* 103 at 105–12.

attitude can be traced to cases dealing with individuals who were charged with attacks on police officers or military personnel in Northern Ireland. Such defendants were brought before what are known as the Diplock courts – special jury-less courts that were established in 1973 to deal exclusively with grave offenses of a terrorist nature ("scheduled offences").[63] When English courts, dealing with "ordinary decent criminals," came to interpret and apply the CJPOA they already found an existing case law that had developed with respect to practically identical provisions in Northern Ireland. The fact that such case law developed against a special security context was mostly left unmentioned.[64]

Interrogation in depth in Finchley?

The early 1970s saw the emergence of persistent allegations of torture and inhuman and degrading conduct against persons undergoing interrogation by the Royal Ulster Constabulary (RUC) and army interrogators in Northern Ireland. Such allegations came on the heels of the government's launching of a massive internment campaign designed to curtail recent waves of violence. Soon after the internment campaign had been initiated, allegations began surfacing that the internees were being systematically tortured. Public outrage over the allegations led the Home Secretary to appoint a committee, headed by the British Ombudsman, Sir Edmund Compton, to investigate allegations of physical brutality by the security forces in one police barracks (Holywood) against persons interned on August 9, 1971. Despite its narrow mandate and in spite of some serious procedural obstacles to its work,[65] the Compton Committee's report concluded that RUC interrogators had resorted to an "interrogation in depth" of some of the internees whose cases were reviewed. "Interrogation in depth" consisted of the combination of some or all of five techniques of disorientation and sensory deprivation. The practice of interrogation in depth was described subsequently as amounting to "physical ill treatment," "brutality," "inhuman and degrading

---

[63] John Jackson and Sean Doran, *Judge without Jury: Diplock Trials in the Adversary System* (Oxford: Clarendon Press, 1995); Dermot P.J. Walsh, *The Use and Abuse of Emergency Legislation in Northern Ireland* (London: Cobden Trust, 1983); Lord Lowry, "National Security and the Rule of Law" (1992) 26 *Israel Law Review* 117.

[64] See, e.g., R v. Cowan (1995) All E.R. 939; Roderick Munday, "Inferences from Silence and European Human Rights Law" (1996) *Criminal Law Review* 370 at 371.

[65] Ian Brownlie, "Interrogation in Depth: The Compton and Parker Reports" (1972) 35 *Modern Law Review* 501.

treatment," and even "torture" by various governmental committees, the European Court and Commission of Human Rights.[66]

What is significant for our purposes here is that interrogation in depth and the five techniques were not invented with the Northern Irish internment campaign. Their origins can be traced to the colonial days of the British empire. The five techniques used against internees in Northern Ireland – i.e., in part of the United Kingdom that is, to paraphrase the words of Margaret Thatcher, "as British as Finchley"[67] – have previously been used in British colonies and dominions such as Kenya, Cyprus, Palestine, Aden, British Cameroon, and Malaya.[68] They were incorporated into the Joint Directive on Military Interrogation in Internal Security Operations Overseas.[69] When military interrogators were faced with the need to perform interrogations in Northern Ireland they had available to them a well-defined set of instructions designed to deal with insurrections, riots, and emergencies abroad. That RUC interrogators resorted to similar techniques is also not at all surprising. The internment campaign was carried out during the period of militarization of the conflict in Northern Ireland.[70] The army rather than the police was in charge and dictated modes of operation against the terrorists. The RUC itself was no ordinary police force to start with. It has always been a semi-military police force with close links to the British army.[71] In addition, the five techniques were considered by interrogators as highly effective (compared with interrogation in which no physical force was used). It would have been surprising to find RUC members resorting to conceivably less effective interrogation techniques than their colleagues from the army when the two were engaged in similar interrogations.

[66] See, e.g., Michael O'Boyle, "Torture and Emergency Powers under the European Convention on Human Rights: Ireland v. United Kingdom" (1977) 71 *American Journal of International Law* 674; Nigel S. Rodley, *The Treatment of Prisoners under International Law* (2nd edn, Oxford: Clarendon Press, 1999), pp. 90–95; Gross, "Entrenched Emergencies," 469–73; Ní Aoláin, "Emergence of Diversity," 115–17.

[67] See http://cain.ulst.ac.uk/othelem/chron/ch81.htm#Nov (quoting a speech delivered by Margaret Thatcher, the British prime minister, in the House of Commons, on November 10, 1981).

[68] Brownlie, "Interrogation in Depth"; Simpson, "Usual Suspects," 706–07.

[69] The full text of the Directive is reproduced as an appendix to the Report of the Committee of Privy Counselors Appointed to Consider Authorized Procedures for the Interrogation of Persons Suspected of Terrorism (the Parker Report) (London: HMSO, Cmnd. 4901).

[70] Ní Aoláin, *The Politics of Force*, pp. 29–44.

[71] Chris Ryder, *The RUC: A Force under Fire* (rev. edn, London: Mandarin, 1997); Michael Farrell, *Arming the Protestants: The Formation of the Ulster Special Constabulary and the Royal Ulster Constabulary* (London: Pluto Press, 1983).

The collaboration of the two organizations and, at the same time, the professional competition between them practically made this outcome inevitable. Thus it came to be that interrogation methods that were originally employed abroad came to be used in the United Kingdom. As Lord Gardiner forcefully put it,

The blame for this sorry story, if blame there be, must lie with those who, many years ago, decided that in emergency conditions in Colonial-type situations we should abandon our legal, well-tried and highly successful wartime interrogation methods and replace them by procedures which were secret, illegal, not morally justifiable and alien to the traditions of what I believe still to be the greatest democracy in the world.[72]

From l'Algérie française to la France algérienne

The phenomenon of torture that has originally been used in the controlled territory coming to be applied in the controlling territory can also be demonstrated in the context of the Algerian War of 1954–62. However, the French continued attempt to maintain dual regimes – normalcy in France and emergency in Algeria during the relevant period – had an even more important effect on the French regime. The French entanglement in the protracted war in Algeria was the main reason not merely for changes in the composition of the French government, but also for a seismic shift in the French constitutional regime, with the demise of the Fourth Republic and the creation of the Fifth Republic and its new constitution, both shaped in the image of General de Gaulle. While it cannot be doubted that the Fourth Republic had its share of internal problems and difficulties, none was as destructive as the Algerian War.[73]

By the end of the 1950s, France had lost most of its assets abroad, being forced to relinquish Vietnam (in 1954), Tunisia and Morocco (in 1955), and its (at least self-perceived) status as a leading global power. The war in Algeria – an area that was considered by most Frenchpeople to be as French as France itself – put much more at stake than actual physical

---

[72] Quoted in Vercher, *Terrorism in Europe*, p. 71.

[73] John Bell, *French Constitutional Law* (New York: Oxford University Press, 1992), pp. 10–12; Walter Laqueur, *Europe in our Time: A History, 1945–1992* (New York: Viking, 1992), p. 370; Alistair Horne, *A Savage War of Peace: Algeria, 1954–1962* (New York: Viking, 1977); Edgar O'Ballance, *The Algerian Insurrection, 1954–62* (London: Faber, 1967); John Talbott, *The War without a Name: France in Algeria, 1954–1962* (New York: Knopf, 1980); Ian S. Lustick, *Unsettled States, Disputed Lands: Britain and Ireland, France and Algeria, Israel and the West Bank-Gaza* (Ithaca, NY: Cornell University Press, 1993).

territory.[74] From a military perspective, Algeria was regarded as protecting the southern flank of France against Islamist threats extending from the Middle East. Losing Algeria was also seen as the last nail driven into the coffin of French grandeur. The existence of one million Frenchpeople in Algeria (the *pieds noirs*) seemed to make a separation all the more improbable. Furthermore, many on the left wing of the political spectrum feared that the loss of Algeria would break the Fourth Republic itself. As Pierre Mendès-France observed in 1957: "[T]he Algerian drama and the crisis of the republican regime are one and the same problem."[75] To keep Algeria French was therefore necessary in order to preserve the regime.[76]

A significant portion of the French population considered Algeria to be an inseparable part of the republic. These sentiments were widely shared and were not merely the domain of right-wing groups such as the Poujadists and the Indépendants or the *pieds noirs* and military personnel stationed in Algeria. Under French law Algeria was an integral part of metropolitan France. It was claimed that "the Mediterranean runs through France like the Seine through Paris."[77] Fighting the war in Algeria, France found itself in a state of acute schizophrenia. On the one hand, it regarded Algeria as French territory, an integral and inseparable part of France. On the other hand, the territory in question was clearly separated from the territory of metropolitan France. The majority of the population involved, more than eight million Muslims, was fundamentally different in its ethnicity, culture, tradition, and religion. The perceived necessities of the conflict, augmented by feelings of superiority over the "enemy," often led the authorities to treat Algerians in a manner starkly at odds with entrenched French values.[78] Actions and activities that would not have been thinkable in France proper were implemented routinely in Algeria. Algeria may have been considered French; the Algerians were not. This distinction between territory and its residents made it possible to justify the panoply of harsh measures taken by the French army as designed to ensure that Algeria remained a part of France.

[74] Tony Smith, *The French Stake in Algeria, 1945–1962* (Ithaca, NY: Cornell University Press, 1978); Raymond Aron, *France, the New Republic* (New York: Oceana Publications, 1960), p. 44.
[75] Lustick, *Unsettled States*, p. 253.   [76] Ibid., pp. 252–58.
[77] Hugh Roberts, *Northern Ireland and the Algerian Analogy* (London: Athol Books, 1986), p. 49.
[78] Rita Maran, *Torture: The Role of Ideology in the French Algerian War* (New York: Praeger, 1989), p. 76.

In the first years of the conflict the French official position that Al-geria was an integral part of the republic and would never be given up remained unchanged regardless of the political and ideological composition of the government of the day.[79] The prophecy made by Marshal Bugeaud – the French commander whose forces captured Algeria in 1830 – that although France ought to leave Algeria, no French government would be "strong enough" to make such a move, leaving it with only one option, i.e., subjugating and completely dominating that territory, described perfectly the situation more than a century later.[80]

On April 3, 1955, responding to internal political considerations as much as to the situation in Algeria itself, the government of Edgar Faure applied an emergency regime to Algeria.[81] A policy of repression ensued and was maintained by the Socialist government of Guy Mollet which adopted such policies as "pacification" and "intégration" (of Algeria into metropolitan France). The three governments that followed until the turn from the Fourth Republic to the Fifth Republic did not change that policy.

As repression and pacification continued, the French schizophrenia concerning Algeria intensified. While the French government sought to keep Algeria French, its agents – the armed forces – used methods and actions, most notoriously torture and extra-judicial killings of prisoners, in complete contradiction of French values and established practices.[82]

As allegations of systematic use of torture and ill-treatment by the French forces in Algeria intensified, so too did criticisms against such practices. Much of the criticism concentrated on the fear that the meth-ods used in Algeria would come to be applied in France against politi-cal adversaries.[83] Reflective of this sentiment is the following warning, sounded in December 1957 by Robert Delavignette, a former member of the Committee for the Safeguard of Rights and Freedoms that the French government had established to ensure the legality of military operations in Algeria:

That which is true for Algeria may very soon be true for France... The most serious problem is not the atrocities themselves, but that as a result of them the state is engaged in a process of self-destruction. What we are witnessing in

---

[79] Lustick, *Unsettled States*, pp. 242–52.   [80] Ibid., p. 239.   [81] Ibid., p. 243.

[82] See, e.g., Paul Aussaresses, *The Battle of the Casbah: Terrorism and Counter-terrorism in Algeria, 1955–1957* (New York: Enigma, 2005).

[83] Lustick, *Unsettled States*, p. 253.

Algeria is nothing short of the disintegration of the state; it is a gangrene which threatens France herself...[84]

The use of torture by the French army especially during the Battle of Algiers was openly admitted by General Jacques Massu – the military commander who conducted the French military operations – after the war.[85] Despite orders issued from Paris condemning excesses against human dignity, and although Massu himself argued that torture had never been institutionalized in Algeria, persistent reports and personal accounts depicted a different picture. One indication of the actual state of affairs was given in a report prepared in March 1955 by Roger Wuillaume, Inspector General in Algiers, where it was suggested that some forms of violence that had been employed by the security forces in Algeria ought to be institutionalized to reflect a reality where their employment during interrogation had become prevalent.[86] While this suggestion had not been adopted by the authorities, it was quite apparent that torture continued to be widely exercised in Algeria. Accounts of gruesome methods of interrogation used by French forces as well as reports concerning the "disappearance" of large numbers (according to some accounts several thousands) of detainees who died under interrogation or who refused to talk[87] were added to several individual cases that came to be known to the public – most notably the "suicides" of Ben M'hidi and Ali Boumendjel, the interrogation under torture of Henri Alleg, and the disappearance of Maurice Audin,[88] the last two being particularly disturbing to the French public as the victims were Europeans rather than Algerian Muslims. Torture practices that had been used against Algerian Muslims were thus extended to Europeans in Algeria suspected of supporting the FLN.

Yet, the effect of torture did not remain geographically bound. Once the threshold of violence and dehumanization had been crossed it was extremely hard to step back. An intoxicating sense of power, coupled with a growing sense of frustration at the inability to stop the FLN in its tracks and at the lack of gratitude by the French people and their government for the work carried out by the army in Algeria, and a growing disrespect for legal niceties were the legacies of that part of

---

[84] Quoted in Horne, *A Savage War of Peace*, p. 234.
[85] Ibid., p. 196. See also Jacques Massu, *La vraie bataille d'Alger* (Paris: Plon, 1971); Maran, *Torture*, p. 98.
[86] Horne, *A Savage War of Peace*, p. 197.   [87] Ibid., pp. 198–202.
[88] Aussaresses, *Battle of the Casbah*, pp. 132–47; Horne, *A Savage War of Peace*, pp. 202–03; Henri Alleg, *The Question* (New York: Braziller, 1958).

the Algerian experience. They led eventually to the permeation of the practice of torture into France itself. The French police, locked in a fierce struggle with the Algerian community in France and L'organisation de l'armée secrete (the OAS) – a secret right-wing organization, established in January 1961 in order to resist granting independence to Algeria, which employed terrorist acts such as assassinations (including several failed attempts on the life of Charles de Gaulle) to further its cause[89] – resorted increasingly to violent methods, including torture and murder, against its "enemies" in France itself.[90]

Use of torture was not the only element of lawlessness to spill over from Algeria into France. The Algerian conflict bred an atmosphere of lawlessness in the ranks of the French army. The army was given, practically, a free hand to implement its policies. Every aspect of daily life in Algeria was deemed to affect French national security, and a legitimate subject for military control. The revolutionary struggle in Algeria was to be subdued by means of total war and total strategy. French career officers serving in Algeria believed that theirs was a mission to save not only Algeria, but France itself from the suicidal policies made by cowardly politicians who cared more about world opinion than about the security and the needs of the republic. For many military officers the government in Paris was not only remote but also out of touch with reality. For them, Algeria, not France, was reality and their term of reference. Parliamentary debates and political quibbles were unreal and unnecessary. Force, decisiveness, power, and ruthlessness were the solution to France's malaise.[91]

In early 1958 it seemed that a coup to overthrow the government and do away with the invertebrate Fourth Republic was imminent. Reflective of the spirit of the times was an article written in December 1957 by Michel Debré – who later became prime minister under de Gaulle and the primary drafter of the constitution of the Fifth Republic – in which he stated that. "To abandon French sovereignty is to commit an illegal action, in other words such an action places all those who take a part in it in the category of outlaws, and all those who oppose those outlaws by whatever means are acting out of legitimate defence."[92] When the government of Pierre Pflimlin was invested on May 13, 1958, a violent riot broke out in Algiers, staged by French *pieds noirs* assisted by military

---

[89] Alexander Harrison, *Challenging de Gaulle: The OAS and the Counterrevolution in Algeria, 1954–1962* (New York: Praeger, 1989).

[90] Horne, *A Savage War of Peace*, p. 500.   [91] Lustick, *Unsettled States*, pp. 259–60.

[92] Quoted in ibid., p. 263.

commanders. The riot resulted in the forming of a Committee of Public Safety headed by the top commanders of the French forces in Algeria, Generals Massu and Salan. This unchallenged revolt was soon followed by the establishment of similar local committees throughout mainland France. On May 24–25, the Algerian rebellion spread to Corsica, as Committees of Public Safety replaced the ordinary civilian authorities on the island. Invasion of the mainland by paratroopers seemed to be a matter of days away. This threat of imminent invasion and the realization that the army would not defend Paris led to the submission to the rebels' demands. On June 1, 1958, de Gaulle was invested as prime minister and was given emergency powers (including the power to prepare the new constitution for the Fifth Republic) for a period of six months during which the National Assembly was dissolved.[93] Crisis did not lead to the assumption of emergency measures in order to protect the existing regime, but rather contributed to the replacement of that regime in a process that reflected a spirit of unconstitutionality. The army, used to getting its way in Algeria, attempted to import its policies of coercion to the mainland. More importantly, the Algerian exigency left its fingerprints on the new constitutional and political arrangement carved out for France.

The apparent difficulties inherent in the party politics of the Fourth Republic, the perceived necessities of the Algerian struggle, and the unique personality of General de Gaulle combined together to shift the constitutional focus under the new constitution of 1958 to the president of the republic. The war in Algeria returned de Gaulle to the political forefront and paved the way to vesting the executive with substantially more powers than before. "[T]he main innovation constituted by 'the wholly unprecedented regime' of the Fifth Republic [was] the re-establishment of state prerogative power, embodied in the President of the Republic."[94] The overall effect of the constitutional change was

---

[93] Ibid., p. 271.

[94] Jack Hayward, "The President and the Constitution: Its Spirit, Articles and Practice" in Jack Hayward (ed.), *De Gaulle to Mitterrand: Presidential Power in France* (New York: New York University Press, 1993), pp. 36, 38, 73. See also John A. Rohr, *Founding Republics in France and America: A Study in Constitutional Governance* (Lawrence, KS: University Press of Kansas, 1995), p. 46; Dorothy Pickles, *The Fifth French Republic: Institutions and Politics* (3rd edn, London: Methuen, 1965); Ben Clift, "Dyarchic Presidentialization in a Presidentialized Polity: The French Fifth Republic" in Thomas Poguntke and Paul Webb (eds.), *The Presidentialization of Politics: A Comparative Study of Modern Democracies* (Oxford: Oxford University Press, 2005), p. 219; Nicholas Atkin, *The Fifth French Republic* (New York: Palgrave Macmillan, 2005).

the strengthening of the president at the expense of the National Assembly, giving the former additional powers and facilitating executive initiative in policy-making and shaping the direction of the republic in internal as well as external affairs. The presidency of de Gaulle, in whose image the constitution was drafted, crystallized these abstract constitutional concepts into concrete practical examples. The Algerian War did not create the apparent weakness of the French executive under the Fourth Republic, nor was it the first demonstration of the instability of the French government. After all, in the twelve years of the Fourth Republic no fewer than twenty-three governments served in France, with the longest term in office of any of them being just short of seventeen months.[95] Yet, the war emphasized these institutional and structural inadequacies. In that sense it served as a catalyst for change.[96] The problem of Algeria, seen against the background of a prolonged inability to take decisive actions because of sharp political schisms, led to the sense that, "in order to solve the Algerian mess, a sort of dictatorship [was] necessary."[97] When the constitution of the Fifth Republic was drafted, the place of the president in the political life of France was still indeterminate. Whether France would be ruled by a sort of modern constitutional monarch or whether the president would become merely "a sort of supreme adviser and supreme arbiter" was unclear.[98] The personality and prestige of Charles de Gaulle and the circumstances of the war in Algeria led the republic toward the former. As Raymond Aron put it, "As long as de Gaulle is there, the time is not normal...When a man has full power, when he is accepted by everybody, when he is recognized by everybody as being a man of wisdom and virtue and greatness and all the rest, he can do anything, even draft the Constitution of the Fifth Republic."[99] The constitution of the Fifth Republic introduced into France a "Roman dictatorship with full freedom [for the citizens]."[100] Yet, this dictatorship was understood to be a temporary, exceptional arrangement "because it require[d] a dictator and an abnormal situation, that is, a situation in which the crises [were] so acute that the deputies [were] pleased to leave the responsibility to someone else. Acute crisis, however, is not a permanent feature of French political life..."[101] However, the strong magistracy, reintroduced in France as a direct result of the

---

[95] Bell, *French Constitutional Law*, pp. 10–12.
[96] Aron, *France*, pp. 19–20.   [97] Ibid., p. 38.
[98] Ibid., pp. 24–25; Bell, *French Constitutional Law*, pp. 14–15; Hayward, "The President and the Constitution," 42–50.
[99] Aron, *France*, p. 25.   [100] Ibid., p. 30.   [101] Ibid., pp. 30–31.

Fourth Republic's difficulties in dealing with an external crisis, became a permanent feature of the French political and constitutional systems. This crisis element of government became an enduring invariable even when "normalcy" was restored to France.

Nowhere is this clearer than in the context of article 16 of the constitution of the Fifth Republic. Article 16 invests sweeping emergency powers in the president of the republic.[102] The president is empowered to take "any measures required" in the event that the "institutions of the Republic, the independence of the nation, the integrity of its territory or the fulfillment of its international commitments are gravely and immediately threatened and the regular functioning of the constitutional public authorities is interrupted."

In an attempt to mitigate the extreme nature of article 16, several conditions for its exercise were introduced. First, resort to the expansive presidential powers under article 16 was to be made only in abnormal situations. In its original draft, article 16 (then 14) could only be invoked in the context of external threats to the nation. However, as it now stands article 16 applies to all threats, whether international or domestic.[103] Second, to invoke his powers under article 16 the president must identify serious and immediate threats to the nation and act to overcome those threats. However, the decision on what constitutes such a threat is left to the sole discretion of the president. The exercise of these extremely broad presidential powers is not dependent upon a prior declaration of a state of siege and makes such a declaration legally unnecessary. The president alone is the judge of the circumstances under which article 16 powers may be invoked and put to use.[104] Nor does article 16 incorporate any interdiction against using the powers granted under it in order to suspend or even change the constitution. Again, what measure ought to be taken in any given case is a matter left to the president. Such actions, it would seem, are not reviewable by any of the judicial authorities.[105] Third, the functioning of the constitutional

---

[102] Francis Hamon, *L'article 16 de la constitution de 1958: documents réunis et commentés* (Paris: La Documentation Française, 1994); Michèle Voisset, *L'article 16 de la constitution du 4 Octobre 1958* (Paris: Librairie Générale de Droit et de Jurisprudence, 1969); Paul Leroy, *L'organisation constitutionnelle et les crises* (Paris: Librairie Générale de Droit et de Jurisprudence, 1966).

[103] Voisset, *L'article 16*, p. 22.

[104] Rohr, *Founding Republics*, p. 49; François Saint-Bonnet, *L'état d'exception* (Paris: Presses Universitaires de France, 2001), p. 15; Joseph B. Kelly and George A. Pelletier, Jr., "Theories of Emergency Government" (1966) 11 *South Dakota Law Review* 42 at 48.

[105] See, e.g., decision by the Conseil d'État in Arrêt Brocas, October 19, 1962.

organs is interrupted. However, interruption may mean no more than partial interruption, and perhaps even less than that as the only use to date of article 16 demonstrates.[106] Fourth, article 16 provides that measures used under it "must stem from the desire to provide the constitutional public authorities, *in the shortest possible time*, with the means to carry out their duties." Yet, on the only occasion in which article 16 was invoked (see below) it remained active for more than five months despite the fact that the threat that gave reason for its initial invocation was over within a matter of a few days. Indeed, the decision of when to terminate the resort to article 16 is left to the sole discretion of the president.[107] Fifth, article 16 imposes on the president a duty of consultation with the prime minister, the presidents of the assemblies and the Constitutional Council. Yet again, this duty is merely to consult, not to accept the opinions of those consulted with.[108] Thus, article 16 allows the president to attain broad powers similar to those that he would have under a regime of a state of siege, while bypassing the procedural and substantive requirements of that regime. Finally, article 68 of the constitution makes it possible to impeach the president for high treason. This, however, is a highly unlikely option.

Article 16 was invoked only once, on April 23, 1961, as a means to contain a military coup in Algeria – organized after a referendum on independence for Algeria received overwhelming support by the French public – and prevent it spreading into the mainland. President de Gaulle invoked his constitutional emergency powers for an unspecified period of time.[109] He eventually relinquished those powers on September 29, 1961. Even assuming that there had been an objective justification for invoking the provisions of article 16 in the circumstances then prevailing, the necessity to retain such emergency powers until September was heavily criticized, especially in light of the fact that the military coup was over within a few days.[110] Exercising the special emergency powers, the president established special military tribunals, instituted censorship, granted expanded powers of search, seizure, and arrest to the French police, modified parts of the criminal procedure, suspended the

---

[106] Rohr, *Founding Republics*, p. 49.   [107] Voisset, *L'article 16*, p. 26.

[108] Friedrich, *Constitutional Government and Democracy*, p. 566; Bell, *French Constitutional Law*, p. 31.

[109] Address by President Charles de Gaulle after the military insurrection in Algeria, April 23, 1961, available at http://www.charles-de-gaulle.org/article.php3?id_article=526 (last visited on August 8, 2005).

[110] See, e.g., Geneviève Camus, *L'état de nécessité en démocratie* (Paris: Librairie Générale de Droit et de Jurisprudence, 1965), pp. 77–78.

life-tenure appointment of judges, and dismissed thousands of military and police officers and personnel. Significantly, President de Gaulle prohibited the parliament from voting a motion of censure or legislating altogether. In line with their general attitude of deference to the political branches on such matters, both the Conseil d'État and the Constitutional Council refused to review the powers employed by the president on their merits, proclaiming those questions to be outside their scope of jurisdiction.[111]

The conceptual significance of article 16 runs much deeper than the single occasion of its implementation. Article 16 represents a sharp break with the French tradition of the state of siege. Its sweeping language and the loose and open-ended guidelines that it sets for the exercise of emergency powers by the president, together with the concomitant impracticality of effective constitutional checks on presidential exercise of such immense powers, stand in clear contrast to the detailed arrangements incorporated in such pieces of legislation as the laws of 1849 and 1878. Article 16 does not establish any more normative guidelines for governmental conduct in the face of future emergencies than martial law does in the English system. Article 16 represents de Gaulle's "grandiose conception" of the presidency according to which the president's judgment as to what the nation needs in any given situation, including a state of emergency, ought always to take precedence and not be limited by purely legalistic constraints and considerations.[112] And while it may be based on an "existential rationale," allowing the president to take extraordinary measures when the republic faces a "life-and-death struggle for survival,"[113] article 16 is in no way limited to such extreme occasions. Large segments of the French population on all sides of the political spectrum, at the first stages of the Algerian conflict, and parts of the right wing all the way to the very end of the conflict and beyond, believed that control over Algeria was compatible with maintenance of normalcy in France itself. France could keep Algeria French and at the same time maintain the French soul of fundamental values of democracy, liberty, freedom, and individual dignity, intact. They were wrong. Norms of conduct and values prevailing among the French forces and settlers in Algeria could not be stopped from flowing back into metropolitan France. If France was normalcy, and Algeria the exception of crisis,

---

[111] Ibid.
[112] Hayward, "The President and the Constitution," 46.
[113] Ackerman, "The Emergency Constitution," 1037–38.

attempts to distinguish between the two domains, applying norms of normality in one while adhering to concepts of emergency in the other, failed. Moreover, in so far as the two spheres grew closer together, it was the sphere of exigency that set the tone and prevailed over notions of normality. Events in Algeria set the national mood in France and were prominent on the political agenda of that country. In order to gain the upper hand in the "savage war of peace" in which the country found itself embroiled, France cast off some of its constitutional, political, and legal traditions, replacing them with others that were derived from the realities of the struggle. France became as much a part of "Algeria" as Algeria was a part of France.

The extent to which Algeria has become part of France has been demonstrated again as this book went to print. On October 27, 2005 the city of Paris witnessed the eruption of ethnic riots following the accidental death of two teenagers in an electrical sub-station in a Paris suburb. The riots soon spread to 300 cities and towns across France – the worst domestic disturbances in that country since the student riots of 1968. By November 14, more than 8,000 vehicles had been burnt by the rioters and more than 2,760 individuals arrested.[114] The riots have clearly manifested the failure of France to integrate second- and third-generation African and Arab immigrants, many of whose families came over to France from Algeria and other parts of North Africa. For a country that had previously refused to accept cultural, racial, and ethnic differences among its citizens, the recent crisis became, fundamentally, a crisis of identity.[115]

On November 8, two days after the worst night of rioting, which left more than 1,400 burnt cars across France, the French cabinet declared a state of emergency, empowering departmental prefects to impose curfews, allow the police to set up roadblocks, conduct house searches, prohibit public assembly, and put people under house arrest. Curfew breakers would be liable to up to two months' imprisonment.[116] The legal basis for the new decree was the April 3, 1955 law that had been introduced in the context of the Algerian war.[117] That law has been

---

[114] Philippe Naughton, "France Extends Emergency Powers to Contain Riots," *Times Online*, November 14, 2005.

[115] Adam Sage and Charles Bremner, "France Tries to Restore its Image after Ethnic Revolt," *Times Online*, November 15, 2005.

[116] Simon Freeman and Charles Bremner, "France Declares State of Emergency," *Times Online*, November 8, 2005.

[117] See supra note 81 and the accompanying text.

rarely used and then mostly outside France proper, as in 1984 when it was employed to counter violence in New Caledonia. The 1955 law was invoked in France itself only once, in 1961, and then too in the context of the Algerian war and the Generals' rebellion. Yet, fifty years after its enactment, the *Loi instituant un état d'urgence* was used to introduce an emergency regime in large parts of France itself, including the capital. Denouncing the new measures, an editorial in *Le Monde* suggested: "Exhuming a 1955 law sends to the youth of the suburbs a message of astonishing brutality: that after 50 years France intends to treat them exactly as it did their grandparents."[118]

Under article 2 of the law of 1955, a declared state of emergency can be in effect for an initial period of up to twelve days. That period can be further extended only by law. Thus, on November 14, less than one week after the introduction of the state of emergency, the French cabinet decided to seek legislative approval for the extension of the emergency police powers for an additional period of three months.[119] Both the National Assembly (on November 15) and the Senate (two days later) swiftly passed the necessary legislation.[120] According to the French government's spokesman, President Chirac had told the cabinet that the emergency powers were "strictly temporary and will only be applied where they are strictly necessary."[121] These powers were, however, necessary in order to "accelerate the return to calm."[122] In fact, both claims are questionable. First, as suggested above, experience has demonstrated that temporary emergency measures have the proclivity of becoming permanent and normalized. Second, the claim that the emergency measures (and their extension) were necessary runs contrary to statements made as early as November 8 (before the new emergency decree went into effect) by the Chief of the National Police, Michel Gaudin, announcing that "the intensity of this violence is on the way down,"[123] and to clear evidence that showed a marked fall-off in the level of violence. Indeed, despite the fact that some thirty municipalities were

---

[118] Quoted in Graeme Smith, "France's Moment of Truth," *Globe and Mail*, November 9, 2005, p. A1.

[119] Agence France Presse Wire, "French Emergency Powers must be Extended by New Law," November 14, 2005.

[120] Craig S. Smith, "World Briefing: Europe: France: Parliament Extends State of Emergency," *NY Times*, November 17, 2005, p. A12.

[121] Naughton, "France Extends Emergency Powers."

[122] Sebastian Rotella, "France: State of Emergency Imposed to Quell Unrest," *Miami Herald*, November 9, 2005, p. A17 (quoting President Chirac).

[123] Associated Press, "French Cabinet Sets a State of Emergency," November 8, 2005.

placed under nightly curfews for unaccompanied children under 16, and two temporary banning orders for public gatherings were imposed in Paris and Lyon, most prefects had not used their new emergency powers, casting doubts about the necessity of extending those extreme measures.[124]

The war on terror: Guantanamo and beyond

Separation between normalcy and emergency along geographic lines has once again been resorted to in the wake of the terrorist attacks of September 11, 2001.

Operation Enduring Freedom resulted in several hundred individuals suspected as al Qaeda or Taliban fighters being detained by the United States at its naval base at Guantanamo Bay. The base is leased by the United States from Cuba. Some of the detainees petitioned for writs of habeas corpus. For the most part, district courts hearing the cases ruled that they lacked jurisdiction to hear such claims. The courts anchored their position in the fact that the plaintiffs were non-resident aliens and that the military base at Guantanamo Bay was outside the territorial jurisdiction of the United States. Aliens detained outside the sovereign territory of the United States could not use American courts to pursue claims brought under the constitution.[125] Such decisions were also held up on appeal.[126] Eventually, the United States Supreme Court held that aliens captured abroad and detained at Guantanamo Bay may challenge their detention under the federal habeas statute, ruling that individuals held in custody "in violation of the Constitution or the laws and treaties of the United States" may apply to the courts for a writ of habeas corpus to secure judicial review of their detention.[127] The court did not clarify, however, the nature of the relief that they may receive and what rights they may have that can be protected by such proceedings.[128] For our purposes here the significant element is the Bush administration's argument that foreign nationals held at Guantanamo, who were captured by the military outside the United States, were not entitled to the protections of the constitution as they were held by the US military outside

---

[124] Agence France Presse Wire, "French Emergency Powers."

[125] Rasul v. Bush, 215 F.Supp.2d 55 (D.D.C. 2002); Coalition of Clergy v. Bush, 189 F.Supp.2d 1036 (C.D. Cal. 2002); Hamdi v. Rumsfeld, 296 F.3d 278 (4th Cir. 2002).

[126] Al Odah v. United States, 321 F.3d 1134 (D.C. Cir. 2003).

[127] Rasul v. Bush, 542 US 466 at 473–74 (2004).

[128] Compare, for example, Khalid v. Bush, 355 F.Supp.2d 311 (D.D.C. 2005) and In Re Guantanamo Detainee Cases, 355 F.Supp.2d 443 (D.D.C. 2005).

the sovereign territory of the United States.[129] This argument, which was accepted by the lower courts, disregarded the fact that the United States exercised complete effective control over its military base at Guantanamo Bay, adopting instead the view that Guantanamo Bay was foreign territory. Thus, the anomalous nature of Guantanamo – demonstrated in the 1990s in the context of detention of Haitian and Cuban refugees[130] – has been invoked once again. The argument was that different rules applied to the territory of the United States and to Guantanamo and that no American court could review actions taken in Guantanamo, leading Lord Steyn to characterize Guantanamo as a "legal black hole."[131]

The war on terror has also sparked debate about the desirability of using torture to obtain information from suspected terrorists when such information may be critical to foiling future terrorist acts.[132] One set of particular allegations that have surfaced in this context, and which invokes, again, geography, as a means to separate normalcy from emergency and counter-terrorism, concerns the practice of rendition. Such torture-by-proxy entails contracting the torture services of other countries by sending suspected terrorists to countries where they would be subjected to torture and the information extracted as a result would then be made available to intelligence agencies of Western countries, without having those countries' agents getting their hands dirty in the process.[133] A former CIA Inspector General, Fred Hitz, was quoted to say that: "We don't do torture, and we can't countenance torture in terms

[129] See, e.g., Neil A. Lewis, "Judge Extends Legal Rights for Guantánamo Detainees," *NY Times*, February 1, 2005, p. A12.

[130] Steven Greenhouse, "As Tide of Haitian Refugees Rises, US Uses Cuban Base," *NY Times*, June 30, 1994, p. A3; John Kifner, "Flight from Cuba: The Refugees," *NY Times*, August 23, 1994, p. A17.

[131] John Steyn, "Guantanamo Bay: The Legal Black Hole" (2004) 53 *International and Comparative Law Quarterly* 1.

[132] See, e.g., Sanford Levinson (ed.), *Torture: A Collection* (New York: Oxford University Press, 2004); Alan M. Dershowitz, *Why Terrorism Works: Understanding the Threat, Responding to the Challenge* (New Haven, CT: Yale University Press, 2002), pp. 131–63; Oren Gross, "Are Torture Warrants Warranted? Pragmatic Absolutism and Official Disobedience" (2004) 88 *Minnesota Law Review* 1481; Harold H. Koh, "A World without Torture" (2005) 43 *Columbia Journal of Transnational Law* 641; Marcy Strauss, "Torture" (2004) 48 *New York Law School Law Review* 201; Louis Michael Seidman, "Torture's Truth" (2005) 72 *University of Chicago Law Review* 881; Jeremy Waldron, "Torture and Positive Law: Jurisprudence for the White House" (2005) 105 *Columbia Law Review* 1681.

[133] Duncan Campbell, "September 11: Six Months on: US Sends Suspects to Face Torture," *Guardian*, March 12, 2002, p. 4; Rajiv Chandrasekaran and Peter Finn, "US Behind Secret Transfer of Terror Suspects," *Washington Post*, March 11, 2002, p. A1; Vicki Haddock, "The Unspeakable: To Get at the Truth, is Torture or Coercion Ever Justified?" *San Francisco Chronicle*, November 18, 2001, p. D1; Walter Pincus, "Silence of

of we can't know of it. But if a country offers information gleaned from interrogations, we can use the fruits of it." A more candid statement was made by a soldier who said that: "We don't kick the shit out of them. We send them to other countries, so they can kick the shit out of them."[134]

The attempt to maintain a veneer of legitimacy while also separating the two realities – at home and abroad – in this context can also be seen in two legal opinions given on either side of the Atlantic. A memo written on March 19, 2004, by Jack Goldsmith, an assistant Attorney General and today a Harvard Law School professor, to Alberto Gonzales, then the counsel to the president and today the US Attorney-General, concluded by suggesting that article 49 of the Fourth Geneva Convention Relative to the Protection of Civilian Persons in Time of War, of August 12, 1949, did not preclude "the temporary relocation of 'protected persons' (whether illegal aliens or not) who have not been accused of an offense from occupied Iraq to another country, for a brief but not indefinite period, to facilitate interrogation."[135] Clean language that masks the illegal reality of torture by proxy. Similarly, the British Court of Appeals ruled that the Secretary of State was entitled to rely on evidence which might have been obtained through torture "by agencies of other states over which [the Secretary] had no power of direction" when deciding whether to certify a foreign national as a terrorist suspect subject to detention

4 Terror Probe Suspects Poses Dilemma for FBI," *Washington Post*, October 21, 2001, p. A6; Dana Priest and Barton Gellman, "US Decries Abuse but Defends Interrogations," *Washington Post*, December, 26, 2002, p. A1; Stephen Grey, "America's Gulag," *New Statesman*, May 17, 2004, p. 22; Douglas Jehl, "Rule Change Lets CIA Freely Send Suspects Abroad," *NY Times*, March 6, 2005, p. A1; Jane Mayer, "Outsourcing Torture: The Secret History of America's Secret 'Rendition' Program," *New Yorker*, February 14, 2005, p. 106; Philip B. Heymann, "Civil Liberties and Human Rights in the Aftermath of September 11" (2002) 25 *Harvard Journal of Law and Public Policy* 441 at 453–54; Ruth Jamieson and Kieran McEvoy, "State Crime by Proxy and Juridical Othering" (2005) 45 *British Journal of Criminology* 504 at 516–17; Association of the Bar of the City of New York and Center for Human Rights and Global Justice, New York University School of Law, *Torture by Proxy: International and Domestic Law Applicable to "Extraordinary Renditions"* (October 29, 2004), available at http://www.abcny.org/pdf/report/Torture%20by%20Proxy%20-%20Final%20(PDF).pdf (last visited on August 8, 2005). Also compare O.K. v. Bush (D.D.C., July 12, 2005), available at 2005 WL 1621343 and Al-Anazi v. Bush, 370 F.Supp.2d 188 (D.D.C. 2005) with Abdah v. Bush (D.D.C., Mar. 12, 2005), available at 2005 WL 589812.

[134] Both quoted in Priest and Gellman, "US Decries Abuse."

[135] Memorandum for Alberto Gonzales on "Permissibility of Relocating Certain 'Protected Persons' from Occupied Iraq," March 19, 2004, reproduced in Karen J. Greenberg and Joshua L. Dratel (eds.), *The Torture Papers* (Cambridge, UK: Cambridge University Press, 2005), p. 367 at 380.

under the Anti-terrorism, Crime and Security Act of 2001, provided that the minister "neither procured the torture nor connived at it.[136]

It's a bad world out there (II): domestic and foreign affairs

It is often asserted that the area of foreign affairs is "constitutionally different" in the sense that ordinary constitutional schemes are relaxed and greater deference than usual is, and some also say ought to be, accorded to the decisions and policies of the executive.[137] The realm of foreign policy is one in which democratic accountability is diminished.[138] In the United States, for example, "the President (almost) always wins in foreign affairs," among other things, because he enjoys the advantages of secrecy, dispatch, unity, and access to broad sources of information.[139] Thus, it is often claimed that the executive enjoys inherent powers to act in matters of foreign affairs that may not be available to it in the domestic context. Such positions assume that a clear separation between the "foreign" and the "domestic" is maintainable and the two spheres can be held apart. Presidential inherent powers in foreign affairs are recognized precisely because of the special nature of the subject matter and its distinctiveness. This, too, is a concept that can be traced back to the Roman republic for, as we saw in chapter 1, the Roman dictatorship, as originally conceived, was designed to enable the republic to respond effectively to external military threats. The awesome powers

---

[136] A. v. Secretary of State (2004) H.R.L.R. 38 (CA Civ. Div.); A. and others v. Secretary of State for the Home Department (No. 2) (2005) 1 W.L.R. 414 (CA Civ. Div.).

[137] See, e.g., Thomas M. Franck, *Political Questions/Judicial Answers: Does the Rule of Law Apply to Foreign Affairs?* (Princeton: Princeton University Press, 1992), p. 11; Louis Henkin, "The United States Constitution in its Third Century: Foreign Affairs" (1989) 83 *American Journal of International Law* 713 at 716; Peter J. Spiro, "Foreign Relations Federalism" (1999) 70 *University of Colorado Law Review* 1223; Joel R. Paul, "The Geopolitical Constitution: Executive Expediency and Executive Agreements" (1998) 86 *California Law Review* 671; Alan I. Bigel, *The Supreme Court on Emergency Powers, Foreign Affairs, and Protection of Civil Liberties 1935–1975* (Lanham, MD: University Press of America, 1986).

[138] Martin S. Flaherty, "The Most Dangerous Branch" (1996) 105 *Yale Law Journal* 1725 at 1821–28.

[139] Harold H. Koh, "Why the President (Almost) Always Wins in Foreign Affairs: Lessons of the Iran–Contra Affair" (1988) 97 *Yale Law Journal* 1255; Harold H. Koh, *The National Security Constitution: Sharing Power after the Iran–Contra Affair* (New Haven, CT: Yale University Press, 1990), pp. 134–49; Clinton Rossiter (ed.), *The Federalist Papers* (New York: New American Library, 1961), No. 64, pp. 392–93 (John Jay), No. 75, pp. 451–52 (Alexander Hamilton).

of the dictator were justified as necessary to meet foreign rather than domestic threats.

Trying to garner support for the proposed constitution and alleviate fears of a strong central government, James Madison suggested that, "The powers delegated by the proposed Constitution to the federal government are few and defined...[They] will be exercised principally on *external objects*, as war, peace, negotiation, and foreign commerce..."[140] A similar idea is conveyed by John Locke's separation between the "executive power" and the "federative power."[141] Although both powers are to be held by the same organ (or organs) of the community, they are distinct and separate. The executive power is the power to "see to the *Execution* of the Laws that are made, and remain in force."[142] The federative power contains "the Power of War and Peace, Leagues and Alliances, and all the Transactions, with all Persons and Communities without the Commonwealth."[143] Locke also notes that

> though this *federative* Power in the well or ill management of it be of great moment to the commonwealth, yet it is much less capable to be directed by antecedent, standing, positive Laws than the *Executive*; and so must necessarily be left to the Prudence and Wisdom of those whose hands it is in, to be managed for the public good. For the *Laws* that concern Subjects one amongst another ... may well enough *precede* them. But what is to be done in reference to *Foreigners*, depending much upon their actions, and the variation of designs and interests, must be *left* in great part to the *Prudence* of those who have this Power committed to them, to be managed by the best of their Skill for the advantage of the Commonwealth.[144]

In *United States v. Curtiss-Wright Export Corp.*, Justice Sutherland stated that the federal government enjoyed extra-constitutional inherent powers in the realm of foreign affairs. These powers are connected to conceptions of nationality and external sovereignty and are not limited to specific affirmative grants of authority found in the constitution. Moreover, within the federal government it is the president who is invested with these inherent powers.[145] The president not only enjoys express constitutional grants of power and statutory delegations of authority, but is also vested with "The very delicate, plenary and exclusive power...as

---

[140] Rossiter, *The Federalist Papers*, No. 45, p. 292 (James Madison).
[141] John Locke, *Two Treatises of Government*, ed. Mark Goldie (London: Tuttle, 1994), para. 148.
[142] Ibid., para. 144.   [143] Ibid., para. 146.   [144] Ibid., para. 147.
[145] 299 US 304 at 315–22 (1936).

the sole organ of the federal government in the field of international relations."[146]

Justice Sutherland's opinion has been the subject of much heated debate.[147] Yet, whatever the criticisms against it, the notion of inherent plenary foreign affairs powers continued to appeal to the executive and has had significant impact upon subsequent judicial decisions.[148] *Curtiss-Wright* came to stand for the proposition that, in the area of foreign affairs, the president was not only the leading branch of government but, in fact, was the *sole* branch vested with powers and authority to act. As Thomas Franck suggests: "Sutherland's words succeeded in capturing a widely shared public preference for rallying around the president in the face of foreign threats. Many Americans ... may still believe that not only politics but also the writ of the law should stop at the water's edge."[149]

Precisely because of the great influence that *Curtiss-Wright* has had in the area of foreign affairs, it is interesting to note the pains to which Justice Sutherland went in order to distinguish between issues of foreign affairs and foreign policy, and the realm of domestic affairs. He starts by noting: "It will contribute to the elucidation of the question if we first consider the differences between the powers of the federal government in respect of foreign or external affairs and those in respect of domestic or internal affairs. That there are differences between them, and that these differences are fundamental, may not be doubted."[150] He then goes on to state, more than once, that the powers of the federal government with respect to "external affairs" are wholly different than the powers it may exercise in "internal affairs." Thus, "The broad statement that the federal government can exercise no powers except those specifically enumerated in the Constitution, and such implied powers as are necessary and proper to carry into effect the enumerated powers, is categorically true only in respect of our internal affairs."[151] Federalism, separation

---

[146] Ibid., p. 320.

[147] Youngstown Sheet & Tube Co. v. Sawyer, 343 US 579 at 635 n.2 (1952) (Jackson, J., concurring); David M. Levitan. "The Foreign Relations Power: An Analysis of Mr Justice Sutherland's Theory" (1946) 55 *Yale Law Journal* 467 at 490; Franck, *Political Questions/Judicial Answers*, pp. 14–18; Louis Henkin, *Foreign Affairs and the United States Constitution* (2nd edn, Oxford: Clarendon Press, 1996), pp. 19–26; Koh, *The National Security Constitution*, pp. 93–95; Charles A. Lofgren, "*United States v. Curtiss-Wright Export Corporation:* An Historical Reassessment" (1973) 83 *Yale Law Journal* 1.

[148] Koh, *The National Security Constitution*, pp. 72–100, 134–46.

[149] Franck, *Political Questions/Judicial Answers*, p. 16.

[150] Curtiss-Wright, 299 US at 315.   [151] Ibid., at 315–16.

of powers, and the delegation of powers doctrine do not apply to the powers of the president over the whole range of foreign affairs issues.[152] *Curtiss-Wright* recognized the existence of two parallel, coexisting legal realities: the reality of domestic affairs, where the three branches of government participated in the processes of government and equilibrium was retained between them through an elaborate system of checks and balances, and the reality of foreign relations, where the president was the sole organ of the federal government.

However, once again, a bright-line separation between foreign and domestic affairs has proved problematic. The external and the internal have increasingly converged. In an era of globalization, the interdependence between nations causes virtually every issue of domestic affairs to bear on the external affairs of the nations and on their national security policies. The significance of geographical boundaries, of the "water's edge," is greatly diminished. At the same time, states are increasingly undertaking international legal commitments in areas that have traditionally been considered as domestic and local.[153] In his 1993 inaugural address, President Clinton expressed this idea when he said that "There is no longer a clear division between what is foreign and what is domestic. The world economy, the world environment, the world AIDS crisis, the world arms race – they affect us all."[154] Similarly, in the 2002 National Security Strategy of the United States of America, President Bush stated that "Today, the distinction between domestic and foreign affairs is diminishing. In a globalized world, events beyond America's borders have a

---

[152] See, e.g., United States v. Pink, 315 US 203 at 233 (1942); United States v. Belmont, 301 US 324 (1937); Rossiter, *The Federalist Papers*, No. 42, p. 264 (James Madison); Senate Foreign Relations Committee Report on National Commitments, S. Rep. No 91-129 (1969), p. 7.

[153] Stephen Breyer, "Keynote Address" (2003) 97 *American Society of International Law Proceedings* 265 at 267; Robert Knowles, "Starbucks and the New Federalism: The Court's Answer to Globalization" (2001) 95 *Northwestern University Law Review* 735 at 749–50; Ernest A. Young, "The Rehnquist Court's Two Federalisms" (2004) 83 *Texas Law Review* 1 at 151; Ernest A. Young, "Dual Federalism, Concurrent Jurisdiction, and the Foreign Affairs Exception" (2001) 69 *George Washington Law Review* 139 at 141; John C. Yoo, "Laws as Treaties?: The Constitutionality of Congressional–Executive Agreements" (2001) 99 *Michigan Law Review* 757 at 848; Nicholas Quinn Rosenkranz, "Executing the Treaty Power" (2005) 118 *Harvard Law Review* 1867 at 1869–70; Jack L. Goldsmith, "Federal Courts, Foreign Affairs, and Federalisms" (1997) 83 *Virginia Law Review* 1617 at 1671.

[154] William J. Clinton, "We Force the Spring," Presidential Inaugural Address (January 20, 1993), quoted in Anne-Marie Slaughter Burley, "Are Foreign Affairs Different?" (1993) 106 *Harvard Law Review* 1980 at 1980. See also Franck, *Political Questions/Judicial Answers*, pp. 8–9.

greater impact inside them."[155] Even prior to September 11, 2001, modern terrorism, such as narcoterrorism, organized international crime, and cyberterrorism, as well as the more traditional forms of terrorism, have been greatly facilitated by the blurring of geographical boundaries and the increasing difficulties facing nation-states in regulating and controlling their environments under conditions of globalization.[156] The compression of time and space brought about by technological innovation, the communications revolution, and advancements in transportation brings new challenges and threats to states while significantly reducing the state's available time for response.[157] Bayless Manning, a former dean of Stanford Law School, suggested the term "intermestic" to describe the large array of issues that are at the same time domestic and international, noting that while in the past these types of issues, although existing, formed a mere exception within the foreign relations agenda, "the exceptional has now become preponderant."[158]

This convergence of foreign and domestic affairs has led, among other things, to the increasing use of quasi-legislative authority of the president in matters of domestic concern through his foreign affairs powers. The Constitution of the United States envisions shared (not necessarily equal) participation by both president and Congress in the treaty-making process.[159] This is of special significance since treaties become part of the law of the land and may enjoy the same status as a congressionally enacted statute.[160] However, since the end of the 1930s, treaties have been replaced by executive agreements as the main form of

---

[155] The White House, *The National Security Strategy of the United States of America* (September 17, 2002), p. 31, available at http://www.whitehouse.gov/nsc/nss.pdf (last visited on August 8, 2005).

[156] See, e.g., Joseph Kahn and Judith Miller, "Getting Tough on Gangsters, High Tech and Global," *NY Times*, December 15, 2000, p. A9.

[157] See, e.g., Anthony Giddens, *Runaway World: How Globalization is Reshaping our Lives* (2nd edn, New York: Routledge, 2003); David Harvey, *The Condition of Postmodernity: An Enquiry into the Origins of Cultural Change* (Cambridge, MA: Blackwell, 1990), pp. 240, 284–307; William E. Scheuerman, *Liberal Democracy and the Social Acceleration of Time* (Baltimore: The Johns Hopkins University Press, 2004).

[158] Bayless Manning, "The Congress, the Executive and Intermestic Affairs: Three Proposals" (1977) 55 *Foreign Affairs* 306 at 309.

[159] Rossiter, *The Federalist Papers*, No. 75, pp. 450–52 (Alexander Hamilton); United States Constitution, art. II, sec. 2, cl. 2.

[160] United States Constitution, art. VI, sec. 2; Cook v. United States, 288 US 102 (1933); United States v. Postal, 589 F.2d 862 (5th Cir. 1979); Diggs v. Shultz, 470 F.2d 461 (1972).

international agreements entered into by the United States.[161] Although many of those executive agreements are congressional–executive agreements, namely agreements that are based on congressionally delegated or statutory authority, the growing web of statutory delegations of powers and the broadening of the scope of such delegations have given the president almost a free hand in concluding international agreements, making it relatively easy to anchor such agreements in the sweeping language of statutory delegations. A wide range of issues, many of which have been traditionally regarded as "domestic," are now regulated by way of international agreements. The classical topics on the agenda of foreign affairs and policy, such as war and peace, diplomatic relations, boundaries, and national security, became overshadowed by economic, cultural, and technological matters. The net result has been the application of the president's expansive scope of foreign affairs powers to an ever-growing number of matters previously considered to be well within the realm of domestic affairs.[162]

James Madison was aware of the difficulties associated with over-reliance on a separation between "foreign" and "domestic." "Perhaps it is a universal truth," he wrote in May 1798 to Thomas Jefferson, "that the loss of liberty at home is to be charged to provisions against danger, real or pretended, from abroad."[163] Indeed, not only are foreign and domestic affairs entangled,[164] but often the realities of foreign affairs (and national security policy) have the more pronounced impact upon the ultimate outcome of the interaction. The movement of expansive presidential powers in the United States from the area of foreign to domestic affairs has been well documented. In *The Imperial Presidency*, Arthur Schlesinger, Jr., notes: "[T]he imperial Presidency received its decisive impetus, I believe, from foreign policy...[I]f the President were conceded these life-and-death decisions abroad, how could he be restrained from gathering unto himself the less fateful powers of the national polity? For the claims of unilateral authority in foreign policy soon began to

---

[161] Loch K. Johnson, *The Making of International Agreements: Congress Confronts the Executive* (New York: New York University Press, 1984), pp. 3–19; Lawrence Margolis, *Executive Agreements and Presidential Power in Foreign Policy* (New York: Praeger, 1986), pp. 101–39.

[162] Paul, "The Geopolitical Constitution," 722–61.

[163] Letter from James Madison to Thomas Jefferson (May 13, 1798), quoted in Saul K. Padover (ed.), *The Complete Madison: His Basic Writings* (New York: Harper & Row, 1953), p. 258.

[164] Robert D. Putnam, "Diplomacy and Domestic Politics: The Logic of Two-Level Games" (1988) 42 *International Organization* 427; Robert J. Schmidt, "International Negotiations Paralyzed by Domestic Politics: Two-Level Game Theory and the Problem of the Pacific Salmon Commission" (1996) 26 *Environmental Law* 95.

pervade and embolden the domestic Presidency."[165] Rather than mutual cooperation between the president and Congress, the presidency appropriated an increasing number of powers and aggrandized its authority over foreign policy and foreign affairs.[166] As nations become increasingly interdependent, there are growing domestic pressures on national governments to protect the public against the perceived deleterious effects of globalization on jobs, security, and national identity. Interdependence also accelerates the pace of the shifting of crises from one nation to another, carried over the transmission belts of global trade and commerce, as powerfully demonstrated by the East Asian currency crisis of 1997. As crises move more rapidly from one country to another, the time available to national governments to respond to such exigencies is dramatically reduced. Events such as the attacks of September 11 strengthen the sense that the world has become a less secure place. If in the past the enemy was clearly known, today's foes are invisible and may be lurking anywhere. They may strike at any time and at any place. Their actions are not confined to activities against targets abroad. Thus, secrecy, unity, dispatch, and access to broad sources of information – the attributes that, as noted above, have traditionally been considered to put the executive in the best position with respect to the conduct of foreign and national security policies – are thus more likely to be introduced into the domestic scene, subverting, in the process, the notion that a constitution may be designed not "to promote efficiency but to preclude the exercise of arbitrary power."[167]

Indeed, Christopher Eisgruber and Lawrence Sager suggest that the events of September 11 and the subsequent war on terror have "made hash" of the boundaries and distinctions between domestic law and the international arena by "blend[ing] criminal law enforcement with immigration policy, foreign intelligence operations, and military force,"[168]

---

[165] Arthur M. Schlesinger, Jr., *The Imperial Presidency* (Boston: Houghton Mifflin, 1989), p. ix. For a different assessment, see Franck, *Political Questions/Judicial Answers*, p. 126; Laurence H. Tribe, *American Constitutional Law* (3rd edn, New York: Foundation Press, 2000), p. 636.

[166] Schlesinger, *The Imperial Presidency*, pp. 299, 498; Jules Lobel, "Foreign Affairs and the Constitution: The Transformation of the Original Understanding" in David Kairys (ed.), *The Politics of Law: A Progressive Critique* (rev. edn, New York: Pantheon Books, 1990), p. 273 at 286.

[167] Myers v. United States, 272 US 52 at 293 (1926) (Brandeis, J.).

[168] Christopher L. Eisgruber and Lawrence G. Sager, "Civil Liberties in the Dragons' Domain: Negotiating the Blurred Boundary between Domestic Law and Foreign Affairs after 9/11" in Mary L. Dudziak (ed.), *September 11 in History: A Watershed Moment?* (Durham, NC: Duke University Press, 2003), p. 163 at 163.

and creating a "new, mixed regime."[169] In this context they note the growing use of immigration laws and regulations to detain and deport individuals – indeed, to engage in mass preventive detentions – bypassing ordinary criminal law procedures and protections.[170] They also suggest that trials of suspected terrorists before special military tribunals and "indefinite detentions" lead to further disappearance of the lines demarcating foreign and domestic.[171]

Another example that Eisgruber and Sager note is the blurring of distinctions between foreign intelligence gathering and domestic law enforcement operations in the United States.[172] Traditionally, a clear distinction existed between the government's powers to gather intelligence abroad – to which the constitution, and particularly the Fourth Amendment, was (mostly) inapplicable[173] – and its authority to act domestically – which was subject to constitutional limitations and statutory regulation. Thus, for example, the United States Supreme Court rejected the arguments made by the Nixon administration that the president enjoyed inherent powers to conduct warrantless domestic wiretapping for reasons of "national security."[174] That distinction was modified with the passage in 1978 of the Foreign Intelligence Security Act (FISA). FISA, applicable only to "foreign powers" or their "agents," expanded the surveillance authority of the government in the United States when "the purpose" of such surveillance was the gathering of "foreign intelligence information."[175] Thus, while the abroad–domestic distinction eroded, distinctions were still maintained between "foreign" intelligence gathering and "domestic" law enforcement activities.[176] Further erosions of the once-clear distinctions occurred as a result of the passage of the USA PATRIOT Act in 2001. Section 218 of the USA PATRIOT contains the following language: the relevant sections of FISA "are each amended by

---

[169] Ibid., p. 164.

[170] Ibid., p. 165. See also David Cole, *Enemy Aliens: Double Standards and Constitutional Freedoms in the War on Terrorism* (New York: New Press, 2003), pp. 26–27.

[171] Eisgruber and Sager, "Dragons' Domain," 164–65. See also Erwin Chemerinsky, "Losing Liberties: Applying a Foreign Intelligence Model to Domestic Law Enforcement" (2004) 51 *UCLA Law Review* 1619 at 1630–43.

[172] Eisgruber and Sager, "Dragons' Domain," 164.

[173] See, e.g., United States v. Verdugo-Urquidez, 494 US 259 (1990).

[174] United States v. United States Dist. Court, 407 US 297 (1972).

[175] Foreign Intelligence Surveillance Act of 1978, Pub. L. No. 95–511, 92 Stat. 1783. See also Americo R. Cinquegrana, "The Walls (and Wires) Have Ears: The Background and First Ten Years of the Foreign Intelligence Surveillance Act of 1978" (1989) 137 *University of Pennsylvania Law Review* 793.

[176] See, e.g., United States v. Cavanagh, 807 F.2d 787 (9th Cir. 1987).

striking 'the purpose' and inserting 'a significant purpose.'" What this seemingly innocuous change achieves is the extension and expansion of FISA, with its lower thresholds, to domestic law enforcement activities, provided that "foreign intelligence" is a "significant" (but no longer the sole) purpose of such activity. That shift means that standards, once reserved for activities that were exclusively aimed at "foreign" intelligence gathering, are incorporated into law enforcement activities in the United States. Moreover, since FISA warrants are subject to authorization by a special court – the Foreign Intelligence Surveillance Court (FISC) – operating under special procedures, the extension of FISA's scope also means extension of FISC's jurisdiction and the potential transfer of warrant applications from the ordinary courts to FISC.[177]

The distinction between foreign and domestic has also been a focal point in defining the powers and authority of the Central Intelligence Agency (CIA). Established as part of the National Security Act of 1947, the CIA charter prohibits the agency from engaging in "police, subpoena, or law enforcement powers or internal security functions."[178] The traditional understanding – although not set out in so many words in the National Security Act itself – was that the CIA would deal exclusively with "foreign" intelligence matters while the Federal Bureau of Investigation (FBI) would continue to be charged with conducting domestic law enforcement activities.[179] The two spheres were not to be mixed. Yet, practice proved the division between the CIA's and FBI's respective spheres of operations hard to define. The involvement of the CIA in domestic surveillance of American citizens in the United States became public in the 1970s.[180] But if such revelations strengthened the belief

---

[177] See, e.g., Chemerinsky, "Losing Liberties"; Peter P. Swire, "The System of Foreign Intelligence Surveillance Law" (2004) 72 *George Washington Law Review* 1306; Richard H. Seamon and William D. Gardner, "The Patriot Act and the Wall between Foreign Intelligence and Law Enforcement" (2005) 28 *Harvard Journal of Law and Public Policy* 319; Seth F. Kreimer, "Watching the Watchers: Surveillance, Transparency, and Political Freedom in the War on Terror" (2004) 7 *University of Pennsylvania Journal of Constitutional Law* 133.

[178] 50 U.S.C. §403-3(d)(1) (2000) (amended 2004). See also Executive Order 12,333, 46 Fed. Reg. 59,941, at 59,953 (Dec. 4, 1981).

[179] See, e.g., Grant T. Harris, "The CIA Mandate and the War on Terror" (2005) 23 *Yale Law and Policy Review* 529 at 531–33; "Select Committee to Study Governmental Operations with Respect to Intelligence Activities" (the Church Committee), S. Rep. No. 94–755 (1976), vol. I, p. 136 (1976).

[180] Harris, "The CIA Mandate," 536–39; Church Committee Report, vol. I, pp. 136–39; Halkin v. Helms, 690 F. 2d 977 (DC. Cir., 1982); Hobson v. Wilson, 737 F. 2d 1 (DC Cir., 1984).

in the need to keep the domestic and foreign spheres of operations distinct, the realities of modern threats to national security facilitated the further blurring of any lines between collection of intelligence – domestically or "foreign" – and law enforcement, and between "foreign" and domestic in general.[181] It has been noted that post–September 11 "the fight against terrorism and other transnational threats has dawned an era of co-location, cooperation, and combined resources" between the CIA and FBI, with national centers established to pool resources of the intelligence community and share information throughout the federal government.[182] Such sharing of information is a manifest example of the "tearing down of the wall" that in the past separated intelligence and law enforcement activities.[183]

The distinct sphere of "national security"

The special treatment of issues pertaining to "national security," and the heightened level of deference that courts and legislators give to decisions and actions of the executive branch of government in those areas, are linked primarily to the notion that when the security and safety of the state are at stake, special rules must apply.[184] Whether explicitly stated or not, the prevailing sense is that matters of national security are "different."

"National security" is an inherently vague concept that is hard to define.[185] Existing definitions include many variables, vague terms,

---

[181] Congressional Research Service, "Intelligence and Law Enforcement: Countering Transnational Threats to the US" (2001), p. 2 available at http://www.fas.org/irp/crs/ RL30252.pdf (last visited on August 8, 2005); Tyler Raimo, "Winning at the Expense of Law: The Ramifications of Expanding Counter-Terrorism Law Enforcement Jurisdiction Overseas" (1999) 14 *American University International Law Review* 1473.

[182] Harris, "The CIA Mandate," 551.

[183] The 9/11 Commission Report, pp. 78–80.

[184] See, e.g., Zadvydas v. Davis, 533 US 678 at 696 (2001); NY Times Co. v. United States, 403 US 713 at 727 (Stewart, J., concurring); John Hart Ely, *War and Responsibility: Constitutional Lessons of Vietnam and its Aftermath* (Princeton, NJ: Princeton University Press, 1993), pp. 54–60; Franck, *Political Questions/Judicial Answers*, pp. 10–30; Koh, *The National Security Constitution*, pp. 117–49; Laurence Lustgarten and Ian Leigh, *In from the Cold: National Security and Parliamentary Democracy* (Oxford: Clarendon Press, 1994), pp. 320–59; George J. Alexander, "The Illusory Protection of Human Rights by National Courts during Periods of Emergency" (1984) 5 *Human Rights Law Journal* 1 at 15–63; Halperin v. Kissinger, 807 F.2d 180 at 187 (D.C.C. 1986) (Scalia, J.).

[185] See, e.g., United States v. United States Dist. Court, 407 US 297 at 320 (1972); Thomas I. Emerson, "National Security and Civil Liberties" (1982) 9 *Yale Journal of World Public Order* 78; Peter Hanks, "National Security – A Political Concept" (1988) 14 *Monash*

uncertainty, great leeway for discretion, and flexibility of implementation. "National security" is linked to perceptions of threats by the citizenry and leadership of any particular nation. For their part, perceptions of threat are intertwined with perceptions of the interests that are endangered and threatened. The more vital and essential the threatened national interest is, the more likely that lesser dangers would be deemed to pose grave threats to the security of the state. National interests, in general, and the prioritization of those interests, in particular, vary greatly from one nation to another. As a result, "national security" is an amorphous, open-ended concept that is amenable to legal and political manipulation.[186] Yet, as is the case with the distinction between foreign and domestic affairs, separating "national security" cases from "normal" ones is critical in order to ensure that the special rules that apply to the former do not permeate the latter.

The context in which "national security" is used has undergone significant changes. The crux of this transformation has been the shift in the understanding of national security from a purely military to a much broader concept, which encompasses almost all areas of human endeavor.[187] If, in the past, it was possible to discuss national security as a distinct, exceptional area, modern times have witnessed the blurring of such separation, as the concept of national security has become increasingly intertwined with areas previously considered outside its scope. In the post-World War II era, identifying national security with the "freedom from foreign dictation" has led many to view national security policy as combining ingredients of foreign and domestic policy

---

University Law Review 114 at 117–18; J.A. Tapia-Valdés, "A Typology of National Security Policies" (1982) 9 *Yale Journal of World Public Order* 10.

[186] Lustgarten and Leigh, *In from the Cold*, pp. 20–23.

[187] See, e.g., R.N. Berki, *Security and Society: Reflections on Law, Order and Politics* (New York: St. Martin's Press, 1986); Robert Mandel, *The Changing Face of National Security: A Conceptual Analysis* (Westport, CT: Greenwood Press, 1994); Oren Gross, "The Normless and Exceptionless Exception: Carl Schmitt's Theory of Emergency Powers and the 'Norm–Exception' Dichotomy" (2000) 21 *Cardozo Law Review* 1825 at 1857–63; Daniel J. Kaufman, "How to Analyze National Security: A Conceptual Framework" in Daniel J. Kaufman, Jeffrey S. McKitrick, and Thomas J. Leney (eds.), *US National Security: A Framework for Analysis* (Lexington, MA: Lexington Books, 1985), p. 3 at 3–26; Moshe Lissak, "Civilian Components in the National Security Doctrine" in Avner Yaniv (ed.), *National Security and Democracy in Israel* (Boulder, CO: Lynne Reinner, 1993), p. 55; Dan Horowitz, "The Israeli Concept of National Security" in Avner Yaniv (ed.), *National Security and Democracy in Israel* (Boulder, CO: Lynne Reinner, 1993), p. 11; Frank N. Trager and Frank L. Simonie, "An Introduction to the Study of National Security" in Frank N. Trager and Philip S. Kronenberg (eds.), *National Security and American Society: Theory, Process and Policy* (Lawrence, KS: University of Kansas Press, 1973), p. 35.

on a wide range of topics.[188] As one author noted in the *Harvard Law Review*:

"National security" is not a term of art, with a precise, analytic meaning. At its core the phrase refers to the government's capacity to defend itself from violent overthrow by domestic subversion or external aggression. But it also encompasses simply the ability of the government to function effectively so as to serve our interests at home and abroad. Virtually any government program, from military procurement to highway construction and education, can be justified in part as protecting the national security.[189]

This evolution of national security from a military concept to a broader strategic concept may be attributed to a wide variety of causes. The two world wars signaled a fundamental change in the scale and nature of warfare. The introduction of total war and the demands it made on the warring communities with respect to the mobilization of manpower and industry injected civilian elements into the discussion of national security. The totality of war also served to blur the distinction between the battle front and the home front, as well as between combatants and non-combatants.[190]

A sense of permanent, international insecurity has also encouraged the rise of the rhetoric of national security in a wider range of issues. A state-centric conception of national security is contrasted with global trends of interdependence, globalization, and internationalism. This combination broadens the scope of "the security dilemma."[191] When a state considers its security to be jeopardized and endangered it will take what it feels are the necessary steps to preserve and maintain its security. Yet, these very measures may invoke a sense of insecurity in other countries that will take their own measures to counter the newly perceived threats. Once again, such measures may stir a sense of danger in the first actor, leading to the creation of a vicious circle of escalation in pursuit of an illusory security. This security dilemma cannot be confined to that which is military; it applies to a much more general range of issues perceived to be essential to the national security of states.

---

[188] Lasswell, *National Security*, pp. 51 and 50–75.
[189] "Note: Developments in the Law: The National Security Interest and Civil Liberties" (1972) 85 *Harvard Law Review* 1130 at 1133. See also Peter M. Sanchez, "The 'Drug War': The US Military and National Security" (1991) 34 *Air Force Law Review* 109 at 151.
[190] Edward S. Corwin, *Total War and the Constitution* (New York: A.A. Knopf, 1947).
[191] John H. Herz, "Idealist Internationalism and the Security Dilemma" (1950) 2 *World Policy* 157; Robert Jervis, "Security Regimes" in Stephen D. Krasner (ed.), *International Regimes* (Ithaca, NY: Cornell University Press, 1983), p. 173.

The fear of armed conflict with global implications has led to alternative ways of pursuing international conflicts. On the military front, large-scale international armed conflicts have been replaced since World War II by armed conflicts waged indirectly between the great superpowers by proxy. Civil wars, revolutions, and wars between relatively small neighboring states came to play a part in the global tug-of-war.[192] In addition, economic, cultural, and political "warfare" became viable alternatives to actual wars. This was compounded by an ideological East–West conflict during the Cold War. Under the Communist agenda, all aspects of society – military as well as civilian – were to be harnessed in the fight against the West for global domination. The Western powers did not lag far behind. As the perception of threats has expanded geographically, with threats to national security identified with events taking place all over the globe,[193] and broadened to encompass more than purely military perils, so, too, has the scope of measures deemed necessary to confront such threats. Defensive strategies could not be limited to the military realm; they called for a total strategy. Thus, for example, President Truman declared: "[W]e live in an age when...there are no longer sharp distinctions between combatants and noncombatants, between military targets and the sanctuary of civilian areas. Nor can we separate the economic facts from the problems of defense and security. [The] President... must be able to act at all times to meet any sudden threat to the nation's security."[194]

Not surprisingly, concepts of "total strategy" were readily adopted by many totalitarian regimes around the world. Many Latin American countries have seen the implementation of a "national security doctrine" by ruling military junta.[195] Under this doctrine, the East–West conflict was waged not only on the international, but also on the domestic level. Upon "identifying" grave internal threats to the nation, the military would proceed to overthrow the incumbent government and replace it

---

[192] Kalevi J. Holsti, *Peace and War: Armed Conflicts and International Order 1648–1989* (New York: Cambridge University Press, 1991), pp. 285–305.

[193] Koh, *The National Security Constitution*, pp. 84–100; Jules Lobel, "Emergency Power and the Decline of Liberalism" (1989) 98 *Yale Law Journal* 1385 at 1397–409; Daniel Yergin, *Shattered Peace: The Origins of the Cold War and the National Security State* (Boston: Houghton Mifflin, 1977), p. 196.

[194] Harry S. Truman, *Memoirs: Years of Trial and Hope* (2 vols., New York: Da Capo Press, 1956), vol. II, p. 478.

[195] Tapia-Valdés, "Typology," 28–35; Kathryn J. Zoglin, "The National Security Doctrine and the State of Siege in Argentina: Human Rights Denied" (1989) 12 *Suffolk Transnational Law Journal* 265.

with a military rule whose main, self-professed, goals were to restore and safeguard the nation's security. The fight against subversive elements within the domestic community would then be waged with a vengeance on all fronts, military and civilian, since every aspect of society would be considered essential for that nation's security, bar none.[196]

Another cause for the transformation of the concept of national security is the reality of increasing global interdependence. As states become increasingly interdependent, tension builds between international and global considerations and national and domestic considerations. No state is currently willing to depend fully on others in any aspect related to the well-being of its citizens and the protection of its vital national interests. Fears of political, military, economic, cultural, and social domination invoke an internal drive toward the maintenance of a core of independence and self-sufficiency. Any impairment of this core, whether actual or perceived, is regarded as posing a serious threat to the security of the state.

National security considerations have carried special weight in debates concerning free trade, where the argument for exceptions to otherwise liberal trade policies is often heard.[197] Thus, it is argued that restrictions on imports may be required in order to protect domestic industries that are deemed important for national security. It is also the case that national security considerations are used to restrict exports of "sensitive products," or to limit foreign investment possibilities. The economic validity of such policies aside,[198] it has been noted that "the concept of national security has proven highly elastic, being invoked to justify restrictions on such unlikely imports as clothes pegs from Poland on the grounds that domestic productive capabilities in clothes pegs would be required in the event of hostilities with the (former) Communist Bloc countries."[199] National security constitutes one of the general exceptions to international trade agreements such as the General Agreement on Tariffs and Trade (GATT)[200] and the North American Free Trade Agreement

---

[196] Zoglin, "Argentina," 274–75.

[197] John H. Jackson, *The World Trading System: Law and Policy of International Economic Relations* (2nd edn, Cambridge, MA: MIT Press, 1997), pp. 229–32.

[198] Ibid., pp. 21–25.

[199] Michael J. Trebilcock and Robert Howse, *The Regulation of International Trade* (2nd edn, New York: Routledge, 1999), p. 11.

[200] General Agreement on Tariffs and Trade, Oct. 30, 1947, article XXI, 55 U.N.T.S. 194. See also Jackson, *The World Trading System*, pp. 229–32; John H. Jackson, William J. Davey, and Alan O. Sykes, Jr., *Legal Problems of International Economic Relations: Cases, Materials, and Text on the National and International Regulation of Transnational Economic*

(NAFTA).[201] In both contexts, the language used has been described as "broad, self-judging, and ambiguous"[202] – undoubtedly the result of the definitional difficulties alluded to above, and the permeation of national security rhetoric and thinking in many aspects of traditionally civilian activity.

In the context of international instruments, a mention should also be made of the major human rights conventions. Many of the limitation clauses found in these documents include national security as a permissible ground for restricting certain rights and freedoms otherwise guaranteed under the relevant instruments. Cases coming before the European Court of Human Rights thus far have demonstrated the wide discretion left to governments in determining the legitimacy and sufficiency of national security considerations as grounds for limiting protected rights.

An important result of the patterns described above, which, in turn, has helped to strengthen the trend of expanding the scope of national security, has been the growing role of the military in traditionally civilian affairs.[203] Clear trends of "role expansion" of the military and convergence between the military and civilian sectors can be detected.[204] This can lead to the somewhat peculiar result that, in societies such as the United States, the military's role in the civilian aspects of the community's life expands while the former continues to be treated as a "separate community."[205] While the "separate community" doctrine has,

Relations (4th edn, St. Paul, MN: West Group, 2002), pp. 1045–52; Michael J. Hahn, "Vital Interests and the Law of GATT: An Analysis of GATT's Security Exception" (1991) 12 *Michigan Journal of International Law* 558; Hannes L. Schloemann and Stefan Ohlhoff, "'Constitutionalization' and Dispute Settlement in the WTO: National Security as an Issue of Competence" (1999) 93 *American Journal of International Law* 424.

[201] See North American Free Trade Agreement, Dec. 17, 1992, 32 *International Legal Materials* 296.

[202] Jackson, *The World Trading System*, p. 230.

[203] See Lissak, "Civilian Components," 58–63, 72–80; J.R. Dutton, "The Military Aspects of National Security" in Michael H.H. Louw (ed.), *National Security: A Modern Approach* (Pretoria: Institute for Strategic Studies, 1978), pp. 100, 102–03, 114.

[204] Lissak, "Civilian Components," 58–63.

[205] For criticisms of the "separate community" treatment of the military in other contexts, see, for example, Kirstin S. Dodge, "Countenancing Corruption: A Civic Republican Case against Judicial Deference to the Military" (1992) 5 *Yale Journal of Law and Feminism* 1; Stephanie A. Levin, "The Deference that is Due: Rethinking the Jurisprudence of Judicial Deference to the Military" (1990) 35 *Villanova Law Review* 1009. For a view supporting the "special community" concept, albeit in the somewhat more limited sphere of servicemen's rights, see James M. Hirschhorn, "The Separate Community: Military Uniqueness and Servicemen's Constitutional Rights" (1984) 62

for the most part, been directed at issues arising within the military,[206] an argument can be made that the growing convergence between military and civilian sectors, resulting, inter alia, in the adoption of similar structural and operational modes as well as social norms,[207] may lead to attempts to apply the same approach in those points of contact between the two spheres.[208]

Communal divisions: us vs. them

Counter-terrorism measures and emergency powers are often perceived as directed against a clear enemy of "others." The contours of conflict are drawn around groups and communities rather than individuals. Such communal distinctions need not be taken as given; counter-terrorism measures often actively produce and construct a suspect community.[209] One is either with "us" or with "them."[210] There is no middle way.

In times of crisis, when emotions run high, the dialectic of "us versus them" serves several functions. It allows people to vent fear and anger in the face of actual or perceived danger, and direct negative emotional energies toward groups or individuals clearly identified as different. The same theme also accounts for the greater willingness to confer emergency powers on the government when the "other" is well defined and clearly separable from the members of the community.[211] The clearer the distinction between "us" and "them" and the greater the threat "they"

North Carolina Law Review 177. For other implications of "separate community" thinking, see Barry Kellman, "Judicial Abdication of Military Tort Accountability: But Who is to Guard the Guards Themselves?" (1989) *Duke Law Journal* 1597; Stanley Levine, "The Doctrine of Military Necessity in the Federal Courts" (1980) 89 *Military Law Review* 3; John B. McDaniel, "The Availability and Scope of Judicial Review of Discretionary Military Administrative Decisions" (1985) 108 *Military Law Review* 89; Darrell L. Peck, "The Justices and the Generals: The Supreme Court and Judicial Review of Military Activities" (1975) 70 *Military Law Review* 1; Gabriel W. Gorenstein, "Judicial Review of Constitutional Claims against the Military" (1984) 84 *Columbia Law Review* 387.

[206] *Parker v. Levy*, 47 US 733 at 758 (1974).

[207] Lissak, "Civilian Components," 58–63.

[208] For a similar argument, see Kellman, "Judicial Abdication," 1606.

[209] Paddy Hillyard, *Suspect Community: People's Experience of the Prevention of Terrorism Acts in Britain* (London: Pluto Press, 1993), p. 257; Leti Volpp, "The Citizen and the Terrorist" (2002) 49 *UCLA Law Review* 1575.

[210] "President Bush's Address on Terrorism before a Joint Meeting of Congress," *NY Times*, Sept. 21, 2001, p. B4; David W. Chen and Somini Sengupta, "Not Yet Citizens but Eager to Fight for the US" *NY Times*, October 26, 2001, p. A1.

[211] W.A. Elliott, *Us and Them: A Study of Group Consciousness* (Aberdeen: Aberdeen University Press, 1986), p. 9; Vincent Blasi, "The Pathological Perspective and the First

pose to "us," the greater in scope the powers assumed by government and tolerated by the public become.

The fact that the targets of emergency and counter-terrorism measures are perceived as outsiders, frequently foreign ones, has important implications when communities set out to strike a proper balance between liberty and security in times of crisis. Targeting outsiders may also be seen as bearing relatively little political cost. In fact it may be considered as politically beneficial: while the benefits (perceived or real) of fighting terrorism and violence accrue to all members of a society, the costs of such actions seem to be borne by a distinct and ostensibly well-defined group of people. Moreover, in as much as violent emergencies may lead to the targeting of "foreigners," as the post-September 11 measures have, those targeted may lack the most basic of requirements for a meaningful political leverage – the right to vote political officials out of office. As William Stuntz notes, violent emergencies tend to result in situations where the cost bearers are sufficiently few and powerless, or have certain substantial (perhaps even insurmountable) barriers to their coalescing to fight the government's actions.[212] Under such circumstances, the danger is that political leaders will tend to strike a balance disproportionately in favor of security and impose too much of a cost on the target group without facing much resistance (and, in fact, receiving strong support) from the general public.[213]

Amendment" (1985) 85 *Columbia Law Review* 449 at 457; David Cole, "Enemy Aliens" (2002) 54 *Stanford Law Review* 953 at 955; Cole, *Enemy Aliens*; Gross, "On Terrorists and Other Criminals"; Oren Gross, "Chaos and Rules: Should Responses to Violent Crises Always Be Constitutional?" (2003) 112 *Yale Law Journal* 1011 at 1082–85; Ileana M. Porras, "On Terrorism: Reflections on Violence and the Outlaw" (1994) *Utah Law Review* 119; Taylor Natsu Saito, "Crossing the Border: The Interdependence of Foreign Policy and Racial Justice in the United States" (1998) 1 *Yale Human Rights and Development Law Journal* 53 at 57–59; Leti Volpp, "The Citizen and the Terrorist" (2002) 49 *UCLA Law Review* 1575; "Note: Blown Away? The Bill of Rights After Oklahoma City" (1996) 109 *Harvard Law Review* 2074 at 2091; Huong Vu, "Us against Them: The Path to National Security is Paved by Racism" (2002) 50 *Drake Law Review* 661 at 663; Ronald Dworkin, "The Threat to Patriotism," *New York Review of Books*, February 28, 2002, p. 44.

[212] William J. Stuntz, "Local Policing after the Terror" (2002) 111 *Yale Law Journal* 2137 at 2165.

[213] Blasi, "The Pathological Perspective," 457; Cole, "Enemy Aliens," 957; Juan E. Méndez, "Human Rights Policy in the Age of Terrorism" (2002) 46 *St. Louis University Law Journal* 377 at 383; Stuntz, "Local Policing," 2165; Volpp, "The Citizen and the Terrorist," 1576–77; Geoffrey R. Stone, *Perilous Times: Free Speech in Wartime from the Sedition Act of 1798 to the War on Terrorism* (New York: W.W. Norton, 2004), p. 545; Henry P. Monaghan, "The Protective Power of the Presidency" (1993) 93 *Columbia Law Review* 1 at 26.

A bright-line separation between "us" and "them" allows for piercing the veil of ignorance.[214] We allow for more repressive emergency measures when we believe that we are able to peek beyond the veil and ascertain that such powers will not be turned against us. Furthermore, the portrayal of the sources of danger as "foreign" and terrorists as "others" who are endowed with barbaric characteristics and who are out to destroy us and our way of life is used to prove the urgent need for radical measures to meet the threat head on.[215]

Take, for example, the issue of racial and ethnic profiling. In the past, an overwhelming majority of the American public considered profiling wrong. The terrorist attacks of September 11 brought about a dramatic reversal in public opinion on this issue. This change in public attitude is attributed to the fact that the September 11 terrorists were all Arab Muslims. That fact, coupled with the high stakes involved in foiling future terrorist attacks, persuaded many that "it [was] only common sense to pay closer attention to Arab-looking men boarding airplanes and elsewhere."[216] The belief that profiling practices were only going to be targeting "Arab-looking" persons, or more broadly, foreigners, made easier the shift from objection to support of profiling. After all, most Americans did not need to worry about such measures. They were not the intended targets and their rights were unlikely to be infringed. If ordinary Americans considered themselves potential targets of such measures, their willingness to support them might have been mitigated.[217]

The distinction between us and them is not unique to the sphere of emergency powers. Such notions are fundamental to the understanding of both our individual and group consciousness. An integral part of our definition as individuals or as members of certain distinct groups is tied to drawing boundaries between the ins and the outs. Group

---

[214] John Rawls, *A Theory of Justice* (Cambridge, MA: Belknap, 1999), pp. 102–07.

[215] Porras, "Violence and the Outlaw," 121–22.

[216] See, e.g., James X. Dempsey and David Cole, *Terrorism and the Constitution: Sacrificing Civil Liberties in the Name of National Security* (2nd edn, New York: New Press, 2002), p. 168; Samuel R. Gross and Debra Livingston, "Racial Profiling under Attack" (2002) 102 *Columbia Law Review* 1413: Bernard E. Harcourt, "Rethinking Racial Profiling: A Critique of the Economics, Civil Liberties, and Constitutional Literature, and of Criminal Profiling More Generally" (2004) 71 *University of Chicago Law Review* 1275; R. Richard Banks, "Racial Profiling and Antiterrorism Efforts" (2004) 89 *Cornell Law Review* 1201; David A. Harris, "New Risks, New Tactics: An Assessment of the Re-Assessment of Racial Profiling in the Wake of September 11, 2001" (2004) *Utah Law Review* 913.

[217] Stuntz, "Local Policing," 2165–66. See also W. Kip Viscusi and Richard J. Zeckhauser, "Sacrificing Civil Liberties to Reduce Terrorism Risks" (2003) 26 (2–3) *Journal of Risk and Uncertainty* 99.

COMMUNAL DIVISIONS: US VS. THEM   223

consciousness is, to a large extent, about an affirmative, internal, organizing, communitarian symbol that serves as the core around which the identity of the group is constructed. It is also about distinguishing those who are in – members of the group – and those left outside.[218] However, crises lead to heightened individual and group consciousnesses. Allegiance to the community and the willingness to sacrifice for the community's sake – in certain situations, the willingness to make the ultimate sacrifice of one's own life – receive a higher premium and attention in times of peril that endanger the group. The lines of ins and outs are more clearly and readily drawn.[219] Stereotyping is often employed with respect both to insiders and to outsiders, emphasizing good, noble, and worthy attributes of the former, and negative traits of the latter. Collective derogatory name-calling and identification of the others as "barbarians" are symptoms of that trend.[220] Internal conformities within the community are exaggerated, while divergence from "outsiders" is emphasized.[221] For that matter, "outsiders" need not necessarily be (although they primarily are) non-citizens. Crises tend to lead to focus on identity and solidarity, rather than the formal legal characteristics of citizenship.[222] Thus, citizens who are somehow identified with the enemy are also seen as outsiders, as the internment of American citizens (together with non-citizens) of Japanese ancestry during World War II demonstrates.

A special feature of group-construction in this context is "the element of foreignness." In his seminal study, *Strangers in the Land*, John Higham analyzes the phenomenon of American nativism, which he defines as "intense opposition to an internal minority on the ground of its foreign (i.e., 'un-American') connections."[223] Higham finds patterns of nativistic attitudes throughout American history, focusing, in particular, on anti-Catholicism, anti-radicalism, and racial nativism. Yet, he also notes that

---

[218] Frederick Schauer, "Community, Citizenship, and the Search for National Identity" (1986) 84 *Michigan Law Review* 1504 at 1513–17; Elliott, *Us and Them*, pp. 6–10.

[219] Schauer, "Community," 1504; E.L. Quarantelli and Russell R. Dynes, "Community Conflict: its Absence and its Presence in Natural Disasters" (1976) 1 *Mass Emergencies* 139 at 143–44.

[220] Elliott, *Us and Them*, p. 9; J. Glenn Gray, *The Warriors: Reflections on Men in Battle* (New York: Harper & Row, 1973), pp. 157–202; Volpp, "Citizen and Terrorist," 153–54.

[221] Elliott, *Us and Them*, p. 9.

[222] Volpp, "Citizen and Terrorist," 156. See also Linda Bosniak, "Citizenship Denationalized" (2000) 7 *Indiana Journal of Global Legal Studies* 447.

[223] John Higham, *Strangers in the Land: Patterns of American Nativism, 1860–1925* (New York: Atheneum, 1983), p. 4.

"nativism usually rises and falls in some relation to other intense kinds of national feeling."[224] Intense moments, such as the Haymarket Affair of May 1886,[225] while not creating nativism, certainly flared up such emotions and attitudes and led to the intensification and polarization of preexisting nativistic sentiments.

The stigma of foreignness, of un-Americanism, is not limited to the distinction of citizenship. "Foreign" connotes, in a real sense, anything that threatens the "American way of life." The links to things and influences from abroad can then be easily made. Race, religion, and eventually ideas and beliefs and associations can, and have been, described as "foreign," mobilizing significant popular forces against particular groups. As William Wiecek notes: "Since the early nineteenth century, Americans have nurtured a consistent fear that alien ideologies, as well as the foreigners who were thought to be their vectors, were invading the pristine American republic."[226] In the aftermath of September 11, the identification of the terrorists as foreigners has followed this pattern. It also serves to explain the shock that seized the British upon discovering that the terrorists who attacked the London public transportation system on July 7, 2005, were British born.[227]

Yet, reliance on the separation between "us" and "them" may run foul of constitutional requirements.[228] It is also far from clear that applying double standards to citizens and non-citizens actually promotes security. Such double standards may, in fact, undermine security because they alienate precisely those segments of the population whose assistance in identifying terrorists and rejection of the terrorists themselves is critical, namely those communities among whom terrorists are likely to hide and who may have greater ability to affect the actions of would-be terrorists.[229] Such alienation may not only push more people to support (actively or passively) the terrorists and their goals, but would

---

[224] Ibid., p. 4.   [225] Ibid., pp. 52–63.

[226] William M. Wiecek, "The Legal Foundations of Domestic AntiCommunism: The Background of Dennis v. United States" (2001) *Supreme Court Review* 375 at 381.

[227] Russell Jenkins, Dominic Kennedy, David Lister, and Carol Midgley, "The London Bombers," *The Times*, July 15, 2005, available at http://www.timesonline.co.uk/article/0,22989-1693739,00.html (last visited on August 8, 2005); Jonathan Guthrie and Chris Tighe, "The Eerily Ordinary Extremists," *Financial Times*, July 16, 2005, p. 13; "The Chilling Challenge of Home-Grown Jihadis: We Need to Confront the Message, not just the Bombers," *Financial Times*, July 14, 2005, p. 18.

[228] Cole, *Enemy Aliens*, pp. 211–27.

[229] Ibid., pp. 183–208. See also Alan Cowell, "Seeking Moderate Support, Blair Meets Muslim Leaders," *NY Times*, July 20, 2005, p. A10.

also lead to further waste of critical resources in the fight against terrorism. Posner and Vermeule have recently rejected this claim, arguing that "terrorists succeed or not in obtaining public support to the extent that the public prefers the terrorists' goals to the government's. Liberals who object to their own government's use of repressive tactics are hardly likely to switch their allegiance to the terrorists who deliberately provoked them.[230] However, their position seems to rely exclusively on a situation in which terrorism is an entirely external threat to society and where that society is, relatively speaking, homogeneous. Notably, this view neglects to consider the effects of repressive governmental measures, taken in the name of fighting terrorism, on specific minority groups that have ethnic, religious, or other close connections to the terrorists. It also runs contrary to much historical experience. Thus, for example, it is widely accepted that the internment campaign initiated by the British in Northern Ireland on August 9, 1970, led to the revival of the IRA and to the creation of the Provisional IRA.[231] Similarly, there is little doubt that the repressive measures taken by the French army during the Battle of Algiers "proved to be a most effective recruiting sergeant for the FLN which managed ... to transform Algerian political life into a military situation thereby alienating the previously quiescent Muslim population against the French state."[232] A closely related danger of reliance on us–them distinctions pertains to the possibility that the growing schism between "us" and "them" will result not only in the alienation of different groups in the population, but in the dehumanization of the outsider or consideration of him or her as inferior.[233] A dichotomy may be created where the enemy is regarded as immoral, cruel, and evil, while "our" people are of the highest morality and fight for a just cause. This may lead, as the French experience in Algeria shows, to debasement of the fundamental values of the community and its members, as they come to ignore the same values when dealing with those who are not part of their own group.[234] Double standards may also undermine the moral standing of the nation among the nations of the world. And since no country, not even the United States, can go

---

[230] Eric A. Posner and Adrian Vermeule, "Accommodating Emergencies" (2003) 56 *Stanford Law Review* 605 at 628, n. 51.

[231] See, e.g., Finn, *Constitutions in Crisis*, pp. 68–71.

[232] Malcolm D. Evans and Rod Morgan, *Preventing Torture: A Study of the European Convention for the Prevention of Torture and Inhuman or Degrading Treatment or Punishment* (Oxford: Clarendon Press, 1998), p. 28.

[233] Dempsey and Cole, *Terrorism and the Constitution*, p. 170; Elliott, *Us and Them*, p. 96.

[234] Elliott, *Us and Them*, p. 97.

it alone where the war on terrorism is concerned, such loss of legitimacy may further be critical for the success of the overall project.[235] Since September 11, 2001, much has been said about the threats posed by "global" terrorism and the need to meet the challenge of terrorism by a coordinated global response.[236] Legitimacy has a major role to play in ensuring the much needed successful coordination.

Of even greater significance for the purposes of our argument here is the fact that such communal distinctions may well prove illusory. Natural as the "us–them" discourse may seem to be, the dangers that it presents are disregarded too easily and its long-term costs are often ignored. A search for an appropriate trade-off between individual liberties and security needs may lead to results that do not reflect adequately the true social costs and benefits. The balance is not between security and civil rights and liberties, but rather, as David Cole put it, between our security and their liberties.[237] There is also the additional danger that extraordinary measures that are employed at present against "them" will be turned against "us" in the future. With time there may be a redefinition of the boundaries of the relevant groups. Some who are today an integral part of the "us" group may find themselves outside the redefined group tomorrow, leaving within its circumference a smaller number of people. Exceptional emergency measures may be acceptable when premised on the understanding that they will only be exercised outward, outside the boundaries of the group consensus. However, in the rush to avail the group of such measures, it is oftentimes the case that no adequate guarantees are installed to ensure that the tide does not turn and that the same mechanisms do not operate inward, i.e., against "us." Indeed, that such measures ought to be used solely against outsiders may be so clear to everyone within the community that there will seem to be no real need to express that consensus explicitly. Moreover, even if current emergency measures do explicitly refer, for example, to foreignness as an operative term for the applicability of legal provisions, it may well be that with time such limitations

---

[235] Cole, *Enemy Aliens*, pp. 194–97; Joseph S. Nye, Jr., *The Paradox of American Power: Why the World's Only Superpower Can't go it Alone* (Oxford: Oxford University Press, 2002).

[236] The White House, *National Security Strategy*, pp. 5–7; W. Michael Reisman, "Editorial Comments: In Defense of World Public Order" (2001) 95 *American Journal of International Law* 833 at 833; David Schneiderman, "Terrorism and the Risk Society" in Ronald J. Daniels, Patrick Macklem, and Kent Roach (eds.), *The Security of Freedom: Essays on Canada's Antiterrorism Bill* (Toronto: University of Toronto Press, 2001), p. 63 at 65–67.

[237] Cole, *Enemy Aliens*, pp. 4–5.

on the scope of the measures will be removed and abandoned, with the measures applying to a much larger group than had been originally intended.

David Cole has demonstrated persuasively the illusory nature of the us–them distinction and the danger of spillover by closely analyzing several historical examples.[238] He draws a line directly between the Red Scare of 1918–21, in which aliens were the target, and the persecution of American citizens during the McCarthy era. He notes specifically the role of J. Edgar Hoover in both periods. As head of the Justice Department's Alien Radical Division, Hoover masterminded the infamous "Palmer Raids" of 1919–20 and maintained lists of radical aliens. As director of the FBI, Hoover applied what he had learned in the years after World War I to the post-WWII era, only this time many of his targets were American citizens. Similarly, Cole argues that the internment of US citizens of Japanese ancestry during World War II could be seen as a perverse logical extension of the rationale that had previously led to according to the president, under the Enemy Aliens Act of 1798, the powers, during wartime, to arrest, detain, deport, or otherwise restrict the freedom of enemy aliens without the need to show evidence of danger from the individual. History teaches us that the distance between a presumption that in time of war citizens of the enemy are loyal to their country and therefore dangerous per se, and General John L. DeWitt's notorious statement that the WWII internment was justified because "a Jap is a Jap,"[239] may be much shorter than most people think.

The war on terrorism has already supplied similar examples. Consider, for instance, the designation of individuals as "enemy combatants" and the use of special military tribunals. These measures were initially described and marketed by the Bush administration as an application of a military model of counter-terrorism measures to aliens, whereas it was widely understood that US nationals would be dealt with under the normal criminal justice system.[240] However, the military model has been later extended and employed in the case of two US citizens, Yaser Hamdi and José Padilla.[241]

---

[238] Ibid., pp. 85–179.

[239] See, e.g., Orville Schell, "Rounding Up Americans," *NY Times*, January 1, 1984, Section 7, p. 22.

[240] Cole, *Enemy Aliens*, pp. 2–3.

[241] Hamdi v. Rumsfeld, 542 US 507 (2004); Rumsfeld v. Padilla, 542 US 426 (2004).

The normalization of the exception

Emergency powers and authorities that are granted to, and exercised by, government and its agents during a crisis create precedents for future exigencies as well as for "normalcy." Whereas in the "original" crisis, the situation and powers of reference were those of normalcy and regularity, in any future crisis government will take as its starting point the experience of extraordinary powers and authority granted and exercised during previous emergencies. What might have been seen as sufficient "emergency" measures in the past (judged against the ordinary situation) may not be deemed enough to deal with further crises as they arise. Much like the need gradually to increase the dosage of a heavily used medication in order to experience the same level of relief, so too with respect to emergency powers: the perception may be that new, more radical powers are needed to fight impending crises. In turn, new extraordinary emergency measures confer an added degree of ex post legitimacy and respectability, as well as a sense of normality, to previously used, less drastic emergency measures.[242] What were deemed exceptional emergency actions in the past may now come to be regarded as normal, routine, and ordinary, in light of more recent and more dramatic emergency powers.[243] As our understanding of normalcy shifts and expands to include measures, powers, and authorities that had previously been considered special, exceptional, and extraordinary yet necessary to deal with emergency, the boundaries of new exceptions are pushed further to include new and more expansive powers and authorities.

As the boundaries of normalcy and exception are redefined and reshaped, the previously unthinkable may transform into the thinkable. We have already noted the shift in public opinion in the United States with respect to racial and ethnic profiling as a result of September 11. This is but one example of a more general pattern. When faced with an acute exigency, public officials and decision-makers, as well as the general public, are often willing to resort to measures and mechanisms that they themselves had strongly rejected in the past. Consider the following example.

---

[242] Woodward, "Cheney," p. A1.
[243] Lawyers Committee for Human Rights, *Assessing the New Normal: Liberty and Security for the Post-September 11 United States* (New York: Lawyers Committee for Human Rights, 2003) available at http://www.humanrightsfirst.org/pubs/descriptions/Assessing/AssessingtheNewNormal.pdf (last visited on August 8, 2005).

In September 1945, the British Mandatory Power in Palestine promulgated the Defence (Emergency) Regulations (DER), which established "a virtual regime of martial law."[244] The Jewish community in Palestine, against whom the brunt of the regulations was directed, decried the measures as creating a "police state" in Palestine[245] and as "undermining the foundations of the law and constituting a grave danger to an individual's life and freedom and imposing an arbitrary regime."[246] When the State of Israel was established much of the mandatory legislation then in effect stayed on as part of the Israeli legal system, including the DER.[247] The challenges to the DER did not stop in 1948. On several occasions these regulations were denounced by leading figures across the political spectrum. For example, in 1951, the then opposition leader, Menachem Begin argued, referring to the DER, that "the law that [the government] used[,] is Nazi, it is tyrannical, it is immoral: and an immoral law is also an illegal law."[248] Yet, the DER have remained in effect almost in their entirety to this day. Almost all the attempts to abolish the regulations, in whole or in part (including, early on, a government proposal to that effect), have failed. The continued use of the DER became acceptable; it came to be considered as an evil perhaps, but an evil that one had to live with because of external circumstances imposed on the nation. At first the regulations were considered a necessary stopgap measure allowing the new state to deal with the critical situation it faced. At later stages, different reasons militated against abolishing the regulations.[249] It is interesting to note that in the official commentary to the Emergency Powers (Detention) Bill – which, as a law passed by the Knesset, is still the most significant reform of the DER since 1948[250] – Menachem Begin's government declared: "[I]n the state of siege to which the State is subject since its establishment, one cannot relinquish special measures designed to ensure adequate defense

---

[244] Alan Dowty, "The Use of Emergency Powers in Israel" (1988) 21 *Middle East Review* 34 at 35.

[245] Bernard Joseph, *British Rule in Palestine* (Washington: Public Affairs Press, 1948), p. 222.

[246] "Resolutions accepted by the Assembly of Jewish Lawyers in Palestine (Feb. 7, 1946)" (1946) 3 *Hapraklit* 62.

[247] Amnon Rubinstein, *Ha-Mishpat Ha-Konstitutsyoni Shel Medinat Israel* (2 vols., 5th rev. edn, Jerusalem: Shoken, 1996), vol. I, pp. 63–82; H.C. 5/48, Leon v. Gubernik, 1 P.D. 58 (1948).

[248] (1951) *Divrei ha-Knesset* 1807.

[249] Amos Shapira, "Judicial Review without a Constitution: The Israeli Paradox" (1983) 56 *Temple Law Quarterly* 405 at 450–52.

[250] Rubinstein, *Ha-Mishpat Ha-Konstitutsyoni*, pp. 263–70.

of the State and the public against those who conspire to eliminate the State. Still, one should not be content with the existence of those radical regulations."[251]

As noted in chapter 1, it may be easier to pass new legislation than to examine why it is that the existing legislation, and the powers granted under it to government and its agencies, was not sufficient. The result is a piling up of legislative measures into a complex state of emergency that is characterized by "the great number of parallel or simultaneous emergency rules whose complexity is increased by the 'piling up' of provisions designed to 'regularize' the immediately preceding situation and therefore embodying retroactive rules and transitional regimes."[252] This is related to two other phenomena. First, government and its agents grow accustomed to the convenience of emergency powers. Once they have experienced the ability to operate with fewer restraints and limitations they are unlikely to be willing to give up such freedom. "So it always happens that whenever a wrong principle of conduct, political or personal, is adopted on a plea of necessity, it will be afterwards followed on a plea of convenience."[253] The second related phenomenon concerns the use of emergency and counter-terrorism legislation for purposes other than those for which it was originally promulgated. The likelihood of such use directly correlates with the age of that particular piece of legislation. The farther we get from the original situation that precipitated its enactment, the greater are the chances that the norms and rules incorporated therein will be applied in contexts not originally intended. The use of the Feed and Forage Act of 1861 to allocate funds for the invasion of Cambodia in 1971 is but one such example.[254]

In 1984, the Republic of Ireland's criminal justice system underwent a momentous paradigm shift, when it replaced the Offences against the State Act of 1939 with the Criminal Justice Act of 1984. The move signified a shift from a "due process" model – emphasizing defendant's rights – to a "crime control" model – vesting the police with significantly more expansive powers and becoming more prosecution-friendly – of the

---

[251] Ibid., p. 263 (quoting Minister of Justice, Shmuel Tamir).

[252] "Study of the Implications for Human Rights of Recent Developments Concerning Situations Known as States of Siege or Emergency," UN Commission on Human Rights, 35th Sess., Agenda Item 10, at 29, UN Doc. E/CN.4/Sub.2/1982/15 (1982).

[253] Julliard v. Greenman, 110 US 421 at 458 (1884) (Field, J., dissenting).

[254] 41 USC para. 11 (a) (1994 and Supp. 1999). The Feed and Forage Act was also invoked on September 14, 2001, by the President. Exec. Order No. 13,223, 66 Fed. Reg. 48,201 (September 14, 2001). See also Fuller, "National Security Dilemma," 1453, n. 4.

criminal process.[255] Regardless of the substantive merits of such a shift, what is important to note here is that it was prompted by the reality of longstanding, special emergency legislation – which was put in place to deal with terrorist threats – existing side by side with ordinary criminal law and procedure. Under the special legislation the police enjoyed the benefit of powers that were not available to it under the ordinary criminal legislation. Thus, for example, section 30 of the Offences against the State Act gave the police special powers to arrest and detain suspects. Under this section police could arrest an individual based on mere (that is not "reasonable") suspicion and hold her for purposes of investigation and interrogation for a period of forty-eight hours without bringing her before a judge. As Dermot Walsh explains:

> It is this feature in particular which makes section 30 so attractive to the police. If they proceed under their ordinary powers they must build up a case against the suspect by painstaking investigations prior to the arrest. By using section 30, however, they can effect an arrest at a much earlier stage, where they have a mere, honest suspicion, and use the forty-eight hour period of questioning, searching, fingerprinting, and photographing to build up their case. If this fails to provide sufficient evidence for charging they can simply release the suspect without charge and rearrest him again under section 30 at a later date.[256]

Moreover, the same provision enabled the police to arrest an individual who was suspected of having information about a relevant offense, even if there was no suspicion that she herself was involved in that crime in any way. However, section 30 was not designed to apply to all ordinary crimes. Rather, it was intended to be applied only in exceptional circumstances and in the context of crimes that were considered to undermine the security of the state.[257] However, as the Irish Garda officers became used to exercising their section 30 powers, they sought to extend their application to other criminal offenses by making the argument that those powers ought to be available to them for dealing with all serious crimes, regardless of the circumstances of their commission. In practice, the police invoked section 30 as a routine matter in an increasing number of criminal investigations. Police officers exercised their broad emergency powers in contexts that were non-emergency, dealing with

---

[255] Dermot P.J. Walsh, "The Impact of the Antisubversive Laws on Police Powers and Practices in Ireland: The Silent Erosion of Individual Freedom" (1989) 62 *Temple Law Review* 1099 at 1128. See also A. Kenneth Pye and Cym H. Lowell, "The Criminal Process during Civil Disorders" (1975) *Duke Law Journal* 581 at 589–603.

[256] Walsh, "Antisubversive Laws," 1113.

[257] Ibid., p. 1106.

"ordinary decent criminals." The pressures on the system led eventually to the merger of emergency and normalcy and to the transformation of exceptional powers into the norm. When the "normal" Criminal Justice Act was enacted in 1984, section 4 incorporated much of the exceptional powers of arrest under section 30. This move was justified as the mere implementation of "the situation that had developed in practice."[258] By this enacting of reality, the legislature normalized the special powers and "has adopted the exception as the norm."[259]

The past few years demonstrate that the practice under the USA PATRIOT is following similar patterns. We have already noted the act's expansion of the scope of the Foreign Intelligence Surveillance Act (FISA) so that it may be used in the context of domestic law enforcement where "foreign intelligence" is also a significant purpose as opposed to the previous requirement that gathering such intelligence be the sole purpose. In addition, while the USA PATRIOT Act's *raison d'être* is the fight against terrorism, the definition of "domestic terrorism" that is provided in section 802 of the act is extremely broad. Such expansive definition, together with the enhanced powers that the act gives to the government, is likely to lead to the use of the act in the context of domestic law enforcement that is removed from the ordinary and common understanding of terrorism. Thus, it has already been noted that "The government is using its expanded authority under the far-reaching law to investigate suspected drug traffickers, white-collar criminals, blackmailers, child pornographers, money launderers, spies, and even corrupt foreign officials."[260]

In Israel, the authority to issue emergency regulations under article 9(a) of the Law and Administration Ordinance of 1948 was originally used mainly in the context of security issues and in a relatively restrained fashion.[261] During the period spanning the 1950s through the early 1970s, there were few cases in which article 9(a) powers were used. This pattern changed dramatically after the Yom Kippur War of 1973. Since then emergency powers have been exercised in an almost routine fashion in situations relating to labor disputes and monetary issues.[262] After surveying the history of applying article 9(a) in the context of labor

---

[258] Ibid., p. 1114.   [259] Ibid., p. 1113.

[260] Eric Lichtblau, "US Uses Terror Law to Pursue Crimes from Drugs to Swindling," *NY Times*, September 28, 2003, p. A1; Chemerinsky, "Losing Liberties," 1623–24.

[261] I. Hans Klinghoffer, "On Emergency Regulations in Israel" in Haim Cohen (ed.), *Sefer yovel le-Pinhas Rozen (Jubilee to Pinchas Rosen)* (Jerusalem: Hebrew University, 1962), p. 86.

[262] Hofnung, *Democracy, Law and National Security in Israel*, pp. 55–60.

disputes, one scholar concluded that the emergency-related mechanism of compulsory work orders had been frequently used in situations where no special urgency was present or when other, less drastic means had been available. The availability of such a relatively easy-to-use mechanism to solve labor disputes has had a "narcotic effect" on government officials, allowing them to bypass the more burdensome process of negotiations between employers and employees.[263]

As noted above, the Defence of the Realm Act (DORA) of 1914 empowered the British government "during the continuance of the present war to issue regulations for securing the public safety and the defence of the realm."[264] It was, in fact, a sweeping enabling act that granted the government not only executive-type emergency powers but also legislative-type powers. With the power to make regulations that were different from parliamentary legislation in name only, cabinet dictatorship substituted parliamentary democracy without much resistance. Law-making became a matter for cabinet rather than parliament. As the war went on, additional broad delegations of power from parliament were made available to the government. Throughout the war the vast majority of British legislation came in the format of governmental regulations promulgated under DORA, leading Clinton Rossiter to conclude that "the fiat of the Cabinet was the law of England."[265] Governmental regulations sought to regulate such areas as dog shows, supply of cocaine to actresses, and the opening hours of pubs.[266] DORA ushered into British history the first example of a "delegated dictatorship."[267]

The increased powers vested in the cabinet and the limited supervision over its actions led to a previously unheard of invasion of individual liberties and freedoms by the government using its powers of arrest without warrant and of detention of persons of "hostile origin or associations"[268] power of search and seizure without a warrant based on the existence of a "reason to suspect" the use of premises for any purpose

---

[263] Mordechai Mironi, "Back-to-Work Emergency Orders: Government Intervention in Labor Disputes in Essential Services" (1986) 15 *Mishpatim* 350 at 380–86.

[264] 4 and 5 Geo. V, c. 29 (Aug. 8, 1914); Rossiter, *Constitutional Dictatorship*, pp. 153–70; John Eaves, Jr., *Emergency Powers and the Parliamentary Watchdog: Parliament and the Executive in Great Britain 1939–1951* (London: Hansard Society, 1957), pp. 8–9.

[265] Rossiter, *Constitutional Dictatorship*, p. 157.

[266] Colm Campbell, *Emergency Law in Ireland, 1918–1925* (Oxford: Clarendon Press, 1994), p. 11.

[267] Rossiter, *Constitutional Dictatorship*, pp. 156–59.

[268] Simpson, *Odious*, pp. 15–26; J. C. Bird, *Control of Enemy Alien Civilians in Great Britain, 1914–1918* (London: Garland Publishing, 1986).

contrary to public safety or to the defense of the realm; strict control over public assemblies; voluntary self-censorship by the press induced by severe punishments prescribed for speech or publication considered as obstructing the prosecution of the war and by the creation of a press bureau in the Home Office; conscription; postponing general, local, and by-elections for the duration of the war; competence to try civilians as well as military personnel before courts martial applying military law to the civilian population and in the process doing away with the centuries-old rights of trial by jury and habeas corpus; and exerting almost full control over the economic life of the nation. Yet, analyzing the British experience during and after World War I, Clinton Rossiter argues that "the return of peace was followed shortly by the re-establishment of the normal pattern of British government."[269] He notes that governmental structures and institutions returned to their prewar character, as did most individual freedoms and liberties. Regulations made under DORA were either repealed or allowed to expire without being extended or incorporated in a subsequent statute and given permanent character. DORA itself lapsed with the declaration on the termination of the war, made official on August 31, 1921.

Despite this optimistic assessment, the British experience during the war dealt the final blow to the traditional common law conception of non-institutionalized emergency powers. It also established a precedent that became the benchmark for future emergency legislation not only in wartime but also in times of peace. Whereas in 1914 the situation and powers of reference for governmental emergency powers had been those of normalcy and regularity and the relatively limited use of martial law, DORA and the broad authority granted to, and exercised by, the cabinet during the war became the reference for future crises.

The attraction of DORA to the government and its agencies did not disappear with the end of the war. On October 29, 1920, before DORA expired, parliament passed the Emergency Powers Act (EPA), dealing with the production, supply, and distribution of essential materials and services.[270] EPA allowed the Crown to proclaim a state of emergency. The government was empowered "to make regulations for securing the essentials of life to the community" that might confer upon the agents of the Crown "such powers and duties as His Majesty may deem necessary

---

[269] Rossiter, *Constitutional Dictatorship*, p. 171.

[270] Emergency Provisions Act, 10 and 11 Geo. V.C. 67. David Bonner, *Emergency Powers in Peacetime* (London: Sweet & Maxwell, 1985), pp. 223–70.

for the preservation of the peace, for securing and regulating the supply and distribution of food, water, fuel, light, and other necessities,
for maintaining the means of transit or locomotion, and for any other
purposes essential to the public safety and the life of the community."
The government was empowered to provide, by way of subsequent regulations, for trial by courts of summary jurisdiction of persons who
violated the provisions included in such regulations. EPA explicitly provided that "The regulations so made shall have effect as if enacted in
this Act..." Apart from a loose limitation on the power to issue regulations under EPA, concerning the purposes for which such regulations
may be issued, EPA included few limitations on the broad governmental
law-making power. With the passage of EPA, Britain came to have its
own permanent legal institution of constitutional dictatorship.

EPA's significance went far beyond the scope of regulating economic
activity since, with its enactment, peacetime Britain institutionalized
governmental crisis management.[271] Like DORA, EPA was not the result
of calm discussion, calculation, and assessment. The government of the
day was faced with the prospect of a general strike and with an ongoing coal-miners' strike. At that moment the government invoked its
successful experience with emergency powers during the war and suggested that parliament adopt a "peacetime DORA."[272] The precedent set
by DORA made the passage of EPA seem more "natural," less threatening, and less revolutionary. A wartime measure set the legal and political
precedent, and no less importantly set the state of mind of the citizenry,
legislators, and government members, so that a similar measure could
be adopted during a time of relative tranquility. Prime Minister Lloyd
George explicitly argued that the new act would be a substitute for
DORA.[273] The passage from DORA to EPA, from a wartime emergency
legislation to a statutory emergency mechanism operating in time of
peace, was a very smooth one.

The economic depression of 1931–32 was another catalyst to the transformation of emergency powers. Invoking yet again the memory of
DORA, while also relying on EPA, Ramsay MacDonald's "National Government" requested parliament to pass broad enabling acts that would
delegate to government a broad spectrum of legislative powers. Parliament did pass five statutes that empowered the government to regulate

---

[271] Rossiter, *Constitutional Dictatorship*, p. 175; Westel W. Willoughby and Lindsay Rogers,
An Introduction to the Problem of Government (Garden City, NY: Doubleday, 1921), p. 97.
[272] Rossiter, *Constitutional Dictatorship*, p. 174.
[273] Ibid., p. 174.

and adopt all the necessary measures with regard to a wide range of issues.[274]

The story repeated itself after World War II. The grave economic difficulties that faced postwar Britain and the Labor Party's market-interventionist policies led to the retention of a substantial number of emergency powers that were designed to give government the power to continue and exercise broad economic control over commerce, industrial life, labor, and the prices of goods and services.[275] Throughout the first several years after the end of the war, parliament was repeatedly asked by government to extend emergency powers of a socio-economic character and, at times, to expand the list of purposes for which exercise of such powers was permissible. Other emergency powers were made part of the ordinary permanent legislation. As John Eaves notes: "[T]he ramifications of the term 'economy' have become so great . . . that, during the post-war period . . . the executive was empowered to legislate on important matters closely affecting the life of the individual."[276]

In a somewhat similar vein to the Israeli and British examples noted above, in the United States martial law has typically been used – mostly on the state level – against the American labor movement in the context of labor strikes and as a means for maintaining the economic status quo.[277]

The effects of the "getting used to" phenomenon are not confined to the state and its agents. While those may seek to expand their powers and authorities and reduce the external supervision on their actions, they are not the only ones who get used to the new normalcy that is brought about by the normalization of the exception. Such normalization also carries with it a tranquilizing effect on the public's critical approach toward emergency regimes. As John Stuart Mill warns:

Evil for evil, a good despotism, in a country at all advanced in civilization, is more noxious than a bad one; for it is far more relaxing and enervating to the thoughts, feelings, and energies of the people. The despotism of Augustus

---

[274] Ibid., pp. 178–80.
[275] Eaves, *Parliamentary Watchdog*, pp. 123–46.   [276] Ibid., pp. 123–24.
[277] Jason Collins Weida, "A Republic of Emergencies: Martial Law in American Jurisprudence" (2004) 36 *Connecticut Law Review* 1397 at 1412–16; William E. Scheuerman, "The Economic State of Emergency" (2000) 21 *Cardozo Law Review* 1869 at 1876; Robert S. Rankin and Winifried Dallmayr, *Freedom and Emergency Powers in the Cold War* (New York: Appleton-Century-Crofts, 1964), pp. 172–87; Charles Fairman, "Martial Rule, in the Light of Sterling v. Constantin" (1934) 19 *Cornell Law Quarterly* 29; Garrett Logan, "The Use of Martial Law to Regulate the Economic Welfare of the State and its Citizens: A Recent Instance" (1931) 17 *Iowa Law Review* 40.

prepared the Romans for Tiberius. If the whole tone of their character had not first been prostrated by nearly two generations of that mild slavery, they would probably have had spirit enough left to rebel against the more odious one.[278]

Consider again the example of article 48 of the Weimar Constitution which we have already discussed in chapter 1. By desensitizing politicians and the public at large, the extensive use, by the different governments of the Weimar republic, of article 48 as a constitutional source of emergency powers to respond to economic crises facilitated the normalization of the exception. Gradually removing all limitations and constraints over governmental emergency measures it set the stage for the complete destruction of democracy through the use of government by decree. During the life of the Weimar republic, article 48 came to be a constitutional source for the promulgation of an extensive array of executive decrees in the context of economic disturbances and eventually became the source of unlimited dictatorial powers exercised by the president. The extensive use of article 48 during the Weimar years led to a broad construction of the range of circumstances in which article 48 powers could be employed. At the same time, while the use of article 48 was, theoretically, subject to certain limitations that were either explicitly prescribed in the constitution or were implicit in the nature of the constitutional order, as a matter of practice none of these limitations proved a meaningful obstacle to the exercise of unfettered dictatorial powers during the 1920s and early 1930s. And so it came to be that when Hitler became the chancellor in 1933, article 48 lay ready to be used by the Nazis in order to finish off the republic.

Another brick in the wall of normalization of the exception is laid by the courts. Court rulings in emergency-related issues may be subsequently used as precedents and their impact expanded to other matters. "Concessions made to necessity in a special, largely unknown context might be later generalized to apply to other contexts."[279] Emergency-related precedents may be generalized and applied to "normal" cases.

---

[278] John Stuart Mill, *Three Essays – On Liberty, Representative Government, the Subjection of Women* (1861) (Oxford: Oxford University Press, 1975), p. 185.

[279] Harold Edgar and Benno C. Schmidt, Jr., "*Curtiss-Wright* Comes Home: Executive Power and National Security Secrecy" (1986) 21 *Harvard Civil Rights–Civil Liberties Law Review* 349 at 389. See also Alexander, "The Illusory Protection of Human Rights," 26–27; Kingsley R. Browne, "Title VII as Censorship: Hostile-Environment Harassment and the First Amendment" (1991) 52 *Ohio State Law Journal* 481 at 538. But see, for example, David Cole, "Judging the Next Emergency: Judicial Review and Individual Rights in Times of Crisis" (2003) 101 *Michigan Law Review* 2565 at 2571–77.

Considering that the scope of "national security" and "emergency" has increased substantially and that "It would, it seems, have to be a manifestly hopeless claim to national security before the courts would turn nasty,"[280] the potentially vast impact of such precedents can be fully appreciated.

The link between emergency-related precedents and ordinary legal rules is even more pronounced and direct where the same rules and norms are applied in both ordinary and emergency contexts. The "transsubstantive" nature of many constitutional limitations – the fact that they apply to "ordinary" criminals and to suspected terrorists, for example – has two important implications in this context. First, judicial decisions made in the context of fighting terrorism will also apply in the more general context of criminal law and procedure. Second, when judges decide "ordinary" criminal cases, they will take into consideration the impact of their rulings on the fight against terrorism. As William Stuntz notes: "One cannot read Fourth Amendment cases from the 1980s without sensing judicial attention to the pros and cons of the war on drugs – even when the cases did not involve drug crime. Crack dealers were the most salient crime problem a dozen years ago; now, terrorists occupy that place."[281]

Institutional and structural modifications that are installed as essential for crisis management may continue long past the termination of the original crisis. In times of emergency governments enjoy unparalleled concentration and expansion of powers. More often than not the executive enjoys substantial, if not overwhelming, support from the public and from the other branches of government. Such aggrandizement of executive power is not solely the product of emergency. The growing complexity of modern society and the needs of its members have played an important role in the expansion of executive authority, as has the inability to regulate the multifaceted aspects of modern life solely through legislative action. However, emergencies have led to quantum leaps in this process of aggrandizement. Special emergency mechanisms may be institutionalized and made into part of the ordinary constitutional terrain either as part of a new "normal" institution or as an expansion and extension of powers and authorities of existing regular institutions.

---

[280] Graham Zellick, "Official Information, National Security and the Law in Britain" (1986) 98 *Studi Senesi* 303 at 317.

[281] Stuntz, "Local Policing," 2140–41.

Consider, once again, the Roman example. As we saw in chapter 1, one of the main organizing principles of the Roman dictatorship was the temporary nature of any use of emergency regimes and the exclusive goal of returning to normalcy as soon as possible. However, with the transformation of Rome from a city-state into an empire, what used to be no more than exceptional threats became integral parts of the normal life of the republic. Normalcy was redefined to account for prolonged wars waged over more extended frontlines and farther away from Rome. Short wars ending in a decisive single battle had given way to lengthy campaigns against strong opponents.[282] The fact that most wars were now waged farther away from Rome and over larger territorial expanses contributed to their prolongation. The need arose, especially in the distant theaters of war, for experienced officers who would not have to step down after a relatively short period in office. This need was met by the development of the office of proconsul: a consul who commanded an army away from Rome remained as commander of that army with the full powers given a consul after his term as consul expired, thus bypassing the constitutional one-year term limit for consuls.[283] A constitutional custom also developed that a person elected to serve as consul could be re-elected in the following year to the same position. Military commanders such as Scipio Africanus, who during the second Punic War (215-201 BC) held supreme command as proconsul for a period of ten years, accumulated immense power.[284] In addition, Rome had also become more aggressive and ready to charge its enemies rather than engage in wars of a defensive nature. The dictatorship – a defensive mechanism – was no longer adequate to the needs of the republic. At the same time, military threats of invasion of, and attack on, Rome itself were reduced substantially.[285] Safe from invasion and attacks, secure in its military might, unparalleled in the region, Rome no longer needed the dictatorship.

Socio-political crises – the struggle of the Orders and the continued conflicts between the aristocracy and the Popular party – had become part of ordinary life in the republic. With the Licinian Laws of 367 BC,

---

[282] William E. Heitland, *The Roman Republic* (3 vols., Holmes Beach, FL: Gaunt, 1969), vol. I, para. 399; Max Cary and Howard H. Scullard, *A History of Rome down to the Reign of Constantine* (3rd edn, New York: St. Martin's Press, 1975), p. 97.

[283] Heitland, *The Roman Republic*, vol. I, para. 147.

[284] George Anastaplo, "The Constitution at Two Hundred: Explorations" (1991) 22 *Texas Tech Law Review* 967 at 979–85; Cary and Scullard, *A History of Rome*, p. 181.

[285] Cary and Scullard, *A History of Rome*, p. 87.

which guaranteed that the consuls would be elected and that one of them would be a Plebeian, the consulship and the dictatorship became open to the Plebs. As a result, the Patricians, who, during the struggle of the Orders, often resorted to the appointment of dictators to preserve their own interests, changed their mind since the dictatorship could no longer serve their own class interests.[286] For their part, the Popular party and its supporters were also suspicious of the dictatorship, recalling its use in the fight against the Plebs' claims during the struggle of the Orders. The contemporaneous strengthening of the Senate, still controlled by the nobility, presented the aristocracy with a suitable institution for continued social and political control. As the power of the Senate grew stronger so did the value of the dictatorship as a viable emergency institution decline. Dictatorship could not live together with senatorial supremacy.[287] The control of the Senate over the appointment of a dictator ensured that no dictator would ever be nominated without its approval, and the growing stature and experience of the Senate led it to assume the power to conduct and direct wars and establish its leadership in times of extreme peril.[288]

Thus, following the Roman victory in the second Punic War, the dictatorship became unnecessary.[289] In those rare cases where it felt that emergency measures might be necessary to preserve the internal structure of the republic or to maintain or restore public order, the Senate opted for the *senatus consultum ultimum* ("resolution of last resort").[290] Such a resolution, calling upon the consuls to save the republic and see that it comes to no harm, was understood to confer dictatorial powers on the two chief magistrates – although in strict legal terms it was no more than a senatorial recommendation to the consuls – allowing them freedom of action (including the use of force against citizens) unobstructed

---

[286] Heitland, *The Roman Republic*, vol. I, para. 112; vol. II, para. 613; Barthold G. Niebuhr, *The History of Rome*, trans. Julius C. Hare and Connop Thirlwall (3 vols., London: Taylor, Walton and Maberly, 1851), vol. I, p. 564; Rossiter, *Constitutional Dictatorship*, p. 21; Oren Gross, "The Concept of 'Crisis': What Can we Learn from the Two Dictatorships of L. Quinctius Cincinnatus?" in *Diritti Civili ed Economici in Tempi di Crisi* (forthcoming).

[287] Rossiter, *Constitutional Dictatorship*, p. 27.

[288] Heitland, *The Roman Republic*, vol. I, para. 397.

[289] Andrew Lintott, *The Constitution of the Roman Republic* (Oxford: Clarendon Press, 1999), p. 112.

[290] Michael H. Crawford, *The Roman Republic* (Cambridge, MA: Harvard University Press, 1993), p. 122; Joseph A.C. Thomas, *Textbook of Roman Law* (New York: North Holland, 1976), p. 17; Giorgio Agamben, *State of Exception*, trans. Kevin Attell (Chicago: University of Chicago Press, 2005), pp. 41–51; Heitland, *The Roman Republic*, vol. II, para. 740.

by existing laws, without risking eventual punishment for their actions or for violating the citizens' right of *provocatio*.[291]

The "normalization of emergency" led, in turn, to the gradual abandonment of some of the most important mechanisms that had originally been designed to curb the accumulation of power – with the attendant danger of abuse and misuse of such powers – in the hands of a few public officials. The prolongation of armed conflicts had paved the way to the creation of the office of proconsul, and to the possibility for consuls to be re-elected. Both institutional changes were patently unrepublican. Machiavelli explicitly identifies the "prolongation of commands" as "the cause of the dissolution of that republic," and that it "in time made Rome servile."[292] He acknowledges that the prolongation of the terms of office was made necessary by the nature of Roman wars and conquests, which moved the theater of war farther away from the city. Yet, "if the Romans had never prolonged magistracies and commands, if they would not have come so soon to so much power, and if their acquisitions had been later, they would have come later still to servitude."[293] Similarly, the continuous fighting contributed to the rise of senatorial power. The Senate, as the only organ in the republican system to acquire and accumulate experience in the affairs of state over time ("institutional memory"), assumed an increasingly larger role in conducting the state's policy both in times of peace and in times of war. Indeed, the power of the Senate grew to such an extent that it could dictate strategic, and oftentimes even tactical, considerations and goals for the armed forces.

The decline of the dictatorship did not signal the disappearance of emergency powers from the life of the republic. Rather, such powers came to be institutionalized and normalized. Indeed, the dictatorship, as an emergency measure, disappeared precisely because it became the norm. The dictators were, for all practical purposes, replaced by proconsuls – mostly in Rome's numerous provinces – and senatorial supremacy and control in Rome proper. If in the past, emergency powers, necessary

---

[291] Lintott, *Roman Republic*, pp. 90–91; Ernest George Hardy, *The Catilinarian Conspiracy in its Context: A Re-Study of the Evidence* (Oxford: Basil Blackwell, 1924), pp. 98–99; Niccolò Machiavelli, *Discourses on Livy*, trans. Harvey C. Mansfield and Nathan Tarcov (Chicago: University of Chicago Press, 1996), p. 196; Lintott, *Roman Republic*, pp. 90–92.

[292] Machiavelli, *Discourses*, pp. 269–70; Roger B. Oake, "Montesquieu's Analysis of Roman History" (1955) 16 *Journal of Historical Ideas* 44.

[293] Machiavelli, *Discourses*, p. 270. For similar arguments in the context of the history of the United States see, for example, Lobel, "Decline of Liberalism," 1385; Koh, *The National Security Constitution*, pp. 74–100.

to "deliver the republic," were exercised by a dictator – an exceptional and temporary position – they now came to be folded into the "normal" functions of ordinary constitutional institutions, or, as in the case of the newly created position of proconsul, institutions that resembled, and invoked the image of, such ordinary institutions. For while the proconsulship constituted a significant deviation from previous constitutional practices and from the underlying logic at the foundation of the republican constitution, its institutional name was designed to tie it to a well-established constitutional institution, conferring upon it an air of respectability, legality, and legitimacy while downplaying its revolutionary nature. From a starting point of a temporary, constitutionally limited emergency institution directed at maintaining the existing constitutional order and ensuring the survival of the republic, Rome moved to incorporate permanent, virtually unfettered, institutionalized powers, applicable both in "normal" and "extraordinary" times.

Modern notable examples of institutional and structural shifts and changes include the explosions of executive powers accompanying the "economic war" against the Great Depression and later on World War II in the United States, where the expansion of the powers and authority of the executive were facilitated by expansive presidential claims of inherent constitutional emergency powers, broad delegations of power from Congress to the president, and the establishment of a complex web of war agencies under the president's assumed constitutional war powers;[294] the transformation from the Fourth to the Fifth Republic in France; and the fundamental changes in the governmental structure of Great Britain during World War I, which continued to leave their mark even after the war was over, such as the ascendance of the cabinet and the concomitant decrease in the power and status of parliament, significant changes in the operation and the structure of the cabinet, substantial contraction of civil liberties as a result of increased governmental powers, and governmental regulation of, and control over, a wide spectrum of economic activity.[295]

September 11, 2001 provides yet another example of significant institutional and structural changes. In the aftermath of the attacks, the largest US governmental reorganization in fifty years took place with the establishment of the Department of Homeland Security under the Homeland

[294] Corwin, *Total War*, pp. 35–77; Rossiter, *Constitutional Dictatorship*, pp. 265–87.
[295] Rossiter, *Constitutional Dictatorship*, pp. 151–70; Campbell, *Emergency Law in Ireland*, p. 11.

Security Act of 2002.[296] The new department, which is composed of four directorates – Science and Technology, Border and Transportation Security, Information Analysis and Infrastructure Protection, and Emergency Preparedness and Response – consolidates under one roof some twenty-two federal agencies such as the Coast Guard, Customs Service, Transportation Security Administration, the Federal Emergency Management Agency, Secret Service, and parts of the Immigration and Naturalization Service.[297]

[296] 6 U.S.C. paras. 101–557.
[297] Harold C. Relyea, *Homeland Security: Department Organization and Management – Implementation Phase* (Washington, DC: Cong. Res. Serv. RL 31751, 2004).

Part II

5   International human rights and emergencies

This chapter evaluates how international human rights law oversight interfaces and affects the domestic regulation of crisis and where human rights norms regulating the experience of emergencies "fit" within the scheme presented in the first three chapters. In doing so, we examine the interaction between international human rights law and the experience of emergencies at the domestic level. We also offer a critique of the failures of the international system to provide consistent and stringent oversight of state recourse to crisis powers. The consequences of this failure are explored further in chapter 7 where we look at the effects of September 11, 2001 on international and national practices.

International human rights law is a recent legal and political phenomenon, created largely by treaty norms put in place after World War II. The postwar period produced a flurry of aspirational and binding documents and treaties, including the Universal Declaration on Human Rights, the Genocide Convention, the European Convention on Human Rights (hereinafter European Convention), the International Covenant on Civil and Political Rights (ICCPR), and the International Covenant on Economic, Social, and Cultural Rights.[1] Additional regional treaties such as the African (Banjul) Charter on Human and Peoples' Rights (African

---

[1] Universal Declaration of Human Rights, GA res. 217A (III), UN Doc A/810 at 71 (1948); Convention on the Prevention and Punishment of the Crime of Genocide, 78 UNTS 277, entered into force Jan. 12, 1951; Convention for the Protection of Human Rights and Fundamental Freedoms, Nov. 4, 1950, 213 UNTS 221, entered into force Sept. 3, 1953 ("European Convention"); International Covenant on Civil and Political Rights, Dec. 16, 1966, 999 UNTS 171, 6 *International Legal Materials* 368; International Covenant on Economic, Social and Cultural Rights, GA res. 2200A (XXI), 21 UN GAOR Supp. (No. 16) at 49, UN Doc. A/6316 (1966), 993 UNTS 3, entered into force Jan. 3, 1976.

Charter) and the American Convention on Human Rights (American Convention) were added later on to the international complement of protections.[2] A driving feature of many of these treaties, regional and international, is that they explicitly acknowledge the need to make provision for the experience of crisis. Notable exceptions are the Genocide Convention and the Convention Against Torture to which no exceptions on protections are permitted.[3]

Chapters 1–3 outlined three general models of emergency powers: the Business as Usual model, models of accommodation, and the Extra-Legal Measures model. We now examine the extent to which these graft on to the international regulation of emergencies. Because, as we discuss below, international human rights law incorporates an accommodation regime, the thrust of our analysis here looks specifically to the workings and limitations of the primary regional and UN enforcement/accommodation bodies, namely the European Court of Human Rights, the Inter-American Court of Human Rights, and the United Nations Human Rights Committee. Before commencing this analysis, we explore briefly the definitions of emergency that have been developed through policy and judicial analysis since the inception of the various human rights systems. We then follow with (1) an analysis of the Business as Usual model as it applies to the human rights regime; (2) a detailed assessment of the mechanisms facilitating legal accommodation that are offered by international human rights law and a review of interpretive accommodation as undertaken by international courts and tribunals; and (3) a review of the interface of extra-legal responses with international human rights law. This chapter concludes with an analysis of what we consider to be a gap between the theory and practice of emergency powers in international law.

---

[2] African Charter on Human and Peoples' Rights, June 26, 1981, OAU Doc. CAB/LEG/67/3 rev. 5 (entered into force Oct. 21, 1986), (1982) 21 *International Legal Materials* 59; American Convention on Human Rights, Nov. 22, 1969, OAS Official Records OEA/ser. K/XVI/1.1, doc. 65 rev. 1 corr. 1, entered into force July 18, 1978, (1970) 9 *International Legal Materials* 673. See also Malcolm D. Evans and Rachel Murray, *The African Charter on Human and Peoples' Rights: The System in Practice, 1986–2000* (New York: Cambridge University Press, 2002); David J. Harris and Stephen Livingstone (eds.), *The Inter-American System of Human Rights* (New York: Oxford University Press, 1998).

[3] Convention against Torture and Other Cruel, Inhuman or Degrading Treatment or Punishment, GA res. 39/46, annex, 39 UN GAOR Supp. (No. 51) at 197, UN Doc. A/39/51 (1984), entered into force June 26, 1987.

Definitions of emergency

In *Lawless v. Ireland*,[4] a nine-member majority in the European Commission of Human Rights defined a "public emergency" for the purposes of article 15 of the European Convention as "a situation of exceptional and imminent danger or crisis affecting the general public, as distinct from particular groups, and constituting a threat to the organised life of the community which composes the State in question."[5] Some of the five dissenters proposed a more rigorous reading of the term "public emergency." One alternative reading suggested that the linkage between war and public emergency in article 15 – "[i]n time of war or *other* public emergency" – indicated that "public emergency" must be construed as "tantamount to war" or as analogous to circumstances of war.[6] Another dissenting opinion suggested that a public emergency existed only when the constitutional order of the state had completely broken down – when the different branches of government could no longer function.[7] However, the European Court of Human Rights merely affirmed the Commission's decision without attempting to provide a definition of its own.

In the *Greek* case,[8] the majority of the Commission's members identified four characteristics of a "public emergency" under article 15: the emergency must be actual or imminent; its effects must involve the whole nation; the continuance of the organized life of the community must be threatened; and the crisis or danger must be exceptional, in that the normal measures or restrictions, permitted by the convention for the maintenance of public safety, health, and order, are plainly inadequate.[9] In its General Comment 5/13 on article 4 of the ICCPR, the UN Human Rights Committee indicated that an alleged emergency will justify derogation under that article only if the relevant circumstances are of an exceptional and temporary nature.[10] Furthermore, the committee determined that in cases coming before it in accordance with the mechanism set forth in the Optional Protocol, the state bears the burden of showing

---

[4] See *Lawless v. Ireland*, 1 Eur. Ct HR (ser. B) at 56 (1960–1961) (Commission report) (hereinafter *Lawless* [Commission]); *Lawless* (Court), 3 Eur. Ct HR (ser. A) (1960–1961).

[5] *Lawless* (Commission), para. 90, at 82.

[6] Ibid., para. 93, at 95 (Commission member Süsterhenn, dissenting).

[7] Ibid., para. 96, at 101 (Commission member Ermacora, dissenting).

[8] 1 European Court of Human Rights, *The Greek Case*: Report of the Commission (1969).

[9] See ibid., para. 153, at 81.

[10] See *Report of the Human Rights Committee*, UN GAOR Human Rights Comm., 36th Sess., Annex VII, General Comment 5/13, at 110, UN Doc. A/36/40 (1981).

that these requirements have been fulfilled.[11] The principles identified in General Comment 5/13 have recently been revised and extended in the new General Comment 29, again stressing both the temporary and exceptional nature of emergencies.[12] Similarly, both the Inter-American Commission on Human Rights (IACHR) and the Inter-American Court of Human Rights have accepted the requirement that the emergency be exceptional and temporary. The IACHR has often expressed its opinion that governmental emergency measures may only be carried out in "extremely serious circumstances" and may never suspend certain fundamental rights.[13] In its advisory opinion on *Habeas Corpus in Emergency Situations*,[14] the Inter-American Court stated that article 27 of the American Convention was "a provision for exceptional situations only."[15] Similar definitions, underscoring the provisional and exceptional nature of "public emergencies," appear in studies prepared by international and non-governmental organizations. Thus, for example, a report submitted in 1982 to the UN Subcommission on Prevention of Discrimination and Protection of Minorities refers to "states of emergency" as a generic juridical term reflecting the use of emergency powers in exceptional circumstances. "Exceptional circumstances" exist when there are

[T]emporary factors of a generally political character which in varying degrees involve extreme and imminent danger, threatening the organized existence of a nation, that is to say, the political and social system that it comprises as a State, and which may be defined as follows: "a crisis situation affecting the population as a whole and constituting a threat to the organized existence of the community which forms the basis of the State"... When such circumstances arise, then both municipal law, whatever its theoretical basis, and international law on human rights allow the suspension of the exercise of certain rights with the aim of rectifying the situation, and indeed protecting the most fundamental rights.[16]

---

[11] See Jaime Oraá, *Human Rights in States of Emergency in International Law* (Oxford: Clarendon Press, 1992), p. 21.

[12] Human Rights Committee, *General Comment No. 29. States of Emergency (Article 4)*, CCPR/C/21/Rev. 1/Add. 11 (Aug. 31, 2001).

[13] *Report on the Situation of Human Rights in Argentina*, Inter-Am. CHR, OEA/ser. L./V./II.49, doc. 19 corr. 1, at 25–27 (1980).

[14] *Habeas Corpus in Emergency Situations*, Advisory Opinion, (1987) 8 Inter-Am. Ct HR (ser. A) at 33, OEA/ser.L/V/111.17. doc. 13 (1987).

[15] Ibid., at 23.

[16] Nicole Questiaux, *Study of the Implications for Human Rights of Recent Developments Concerning Situations Known as States of Siege or Emergency*, UN ESCOR, 35th Sess., UN Doc. E/CN. 4/Sub. 2/1982/15 (1982), para. 23, at 8.

The International Law Association (ILA) adopted another definition of "public emergency." Their Paris Minimum Standards of Human Rights Norms in a State of Emergency (Paris Standards) prescribe the following:

(a) The existence of a public emergency which threatens the life of the nation, and which is officially proclaimed, will justify the declaration of a state of emergency.

(b) The expression "public emergency" means an exceptional situation of crisis or public danger, actual or imminent, which affects the whole population or the whole population of the area to which the declaration applies and constitutes a threat to the organized life of the community of which the state is composed.[17]

Yet another definition of "public emergency" was suggested by a group of international law experts who convened in 1984 in Siracusa, Italy, to formulate a list of seventy-six principles concerning the limitation and derogation provisions in the ICCPR.[18] Principles 39–41 deal with the concept of "public emergency threatening the life of the nation":

39) A state party may take measures derogating from its obligations under the International Covenant on Civil and Political Rights pursuant to Article 4 (hereinafter called "derogation measures") only when faced with a situation of exceptional and actual or imminent danger which threatens the life of the nation. A threat to the life of the nation is one that: affects the whole of the population and either the whole or part of the territory of the State, and threatens the physical integrity of the population, the political independence or the territorial integrity of the State or the existence or basic functioning of institutions indispensable to ensure and protect the rights recognized in the Covenant.

40) Internal conflict and unrest that do not constitute a grave and imminent threat to the life of the nation cannot justify derogations under Article 4.

41) Economic difficulties per se cannot justify derogation measures.[19]

These definitions point to a broad international consensus on the general contours of the term emergency, particularly with respect to its contingent and exceptional nature. Notwithstanding differences in nuance

---

[17] See Subrata Roy Chowdhury, *Rule of Law in a State of Emergency* (London: Pinter, 1989), p. 11.

[18] The Siracusa Principles on the Limitation and Derogation Provisions in the International Covenant on Civil and Political Rights (1984), reprinted in (1985) 7 *Human Rights Quarterly* 3 at 7–8.

[19] Ibid.; see also Daniel O'Donnell, "Commentary by the Rapporteur on Derogation" (1985) 7 *Human Rights Quarterly* 23 at 23–25 (restating principles).

and emphasis, they accentuate the capacity for definitional agreement and the possibility for meaningful and robust oversight and accountability by law over claims of "public emergency."

Application of the models: Business as Usual

Under the Business as Usual model in its purest expression, a state of emergency is not deemed to justify a deviation from the "normal" legal system. The ordinary legal system is presumed to provide the necessary answers to any crisis without the need to resort to extraordinary governmental powers. We acknowledge here that the term "ordinary" may have multiple meanings and a lack of new powers does not mean that the coercive power of the state is necessarily limited.

Only the African Charter comports formally to this approach, in that it contains no stand-alone derogation provision and offers a unitary vision of response to crisis. Thus, the African Commission on Human and Peoples' Rights has noted that, "In contrast to other international human rights instruments, the African Charter does not contain a derogation clause. Therefore limitations on the rights and freedoms enshrined in the Charter cannot be justified by emergencies or special circumstances."[20] This would seem to suggest that the African human rights system effectively holds states to higher standards of enforcement than its regional counterparts in Europe and the Americas. However, commentaries on the theory and observance of rights protection in Africa have demonstrated that littered throughout the charter's rights provisions are numerous and multiple internal limitation clauses. These clauses outline the ability of the state to limit the protection of rights on various grounds. Thus, for example, article 10 of the charter – concerning freedom of association – states that individuals have the right to free association, provided that they "abide ... by the law." Also prominent are various forms of duties that are imposed on individuals and whose wording suggests a strong bent against an individual rights-based approach. Specifically, article 29 lays down a series of requirements including duties to the family, community, and state, as well as obligations of solidarity, unity, and positive disposition.[21] Thus, while lacking a formal provision for emergency powers, the internal limitation clauses on their

---

[20] "Media Rights Agenda and Constitutional Rights Project Case", Comm. No 105/93, 128/94, 130/94, 152/96, 12th Annual Activity Report 1998–1999, paras. 67–70.

[21] For example, "The individual shall also have the duty: 1. To preserve the harmonious development of the family and to work for the cohesion and respect of the family; to

own, specifically those with reference to national security and social and national solidarity, serve as strong platforms for the state when a departure from the full protection of rights is deemed desirable. The African Commission on Human and Peoples' Rights has stated that the only legitimate basis for limiting rights under the charter is found in article 27(2), and that such limitations should be founded on legitimate state interest, and must be both proportionate and absolutely necessary.[22] They have also proclaimed that limitations should never function to make the restricted right illusory. The commission's enforcement capacity is virtually non-existent and thus the practical value of such pronouncements is limited. It remains to be seen whether the creation of two new judicial institutions in Africa, the African Court on Human and Peoples' Rights and the African Court of Justice, will affect the quality of rights oversight or practice in the region.[23]

Thus, the African system is not truly based on a business as usual approach. It is not a system working from the hypothesis that the regular legal system is suited to provide the necessary answers to any exigency without legislative or executive assertion of new or additional governmental powers. As country-specific examples illustrate, there are multiple instances of both the Legislative and Interpretive Accommodation models to be found on the African continent. While rhetorically many states claim that emergencies are regulated by a Business as Usual approach, in fact, this is far from being the case.

Kenya, for example, ratified the African Charter in 1992. It has before and since that time experienced one-party authoritarian government. There are multiple examples of legislative accommodation that are presented politically as ordinary legislation with no formal emergency title. In 2003 Kenya passed the Suppression of Terrorism Bill, which included provisions allowing persons to be held incommunicado for thirty-six hours, on its face in conflict with the provisions of the African Charter but justified by the discretion inherent in the charter's limitation clauses. In addition many ordinary legislative acts operate to curtail individual freedom substantially, including the Access to Information and

respect his parents at all times, to maintain them in case of need; 2. To serve his national community by placing his physical and intellectual abilities at its service; 3. Not to compromise the security of the State whose national or resident he is." Article 29, African Charter.

[22] See "Media Rights Agenda and Constitutional Rights Project Case," paras. 67–70.

[23] Frans Viljoen and Evarist Baimu, "Courts for Africa: Considering the Co-Existence of the African Court on Human and Peoples' Rights and the African Court of Justice" (2004) 22 *Netherlands Quarterly of Human Rights* 241.

Protection of Privacy Act (Media Law) (2002), which extends the payment publishers are required to make to register with the government, and requires copies of every publication to be submitted to a government register.[24] Zimbabwe provides us with multiple examples of state over-reach in the area of emergency powers undertaken through the guise of ordinary law, operating as if normal legislative mechanisms were in place and not affected by the context of national security or other stated political threats. The Public Order and Security Act of 2002 prohibits a broad range of speech acts, including any public statements "likely to undermine public confidence,"[25] and requires organizers of meetings to inform the police four days in advance. Other problematic legislation includes the Access to Information and Protection of Privacy Act of 2002 (requiring all journalists and media entities to register with the government); the Private Voluntary Organizations Act of 1996 (requiring all organizations providing welfare services to register with the government); and a proposed Non-Governmental Organization Act (requiring all non-governmental organizations to register with a government-appointed Council of Non-Governmental Organizations).[26] None of these provisions has the formal title of emergency laws, but all are better understood as de facto forms of special powers that are introduced by way of legislative accommodation, rather than ordinary law in its pure sense.

One particularly common feature of the manner in which African states respond to crisis is that the accommodation is not achieved by way of explicit rule modification but rather by way of interpretive moves concerning existing norms. Both government actors and courts are involved in this process, in which existing rules are given emergency-sensitive interpretation. This form of accommodation on the African continent has been strongly associated with the rule interpretation of authoritarian governments. In a universe where the state is virtually omnipotent, the capacity of the rule-maker to have all the rules (both ordinary and extraordinary) operate as an exercise of will makes it inappropriate to view such manipulation as a genuine example of the capacity of "ordinary"

---

[24] For the full text as amended in 2003 see http://www.kubatana.net/html/archive/legisl/ 030611aippaamd.asp?sector=LEGISL&range_start=1 (last visited Aug. 8, 2005).

[25] Public Order and Security Act, promulgated by Extraordinary Government Gazette on Jan. 22, 2002.

[26] The Access to Information and Protection of Privacy Act, passed by Parliament Jan. 31, 2002, entered into force Mar. 15, 2002; the Private Voluntary Organizations Act, passed and entered into force 1995; the Non-Governmental Organization Bill, proposed 2004, which is pending presidential approval.

law to accommodate the extraordinary. In such states, the terms "ordinary" and "extraordinary" are interchangeable, given that the rule of law itself is both precarious and almost entirely subjective.

Application of the models: accommodation

The most relevant category of analysis for international human rights law is that of the models of accommodation. To recap briefly, we have previously outlined that several models may be grouped together under this general category. They all countenance a certain degree of accommodation for the pressures exerted on the state in times of emergency while, at the same time, maintaining that normal legal principles and rules should be adhered to as much as possible. These models insist upon the maintenance of a *legal* emergency system so that legal mechanisms and rules control the measures implemented by the authorities in response to a crisis. The models acknowledge that the existing "normal" rules do not supply adequate responses to the acute problems facing a community in crisis, but there remains a commitment to a response within the confines of a legal framework. We have previously identified three dominant modes of accommodation. First, constitutional accommodation, which, simply put, refers to the inclusion of emergency provisions in the constitutional document. As we have outlined in chapter 1, different constitutional systems diverge significantly in their treatment of emergency powers. Most modern constitutions make explicit provision for emergencies, though this approach is not universally followed. The second accommodation model is that of legislative accommodation, which is achieved by introducing legislative amendments and modifications to existing ordinary laws, or by creating new legal rules in times of emergency, such as special emergency legislation. Finally there is interpretive accommodation, which focuses on the interpretation of existing legal rules in a way that is emergency-sensitive. The need for special emergency powers is accommodated through an expansive, emergency-minded interpretive spin given to existing norms. In practice this means that ordinary norms may have their scope substantially expanded in the context of crisis. We have examined in chapter 1 how these models map onto the exercise of power by different branches of government and the range of issues that arise in relation to achieving accommodation and balance in the domestic sphere. We now turn to mapping how the models of accommodation "fit" the regulatory framework of international human rights law.

International accommodation: constitutional and legislative

By applying a broad notion of "legislative" accommodation, we draw a parallel between agreed and enforceable treaty norms and what we define as legislative accommodation in a domestic legal setting. However, certain international human rights treaties, specifically the European Convention, through the process of domestic incorporation as well as the garnering of "constitutional-like" status through its influence on domestic judicial thinking, should also be categorized as a form of constitutional rather than legislative accommodation.

The European Convention was opened for signature in November 1950. Its enforcement structure was initially three pronged, comprising a part-time court, a full-time commission, and the overarching political structure of the Council of Europe. Protocol 11 to the European Convention modified this structure significantly by replacing the commission with a full-time court.[27] The American Convention was adopted in 1969, and provides for two significant procedural bodies to safeguard the implementation of the rights contained in the convention. Chapter VII of the convention outlines the structure of the IACHR, while the role and composition of the Inter-American Court is outlined in Chapter VIII. It is also useful to note that by virtue of the Charter of the Organization of American States (OAS), all member states are bound by the human rights obligations contained in that instrument, which the political and human rights organs of the OAS have recognized are expressed in the American Declaration on the Rights and Duties of Man.[28] As regards the UN Human Rights Committee, its existence was first approved in 1950, after an extended debate within the Human Rights Commission. It was given the task of drafting the International Bill of Rights by the Economic and Social Council.[29] The adoption of the Optional Protocol to the International Covenant on Civil and Political Rights guaranteed the right of individual petition to the committee.[30] What is important to

---

[27] See http://www.echr.coe.int/ECHR/EN/Header/The+Court/The+Court/History+of+the+ Court/ (last visited Aug. 8, 2005): Andrew Drzemczewski and Jens Meyer-Ladewig, "Principal Characteristics of the New ECHR Control Mechanism, as Established by Protocol 11" (1994) 15 *Human Rights Law Journal* 81 (describing basic features of reform).

[28] Not all states agree with this interpretation of the breadth of their legal obligations under the OAS Statute, specifically the United States.

[29] The General Assembly adopted Resolution 2200 (XI) and on December 16, 1966 opened for signature both the International Covenant on Economic, Social and Cultural Rights, and the International Covenant on Civil and Political Rights.

[30] Optional Protocol to the International Covenant on Civil and Political Rights, GA res. 2200A (XXI), 21 UN GAOR Supp. (No. 16) at 59, UN Doc. A/6316 (1966), 999 UNTS 302, entered into force Mar. 23, 1976.

note here is that the legal status of the committee is much lower than that of its regional counterparts. It plays a more constrained and limited role in the application of individual complaints. This role should be understood in relation to its less expansive complaints procedure and the complex political underpinnings of the United Nations structure.[31] All of these bodies are responsible substantively for dealing with derogation review (which comes either by means of individual complaints or by reports) from states that are parties to the relevant treaty and have exercised that privilege.

Derogation thus refers to the legally mandated authority of states to allow suspension of certain individual rights in exceptional circumstances of emergency or war. A variety of terms is used to describe these exceptional circumstances. For the European Convention the operative phrase is "time of war or other public emergency threatening the life of the nation." The American Convention outlines a wider variety of situations including "time of war, public danger, or other emergency that threatens the independence or security of a State Party." For the ICCPR the requirement is simply a "time of public emergency which threatens the life of the nation." We note that a state need not enact specific emergency legislation for derogation to follow; ordinary law or practice sufficiently encroaching on rights can require a state to derogate from its international treaty obligations.

Considerable effort has been spent illuminating the treaty language, and we have traversed some of that territory above.[32] Further and extensive specificity has been given to the emergency concept in the jurisprudence of the European Court of Human Rights.[33] Its core definition gives particular weight to the effects of the emergency on the physical territory of the state, its population, and the basic functioning of state institutions.[34]

The events of September 11 and the domestic legislative responses by many states which involve invoking derogation pose particular challenges to the territorial requirement of threat. There is a genuine question as to whether events that occurred in one state can be interpreted as acts that threaten the life of many nations. Even if that requirement

---

[31] Dominic McGoldrick, *The Human Rights Committee: Its Role in the Development of the International Covenant on Civil and Political Rights* (Oxford: Clarendon Press, 1991).

[32] See pp. 249–52 above.

[33] See, e.g., *Lawless* (Court), at 55; Welfare Party v. Turkey, App. Nos. 41340, 42–44/98, 35 *European Human Rights Reports*, (2002) 3 at 89; Djavit An v. Turkey (20652/92) (2003) ECHR 91; Ireland v. United Kingdom, 23 Eur. Ct HR (ser. B) (1976).

[34] *Lawless* (Court), at 55.

is satisfied there is still a question as to whether the danger is imminent.[35] Legitimacy for state derogation in such cases might be based on
the *Lawless v. Ireland* case in which the European Court of Human Rights
accepted that the activities of the Irish Republican Army (IRA) could give
rise to a state of emergency in the Republic of Ireland even though the
activities of the IRA had largely been directed at the United Kingdom
in the territory of Northern Ireland.[36] Resolution 1373, the Security
Council's executive response to the events of September 11, does not
state explicitly that derogation is required to conform to the suppression
duties contained in the resolution.[37] It simply outlines that states should
take "appropriate measures in conformity with the relevant provisions
of national and international law, including international standards of
human rights" in furtherance of the resolution's requirements. However,
there are unresolved quandaries as to whether the objectives and mandates of resolution 1373 can be carried out without resort to derogation
or at least a substantial infringement on human rights.[38] These issues
will be further examined below when we assess the post-September 11
effects on the international human rights treaty system.

The privilege of derogation is not unlimited, and there are restrictions
and limitations on its use (found in the "legislative" framework). First,
non-derogable rights cannot be limited or suspended whatever the circumstances, i.e., even in the face of public emergencies. For example, the
non-derogable rights under the European Convention include the right
to life (except in respect of deaths resulting from lawful acts of war), freedom from torture, inhuman, and degrading treatment, freedom from
slavery, and the right not to be subject to ex post facto application of
law. By comparison, article 27(2) of the American Convention does not
allow derogation from a fuller and far more extensive list of rights.[39] The
relationship between derogable and non-derogable rights has become a

---

[35] See Sarah Joseph, "Human Rights Committee: General Comment 29" (2002) 2 *Human Rights Law Review* 81 at 84.

[36] For critique of this see Oren Gross, "Chaos and Rules: Should Responses to Violent Crisis Always Be Constitutional?" (2003) 112 *Yale Law Journal* 1011.

[37] Adopted by the Security Council at its 4385th meeting, on Sept. 28, 2001.

[38] Ibid., at para. 3(f).

[39] See article 3 (Right to Juridical Personality), article 4 (Right to Life), article 5 (Right to Humane Treatment), Article 6 (Freedom from Slavery), article 9 (Freedom from Ex Post Facto Laws), article 12 (Freedom of Conscience and Religion), article 17 (Rights of the Family), article 18 (Right to a Name), article 19 (Rights of the Child), article 20 (Right to Nationality), and article 23 (Right to Participate in Government), or of the judicial guarantees essential for the protection of such rights.

site of considerable judicial activity. The UN Human Rights Committee's recent General Comment on derogation provides that the committee has a duty to "conduct a careful analysis under each article of the Covenant based on an objective assessment of the actual situation."[40] The committee makes particular reference to derogations from derogable rights, stressing that the status of derogable rights does not mean that these rights can be derogated from "at will."[41] Here the committee has taken the view that derogable rights which also constitute peremptory norms of international law are effectively non-derogable. Moreover, the committee seems to indicate that derogations from certain rights could never be proportionate. Thus the committee states:

> States parties may in no circumstances invoke article 4 of the Covenant as justification for acting in violation of humanitarian law or peremptory norms of international law, for instance by taking hostages...through arbitrary deprivations of liberty or by deviating from fundamental principles of fair trial, including the presumption of innocence.[42]

The application of these views to state reporting and individual complaints will make for interesting watching, particularly in the light of state responses to September 11. This approach has an interesting cross-application to the approach of the Inter-American Court which, in two important advisory opinions, found that certain derogable rights under the American Convention were effectively rendered non-derogable by expansive interpretation of the term "judicial guarantees" as used in article 27 of the American Convention.[43]

Second, there are procedural limitations contained in all the treaty documents, which are all quite similar. This maps onto many of the procedural obligations that we find in domestic legal statutes governing the resort to emergency powers. States are obliged to inform the relevant treaty bodies when they have taken legal measures entailing derogation from their treaty obligations.[44] The European Convention requires a state party to provide full information on "the measures which

---

[40] Human Rights Committee, General Comment 29, States of Emergency (article 4). UN Doc. CCPR/C/21/Rev. 1/Add. 11 (2001), para. 6.

[41] Ibid.   [42] General Comment 29, para. 11.

[43] See *Judicial Guarantees in States of Emergency*, 9 Inter-American Ct HR (ser. A) at 40, OEA/ser. L/VI/111.9 doc. 13 (1987); *Habeas Corpus in Emergency Situations*, 8 Inter-Am. Ct HR (ser. A) at 33, OEA/ser. L/V/111.17. doc. 13 (1987).

[44] Article 15(3) of the ECHR requires that "Any High Contracting Party availing itself of this right of derogation shall keep the Secretary General of the Council of Europe fully informed of the measures which it has taken and the reasons therefor. It shall also inform the Secretary General of the Council of Europe when such measures have

it has taken and the reasons therefor." States are also generally required to notify the treaty body when the measures cease to be used and the full protection of rights is again guaranteed. Both the ICCPR and the American Convention require that notice of derogation by any contracting state also be communicated to other state parties that have ratified the covenant and the convention.[45] The American Convention and the ICCPR also mandate that reasons for the derogation will be provided by the derogating state. The ICCPR, European Convention, and American Convention all require that states report termination of the emergency and full restoration of rights protection. States are required to articulate the reasons for their derogation. By and large this requirement has little substance. It provides some clues to troubles that may lie ahead with recalcitrant states, indicating that the resort to crisis powers may be sub-text for other unsanctioned governmental goals. It may even provide the primary indication that a government is resorting to the use of emergency powers as a means to circumvent external scrutiny and internal political instability. Thus, the process of derogation itself may operate as a basis for disingenuous resort to crisis powers. That said, we still accept that the process of derogation can incur a significant cost for any state and that derogation can create a context of oversight and accountability on state actions in times of crisis.

The problem in practice with the twin procedures of notification and proclamation is that once they are externally validated and internally acquiesced to (either by force or by consent) they play little further active role in the development of the emergency regime. The longer the emergency regime lasts the further the state may move away from the objective criteria that may have validated the use of emergency powers in the first place. This may happen for a number of reasons. In some cases the declared emergency becomes part of the problem, not an inherent means for its resolution. Such a situation in effect contravenes the basis for the use of extraordinary powers in the first place. Questiaux

---

ceased to operate and the provisions of the Convention are again being fully executed." See Castillo Petruzzi et al. Case, Judgment of May 30, 1999, Inter-Am. Ct HR (ser. C) No. 52, at paras. 50–51.

[45] Article 4(3) of the ICCPR states that "Any State Party to the present Covenant availing itself of the right of derogation shall immediately inform the other States Parties to the present Covenant, through the intermediary of the Secretary-General of the United Nations, of the provisions from which it has derogated and of the reasons by which it was actuated. A further communication shall be made, through the same intermediary, on the date on which it terminates such derogation." See, OEA/Ser. L/V/II.19 Doc. 32.

argues that "the measure should – at the very least – apparently make it possible to abate or bring an end to the specific situation of danger."[46] The assumption is that the short-term use of emergency powers, the "short sharp shock" therapy, will ensure the return to a normal functioning for society and the restoration of normality. The theory does not take account of the manner in which the exercise of these powers can add to societal insecurity and potentially augment the political roots of instability. In theory, these mechanisms are reasonably well equipped to cope with the inception of an emergency. Their fundamental weakness revolves, however, around the willingness of states to be constrained by such procedures, and the willingness of international (and domestic) judicial and quasi-judicial bodies to enforce them robustly at that preliminary juncture. Notwithstanding these difficulties, we argue that it is the middle and end of emergencies that pose the most difficult evaluative problems, both substantively and procedurally. The point becomes most evident when we examine the international judicial response to emergencies and emergency powers.

Notably the recent General Comment by the UN Human Rights Committee concerning derogations under article 4 of the ICCPR amplifies procedural requirements for the covenant, viewing them as safeguards against the unnecessary use of derogation.[47] The committee confirmed that an emergency must be "officially proclaimed,"[48] and expressed the view that notification of derogation should "include full information about the measures taken and a clear explanation of the reasons for them, with full documentation attached regarding their law."[49] Interestingly, the first notice of derogation by a state following September 11 – and presumably based on these new guidelines (United Kingdom) – is the most detailed notice submitted to date.[50]

A final requirement of all the treaty provisions is that measures taken are proportional and consistent with the state's other international legal obligations. The European Convention, ICCPR, and the American Convention mandate that derogations by states must be proportionate and not inconsistent with the derogating state's other obligations under international law. Concerning proportionality, the Inter-American Commission has noted that "any restrictions [must be] necessary for the security of all and in accordance with the just demands of a democratic society and

---

[46] Questiaux, "Study of the Implications for Human Rights," para. 63.
[47] UN doc. CCPR/C/21/Rev. 1, Add. 11, Aug. 13, 2001 (adopted July 24, 2001).
[48] Ibid.   [49] Ibid.   [50] See Joseph, "General Comment 29."

must be the least restrictive of possible means to achieve a compelling public interest."[51] All three derogation provisions imply that derogation is not a blanket mechanism. States must reach the same threshold of necessity and proportionality for each measure taken, and each measure shall be "directed to an actual, clear, present or imminent danger."[52]

The implementation of this proportionality requirement has been varied across the treaty bodies. We have been critical of the European Court of Human Rights in this context, arguing that the application of the margin of appreciation doctrine to article 15 of the European Convention has been extremely problematic.[53] That doctrine stands for the notion that the authorities of each state ought to be allowed a certain measure of discretion in the enforcement of human rights or in the choice of measures taken to implement their human rights obligations. The court has ceded a "wide margin of appreciation" to states over the assessment of, and response to, emergencies.[54] Despite the critique of the expansive use of the doctrine in the context of derogations, it is still fair to say that as a general matter states are required to demonstrate some necessity requirements.[55]

As chapter 6 regarding the interface between emergencies and the laws of war illustrates, the relationship between these two bodies of law is crucial in defining what a state's other international obligations amount to in times of crisis. It also raises a key issue, namely that of which particular legal regime applies *within* the general legal framework of accommodation. The UN Human Rights Committee stated in its 2001 General Comment that it was "not the function of the Human Rights Committee to review the conduct of a State party under other treaties."[56] However, this reticence is abandoned when the committee goes on, controversially, to state that when examining a derogation it has the competence to, and may "take a State party's other international obligations into account when it considers whether the Covenant allows the State party to derogate from specific provisions of the Covenant."[57] A recent report by the Inter-American Commission examining the relationship

---

[51] Inter-American Commission Report, OEA/Ser. L/V/II.116, at para. 34.
[52] See Siracusa Principles, 9.
[53] Oren Gross and Fionnuala Ní Aoláin, "From Discretion to Scrutiny: Revisiting the Application of the Margin of Appreciation Doctrine in the Context of Article 15 of the European Convention on Human Rights" (2001) 23 *Human Rights Quarterly* 625.
[54] Ibid., at 630–34.
[55] See James v. United Kingdom, 8 Eur. HR Rep. 123 (1986) at para. 50; Refah Partisi (Welfare Party) v. Turkey, 37 Eur. HR Rep. 1 (2003) at para. 133.
[56] General Comment 29.   [57] Ibid.

between terrorism and human rights holds that, while states can derogate from certain due process rights in times of emergency, a state cannot deny an individual more favorable protection that is non-derogable under other applicable international instruments.[58] Moreover, this report has stated the IACHR's view that anti-terrorism initiatives do not lessen the obligation of states to remain in *strict* compliance with their other international obligations, specifically those set out in international human rights and humanitarian law.[59] This question was also raised in the *Brannigan and McBride* case where the European Court confirmed that derogation under article 15 of the European Convention must not be inconsistent with a state's obligation under international law. In this context, the European Court rejected the applicants' arguments that the United Kingdom was barred from derogation under the European Convention by virtue of its ICCPR obligations.[60] The Inter-American Commission has forayed into this overlap territory quite considerably, by giving consideration to the international humanitarian law obligations of states in situations where both bodies of law – namely human rights and international humanitarian law – seem to be applicable.[61]

The general thrust of international human rights law's "legislative" approach to accommodating emergencies has been to acknowledge the need for states to have resort to extraordinary powers in times of crisis; to seek to regulate that resort by means of external oversight that is facilitated by access by individuals to supra-national complaints procedures; to impose reporting requirements on states; and to create the capacity for states to call one another to account through the inter-state complaint mechanism.

Models of accommodation: interpretive accommodation

An overview of the international human rights case law related to emergency powers demonstrates the critical role played by interpretive accommodation in the international regulation of emergencies. It also

---

[58] Report on Terrorism and Human Rights, OEA/Ser. L/II.116 Executive Summary, at para. 20.

[59] Ibid., Introduction, at para. 4.

[60] See Brannigan and McBride v. United Kingdom, 258 Eur. Ct HR (ser. A) at 34 (1993), paras. 67–73.

[61] See Inter-American Commission on Human Rights, "Third Report on the Situation of Human Rights in Colombia," OEA/Ser. L/V/II.102 doc. 9 rev. 1, Feb. 26, 1999.

gives a more complete understanding of why accommodation models constitute the best means to understand this regulatory framework.

We have identified a number of strategic concentrations in juridical thinking about emergencies across regional courts and international committees, and our analysis tracks these approaches through the case law of the European Court of Human Rights, the Inter-American Court of Human Rights, and the UN Human Rights Committee. We identify these as primary markers of judicial thinking (though there are evidently many sub-strains on particular issues not covered by this broad assessment).

First, international courts and tribunals give greater leeway in derogation cases to democratic states than to non-democratic or illiberal states. This leeway is not merely a matter of nuance with political consequences but profoundly affects rule integrity and legitimacy. This is a particular trait of the European human rights system, and we identify the problems that this creates for rule consistency as well as general accountability for the use of crisis powers. At first glance, granting greater leeway to democratic than to non-democratic states may not seem particularly awkward or deserving of disparagement. Democratic states may be assumed to act with greater bona fides than their authoritarian counterparts. It may also be assumed that democratic states have internal capacity for self-correction when legal rules are disregarded or abused. We suggest that both assumptions are somewhat naive. The historic experience and practice of emergency powers by democratic states (as noted in Part I) illustrate the capacity of such states to abuse and manipulate the existence of crises in ways that sometimes leave little light between them and formally acknowledged authoritarian states. Moreover, the term "democratic" here requires some critical application, as the quality of democracy in many states thus designated does not always correspond to the expectations of the title. Finally, as one of us noted elsewhere, one peculiar aspect of democratic states is a particular blindness to their own limitations with regard to the abuse of legal and political powers and the human rights abuses that follow.[62]

Second, international courts and tribunals are unable to deal with "problem" emergencies, particularly permanent or enduring emergencies. This inability is linked to a profound conceptual lacuna in international human rights law regulation (explored below), namely that the

---

[62] Fionnuala Ní Aoláin and Colm Campbell, "The Paradox of Transition in Conflicted Democracies" (2005) 27 *Human Rights Quarterly* 172.

treaty regimes presume the existence of an "ideal type" emergency that conforms to practice. Yet, this ideal type emergency hardly exists, and in practice, courts encounter permanent, complex, and de facto emergencies. This encounter is consistent across treaty regimes, as has been the inability of courts to come to terms with it jurisprudentially.

Third, judicial examination of emergency powers (taking into account general early hesitancy connected to internal concerns of establishing court legitimacy) has tended to focus on a secondary issue rather than on the primary question concerning the validity of emergency powers. The primary question focuses on the beginning of emergencies, namely whether the derogation invoked was justified per se. The secondary question is whether the measures taken in response to the perceived emergency are justified. Courts have generally been robust on the second question and quite ineffectual when dealing with the first. We argue that this occurs because courts have not rigorously probed states' asserted rationales for resorting to emergency powers. The reasons for this lack of traction are related to a broader set of social and political dynamics that define the ways in which judicial oversight and emergency review collide. This problem has been rigorously examined at the domestic level, where it was shown that national courts consistently fail to live up to the challenge of being particularly vigilant in protecting rights in times of emergency.[63] Nor is such failure unique to any one country or to any particular period in a nation's history.[64] As we discuss in chapter 1, when faced with national crises, domestic judicial institutions tend to "go to war," and much like the community in which they operate, they, too, "like to win wars." This pattern is not confined to domestic judicial responses.[65]

Some suggest that international judicial institutions can deal more effectively with national predicaments because they enjoy both a detachment and independence from the immediate effects of national emergencies.[66] We suggest that international judges evidence similar faultlines to their domestic counterparts with regard to their oversight

---

[63] Gross, "Chaos and Rules," 1034 and sources cited there.

[64] Arnon Gutfeld, "'Stark, Staring, Raving Mad': An Analysis of a World War I Impeachment Trial" (1995) 30 *Yearbook of German-American Studies* 57 at 69.

[65] Thomas M. Franck, *Political Questions/Judicial Answers: Does the Rule of Law Apply to Foreign Affairs?* (Princeton: Princeton University Press, 1992).

[66] See, L. C. Green, "Derogation of Human Rights in Emergency Situations" (1978) 16 *Canadian Yearbook of International Law* 92 at 99; see George J. Alexander, "The Illusory Protection of Human Rights by National Courts during Periods of Emergency" (1984) 5 *Human Rights Law Journal* 1 at 3; see Aisling Reidy, Françoise Hampson, and Kevin Boyle,

of emergencies. There are a number of reasons for this. The first relates to delays. Although some measure of delay is a feature of every judicial process – some have even argued that it is a positive element when issues of emergency and national crisis are involved – it has certain undesirable effects on the development of an *international* public emergency jurisprudence.[67] Significantly, delay may result in the loss of public interest in the issues and the entrenchment of a "business as usual" attitude that downplays the gravity of derogation measures in a particular case. This is of special significance in light of the important role that public opinion plays in the enforcement of international legal norms. Another result of the delay may be a willingness by the international tribunals to accord a wider margin of appreciation to national governments because of the courts' recognition of the difficulty in replicating the conditions that the government faced in dealing with the exigencies of the time.

Furthermore, both inter-state and individual applications present particular procedural problems. Most international human rights adjudicatory bodies cannot initiate an investigation into a specific situation in a state and must await a formal application by another state party to the treaty or by an individual. Practice shows that inter-state cases are extremely rare, owing mainly to such political considerations as good relations, fear of retaliation, and competing political interests. Individual applications have their own inherent difficulties. These are especially apparent when individual applicants allege that human rights violations have become "administrative practice," as in the series of Turkish cases that have come before the European Court of Human Rights, or when "any individual case brought to the knowledge of the monitoring bodies is representative of a general phenomenon with much larger dimensions."[68] In all these complex instances judicial activism has generally been lacking.

"Gross Violations of Human Rights: Invoking the European Convention on Human Rights in the Case of Turkey" (1997) 15 *Netherlands Quarterly of Human Rights* 161 at 162.

[67] See Brendan Mangan, "Protecting Human Rights in National Emergencies: Shortcomings in the European System and a Proposal for Reform" (1988) 10 *Human Rights Quarterly* 372 at 379–82; Michael P. O'Boyle, "Emergency Situations and the Protection of Human Rights: A Model Derogation Provision for a Northern Ireland Bill of Rights" (1977) 28 *Northern Ireland Legal Quarterly* 160 at 182–83; Christopher N. May, *In the Name of War: Judicial Review and the War Powers since 1918* (Cambridge, MA: Harvard University Press, 1989), pp. 268–70.

[68] Christian Tomuschat, "Quo Vadis, Argentoratum? The Success Story of the European Convention on Human Rights and a Few Dark Stains" (1992) 13 *Human Rights Law Journal* 401 at 406; Reidy et al., "Gross Violations," 164–65.

Another reason why governments fare well when their decisions concerning the existence of a situation of emergency are reviewed by international judicial institutions is linked to the notion of "explosive situations." If international human rights adjudication is "essentially a question about the impact of human rights law on national sovereignty,"[69] the issues involved in emergency-related cases go to the very heart of a state's autonomy. These cases raise extremely sensitive and complex political questions, and therefore require the courts to examine such explosive extra-legal issues as the socio-economic, cultural, political, and historical backgrounds of various conflicts.[70] The evidence to date is that these issues (critical to answering the primary justification question we identify) are beyond the pale of self-defined judicial boundaries when emergencies come before either international, regional, or domestic courts. It should also be obvious that there is a unique challenge for international courts in establishing the facts of an emergency and whether this can be facilitated by on-site visit to the jurisdiction under review. Given the systemic lack of a truly effective fact-finding mechanism, international courts hesitate to interfere with the discretion of national governments, and particularly with their call on the emergency justification question.[71] All of these composite factors illustrate some of the complexities of judicial interface with emergencies and go part of the way to explaining some of the structural reasons for a lack of judicial activism on the question of emergency justification.

A fourth strategic concentration in juridical thinking about emergencies identifies a difference of approach between regional systems and suggests that, generally speaking, the Inter-American Court of Human Rights has taken a more robust approach to determining both substantive and procedural questions about emergencies than its European and United Nations counterparts. We also note in this context the substantially different structural capacity of the UN Human Rights Committee as compared with the regional human rights courts.

Fifth, we suggest that the derogation case law of all systems is substantially concerned with violations of due process rights. This indicates the centrality of this set of rights to the exercise of emergency powers.

---

[69] J.G. Merrills, *The Development of International Law by the European Court of Human Rights* (2nd edn, Manchester: Manchester University Press, 1993), p. 9.

[70] Clovis C. Morrisson, Jr., "Margin of Appreciation in European Human Rights Law" (1973) 6 *Human Rights Journal* 263 at 269; Joan F. Hartman, "Derogation from Human Rights Treaties in Public Emergencies" (1981) 22 *Harvard International Law Journal* 1 at 2.

[71] See Hartman, "Derogation," 2.

An important assessment of judicial prowess is the extent to which the courts are prepared to be robust in defense of derogable rights. Finally, all systems have in common a limited supply of effective and genuinely responsive remedies when states overstep the boundaries of acceptable emergency regulation. One conclusion to be garnered here is that even where states are found to breach the legal norms of derogation the costs to the state are not high, and not sufficiently damaging for the state to withdraw from the oversight systems.

Broadly what all these themes tell us about the interpretive model of accommodation as it operates through the human rights system is that there are distinct and identifiable limits of accountability in the accommodation context. They are also clearly indicative of the extent to which the accommodation model favors in practice the needs of states over individuals. That may suggest that democratic states need not violate the law in order to defend their interests in times of crisis, since international human rights norms and their subsequent interpretation are generally flexible and multi-textured enough for state action to fall within the realm of that which is legal. Yet the derogation regime is not valueless from the vantage point of emergency oversight and review. The requirements of procedure and the information drawn from the judicial process can act as a brake on the worst of state excesses and have, as the case law demonstrates, clearly required states to modify or abandon particular regulatory approaches. We suggest that if there is a move to augment accountability for state resort to exceptional powers, it might need to focus on the primary question, i.e., whether the resort to emergency powers was per se justified, over the secondary question, whether the measures were proportionate and necessary.

The European human rights jurisprudence

The European human rights system presents the most comprehensive case law on emergencies. The relatively large number of European cases (compared with other regional and international systems) can be explained, to some degree, by the fact that the democratic character of the derogating states affords greater access to legal mechanisms in the region, while also offering greater scope for meaningful scrutiny by the adjudicatory body. More obviously the European Convention has been operational for longer than any of the other major human rights treaties.

The first case concerning derogation to come before the European Court – which was also the very first case to be decided by the court – illustrates a number of the key themes that we identified above. The

Lawless case exhibits the dynamics of a new supra-national court anxious to establish its legitimacy, offer a meaningful review of states' actions, while anxious not to overstep the boundaries of state consent to be subject to external oversight.[72] While the European Court of Human Rights demonstrates a willingness to establish the theoretical boundaries of the primary question of whether an emergency exists, its decision also shows an unwillingness to verbalize a negative assessment of the state's action that was clearly sustainable on the facts before the court.

In this case, the European Court was asked to examine the validity of a derogation entered by the Irish government.[73] Gerard Lawless, an Irish citizen, was arrested on July 11, 1957, in the Republic of Ireland on suspicion of membership of the illegal Irish Republican Army (IRA). He was detained without trial from July 13 to December 11, 1957, in a military detention camp. On July 20, the Irish Minister for External Affairs informed the Secretary-General of the Council of Europe of the entry into force of the special powers of arrest and detention that served as the legal basis for Lawless's detention and notified him of a derogation to that extent under the provisions of article 15 of the European Convention.[74] Lawless filed a complaint with the European Commission of Human Rights alleging numerous violations of his rights under the convention. Both the commission and the court found that detaining Lawless without trial for a five-month period violated the obligations of the Irish government under the European Convention.[75] Thus, it became necessary to examine whether the detention could be justified under the provisions of the derogation clause.

Lawless is the first critical judicial step taken toward placing the resort to emergency powers by states within an accommodation framework. The Irish government had contested the right of the European Court (and Commission) of Human Rights to scrutinize the government's actions – arguing effectively that while the government used the framework of derogation it was nonetheless entirely in its discretion to determine that a state of "public emergency" existed and what measures were needed to overcome the exigency and in what proportion. The court paid close attention to the need for a thorough procedural examination of the claim

---

[72] *Lawless* (Court).   [73] Ibid., at para. 195.

[74] *Lawless* (Commission), para. 72. For a description of the factual basis of the case see ibid., para. 54; and *Lawless* (Court), paras. 15–25.

[75] The court held that the detention violated the provisions included in articles 5 and 6 of the European Convention but did not conflict with article 7. *Lawless* (Court), paras. 8–22.

before it. It stated categorically, "it is for the Court to determine whether the conditions laid down in Article 15 for the exercise of the exceptional right of derogation have been fulfilled."[76] At least at the rhetorical and symbolic level the *Lawless* decision reflects the willingness of the court to review on its merits the question of whether a situation of public emergency did exist that would allow a state to use the power of derogation set out in article 15. Expounding a definitive "right to scrutiny" doctrine the court rejected the proposition that the resolution of such an issue ought to be left to the sole discretion of the government concerned – a significant decision indeed, especially in light of the fact that *Lawless* was the first case to come before the court. Following the definition of "public emergency" for the purposes of article 15, as set out by the commission's majority in this case, the European Court declared that: "[I]n the general context of Article 15 of the Convention, the natural and customary meaning of the words 'other public emergency threatening the life of the nation' is sufficiently clear . . . they refer to an exceptional situation of crisis or emergency which affects the whole population and constitutes a threat to the organised life of the community of which the State is composed."[77] Thus, the court went some way toward developing criteria to evaluate whether a situation of emergency could be said to exist. Unanimously affirming the commission's conclusion that a state of public emergency had in fact existed in the Republic of Ireland as of July 5, 1957, the court based its judgment on three factual elements that validated in the court's opinion the Irish government's resort to the mechanism of derogation under article 15: the existence of an illegal and secret military organization operating within the territory of the Irish Republic that resorted to violent actions to further its goals; the detrimental impact of this organization's operations on the foreign relations of the Republic because of its activities in Northern Ireland; and finally, the "steady and alarming" escalation in the intensity and scale of its terrorist campaign from the autumn of 1956 through the first

[76] Ibid., para. 22, at 55. The European Commission of Human Rights had previously established its competence to review and rule on the compliance of a derogating state with its obligations under article 15 in Greece v. United Kingdom, 1958–1959 YB Eur. Conv. on HR 174 (Eur. Comm'n on HR).

[77] *Lawless* (Court), para. 28, at 56. In his concurring opinion, Judge Maridakis wrote that: "By 'public emergency threatening the life of the nation' it is to be understood a quite exceptional situation which imperils or might imperil the normal operation of public policy established in accordance with the lawfully expressed will of the citizens, in respect alike of the situation inside the country and of relations with foreign Powers." Ibid., at 64.

six months of 1957.[78] Remarkably, though, the portion of the court's decision concerning the question of the existence of a public emergency threatening the life of the nation is less than two pages long.

The court's conclusory language is problematic both with respect to the particular facts presented in this case and, more significantly, for its long-term effects on the jurisprudence under article 15. It is questionable whether, on the facts of the case, the court's answer to the primary question as to the existence of a public emergency in Ireland could be sustained.[79] Thus, for example, the existence of a state of emergency was closely linked to the continuance of unlawful activities in Northern Ireland by the IRA. Northern Ireland, however, was neither part of the Irish Republic's territory nor under its control. The IRA's terrorist activities across the border did not threaten the life of the Republic and affected the day-to-day lives of its citizens only marginally, if at all.[80] Of course, it could be imagined that continued terrorist activity might lead to such actions as closure of the border between the North and the Republic or might otherwise detrimentally impact Anglo-Irish relations. Yet, even assuming that such effects could be considered a "public emergency," there was no indication that they had been anything more than a remote possibility, much less an imminent or actual threat to the normal life of the Irish nation.[81]

The decisions of both the commission and the court reflect strong deference to the government's assessment of crisis. Although they have not completely abdicated their judicial review responsibility to decide a derogation case on its merits, both the commission and the court adopted a markedly deferential attitude toward the national governments as to whether a "public emergency" existed, employing (and extending) for this purpose the "margin of appreciation" doctrine. This doctrine was initially formulated by the commission in the *(First) Cyprus* case when it stated that a state exercising the derogation power under the European Convention enjoyed "a certain measure of discretion in assessing

---

[78] Ibid., para. 28, at 56.

[79] Oren Gross, "'Once More unto the Breach': The Systematic Failure of Applying the European Convention on Human Rights to Entrenched Emergencies" (1998) 23 *Yale Journal of International Law* 437 at 462–64; Hartman, "Derogation," 24–27.

[80] *Lawless* (Commission), para. 90, at 85; *Lawless* (Court), para. 36, at 57–58.

[81] *Lawless* (Commission), para. 93, at 97–98 (Commission member Süsterhenn, dissenting); see also Francis G. Jacobs and Robin C.A. White, *The European Convention on Human Rights*, eds. Clare Ovey and Robin White (3rd edn, Oxford: Oxford University Press, 2002), pp. 369–73.

the extent strictly required by the exigencies of the situation."[82] This "measure of discretion" applied only to the secondary question arising from article 15, namely whether the emergency measures taken by the government were limited to the extent strictly required by the exigencies.[83] In *Lawless*, the commission extended the notion of a measure of discretion, applying it not only to the question of whether the measures taken by the government were "strictly required" by the exigencies but also to the determination of whether a "public emergency threatening the life of the nation" existed. Thus, the commission stated:

> [H]aving regard to the high responsibility which a government has to its people to protect them against any threat to the life of the nation, it is evident that a certain discretion – a certain margin of appreciation – must be kept to the Government in determining whether there exists a public emergency which threatens the life of the nation and which must be dealt with by exceptional measures derogating from its normal obligations under the Convention.[84]

Although the court made no specific mention of the margin of appreciation doctrine in *Lawless*, its opinion contains similar language, as when it concluded that "the existence at the time of a 'public emergency threatening the life of the nation', was *reasonably deduced* by the Irish Government from a combination of several factors."[85]

Thus, *Lawless* presents a cocktail of robustness and timidity on both the primary and secondary questions. On one reading, *Lawless* represents a high point of judicial activism, simply because a court was asserting a legitimate authority to set judicially constructed criteria and measure whether an emergency existed in fact. However, this primary question lacked traction throughout the judgment, and the secondary question (the validity of the measures taken) also gave substantial leeway to the state. While the high moral ground was occupied on the issue of the

---

[82] Greece v. United Kingdom, at 176. See Gross and Ní Aoláin, "From Discretion to Scrutiny"; *Lawless*, at para. 28; Chowdhury, *Rule of Law in a State of Emergency*, p. 32.

[83] The *Greek* Case, paras. 180–84, at 92–99 (commission member Eustathiades, dissenting).

[84] *Lawless* (Commission), para. 90, at 82. See also ibid., at 395–96, 408. A minority of the commission members rejected adamantly the margin of appreciation doctrine, arguing that evaluation of the existence of a public emergency ought to be based solely on existing facts without regard to any "account of subjective predictions as to future development." Ibid., para. 92, at 94 (commission member Eustathiades, dissenting).

[85] *Lawless* (Court), para. 28, at 56 (emphasis added). With respect to the issue of the proportionality of the measures taken by the government, however, the court seemed to engage in an independent evaluation of possible alternatives.

court's competence and authority to scrutinize, the substance of the examination was made meaningless by the use (implicitly in the case of the court and explicitly by the commission) of the "margin of appreciation" doctrine. Ultimately, one of the major weaknesses of the European oversight system was given its genesis by the court's judicial deference to the state's assessment of risk. In this we see the faultline for a consistent tendency to avoid answering hard questions about the legitimacy of the emergency per se. It also set a weak beginning for the court's approach to the violations of due process rights, a weakness which has since been evident in the case law under the European Convention. Finally, precisely because the commission and the court adopted the rhetoric of judicial activism, their decisions carried significant legitimating value for the actions of the government.

Following *Lawless* came an exceptional case brought to the European Commission by Denmark, Sweden, Norway, and the Netherlands against Greece, on October 2, 1967. At first blush the decision by the European Commission – determining that no public emergency existed in Greece at the time derogation occurred – might suggest that none of the thematic patterns and flaws that we identified above is true of the judicial accommodation approach advanced by the European system. However, this case is an anomaly. Its outcome is explained by the need of the Council of Europe (and by implication its judicial organs) to self-define politically in terms of democratic identity and institutions. The imposition of an authoritarian military regime in Greece was a direct challenge to that political self-identity and was therefore met by a staunch judicial response. The eventual consequence of that response was the withdrawal of Greece from the Council of Europe, a result that might not have been unintended by the commission's own reasoning.[86]

In April 1967, a group of military officers carried out a successful *coup d'état* in Greece. In the name of "The National Revolution" constitutional guarantees protecting human rights were suspended. Mass arrests, purges of the intellectual and political community, censorship, and martial law followed. Clearly due process rights alone were not the sole or most significant response in the arsenal of the authoritarian regime. In May 1967, the new government informed the Secretary-General of the Council of Europe that it was invoking article 15 of the European

---

[86] The case never came before the European Court as the Greek government denounced the European Convention and withdrew its membership in the convention after the commission's report was made public.

Convention to allow for the suspension of certain constitutional rights, arguing that a "public emergency threatening the life of the nation" existed in Greece because of the threat of a violent Communist overthrow of the military government, a crisis of constitutional government, and a crisis of public order.

In contrast to *Lawless*, the commission assessed both procedurally and substantively whether a state of emergency actually existed in Greece at the relevant time. It concluded that the evidence supplied by the Greek government was not persuasive. Thus, for example, after carefully reviewing the facts, the commission found that not only did the Greek government not show that the threat of a Communist coup was imminent, but rather the evidence actually indicated that a violent takeover was "neither planned at that time, nor seriously anticipated by either the military or police authorities."[87] Although the commission paid its rhetorical respect to the "constant jurisprudence" concerning the margin of appreciation doctrine, it did not grant any such margin to the Greek revolutionary government in what constituted a virtual de novo review of the factual basis of the case and the Greek government's submissions.[88] The case demonstrates the capacity to answer the primary emergency question based on the criteria developed by the court and commission. This capacity was further strengthened by an emphasis on independent fact-finding.[89] The commission's approach in this case is characterized by objective assessment, non-deference to state justification, and the streamlining of categories within which to assess state action. It set a positive example of robust international judicial oversight. However, this approach has not been adopted in relation to other assessments of valid derogations and it has been typecast by many as simply a response to the anti-democratic character of the Greek

[87] The *Greek Case*, para. 159, at 83. The commission similarly rejected the Greek government's claim that the circumstances prevailing in Greece at the relevant time constituted a constitutional crisis that put public order in serious jeopardy. Ibid., paras. 126–32, at 67–71; paras. 163–64, at 85–86. Similarly, while acknowledging that great tension existed in Athens and Salonica, particularly among students and building workers, the commission nonetheless found that "there [was] no evidence that the police were not in both cities fully able to cope with the situation; there [was] no indication that firearms were used or their use planned and still less was there any suggestion that the army should be called in to assist the police." Ibid., para. 149, at 78–79. Thus, the government "was in effective control of the situation." Ibid., para. 160, at 84.

[88] Cora S. Feingold, "The Doctrine of Margin of Appreciation and the European Convention on Human Rights" (1977) 53 *Notre Dame Law Review* 90 at 91–94.

[89] Hartman, "Derogation," 37.

government.[90] The non-democratic nature of the Greek government enabled the commission to assume an uncompromising stance: not only would such a decision enjoy moral and political support, but it would be easily distinguishable from any future case involving a democratic regime, thus alleviating member states' fears that a strong decision might be used against them in the future. In so far as the commission's decision opposed the self-proclaimed interests of the Greek junta, it was all the more palatable to established regimes, as it worked against an unconstitutional overthrow of a lawful government. The clear signal was that the use of the convention and its processes to legitimate usurping the democratic order was intolerable. In the more generally litigated area of democratic governments' resort to emergency powers, the commission and court's response has proved less robust. Thus, where ostensibly democratic states have engaged in the suspension of certain rights guaranteed under the convention, the commission and court have been less exacting in their requirements. This pattern is exacerbated when dealing with long-term or permanent emergencies. The nexus is most evidently shown in contexts where democratic states introduce temporary legislation limiting rights protection in order to confront finite crises, but subsequently allow such legislation to become entrenched and survive as an integral component of the state's legal regulation.[91] Here the boundaries between emergency and "ordinary" law become extremely tenuous, and the weakness (from an accountability standpoint) of international judicial accommodation is most evident.

The consistent approach taken by the court and commission to frequent derogations by the United Kingdom is a prime example of these themes.[92] Employing a legislative model of accommodation, the United Kingdom has both utilized special emergency legislation and modified ordinary law (sometimes simultaneously) in its domestic resort to emergency powers. However, some aspects of the United Kingdom's

---

[90] James Beckett, "The *Greek Case* before the European Human Rights Commission" (1970–71) 1 *Human Rights* 91 at 113; Hartman, "Derogation," 29.

[91] The Prevention of Terrorism (Temporary Provisions) Act 1974, 48 Halsbury Stat. 972 (3rd edn, 1978) (Eng) is the classic example of this phenomenon.

[92] Derogation of Aug. 20, 1971, 1971 YB Eur. Conv. on HR 32 (Eur. Comm'n on HR); Derogation of Jan. 23, 1973, 1973 Eur. Conv. on HR 24 (Eur. Comm'n on HR); Derogation of Aug. 16, 1973, 1973 YB Eur. Conv. on HR 26 (Eur. Comm'n on HR); Derogation of Dec. 18, 1978, 1978 YB Eur. Conv. on HR 22, (Eur. Comm'n on HR); Derogation of Dec. 23, 1988, 1988 YB Eur. Conv. on HR 15 (Eur Comm'n on HR); Derogation of Mar. 23, 1989, 1989 YB Eur. Conv. on HR 8 (Eur. Comm'n on HR). Most recently see Human Rights Act (Designated Derogation) Order 2001, which came into effect on Nov. 13, 2001.

response – including the unregulated or unproclaimed use of martial law,[93] and the patterns of state behavior exhibited in the use of lethal force by law enforcement agencies throughout the conflict in Northern Ireland[94] – shade into the realm of extra-legality.

On August 9, 1971, the British government reintroduced into Northern Ireland such measures as detention and internment. At least some of the detainees were subjected to the "five techniques" – hooding, standing against a wall, subjection to noise, deprivation of food and water, and deprivation of sleep – during their interrogation.[95] In *Ireland v. United Kingdom*,[96] the Irish government contended that the detention and internment without trial violated articles 5 and 6 of the European Convention. It also argued that these measures were not "strictly required by the exigencies of the situation" and that the British government's detention and internment policy discriminated against Northern Ireland's minority Catholic community. Finally, the Irish government claimed that the use of the five techniques violated the British government's obligations under article 3 of the European Convention, which is included in the list of non-derogable rights. Notably, the Irish government did not dispute the existence of an emergency situation in Northern Ireland.[97]

The European Commission concluded that, as implemented under the domestic emergency legislation, the powers of detention and internment without trial did, in fact, violate the provisions of article 5 of the European Convention.[98] Thus, it then had to examine whether these measures could be justified under article 15. On this question, the commission was unanimous in determining that at any point during the period relevant to the case, detention without trial was indeed "strictly required by the exigencies of the situation."[99] Again by a unanimous vote, however, the commission concluded that the combined use of the five techniques during the interrogations of several detainees amounted to torture within the meaning of article 3 of the European

---

[93] Colm Campbell and Ita Connolly, "A Model for the War against Terrorism? Military Intervention in Northern Ireland and the 1970 Falls Curfew" (2003) 30 *Journal of Law and Society* 341.

[94] Fionnuala Ní Aoláin, *The Politics of Force: Conflict Management and State Violence in Northern Ireland* (Belfast: Blackstaff Press, 2000).

[95] See discussion in chapter 4.

[96] Ireland v. United Kingdom, 1976 YB Eur. Conv. on HR (Eur. Comm'n on HR).

[97] Ibid., at 542–44.   [98] Ibid., at 578–80.

[99] Ibid., at 602. For critique of the commission's approach see, for example, Hartman, "Derogation," 33–34; Rosalyn Higgins, "Derogations under Human Rights Treaties" (1976–1977), 48 *British Yearbook of International Law* 281 at 304.

Convention.[100] Yet, neither the court nor the commission paid significant attention to its obligation meaningfully to examine whether, in fact, a situation of emergency existed, as opposed to examining whether the specific measures were "strictly required" by the situation.[101] In fact, although the Republic of Ireland did not contest the existence of a "public emergency threatening the life of the nation" in Northern Ireland at the relevant times, the commission affirmatively found that such an emergency did exist.[102] Yet, the circumstances of the Northern Irish conflict, so well depicted by the commission in its report, strongly challenge the fundamental premises upon which the derogation system is based. The commission began its report by stating that "[t]he *lasting crisis* in Northern Ireland gave rise to the present application...The present emergency is not as such in dispute between the parties. *It began in 1966* with the first use of violence for political ends in Northern Ireland in recent years."[103] It is difficult to reconcile this statement with the commission and court definitions of "public emergency threatening the life of the nation," which emphasize that a state of "public emergency" is an exceptional phenomenon and a temporary deviation from the normal state of affairs. Yet neither the commission nor the court acknowledged the strain that such a "prolonged crisis" put on the derogation regime. Similarly, neither institution addressed the fact that the United Kingdom has practically maintained an ongoing derogation notice with respect to Northern Ireland. That, too, ran against the theoretical underpinnings of the derogation system. The formalistic approach taken by both the court and the commission to the emergency justification question gave the United Kingdom evident judicial approval within which it could maintain both a legal and political narrative about the bona fide use of a legislative accommodation model to contain a bona fide emergency. It presents a real danger that derogation merely becomes another form of international rubberstamping for the state, which can be compounded by the failure of domestic legal and political institutions to perform

---

[100] Ireland v. United Kingdom (Commission), at 794, 930. For its part, the court refused to rule that each of the five techniques amounted to "torture," instead labeling each of them "inhuman or degrading treatment." Ireland v. United Kingdom (1978) 25 Eur. Ct HR (ser. A), paras. 167–68.

[101] See Pieter Van Dijk and Godefridus J.H. Van Hoof, *Theory and Practice of the European Convention on Human Rights* (3rd edn, Boston, MA: Kluwer Law International, 1998), pp. 552–53 (noting that preliminary determination of "public emergency" is essential to determining whether derogations applied are "strictly required").

[102] Ireland v. United Kingdom (Commission), at 584–86.

[103] Ibid., at 512 (emphasis added).

their oversight and monitoring functions during times of crisis. Two subsequent judgments, both dealing with the United Kingdom, follow a similar pattern of deference to a democratic state that asserts a state of emergency. Both cases involve violations of article 5 of the European Convention, protecting due process rights under the convention.

Brogan and Others v. United Kingdom concerned the arrest and detention of four persons under Section 12 of the Prevention of Terrorism (Temporary Provisions) Act 1984. All were held in detention centers for periods ranging from four days and six hours to six days and sixteen-and-a-half hours. All were subsequently released without criminal charge. Technically this was not a derogation case, as the United Kingdom had in fact withdrawn its notice of derogation. Thus, the respondent government made no claim for derogation with respect to the factual or legal circumstances giving rise to this case. We review the case nonetheless because, while the court concluded that a breach of article 5 had occurred, it also posited its views that such a breach could be contextualized in relation to the ongoing terrorist campaign in Northern Ireland.[104] This suggests a "derogation through the back door approach," one which confirms a more lax judicial review for democratic states over those with less convincing political credentials. Moreover, *Brogan* illustrates classic interpretive accommodation (which may also be read as the "soft" version of the Business as Usual model), whereby the rule stays the same but the outcome may vary dependent on context (here the assertion of the crisis created by terrorism).

This contextualized approach is illustrated by the fact that though the court specifically recognized that the United Kingdom had withdrawn its notice of derogation, its reasoning is contextual and crisis-influenced. Thus, for example, the court's majority opinion states that the exclusion of a derogation examination "does not, however, preclude proper account being taken of the *background circumstances* of the case."[105] Referring to an earlier court decision, the majority opinion continues to remark that "having taken notice of the growth of terrorism in modern society, [the court] has already recognised the need, inherent in the Convention system, for a proper balance between the defence of the institutions of democracy in the common interest and the protection of individual rights."[106] Such language could, without any need

---

[104] Brogan and Others v. United Kingdom, 145-B Eur. Ct HR (ser. A) at 16 (1988).

[105] Ibid., at 27 (emphasis added).

[106] Ibid., para. 48, at 27. The opinions written by the seven dissenting judges of the court resonated with explicit, derogation-like language. Ibid., at 39–40.

for modification, be transplanted into any emergency-related judicial decision.

The court (and the commission) recognized the possibility of "context justification" for governmental actions that in fact derogated from otherwise protected rights and permitted derogation treatment in circumstances in which none of the parties coming before the court or the commission formally requested it. Essentially, the position adopted in *Brogan* enabled the British government to enjoy the fruits of derogation without having to incur the legal and political costs of such a formal act. The long-term imprint of this has a contemporary reading, where many states have extended their emergency powers or reformulated their ordinary laws with an emergency spin as a result of the events of September 11, but have not entered derogation notices based on the measures taken. *Brogan* constitutes a prime example of a court finding that a democratic government is making a good-faith effort to preserve human rights, and de facto giving the state a wider margin of appreciation than those states with lesser reputations for rights enforcement.[107] Setting the balance of discretion in favor of democratic states is directly aided by the use of context justification. The context is the full acceptance of the state's assessment of the existence of a terrorist or other political threat, imported into the core of the judicial argument which then becomes the baseline from which legal justifications follow. The sub-text of this justification is an unwillingness to impute to democratic states the negation that regularly occurs in respect of rights in situations where the government perceives threats to the democratic or public order, whether objectively based or not. Given that the derogation was not an issue, as it had been withdrawn by the United Kingdom four years earlier, its mention, despite its subsequent exclusion, highlights the positioning of its potential permissibility. As noted above, the judgment contains pervasive references to the ongoing campaign of terrorist violence in Northern Ireland.[108] This is used, in turn, to give a judicial interpretive emergency spin to "ordinary" norms (in this case human rights treaty provisions). The timbre of this language post-September 11 is particularly compelling where nebulous references to the pervasiveness of terrorist threat have fundamentally affected the manner in which states contextualize the extension of anti-terrorist and criminal legislation to combat a variety of behaviors. This is not unexpected. However, those who place

---

[107] Mangan, "Protecting Human Rights," 379–82.
[108] Brogan, at 21–24, 27, 33.

some faith in the capacity of international judicial oversight to balance out the overreaction of states may be disappointed. Hence, while in *Brogan* the United Kingdom was found to be in breach of article 5(1) of the European Convention, the approach taken was potentially a backwards step.[109] The court was fulsome on the question of proportionate measures interpreted in a manner that extended a rationale containing emergency-like justification into the core of decision-making in a non-emergency context.

Immediately following the decision of the European Court of Human Rights in *Brogan*, on November 28, 1988, the United Kingdom, in December 1988, issued a further notice of derogation in respect of article 5(3).[110] Yet the derogation notice did not include any mention of events or developments taking place after August 22, 1984 (the date on which the previous derogation notice was withdrawn) that might justify the conclusion that a state of emergency had developed in the United Kingdom since that date, except for a brief reference to the court's adverse judgment in *Brogan*. Thus, there is a cogent argument that the derogation was issued as a direct response to the judgment rather than to any upsurge in violence or increased threat to the security of the state.[111] The accommodation sought by the state was thus in response to an external legal decision, rather than to the facts on the ground. Under these circumstances, one could question whether a "public emergency threatening the life of the nation" did in fact exist in Northern Ireland in December 1988, as compared with the situation prevailing in that area in August 1984, which, by the British government's own admission, did not constitute a public emergency. We suggest that the challenge for the European Court ought to have been whether it had the capacity

---

[109] See de Jong, Baljet, and van den Brink, 77 Eur. Ct HR (ser. A) at 21–22.

[110] See European Commission of Human Rights, Minutes of the Plenary Session, Strasbourg Jan. 16–20, 1989, DH (89) (Déf), Appendix VI at 10.

[111] Note the statement of Douglas Hogg, at the time under-secretary of state for the Home Department, to the House of Commons on Dec. 13, 1998: "The case of Brogan and Others has rightly exercised Honourable Members' minds. The Committee will recall that my right honourable friend the Home Secretary told the House on 6 December that we shall bring forward our proposal for responding to the judgement in the Brogan case as soon as possible and before the Bill leaves the House. The matter is complex, and whether we opt for derogation or some sort of judicial control, the implications are obviously far reaching." Quoted in UNHCR, US Lawyers Committee Country Reports, "At the Crossroads: Human Rights and the Northern Ireland Peace Process" (Dec. 1, 1996), available online at http://www.unhcr.ch/cgibin/texis/vtx/print?tbl=RSDCOI&id=3ae6a5944 (last visited Aug. 8, 2005).

and willingness to enquire fully into the reasons for the government's legal response, and thus probe the primary question of emergency justification.

Brannigan and McBride, which followed *Brogan*, confirmed the trend that democratic states resorting to the use of emergency powers in the European system experenced an "easier ride" than their newer or less ostensibly liberal counterparts. It also verified the unwillingness of the court to look behind the stated rationale for formal accommodation by states whether in legislative or executive form. A critical analysis of the case reveals that the court failed to examine the possibility that the United Kingdom's derogation was simply a response to an adverse court decision.[112]

The facts of *Brannigan and McBride* were substantially similar to those of *Brogan*. This time, however, the British government conceded that article 5(3)'s promptness requirement had not been met. However, the government invoked as a defense the derogation notice it had submitted in December 1988, claiming that the article 5(3) violation was justified under article 15. The issue, then, was whether the derogation was a valid one under article 15, namely the very question that the court did not have to deal with in *Brogan*.[113] The applicants in this case contended specifically that the derogation entered by the state was merely a mechanical response to the finding in *Brogan*. Amicus briefs stressed to the court that there existed empirical evidence to dispute the claim that a truly exceptional situation existed justifying a continued state of emergency.[114] Yet both the court and the commission maintained that while the judgment in *Brogan* "triggered off"[115] the derogation, there was no reason to conclude that the derogation of 1988 was anything other than a "genuine response" to a persistent emergency situation.[116]

The unwillingness of the court to examine whether the state was actually experiencing such a level of violence and threat that necessitated a resort to emergency powers is a clear manifestation of an unwarranted non-interference principle. It points to the dangers we have illustrated in chapter 1 that accommodation models do not necessarily encourage the judicial branch to act as a meaningful guardian of individual rights and liberties. It demonstrates timidity on the part of the court, which parallels the general responses of domestic courts to review of crisis

---

[112] Brannigan and McBride, at 37.   [113] Brogan, para. 48, at 28.
[114] Brannigan and McBride, at 36.   [115] Ibid., para. 51 at 34.   [116] Ibid.

powers by the state.[117] It shows that while accommodation models keep the state's regulation of emergency within the frame of law, this may not actually be synonymous with meaningful legal oversight of crisis powers. Moreover, the court's statement that there was no indication that the derogation was other than a genuine response seems to mean that the applicants had to demonstrate that the derogation was not genuine. This illustrates the danger of the burden of proof shifting silently in favor of the state in a way that circumvents the rationale behind the accommodation model's legal foundations and creates the danger that it functions only as an edifice for accountability.

The *Brannigan and McBride* decision also serves to illustrate another theme we have highlighted in respect of international judicial oversight, namely, the particularly difficult problem that international courts encounter when they seek to confront permanent emergencies. As noted above, one of the "four basic elements" of an emergency is its provisional and temporary character.[118] We have argued elsewhere that, all other things being equal, the longer an emergency persists the narrower, not wider, the margin of appreciation to the state should be.[119] Yet, in *Brannigan and McBride*, the court adopted an extremely broad conception of the margin of appreciation, stating that:

> By reason of their direct and continuous contact with the pressing needs of the moment, *the national authorities are in principle in a better position than the international judge* to decide both on the presence of such an emergency and on the nature and scope of derogations necessary to avert it. Accordingly, in this matter *a wide margin of appreciation should be left to the national authorities.*[120]

More generally, in the Northern Ireland cases and in a series of cases emanating from the conflict in Turkey, the European Court and Commission have consistently sidestepped the issue of permanent emergencies by regarding each derogation case as a singular exception. By doing so the court ignores the fact that the same respondent government may be appearing frequently before it with respect to the same situation of exigency. By refusing to regard the history or frequency of previous derogations as relevant to the arbitration of the particular issue before

---

[117] Alejandro M. Garro and Henry Dahl, "Legal Accountability for Human Rights Violations in Argentina: One Step Forward and Two Steps Backward" (1987) 8 *Human Rights Law Journal* 284.

[118] Chowdhury, *Rule of Law in a State of Emergency*, pp. 24–29.

[119] Gross and Ní Aoláin, "From Discretion to Scrutiny."

[120] Brannigan and McBride, para. 43, at 49 (emphases added); see also ibid., para. 59, at 54.

the court, the issue is never addressed. This makes evident in the international context the problems of separation between normalcy and emergency that arise in the regulation of emergencies, as outlined in chapter 4. This also serves to illustrate a wider point, explored further below, that the conceptualization of emergencies in international legal thinking is limited. Accommodation models match the "ideal" form of derogation, where the state derogates for a finite period of time and then following the emergency's end returns to the status quo ante. However, in practice accommodation models are ill-tested in coming to terms with the "aberrational emergency," i.e., that emergency which is permanent, undisclosed, or complex in nature. The point becomes particularly apparent when one examines the Turkish cases concerning article 15 which have come to the court. A common thread of these cases is the allegations of ongoing human rights abuses in the struggle against the Kurdistan Workers Party (PKK). Turkey has invoked article 15 derogations for much of the time since 1970. Domestically, most of the provinces of south-eastern Turkey have been continuously subjected to an emergency regime.

The Turkish cases highlight a number of the general themes we have identified in earlier cases. First, concerning the variance in the court's approach to the primary justification question contrasted with the secondary question regarding the proportionality of emergency measures, the Turkish cases provide some interesting interpretive nuances. We suggest that these cases prove that the court can be fairly robust when it comes to measuring the necessity and proportionality of particular measures taken by a derogating state. Second, the court demonstrates a markedly more activist jurisprudence when faced with a recalcitrant state whose democratic credentials are suspect. Third, the cases reveal a structural inability to deal credibly with permanent emergencies. Finally, due process rights remain consistently and flagrantly violated by states resorting to emergency powers and practices, whether they are derogating formally from their treaty obligations or not.

In *Aksoy v. Turkey*, the commission and the court examined the validity of the Turkish derogation from article 15 in the context of the applicant's detention and alleged ill-treatment in custody for approximately fourteen days in November 1992.[121] The derogation in place was limited

---

[121] Aksoy v. Turkey, 23 Eur. HR Rep. 553 (Dec. 18, 1996). There was dispute as to the length of detention time. The commission, based on its fact-finding mission to the region, concluded that the applicant was held for at least fourteen days. Ibid., at para. 23.

to article 5 protections only. Both commission and court demonstrated again their reluctance to examine substantively the emergency justification question. Thus, the commission briefly disposed of the question, concluding that: "There is no serious dispute between the parties as to the existence of a public emergency in South-East Turkey threatening the life of the nation. In view of the grave threat posed by terrorism in this region, the Commission can only conclude that there is indeed a state of emergency in South-East Turkey which threatens the life of the nation."[122] For its part, the court examined the issue only perfunctorily, ruling that "in the light of all the material before it...the particular extent and impact of PKK terrorist activity in South-East Turkey has undoubtedly created, in the region concerned, a 'public emergency threatening the life of the nation.'"[123] The court repeated its consistent assertion that states had a "wide margin of appreciation" in deciding whether they were facing a public emergency.[124] It did not second guess the state's call that an emergency was in play, nor seek to tease out the role of the state versus the role of non-state actors (if any) in the circumstances which created the emergency. This approach is striking when contrasted with three other elements of the court's decision. First, the court asserted that in exercising its supervision over states' actions, it "must give appropriate weight to such relevant factors as the nature of the rights affected by the derogation and the circumstances leading to, *and the duration of*, the emergency situation."[125] Second, discussing the Turkish government's compliance with the notification requirements of article 15(3), the court pointed out that it was competent to examine this issue of its own motion, although none of those appearing before it had contested that Turkey's notice of derogation complied with the formal requirements of article 15(3).[126] Finally, as regards the secondary question of proportionality of measures the court was markedly more interventionist. Reiterating its view that seven-day detention accompanied by derogation (the *Brannigan* situation) was within the bounds permissible under the European Convention, it went on to state that fourteen-day detention was outside that perimeter.[127] Thus, an article 5 violation was upheld notwithstanding the state's derogation.

Regarding the difference of approach toward democratic states and those with more suspect credentials, the *Sakik and Others v. Turkey* case is

---

[122] Ibid., at 572 (Commission report).   [123] Ibid., at 587.   [124] Ibid., at 571, 586–87.
[125] Ibid., at 587 (emphasis added).   [126] Ibid., at 590.   [127] Ibid., at para. 84.

instructive.[128] The case concerned the arrest and detention of six former members of the Turkish National Assembly who were prosecuted in a national security court. At issue was extended detention (fourteen days) and all the detainees had been charged with terrorist offenses. The court showed a markedly less deferential stance to the state's views than was evident in the Northern Ireland cases. The applicable derogation had been submitted in August 1990. The notice was highly specific both in its geographical scope of application and the rights affected (article 5).

The judgment is particularly illuminating as the court made some substantial inroads on meaningfully assessing the primary question of emergency justification. The court reviewed whether the derogation in force at the time of the alleged violation was in fact applicable to the facts of the case. It found that the derogation applied only to the region where a state of emergency had been proclaimed, and did not include the city of Ankara (where the applicants were arrested, detained, and subjected to trial). Thus, the court forcefully held that it would be working against the purpose of article 15 if the territorial scope of the provision were to be extended judicially to a part of the state not explicitly named in the notice of derogation. The court here was working through and applying spatial distinctions to the exercise of emergency powers, and on some level seeking to make legally meaningful the political and legal characteristics held by the state itself, which maintained that two legal regimes could be contemporaneously applied within the territory controlled by the state. In this case the court held that article 15 did not apply to the facts of the case.

The procedural point marks a neat but substantial barrier created by the court to state use of the derogation mechanism. Instead of accepting the government's position that the terrorist threat was not confined to any particular part of the state and that an expansive reading was required to ensure a return to normality in the jurisdiction, the court required the state to live with the consequences of its own political assessment of the threat as expressed in the notice of derogation. While setting a strong procedural precedent, the approach holds some dangers in that the state might simply respond by reformulating the derogation to have wider territorial scope. Yet, this is a court setting limits on the boundaries of interpretive accommodation. The court's language and tone are entirely different from that of its *Brogan* and *Brannigan and*

---

[128] Sakik and Others v. Turkey [1997] ECHR 95 (Nov. 26, 1997), 58 Reports of Judgments and Decisions 2609, 2628, Holding PP 2, 5, 7 (1997-VII).

McBride jurisprudence where the court demonstrated little willingness to second guess the bona fides of the state in its choice of executive response to an adverse derogation decision. Obviously, the democratic credentials of the state under scrutiny may affect this assessment. This again highlights the difference of judicial analysis with respect to the lesser established democracies, one that is not always positive for the overall standards set in derogation review.

The *Sakik* judgment also has a number of contributions to make concerning the violation of due process rights. The court's views have strong contemporary resonance in light of the procedures put in place by the United States with respect to persons detained in Afghanistan and Iraq.[129] These views are particularly important given our contention that the case law demonstrates that the first port of call for states when faced with a crisis is to modify or limit the application of due process rights. The Turkish government argued that the scale and nature of the terrorist threat had made it particularly difficult to obtain evidence, thereby making it difficult to proceed with trials in a speedy fashion. While acknowledging that terrorist offenses presented meaningful difficulties for the state, the court trenchantly held that "This does not mean, however, that the investigating authorities have *carte blanche* under Article 5 to arrest suspects for questioning, free from effective control by the domestic courts and ultimately, by the Convention supervisory institutions, whenever they choose to assert that terrorism is involved."[130] The court went on to state that the time the applicants were held in police custody (twelve and fourteen days respectively) fell outside the strict constraints of article 5(3). Most compelling was the court's statement that even "supposing that the activities...were linked to a terrorist threat," the court could not accept that it was necessary to detain the applicants for the time periods in question without judicial intervention.[131] One can again speculate as to whether the democratic credentials of the state have some bearing on the robustness of the judicial analysis.

These themes of heightened scrutiny in respect of suspect democracies allied with the frailty of due process rights in times of emergency are also evident in *Demir and Others v. Turkey*.[132] The decision in this case

---

[129] See, for example, Executive Order of Nov. 13, 2001: Detention, Treatment, and Trial of Certain Non-Citizens in the War against Terrorism, 66 Fed. Reg. 57, 833 (Nov. 13, 2001), para. 4.

[130] Sakik and Others v. Turkey, at para. 44.

[131] Ibid., at para. 45.

[132] Demir and Others v. Turkey (21380/93) (1998) ECHR 88 (Sept. 23, 1998).

also confirms the court's activism regarding the proportionality aspects of derogation. The three applicants were politically active, holding positions in the People's Social Democratic Party. All three were arrested in 1993, and were held for between sixteen and twenty-three days.[133] They were subsequently charged and convicted of offenses under the Criminal Code and Terrorism Act. At the time of the arrests the Turkish derogation was expressly limited to article 5.

The court briskly held, with reference to *Brogan v. United Kingdom*, that the periods of detention in *Demir* failed to satisfy the requirement of "promptness" laid down in article 5(3).[134] This was notwithstanding the government's insistence that the measures were taken to protect the community from terrorism. Without elaboration the court noted that, where necessary, the authorities facing terrorist threats could "develop forms of judicial control which are adapted to the circumstances but compatible with the Convention."[135] It then examined the government's contention that the derogation absolved it of any convention violation. The court affirmed that states enjoyed a "wide" margin of appreciation in deciding the presence of an emergency and the nature and scope of the derogation necessary to deal with it, confirming its generally deferential approach to the emergency justification question. In deciding whether the state had overstepped the bounds of derogation, the court weighed such factors as the nature of the rights affected by the derogation as well as the circumstances leading to, and the duration of, the emergency.[136] Once again, the court accepted that a public emergency "threatening the life of the nation" existed in south-east Turkey.

The court was more stringent in its requirements when reviewing the specific measures that Turkey had invoked. It seemed particularly struck by the state's failure to show why "the fight against terrorism in south-east Turkey rendered any judicial intervention impracticable."[137] It noted that the mere fact that a detention is in conformity with domestic law does not fireproof it from an article 15 review.[138] Nor was the court prepared to agree with the government's position that article 5(3) could not be applied when investigations were ongoing. Instead it asserted that this was precisely when article 5(3) was enforceable.[139] It further held that subsequent conviction for terrorist offenses had no bearing on the question of whether there was a "situation which necessitated

---

[133] The exact length of detention was disputed by the parties. Ibid., at 13.
[134] Ibid., at paras. 39–41.   [135] Ibid., at para. 41.   [136] Ibid., at para. 43.
[137] Ibid., at para. 51.   [138] Ibid., at para. 52.   [139] Ibid.

the detention of suspects incommunicado for such lengthy periods."[140] In short, the applicants' subsequent terrorism-related convictions did not retroactively justify lengthy periods of prior detention. The court was also concerned about the lack of safeguards during the detention, especially lack of access to counsel and the insufficiency of medical oversight. In conclusion the court held that the length of detention was not strictly required by the crisis.

The *Demir* case arguably demonstrates how a lack of scrutiny on the primary question – does an emergency exist that could justify a derogation? – was traded off against the narrower question of the necessity and proportionality of the specific emergency measures taken by the respondent state. This reflects the regional political balancing of the court: a necessary degree of deference to the contracting states, while leaving enough space to mount a credible defense of convention-protected rights around it. It also reflects a central tension of accommodation models and more specifically of their oversight, namely, that while one can tinker within the models to measure the breadth and scope of legal conformity within the assigned legal space, this rarely extends to allow for the core regulatory aspects of the models themselves to come under scrutiny. That is to say, it generally operates on the assumption of the general necessity for a legally regulated crisis response, but has a limited legal and political vocabulary to challenge the reality of the crisis assertion in the first place.

This approach has continued in the court's case law since the events of September 11, 2001. For example, in *Ocalan v. Turkey* the court found that while the investigation of terrorist offenses undoubtedly presented the authorities with special problems, "this does not mean that the investigating authorities have *carte blanche* under Article 5 to arrest suspects for questioning, free from effective controls by the domestic courts."[141] In *Al-Nashif v. Bulgaria*, a case concerning deportation and detention, the court determined that national authorities could not "do away with" effective control of the lawfulness of detention by choosing to assert that national security and terrorism were involved.[142] Yet, a thorough review of whether invoking an emergency is per se justified remained consistently

---

[140] Ibid., at para. 53.

[141] Ocalan v. Turkey (46221/99) (2003) ECHR 125 (Mar. 12, 2003), para. 106; Filiz and Kalkan v. Turkey (34481/97) (2002) ECHR 504 (June 20, 2002), paras. 25–26.

[142] Al-Nashif v. Bulgaria (50963/99) (2002) ECHR 497 (June 20, 2002), paras. 94, 123–24. A more thorough examination of the court's review of terrorism-related cases is contained in chapter 7.

off limits. This means that states can rest assured, to some degree, that their overall sovereign rights to resort to exceptional measures in times of crisis are not affected, nor will their political reactions and measurements be undercut. However, at the point of exercising these limitations states also know that the court will operate as if it is applying the twin tests of proportionality and necessity to their assessment of state behavior. This is classic accommodation being practiced by an international court. This supervision is not meaningless, and certainly not without effect. However, it generally fails to deal with the wider problems that accompany emergencies, namely, the tendency for emergencies to be prolonged and to become permanent; the capacity of emergency powers to be subsumed into the ordinary law; and the capacity of emergency powers to distort the normal functions of executive, legislative, and judicial power within states. These problematic characteristics will be dealt with below.

Judicial accommodation at the Inter-American Court

The Inter-American human rights enforcement system tracks the twin accommodation structures along similar lines to the European Convention. The American Convention itself acts as a form of international legislative authority for contracting states to derogate, and the case law of the Inter-American Court provides an interpretive accommodation mechanism for states in times of crisis. However, while many of the issues that we have highlighted in respect of the European Court of Human Rights are duplicated by its Inter-American counterpart, there are some notable differences.

The jurisprudence of the Inter-American Court of Human Rights is markedly sparser than that of the European Court. This is in part explained by the fact that the role of the Inter-American Commission on Human Rights is different from that fulfilled in the past by the European Commission. The IACHR plays a prominent part in regulating the recourse to emergency powers in the region. As we trace below, the court has been extremely activist in its emergency-related jurisprudence, a product of the hemisphere's long and tragic experiences with dictatorships, authoritarian regimes, and the profound abuse of emergency powers. We also suggest that the suspect quality of many of the region's democracies, particularly in the early years of the court's existence, confirms the pattern of more stringent review with problematic democracies. The court's jurisprudence also affirms the pressure that due process rights experience in times of crisis. Finally, there is also strong evidence of structural and jurisprudential limitations when confronting permanent states of emergency.

Many of these themes are highlighted in the first and most significant case before the Inter-American Court, namely the advisory opinion in *Judicial Guarantees in a State of Emergency*.[143]

As we noted above, limitations on due process rights are often the first port of call for states limiting rights protections in times of crisis. The European Convention, the American Convention, and the ICCPR all allow for derogation of due process rights. A significant test for the enforcement and monitoring bodies that operate under these treaties is the extent to which they are prepared to defend robustly limitations on such crucial rights. The *Judicial Guarantees* decision demonstrates the strengths of the Inter-American Court in this respect. In finding an expansive scope for the non-derogable character of judicial guarantees the court recognized that the exercise of emergency powers was potentially fraught with abuse and could lead to subversion of the democratic order.[144] The court was clearly setting limits on its willingness to accommodate, essentially limiting the expansion of state powers in times of crisis. The court took a far-reaching view on interlinking rights in emergency contexts rather than narrowing its focus on non-derogable rights per se. It examined the extent to which judicial guarantees and remedies could be minimized in a period of emergency in accordance with article 27 of the American Convention.[145] Here the court concluded that some fundamental guarantees may never be excluded and that "judicial guarantees essential for the protection of such rights" are immune from limitation.[146] It held that the due process guarantees of article 8 – which protect the right to fair trial, and which include the right to a hearing by a competent, independent tribunal; the right to be presumed innocent; the right to notification of pending criminal charges; the right to counsel of choice; the right to examine witnesses; and the right of appeal to a higher court – could not be suspended in times of emergency in so far as they are prerequisites for the necessary functioning of judicial safeguards.

Unique about this judgment is the court's multi-layered approach, recognizing rights as knitted into one another, interdependent and inseparable. Thus, to speak of rights protection in situations of emergency is to weave together the rights that guarantee protection rather than

---

[143] Judicial Guarantees in States of Emergency, at 24.
[144] Ibid., at 98.   [145] Ibid., at 24.   [146] Ibid.

to isolate certain non-derogable rights as being sufficient per se to protect the individual against potential excesses by the state. This is an approach that recognizes that the core and the penumbra of derogable and non-derogable rights are interlinked and mutually significant. It offers not only substantive appraisal within an accommodation model but a significant maneuvering by the court to expand its oversight capacity in the context of acute crises. The approach is partly explicable by reference to the abuse of emergency powers in the region. The *Judicial Guarantees* judgment and the cases that follow it draw directly from the experience of the hemisphere.[147] The court recognizes that the exercise of emergency powers is inherently fraught with abuse and leads to the subversion of the democratic order.[148] Again, there is an evident link to our thesis articulating the view that human rights courts are far more prepared to be vigorously defensive of rights violated by non-democratic or suspect states. Yet, the court's approach also demonstrates what an activist-minded tribunal can do within the overall accommodation model expressly to limit the range of legitimate actions by the state in times of emergency.

The court's views highlight a strong regional variance in approach to emergency powers. The *Judicial Guarantees in a State of Emergency* decision affirms that the nature, and therefore the appropriate examination, of emergencies can vary. The court states that "what might be permissible in one type of emergency would not be lawful in another."[149] This distinction illustrates the subtlety and depth needed to address different kinds of crises that are subsumed under the "emergency" label. The court recognizes the differences in intensity and length of emergency. Its opinion develops, potentially, a tailored complex approach to international judicial intervention. It offers the possibility that the court might be prepared to examine the totality of recourse to emergency powers, including the fraught question of whether resort to derogation was justified by the exigencies that the relevant state experienced. This is ultimately the most far-reaching tool in the accommodation kit, allowing

---

[147] C.G. Brown, *Chile since the Coup: Ten Years of Repression* (New York: Americas Watch, 1983); Juan E. Méndez, *Truth and Partial Justice in Argentina* (New York: Americas Watch, 1987); Lawyers Committee for Human Rights, *Uruguay: The End of a Nightmare?* (New York: Lawyers Committee for Human Rights, 1984); David Bitel, *The Failed Promise: Human Rights in the Philippines since the Revolution of 1986* (Geneva: International Commission of Jurists, 1991); Amnesty International, *Nicaragua: The Human Rights Record* (London: Amnesty International Publications, 1986).

[148] Judicial Guarantees in States of Emergency, at 98.

[149] Ibid., at 99.

the court a meaningful opportunity to declare that a government's views on the nature and extent of the emergency are not justified and cannot be accommodated or legitimated.

The court's approach was confirmed subsequently in the *Habeas Corpus in Emergency Situations* decision.[150] Here the court was asked to express its views on the question of whether the writ of habeas corpus constituted an "essential judicial guarantee" that could not be suspended by a state party in a time of emergency. The court gave detailed consideration to the nature of an emergency situation as well as to the scope of the non-derogable judicial guarantees language contained in article 27(2) of the American Convention.

The regional variance is clearly evident, as is the strong emphasis on substantive defense of due process rights. The court made it clear that the derogation privilege did not allow for rights to be absolutely suspended in an emergency situation. Rather, only their "full and effective" exercise could be limited.[151] Even in times of crisis the state operates within the rule of law and cannot operate outside the law to protect the legal and political order.[152] The court says that the right to derogate "does not mean ... that the suspension of guarantees implies a temporary suspension of the rule of law, nor does it authorize those in power to act in disregard of the principle of legality by which they are bound at all times."[153]

As with the *Judicial Guarantees* decision the court strongly emphasized the regional experience of emergencies and emergency powers, and forcefully argued that exercise of derogation could only be legally valid when operating in tandem with the "effective exercise of representative democracy."[154] The court stressed the exceptional nature of a resort to emergency powers, and confirmed that the lawfulness of measures taken would depend upon the "character, intensity, pervasiveness, and the particular context of the emergency and upon the corresponding proportionality and reasonableness of the measures."[155]

With respect to the particular question before it in this case, the court explained that the determination as to what judicial remedies were essential would differ depending on the rights that were at stake. The

---

[150] Habeas Corpus in Emergency Situations, Advisory Opinion, OC-8/97 (Ser. A), Jan. 30, 1987.

[151] Ibid., at para. 18.

[152] Notably here the court quibbles with the use of the term "suspension" in the treaty language while effectively limiting its meaning: "Nevertheless, the Court will use the phrase 'suspension of guarantees' that is found in the Convention." Ibid., at para. 18.

[153] Ibid., at para. 24.   [154] Ibid., at para. 20.   [155] Ibid., at para. 24.

court then proceeded to characterize the active component of habeas corpus (literally bringing the person before the court) as performing a vital role in ensuring the physical safety and integrity of the person, relevant both to freedom from torture and to liberty rights. The court also found the procedural aspect of habeas corpus necessary to facilitate the verification of whether in fact emergency legislative measures authorizing detention were lawful. In such a context, habeas corpus performed a dual oversight function. Following these statements the court held that the writs of habeas corpus and amparo (defined as the right of any individual to procedural protection by means of effective recourse to a court or tribunal) were among the judicial remedies that were essential for the various rights whose derogation was prohibited by article 27(2) of the American Convention. This is a robust application of oversight to a state's potential use of emergency powers, confirming both the presumption of legal means to regulate the resort to crisis and the right of the regional human rights court to oversee the process.

A strong concern about due process rights has continued to define the Inter-American Court's jurisprudence. While the court has relied heavily on the general approach of the European Court as regards the justification of emergency question, allied with a very activist approach to the proportionality of measures enquiry, there are indications in the judicial language of a willingness to go further than the European Court with respect to the primary question.

In *Neira Alegria et al. v. Peru*[156] the court examined the disappearance of three prisoners, all alleged terrorists held at El Frontón – a Peruvian prison – following armed intervention by special state forces to quell a riot between June 18 and 19, 1986.[157] The court decision was particularly forceful on the question of due process violation, although a violation of the right to life (article 4(1)) was also found. The court concluded that by its emergency declaration the state effectively suspended habeas corpus remedies, and thereby brought about a situation in which no effective judicial remedy existed to protect the victims of state actions in the emergency context. The court held further that Peru violated article 27(2) by declaring a state of emergency and applying the status of Restricted Military Zone to three correctional facilities.[158]

---

[156] Neira Alegria et al. v. Peru, Judgment of Jan. 19, 1995, Inter-Am. Ct HR (ser. C) No. 20 (1995).

[157] The state of emergency was alleged to have been declared by the government on June 2, 1986. Ibid.

[158] Ibid., at para. 77.

A steadfast retort to state practices in relation to limitations on due process rights, also indicative of consistency in relation to the court's concern with the proportionality of measures in times of emergency, is evident in the case of *Loayza Tamayo v. Peru*.[159] The applicant was tried and convicted in a "faceless" civil court, where the identity of the judges was kept secret. She alleged multiple due process violations as well as being subjected to torture and sexual violence while she was detained by the state, both before and after her trial. The Inter-American Court swiftly and firmly found that the provision in Peruvian emergency law that suspended the writ of habeas corpus constituted a flagrant violation of articles 5 and 27(2) of the American Convention.[160] The court also concluded that Professor Loayza Tamayo had suffered inhuman and degrading treatment. It concluded that "The exigencies of the investigation and the undeniable difficulties encountered in the anti-terrorist struggle must not be allowed to restrict the protection of a person's right to physical integrity."[161] The centrality of due process rights to individual protection in times of emergency was underscored throughout the court's opinion as was the court's insistence that no special deference was due to states' national security assertions.[162] Notably, while refusing to rule on the compatibility of military courts with the convention as a general matter, the court found that Peru's use of a military court in this case had breached article 8(2) of the convention.[163]

The legal status of military tribunals was revisited in *Castillo Petruzzi*, a case that reflects, once more, the court's consistency and deep-rooted views on the protection of procedural rights in times of emergency.[164] Again, the court's decision, like those of the European Court, does not deal directly with the primary question, namely whether the emergency was per se justified. At the same time the decision is consistent and demanding in its measurement of the proportionality of the state's responses to the claimed emergency. A number of Chilean nationals had been charged and convicted of treason.[165] The court took an extremely robust approach in a context resonating with contemporary legal and

---

[159] Loayza Tamayo v. Peru, Case 33, Inter-Am. CHR at P 57 (ser. C) (1997).
[160] Ibid., at paras. 50–55.   [161] Ibid., at para. 57.   [162] Ibid.
[163] Ibid., at para. 63. The court concluded further that the fact that Loayza Tamayo had been convicted in the civil courts on the basis of evidence that had acquitted her in the military courts, meant that she was subjected to unfair trial procedures in the civil courts in violation of article 8(4) of the convention.
[164] Castillo Petruzzi et al., Judgment of May 30, 1999, Inter-Am. Ct HR (ser. C) No. 52 (1999).
[165] The applicable domestic law was Decree-Law No. 25, 659.

political dilemmas about the rights of persons suspected of the most heinous offenses:

> [T]here can be no doubt that the State has the right and the duty to guarantee its own security. Nor is there any question that violations of the law occur in every society. But no matter how terrible certain actions may be and regardless of how guilty those in custody on suspicion of having committed certain crimes may be, the State does not have a license to exercise unbridled power or to use any means to achieve its ends, without regard for law or morals. The primacy of human rights is widely recognised. It is a primacy that the State can neither ignore nor abridge.[166]

As regards article 7 of the American Convention the court was particularly strong in its views. This illustrates the centrality of proportionality of measures to the court's thinking and confirms its willingness to be robust in defense of a derogable right. Thus, while acknowledging that article 7 incorporates a derogable right, the court effectively found that the state could not ignore its applicability in an emergency. Rather, the court confirmed that "the suspension of guarantees must not exceed the limits strictly required and that 'any action on the part of the public authorities that goes beyond those limits, which must be specified with precision in the decree promulgating the state of emergency, would ... be unlawful."[167] It held that a fifteen-day detention constituted a breach of article 7(5).

The final substantive issue that the court addressed was whether the trials of civilians, albeit as suspected terrorists, by faceless military courts constituted a violation of article 8 of the American Convention protecting the rights of persons to hearings by independent and impartial tribunals. The resonance of this judgment with current events in Guantanamo Bay is self-evident. Peru argued for the need to allow states to derogate and adopt extraordinary measures as permitted by article 27 of the convention when faced with "war, public danger or other emergency threatening the independence and security of a State Party." The court commenced its analysis by noting that military tribunals had very specific functions within Peru's Code of Military Justice. Specifically, such courts were permitted to try civilians for treason, but only when the country was at war abroad. In addition the military courts had jurisdiction for maintaining order and discipline within the ranks of the armed forces. The court resolved that "Transferring jurisdiction from civilian courts to military courts, thus allowing military courts to

---

[166] Castillo Petruzzi, at para. 204.   [167] Ibid., at para. 109.

try civilians accused of treason, means that the competent, independent and impartial tribunal previously established by law is precluded from hearing these cases."[168] In such contexts the right to due process was violated. Furthermore, the court found that under article 8(1) of the convention, presiding judges were required to be independent and impartial. Because the armed forces in Peru were simultaneously involved in counterinsurgency and prosecuting those charged with actions resulting from alleged insurgency, there was a clear absence of judicial impartiality.[169] Most significant was the court's insistence that the demands of fair trial in a situation of emergency required "the active involvement of an independent and impartial judicial body having the power to pass on the lawfulness of measures adopted in a state of emergency."[170] The court found that the state had violated article 8(1) as well as article 8(2)(b) (prior notification of charges), 8(2)(c) (adequate time and means to prepare defense), and 8(2)(d) (the right to counsel of choice). Finally and perhaps most pertinently, the court decided that the military proceedings in their faceless and secret form constituted a violation of article 8(5) which guarantees the right to public proceedings.[171]

Concluding our overview of the case law of the Inter-American system we note the strength of review and accountability of governmental response to crisis in the region is not solely dependent on the strength of the court's jurisprudence. One of the unique features of the Inter-American enforcement system is the operation and functioning of the Inter-American Commission. In particular, the commission has extremely well-developed procedures for on-site fact-finding that provides an extraordinarily useful tool in emergency contexts facilitating responsive international oversight.[172] Thus, for example, the commission's visit to Colombia in 1997 provided a timely opportunity for assessment of the internal conflict in, and the responses of, the state.[173] The breadth of access and issues identified is striking. Even more striking is the

---

[168] Ibid., at para. 128.   [169] Ibid., at para. 129.

[170] Ibid., at para. 131, citing *Habeas Corpus in Emergency Situations*, at para. 30.

[171] Also of note is the finding by the court that the guarantees of article 25 (Right to a Remedy) had been breached by the Peruvian authorities, by the lack of effective enforcement for the writ of habeas corpus. The court reiterated its view that remedies in this context were not only "paper" remedies but had to be truly effective in both ordinary and extraordinary times. Ibid., at para. 186.

[172] Provided for by the Statute of the Commission, article 18(g).

[173] Inter-American Commission on Human Rights, "Third Report on the Human Rights Situation in Colombia."

willingness of the commission to acknowledge and apply not only the standards of international human rights law but also norms that flow from international humanitarian law. This interlinking is critical in those situations where the emergency flows directly from some form of armed conflict taking place within the state, and where bifurcation of legal norms can actually serve to limit rather than to expand oversight. This is taken up further in the next chapter.

Accommodation at the United Nations: the Human Rights Committee

The interpretive capacity of the United Nations Human Rights Committee (HRC) is more limited than that of its regional counterparts. As such the HRC has a narrower capacity to pass judgment on the nature, form, and limitations to be imposed on states within the accommodation model that is set out in article 4 of the ICCPR. The limited format of HRC communications makes it difficult to draw general conclusions from the committee's case law.

The HRC has considered very few cases in which derogation under article 4 formed a substantive issue.[174] This fact is linked to the limited number of state parties to the ICCPR that have also signed the Optional Protocol, as well as to limited financial resources for applicants and a myriad other procedural obstacles. A particular problem is the status of HRC decisions after consideration of communications on their merits. Article 5(4) of the Optional Protocol states only that the committee "shall forward its views to the State Party concerned and to the individual." The legal status of the decision is not mentioned nor is any follow-up to the communication envisaged. Because of the relatively limited status of the HRC, there may be less adverse consequences for states for non-compliance with its communications. More recently the HRC has appointed a Special Rapporteur to seek and evaluate information concerning state compliance with adopted committee views.[175] The issue of the status of HRC decisions reflects a more general phenomenon across regional and international systems, namely the lack of enforcement "bite" for decisions by human rights bodies that have

---

[174] Rein Mullerson, "The Efficiency of the Individual Complaint Procedures: The Experience of the CCPR, CERD, CAT, and ECHR" in Arie Bloed, Liselotte Leicht, Manfred Nowak and Allan Rosas (eds.), *Monitoring Human Rights in Europe: Comparing International Procedures and Mechanisms* (Boston, MA: M. Nijhoff Publishers, 1993), p. 25.
[175] *Report of the Human Rights Committee*, UN GAOR, 47th Sess., Supp. 40, at 142, UN Doc. A/47/40 (1992).

adverse effects for respondent states. Thus, for example, in the recent case of *Kavanagh v. Ireland*, despite a finding that the procedures of the Special Criminal Court (through its lack of a jury trial) were in breach of the due process guarantees of the ICCPR, the only remedy offered to the complainant was a paltry amount of financial compensation which he rejected.[176]

Some general thematic approaches can be drawn from the HRC's views regarding its role in individual applications. First, there is a consistent hesitancy on the committee's part to address the primary – emergency justification – question coupled with a far greater willingness to look into the secondary question concerning the proportionality of emergency measures that had been taken by the state concerned. Second, the committee has been similarly unimaginative with respect to its capacity to confront problem emergencies, particularly situations of permanent emergency. Third, there is a preponderance of cases concerning individual violations of due process rights in times of emergency coming before the committee in the derogation context. Finally, the committee has demonstrated, within the limitations noted above, some willingness to confront state overreaction to perceived internal threats, allegedly undermining public order and security.[177]

On some occasions the committee has gone further than might be anticipated in its approach to emergency review and has shown some willingness to address the primary question of emergency justification. For example, in its *Landinelli* decision[178] the HRC confirmed its competence to make an independent determination of whether a specific derogation measure was "strictly required." The committee noted that the government of Uruguay had sent a note to the Secretary-General of the United Nations, confirming a state of public emergency by reference to a number of "institutional acts" taken at the domestic level. The government's

---

[176] Kavanagh v. Ireland (No. 1) Case No. 818/1998, Views adopted on Apr. 4, 2001.

[177] *Report of the Human Rights Committee*, UN GAOR, 37th Sess., Supp. No. 40, Annex XV, at 168, UN Doc. A/37/40 (1982) (Consuelo Salgar de Montejo v. Colombia, Communication No. R/15/64; Jorge Landinelli Silva et al. v. Uruguay, Communication No. 34/1978, in *Selected Decisions of the Human Rights Committee Under the Optional Protocol* (1985) 65–66; *Report of the Human Rights Committee, supra*, Annex XVIII, at 187 (Carmen Amendola Massioti v. Uruguay, Communication No. R6/25); *Report of the Human Rights Committee*, UN GAOR, 38th Sess., Supp. No. 40, Annex XXII, at 216, UN Doc. A/38/40 (1983) (María del Carmen Almeida de Quinteros v. Uruguay, Communication No. 107/1981); *Report of the Human Rights Committee*, UN GAOR, 40th Sess., Supp. No. 40, Annex IX, at 179, UN Doc. A/40/40 (1985) (Monja Jaona v. Madagascar, Communication No. 132/1982).

[178] Landinelli Silva, at 65–66.

note claimed that the existence of the emergency was a "matter of universal knowledge," without making any further attempt to indicate the nature and the scope of the derogation. The committee accepted that the sovereign state had the right to declare an emergency, but stated that such right was not absolute. Rather, the government was told that it could not evade responsibility for rights enforcement by "merely invoking the existence of exceptional circumstances," without supplying sufficient information to confirm the necessity of emergency measures.[179]

The *Salgar de Montejo* case, concerning the Colombian government's recourse to a state of siege, contains a more detailed commentary by the HRC on the procedural aspects of derogation as well as on the requirement of proportionality.[180] The case concerned the imprisonment of a newspaper director by a military tribunal for the offense of illegally selling a weapon contrary to the domestic Statute of Security. The applicant contended violation of article 14(5) of the ICCPR, alleging that the military tribunals were neither independent nor impartial. The government's communications alluded consistently to a state of siege, and contained express reference to the application of articles 19(2) and 21 of the ICCPR. In a pithy and assertive commentary the committee declined to countenance that article 14(5) of the ICCPR was derogated from in accordance with article 4. While the committee did not second guess the very existence of an emergency it was not prepared to accept the necessity of the particular measures that the state had used. By refusing to accept that derogation is a general provision creating leeway for any governmental action in a state of emergency, the committee was confirming the limited nature of the derogation provision. Thus, the committee stated that it was "of the view that the State Party, by merely invoking the existence of a state of siege, cannot evade the obligations which it invokes by ratifying the Covenant."[181] This case confirms a solid commitment on the part of the HRC with respect to the secondary question and a willingness to be assertive with states as regards the internal requirements of derogation. At the same time it also follows the general unwillingness of the European and Inter-American Courts to question the bona fides of the state's resort to the emergency.

A robust approach to the secondary question is also evident in a small number of cases where, although derogation was not applicable, the relevant state sought to rely on an internal state of exception as a justification for its actions, asking the committee, effectively, for a judicial

---

[179] Ibid.   [180] Salgar de Montejo.   [181] Ibid., at 173.

emergency "spin" in a situation where in theory the ordinary law of the land applied. The committee has not shown itself to be as pliant as the European Court in this context. Thus, in the *Camarago de Guerro* decision, which concerned the killing by Colombian police of seven individuals suspected of kidnapping a former Colombian diplomat,[182] the HRC took a forceful line on individual protection and subjected state justifications for limitations on individual rights to rigorous scrutiny.[183] A core element of the application was the allegation that the passing of a domestic legislative decree,[184] creating police immunity for certain forms of action, related to the assessment that the national territory was under a state of siege. The applicants further argued that the decree was in violation of articles 6, 7, 9, 14, and 17 of the ICCPR.

The Human Rights Committee accepted that the Colombian government had complied with the formal requirements of notice for derogation regarding domestic legislative changes to confront the situation of disturbed public order in the jurisdiction.[185] It went on to observe that there were certain provisions of the ICCPR that could never be derogated from under any circumstances. The committee unequivocally concluded further that there had been a violation of the right to life protected under article 6(1), declining to give the state an interpretive leeway on the violation of a non-derogable right notwithstanding the existence of a derogation.[186] The case presents a useful example of an enforcement mechanism (albeit a weak one) grafting onto the interpretive accommodation model set out in article 4 of the ICCPR.

As regards violations of due process rights by derogating states the HRC has been, following its precedents on proportionality of measures, generally activist and strongly affirmative of rights protections. Cases of contemporary interest include *Polay Campos v. Peru*, where the committee examined detention practices in the context of alleged terrorist activity,[187] and *Fals Borda v. Colombia*.[188] In *Polay Campos* the applicant had been detained incommunicado from the time of his arrest and had also been denied access to legal counsel. The committee held that this form of detention, despite the terrorism context offered by the government,

---

[182] Report of the Human Rights Committee (1982), at 137.
[183] Ibid., at 137–38.
[184] Colombian Legislative Decree No. 0070 of 1978.
[185] *De Guerro*, at para. 146.   [186] Ibid., at paras. 146–47.
[187] Polay Campos v. Peru, Case No. 577/1994, Views adopted on Nov. 6, 1997 (paras. 8.4, 8.6, and 8.7).
[188] Fals Borda v. Colombia, Case No. 46/1979, Views adopted on July 27, 1982, para. 12.3.

violated article 10(1) of the covenant. The denial of access to correspondence from family members was similarly found to violate the provisions of article 10(1). The committee was not prepared to accommodate interpretively the state's approach despite the crisis contextualization offered and the derogable status of the rights in question. In *Fals Borda* the applicant and his wife had been arrested under state emergency laws and detained incommunicado for two months and one year, respectively. No domestic procedure was in place at the time to test the lawfulness of the applicants' detention and the committee found a violation of article 9(4) on that basis.

Claims of emergency have also been invoked outside the context of individual applications, namely in country reports made to the committee by states in compliance with their reporting duties under article 40 of the ICCPR.[189] We survey some of the committee's views on practices of emergency powers as outlined in its Concluding Comments on state reports under article 40(4). While the committee has used the report review sessions as a means to create and encourage dialogue with state parties about the validity and status of, and measures taken in the context of, emergencies, this procedure is not a validation of the derogation's legality.[190]

The article 40 review process has been the subject of much criticism. Joan Fitzpatrick's cogent critique is as relevant today as it was when it was first made in 1981: "The article 40 report process fails as a device for fact-finding in derogation situations because it is unfocused, subject to substantial delays, and unequipped either to produce or test the veracity of relevant information."[191]

---

[189] See *Consideration of Reports Submitted by States Parties under Article 40 of the Covenant*, UN Human Rights Committee, 3rd Sess., UN Doc. CCPR/C/1/Add. 17 (1977) (discussing report filed by the United Kingdom under article 40 of the covenant); *Consideration of Reports Submitted by States Parties under Article 40 of the Covenant*, UN Human Rights Committee, 4th Sess., UN Doc. CCPR/C/1/Add. 25 (1978) (discussing report filed by Chile under article 40 of the covenant); *Summary Record of the 221st Meeting*, UN Human Rights Committee, 10th Sess., UN Doc. CCPR/C/1/SR.221 (1980) (discussing report filed by Colombia under article 40 of the covenant): *Report of the Human Rights Committee*, UN GAOR, 37th Sess., Supp. No. 40 at 58, UN Doc. A/37/40 (1982) (discussing report filed by Uruguay under article 40 of the covenant).

[190] See Jaap A. Walkatee, "The Human Rights Committee and Public Emergencies" (1982) 9 *Yale Journal of World Public Order* 134.

[191] Hartman, "Derogation," 41. See also Joan Fitzpatrick, *Human Rights in Crisis: The International System for Protecting Rights during States of Emergency* (Philadelphia: University of Pennsylvania Press, 1994).

The HRC has traditionally failed to assess the existence of emergency in certain states and has frequently declined to endorse the principle of proportionality in its examination of state practice.[192] While the committee has shown greater gumption in this area in the past few years,[193] its room for maneuver remains limited. Each country report is limited to the matters contained therein and to a specific territory. Therefore each derogation is examined within its own frame of reference, without any institutional method for linking it to continuous state resort to emergency powers. The examination process is akin to stopping a marker at one point on a long continuum and merely looking left and right at the moment of pause, rather than assessing the whole. In this way, problem emergencies, and specifically permanent emergencies, have always managed to escape the net of thorough examination. States have learnt, as country reporting encourages, to reflect on the present and evaluate what room for growth and rights enforcement exists in the future. The limited time for discussion on country reports facilitates further an avoidance of a hard critical examination of the extended past. Such a dialogue is not fully constructive and in some ways not completely relevant to the committee's concern with present protection and adherence to the covenant. Only with a willingness to survey thoroughly past and persistent state recourse to emergency powers can the entrenched emergency be evaluated for what it is.

With that critique in mind, we note that the committee has issued some positive comments. While it has been generally unwilling to hold prolonged emergencies as per se unjustified, the committee has posed awkward questions to the relevant countries. Thus, for example, in examining a twenty-one-year emergency, the committee urged Egypt to "consider reviewing the need to maintain the state of emergency."[194] In another case considering the thirty-eight-year emergency in Syria, the committee recommended that the legal emergency be "lifted as soon as possible."[195] It has also on occasion been willing to identify the use of de facto emergency power, expressing its "regret" in one instance that

---

[192] Fitzpatrick, *Human Rights in Crisis.*

[193] See *Report of the Human Rights Committee*, UN GAOR, 36th Sess., Supp. No. 40, Annex VII, at 110, UN Doc. A/36/40 (1981). This was a General Comment by the committee on the derogation process under article 4, where the committee emphasized its particular concerns about the problems of notification and proclamation.

[194] "Concluding Observations of the Human Rights Committee: Egypt," Nov. 28, 2002, CCPR/CO/76/EGY, para. 6.

[195] "Concluding Observations of the Human Rights Committee: Syrian Arab Republic," Apr. 24, 2001, CCPR/CO/71/SYR, para. 6.

"some parts of India have remained subject to declaration as disturbed areas for many years – for example – the Armed Forces (Special Powers) Act has been applied throughout Manipur since 1980 and in some areas of that state for much longer – and that, in these areas, the State party is in effect using emergency powers without resorting to article 4, paragraph 3 of the Covenant."[196] The committee recommended that the application of these emergency powers should be closely monitored so as to ensure its strict compliance with the provisions of the covenant.[197] The committee has also stated that it "deplores the lack of clarity of the legal provisions governing the introduction and administration of the state of emergency."[198] It expressed its concern about the proliferation of emergency forms within a state's legal structure and about the compatibility of multiple legal regimes with the covenant's derogation requirements.[199]

The HRC has further found that the principle of proportionality should not be considered *in abstracto*, and that it was intimately connected with appraising the practical steps taken by governments facing crises.[200] An interesting example in this regard is the decision of Cyprus to inform the committee that it had not declared a state of emergency even after the occupation of a portion of its territory by Turkey in 1974 as "it has been considered more appropriate not to take any measures which would in any way adversely affect the enjoyment of human rights."[201]

It is also worth noting that, seeking to augment its oversight capacity while recognizing its own remedial limitations, the HRC decided in 1979 that it could take into account, when examining emergency and derogation, information from other United Nations organs including

---

[196] "Concluding Observations of the Human Rights Committee: India," Aug. 4, 1997, CCPR/C/79/Add. 81, para. 19.

[197] Ibid.

[198] "Concluding Observations of the Human Rights Committee: Nepal," Nov. 10, 1994, CCPR/C/79/Add. 42, para. 9: see also "Concluding Observations of the Human Rights Committee: Zambia," Apr. 3, 1996, CCPR/C/79/Add. 62, para. 11. "Concluding Observations of the Human Rights Committee: Uruguay," CCPR/C/79/Add. 90, para. 8 (1998).

[199] "Concluding Observations of the Human Rights Committee: Guatemala," Aug. 27, 2001, CCPR/CO/72/GTM, para. 11.

[200] *Report of the Human Rights Committee*, General Assembly, Official Records, 34th Sess., Supp. No. 40 (A/30/40), United Nations, para. 73, p. 18, report of Chile.

[201] *Report of the Human Rights Committee*, 34 UN GAOR Supp. No. 40, UN Doc. A/34/40 (1979), at para. 383.

information received through the 1503 and 1235 procedures.[202] Despite some practical administrative difficulties in making this as useful a device as it might be, the committee's position evidences an intention to strengthen oversight procedures. A simple if practical reform that might encourage more thorough understanding of the permanent and complex emergency phenomena would be structured and administratively supported information-sharing between treaty and non-treaty examination processes.

The gap between the theory and practice of emergency powers

Chapter 4 discussed the profound gap which exists between the theory and practice of the resort to emergency powers by states and corresponding oversight by domestic legal mechanisms. The same analysis is equally applicable to the practice of states with regard to derogation and the oversight offered by international legal bodies. We now turn to these anomalies.

In common linguistic understanding, an emergency supposes a sudden, urgent, and usually unforeseen occurrence requiring immediate action. A clear premise underlying the international legal treaty standards discussed above was that derogation (the means for dealing with emergencies) was conceived of as a finite concept – temporary and exceptional – and was never envisaged as creating the means for the permanent operation of emergency powers. However, numerous examples of state practice demonstrate that the exception has, in fact, become the norm. The emergency deviation has become systematically entrenched in state legal and political systems and culture. The "ideal emergency" rarely exists in practice. At this point we wish to illustrate and expand upon some of the general gaps that we identify in international human rights law's conceptualization and regulation of emergencies.

A study conducted in 1978 estimated that, at the time, at least thirty countries experienced a state of emergency.[203] Similarly, a substantial number of states have entered a formal derogation notice under

---

[202] ESC Res. 1235 (XLII), 42 UN ESCOR Supp. No. 1 at 17, UN Doc. E/4393 (1967). ECOSOC granted its approval under the procedure to authorize the Human Rights Commission to make a "thorough study" and to report on situations of violations of human rights.

[203] See Daniel O'Donnell, "States of Exception" (1978) 21 International Commission of Jurists Review 52.

article 4(3) of the ICCPR.[204] It should be noted that this number does not take into account states that are not signatories to the ICCPR or which experience de facto emergencies that are not officially proclaimed and notified. Equally, this does not take account of those states that have routinized and institutionalized emergency measures in their ordinary legal system. Further studies have confirmed the persistent resort to emergency powers by a significant number of countries. Thus, for example, in 1983, the International Commission of Jurists undertook a comprehensive analysis of states of emergency throughout the world.[205] The study examined in depth the practices of nineteen countries that had experienced states of emergency in the 1960s and 1970s.[206] The commission outlined from the outset the premise that there was a frequent link between states of emergency and situations of grave violations of human rights.[207] It also clearly enunciated the principle that many governments regarded any challenge to their authority as a "threat" facilitating the use of derogation provisions, allowing for the dismantling of existing legal machinery for the protection of individuals.[208]

The commission's conclusions recognized the frequency with which emergency powers had been utilized and emergency regimes created. The report identifies a number of patterns that are useful to our analysis. First, a distinction can be made between "transitional regimes of exception with democratic goals" and "transitional regimes of exception with authoritarian goals."[209] Second, recourse to a state of emergency corresponds in many situations to a government's desire for legalism.[210] Third, states of emergency are frequently hidden by the exercise of repressive powers without formal acknowledgment of the existence of an emergency (de facto states of emergency).[211] Fourth, empirical evidence

---

[204] For a list of derogation notices so entered see The United Nations Treaty Collection: International Covenant on Civil and Political Rights, http://untreaty.un.org/humanrightsconvs/Chapt_IV_4/CovenantCivPo.pdf (last visited Aug. 8, 2005).

[205] International Commission of Jurists, *States of Emergency: Their Impact on Human Rights* (Geneva: International Commission of Jurists, 1983).

[206] The case studies examined were Argentina, Canada, Colombia, Ghana, Greece, India, Malaysia, Northern Ireland, Peru, Syria, Thailand, Turkey, Uruguay, and Zaire. Additionally, one chapter – devoted to eastern European countries – examined the practices of the Soviet Union, Hungary, Czechoslovakia, Yugoslavia, and Poland. In addition to the case studies, two questionnaires were circulated to 158 governments. To these, replies were received from 34 countries of which 28 were not subjects of the in-depth studies.

[207] International Commission of Jurists, *States of Emergency*, p. 1.

[208] Ibid.   [209] Ibid., pp. 311–12, 315, 317, and 413.

[210] Ibid., p. 413.   [211] Ibid., p. 413.

demonstrates the tendency for a state of emergency to become perpetual or to effect far-reaching authoritarian changes in preexisting ordinary legal norms.[212] Fifth, in some cases excessive use of emergency powers is partially explained by the persistence of absolutist moral values and political habits.[213] Sixth, the abuse of emergency powers is frequently a result of disregard for constitutional and legal safeguards rather than inadequacies in the law per se.[214] Finally, what is most notable about the study is that of the fourteen countries considered in the in-depth examination (excluding the eastern European states) nine fall into the category of permanent emergencies. Only two countries, Canada and India, fit the exemplary emergency model that is the working assumption of the major studies on emergency norms.

The Questiaux Report

Subsequent research principally undertaken to assist in the monitoring, supervision, and movement toward ending of emergency regimes also shed much light on the concurrent practices of states during emergency rule.[215] The Questiaux Report[216] was undertaken at the behest of the United Nations Sub-Commission on Prevention of Discrimination and Protection of Minorities,[217] concerned at the general risks to rights protection that emanated from emergency regimes.[218] The report offers a profile of patterns evidenced by national legislation concerning emergency powers, postulating a "reference model"[219] with a high degree of formality. Chapter 1 of the study opens with the premise that the fundamental precept on limiting states in bringing situations of emergency into effect is consistency between emergency legislation and democratic principles. This is subject to three conditions: (1) that the legislation pre-date the occurrence of the crisis; (2) that it contain a priori or a

---

[212] Ibid., p. 415.   [213] Ibid., p. 416.   [214] Ibid., p. 417.

[215] International Law Association, *Report of the 64th Conference Held at Queensland*; James Crawford (ed.), *International Law Association, Report of the 64th Biennial Conference Queensland, 19–25 August 1990* (London: ILA, 1991); Chowdhury, *Rule of Law in a State of Emergency*.

[216] Questiaux, "Study on the Implications for Human Rights."

[217] Resolution 10 (XXX) of Aug. 31, 1977.

[218] Reports of the Special Rapporteur for the UN Commission on Human Rights' Sub-Commission on Prevention of Discrimination and Protection of Minorities should also be noted in this context. Leandro Despouy, "Tenth Annual Report and List of States which, since 1 January 1985, have Proclaimed, Extended or Terminated a State of Emergency," June 23, 1997, E/CN.4/Sub. 2/1997/19.

[219] It is Joan Fitzpatrick who describes Questiaux's standard reference point in this manner. Fitzpatrick, *Human Rights in Crisis*, p. 21.

posteriori control procedures; and (3) that it is to be applied as a provisional or, more correctly, a temporary measure.[220] Thus, the term "state of emergency" is referred to in the report as a generic juridical term reflecting the use of emergency powers in exceptional circumstances. The exceptional character of the situation is measured by certain temporary factors as well as by the extremity and imminence of the danger facing the nation.[221]

In her report, Questiaux offers a typology of state acts outside the norm, or "deviations" from the reference model of emergency regime,[222] which, in turn, is taken as the consensual and generally applied starting point for states. Joan Fitzpatrick provides a synopsis of the five enunciated "deviations" as follows:

(1) the formal emergency not notified to treaty implementation bodies; (2) the *de facto* emergency, during which rights are suspended without proclamation or notification, or suspension of rights is continued after termination of a formal emergency; (3) the permanent emergency arising out of continual and decreasingly valid formal extensions of the emergency; (4) the complex emergency involving overlapping and confusing legal regimes through partial suspension of constitutional norms and issuance of a large volume of far-reaching decrees; and (5) the institutionalized emergency under which an authoritarian government prolongs an extended transitional emergency regime with the purported, but questionable, aim of returning to democracy and the full reinstitution of constitutional guarantees.[223]

While the models outlined as "deviations" are well defined within their own terms of reference, the choice of terminology is problematic. The Questiaux Report seems to miss an essential conundrum, namely that most emergencies fail to conform to the formal typology. This is particularly noticeable with regard to de facto states of emergency in municipal practice. Questiaux certainly notes their existence but her study seems to understate their widespread use by states. Questiaux's opening remarks on the scope of the study underscore its formalistic approach, and thus its inherent limitations: "In theory, the *de facto* situation which constitutes the exceptional circumstances is thus without legal validity (a) in municipal law, as long as a state of emergency has not been proclaimed, and (b) to a lesser degree in international law, as long as the state of emergency has not been the subject of communication

---

[220] Questiaux, "Study on the Implications for Human Rights," paras. 34–35.
[221] Ibid., at para. 23.   [222] Ibid., at para. 97.
[223] Fitzpatrick, *Human Rights in Crisis*, pp. 21–22.

to the competent international bodies."[224] There is no subsequent recognition that such de facto emergencies may, in fact, endure and flourish without explicit legal validation, and that as a result, the process of formally authenticating their existence might require critical assessment. Yet, naming a situation as a de facto emergency is not merely a matter of pedantic academic quibbling over terms. Rather, the manner in which emergencies have been typecast in key academic and policy studies (in tandem with the jurisprudence of the relevant international courts) has profoundly shaped the way in which states and others understand and thus regulate the emergency phenomenon.

Questiaux's theorizing has a significant focus on the procedural mechanisms that allow for emergencies to be legally validated by municipal law. These include formal procedural guarantees, substantive guarantees, and the actual implementation of guarantees.[225] These procedural mechanisms presume the operation of a model of accommodation, but underestimate its limitations. These include, first, an assumption that the existence of these formal requirements is per se sufficient to assure protection of human rights in situations of exigency.[226] Second, the conceptual framework does not give sufficient weight to the widespread phenomenon of permanent emergencies, relegating it to a side-discussion about emergencies that are "deviations," rather than treating it as central to our understanding of how emergencies have developed since the inception of the international human rights regime.[227] The Questiaux study assumes, like much of the policy and legal analysis that followed it, that positive legal norms reflect and shape the practice of emergencies. It fails to examine the extent to which practice circumvents and subverts such norms.

The Questiaux Report does not completely ignore the permanent emergency problem. It addresses the development of permanent emergencies as a phenomenon which arises "with or without proclamation ... either as a result of *de facto* systematic extension or because the Constitution has not provided any time limit a priori."[228] The study's definition is premised on the assumption that a formal constitutional limitation will

---

[224] Questiaux, "Study on the Implications for Human Rights," para. 24.
[225] Ibid., at paras. 40–63.
[226] Fitzpatrick, *Human Rights in Crisis*, p. 21 (highly critical of Questiaux's methodology).
[227] The International Law Association's (ILA) Warsaw Report (1988) confirms this: "an exclusive focus on formal states of emergency barely scratches the surface of the widespread phenomenon of human rights abuses associated with states of emergency." Ibid., p. 14.
[228] Questiaux, "Study on the Implications for Human Rights," para. 112.

be sufficiently persuasive to prevent the creation of a permanent emergency. Yet, the study does not address those systems without formal constitutional guarantees that have nonetheless entrenched a permanent emergency by formal legal means. The study's assumption that the creation of a permanent emergency would distinctly result from formal failings by the legal regime also fails to take into account the possibility that permanent emergencies could be facilitated expressly by the correct and intended functioning of the legal regime. However, the study usefully and positively identifies three common features of permanent emergencies. These are: (1) the fact that, as the emergency progresses over time, less account is taken of the imminence of the danger facing the state (the "one can get used to this" phenomenon); (2) the longer the emergency lasts the less important the principle of proportionality is considered to be (the "increasing dosages" phenomenon); and (3) as the emergency entrenches, time limits are ignored and no longer even envisaged by the state.[229]

In some respects it is difficult to draw the dividing line between the normal and the permanent emergency. By definition, emergencies do not commence in permanent form and states rarely (if ever) defend the choice of using emergency powers in terms of their permanent imposition. Moreover, permanent emergencies have an increasingly unhealthy cross-pollination with complex states of emergencies. The latter are defined by Questiaux as "A great number of parallel or simultaneous emergency rules whose complexity is increased by the 'piling up' of provisions designed to 'regularise' the immediately preceding situation and therefore embodying retroactive rules and transitional regimes."[230] The "piling up" effect is often one of the practices that facilitate the creation of a legal and political culture which supports an extended emergency regime. The system becomes self-defined and reliant upon the legislative support structures created by the emergency, and "normal" supports are lost in the process, thus making the return to normality more difficult. Complex states of emergency also sustain the enactment of repressive laws assuming the features of ordinary law. Thus, the emergency is hidden. In this manner, its permanent creation is easily facilitated in political terms and is less amenable to legal challenge.

One example of this form of silent emergency existed in the Irish Republic for more than five decades.[231] In 1939, the submersion of emergency measures inside ordinary laws was commenced by the enactment

---

[229] Ibid., at para. 117.   [230] Ibid., at para. 118.

[231] Mary Robinson, *The Special Criminal Court* (Dublin: Dublin University Press, 1974).

of the Offences against the State Act, where the legislature used its ordinary, as opposed to emergency, legislative power while simultaneously declaring a state of emergency. The centerpiece of the legislation was the establishment of a Special Criminal Court, conducting jury-less trials. The Special Criminal Court sat from 1939 to 1946. It stopped hearing cases in 1946 but was not abandoned. The proclamation authorizing it was not rescinded and the appointments of the military officers who made up the court were never terminated. The court operated again for a brief period in 1961–62, following an IRA campaign, but in October 1962 the Irish government formally rescinded the 1939 proclamation. The court's permanent rehabilitation came in 1972 with another proclamation in response to the violence in Northern Ireland. It has remained in place since that time. To date, more than two thousand people have been tried by this court.

Questiaux makes a positive addition to the literature by attesting to the difficulties in contesting the legality of overlapping (emergency and ordinary) legislation which facilitates de facto emergencies. The politically defended normality of the legislation masks its emergency character and allows for its long-term retention with few of the international repercussions that might follow legislation that is specifically designated to have an "emergency" title or character. Thus, these normalized emergencies become a prime means to circumvent international control and scrutiny. What we have argued elsewhere and reiterate here is that it is imperative that international courts and tribunals become more sophisticated in their judicial supervision of such emergencies. It is not enough that the positive laws of notification, proclamation, and proportionality be applied only to those situations whose regime title is deemed to fall within the perimeters of supervision. Instead, empirical assessment of the effect and scope of the regime must be firmly focused, recognizing that domestic political rhetoric may mask the reality of repressive regimes that are unprotective and dismissive of individual rights.

Paris Minimum Standards

Another relevant reference point for an understanding of policy thinking in the human rights field concerning emergencies is the Paris Minimum Standards of Human Rights Norms in a State of Emergency. They reflect eight years of study by the International Law Association (ILA) from 1976 to 1984, setting out a consensus on a set of minimum standards to govern the declaration and administration of states of emergency that threaten the life of a nation.[232] In this comprehensive study of the regulation and limits of governmental exercise of emergency powers, "aberrations" from the reference model are stated to include the de facto state of emergency, the permanent state of emergency, institutionalization of the emergency regime, and complex states of emergency, following the pattern and conceptual model outlined in the Questiaux Report.[233] In following the theoretical framework laid down by Questiaux, the ILA's inquiry assumes that the "ideal" emergency type is the norm and that aberrations are neither widespread nor indicative of general practice.[234] The weakness of the approach should be obvious by now.

There is a consistent unwillingness to examine whether the patterns of emergency behavior by governments reflect a move toward the aberration being normalized. It is difficult to let go of the assumption that governments behave as they are required to by treaty standards. This is the case for at least two reasons. First, there is the apprehension (fundamentally a psychological one) that if the treaty standards are not indicative of behavioral patterns, control and accountability of government action may be lost. Second, many governments' actions have the veneer of procedural lawfulness. Notification and proclamation procedures may be adhered to in the formal sense, but the actual substantive practice of the emergency may deviate substantially from its envisioned international legal parameters. This is not simply a matter of governments violating rights in an emergency regime. It is also a matter of the form in which those violations occur. When a government adheres to procedural requirements to some extent "the heat is off." As noted above, international courts and tribunals have been historically wary of intervening and interposing their own judgments on whether a government is prima facie justified in calling an emergency. When the state opts into the process by playing by the procedural rules, the form of the emergency may in fact escape detailed scrutiny. Thus, in *Ireland v. United Kingdom*, where both governments conceded that an emergency existed, the European Court of Human Rights did not undertake any meaningful

---

[232] The discussion on the Minimum Standards in this chapter is drawn principally from Chowdhury, *Rule of Law in a State of Emergency*.

[233] Ibid., pp. 45–55; Questiaux, "Study on the Implications for Human Rights," paras. 103–45.

[234] Richard B. Lillich, "Paris Minimum Standards of Human Rights Norms in a State of Emergency" (1985) 79 *American Journal of International Law* 1072.

independent assessment as to whether that in fact was the case.[235] The focus thus became the nature of the measures that had been employed, a proportionality issue, rather than the emergency itself. International courts have also been reluctant to use language that suggests that there may be a range of emergency regimes, or that emergency regimes have complex features that may change and evolve over time. Chowdhury examines the phenomenon of institutionalized emergencies as a discrete sub-set of crisis aberration, but does not investigate the clear link between institutionalized and permanent emergencies. The former are defined as "an extended transitional emergency regime with a veneer of legitimacy by professing to return to some form of democracy – which may be variously described as 'authoritarian,' 'restricted' or 'gradual.'"[236] The latter are described as the "systematic extension of a state of emergency, which results in giving it permanent status."[237] Extended transitional regimes have illustrated the strong capacity for continuity (at least by political rhetoric) thereby facilitating permanent emergencies. The links between these various phenomena are little explored in the ILA's and Chowdhury's work, leaving a lacuna in conceptualizing the organic nature of exigency and crisis. This ultimately has the effect of limiting the manner in which crises are addressed by courts as well as by political and legal decision-makers.

As we noted in chapter 4, the subversion of emergency practice as outlined above affects the various models of emergency regimes that are the subject of Part I of this book. In terms of the business as usual approach, even where the argument is made that "ordinary" law is coping adequately with the exception, a far more probing account of practice is required. Categories such as "complex" or "institutionalized" emergencies, especially where they have become entrenched over time, may display the appearance of normality, but actually mask a slow and damaging erosion of rights' protection over time. Often too the practice of governance has been markedly affected, with power centralization and a lack of genuine representativeness. When faced with situations of entrenched, complex, or prolonged emergencies, the Business as Usual model will come under strong pressures. The longer people live under the shadow of emergency, the more likely they are to demand that the legal system accommodate the necessities of the situation. Continued adherence to the Business as Usual model in those circumstances may

---

[235] Ireland v. United Kingdom, paras. 204–05.
[236] Chowdhury, *Rule of Law in a State of Emergency*, pp. 49–50.
[237] Ibid., p. 49.

lead to adjustments to the system that are made in ways that lack transparency. Eventually the system will reach a position where significant portions of the "ordinary" legal system have been formulated and reformulated in response to crises. As emergencies become more prolonged and less exceptional it becomes harder to argue for a business as usual approach since it is clear that much is not "as usual." The categorizations offered and critiqued in this chapter pose a profound challenge also to the various models of accommodation. If, as we suggest, emergencies do not generally conform to an "ideal" type and international legal systems are failing to comprehend the true nature of state practice and to respond accordingly, then it is not clear that the "fix" for international oversight mechanisms is through accommodation of the actual practices of states, particularly in the permanent emergency category. Accommodation might then regulate for the long-term perpetuation of emergencies. The danger is that emergency-specific accommodation will become an integral part of the regular legal system. Rather, by acknowledging that states' practice is out of step with the concept underpinning the accountability models contained in international human rights law, we are instead calling for greater robustness in constraining states along the lines that they have already agreed to in treaty form. This means developing measurements for permanent emergencies, naming them when they are found, and asking the difficult questions about whether they are actually justified in form and length.

Finally, any model that recognizes the possibility of extra-legal action in times of emergency is, arguably, premised on a notion of impermeable boundaries between normalcy and emergency. It is that separation which enables proponents of such models to claim that the ordinary legal system will not be tarnished by the necessities of emergency and the extra-legality that they bring about, and will remain intact and ready to resume its fullest extent when the emergency is over. Again, the identification of entrenched, complex, and prolonged emergencies requires recalibration if the model is to function properly.

The Siracusa Principles: an attempt at concrete rules to limit abuse of emergencies

In this context it is useful to recall the Siracusa Principles[238] which resulted from the work of international experts coming together to interpret and give meaning to the concepts of limitations and derogation

---

[238] The Siracusa Principles on the Limitation and Derogation Provisions in the International Covenant on Civil and Political Rights (1984), reprinted in (1985) 7 *Human Rights Quarterly* 3.

under the ICCPR.[239] As one commentator notes: "The devotion of a week's labor by one-half of the experts attending the Siracusa Conference to the interpretation of a single article (Art.4) reflects the central importance of states of exception for efforts to promote respect for human rights."[240] The Siracusa Principles were created in an attempt to respond to perceived weaknesses in the oversight of emergencies by the Human Rights Committee. The Principles address both the substantive limits and procedural requirements of article 4 of the covenant. In tandem with the work of the International Commission of Jurists, and the International Law Association and the Questiaux Report they constitute a benchmark for international policy thinking on the nature and control of emergencies.

The definition of "public emergency" draws heavily on the terminology adopted by the European Court in the *Lawless* case.[241] Concrete steps are outlined to fulfill proclamation, notification, and termination requirements.[242] The Principles recognize the inherent dangers in the perpetuation of the state of emergency. This concern is manifested in the emphasis on the severity and scope of each individual emergency measure,[243] the unwillingness to accept national determinations of facts as the sole definer of authenticity,[244] and the stress laid on the short-term and limited nature of derogation.[245] The additional commentaries to the Principles stress that the sole legitimacy for derogation lies in the preservation of and return to full democratic governance.[246] The Principles are a useful guide to the augmentation of procedural matters for the HRC and offer practical guidelines to assist it in dealing with states of emergency. Yet, while useful they do not go as far as is required to come to terms with the consistent practice of states in abusing the emergency regime and the derogation process.

Strong procedural requirements may well make it more difficult for states to invoke emergency powers without good cause. If a state must

---

[239] The conference of experts was organized by several non-governmental organizations in 1984.

[240] Joan F. Hartman, "Working Paper for the Committee of Experts on the Article 4 Derogation Provision" (1985) 7 *Human Rights Quarterly* 89 at 90–91.

[241] "Siracusa Principles," Principle 39.

[242] Ibid., Principles 42–50.   [243] Ibid., Principles 51, 53, and 54.

[244] Ibid., Principle 57.   [245] Ibid., Principle 64.

[246] Hartman, "Working Paper"; Bert B. Lockwood, Jr., Janet Finn, and Grace Jubinsky, "Working Paper for the Committee of Experts on Limitation Provisions" (1985) 7 *Human Rights Quarterly* 35; Daniel O'Donnell, "Commentary by the Rapporteur on Derogation" (1985) 7 *Human Rights Quarterly* 23; Alexandre Kiss, "Commentary by the Rapporteur on the Limitation Provisions" (1985) 7 *Human Rights Quarterly* 16.

qualify its recourse to extraordinary powers, the articulation of cause – "giving reasons" – may have a braking effect on the arbitrary or non-transparent resort to extreme measures.[247] Yet, the prospect of account-ability offered by procedures works best if states invoke emergency pow-ers along the lines envisioned by international treaty law. However, as applied, those do not account currently for the absorption of emergency powers into ordinary law, the increasing tendency of many states to elec-tive dictatorships, the appropriate response of international law to the failure to end emergencies (even when the state has fulfilled all the tech-nical obligations imposed upon it), and the legitimizing effect that the rules themselves have in validating long-term emergencies.

The Siracusa Principles and similar studies are partly responsible for perpetuating the gap that exists between the "ought" and the "is" of emergency regimes. The experts who drafted the Principles recog-nized the existence of deviations and aberrations from the model emer-gency.[248] Nonetheless they continued to cling to the model hypothesis and demonstrated unwillingness to question whether the widespread proliferation of such deviations ought to prompt a fundamental re-think about the viability of orthodox academic conceptualizations of "emergency."

Weakness of the "aberration" hypothesis

A common thread going through the various studies discussed above is the fundamental premise that the "model" emergency type is the archetypal emergency experience and that flowing from this are the "problem" emergencies that fail to conform to type. Questiaux and the International Law Association replicate one another's stated "devia-tions" from the model emergency formula. Both list de facto, permanent, complex, and institutionalized emergencies in this manner.[249] Questi-aux adds one additional category, that of unnotified emergencies. Using

---

[247] Rene Cassin, one of the drafters of the covenant, was particularly convinced of the importance of notification as a restriction on the use of emergency powers. He stated: "the real purpose of article 4 was to require States to take a decision in public when they were obliged to restrict such rights." UN Doc. E/CN.4/SR 127, 14.6 (1949).

[248] Hartman concedes that the Questiaux Report distinguishes categories of deviations from the model emergency which she accepts as valid proof of the capacity of governmental abuse. Nonetheless, instead of following this practice through its direct implications on the relevance of the treaty standards, the response is simply to stress the importance of bona fide derogations. Hartman, "Working Paper," 92.

[249] Questiaux, "Study on the Implications for Human Rights," paras. 99–147; Chowdhury, Rule of Law in a State of Emergency, pp. 45–55.

these categories in addition to the "model" emergency type, the empirical data show that the aberration comes closer to being the norm of practice than does the "model." The "official" approach is understandable when one starts the evaluative assessment of emergencies from the treaty standards downwards using those standards as yardsticks for examining states' practice.[250] There is a tautological aspect to the inquiry, when the treaty standards shape the way in which one comes to examine the empirical examples of government practices preceding, during, and after crisis. The fallacy of the traditional approach is amply depicted by a close examination of government practice. To illustrate this we reappraise the experience of fourteen of the nineteen states examined by the International Commission of Jurists' study.[251] We exclude the five Eastern European countries since they present a special case to be examined in light of the political regime of the day spawning a particular use of emergency powers that should not be detached from commentary on the political administration itself. However, we note in passing that in abstract terms, those five countries demonstrate many of the same problematic elements that arise in the other fourteen country studies.[252] The aim of the exercise is simply to demonstrate that the choice of categorization is crucial to making any conjectural appraisals that may follow.

Of the fourteen states examined, nine fall into the category of the permanent emergency type. Only two – India and Canada – fit the exemplary emergency model which serves as the working assumption of the major studies on emergency regimes. Two other countries demonstrate complex emergency types (Thailand also falls into the permanent emergency classification). One state – Ghana – falls into the institutionalized emergency classification. Finally, Greece presents an example of a "bad" classic emergency type. While conforming to the notification and proclamation requirements of the model emergency, it failed to demonstrate

---

[250] Legal realism has a significant jurisprudential value to this discussion. See Karl N. Llewellyn, *The Bramble Bush: On our Law and its Study* (New York: Oceana Publications, 1951).

[251] International Commission of Jurists, *States of Emergency*.

[252] All five states – the Soviet Union, Hungary, Czechoslovakia, Yugoslavia, and Poland – demonstrate elements of the complex emergency model, finding original basis in the subordination of individual and civil rights under the constitutional framework of the system to collective and social rights. See Peter Juviler and Bertram Gross, *Human Rights for the 21st Century: Foundations for Responsible Hope* (Armonk, NY: M.E. Sharpe, 1993), pp. 28–50. Poland presents a prime example of the permanent emergency, having experienced two decades of formal emergency at the time the study was written. International Commission of Jurists, *States of Emergency*, p. 69.

Table 1

Country	Emergency type	Relevant details
Argentina	Permanent	Emergency 1974–83
Canada	Fits within model	Issue of Proportionality (Oct. 1970–April 1971)
Colombia	Permanent (with complex elements)	State of siege 1958–83 (intermittent normality)
Ghana	Institutionalized (with complex elements)	Military regime/two formal declarations
Greece	Classic "bad" emergency	Notification but no proportionality
India	Fits within model (generally)	Third emergency (1975–78), proportionality issue
Malaysia	Complex emergency (some fit with model)	Ordinary law containing emergency powers
Northern Ireland	Permanent (with complex elements)	Emergency 1922–83
Peru	Permanent	Emergency 1932–83
Syria	Permanent (with unnotified elements)	Emergency 1923–83
Thailand	Permanent and complex emergency	Emergency 1932–83
Turkey	Quasi-permanent emergency (regime of exception)	Emergency 1960–80
Uruguay	Permanent emergency (with unnotified elements)	Emergency 1969–83
Zaire	Permanent emergency	Emergency 1960–80

Notes: Time-spans for emergency relate to the relevant time-frame for the study. However, it should be noted that many of the identified permanent emergencies are still in place twenty years on.
Source: International Commission of Jurists, *States of Emergency*, pp. 1, 31, 43, 99, 133, 169, 193, 217, 247, 277, 289, 309, 337, and 371, respectively, for individual countries.

a justified resort to emergency powers. Table 1 illustrates the position of each of the fourteen countries on the spectrum at the time of the study.

As this brief example shows, the assumption that emergency powers are described adequately by setting out a standardized model and deviations thereto is misguided and ineffectual as a means of assessing both practice and control of emergency regimes. The emergency phenomenon is not static. Traditional discussions assume that exigencies are short-lived, finite phenomena, and that they are co-related in response and substance to the nature of a threat that is verifiable objectively and is widespread in extent. The "ideal type" emergency model presupposes that the length of an emergency will have no effect on its defining characteristics. The issue is not whether the model is incorrect per se as the legal and political basis upon which an emergency should be legitimized and enforced with domestic and international consent. Rather, the issue is whether that standard is undermined by a recognition that state practice is failing to conform to the ideal and that the experience of emergencies is significantly different.

By perpetuating the myth that emergencies follow a static pattern, and by failing to identify shifting patterns of crisis management, academic commentary, courts' jurisprudence, and international institutions fail to come to terms adequately with the emergency phenomenon. Emergencies weave peculiar and frequently inconsistent patterns. For example, the longer the emergency lasts the more likely it is that the nature of the power exercised will be transformed. Thus, institutionalized emergencies may take on aspects of complex emergencies over time. While institutionalized emergencies are the product of political upheaval or transformation, as that *raison d'être* wanes many governments have turned to ordinary law as a means to absorb and regularize the use of extraordinary powers and measures, affecting a creeping permanent emergency. Such shifts pose substantial obstacles to genuine accountability for the use of emergency powers.

Artificiality of formal emergencies

Following the Questiaux Report, the Second Interim Report of the International Law Association's Committee on the Enforcement of Human Rights recognized explicitly the potential artificiality of the notion of a formal emergency regime.[253] This report places much emphasis on defining de facto states of emergency. It sets out a detailed analytical framework to assist in the task of categorizing emergency regimes. The report makes a basic distinction between formal and non-formal emergencies. The formal emergency has two sub-sets: the "good de jure emergency" and the "bad de jure emergency."[254] The former is characterized

---

[253] "Warsaw Report," p. 3.

[254] The report states categorically that the phrase "good" is in some sense a euphemism: "Emergencies by nature imply that human suffering of some kind is inevitable when a menace of sufficient magnitude exists to threaten the life of the nation. Further,

by the existence and verification of actual emergency conditions and formal declaration/notification to the appropriate legal and political organs that a situation of exigency exists. The latter comprises a situation where the actual conditions justifying an emergency are absent but nonetheless notification/declaration has taken place.

The second broad category where no formal emergency is declared has four separate sub-categories. The first is the "classic" de facto emergency. This involves all the necessary factual elements that empirically formulate an emergency but the complete absence of any formal declaration/notification of the same. The second is the "ambiguous or potential" de facto emergency, where no actual emergency conditions exist, notification/declaration is absent, but there is a sudden shift in the application of permanent, "ordinary" internal security laws within the state. The third is the "institutionalized" emergency. Here again the actual conditions justifying an emergency are absent. However, while there is no formal declaration of emergency, emergency provisions are incorporated simultaneously into ordinary law. Finally, there is the category of "ordinary" repression, where there are no conditions that justify a declaration of emergency and no formal declaration or notification of emergency exists. Notwithstanding this, permanent laws severely restricting individual rights and civil liberties are the norm without formally invoking emergency powers. While the drafters of the international major human rights treaties envisioned both the "good" and "bad" de jure emergency types and provided for derogation provisions covering situations that would arise in respect of such emergencies, the de facto emergency types were not dealt with.

As noted above, the Warsaw Report focuses on de facto emergencies, in both definitional and substantive terms. However, missing once again is a detailed examination of the permanent emergency phenomenon, which is only mentioned peripherally in the context of the discussion of both formal and non-formal emergencies. Prolonged formal emergencies are recognized as "gray" areas in the formal emergency category[255] and as potential manifestations of non-formal emergencies. Thus, for example, illustrations given of the classic de facto emergency type include government rule by decree without formal declaration of crisis, noting Afghanistan and Angola as specific examples.[256] The examples given

---

human rights abuses (unjustified by the emergency) can and do occur under 'good' *de jure* emergencies." Ibid., pp. 15–16.
[255] Ibid., p. 12.   [256] Ibid., p. 17.

illustrate a wider point, that this is an example not only of an undeclared and unjustified emergency but of the permanent and normalized use of crisis powers.

In the report's discussion of institutionalized emergencies, the specter of permanent emergencies occurs once again.[257] The definition adopted in the report limits institutionalized emergencies to "a narrowly defined range of situations in which a government chooses to abandon the formal state of emergency in favor of incorporating similar powers and provisions into its ordinary legislation."[258] A prime example of this type of emergency is South Africa before the ending of the apartheid regime. During 1986, the South African government transplanted large segments of the then existing emergency legislation into ordinary legislation in an apparent attempt to ease international pressure. A more contemporary example is the decision by the British government to consolidate emergency powers under a unified umbrella of ordinary legislation following the transitionary process in Northern Ireland that had been initiated by the Good Friday Peace Agreement.[259] The Warsaw Report poses the question of whether such situations should be classified as states of emergency. It concludes that if draconian internal laws "are not applied too extensively,"[260] they should not be so classified. Such a cursory conclusion is problematic as it allows governments the luxury of resort to emergency powers with little oversight as long as they are careful about the extent of violations that they actually commit. This gives rise to further serious questions about where the boundary is to be drawn on the use of such powers and by whom. Giving governments the go-ahead to use extraordinary powers through ordinary law without accepting that any inappropriate manipulation pushes the state into the broad states of emergency category is a virtual opt-out on scrutiny.

The hidden emergency

The Warsaw Report also illustrates the danger that many states will resort to emergency powers by incorporating draconian national security laws into their ordinary legislation as an alternative to proclaiming a state of emergency and dealing with the consequences (both domestic

---

[257] Ibid., pp. 22–25.   [258] Ibid., p. 22.

[259] See the Terrorism Act 2000 and the Anti-Terrorism, Crime and Security Act 2001. See also Clive Walker, "Terrorism and Criminal Justice: Past, Present and Future" (2004) *Criminal Law Review* 311.

[260] "Warsaw Report," p. 23.

and international) of such a declaration. The report concludes by suggesting that

> The primary drawback to treating states of emergency as a discrete phenomenon is the possibility that governments will simply re-label and entrench emergency measures as ordinary laws and restrict the actual enjoyment of rights in less easily visible ways. This trend is already perceptible among governments that have institutionalized their emergency powers or follow the model of duplicative emergency/internal security measures.[261]

Thus, "normalization" of the emergency hinders international scrutiny. It is this normalization process which frequently conceals the existence and proliferation of permanent emergencies. A number of elements coincide here, limiting appropriate monitoring and recognition of such situations.

The derogation provisions of the major international human rights instruments were not designed to be mechanisms to confront "ordinary" sovereign legislation. "Ordinary" repressive laws that are used as a means to limit rights protected by the international or regional instruments will usually invoke emergency and derogation claims internationally only where the scope and extent of rights' infringement extends beyond the limits allowed by the jurisprudence on the limitation of a particular right. Only under such circumstances will the relevant state need to derogate if it wishes to maintain such powers. An example of this is the use of seven-day detention by the British government in Northern Ireland under section 14 of the Prevention of Terrorism (Temporary Provisions) Act 1974.[262] As the discussion of *Brogan* and *Brannigan and McBride* reveals, governments faced with adverse judicial findings in respect of derogable rights have viewed the maintaining of the relevant extraordinary powers as a matter of free choice in electing to derogate, in order to maintain the power, rather than assessing whether or not an objective right to derogate exists under international legal obligations. The long-term use of such "extraordinary" ordinary powers has a keen effect on societal constructs of the rule of law. Where emergency powers become the norm over an extended period of time, the reference point for legal normality may be lost or diluted, helping ultimately to create and entrench a hidden permanent emergency. As chapter 4 demonstrates, the effects of the long-term application of "ordinary" crisis powers for

---

[261] Ibid., p. 44.
[262] Prevention of Terrorism (Temporary Provisions) Act, 1974, 48 Halsbury Stat. 972 (3rd edn, 1978).

both state actors and citizens alike are severe, legitimizing extraordinary regimes and transforming them into ordinary benchmarks for the legal system as a whole.

A similar situation in which "normalized" emergencies arise is where there is an apparent transition from a formal state of emergency to rule by ordinary law. While external notification and positive law may portray metamorphosis – for example, as a result of internal political recognition that the international community equates emergency with insecurity, high potential for human rights abuses, and political instability – actual emergency conditions may continue to prevail. Formally disavowing emergency suggests progress and stability regained, while, in fact, the government may seek to conceal the true nature of the regime. This suggests that scrutiny ought not to focus solely on the government's own rhetorical statements of change but take into account solid factual assessment of whether emergency laws have in fact disappeared from the legal terrain.

As suggested above, while many of the studies on emergency regimes recognize the phenomenon of permanent emergencies, their framework for analysis is rather limited. Permanent emergencies are often conceived of as a spin-off from other factors, insufficient internal accountability, failure of external scrutiny, the result of the left-over apparatus of colonial regimes designed to protect hegemony, or the creation of paranoid governments. They have rarely been examined as manifestations of regime illegitimacy, representing a loss of consensus in government and the imposition of force as the sole means to control power. Furthermore, permanent emergencies are examined solely (if at all) through the prism of human rights, as they arise either in the context of state derogation or from the massive violations of individual rights that generally tend to accompany extended loss of rights' protection. A fundamental question is whether the examination of permanent emergencies belongs in the human rights framework at all, or whether its very existence should spark a wider discussion about the nature of the problem creating the crisis, and consequently the legal backdrop against which it is investigated.

Concluding assessment

Highly circumscribed thinking dominates academic, judicial, and policy analysis of emergencies. However, in practice there are substantial deviations from the core regulatory model that is incorporated into the derogation regime and what is missing is a more provocative profile of emergencies taking into consideration the failure of conventional thinking to account for the practice of states in this sphere. A more comprehensive approach to the multifaceted phenomena of emergency is needed.

There is also a need to think openly and creatively about where the boundaries of emergency doctrine begin and end. As the next chapter explores in the context of the application of international humanitarian law, there is a need to ask whether and when an emergency ceases to be such and is transformed into something else. The identification of such boundaries, to the extent that they exist, is crucial to a more comprehensive understanding of how an emergency operates and evolves. Detailing the line of demarcation between states of emergency, non-emergency, and grave civil strife (all of which are currently grouped together under the unified umbrella of the emergency doctrine) is a means to ensure greater accountability and transparency when emergency powers are activated. It is also a means to check the abuse of the privileges of derogation and crisis management by governments. Courts, both international and domestic, have been uniformly unwilling to perform this task, either considering it to lie outside the scope of their powers, or assuming the bona fides of the state when it comes before them.

One may wonder why it is that states choose to comply with the dictates of the derogation regime which lacks any truly effective structures of enforcement, and particularly where compliance may work against perceived national self-interest. This goes, obviously, to the heart of the broader question about the relevance of international legal rules and norms in general (which is outside the scope of this study). Here we would note two factors that are relevant in this context. The first concerns the legitimizing aspect of opting for and remaining part of international rule systems, which is marked by dual perceptions of the rules themselves as legitimate, and by their effects of legitimization.[263] Choosing to "play by these rules" revolves around the recognition of the role of legitimacy. As Habermas argues:

Legitimacy means that there are good arguments for a political order's claim to be recognized as right and just; a legitimate order deserves recognition. *Legitimacy means a political order's worthiness to be recognized.* This definition highlights the fact that legitimacy is a contestable validity claim; and the stability of the

---

[263] See Oscar Schachter, "Towards a Theory of International Obligation" (1968) 8 *Virginia Journal of International Law* 300; Abram Chayes and Antonia Handler Chayes, *The New Sovereignty: Compliance with International Regulatory Agreements* (Cambridge, MA: Harvard University Press, 1995).

order of domination (also) depends on its (at least) de facto recognition. Thus, historically as well as analytically, the concept is used above all in situations in which the legitimacy of an order is disputed, in which, as we say, legitimization problems arise.[264]

Coercion is not essential in order to ensure the efficacy of compliance. Compliance within the legal limits of derogation is valuable for states. But to be meaningful it depends on the rule-making bodies fully enforcing the demands of the relevant legal norms. Compliance also serves other functions for states. Thomas Franck maintains in his work on legitimacy in international law that "the international community more closely resembles a membership club with house rules."[265] This membership confers a desirable status, which results in members internalizing social functions and status-rooted privileges and duties. "Membership," Franck argues, is "reinforced by valid governance, shared experience, reciprocal gestures of deference and recognition, common rituals, mature common expectations and the successful pursuit of shared goals."[266] It is this "club" membership that confers the dual benefits of symbolic validation and recognition. This is true even in a context in which the single superpower shows a certain preference for unilateral actions.

The flip side of the legitimacy argument is that derogation can serve domestic and international political purposes for governments. Domestically, it supports the perception that the nature of the particular crisis is transient and limited and that the declaration of emergency, as well as the scope of the particular measures taken by the government, is subject to rigorous examination by external, neutral, and objective judicial bodies. As these bodies have demonstrated themselves manifestly incapable of dealing with the prolonged emergency syndrome, the government reaps tangible benefits from following the derogation procedures. Similarly, when "playing by the rules" of the derogation regime governments may obtain a seal of approval and further legitimacy from such international tribunals to be used as a shield against external criticisms by other states, NGOs, and international organizations. The acceptance of

---

[264] Jürgen Habermas, "Legitimation Problems in the Modern State" in *Communication and the Evolution of Society*, trans. Thomas McCarthy (Boston: Beacon Press, 1979), pp. 178–79.

[265] Thomas Franck, "Legitimacy in the International System" (1988) 82 *American Journal of International Law* 705. This article is a masterful analysis of how traditional doctrine relaying misgivings about the validity of international law is misplaced because of an overemphasis on the role of coercion in compliance. It also forcefully undermines the assumption that the community of states is a small and primitive entity. See H.L.A. Hart, *The Concept of Law* (Oxford: Clarendon Press, 1961), ch. 10.

[266] Franck, "Legitimacy," 711.

the derogation, and indeed consideration (even if negative in tone), is a form of symbolic validation for a government invoking emergency powers. If reporting and individual complaints processes are entertained and complied with, the examination of state derogation comes in a straitjacket formula that allows a government contending with a real crisis of its own legitimacy to avoid any scrutiny of this matter. The act of examination furthers, in a discrete sense, the act of pedigreeing in the international system, assisting the overall aim of continued recognition for governments, whose use of extensive crisis powers might otherwise exclude them from the fringe benefits of the global collective formalized in organizations such as the United Nations. Given this rather bleak assessment, a positive way forward is not immediately apparent. Though the function of this book is not to offer a reform program for international and national institutions overseeing emergencies, it is evident in our view that two important areas demand oversight attention. First, a willingness by oversight mechanisms to ask the fundamental question of whether an emergency is per se justified. This question is all the more pertinent in the post-September 11 context where state resort to emergency powers has been amplified on grounds that do not appear to be justifiable in all cases. The second is a willingness to examine the phenomenon of emergencies more robustly. This means acknowledging the failure of emergencies to conform to ideal type and then amending/reviewing oversight strategies accordingly. Neither of these tasks is simple, but they start from the premise upon which this book is based, namely the need to take a more critical look at the form and practices of emergencies as currently conceived by domestic and international law.

6   Emergencies and humanitarian law

The compacted relationship between war and emergency is under-explored theoretically. This chapter examines that relationship in the context of classic inter-state war and also explores it with respect to nebulous and underdefined situations of internal armed conflict. We set out three principles that shape our thinking in this context, and then move to assess some of the quandaries which arise when situations of war or conflict intersect with emergencies. First, international humanitarian law is prima facie an accommodation model.[1] Second, its genesis was located in the understanding that war required legal limits, understood and internalized by both combatants and states. Finally, war fulfills the classic definition of an "emergency" as set out by international human rights law norms. This is specifically recognized by the language of some of the derogation provisions that allow for derogation "in times of war or other emergency."[2]

In identifying "war" and unpacking the effects of its practices in the legal sphere a number of observations can be made. First, that the experience of war is an acute actualization of the breaking down of dichotomies and clear-cut distinctions between the normal and the extreme. Second, we identify the fallacy of basic assumptions underlying

---

[1] In this sense the principle has a surprising echo in the recent dissent by Justice Scalia in the *Hamdi* case. He forcefully stated: "Many think it not only inevitable but entirely proper that liberty give way to security in times of national crisis – that, at the extremes of military exigency, *inter arma silent leges*. Whatever the general merits of the view that war silences law or modulates its voice, that view has no place in the interpretation and application of a Constitution designed precisely to confront war and, in a manner that accords with democratic principles, to accommodate it." Hamdi v. Rumsfeld, 542 US 507 at 579 (2004).

[2] Convention for the Protection of Human Rights and Fundamental Freedoms, Nov. 4, 1950, 213 UNTS 221 (entered into force Sept. 3, 1953), art. 15.

the conceptualization of "war" and "emergency," and the attempts to separate them as unique and distinct phenomena. In particular, as we have done throughout this book, we wish to test the perceived wisdom that normalcy is the general rule while emergency constitutes the exception to that rule.[3] Rather, we suggest that emergency and its associated practices are a far more widespread and pervasive aspect of state experience and action than has generally been accepted by legal scholars and political thinkers. Moreover, we are convinced that the way in which governments conceptualize emergency responses is not limited to the classic emergency situation, but spills over to other critical aspects of state action. This should lead, in turn, to rethinking some of the foundational concepts that artificially separate certain strains of international law from each other.

In breaking down separation myths this chapter also demonstrates that certain patterns associated with the exercise of emergency powers at the domestic level are also reflected on the international plane. In particular, the breaking down of dichotomies and clear-cut distinctions between normalcy and emergency appears also on the international level and is by no means unique to national jurisdictions. This understanding has been missing from the conceptualization of emergency that is predominant in international law.

By closely analyzing the legal regulation of low-intensity conflict we show how the alleged distinctions between humanitarian law and the derogation regime of international human rights law are in fact more apparent than real. In short, there are multiple situations in which high-intensity emergencies are almost indistinguishable from low-intensity armed conflicts. This raises the important question of what law actually applies to these situations, that is, which legal regime applies within a broader accommodation model. It also questions the appropriateness of framing the discourse in terms of mutually exclusive categories. Here we do not aim to answer the larger questions that arise with respect to the relationship between international humanitarian law and human rights law generally, although analysis of this relationship in the concrete context of "high-intensity" emergencies provides certain important insights that are relevant to, and illuminating of, these more general issues.

Finally, in critically assessing the crossover question, this chapter seeks to answer some of the questions we have so far left unresolved

---

[3] See chapter 4.

concerning oversight of emergency situations as offered by international human rights law.

This chapter addresses these issues by first examining the legal doctrines of self-preservation, necessity, and self-defense in international law. It then explores the relationship between internal armed conflicts and situations of emergency, with particular emphasis on the concept expanded here, i.e., that of a "high-intensity emergency." The chapter follows this with a close analysis of low-intensity armed conflicts and their place in the accommodation model that international humanitarian law provides. Finally we assess the overlap between situations of high-intensity emergency and low-intensity conflict. We then close with a review of accountability mechanisms relevant to situations of crisis that fall within the legal boundaries identified by this chapter.

Self-preservation, necessity, and self-defense in international law

As noted in chapter 4, the main traditional feature of the international legal system has been a highly dichotomized division into two categories of legal rules distinguishing between times of peace and of war. The laws of peace apply in times of peace; the laws of war apply to belligerent states and regulate certain aspects of the relationship between these states and between them and other states not parties to the conflict. It is important to qualify this historical pedigree by noting the growing recognition that international human rights law norms continue to apply throughout the period of any armed conflict.[4] Recent jurisprudence by international courts and bodies undercuts the division, with significant practical consequences. Two pertinent examples illustrating this are the General Comment of the United Nations Human Rights Committee concerning states of emergency,[5] and the decisions of the International Court of Justice in the Nuclear Weapons and "Wall" cases.[6] All emphasize, though in strikingly different ways, the ongoing application

---

[4] See, e.g., Human Rights Committee, General Comment 29, States of Emergency (article 4), UN Doc. CCPR/C/21 Rev. 1/Add. 11 (2001), para. 3; *Legality of the Threat or Use of Nuclear Weapons*, Advisory Opinion (1996) *International Court of Justice Reports* 226, (1997) 35 *International Legal Materials* 809 (*Nuclear Weapons*); *Legal Consequences of the Construction of a Wall in the Occupied Palestinian Territory*, Advisory Opinion, July 9, 2004, available online at http://www.icj-cij.org/icjwww/idocket/imwp/imwpframe.htm (*The Wall*) (last visited on Aug. 8, 2005).

[5] Human Rights Committee, General Comment 29, para. 3.

[6] *Legality of the Threat or Use of Nuclear Weapons*, Advisory Opinion; *Legal Consequences of the Construction of a Wall in the Occupied Palestinian Territories*.

of international human rights law norms throughout the period of any armed conflict.

Until the third decade of the twentieth century[7] the waging of war, whether of an aggressive or defensive nature, was not illegal under international law.[8] States resorted to war in order to protect and defend their legal rights or to increase the state's power and possessions irrespective of its legal rights, as well as to challenge existing rights under international law. The distinction between just and unjust wars, while having a moral weight, did not have a direct impact on the international legal system in so far as wars continued to be a legal recourse regardless of their nature or motivation.[9] The right to go to war was closely attached to the notion of sovereignty and as the latter was deemed to be absolute, so was the former.[10]

Yet, the narratives of international law and international relations reveal a clear trend of states shying away from asserting openly their right to wage war against other states, even in those cases where waging war was precisely what they had, in fact, been doing. Rather than formally declare war,[11] invoking the rules and norms of belligerency and neutrality, states preferred to resort to "hostile measures short of war."[12]

---

[7] The important changes in the legal trend described in the text below came with the establishment of the League of Nations in 1919, and the signing of the Treaty Providing for the Renunciation of War as an Instrument of National Policy, on Aug. 27, 1928, 94 *League of Nations Treaty Series* 57 (the Kellogg–Briand Pact). See also Inter-American Anti-War Treaty of Non-Aggression and Conciliation (Saavedra Lamas Treaty), Oct. 10, 1933, 49 Stat. 3363, 163 *League of Nations Treaty Series* 57.

[8] See, e.g., Peter Malanczuk, *Akehurst's Modern Introduction to International Law* (7th edn, London: Routledge, 1997), pp. 306–09; Geoffrey Best, *War and Law since 1945* (Oxford: Clarendon Press, 1994), pp. 14–59; Ian Brownlie, *International Law and the Use of Force by States* (Oxford: Clarendon Press, 1963), pp. 66–112.

[9] Lassa Oppenheim, *International Law*, ed. Hersch Lauterpacht (7th edn, 2 vols., London: Longman, 1952), vol. II, pp. 177–78; William E. Hall, *A Treatise on International Law* (8th edn, Oxford: Clarendon Press, 1924), p. 82: "International law has no alternative but to accept war, independently of the justice of its origin, as a relation which the parties to it may set up, if they choose, and to busy itself only in regulating the effects of the relation." Cited in J.L. Brierly, *The Law of Nations: An Introduction to the International Law of Peace*, ed. Humphrey Waldock (6th edn, Oxford: Clarendon Press, 1963), p. 398. See also Michael Walzer, *Just and Unjust Wars: A Moral Argument with Historical Illustrations* (3rd edn, New York: Basic Books, 2000).

[10] See A. S. Hershey, *The Essentials of Public International Law* (New York: Macmillan, 1912), p. 349.

[11] Brownlie lists such examples as the Boxers and Chinese troops in 1900 and 1901, and the United States' occupation of Cuba in 1898 as characteristic of this phenomenon. Brownlie, *Use of Force*, pp. 45–46.

[12] Ibid.

Measures such as reprisals, blockade, and intervention were deemed not to invoke the laws of war. While not declaring war a state could use force against another state. The various classifications of these coercive measures "short of war" were not clearly distinguishable from each other. Quite often they were not easily (if at all) distinguishable from a fully fledged war. Thus, even the classical dichotomy of peace and war became tenuous and was practically, albeit not theoretically, replaced by a continuum calibrating the extent to which force was used between states. One may argue, of course, that the peace–war dichotomy merely gave way to another dichotomized classification distinguishing between situations involving the use of physical force and situations where force was not employed in inter-state relations. To the extent that one identifies force only with physical force the distinction may hold even today. However, if one is ready to recognize that economic and political pressures may be no less coercive than exercise of military power it is doubtful to what extent the clear separation is a valid one.[13]

Another result of states' historic hesitation to claim openly the right of war and their desire to coat themselves with a mantle of justification for their use of force has been the invocation of the rhetoric of self-preservation, self-defense, and necessity.[14] During the nineteenth century these three concepts had been mostly indistinguishable, often used interchangeably to express similar ideas.[15] The existence of a general right of self-preservation was widely acknowledged during the nineteenth century and the beginning of the twentieth century. This "natural" right[16] of states could be, and was, invoked by states wishing to conduct their affairs in a manner inconsistent with the dictates of positive international legal norms.[17] However, with the turn of the twentieth century, and especially after World War II, the tide shifted and turned against the recognition of a general right of self-preservation.[18] The prevailing opinion held that the acceptance of such a broad and sweeping

---

[13] Oscar Schachter, *International Law in Theory and Practice* (Boston: Nijhoff, 1991), p. 111.

[14] Brownlie, *Use of Force*, p. 41.

[15] Ibid., pp. 42, 46–47; Brierly, *The Law of Nations*, p. 404.

[16] Brownlie, *Use of Force*, p. 41.

[17] Hall, *International Law*, p. 322. See also *The Wimbledon* (1923) *Permanent Court of International Justice Report*, Aug. 17, 1923, Ser. A, No. 1, at 37 (Anzilotti, Huber, JJ., dissenting) ("The right of a State to adopt the course which it considers best suited to the exigencies of its security and to the maintenance of its integrity, is so essential a right that, in case of doubt, treaty stipulations cannot be interpreted as limiting it, even though these stipulations do not conflict with such an interpretation").

[18] John Westlake, *The Collected Papers of John Westlake on Public International Law*, ed. L. Oppenheim (Cambridge: Cambridge University Press, 1914), p. 115.

doctrine "would destroy the imperative character of any system of law in which it applied, for it makes all obligation to obey the law merely conditional; and there is hardly any act of international lawlessness which it might not be claimed to excuse."[19] Arguments that international law accommodates the right of self-preservation as a general principle of law within the meaning of article 38(1)(c) of the Statute of the International Court of Justice have been squarely rejected by the majority of scholars.[20] Thus, for example, George Schwarzenberger notes that: "If self-preservation were an absolute and overriding right, the rest of international law would become optional, and its observance would depend on a self-denying ordinance, revocable at will by each State, not to invoke this formidable superright."[21] Hence, "The truth is that self-preservation in the case of a state as of an individual is not a legal right but an instinct; and even if it may often happen that the instinct prevails over the legal duty not to do violence to others, international law ought not to admit that it is lawful that it should do so."[22] Considering such a doctrine to be legal when its net effect was to permit unhampered employment of extra-legal measures in the name of necessity and self-preservation – concepts which are, in themselves, too vague[23] – could only be regarded as "a logical and legal absurdity."[24]

In its original form, the doctrine of self-preservation could be regarded as the ultimate form of derogation, allowing states, lawfully, to suspend their observance of all other rules of international law. However, with time that doctrine was pushed outside the boundaries of international law and into the realm of extra-legality. For political realists, for example, the doctrine of self-preservation was nothing more than a different expression of the old adage "necessity knows no law." When a state deemed certain actions to be necessary for its own self-preservation and continued existence, it could take whatever measures it saw fit to end

[19] Brierly, *The Law of Nations*, p. 404.
[20] Bin Cheng, *General Principles of Law as Applied by International Courts and Tribunals* (London: Stevens, 1953), pp. 30–31 (making this argument).
[21] Georg Schwarzenberger, "The Fundamental Principles of International Law" (1955-I) 87 *Receuil de cours de l'Academie de droit international* 191 at 195, quoted in Julio Barboza, "Necessity (Revisited) in International Law" in Jerzy Makarczyk (ed.), *Essays in International Law in Honour of Judge Manfred Lachs* (Boston: Nijhoff, 1984), 27 at 28.
[22] Brierly, *The Law of Nations*, p. 405. See also Westlake, *The Collected Papers*, p. 112.
[23] On the inherent indeterminacy of such concepts as "necessity" and "proportionality," see Oscar Schachter, "Self-Defense and the Rule of Law" (1989) 83 *American Journal of International Law* 259 at 266–67.
[24] Brownlie, *Use of Force*, p. 48. See also Hersch Lauterpacht, *The Function of Law in the International Community* (Oxford: Clarendon Press, 1933), pp. 179–80.

the danger or minimize the damage, regardless of the legality of such measures under international law.

International legal scholars recognized, of course, that the political and military realities facing nations could not be ignored. If international law was to play any meaningful role it had to recognize and consider the special needs of states when confronted with crises. The solution was found by turning to an accommodation model of emergency regimes. The option to use extraordinary powers was left open to states but was limited to exceptional circumstances and required the relevant state to comply with certain preconditions. The legal system was the one to regulate the use of emergency powers under such doctrines as self-defense and, if applied in accordance with the relevant legal rules, to confer legitimacy upon them. The broad concept of self-preservation allowed virtually uninhibited use of force by states. In order to avoid the pitfalls inherent in this doctrine while enabling states to protect and defend themselves and their legal rights, a narrower doctrine, limited within the confines of strict criteria, was put forward.[25] Under the doctrine of self-defense states could be justified, under certain circumstances, in using force.[26] In a move designed to release the doctrine of self-defense from the clinch of the discredited self-preservation doctrine, the former was considered to be a restricted accommodation, well delimited within the confines of certain criteria and conditions.[27] Customary international law[28] sanctioned self-defense measures only when they were necessary to respond to an armed attack and the response was proportionate to the threat.[29] In the famous words of the American Secretary of State, Daniel Webster, a state using force must demonstrate the existence of "necessity of self-defence, instant, overwhelming,

---

[25] Yoram Dinstein, *War, Aggression and Self-defence* (4th edn, Cambridge: Cambridge University Press, 2005), pp. 175–77.

[26] D.W. Bowett, *Self-Defence in International Law* (Manchester: Manchester University Press, 1958), p. 11; D.W. Greig, *International Law* (2nd edn, London: Butterworths, 1976), p. 671.

[27] The doctrine of necessity has been often subsumed in the discussion about the general doctrine of self-preservation or concerning the doctrine of self-defense. Barboza, "Necessity in International Law," 28. But see Robert Ago, "Addendum to the Eighth Report on State Responsibility to the International Law Commission" (1979) 2 *Yearbook of the International Law Commission* 13, UN Doc. A/CN. 4/Ser. A/1980/Add. 1 (the concept of necessity not founded in the notion of self-preservation).

[28] Article 51 of the UN Charter refers to the "inherent right" of individual or collective self-defense. See also Nicaragua v. United States (Merits), at 94, 102–03; see also Oppenheim, *International Law*, p. 418; Robert Y. Jennings, "The Caroline and McLeod Cases" (1938) 32 *American Journal of International Law* 82; Brownlie, *Use of Force*, p. 43.

[29] Nicaragua v. United States (Merits), at 94; Brownlie, *Use of Force*, pp. 433–34.

leaving no choice of means, and no moment for deliberation." It was also necessary to show that the measures taken involved "nothing unreasonable or excessive; since the act justified by the necessity of self-defence, must be limited by that necessity, and kept clearly within it."[30] The principle of necessity means that no other peaceful alternative measures are available or effective. Use of force was to be a measure of last resort.[31] This operates as the functional equivalent of "ordinary law first" in the derogation regime's use of the proportionality test. Equally the principle of proportionality was considered to be the crux of the self-defense doctrine in international law. A third condition which forms part of customary international law on this matter is the principle of immediacy. This principle requires that there will not be "an undue time-lag between the armed attack and the exercise of self-defence."[32] Thus, if the historical model of self-preservation ushered in an element of extra-legality, the doctrine of self-defense was part and parcel of a model of accommodation, internalizing rules concerning use of force into the system of international law and operating within the legal framework of international law rather than outside it. This conceptual distinction, which had been mostly theoretical during the nineteenth century when war was not legally outlawed, became significant with the prohibition on war and use of force. In modern form this prohibition is most cogently and authoritatively expressed in article 2(4) of the United Nations Charter (UN Charter) which provides the general rule prohibiting the use of force in inter-state relations.[33] This general prohibitory rule is subject, in turn, to article 51 of the charter which permits a resort to individual and collective self-defense in certain circumstances as well as to the power of the Security Council to authorize the use of force under Chapter VII of the charter.

A closely linked pattern of moving away from extra-legal claims about the right of self-preservation to claims rooted and defined within the boundaries of international legal rules is demonstrated by the rejection of the "German doctrine" of military necessity.[34] According to this doctrine – which was invoked as justification for German actions during

---

[30] Letter from Daniel Webster to Fox (Apr. 24, 1841) later incorporated in a Note to Lord Ashburton (July 27, 1842), quoted in Brownlie, *Use of Force*, p. 43.

[31] For a critical analysis of this proposition, see Schachter, *International Law in Theory and Practice*, pp. 106–34.

[32] Ibid., p. 202. Dinstein, *Aggression*, p. 210.   [33] Dinstein, *Aggression*, p. 177.

[34] Thomas Erskine Holland, *The Laws of War on Land* (Oxford: Clarendon Press, 1908), para. 2.

World War I – there could have been no obligations whatsoever imposed upon states in times of war concerning the rules of warfare, since *Kriegsraison geht vor Kriegsmanier.* Under circumstances of extreme emergency the rule of law was replaced by a "rule of necessity."[35] If a belligerent deemed it necessary for the success of its military operations to violate a rule of international law, the violation would be permissible. This doctrine was widely rejected as leading to "an end of international law...[and to] a world without law."[36] It is generally accepted that claim of necessity cannot justify or excuse any deviation from the rules and norms of the laws and customs of war unless a particular rule is explicitly qualified by a clear reference to military necessity.[37] "Military necessity or expediency do [sic] not justify a violation of positive rules."[38] Thus, "military necessity" has come to be an integral part of the international legal system, defined and operating within the confines of international law, rather than being an extra-legal measure justifying the suspension of legal norms and rules.

The concepts of "necessity" and "self-defense" are not confined to the area of the laws of war. There is a clearly marked pattern of incorporating these doctrines within the confines of legal discourse and adopting a model of accommodation concerning their application. Thus, for example, these concepts form two of the defenses that a state may seek to invoke against the imposition upon it of responsibility for acts violating international legal rules. In the context of the discussion concerning the desirability of setting an a priori emergency structure, it is instructive to note that during the discussions in the International Law Commission (ILC) concerning the Draft Articles on State Responsibility, an argument was made that the justificatory claim of a "state of necessity" need not be included within the codified list of circumstances precluding the

---

[35] N.C.H. Dunbar, "Military Necessity in War Crimes Trials" (1952) 29 *British Yearbook of International Law* 442 at 446.

[36] Elihu Root (1921 speech in the annual meeting of the American Society of International Law), quoted in William G. Downey, Jr., "The Law of War and Military Necessity" (1953) 47 *American Journal of International Law* 252 at 253.

[37] See, e.g., Gerhard von Glahn, *The Occupation of Enemy Territory: A Commentary on the Law and Practice of Belligerent Occupation* (Minneapolis: University of Minnesota Press, 1957), pp. 225–26.

[38] *United States v. List et al.* (1950) 11 *Trials of War Criminals before the Nuremberg Military Tribunals under Control Council Law* 757 at 1252 (Case VII, also known as the *Hostages trial*). See also *In re Krupp and Others* (1949) 10 *War Crimes Reports* 138–39; *In re von Leeb and Others* (1949) 12 *War Crimes Reports* 1 at 93 (the *German High Command Trial*); Quincy Wright, "The Outlawry of War and the Law of War" (1953) 47 *American Journal of International Law* 365 at 371.

wrongfulness of a state action or omission which does not conform to that state's international obligations. The claim was made that situations amounting to a true "state of necessity" were exceptional and rare, that a codified rule might lend itself more easily to further abuse, and that immense practical difficulties would inhere in any attempt to determine objectively that an "essential" interest of a state had been severely endangered. It was thus thought best not to include an express provision concerning necessity in the articles.[39] In rejecting this position the ILC emphasized a number of considerations.[40] Silence on this matter would not lead to states forgoing the possible use of the necessity claim since this claim was "too deeply rooted in general legal thinking." Fear of potential abuses could not serve as a reason to bar the legitimate resort to the justificatory claim of necessity in adequate circumstances.[41] Moreover, abuses could be minimized by setting out precisely the strict conditions necessary for a claim of a "state of necessity" to be legitimate,[42] and by excluding from the ambit of that doctrine certain matters with regard to which the risk of abuse is considered too large to take.[43] Similar arguments were made with respect to the doctrine of self-defense.[44]

The debate as to whether matters of state security can or ought to be regulated by legal norms and rules is a long-standing one.[45] As noted

---

[39] Report of the International Law Commission on the Work of its Fifty-Third Session, Official Records of the General Assembly, Fifty-Sixth Session, Supplement No. 10 (A/56/10), chp.IV.E.1, Text of the Draft Articles on Responsibility of States for Internationally Wrongful Acts (Nov. 2001). See also James Crawford, *The International Law Commission's Articles on State Responsibility: Introduction, Text and Commentaries* (Cambridge: Cambridge University Press, 2002).

[40] Ibid.

[41] Thus, "This right possessed by all nations, which is based on generally accepted usage, cannot lose its *raison d'être* simply because it may in some cases have been abused." *The Wimbledon*, at 36 (Anzilloti, Huber, JJ., dissenting).

[42] See also Francisco V. Garcia Amador, "Report on Responsibility of the State for Injuries Caused in its Territory to the Person or Property of Aliens" (1959) 2 *Yearbook of the International Law Commission* 53 at para. 13 (the uncertainty surrounding the substantive content of the doctrine of necessity as a significant reason to codify this doctrine and set it within well-defined limits and criteria).

[43] For a discussion on the categories of matters in which states are barred from invoking the claim of necessity see International Law Commission, *Articles on State Responsibility*, pp. 50–51, paras. 37–38.

[44] Schachter, *International Law in Theory and Practice*, pp. 259–63.

[45] Indeed, the debate might be considered as a particular reflection of an even more general debate concerning the ability of legal norms to shape behavior and influence conduct of individuals and states, rather than being a mere ex post justification for such behavior that is originally propelled solely by other, extra-legal considerations.

above, the prevailing position among international legal scholars considers claims of self-defense to be governed and regulated by positive law. In other words, a constitutional model of emergency regime may be said to govern the international legal sphere.[46] An alternative approach considers self-defense to be outside the realm of positive law. Under this position, the right of self-defense is "an autonomous, non-derogable right that 'exists' independently of legal rules."[47] This position is shared by two main schools of thought. First, there are those who regard the right of self-defense as an expression of the natural right of self-preservation applicable both to individuals and to states and who therefore refuse to recognize the possibility of limiting that right by means of positive law.[48] According to Grotius, for example, "The right of self-defence ... has its origin directly, and chiefly, in the fact that nature commits to each his own protection."[49] Under certain exceptional circumstances, necessity may confer a right upon a state to act in contravention of recognized positive rules of law.[50] However, it should be noted that Grotius rejected the view that necessity led to the suspension of all law. Rather he thought that it might result in the suspension of a particular rule or norm.[51] Moreover, Grotius considered the doctrine of necessity to entail certain limitations on its own use, such as that there must not be fault on the part of the state which exercised the right of necessity, that the danger be real, threatening life or property as well as imminent, and that the measures employed would not exceed that which was necessary for removing that danger.[52]

The view of self-defense as an autonomous "right" is advanced even further by those who regard law as subordinate to power in international relations.[53] Those who subscribe to the realist school in international relations (the history of which can be traced back to Thucydides,

---

[46] See, e.g., D.W. Bowett, "The Use of Force for the Protection of Nationals Abroad" in Antonio Cassese (ed.), *The Current Legal Regulation of the Use of Force* (Boston: Nijhoff, 1986), p. 39.

[47] Schachter, *International Law in Theory and Practice*, p. 260.

[48] Hugo Grotius, *De Jure Belli ac Pacis* (1646) (Washington, DC: Carnegie Institution of Washington, 1925), p. 172. On the Grotian concept of necessity see generally Burleigh C. Rodick, *The Doctrine of Necessity in International Law* (New York: Columbia University Press, 1928), pp. 2–8; Hersch Lauterpacht, "The Grotian Tradition in International Law" (1946) 23 *British Yearbook of International Law* 1 at 30–39.

[49] Schachter, *International Law in Theory and Practice*, p. 259.

[50] Rodick, *The Doctrine of Necessity*, p. 4.   [51] Ibid.

[52] Ibid., p. 6; Lauterpacht, "The Grotian Tradition," 32.

[53] Schachter, *International Law in Theory and Practice*, p. 260.

Machiavelli, and Hobbes)[54] reject the belief in the ability of states to cooperate and that international law and institutions can be effective means to bring about world peace. The picture that they paint is one dominated by the twin images of power and anarchy.[55] The question of peace is to be viewed not through the prism of law and international institutions, but rather through the mediating factor of the "balance of power."[56] Under this approach, there is no room for any kind of a "legalistic-moralistic" approach in international relations, in general, and with respect to issues involving state safety and security, in particular. Legal rules and norms are considered too inflexible and rigid to accommodate the security needs of states; each state is and should have the full and unfettered discretion to determine what course of action ought to be taken to promote its vital interests, security and preservation being the most prominent of those interests.

That there is a tension between what states might perceive to be their security needs and the restrictive dictates of international law can hardly be disputed. But an attempt to resolve that tension cannot ignore one part of the equation and focus on the other as a sole factor. "International law" and "state interest" cannot be regarded as totally separate of each other and mutually exclusive; they are both important factors in the overall equation and are interdependent. The "defensist" principle, considering self-defense to be the only legitimate reason to use force in inter-state relations, is not only a legal proposition but is also accepted by many states as a strategic policy.[57] The implementation of such a

---

[54] Thucydides, *History of the Peloponnesian War*, trans. Richard Crawley (Vermont: Everyman, 1993); Thomas Hobbes, *Leviathan* (1651), ed. C.B. Macpherson (Harmondsworth: Penguin, 1968).

[55] See, e.g., Jack Donnelly, *Realism and International Relations* (Cambridge, UK: Cambridge University Press, 2000); Hans J. Morgenthau, *Politics Among Nations: The Struggle for Power and Peace* (6th edn, New York: Knopf, 1985); Hans Morgenthau, "Diplomacy" (1946) 55 *Yale Law Journal* 1067; Edward H. Carr, *Twenty Years' Crisis, 1919–1939: An Introduction to the Study of International Relations* (New York: Palgrave, 2001); George F. Kennan, *American Diplomacy, 1900–1950* (London: Secker & Walburg, 1951); Dean Acheson, "Foreign Policy of the United States" (1964) 18 *Arkansas Law Review* 225; Robert Kagan, *Paradise and Power: America and Europe in the New World Order* (rev. edn, London: Atlantic Books, 2004).

[56] See generally Kenneth N. Waltz, *Theory of International Politics* (New York: McGraw-Hill, 1979); Claude L. Inis, *Power and International Relations* (New York: Random House, 1962); Ernst B. Haas, "The Balance of Power: Prescription, Concept, or Propaganda" (1953) 5 *World Politics* 442; Kenneth N. Waltz, "Realist Thought and Neorealist Theory" (1990) 44 *Journal of International Affairs* 21; A.F.K. Organski, *World Politics* (2nd rev. edn, New York: Knopf, 1968).

[57] Schachter, "Self-defense," 268.

policy calls for active measures by states (for example, considering ways to resolve conflicts and reduce threats without resort to force) that go beyond the negative dictates of the law prohibiting the use of force.[58] This policy leads, in turn, to the strengthening of the international legal prohibition on the use of force by means of bilateral and multilateral treaties, as well as unilateral actions taken by states.[59] Despite contemporary challenges we believe that such steps serve to enhance rather than limit a state's sense of security and stability over the longer term.[60]

As originally understood the concepts of self-preservation, necessity, and self-defense had frequently been used interchangeably. The turn of the twentieth century saw an increasing number of voices in the international legal community expressing doubts as to the viability, in international law, of such broad notions as "self-protection" and "necessity." The two world wars led to an almost complete abandonment of these doctrines. A more strictly defined doctrine of self-defense filled the place once occupied by the broad doctrines of necessity and self-preservation. These sweeping doctrines allowed states to act in contravention of their international legal obligations. They were seen as suspending some of the rules of international law (and, under a radical version, all rules of international law) and justifying acts otherwise considered to be illegal. The clear move was away from an unconstitutional, extra-legal model of emergency powers toward an accommodation/constitutional style model of emergency regime. It was accepted that claims of self-defense and necessity, in their modern, limited sense, ought to be strictly confined to situations that were truly exceptional – the threat had to be directed at the most important interests of the state and the danger to those interests had to be extremely serious and imminent – and could not be legitimate unless the principles of necessity and proportionality were maintained, i.e., the measures taken were necessary to ward off the danger, and no other legal means were available or effective to the achievement of that purpose.

The concept of "exceptional circumstances" informed by the traditional discourse concerning the relationship between normalcy and emergency is also closely linked to the fundamental dichotomy of international law relating to the distinction between peace and war. Special rules and laws were developed to deal with these two separate phenomena. When peace ended and war started a new regime of international legal rules became applicable and vice versa when peace

---

[58] Ibid.   [59] Ibid., pp. 269–70.   [60] Ibid., p. 274.

was reinstituted. Evidently, as we have noted above, this historical distinction has been substantially reformulated by the jurisprudence of the International Court of Justice and the Human Rights Committee, insisting (though with markedly different emphasis) on the continuation of the norms of peacetime (namely human rights norms) throughout any period of armed conflict. But suffice to note here as a historical matter that as the peace–war separation became less clear so too did the distinction between normalcy and emergency, between the boundaries of the rule and the limits of the exception. We observe similar patterns between national and international legal responses to the exception. The same is equally apparent when we examine the relationship between emergency and internal conflict.

Internal armed conflicts and emergencies

This brings us to examine one of the most contentious aspects of international humanitarian law, whose content has remained the subject of much debate among states and scholars, namely classifying the legal status of internal armed conflicts and the rules applicable thereto. Lack of consensus has been most marked on the issue of when the legal criteria establishing the existence of an internal armed conflict are satisfied. Despite, or perhaps because of, lack of such agreement internal armed conflicts have been a persistent feature of the international political landscape for decades. They have been associated with the most egregious human rights violations, characterized by inept and insufficient governance and increasingly leading to various forms of international and regional intervention.

We suggest that there is increasing clarity on the legal and factual requirements that activate the applicability of international humanitarian law to low-intensity internal conflict. In particular, we examine the overlap between situations characterized as "high-intensity" emergencies and situations of low-intensity armed conflict and argue that rigid "emergency–normal" or "emergency–conflict" distinctions are misplaced. In doing so we stress the importance, both symbolic and legal, of identifying which model of accommodation actually applies to a situation of violent crisis. Moreover, we note that such situations can move between legal regimes (and thus, between the various models of accommodation).

To demonstrate this, we propose a series of markers that facilitate the classification of conflicts with emergency characteristics in the legal campground of humanitarian law. We believe that such categorization is not only significant in terms of accountability, but has a substantial impact on the capacity to successfully negotiate the end of conflict as well as the successful transformation of conflicted societies during and after peace agreements have been negotiated. In doing so we set out the means to distinguish between situations of emergency and situations of conflict. In this way, we address the standard response by states confronted with internal insurgency – claiming that the problem they face is one of internal criminal or terrorist behavior, which activates only the application human rights law and domestic emergency responses.[61] We conclude the discussion by suggesting that the pressing question for those concerned with the oversight and control of emergencies is not satisfied simply by applying a model of accommodation to deal with an emergency problem, but rather that it is important within that discussion to decide which model is applied.

We start by examining "high-intensity" emergencies and identifying their characteristics. We then move to clarify and identify what we mean by low-intensity conflict. This discussion sketches the legal standards that are relevant to classifying such situations, as well as addressing the application of such standards in practice. We then address the meeting point of emergency and conflict regimes. Here we look at the form of accommodation model that is applied by international law to internal conflict matters and explore the overlap between human rights and humanitarian law in conflict situations. We propose a series of markers that may be used to chart the movement of situations from emergency to conflict regulation. We also outline the benefits, in terms of accountability and transparency, of regulating low-intensity conflicts by applying international humanitarian law. However, it should be noted that while we make specific claims for the categorization of certain emergency situations under the humanitarian law framework, this does not

---

[61] In this context it is argued that the appropriate regulatory standards are Minimum Humanitarian Standards. See, for example, Declaration of Minimum Humanitarian Standards, reprinted in Report of the Sub-Commission on Prevention of Discrimination and Protection of Minorities on its Forty-Sixth Session, Commission on Human Rights, 51st Sess., Provisional Agenda Item 19, at 4, UN Doc. E/CN.4/1995/116 (1995); Report of the Secretary-General, "Promotion and Protection of Human Rights – Fundamental Standards of Humanity", E/CN.4/2001/91 (Jan. 12, 2001); Peter H. Kooijmans, "In the Shadowlands between Civil War and Civil Strife: Some Reflections on the Standard-Setting Process" in Astrid J.M. Delissen and Gerard J. Tanja (eds.), *Humanitarian Law of Armed Conflict: Challenges Ahead: Essays in Honour of Frits Kalshoven* (Boston: Nijhoff, 1991); Theodor Meron, "Towards a Humanitarian Declaration on Internal Strife" (1984) 78 *American Journal of International Law* 859.

imply that some internal conflicts are not appropriately regulated by both human rights law and humanitarian law. In fact, as noted above, there is an increasing consensus that international human rights law norms continue to apply throughout the experience of conflict. However, we believe that there is still considerable tension over which body of law enjoys primacy in such context. Moreover, many conflict situations are fluid and are capable of moving between these legal regimes.

High-intensity emergencies

As chapter 5 demonstrated, situations of emergency are facilitated and regulated by international human rights law through the mechanism of derogation. The crises that derogation can attach to are varied – being political, economic, or social in nature (though we have generally focused our assessment on political/violent crisis type emergencies).

Recalling chapter 5, an analysis of international human rights law jurisprudence gives us some guidelines as to what constitutes an emergency: "public emergency" was characterized in the *Lawless* case as "an exceptional situation of crisis or emergency which affects the whole population and constitutes a threat to the organized life of the community of which the state is composed."[62] It is also clear that a situation of emergency is conceived of as a temporary phenomenon.[63] Finally the measures taken must be proportionate to the scale of the crisis experienced and must function as a means to bring an end to the crisis, rather than as a mechanism to perpetuate it.

As envisaged by the derogation regime, emergencies were well defined, both in terms of the situations to which they would apply and with regard to the length of time for which "special" legal regulation would be required. However, the real world of derogations and their legal regulation has been markedly different. Emergencies have rarely operated in textbook form, with situations of de facto, complex and institutionalized, and permanent emergencies being common features in practice.[64] These "problem" emergencies are more typical of the experience of emergency powers than the "model" scenario in which a state resorts to emergency powers for a brief period of time in order to contain a specific problem, and having done so successfully returns the

---

[62] Lawless v. Ireland (Court), 3 Eur. Ct HR (ser. A) (1960–61).
[63] Nicole Questiaux, "Study of the Implications for Human Rights of Recent Developments Concerning Situations Known as States of Siege or Emergency," UN ESCOR, 35th Sess., UN Doc. E/CN.4/Sub. 2/1982/15 (1982), para. 69, at 20.
[64] Ibid., para. 103, at 26; para. 118, at 29; para. 112, at 28.

legal situation to the *status quo ante*. These problem emergencies also point to the many limitations of the models of accommodation that are manifested domestically and internationally.

These problem emergencies have, in turn, a high crossover with situations of internal armed conflict. In particular, we suggest that there is a high correlation between what we call "high-intensity" emergencies and situations of low-intensity internal armed conflict. In this we suggest that the emergency typecast can be maneuvered by governments to cover up extreme and fatal internal disorder. The emergency exception becomes a disguise for regime illegitimacy. The prolonged suspension of normal protections for individuals is often inimical to the original rationale for allowing states to limit the exercise of certain rights and liberties. The validated legal exception may further autocratic tendencies, advance strong-arm military tactics, and facilitate the creation of power hierarchies where ultimate control rests with elite political actors. Thus, the hybrid models of accommodation that the derogation procedure offers can function negatively rather than positively to deal with problem emergencies.

High-intensity emergencies are a particular form of emergency that combines features of complex, institutionalized, and permanent emergencies. We suggest that they are characterized by the following elements. First, these emergencies are not short term but permanent. In a variety of jurisdictions including, but not limited to, Northern Ireland, Turkey, El Salvador, and India, a state of emergency may have been proclaimed for decades.[65] Second, normal constitutional or judicial guarantees in these contexts are suspended or rendered inoperable for extended periods of time. Third, the reach and substance of emergency powers are continuously expanded. The effect of emergency powers on due process rights is particularly notable.[66] Fourth, states that

---

[65] For Turkey see Oren Gross, "'Once More unto the Breach': The Systematic Failure of Applying the European Convention on Human Rights to Entrenched Emergencies" (1998) 23 *Yale Journal of International Law* 437; for India see C. Raj Kumar, "Human Rights Implications of National Security Laws in India: Combatting Terrorism while Preserving Civil Liberties" (2005) 33 *Denver Journal of International Law and Policy* 195; for Northern Ireland derogations see http://www.law.qub.ac.uk/humanrts/emergency/ nireland1/INTRO.HTM# declarations (last visited on Aug. 8, 2005).

[66] *Judicial Guarantees in States of Emergency*, 9 Inter-American Ct HR (ser. A) at 40, OEA/ser. L/VI/111.9 doc.13 (1987). Notably in this decision the court decided that the due process protections of article 8 of the American Convention cannot be suspended in situations of emergency, in so far as they are prerequisites for the necessary functioning of judicial guarantees.

experience high-intensity emergencies are consistently and repeatedly in derogation of their human rights treaty obligations. Finally and most significantly, high-intensity emergencies are associated with persistent levels of internal violence. That violence generally emanates from two sources, namely third-party actors whose aim is the destruction of the state, its agents, and institutions, or third-party actors fighting amongst themselves (a civil war situation) or also in conflict with state forces.

Persistent internal conflict is a key aspect of distinguishing high-intensity emergencies from other exigencies. However, ascertaining the nature, quantity, and form of such violence is a difficult exercise. A number of preliminary qualifications are necessary. Generally, protracted internal violence between the state and third parties or intra-third parties has a political component. That is to say, the nature or control of the state itself is disputed to some extent. The legitimacy of such disputes, namely the interference with the state's authority, is a hotly contested issue for sovereign states.[67] As a result, such forms of internal political violence are generally branded as forms of terrorism, and any political legitimacy that might accrue to non-state actors is stripped away.[68]

Second, high-intensity emergencies are generally not containable by a normal policing response. These situations tend to involve the use of military forces or militarized police as a means to combat the violence. Yet, while there are circumstances under which states may be entitled to resort to military means to defend themselves from internal strife, when military forces are used consistently for extended periods of time there is a need to take a closer look at the crisis within the state. In such situations the pertinent question to be asked is whether such violence is merely aberrational criminal activity or whether it is a form of violence of a different nature.

Finally, high-intensity emergencies entail a persistent experience of violence. The state continues to experience internal conflict from the same source(s) over an extended period of time. This, again, is a terrain that is highly contested. Many states experiencing low-level internal violence argue, both domestically and internationally, that the violence is at such a low level that it fails to activate the legal standards of

[67] Louis Rene Beres, "The Meaning of Terrorism – Jurisprudential and Definitional Clarifications" (1995) 28 *Vanderbilt Journal of Transnational Law* 239.

[68] A good example here is Chechnya. For background see Paola Gaeta, "The Armed Conflict in Chechnya before the Russian Constitutional Court" (1996) 7 *European Journal of International Law* 563. This invokes the complex issues concerning the definition of terrorism that are revisited in the next chapter.

international humanitarian law. Rather, they argue that human rights law as modified by the privilege of derogation is the appropriately applicable legal regime. Accordingly, such low-level violence is frequently described as "internal disturbances and tensions,"[69] passing under the radar screens of international humanitarian law. States that experience internal violence and wish to avoid the application of humanitarian law may refer to this formula as a means of deflecting scrutiny and application of humanitarian norms. We examine below how states generally maintain for themselves the prerogative to decide whether the laws that apply to internal armed conflict are applicable to their particular context and circumstances. The obvious question is how we can assess the violence taking place within a state and decide whether it indeed falls inside the threshold of "internal disturbances and tensions." In doing so we also make a legal and political call over the "type" of emergency being experienced and therefore over the appropriate model of accommodation.

Although there is no one entirely satisfactory method of assessing the threshold at which the level of violence moves from "disturbances and tensions" to conflict, some useful pointers can be identified. States experiencing low-level internal violence often argue (correctly) that the level of violence experienced at any particular moment is insufficient to satisfy the criteria of intensity that are required to recategorize the conflict. The test applied to assess such violence is a vertical one. The requirement is that the violence experienced at a given point in time be of sufficient intensity at that moment to ensure legal categorization in one category (humanitarian law) over another (human rights/emergency). We suggest that this snapshot approach is fundamentally flawed and requires rethinking. Attention should also be focused on the experience of violence over time. It is not difficult to envisage a situation in which military assaults are carried out by the government over a long period of time, but the intensity of the conflict at any given point is low.[70] We suggest that the test for intensity of violence should be a horizontal one, taking

---

[69] See *Minimum Standards*, reprinted in Report of the Sub-Commission on Prevention of Discrimination and Protection of Minorities on its Forty-Sixth Session, Commission on Human Rights, 51st Sess., Provisional Agenda Item 19, at 4, UN Doc. E/CN.4/1995/116 (1995).

[70] As Hogan and Walker demonstrate, the nature and extent of political violence in Northern Ireland show huge swings over time. At the height of the conflict (1972) 4,876 persons were killed and injured. In 1983 a total of 210 individuals were similarly hurt or killed. Gerard Hogan and Clive Walker, *Political Violence and the Law in Ireland* (Manchester: Manchester University Press, 1989), p. 170.

into account the consistent intensity of violence, which would account, among other things, for situations that are characterized by persistent but low-intensity violence. By looking at extended emergencies that are characterized by significant and persistent internal violence through the prism of the proposed test we can reassess whether they are regulated appropriately by the human rights/derogation regime. The better view is to have a more critical approach to high-intensity emergencies, combined with a more sophisticated test to assess intensity of violence. In short, high-intensity emergencies constitute a "suspect-class" that merits greater critical attention.

Oversight of high-intensity emergencies

One response to the approach outlined above is that emergency situations are generally overseen by international human rights judicial mechanisms and that this scrutiny is sufficient to ensure that abuse and manipulation do not occur. This section rejects this argument and outlines a series of fault-lines in the structure and jurisprudence of international human rights bodies that facilitate the manipulation by states of the derogation provisions. It also explains why human rights oversight bodies have not viewed themselves as competent to apply another legal regime, that of international humanitarian law, when looking at states' invocation of derogation and emergency claims.[71]

As outlined earlier, the derogation regime was intended to operate as a time-bound, limited, and proportionate response for states experiencing crisis. In practice this has not been the case. The most evident and persistent misuse of the derogation privilege has been the tendency of states to limit individual rights indefinitely and to operate in a context of permanent emergency.[72] Following from the case law analysis in the previous chapter we take our position a step further here and argue that the permanent emergency can be one of the most significant factors in assisting the appropriate classification of an enduring internal conflict. This analysis more generally highlights the point that

---

[71] On the overlap between human rights and humanitarian law norms see generally René Provost, *International Human Rights and Humanitarian Law* (Cambridge: Cambridge University Press, 2002); see also Kenneth Watkin, "Controlling the Use of Force: A Role for Human Rights Norms in Contemporary Armed Conflict" (2004) 98 *American Journal of International Law* 1.

[72] Oren Gross and Fionnuala Ní Aoláin, "From Discretion to Scrutiny: Revisiting the Application of the Margin of Appreciation Doctrine in the Context of Article 15 of the European Convention on Human Rights" (2001) 23 *Human Rights Quarterly* 625 at 644–47.

observers and academics should remain finely attuned to – namely that what happens *within* legal categories of accommodation is as significant as placing a situation within a broad definitional boundary to begin with.

Regional courts and international tribunals have been unable and unwilling to challenge the practice of states in this context. The reasons for this are complex, and testify to the difficulty of reining in state behavior where the state perceives itself to be under threat and is therefore less willing to place limits on its responses. First, the emergency oversight mechanisms created by treaty law are grossly inadequate to confront the permanent emergency situation. All actors in the human rights drama, such as the Human Rights Committee, the European Court and Commission of Human Rights, the Inter-American Court and Commission, and the Human Rights Commission focus on the regulation of state behavior that generally assumes a peacetime context. Humanitarian law invokes a different legal regime that binds, in whole or in part, both state and non-state actors in a context of armed conflict. While a number of these bodies, notably the Inter-American Court of, and Commission on, Human Rights have incorporated humanitarian law principles into their oversight of human rights violations, such jurisprudence is still tentative and generally under-developed.[73] The most significant decision in this respect is in the *Tablada* case concerning an attack in 1989 by forty-three armed persons on a military base containing members of the national armed forces at La Tablada, Argentina.[74] The complaint by relatives of those killed to the IACHR alleged both violations of international humanitarian law and human rights law. The commission found that it had the competence to apply humanitarian law directly. Notwithstanding such occasional decisions, human rights tribunals remain wary of applying humanitarian law norms to cases coming before them. In particular, when examining emergency situations they do not consider it appropriate to shift their examination to include humanitarian law

---

[73] See, e.g., Inter-American Commission on Human Rights, *Report on the Situation of Human Rights in Nicaragua*, OEA/Ser. L/V/II.45 (Nov. 17, 1978). See also Aloeboetoe et al. v. Surinam (1994) Inter-Am. Ct HR (Ser. C) No. 15 (Sept. 10, 1993). The European Court of Human Rights has avoided categorization of the situation in south-east Turkey between government security forces and Kurdish separatists as "internal armed coflict." The furthest they have gone in this respect is to describe the situation as "civil strife." See Akdivar v. Turkey (1997) 23 *European Human Rights Reports* 143 at 186.

[74] See Inter-American Commission on Human Rights Report No. 55/97, Case No. 11.137, Argentina, OEA/Ser. L/V/II. 97, Doc. 38, Oct. 30, 1997.

terms of reference. Even when examining repeatedly permanent emergency situations they have not, by and large, applied humanitarian law to these problem situations.[75] In addition, the human rights enforcement bodies remain generally unwilling (conceptually and politically) to recognize within their own boundaries the validation of another phenomenon, namely armed conflict, which seems at odds with the highest standards of protection for human rights. The obvious caveat to this is the formal recognition by a number of derogation clauses that "war" itself is a lawful basis for derogation and the affirmation, under article 15 of the European Convention, that notwithstanding the non-derogable nature of article 2, its provisions are not violated by "lawful acts of war." However, these formal treaty recognitions have had little effect in practice on how judicial bodies treat international humanitarian law and their willingness to acknowledge its potential applicability to issues before them. The recognition that the derogation regime applies to a situation of war has not lessened the separate application of the two legal regimes despite some recent judicial affirmations of the continued application of human rights norms throughout periods of armed conflict. Despite the conceptual similarity of accommodation that is inherent in the two regimes, their specialized oversight mechanisms and particular rule definitions may lead to areas of overlap contributing to lack of legal oversight.

Second, when states appear before human rights tribunals the procedural structure of the interface militates against an assessment of the totality of the derogation or conflict experience. When considered under the individual complaint process each case is treated as being an independent hearing for the state and the party bringing the complaint. Therefore, there is little room for the institutional memory of preceding cases invoking similar (or, indeed, even the very same) derogation. The results can be absurd, in the sense that in certain contexts, such as the one pertaining to Northern Ireland, the state may be in derogation for decades without that fact being considered in the context of the particular case at hand. In a similar and related context the European Court (and, in the past, also the European Commission) has dealt with the numerous Turkish cases coming before it on a case-by-case basis while

---

[75] Gross and Ní Aoláin, "From Discretion to Scrutiny"; Aisling Reidy, Françoise Hampson, and Kevin Boyle, "Gross Violations of Human Rights: Invoking the European Convention on Human Rights in the Case of Turkey" (1997) 15 *Netherlands Quarterly of Human Rights* 161.

ignoring the implications of systematic abuses and rights violations.[76] As several scholars noted in 1997:

[I]n over 60 cases from South East Turkey declared admissible, the Commission has found in each case that the applicants did not have an adequate remedy at their disposal to address their particular complaint. However, the Commission has also always held that as the individual applicants on the particular facts of their complaints had no remedy available to them, the question of a *systematic* failure to provide domestic remedies need not be addressed. The Commission's approach . . . nevertheless prompts the question of how many cases are necessary in which applications, raising essentially similar complaints, are admitted by reason of lack of effective remedies, before the conclusion is reached that there is a practice of violation of the right to an effective domestic remedy?[77]

This judicial approach is particularly striking when measured against the realities of those cases. First, dozens of cases have come from the same jurisdiction, each raising substantially similar allegations against the Turkish security forces. Second, in some cases, the complainants furnished the court and the commission with external evidence accumulated by prestigious NGOs and international organizations pointing to the systematic abuse and violation of rights. For the most part, neither the court nor the commission has sought to use this information as a catalyst to determine whether administrative practice of rights abuses had, in fact, taken place.[78] Similarly, in the immediate context of derogation cases, the fact of an extended derogation or of a series of successive derogations, in and of itself, is both relevant to the question of proportionate response, the overall validity of the derogation, and the responsibility of the state for a particular breach. We note that in the context of the reporting requirements for states under treaties such as the ICCPR there is room, potentially, for more robust assessments by the Human Rights Committee with respect to long-term derogation or a series of derogations, as well as for the initiative of asking whether humanitarian law may be the correct and applicable legal regime. However, such an approach has not generally been followed, possibly because of undue deference to the state's own self-assessment of the applicable regime, as well as an institutional fear of acting outside the legal regime of human rights.

---

[76] See, for example, Christian Tomuschat, "Quo Vadis, Argentoratum? The Success Story of the European Convention on Human Rights and a Few Dark Stains" (1992) 13 *Human Rights Law Journal* 401 at 406.

[77] Reidy et al., "Gross Violations," 165.   [78] Ibid., pp. 171–72.

Third, fluidity of legal regimes creates uncertainty for governments. Courts enforcing human rights law remain attuned to the context of their legitimacy, and the need to keep state parties "on board."[79] There is little judicial interest in forcing a legal position on states far beyond their point of consensus. Situations of emergency and conflict are fraught zones for courts because states are especially sensitive to criticism in these arenas. This makes it highly unlikely that courts and tribunals will seek to validate the application of humanitarian law or the dual applicability of legal regimes without prior state agreement.

Finally, human rights tribunals are not in the business of making assessments about the status of conflict or questioning the bona fides of the state in the sense of the state's actual or perceived legitimacy when adjudicating on allegations of human rights violations. There is the sense of agreed contract between all the parties in these legal dramas about what the frame of reference is for the purpose of adjudication. Moreover, human rights courts can conclude that there are other institutions that are charged with the duty of enforcing and ensuring the observance of humanitarian law. The problem is that such an approach can serve to undermine both the specific protection for human rights sought as well as the broader goal of ensuring that the state is in compliance with its international legal obligations. Moreover, it blurs the overlap between two distinct accommodation regimes in a way which serves to obscure rather than deliver legal clarity and accountability.

All these factors explain why it is that international human rights tribunals do not assess critically which legal regime ought to apply when a signatory state is experiencing a situation of low-intensity conflict. With few notable exceptions, the state's assessment of applicable regime is accepted by the supervisory body. This approach has contributed to the major gap in the legal regulation of low-intensity conflicts since World War II.

---

[79] It bears reminding that states can withdraw from their positive treaty obligations. A recent example is the withdrawal of Trinidad and Tobago from the American Convention on Human Rights and the ICCPR following a decision by the Privy Council that, in any case in which execution was to take place more than five years after the sentence of death, there would be strong grounds for believing that the delay was such as to constitute "inhuman or degrading punishment or other treatment," and the subsequent refusal by the IACHR to give the government of Trinidad and Tobago any assurances that capital cases would be completed by the commission within the relevant time-frame. See Trinidad and Tobago, "Denunciation," Notified May 26, 1998, http://www.oas.org/juridico/english/sigs/b-32.html#Trinidad%20and%20Tobago (last visited Aug. 8, 2005).

Low-intensity conflict

Low-intensity conflicts are not a new phenomenon.[80] What seems new is their widespread proliferation and the host of international and regional problems that accompany them in a globalized community. The legal regulation of low-intensity internal conflicts illustrates a wider and more complicated story for international humanitarian law, which has struggled to keep pace with the forms of conflict that emerge once agreement has been reached on regulation of one variety. There are essentially three substantial legal regimes that regulate the experience of internal armed conflict. All reflect models of accommodation defined by specialized approaches to particular "types" of conflict. This section surveys briefly the content of such regimes and their application. We then outline their links with situations of "high-intensity" emergency.

Protocol I

Protocol I of the Additional Protocols to the Geneva Conventions extends the criteria and status of international armed conflicts to specifically enumerated internal conflicts, deemed "internationalized," by certain inherent characteristics.[81] Fashioning these "privileged" conflicts was a direct corollary to the strong advocacy by developing nations for which "wars of national liberation" and variations thereof were a defining feature of state creation and consolidation. Article 1(4) of Protocol I sets out these favored conflicts as follows:

The situations referred to in [common article 2 of the Geneva Conventions of 1949] include armed conflicts in which people are fighting against colonial domination and alien occupation and against racist regimes in the exercise of their right of self-determination, as enshrined in the Charter of the United Nations and the Declaration on Principles of International Law concerning Friendly Relations and Co-operation among States in accordance with the Charter of the United Nations.

In addition to the categorization requirement outlined in article 1(4), article 96(3) provides that an authority representing a people engaged in the type of conflict covered by Protocol I may undertake to apply the Geneva Conventions and the protocol by means of a unilateral

---

[80] See L.C. Green, "Low-Intensity Conflict and the Law" (1997) 3 *ILSA Journal of International and Comparative Law* 493.

[81] Protocol Additional to the Geneva Conventions of 12 August, 1949, and Relating to the Protection of Victims of International Armed Conflicts (Protocol I), UN Doc.A/32/144 (1977), 1125 UNTS 3, entered into force Dec. 7, 1978.

declaration. This means that application of Protocol I is not solely dependent on recognition by a High Contracting Party, which for obvious reasons might not be forthcoming. Once a conflict is deemed to fall within these confines, all the benefits of international conflict status and combatant standing attach to it. Were a conflict to satisfy the requirements of Protocol I, a sovereign state would be fully entitled to exercise its privilege of derogation. It bears reminding that derogation provisions are also activated by situations of "war," which constitute an extreme form of crisis experience for the state.

The application of Protocol I has little relevance to most of the conflicts experienced today. Its application is largely tied to the colonial context and its material field does not extend to the low-intensity internal armed conflicts that have plagued the international community in recent decades. However, some continuing practical and symbolic value can be ascribed to it. The paucity of Protocol I armed conflicts has meant that there is little or no evidence of states abusing the privilege of derogation in these kinds of conflicts.

Protocol I reflects the acknowledgment by governments of the limitations of traditional definitions of war and combatancy in the patterns of conflict that emerged after World War II. It also facilitates the construction of a continuum to explain the variety of configurations in which internal conflicts can appear, with Protocol I positioned at the upper end of that scale. The protocol's very existence makes the unresolved status of internal armed conflict more conspicuous, drawing attention to the proliferation of conflicts below its threshold. It is also conceptually important in that it tells us that the conflict/emergency experience is not unidimensional. It also indicates the multiple models of accommodation within specific legal regimes.

Protocol II

Discussion of Protocol II of the Additional Protocols to the Geneva Conventions is a crucial part of any analysis about the regulation of internal conflict.[82] The traditional view of Protocol II is that it "develops and supplements Article 3 common to the Conventions of 1949."[83] Such a description belies much of the controversy that surrounded the

---

[82] Protocol Additional to the Geneva Conventions of 12 August 1949, and Relating to the Protection of Victims of Non-International Armed Conflicts (Protocol II), 1125 UNTS 609, entered into force Dec. 7, 1978.

[83] Protocol II, Article 1(1). Frits Kalshoven and Liesbeth Zegveld, *Constraints on the Waging of War* (Geneva: International Committee of the Red Cross, 3rd edn, 2001), p. 132.

protocol's negotiation. The Diplomatic Conferences were split into two camps on the appropriate field of the protocol's application. One camp, whose approach was embodied in the draft for Protocol II of the International Committee of the Red Cross (ICRC), favored limiting its scope to basic humanitarian provisions and applying it broadly to a wide variety of armed conflicts.[84] This approach was strongly resisted by a number of delegations who regarded a protocol with such a low threshold as an unacceptable limitation on the sovereignty of states.[85] In the end, the compromise that was reached – which was criticized by many as a "seriously amputated version" of the original draft[86] – set a high threshold of application. It was agreed to have the protocol apply to all non-international armed conflicts that take place in the territory of a party between its armed forces and dissident armed forces "or other organized armed groups which, under responsible command, exercise such control over a part of its territory as to enable them to carry out sustained and concerted military operations and to implement this Protocol."[87] Protocol II lies somewhere on the continuum between Protocol I and Common Article 3 applicability.

The threshold of Protocol II excludes specifically situations low on the ladder of violence. Those situations of "internal disturbances and tensions such as riots, isolated and sporadic acts of violence and other acts of a similar nature" are excluded from the protocol's ambit as "not being armed conflicts."[88] As noted above, states experiencing internal low-level conflict often maintain that their internal problems fall into the "disturbances and tensions" category. Protocol II's threshold of application is described by the authoritative ICRC commentary as automatic, "once the conditions set out in Article 1(1) exist."[89] Many agree that Protocol II sets a high, if not unreachable, threshold that is unreflective of the general patterns of strife in internal contexts.[90] The protocol requires not

---

[84] See Waldemar A. Solf and W. George Grandison, "International Humanitarian Law Applicable in Armed Conflict" (1975) 10 *Journal of International Law and Economics* 567 at 578.

[85] Ibid., at 579.

[86] See Charles Lysaght, "The Scope of Protocol II and its Relation to Common Article 3 of the Geneva Conventions of 1949 and Other Human Rights Instruments" (1983) 33 *American University Law Review* 9 at 10 (outlining in particular the position of the Norwegian delegation).

[87] Protocol II, article 1(1).   [88] Protocol II, article 1(2).

[89] Theodor Meron, "The Geneva Conventions as Customary Law" (1987) 81 *American Journal of International Law* 348.

[90] Antonio Cassese, "A Tentative Appraisal of the Old and New Humanitarian Law of Armed Conflict" in Antonio Cassese (ed.), *The New Humanitarian Law of Armed Conflict* (Naples: Editoriale Scientifica, 1979), p. 461; Lysaght, "The Scope of Protocol II," 22.

only that the dissident group have a degree of organization that would allow them to implement and disseminate the stipulations of the protocol, but that it must be in control of physical territory. This does little to elucidate what such "control" should amount to.

The question of what constitutes "control" is critical in deciding the kinds of conflicts to which Protocol II applies. After agreement was reached on both protocols many observers felt that the threshold for control of territory contained in Protocol II was a high one. It was assumed to mean that dissident forces would have to have full physical and governmental control of a significant portion of the state's territory for a conflict to be regulated by Protocol II. However, this view ignores the reality of conflict situations where all kinds of complex control and absence of control scenarios are confronted, for example, mixed situations where control of territory is fluid, dependent on territorial gains and losses by combat, or situations where government forces are severely restricted in their access to and movement within a particular territory. It also takes no formal account of situations in which the government may have to resort to extraordinary means over long periods of time to maintain "control" of a territory where the community may be entirely hostile but subdued by state or dissident military presence.[91] The requirement of territorial control also raises the question of how large the territory under control ought to be in order to satisfy the requirement. If control is absolute but minuscule in its territorial scope, is the protocol activated? If a dissident armed group controls one town, is that sufficient? What if the area controlled is tiny but of crucial strategic value to the state? If it is a large territory within the state, is the protocol automatically activated? Other difficulties concern the question of duration, i.e., whether there is a time-frame on the control prerequisite. In other words, does the capacity to control indicate a long-term control rather than a mere blip in time? Control, even if absolute, may not be sufficient if its duration is not long enough to illustrate its stability and prove loss of control by another (state) entity. These questions are indicative of the difficulties that inhere in the application of Protocol II where domination is not exercised consistently by one entity (either dissident or government). It is also noticeable that these are exactly the kinds of

---

[91] This raises a question on the validity of martial control. If martial control is accepted as fulfilling the command criteria, it potentially validates the erroneous conclusion that those individuals living under forced rule must, of necessity, support their rulers. It is also evident that control need not be consent based. It can be imposed by force or threat of force alone. Control does not depend on cooperation by local civilians with either state or dissident groups.

questions that frequently arise in situations of "high-intensity" emergencies. Hence one can reasonably ask what the extent of the Turkish government's control over south-east Turkey might be and whether the dynamics of the "control" question on the ground there implicate the application of international humanitarian law. The same question also implicates the limitations of the emergency law regime in regulating the conflict in that jurisdiction. Once again, this points to the difficulty and, at the same time, importance of assessing the legal crossovers between accommodation regimes.

In recent years substantial case law has been generated by international courts clarifying the meaning of "control." The International Court of Justice in the *Nicaragua* case decided that "effective control" sufficient to hold the United States responsible for the acts of third parties had not been proved despite the fact that the United States helped to finance, organize, equip, and train the Contras. The court stated that those facts alone did not warrant the conclusion that "these forces [were] subject to the United States to such an extent that any acts they have committed are imputable to that State."[92] While this conclusion obviously pertains to control by another state over rebel forces within the "contested" state and does not specifically address the "control" that a rebel group would be required to exercise to activate Protocol II, it is nonetheless useful as an indicator as to the content of "control." The perceived rigidity of the test for effective control has prompted other international courts to adopt a looser test of "overall control" to define the nature of the relationship between a belligerent state and third parties.[93] What is now evident is that the test for control is a variable one dependent on the precise legal question being asked and the consequences for state parties that follow. It is not unreasonable to suggest that our understanding of the legal meaning of "control" is context-specific. There are defensible reasons why a lower standard might be set on its definition in the context of applying the law of armed conflict than might be the case when assessing control for the purposes of defining, for example, state responsibility. Such reasons would include the overall rationale prompting the application of humanitarian law in

---

[92] Nicaragua v. United States, paras. 86–93.
[93] Prosecutor v. Dusko Tadic, Case No. IT-94-1-A, Judgment, PP 172-237 (July 15, 1999), available online at http://www.un.org/icty/tadic/appeal/judgement/tad-aj990715e.pdf (last visited Aug. 8, 2005), paras. 131, 137 ("overall control"); Prosecutor v. Delalic, Mucic, Delic & Landzo, Judgment, No. IT-96-21-T (Nov. 16, 1998), para. 231 ("continuity of control").

the first place, namely the protection of those made vulnerable in times of conflict. There is every reason for this net to be spread widely, a view which is in keeping with the overall object and purpose of Protocol II itself. Furthermore, the more attainable the standard of control is, the more likely it is that violations of the laws and customs of war by dissidents can be called to account.[94] An attainable threshold for the application of Protocol II is highly significant, because there is a significant number of "high-intensity" emergency situations that might be more correctly placed in the framework of Protocol II if a greater consensus on this threshold issue were reached. If thresholds of application are both attainable and responsive to the actuality of conflict experience, then the argument promoted here will reflect the actual experience of conflict where high-intensity emergencies overlap with both Protocol II and Common Article 3 type situations.

Common Article 3

Common Article 3 of the 1949 Geneva Conventions made the first, controversial attempt to incorporate provisions regulating the conduct of parties during civil/internal strife.[95] It is the sole article of the 1949 Conventions that specifically addresses the problem of non-international armed conflicts. It has been variously described as the "mini-convention" or the "convention within a convention," providing rules that parties to an internal armed conflict are "bound to apply as a minimum." The opening paragraph of article 3 states: "In the case of armed conflict not of an international character occurring in the territory of one of the High Contracting Parties, each Party to the conflict shall be bound to apply, as a minimum, the following provisions..."

---

[94] See, e.g., Prosecutor v. Dusko Tadic, Decision on the Defence Motion for Interlocutory Appeal on Jurisdiction (Tadic Jurisdiction Decision), Case No. IT-94-I-AR72 (Oct. 2, 1995) para. 70; Prosecutor v. Dusko Tadic, Trial Chamber Judgment, May 7, 1997, Case No. IT-94-1-AR72, para. 562.

[95] Article 3 common to Geneva Convention for the Amelioration of the Condition of the Wounded and the Sick in Armed Forces in the Field, Aug. 12, 1949, 6 UST 3114, 75 UNTS 31; Geneva Convention for the Amelioration of the Condition of Wounded, Sick and Shipwrecked Members of Armed Forces at Sea, Aug. 12, 1949, 6 UST 3217, 75 UNTS 85; Geneva Convention Relative to the Treatment of Prisoners of War, Aug. 12, 1949, 6 UST 3316, 75 UNTS 135; Geneva Convention Relative to the Protection of Civilian Persons in Time of War, Aug. 12, 1949, 6 UST 3516, 75 UNTS 287 ("Common Article 3"). G.I.A.D. Draper attests to the negotiation difficulties this provoked at the Diplomatic Conference. See G.I.A.D. Draper, "Humanitarian Law and Internal Armed Conflicts" (1983) 13 *Georgia Journal of International and Comparative Law* 253 at 261.

The article contains the lowest threshold of both application and standards. It is intended to provide a minimum basis of protection to persons not participating in hostilities during internal armed conflicts.[96] Article 3 protects those classes of people deemed most vulnerable when conflict occurs. Protection under the article is given on the basis of non-discrimination and non-partisanship, these principles being derived from the then-embryonic human rights regimes, and indeed, ahead of them.[97] Its protections are to ensure that violence against life or person is prohibited;[98] that taking of hostages is unlawful;[99] that outrages against personal dignity, specifically humiliating and degrading treatment, are forbidden;[100] that legal processes enforcing adverse consequences upon persons are carried out by regularly constituted courts affording recognized due process rights;[101] and finally, that all those wounded and sick in conflict be cared for.[102]

The obvious question regards when article 3 becomes applicable. What is not generally acknowledged is that the Diplomatic Conference considered a wide range of criteria that would provoke the applicability of article 3, ranging from de jure to de facto recognition of belligerency. The wider of these criteria would appear to include "every offer of armed force against the authorities of the state that have been met by more than ordinary police measures taken against normal, violent criminal activity."[103] This is a clear sign that, as early as 1949, it was recognized by a number of states that moving beyond a normal policing response was an indicator that the state was facing a crisis that did not fall within the normal realm, and moved along the continuum towards a situation of internal armed conflict. The vagueness of article 3, the price for its broad acceptance, leaves out explicit recognition of such a low-end threshold. But it still is useful to keep in mind that a number of states envisioned this as the starting point of applicability.

---

[96] The norms stated in Common Article 3 may be viewed as applicable to all conflicts, even those of an international character. See Theodor Meron, "International Criminalization of Internal Atrocities" (1995) 89 *American Journal of International Law* 554 at 560 (noting the US adherence to this position regarding the application of law to the international conflict in the former Yugoslavia).

[97] See Draper, "Humanitarian Law," 269.

[98] Common Article 3, section (1)(a).

[99] Ibid., Article 3(1)(b).   [100] Ibid., Article 3 (1)(c).   [101] Ibid., Article 3 (1)(d).

[102] Ibid., Article 3 (2).

[103] See G.I.A.D. Draper, "The Geneva Conventions of 1949" (1965-I) 114 *Recueil des Cours* 59 at 89.

We think that it is useful to note the effect that the agreement of thresholds for Protocol I and II have had on Common Article 3. Noting the existence of a continuum of norms, Common Article 3's point of application has been affected by the agreements for the two protocols. Article 3 now stands as the lowest threshold for the determination that an armed conflict exists, and provides the minimum standards to apply thereafter. There can be little doubt that its threshold for application has shifted, no longer requiring the presence of the classic two-sided civil war.[104]

Critical to deciding which model of accommodation applies (international human rights with derogation or international humanitarian law) is the precise legal question of determining the applicability of Common Article 3. Two broad conclusions are offered at this point which tend to support the existence of an article 3 type conflict. First, it is suggested that when sustained military, as opposed to policing, action is undertaken against rebels or insurgents, even where actual rebel control of territory may be minimal, the burden of proof lies on the state to demonstrate that an article 3 situation is not activated. This parallels the proposal outlined above that when an emergency situation is characterized by the use of military forces, classification ought to be thought of in humanitarian law terms. Evidently this is contrary to current practice. The extended crossover to the use of military forces, rather than the ordinary civilian forces, to contain violence is suggested as one of the primary markers to indicate that the article 3 threshold has been crossed. A Commission of Experts convened some years ago by the ICRC made the following pertinent observation: "The existence of armed conflict is undeniable, in the sense of Article 3, if hostile action against a lawful government assumes a collective character and a minimum of organisation."[105]

It is important to emphasize that short-term use of military forces (often for reasons of expediency) does not necessarily implicate article 3. Extended use of the military to maintain order and control is an entirely different matter and should be viewed as such. We do not argue that on all occasions and for all purposes military deployment in a domestic context means that article 3 is activated. Rather, the suggestion is made

---

[104] See Sylvie Junod, "Additional Protocol II: History and Scope" (1983) 33 *American University Law Review* 29; but see Hamdan v. Rumsfeld, 415 F.3d 33 (DC Cir. 2005).

[105] International Committee of the Red Cross, "Reaffirmation and Development of the Laws and Customs Applicable in Armed Conflict", Report Submitted to the XXIst International Conference of the Red Cross, Istanbul (1969), p. 99.

that in such cases of prolonged military deployment there is a need for the burden of responsibility to shift to the state. The state should be required to demonstrate that article 3 is not activated, rather than the current assumption that such prolonged action has no external legal consequences for the state.

Second, where the state, through its policing and judicial functions, has been required to abdicate enforcement of the criminal and civil law for an extended period of time by reason of armed third-party actions, classification should be thought of in terms of article 3. This is also a sensitive area. Who is to judge when such abdication takes place? And how far must judicial function be impaired in these circumstances? For example, if the judiciary continues to hear and adjudicate cases, though rights such as habeas corpus and constitutional or legislative guarantees are not perfectly enforced, is there a reason to assume a de facto abdication?[106] If judicial function is itself permanently modified, either by the replacement of judicial personnel or the alteration of court structure (special courts/military courts/non-jury trials) is this sufficient to determine abdication? There are no crystal-clear answers. Nonetheless, it can be concluded that severely impaired judicial or policing functioning over extended periods of time is another indicator that suggests that a situation falls within the ambit of article 3.[107] In a sense, these factors are warning flares that something which falls outside normal peacetime state regulation is taking place and requires monitoring on that basis. It also informs us that there may be a shift in the applicable legal regime.

These two criteria have in common the notion of a *sustained* armed interference from a consistent source, preventing the state's normal functioning. This is affirmed by the language contained in the statute of the International Criminal Court, where "protracted" armed conflict is confirmed to activate the application of the statute's war crimes

---

[106] Alejandro Garro, "The Role of the Argentine Judiciary in Controlling Governmental Action under a State of Siege" (1983) 4 *Human Rights Law Journal* 311 for a gloomy assessment of the functioning of domestic judiciary in a state of crisis.

[107] A parallel question, beyond the scope of this work, is whether the usurpation of democratic government itself is an indication that the emergency framework is an inappropriate measuring stick by which to examine low-intensity conflict. The issue of whether a non-democratic government may be allowed to rely on a derogation provision has been well surveyed in the literature. It was also cogently examined in the Report of the European Commission on the "Greek" Case, 1969 YB Eur. Conv. on HR 75. See also Thomas M. Franck, "The Emerging Right to Democratic Governance" (1992) 86 *American Journal of International Law* 46; Thomas M. Franck, *The Power of Legitimacy among Nations* (New York: Oxford University Press, 1990).

provisions.[108] It is also now generally agreed that armed opposition to the state could shift over time and that internal armed dissension could proliferate between rival third-party entities. The sole criterion in respect of such splintering of conflict sources is that the intensity of armed resistance offered to, and disrupting, state activity remain consistent and the parties be in a position to enforce the provisions of article 3. This should clearly distinguish the article 3 situation from short-term interruptions to state order owing to natural calamities, or loss of state control temporarily as envisioned and allowed by the derogation procedures of the international human rights instruments.

Observers may point out that any criterion that links low-intensity conflict status to serious disruption in state life is merely borrowing a yardstick already in place in the derogation jurisprudence and attaching unwarranted significance to it. There can be little doubt that the extent of chaos created within any given state by a true emergency situation might look the same as the chaos created by a low-intensity armed conflict if the two were examined in tandem at specific moments. It is also evident that the legal criteria (drawn from empirical assessments) used to define the true emergency look similar to the criteria that apply to a description of low-intensity armed conflict. However, the key differences between the two phenomena are duration and sustainability. While an emergency may share short-term characteristics with armed conflict, it is sanctioned *only* as a short-term phenomenon. As noted in chapters 4 and 7, this basic supposition is coming under pressure from a long-term, indeterminate "war on terror."

Overlapping regimes: high meets low

There is no doubt that states may be extremely sensitive to any attempt to limit their sovereign rights of response when faced with internal

---

[108] Rome Statute of the International Criminal Court, UN Doc. 2187 UNTS 90, entered into force July 1, 2002, article 8(2)(f): "Paragraph 2(e) applies to armed conflicts not of an international character and thus does not apply to situations of internal disturbances and tensions, such as riots, isolated and sporadic acts of violence or other acts of a similar nature. It applies to armed conflicts that take place in the territory of a State when *there is protracted armed conflict* between governmental authorities and organized armed groups or between such groups" (emphasis added). While Meron is of the view that the provision does not per se create another threshold of applicability, and lacks clarity, it can also be viewed as confirming key aspects of threshold activation. See Theodor Meron, "The Humanization of Humanitarian Law" (2000) 94 *American Journal of International Law* 239.

crisis. Thus, the argument that internal emergencies may constitute armed conflicts remains a controversial one.[109] States have persistently defended the scope of discretionary action under international law that allows them in times of crisis to suspend the protection of certain rights and to expand the scope of executive control. States have also maintained rigorously that few, if any, situations of internal crisis fall to be regulated by Common Article 3 or Protocol II.

Notwithstanding a provision that declares unambiguously that the application of Common Article 3 shall in no way "affect the legal status of the Parties to the conflict," states remain mindful that legal and political effects are potentially divorced entities. In short, the exclusion of legal standing within the terms of Common Article 3 per se does not remove the provisions of article 3 nor those of its more substantial companion Protocol II from the realm of legal implication. Any acknowledgment that Common Article 3 applies is equally an acknowledgment that the state is subject to the threat of armed conflict, which may appear implicitly to acquiesce in a crisis of legitimacy and control within the state. We suggest that as a result both of their unwillingness to appear weak and of the perceived necessity to maintain normality, states have endeavoured successfully to subsume the twilight-zone of low-intensity armed conflict into the more acceptable regime of emergency. The key to understanding this practice lies in the phenomenon of "high-intensity" emergency characterized by a permanent reliance on extraordinary powers.

In many cases, the permanent emergency has become a cloaking device for low-intensity armed conflict. Further, we suggest that the existence of an acknowledged permanent emergency is, in fact, one of the indicators that point to the existence of low-intensity conflict. Emergency itself can be both a symptom of, and a causal factor in, the durability quotient of low-intensity article 3 situations. One prominent example of this comes from the ongoing conflict in Peru. In a report on the jurisdiction the International Commission of Jurists made the following observations:

[W]e think that it is useful to clarify our views on the nature of the ongoing conflict in Peru. This is particularly important since we detected in our discussions,

[109] For example, Tom Hadden and Colin Harvey argue that the substantive norms of both regimes share much in common and could in certain circumstances be encapsulated in a single legally binding construct. They do not, however, seek to pinpoint the precise military and political circumstances that would activate such application. See Tom Hadden and Colin Harvey, "The Law of Internal Crisis and Conflict" (1999) 81 *International Review of the Red Cross* 119.

primarily with Peruvian military personnel, what we regard as a basic misunderstanding of the relevance and applicability of international humanitarian law, i.e., the law of armed conflict, to the conflict in Peru. Moreover, this misunderstanding extended to an unwarranted apprehension about the legal effects that ensue from the law's application to the hostilities. For example, these officials would vigorously assert that the country was engaged in an "internal" war, but, on the other hand, would argue implicitly that since the enemy were mere criminals and terrorists, the situation was not governed by humanitarian law. We disagree with this position and believe without question that a non-international, i.e., internal armed conflict is underway in Peru and, as such, it is directly governed by the terms of Article 3 common to the four Geneva Conventions, to which Peru is a state party.[110]

Many states and commentators will decry any effort to pursue such a line of inquiry. The response is likely to be that emergency is regulated, mandated, and legalized by international human rights law. As such, there can be no slippage between the human rights and the humanitarian law regimes. Such a claim is overcome with careful review of relevant legal and empirical factors. We think it critical that deeper scrutiny be given to the applicability of legal regimes and thus to the specific form and legal content of the applicable model of accommodation. It is also important to recognize that movements within and between models of accommodation are possible and consistent with practice on the ground.

The obvious question is how reclassification of certain emergencies under the rubric of international humanitarian law assists us in regulating conflict, bringing it to a peaceful resolution, and making persons accountable for violations of law committed during conflict. Historically, international humanitarian law was considered weak on the implementation front with few, if any, real mechanisms for enforcement. There are a number of substantial institutional developments that affect that assessment. These include the establishment of the ad hoc International Tribunals for the Former Yugoslavia and Rwanda, the agreement on the International Criminal Court Statute, and the increased willingness of national courts to enforce principles of universal jurisdiction in respect of certain crimes. It is also critical to recall that the application of international humanitarian law does not eclipse the oversight of international human rights law, in terms of both the applicable norms and the oversight of international bodies. Furthermore, there is increased acceptance of the augmentation of humanitarian law oversight through

---

[110] *Report of the Commission of International Jurists on the Administration of Justice in Peru*, Nov. 30, 1993 at 4.

the influence of human rights norms. In this context the International Court of Justice stated in its Advisory Opinion on the *Legality of the Threat or Use of Nuclear Weapons* that:

[T]he protection of the International Covenant on Civil and Political Rights does not cease in times of war, except by operation of Article 4 of the Covenant whereby certain provisions may be derogated from in a time of national emergency. Respect for the right to life is not, however, such a provision. In principle, the right not arbitrarily to be deprived of one's life applies also in hostilities. The test of what is an arbitrary deprivation of life, however, then falls to be determined by the applicable *lex specialis*, namely, the law applicable in armed conflict which is designed to regulate the conduct of hostilities.[111]

Nonetheless, the distinguishing feature of international humanitarian law is that it holds both state and non-state actors accountable for their violations of the laws and customs of war. This is a key aspect of why it is vital that constraints apply to internal armed conflict. The benefits are manifold. First, it may act as inducement through the implicit grant of status to non-state parties to conform to humanitarian law rules.

Evidence of this effect is limited but it can constitute the basis upon which to hold non-state actors and their official counterparts accountable when they violate those rules. The creation of the International Criminal Court holds the promise that this is more than an abstract possibility.[112] Most significant for the present analysis, the Statute of the International Criminal Court confirms that violations of the laws and customs of war include acts committed during internal armed conflict.[113] It is also significant, of course, that recent standard setting allows for certain crimes such as crimes against humanity to be prosecuted without the requirement of an armed conflict present to activate the criminal category. The statute addresses the applicable threshold for the laws of war to situations of internal armed conflict. In article 8(2)(f) the statute defines the kinds of internal conflict that activate the force of war crime responsibilities for participants: "[A]rmed conflicts that take place in the territory of a State when there is a *protracted* armed conflict between governmental authorities and organized armed groups or between such groups" (emphasis added). The language is ambiguous to some degree and may be viewed as an attempt to find some middle ground between the Protocol II threshold of application and that

---

[111] *Nuclear Weapons*, para. 24.
[112] The negotiation of this latter provision was extremely difficult. See Report of the Preparatory Committee, Volume I at paras. 85–90.
[113] Rome Statute of the International Criminal Court, Article 8(2)(c)–(f).

of Common Article 3. Even if there is a widening of threshold here, in practice most of what might be punishable would be caught under the Common Article 3 rubric and the category of crimes against humanity does not require an "armed conflict" to be activated to facilitate prosecution. We take the view that the use of the term "protracted" is significant in drawing attention to the kinds of conflicts on which we particularly focused above, namely where a horizontal rather than a vertical application of the violence threshold would place them in the ambit of humanitarian law regulation. However, pending judicial interpretation, the weight of academic commentary seems to dismiss that possibility, with Meron arguing that article 8(2)(f) "should not be considered as creating yet another threshold of applicability, but it may well exacerbate the previous lack of clarity."[114] The ICRC has stated that "The addition of the word 'protracted' to armed conflict seems to be redundant since protracted violence is a constituent element of an armed conflict not of an international character."[115]

Conclusion

Why is it important to identify which legal regime of accommodation applies and to classify emergency situations correctly? This chapter argues that cloaking low-intensity armed conflict under the mantle of emergency derogation is problematic in multiple respects. First, it creates conceptual confusion over what exactly constitutes an "emergency" as opposed to an armed conflict. The results of such confusion are not merely academic. Despite claims by many commentators that human rights law (or non-binding minimum humanitarian standards) is sufficient and appropriate to respond to these conflicts, we propose a different view. The application of international humanitarian law (in tandem with human rights obligations) clarifies the status of conflict and the role of various actors within it. We believe that its exclusion is highly problematic and suggest that the legal form of accommodation matters in practice. Such classification leads to a clearer basis for political resolution of conflicts

---

[114] Meron, "The Humanization of Humanitarian Law," 239. See also Anthony Cullen, "The Parameters of Internal Armed Conflict in International Humanitarian Law" (2004) 12 *University of Miami International and Comparative Law Review* 189.

[115] International Committee of the Red Cross Working Paper, June 29, 1999, available online at http://www.iccnow.org/documents/prepcom/ papersonprepcomissues/ICRC WorkPaperArticle8Para2e.pdf (last visited Aug. 8, 2005).

in the long run.[116] Moreover, international humanitarian law holds both state and non-state actors accountable for their violations and abuses. This is valuable as both a symbolic and practical matter and one that can agitate positively for states to accept classification of conflicts in the humanitarian law arena. Second, drawing on Abe and Antonia Chayes' analysis of a managerial model of legal compliance with international treaties, we argue that clarity of legal regimes has a specific effect in terms of the possibilities of affecting the modes of state behavior and interaction in the international sphere around internal conflicts.[117]

We accept that states have generally avoided the classification of the kinds of emergency situations we identify in the humanitarian law context. States have guarded jealously that scope of discretionary action which allows them under international law to suspend in times of crisis the protection of certain rights vested in individuals and to expand the scope of executive control. States have also maintained rigorously that few, if any, situations of internal crisis are to be regulated by the laws of armed conflict. Moreover, we accept that states and commentators alike have been generally reluctant to admit the fluidity and exchange between the human rights and the humanitarian law regimes that we identify. We have underlined the importance of understanding that situations of crisis can and do move within and between legal regimes. In addition to suggestions about the appropriate home for certain permanent emergencies, we argue that the relationship between human rights and humanitarian law in this context should be conceived of in terms of a continuum. This continuum acknowledges the malleable aspect of emergency situations as a practical matter and their capacity to move upwards and downwards in intensity and effects. However, the point of such a continuum is to defend clearly the position that accountability for the powers exercised by the state at any point is referenced to a clear set of legal constraints. In short, the continuum is a means not to leave gaps of accountability for the state but rather to map out a set of legal structures that accommodate the varying experiences of state practice.

---

[116] Christine Bell, Colm Campbell, and Fionnuala Ní Aoláin, "Justice Discourses in Transition" (2004) 13 *Social & Legal Studies* 305.

[117] Abram Chayes and Antonia Handler Chayes, *The New Sovereignty: Compliance with International Regulatory Agreements* (Cambridge, MA: Harvard University Press, 1995).

7 Terrorism, emergencies, and international responses to contemporary threats

One fundamental issue encountered by the subject matter of this book and thrown into sharp relief by contemporary events is whether the phenomenon of terrorism creates the material conditions that activate the conceptual and regulatory space of "emergency" or whether terrorism constitutes a fundamentally distinct phenomenon that cannot be captured by the emergency framework (either domestic or international). A follow-on and obvious question is whether terror attacks in a given society can legitimately create a state of emergency. This chapter seeks to explore that terrain by mapping out the features and, where appropriate, the distinctiveness of terrorism. The analysis then seeks to assess how terrorism (in its various guises) fits into the models proposed in Part I of this book. Following from this, the chapter undertakes an analysis of the applicable legal regimes relevant to terrorism. We conclude with an examination of how the events of September 11, 2001 have shaped national and international legal responses to terrorism and how these responses "fit" or not into the general framework of emergency powers.

We start with the caveat that any serious discussion of terrorism as a phenomenon is fraught as both an intellectual and policy enterprise.[1] The current political climate, in which sweeping categorizations about the nature and form of all types of violence directed against states are rife, discourages any attempts to disaggregate the phenomenon of terrorism from other forms of violence. Thus, John Ashcroft, the former United States Attorney-General, has stated: "To those who scare peace loving people with phantoms of lost liberty, my message is this: your

---

[1] See e.g., Ileana M. Porras, "On Terrorism: Reflections on Violence and the Outlaw" (1994) *Utah Law Review* 119; Conor A. Gearty, "Terrorism and Human Rights" (2005) *European Human Rights Law Review* 1.

tactics aid terrorists for they erode our national unity and diminish our resolve. They give ammunition to America's enemies and pause to America's friends."[2] Despite the contemporary chill factor, for many decades the study of terrorism has constituted a separate field of intellectual and policy inquiry and yields sufficient information to draw some general conclusions.

The chapter proceeds in the following manner. We begin by analyzing closely the legal and political difficulties associated with reaching an agreed definition of terrorism among states. This forms the basis for a wider discussion on whether acts of terrorism can constitute a sufficient basis to trigger the application of emergency law, or whether terrorism can or should be contained by ordinary law (whether a crime control or military/national security type model), or, more cogently in recent times, whether the nature and form of terrorist acts require responses that go beyond the constraints of existing domestic and international regimes. We then move to assess how the phenomenon of terrorism can be applied to, and be understood to operate within, the models of emergency powers that form the core conceptual analysis of this book. We then follow with a detailed review of the interface between terrorism and different legal regimes, with particular attention to the relationship between terrorism and international humanitarian law. In this context dissection of the term "the war on terror" is particularly important, and relevant to exposing the inconsistencies between contemporary political rhetoric and the applicability of law to situations on the ground. Finally, the chapter assesses the multiplicity of international legal responses to transnational terrorism post-September 11, and the influence legal obligations created supra-nationally have had on domestic legal and political systems. These responses point to a model of legal accommodation being developed specifically to deal with the challenges of terrorism, premised on a form of international legislative action that triggers, and in some cases mandates, specific legislative responses at the domestic level.

General issues of definition and applicable legal regimes

Defining terrorism

We start by making the general observation that, as with emergency powers, many states have operated under the legal assumption that the

---

[2] Susan Milligan, "Critics Aid Terrorists, AG Argues," *Boston Globe*, Dec. 7, 2001, p. A34.

experience of terrorism was a temporary and finite phenomenon. Thus, it was seen as capable of being controlled by a strong crime control or law enforcement model, or by the modification of existing legal and political structures to give victory against what were generally considered to be containable groups or individuals. As outlined in chapter 5, it is also evident that this "ideal" type terrorism rarely exists in practice, and had a high crossover with the permanent emergencies that populate the terrain of emergency law.

Another generally salient feature of terrorism was its national or nationalistic characteristic, notwithstanding that, in practice, terrorist groups and individuals may have operated outside the state against which their actions were generally directed, and may have directed violence against other states to achieve the ends sought. This parallels the general pattern of emergencies that are largely nationally (or territorially) based but may occasionally affect other states.

But unlike emergencies, there exists deep disagreement within national and international legal communities concerning the legal definitions of terrorism.[3] Terrorism is not a new phenomenon; in fact terrorism has long been experienced in national and international systems, a potent example being the murder of the Austrian Crown Prince that triggered World War I.[4] However, attempting to regulate terrorism through international law is a relatively new enterprise. As early as 1937 the League of Nations drafted the *Convention for the Prevention and Punishment of Terrorism*.[5] Upon its creation the United Nations inherited and sought to advance this work. In parallel, a number of regional international organizations have addressed the manifestations of terrorism at a national and regional level. These include the Council of Europe,[6] the European Union, the Organization for Security and Co-operation in Europe, the

---

[3] Hans-Peter Gasser, "Acts of Terror, 'Terrorism' and International Humanitarian Law" (2002) 84 *International Review of the Red Cross* 547 at 552–54.

[4] See C.A. Russell, C.A. Banker, and B.H. Miller, "Out-Inventing the Terrorist" in Yonah Alexander, David Carlton, and Paul Wilkinson (eds.), *Terrorism: Theory and Practice* (Boulder, CO: Westview Press, 1979), p. 3; Sharon Harzenski, "Terrorism, a History: Stage One" (2003) 12 *Journal of Transnational Law and Policy* 137. We do not suggest that every act of political assassination constitutes a terrorist act, as there may be multiple causalities for such (illegal) actions.

[5] League of Nations, Convention for the Prevention and Punishment of Terrorism, Nov. 16, 1937 (1938) 19 *League of Nations Official Journal* 23 (never entered into force).

[6] Council of Europe, *The Fight against Terrorism – Council of Europe Standards* (3rd edn, Council of Europe, 2005).

African Union, and the Organization of American States.[7] Much of the work by these bodies can be defined as attempts to agree suppression conventions as well as cooperative regional action on a multitude of fronts. The suppression conventions will be discussed in greater detail below. Here suffice it to note that we view the suppression conventions as the natural result of a failure to agree broader definitions of terrorism through enacting a generally agreed multilateral treaty. They represent an interesting international hybrid of a business as usual approach combined with specific accommodation on particular crimes.

A recent report by the Inter-American Commission on Human Rights helpfully breaks down the concept of terrorism in international law into five distinct categories.[8] It includes *Actions* (including forms of violence); *Actors* (including persons or organizations); *Causes or Struggles* (where the cause or the struggle may be so marked by terrorist violence as to be indistinguishable from it, or where isolated terrorist violence may take place as part of the cause or struggle); *Situations* (where terrorist violence is particularly serious or widespread in a state or region); and *Armed Conflicts* (in the sense of terrorism being used during the course of an armed conflict [international or internal] as set out by the Geneva Conventions and Additional Protocols).[9] Notwithstanding these helpful categories it is generally agreed that there has been no consensus on an international legal classification.[10] This lack of consensus is most potently illustrated by the lack of an agreed definition of terrorism within the UN General Assembly's Ad Hoc Committee on terrorism as well as

---

[7] Inter-American Convention against Terrorism, OAS AG Res. 1840, 32nd Sess., OAS Doc. XXXII-O/02 (June 3, 2002), entered into force July 10, 2003; Inter-American Committee against Terrorism, "Declaration of San Salvador on Strengthening Cooperation in the Fight Against Terrorism," OEA/Ser. L/ X.2.3., adopted Jan. 24, 2003. On June 13, 2002, the EU Council of Ministers adopted a Framework Decision on the European Arrest Warrant. See http://europa.eu.int/comm/justice_home/fsj/criminal/extradition/ fsj_criminal_extradition_en.htm (last visited Aug. 8, 2005); OSCE Charter on Preventing and Combating Terrorism, Mc(10). Jour/2, Dec. 7, 2002, Annex 1, available online at http://www.osce.org/documents/odihr/2002/12/1488_en.pdf (last visited Aug. 8, 2005); African Union, "Declaration of the Second High-Level Intergovernmental Meeting on the Prevention and Combating of Terrorism in Africa," Mtg/HLIG/Conv.Terror/Decl. (II) Rev. 2.

[8] Inter-American Commission on Human Rights, "Report on Terrorism and Human Rights," OEA/Ser. L/V/II. 116, Doc. 5 rev. 1 corr. (Oct. 22, 2002).

[9] Ibid., at para. 12.

[10] There is now a regional European agreement on a definition of terrorism, which speaks to the potential for broader international consensus. Protocol Amending the European Convention on the Suppression of Terrorism, *European Treaty Series* No. 190 (May 15, 2003).

within the working group of the General Assembly's Sixth Committee, in the context of a comprehensive treaty regulating state responses to and responsibility for terrorism.[11] At point of writing, a draft convention is available which controversially seeks to provide a comprehensive definition of terrorism, and is still lacking state agreement.[12] More recently the Report of the Secretary-General's High-Level Panel on Threats, Challenges, and Change has focused on the challenges posed to the United Nations by terrorism and has recommended that any definition of terrorism should contain the following elements: a restatement that acts under the twelve suppression conventions are terrorism; reference to the definitions contained in the 1999 International Convention for the Suppression of the Financing of Terrorism and Security Council resolution 1566 (2004); and a description of terrorism as "any action...that is intended to cause death or serious bodily harm to civilians or noncombatants, when the purpose of such an act, by its nature or context, is to intimidate a population, or to compel a Government or an international organization to do or to abstain from doing any act."[13]

Lack of agreement on a comprehensive definition does not mean that there is no consensus at all between states on what constitutes terrorism. In fact, and definitionally jumpstarted by September 11, the international community has identified certain *acts* of violence that are generally considered to be forms of terrorism. In this ever-expanding list are included such acts as the hijacking of civilian airplanes and taking the lives of hostages, acts the primary purpose of which could be said to be to spread terror among the civilian population both in times of armed conflict and in peacetime. Moreover, when we look at the wide range of international definitions (as provided by regional bodies and the United Nations) we can identify certain common characteristics to be seen in incidents of terrorism. For example, the United Nations General Assembly has a working definition of terrorism for general use

---

[11] See also UN General Assembly Ad Hoc Committee on International Terrorism, "Observations of States Submitted in Accordance with General Assembly Resolution 3034 (XXVII)," A/AC.160/1 (May 16, 1973) and A/AC.160/1/Add. 1 (June 12, 1973); see also A/AC.160/2 (June 22, 1973) (study by the Secretary General on the basis of that material).

[12] See, e.g., Report of the Ad Hoc Committee Established by General Assembly Resolution 51/210 of December 17, 1996, Fifth Session (February 12–23, 2001), General Assembly Official Records, 56th Session, Supplement No. 37, UN Doc. A/56/37.

[13] Report of the Secretary-General's High-Level Panel on Threats, Challenges, and Change, *A More Secure World: Our Shared Responsibility* (United Nations, 2004) at para. 164, available online at www.un.org/secureworld/report2.pdf (last visited Aug. 8, 2005).

in resolutions and declarations on terrorism. Namely, "Criminal acts in-tended or calculated to provoke a state of terror in the general public, a group of persons or particular persons, for political purposes [which] are in any circumstances unjustifiable, whether on the considerations of a political, philosophical, ideological, racial, ethnic, religious or any other nature that may be used to justify them."[14] The Inter-American Commission Report again usefully identifies certain common character-istics including the nature and identity of the perpetrators of terrorism, the nature and identity of the victims of terrorism, the objectives of terrorism, and the measures employed to perpetrate terrorism.[15] Key to many of these partially agreed definitions is the understanding that the targeting of civilians is per se unacceptable. It is also useful to point out that while state and non-governmental targets of terrorism have been widespread, democratic communities (and their civilian popula-tions) by virtue of their open societies are particularly vulnerable to terrorism.

Terrorism has not only been a phenomenon associated with the ac-tions of non-state actors, but there is also some acceptance (in some but not all state quarters) that states themselves have used terrorist methods to achieve dubious political ends.[16] Notably, some states have endeavored domestically to proscribe a specific crime of terrorism based on some of these commonly assumed characteristics. Others have chosen not to do so, but rather have used existing definitions of common crimes, such as murder, by adding terrorist intention or variant consequences in pun-ishment.[17] This is one clear example where the ordinary criminal law bears the brunt of processing crimes defined (or not) as terrorist. Finally the absence of agreement on a definition of terrorism under interna-tional law suggests, according to the Inter-American Commission on Human Rights, that the characterization of "an act or situation as one

---

[14] See, e.g., UN Declaration on Measures to Eliminate International Terrorism, annexed to the UN General Assembly Resolution 49/60, 84th Plenary Meeting, UN Doc. A/RES/49/60 (Dec. 9, 1994), article 3.

[15] Inter-American Commission on Human Rights, "Report on Terrorism and Human Rights," at para. 17.

[16] Ibid., at chapter V.

[17] For example, in Canada under Bill C-36 (Anti-Terrorism Act) a prosecutor is required to prove beyond a reasonable doubt that the terrorist activity was committed "in whole or in part for a political, religious or ideological purpose, objective or cause." Criminal Code, s. 80.01(1)(b)(i)(A). For the problems that result from this attempt to criminalize motive, see Kent Roach, *September 11: Consequences for Canada* (Montreal: McGill-Queen's University Press, 2003), pp. 25–29.

of terrorism cannot in and of itself serve as a basis for defining the international legal obligations of states. Rather, each act or situation must be evaluated on its own facts and its particular context." Inherent in this characterization is the view that the methods and means by which states respond to acts of terrorism are not unlimited.[18]

Models of emergency powers as applied to terrorism

All of the acts of violence termed "terrorist" (or at least the core action involved) are generally defined as criminal by the legal systems of functional states. Thus murder, manslaughter, grievous bodily harm, theft, violence to property, hijacking, and corrupt use of earnings to criminal ends are the acts that at the core constitute the mainstream *actus reus* of behaviors that are of a "terrorist" nature. State practices across legal systems illustrate the capacity to use ordinary criminal and civil law to confront such acts of violence. Parallel enforcement examples include the capacity of democratic states to process widespread criminal activity (e.g, Mafia crime) that may contain terrorist-style tactics and actions.[19] This is not to say that the identification and processing of crimes undertaken by closely knit organizational structures that are difficult to penetrate owing to the nature of their associational make-up and their ideological aims are straightforward or without obstacles. However, it should not be assumed that the ordinary law of most democratic states is inherently unable, or the state's actors unwilling, to use substantive criminal law and procedure to confront terrorist actions. This is most pertinent when states first have to respond to terrorist acts. Where it becomes evident that the ordinary law may require additional capacities, or when the utilization of measures that are not available in normal circumstances based on the principles of necessity or proportionality is sought, then the calibration of an "ordinary law first" approach may be different. Nonetheless, at any stage in response to sustained or infrequent terrorist acts the balancing process concerning which law to use should contain a high threshold for moving beyond the ordinary criminal and civil law to emergency powers. We also note that there is

---

[18] Inter-American Commission on Human Rights, "Report on Terrorism and Human Rights," at para. 16; Roach, *Consequences for Canada*, p. 16.

[19] See Bruce Ackerman, "The Emergency Constitution" (2004) 113 *Yale Law Journal* 1029 at 1034; Thomas M. Franck, "Criminals, Combatants or What? An Examination of the Role of Law in Responding to the Threat of Terror" (2004) 98 *American Journal of International Law* 686.

a range of reasons why states may wish to retain their designation of terrorists as criminals, or avoid resort to emergency laws or derogation in the first place. The response of the United Kingdom to the status of politically motivated prisoners in Northern Ireland is a useful example of this approach.[20]

The issue has particular international resonance in the post-September 11 world as a number of states, upon being mandated to expand their anti-terrorism laws by virtue of the demands of the United Nations Security Council Resolution 1373, reported initially to the newly created United Nations Counter-Terrorism Committee ('CTC') that their legal systems made no unique provision for the processing of terrorist crime. Rather, it was presumed that no such modifications were necessary, effectively representing either the application of the "hard" version of the Business as Usual model, a model of interpretive accommodation, or perhaps even occasional examples of legislative accommodation (by way of modifying existing ordinary laws), depending on the circumstances and context.[21] Such states included Mexico, which indicated in its first report to the CTC that it was able to handle all crimes that amounted to terrorism within its current criminal code without explicitly calling terrorism a crime as such. Austria, Brazil, and Belgium also declared that their domestic criminal provisions included no specially defined crime of terrorism.

While ordinary law may be capable of responding to terrorist crime, the general practice of states, particularly Western democracies in recent years, has been to legislate special or emergency laws in response to acts deemed as "terrorist" occurring within their territories. States have also legislated against the background of terrorist threats and activities in neighboring countries which the former consider to undermine their security. As we pointed out in Part I, the models of accommodation dominate state practice and responses to crisis generally and terrorism in particular. Courts have also interpreted existing legal rules and legislation so as to accommodate the experience of terrorism. In chapters 1 and 5 we argued that both domestic and international legal systems allow for, and have validated, emergency powers to confront the experience of terrorism. Thus the models of accommodation of emergency powers

---

[20] McFeeley v. United Kingdom, App. No. 8317/78, (1980) 3 *Eur. HR Rep.* 161, (1980) 20 D.R. 44 (Commission report); Clive Walker, "Irish Republican Prisoners: Political Detainees, Prisoners of War or Common Criminals?" (1984) 19 *Irish Jurist* 189.

[21] Notably all these states were strongly pressed by the CTC to adopt specific domestic legislation in this regard. All complied.

have had a continuous overlap with state and international responses to terrorism (though we note that attaching the label "terrorism" to any act may not be legally neutral but rather constitutes an important symbolic and legal action in itself).

To illustrate this we briefly turn to examine a selection of the case law involving terrorism that has come before the European Convention on Human Rights' system. Much of this case law has been litigated on the basis of the state's appropriate and permissible use of limitation clauses and not in a derogation context. This in itself reveals a germane aspect of state practice as regards legal responses to terrorism (to date), namely state capacity to deal with the threat and violence of terrorism within an accommodation or Business as Usual model.

As Colin Warbrick notes, "There is no definition of terrorism in the European Convention on Human Rights...and the European Court of Human Rights has not developed one in its jurisprudence."[22] Thus, the convention itself does not formally acknowledge terrorism as a unique phenomenon and thus it does not create a special class requiring specific accommodation in dealing with terrorism. Evidently, the more general language of the convention concerning derogation and limitation clauses in respect of national security, public order, and public safety operate to couch claims made by states in terms of their responses to terrorist acts.

This regional example may provide a provisional answer to the question of whether terrorism per se creates unique problems that cannot be dealt with under existing legal arrangements. The case law demonstrates a consistent and vigorous interface at the international level concerned specifically with the oversight of various legal practices and rules deployed by states in response to terrorist acts. There is no obvious state dissatisfaction to be gauged in global responses to this oversight (aside from the displeasure at losing particular cases). A separate question, addressed later in this chapter, is whether the terrorist phenomenon is a markedly different creature, requiring a markedly different legal response, from general "public emergencies."

As stated above the European Convention does not contain any definition of terrorism. However, the court (and in the past also the commission) has proceeded with an unarticulated concept of terrorism, facilitated by two notable features. First, as the court deals only with the

---

[22] Colin Warbrick, "The Principles of the European Convention on Human Rights and the Response of States to Terrorism" (2002) 3 *European Human Rights Law Review* 287 at 287.

acts of states it has not inquired into the "legal consequences of human rights violations by non-State actors."[23] Second, as each case is examined on its own merits relevant to the particular factual circumstances of the state under review, a uniform legal concept of terrorism has not been necessary to facilitate the judicial process.

The court articulated its overall approach in *Fox, Campbell and Hartley*. The court recognized:

[T]he need, inherent in the Convention system, for a proper balance between the defence of the institutions of democracy in the common interest and the protection of human rights...Accordingly...the Court will...take into account the special nature of terrorist crime and the exigencies of dealing with it, as far as is compatible with the applicable provisions of the Convention in the light of their particular wording and the overall object and purpose.[24]

This is the most cogent articulation of judicial accommodation operating at the international level. It is clear across a range of cases dealing with the substantive rights protected by the convention that the court is prepared to take into account a background of terrorism in assessing the counter-terrorism claims of states. However, even within this model of accommodation the discretion of states is not unlimited. In the *Klass* decision the court stated that it was aware "of the danger such [action] poses of undermining or even destroying democracy on the ground of defending it, [and] affirms that the Contracting States may not, in the name of the struggle against espionage and terrorism, adopt whatever measures they deem appropriate."[25]

Under its article 2 jurisprudence the court has considered the amount of, and circumstances within, the use of force that can be utilized against terrorist suspects. In *McCann and Others v. United Kingdom* the court ruled effectively that the existence of a terrorist threat, or the fact that the person killed was a terrorist suspect, does not in and of itself provide a stronger or different justification for the use of lethal force than would have been the case if the victim were an ordinary criminal.[26] Under article 3, while acknowledging the difficulties of interrogating terrorist suspects, the court has absolutely prohibited torture or inhuman

---

[23] Ibid., at 288. See also Ireland v. United Kingdom, 1976 *YB Eur. Conv. on HR* (Eur. Comm'n on HR), para. 19 ("It [the court] is not required to rule on the terrorist activities in the six counties of individuals or groups, activities that are clearly in disregard of human rights").

[24] Fox, Campbell, and Hartley v. United Kingdom (1991) 13 *Eur. HR Rep.* 157 at para. 28.

[25] Klass v. Germany (1978) 28 *Eur. Ct HR* (ser. A) at 5, (1978) 2 *Eur. HR Rep.* 214 at para. 48.

[26] McCann and Others v. United Kingdom (1996) 21 *Eur. HR Rep.* 97 at para. 159.

or degrading treatment or punishment "irrespective of the victim's conduct."[27] In the context of article 5 protections (the right to liberty) the court has examined such matters as preventive detention for terrorist suspects,[28] powers of detention for questioning persons moving within a territory and suspected of terrorism,[29] and bringing suspects arrested under anti-terrorism legislation "promptly" before a judicial officer.[30] As we have set out in chapters 1 and 5, judicial interpretive accommodation may allow states greater latitude – activated by articulation of a specific context (terrorism) – than they would otherwise enjoy. While formally the rule itself, and thus the nature of the state's obligation, remains unchanged, outcomes are modified. This operates as a de facto modification of the state's obligations that is linked to the special characteristics of terrorist crime. Moreover, this interpretive modification is relatively hidden by virtue of the procedural proprieties that are followed with regard to the right of individual petition to the European Court of Human Rights. As each case is considered on its own merits, one can make the claim that, for example, restrictions on expressions of support for terrorist acts are "necessary" within the meaning of article 10 of the European Convention, or that a ban on a political party that supports terrorist groups is proportionate under article 11, and nothing has been done to modify the state's formal obligations. Conversely, we suggest that where states are aware that individual cases will give rise to interpretive accommodation where the outcomes are balanced consistently in the states' favor, the practical outcome is tantamount to a de facto modification of the relevant rules and norms that is facilitated by judicial interpretation.

As regards the right to fair trial the court (and, again, the commission) has examined the use of special courts,[31] looking at whether trials involving persons charged with terrorist offences should be public,[32] and examined the right to silence and the privilege against self-incrimination for all defendants.[33] Here, while there is still clear

---

[27] Chahal v. United Kingdom (1996) 23 *Eur. HR Rep.* 413 at para. 80; Fionnuala Ní Aoláin, "The European Convention on Human Rights and its Prohibition on Torture" in Sanford Levinson (ed.), *Torture: A Collection* (Oxford: Oxford University Press, 2004), p. 213.

[28] Lawless v. Ireland (Court), 3 *Eur. Ct HR* (ser. A) (1960–61).

[29] McVeigh et al. v. United Kingdom (1981) 25 *Eur. Comm'n HR Dec. & Rep.* 15.

[30] Brogan and Others v. United Kingdom (1988) 145–B *Eur. Ct HR* (ser. A) at 16.

[31] Incal v. Turkey (1998) 29 *Eur. HR Rep.* 448, (1998–IV) *Eur. Ct HR* 1547.

[32] Tinnelly & Sons Ltd and McElduff v. United Kingdom (1999) 27 *Eur. HR Rep.* 249.

[33] John Murray v. United Kingdom (1996) 22 *Eur. HR Rep.* 29.

evidence of accommodating the uniqueness of the terrorist context as articulated by states, the court has been robust in its conclusions on the incompatibility of such measures as military trials for terrorist defendants.[34] With respect to the right to silence the court has highlighted the right of access to legal advice and counsel as a key element of a fair procedure where a defendant may incriminate herself by silence.[35] The court has also reviewed closely limitations placed by states on the freedoms of expression and association premised on state categorization of certain forms of speech as unacceptable political expression related to terrorism. The measures that have been so reviewed include broadcasting bans on identified members of political parties (upheld as proportionate)[36] and the banning of political parties. The court has been sensitive to governmental claims as regards limitations on media access by proscribed organizations, applying a proportionality test that was generally weighted in the state's favor. However, the banning of political parties has proved more difficult for states, demonstrating the importance that the court attaches to this kind of political association and its links to the maintenance of effective and participatory democracy.

The overall range of jurisprudential accommodations and bars to state action demonstrates an active legal exchange between international human rights courts and state responses to terrorism over a protracted period. For one of us, this exchange evidences and highlights the capacity of international human rights law to respond to terrorists acts, and partly answers the rhetorical question of whether existing legal arrangements can appropriately respond to terrorism through constitutional models of emergency powers.

Another closely related question is whether special laws are required to deal with the actions of terrorists. The question is broadly stated, recognizing that the response may have a slightly different calibration across legal systems dependent on their terrain of existing laws. However, the need for such special, emergency, and counter-terrorism legislation has been firmly asserted by the Counter-Terrorism Committee in the nature of the legislative obligations placed upon states, without regard to their legal capacity.

---

[34] See also the decision of the UN Human Rights Committee Kavanagh v. Ireland, Communication No. 1114/2002/Rev. 1, UN Doc. CCPR/C/76/D/1114/2002/Rev. 1.

[35] Magee v. United Kingdom (2001) 31 Eur. HR Rep. 822, (2000) Eur. Ct HR 215; Heaney and McGuinness v. Ireland (2000) Eur. Ct HR 675, (2001) 33 Eur. HR Rep. 12.

[36] Purcell v. Ireland (1991) 70 Eur. Comm'n HR Dec. & Rep. 262.

This raises the further and more refined question of whether the form of terrorist violence now being experienced, which is not purely internal to a particular state and by which states do not necessarily face threats to their day-to-day operations, but may be faced with a greater potential for catastrophic (yet relatively isolated) dangers and harms – and the global counter-responses to it, which are transnational in scope – require the activation of special powers.[37] The question is a complex one and is explored further below. For now it may be sufficient to note that perhaps indicative of the complexity of this question is the fact that, while one of us views existing legal regimes as providing sufficient cover to respond adequately to the nature of the threat posed by transnational groupings such as al Qaeda, the other co-author argues that certain catastrophic cases may justify, and indeed call for, the invocation of the Extra-Legal Measures model, which is discussed in chapter 3.

By and large when states experience terrorist actions (the scale is often irrelevant) they resort to the use of emergency powers. Moreover, such powers (and the form of resort) conform generally to certain common patterns across jurisdictions and legal systems.[38] Terrorist actions, actors, causes, struggles, and situations can all theoretically create the material conditions in which extraordinary laws are required.

Empirical evidence as to the relative success of special anti-terrorist laws compared with ordinary law is limited. The work that has been carried out, such as the research undertaken by Brice Dickson in Northern Ireland, has shown persuasively that the use of emergency powers was of limited effectiveness in combating the terrorism experienced in the jurisdiction during the height of the violence.[39] It has often been the case that the capacity of ordinary law to cope with such crises has not been fully tested before employing extraordinary emergency powers. We note that amplified pressure to increase security within and by states in response to the augmented terrorist threats is part of what has been called "a fundamental switch away from reactive policing of incidents to proactive policing and management of risk."[40] The appeal for special laws to

---

[37] Thanks to David Wippman for raising this point.

[38] See United Nations High Commissioner for Human Rights, "Protection of Human Rights and Fundamental Freedoms while Countering Terrorism," UN Doc. A/59/428 (Oct. 8, 2004) at para. 20.

[39] See Brice Dickson, "Northern Ireland's Emergency Legislation – The Wrong Medicine?" (1992) *Public Law* 592 at 597.

[40] See Clive Walker, "Terrorism and Criminal Justice: Past, Present and Future" (2004) *Criminal Law Review* 311 at 315; Ulrich Beck, *Risk Society: Towards a New Modernity* (London: Sage, 1992).

respond to the threat of terrorism is usually made on three grounds. First, the duty of the state, especially the liberal democratic state, is to defend itself, its citizens, and its values from threats. The greater and more acute dangers and threats that are posed by terrorism require more expansive powers and authorities to be employed by the state in order to overcome the challenge. Terrorism interrupts the "normal" balance between security and liberty so that a new balance must be struck that is more "security" oriented and weighted. Second, a morality-based argument that terrorism is an illegitimate form of political expression that necessitates special means to respond to its violent forms. Finally, terrorism is a specialized form of criminal behavior, with characteristics that make it very difficult for police and for the ordinary criminal process to deal with its manifestations. Only distinct antiterrorist laws can capture the organizations and individuals engaged in such activities.

As noted above, one of us believes, however, that an "ordinary law first" approach corresponds to the requirements of proportionality contained in international human rights law norms (see chapter 5). This approach is increasingly under political pressure to give way to the immediacy of an emergency response. The work of Kent Roach, who has assessed methodically the Canadian response to the events of September 11, 2001, is useful in this regard.[41] Roach argues persuasively that there is a new atrocity-driven tempo evident in the use of expanded criminal law regulating anti-terrorism. Rather than fully testing the capacity of existing criminal categories to process perpetrators, political pressure to "name" terrorist crime in a unique manner in order both to demonstrate state response and to inculcate security in target populations actually serves to undermine the liberties that democracies hold dear. Thus, Roach suggests:

Had the September 11 terrorists planned their crimes in Canada and had law enforcement officials been aware of their activities, the existing law would have allowed them to be charged and convicted of serious crimes before they boarded the aircraft. They would have been guilty of conspiracy to hijack the plane, conspiracy to murder, attempted hijacking, or attempted murder when they were still planning their suicide missions. Such offences already carry high maximum penalties, including life imprisonment. The failure of September 11 was one of law enforcement, not of the criminal law.[42]

This patterns a more general phenomenon that Roach identifies, namely the tendency to amend the criminal law to respond to well-publicized

---

[41] Roach, *Consequences for Canada*, pp. 21–55.   [42] Ibid., p. 23.

tragedies and to "govern through crime."[43] Thus, post-September 11 additions to the criminal law reflect an augmentation of a "narrative" and "memorial" style to the criminal law based on the perceived impact of the harm suffered and not on an assessment of the capacity of existing law to respond. We suggest that the use of emergency powers has become a conduit for this narrative style of response to terrorism by states. This has occurred despite (and perhaps precisely because of) the lack of definitional boundaries for the term "terrorism." The emergency category, generally in its accommodation mode, has become the legal facilitator for responses against terrorism in many jurisdictions.

Political rhetoric about a "new form of global terrorism" has ignited a conversation about the capacity of emergency accommodation to respond adequately to terrorism.[44] One view of the derogation regime facilitated under international human rights law is that it was created by states primarily as a means to deal with crises within their own borders that affected the capacity of the state to function fully and protect the rights of all inhabitants. This has been the general context in which derogation reviews, whether involving terrorism or not, have come before regional and international courts. However, it should also be noted that regional courts and international tribunals have considered cases concerning derogation triggered by situations of terrorism in which the threats perceived were primarily taking place in another jurisdiction (most famously in the case of *Lawless v. Ireland*). A contemporary challenge may be that the episodic but catastrophic nature of current terrorist violence (New York, Madrid, and London) means that emergency powers facilitated domestically by international derogation privileges are not sufficient to contain the global threat of terrorism. It might also be argued that the prolonged nature of an indeterminate "war on terrorism" does not fit the conceptual frame of derogation (created to deal with specific and finite emergencies).

We do not subscribe to this view. While recognizing that supplemental measures may be useful, specifically with respect to tailored augmentations of international humanitarian law (see below), we defend the relevance and utility of the accommodation and derogation mechanisms where used appropriately. Two brief points can be made. First, the

---

[43] Ibid., p. 24; Lawrence M. Friedman and George Fisher, *The Crime Conundrum: Essays on Criminal Justice* (Boulder, CO: Westview Press, 1997).

[44] See Tom R. Hickman, "Between Human Rights and the Rule of Law: Indefinite Detention and the Derogation Model of Constitutionalism" (2005) 68 *Modern Law Review* 655.

transnational features of terrorism are not new. Many terrorist organizations (such as the PLO, IRA, and ETA) have operated and trained across jurisdictions for decades, and have been financed accordingly. While there may be a higher intensity (or at least attention) to the transnational operations of groups such as al Qaeda, the phenomenon itself is not new. It has also been addressed actively by robust mutual cooperation and assistance measures agreed between states since September 11. Second, despite our concerns about the prolonged use of emergency powers and derogation by states, the derogation regime has demonstrated substantial capacity to deal with long-term crises. The oversight mechanisms of derogation should remain utilized, albeit a more sophisticated approach to the application of the derogation regime might be called for, as discussed in chapter 5. If change is necessary it is needed most in augmenting the structural capacity of international accountability mechanisms to deal with permanent and complex emergencies.[45]

We would also recall that, from the perspective of individual governments, the emergency construct has generally proved beneficial, in part because international oversight mechanisms were defective in dealing with obvious manipulations of the regime by states. Historically, debates concerning the status and definition of terrorism were more overtly found in the language narrating the extent to which states and non-state actors argued about the application of "armed conflict" status to a particular situation of violence. This language was also usually at the very margins of the human rights discourse of international courts and tribunals, a facet that was not without virtue to state parties. Importantly in these debates the applicability of some legal regime was not contested, although the specific regime to be activated was. This is no longer the case. We note briefly two examples in this context. Both reflect what one of us regards as the appeal of the Extra-Legal Measures model of emergency powers: first, the use of preventive interrogational torture, i.e., torture whose aim is to gain information that would assist authorities in foiling exceptionally grave terrorist attacks, rather than to obtain confessions or other evidence that may be used to bring the subject of interrogation to criminal trial or to punish individuals for past actions;[46] and second, preemptive self-defense.

---

[45] See Joan Fitzpatrick, "Speaking Law to Power: The War against Terrorism and Human Rights" (2003) 14 *European Journal of International Law* 241.

[46] Oren Gross, "Are Torture Warrants Warranted? Pragmatic Absolutism and Official Disobedience" (2004) 88 *Minnesota Law Review* 1481 at 1487–88.

Reflecting strong universal condemnation and reprobation of such practices, torture is absolutely prohibited under all major international human rights and humanitarian law conventions.[47] This absolute ban is considered universal and has become part of customary international law. In fact, it amounts to a preemptory norm of international law. [48] For reasons explained in detail elsewhere we believe that, when considered from both moral and pragmatic perspectives, this absolute legal prohibition on torture must not be relaxed.[49] However, one of us has argued that there may be circumstances – truly catastrophic cases – when the appropriate method of tackling extremely grave national dangers and threats may call for public officials going outside the legal order, at

---

[47] Convention against Torture and Other Cruel, Inhuman or Degrading Treatment or Punishment, GA Res. 39/46, UN GAOR, 39th Sess., Supp. No. 51, at 197, UN Doc. A/RES/39/46 (1984) (entered into force June 26, 1987); African Charter on Human and Peoples' Rights, June 27, 1981, art. 5, OAU Doc. CAB/LEG/67/3/Rev. 5, (1982) 21 *International Legal Materials* 59 (entered into force Oct. 21, 1986); American Convention on Human Rights, Nov. 22, 1969, art. 5, (1970) 9 *International Legal Materials* 673 at 676–77, OAS Official Records OEA/ser. K/XVI/1.1, doc. 65, rev. 1, corr. 1 (entered into force July 18, 1978); International Covenant on Civil and Political Rights, Dec. 16, 1966, art. 7, 999 UNTS 171, 175, 6 *International Legal Materials* 368 at 370; Convention for the Protection of Human Rights and Fundamental Freedoms, Nov. 4, 1950, art. 3, 213 UNTS 221 at 224 (entered into force Sept. 3, 1953). See also Tomasi v. France (1992) 241 *Eur. Ct HR* (ser. A), at 42; Oren Gross, "The Grave Breaches System and the Armed Conflict in the Former Yugoslavia" (1995) 16 *Michigan Journal of International Law* 783 at 801–09; J. Herman Burgers and Hans Danelius, *The United Nations Convention against Torture: A Handbook on the Convention against Torture and Other Cruel, Inhuman or Degrading Treatment or Punishment* (Boston: Nijhoff, 1988).

[48] See, e.g., Kadic v. Karadzic, 70 F.3d 232 at 243 (2nd Cir. 1995); Siderman de Blake v. Republic of Argentina, 965 F.2d 699 at 717 (9th Cir. 1992); Filartiga v. Pena-Irala, 630 F.2d 876 at 890 (2nd Cir. 1980); Council of Europe, *Guidelines on Human Rights and the Fight against Terrorism* (Strasbourg: Council of Europe Pub., 2002); Inter-American Commission on Human Rights, "Report on the Situation of Human Rights of Asylum Seekers within the Canadian Refugee Determination System", OEA/Ser. L/V/II.106, Doc. 40 rev., Feb. 28, 2000, at para. 118; *Restatement of the Law (Third), The Foreign Relations Law of the United States*, para. 702, cmt. n (St. Paul, MN: American Law Institute Pub., 1987); Roland Bank, "International Efforts to Combat Torture and Inhuman Treatment: Have the New Mechanisms Improved Protection?" (1997) 8 *European Journal of International Law* 613; Sanford Levinson, " 'Precommitment' and 'Postcommitment': The Ban on Torture in the Wake of September 11" (2003) 81 *Texas Law Review* 2013 at 2013–17. See also Sissela Bok, *Common Values* (Columbia, MO: University of Missouri Press, 1995), pp. 15–16; Seth F. Kreimer, "Exploring the Dark Matter of Judicial Review: A Constitutional Census of the 1990s" (1997) 5 *William and Mary Bill of Rights Journal* 427 at 510–11; Jeremy Waldron, "How to Argue for a Universal Claim" (1999) 30 *Columbia Human Rights Law Review* 305 at 305.

[49] Gross, "Torture Warrants," 1490–511; Oren Gross, "The Prohibition on Torture and the Limits of the Law" in Sanford Levinson (ed.), *Torture: A Collection* (Oxford: Oxford University Press, 2004), p. 229.

times even violating the otherwise entrenched absolute prohibition on torture, anchoring this position in the framework of the Extra-Legal Measures model of emergency powers.[50] In such extreme situations, denying the use of preventive interrogational torture may be hypocritical, cold hearted, detrimental to long-term notions of the rule of law, and may, in fact, lead to more, rather than less, radical interference with individual rights and liberties.[51]

Article 2(4) of the Charter of the United Nations prohibits "the threat or use of force against the territorial integrity or political independence of any state." The charter contains only two exceptions to this general prohibition. First, the United Nations Security Council can authorize the use of force under Chapter VII of the charter. Second, article 51 of the charter provides that "Nothing in the present Charter shall impair the inherent right of individual or collective self-defence if an armed attack occurs against a Member of the United Nations . . . " The accepted opinion has traditionally been that article 51, by invoking the language of "if an armed attack occurs," precludes the possibility of using force preemptively.[52] Yet, the war on terror, in general, and the war in Iraq, in particular, ushered in the Bush doctrine of preemptive self-defense.[53] On a number of occasions, President Bush announced that the United

---

[50] Gross, "Torture Warrants," 1511–34.   [51] Ibid., pp. 1511–13.

[52] See, e.g., Christine Gray, *International Law and the Use of Force* (2nd edn, Oxford: Oxford University Press, 2004), pp. 129–33; Ian Brownlie, *International Law and the Use of Force by States* (Oxford: Clarendon Press, 1963), p. 278; Hans Kelsen, *The Law of the United Nations: A Critical Analysis of Its Fundamental Problems* (New York: F.A. Praeger, 1951), pp. 797–98; Philip C. Jessup, *A Modern Law of Nations: An Introduction* (Hamden, CT: Archon Books, 1968), p. 166; Yoram Dinstein, *War, Aggression, and Self-Defence* (4th edn, Cambridge: Cambridge University Press, 2005), p. 182, but see ibid., pp. 187–92 (legitimacy of "interceptive" self-defense); Sean D. Murphy, "The Doctrine of Preemptive Self-Defense" (2005) 50 *Villanova Law Review* 699 at 706–11.

[53] The White House, *The National Security Strategy of the United States of America* (Sept. 17, 2002), pp. 6, 13–16, available at http://www.whitehouse.gov/nsc/nss.pdf (last visited on Aug. 8, 2005); Remarks by President George W. Bush to Troops and Families of the 10th Mountain Division, Fort Drum, New York (July 19, 2002), available online at http://www.whitehouse.gov/news/releases/2002/07/20020719.html (last visited Aug. 8, 2005); Remarks by President George W. Bush at 2002 Graduation Exercise of the United States Military Academy, West Point, New York (June 1, 2002), available online at http://www.whitehouse.gov/news/releases/2002/06/20020601-3.html (last visited Aug. 8, 2005). See also Dominic McGoldrick, *From "9/11" to the "Iraq War 2003": International Law in an Age of Complexity* (Oxford: Hart, 2004), pp. 81–85; Harold Hongju Koh, "On American Exceptionalism" (2003) 55 *Stanford Law Review* 1479; Sean D. Murphy, "Assessing the Legality of Invading Iraq" (2004) 92 *Georgetown Law Journal* 173; Murphy, "Preemptive Self-Defense," 701–02, 715–17; Gray, *Use of Force*, pp. 175–86.

States "will act against...emerging threats before they are fully formed" as a matter of "common sense and self-defense." Thus,

We must be prepared to stop rogue states and their terrorist clients before they are able to threaten or use weapons of mass destruction against the United States and our allies and friends...the United States can no longer solely rely on a reactive posture as we have in the past. The inability to deter a potential attacker, the immediacy of today's threats, and the magnitude of potential harm that could be caused by our adversaries' choice of weapons, do not permit that option. We cannot let our enemies strike first...We must adapt the concept of imminent threat to the capabilities and objectives of today's adversaries...To forestall or prevent such hostile acts by our adversaries, the United States will, if necessary, act preemptively.[54]

This expansive notion of the use of preemptive self-defense has been the subject of much heated debate. Some have argued that existing international legal rules on the use of force are sufficient to deal with the fight against terrorism and need not be modified or changed. Others have argued that the rules are inadequate and ought to be changed (or, in a more radical vein, have argued that the existing rules were practically "dead"). Yet others have argued that the meaning and application of the rules have changed in light of state practice. Another perspective that is in line with the Extra-Legal Measures model is that,

[I]n the truly exceptional situation where a serious crisis exists...and the [Security] Council is not prepared to act, it would be better if the United States simply violated international law *without* advancing strained and potentially destabilizing legal justifications. By doing so it would allow its action to be assessed subsequently, not in terms of the law, but in terms of its political and moral legitimacy – with a view to mitigation rather than exculpation.[55]

Similar suggestions have been made in the context of humanitarian intervention, in general, and NATO's actions in Kosovo in 1999, in particular. Thus, it has been argued that, assuming one accepts the position that such actions, while potentially desirable in certain circumstances, are unlawful under existing international legal norms,[56] it would be better to recognize such actions for what they are – extra-legal – while

---

[54] *National Security Strategy*, Introduction and p. 15.

[55] Michael Byers, "Preemptive Self-Defense: Hegemony, Equality and Strategies of Legal Change" (2003) 11 *Journal of Political Philosophy* 171 at 186, 185–88. See also Thomas M. Franck, *Recourse to Force: State Action against Threats and Armed Attacks* (Cambridge: Cambridge University Press, 2002), pp. 174–91.

[56] Both claims – about desirability and about the legal status of such operations – are, of course, subject to much controversy that is beyond the scope of this work.

accepting that they may be justified or excused in the particular circumstances, rather than attempt to modify the existing legal rules to accommodate such actions.[57] As Oscar Schachter suggested:

> [A] state or group of States using force to put an end to atrocities when the necessity is evident and the humanitarian intention is clear is likely to have its action pardoned. But, I believe it is highly undesirable to have a new rule allowing humanitarian intervention, for that could provide a pretext for abusive intervention. It would be better to acquiesce in a violation that is considered necessary and desirable in the particular circumstances than to adopt a principle that would open a wide gap in the barrier against the unilateral use of force.[58]

The "terrorism and law" interface

Despite these contemporary pressures we take the overall view that terrorism occurs in a context of interrelated and mutually reinforcing legal regimes, rather than as a phenomenon that operates to nullify the relevance of those regimes. In this we dispute the notion that terrorism per se constitutes a *sui generis* threat to which existing legal processes, and or notions of crisis, are ill suited. We are not convinced that a coherent legal or policy argument can be made to exempt terrorism from the regulation of crises more generally. Terrorism is, we conclude, one point on a broad spectrum of political, economic, and social occurrences that may challenge profoundly the capacity of the state to operate within the boundaries of the normal. This does not underplay or negate the enormous challenges terrorism poses to democratic societies in particular.

The follow-up to the definitional task in this chapter is to inquire what, if any, international legal regime applies when states react to terrorism. The short answer is that state action is regulated, independently or concurrently, by several legal regimes. Terrorist violence thus may occur in the context of:

1. An otherwise peaceful situation where international human rights law is fully applicable. Here, the Business as Usual model or some form of interpretive accommodation is most relevant.

---

[57] See, e.g., Ian Johnstone, "The Plea of 'Necessity' in International Legal Discourse: Humanitarian Intervention and Counter-Terrorism" (2005) 43 *Columbia Journal of Transnational Law* 337 at 357–66.

[58] Oscar Schachter, *International Law in Theory and Practice* (Boston: Nijhoff, 1991), p. 126. See also Louis Henkin, "NATO's Kosovo Intervention: Kosovo and the Law of 'Humanitarian Intervention'" (1999) 93 *American Journal of International Law* 824.

2. An emergency that threatens the life and security of the state, in which international human rights law applies subject to any allowable derogations that fully comport with the substantive and procedural requirements of derogation. This is most likely to occur in tandem with modes of domestic legislative accommodation.

3. An armed conflict where both international human rights law and international humanitarian law may apply simultaneously, though the latter will constitute the *lex specialis*,[59] suggesting another format for an international model of accommodation.

4. An Extra-Legal Measures context where ex post accountability (legal and otherwise) is sought for unlawful acts by state actors.

We argue that a useful means to conceptualize the relationships between the first three regimes is to think in terms of the principle of complementarity. What we hope to demonstrate is that the legal regimes that apply to crisis situations (terrorist or otherwise) need not be static in nature and that movement between them is both a practical reality and a legal imperative to ensure the maximum responsiveness of legal systems to exigencies. The emphasis of analysis in this context is on the constitutional models of emergency regimes.

The principle of complementarity has come to play a critical role in the advancement of international criminal law,[60] specifically in its regulation of the relationship between international and national jurisdiction over specific crimes and individuals. It contains the expression of the idea that national law and international law play mutually reinforcing and complementary roles in the context of international crimes. The concept is a useful way to think about how the regulation of terrorism can move between the accommodation and Business as Usual models. Regulation may therefore be dependent on the scale of the terrorist action or its increased intensity, and most importantly reflects that the regulation of terrorism can move between legal categories and is not necessarily static.

The regulation of terrorism by international humanitarian law

Chapters 1 and 2 have set out in principle how terrorism is amenable to regulation by ordinary law or through certain models of accommodation. Chapter 6 demonstrated how there can be a clear overlap between

---

[59] We acknowledge the influence of the typologies proposed by the Inter-American Commission on Human Rights in its "Report on Terrorism and Human Rights."

[60] Bartram S. Brown, "Primacy or Complementarity: Reconciling the Jurisdiction of National Courts and International Criminal Tribunals" (1998) 23 *Yale Journal of International Law* 383.

what we term "high-intensity emergencies" and situations of armed conflict (conflict that may include acts of terrorism). However, at this juncture, and given its importance to contemporary legal regulation, we
think it important to address a separate question, namely whether acts
of terrorism alone can create the material conditions that activate the
application of international humanitarian law.[61] This is an important
question in that those who reject the applicability of existing legal structures and rules (national and international) to the actions of groups such
as al Qaeda make the clear supposition that the accommodation model
of humanitarian law is irrelevant or inapplicable to the contemporary
context.

We would suggest that some, though not necessarily all, terrorist acts
can, in principle, activate the application of international humanitarian
law.[62] Applying international humanitarian law to terrorist acts or situations encounters conceptual and political barriers. States have frequently
resisted the application of such law on the general grounds that to do so
would be to give an undeserving status (symbolic and practical) to organizations and individuals engaged in terrorist violence.[63] States have also
been concerned that, because neither Common Article 3 nor Protocol II
contains any specific provisions on criminal responsibility, non-state actors will escape legal process. These latter concerns have been addressed
by the Statute of the International Criminal Court, by a developing jurisprudence of universal jurisdiction, and by the jurisprudence of the
International Criminal Tribunal for the Former Yugoslavia.[64]

At this point we separate out two discrete questions, i.e., whether
terrorism can engage international humanitarian law and whether the
particular acts of al Qaeda, commencing with the attacks of September
11, 2001, activate the laws of armed conflict.

On the first question, there has been a wide variety of academic views
expressed by legal scholars on the core question, as well as on related

---

[61] We specifically imply here the application of the law of armed conflict, which, while
having overlap with the term international humanitarian law, may be narrower in
scope.

[62] See Derek Jinks, "September 11 and the Laws of War" (2003) 28 *Yale Journal of
International Law* 1; Christopher Greenwood, "War, Terrorism and International Law"
(2003) 56 *Current Legal Problems* 505.

[63] Fionnuala Ní Aoláin, *The Politics of Force: Conflict Management and State Violence in
Northern Ireland* (Belfast: Blackstaff Press, 2000), pp. 224–30.

[64] Prosecutor v. Tadic, Case No. IT-94-1-AR72, Decision on the Defense Motion for
Interlocutory Appeal on Jurisdiction, reprinted in (1996) 35 *International Legal Materials*
32 (Int'l Crim. Trib. for Former Yugoslavia Appeals Chamber, Oct. 2, 1995).

matters such as the right of self-defense, the status and legitimacy provided (or not) by the Security Council, and the status of non-state actors engaged in terrorist activity.[65] The general threshold question as to
whether an act (or acts) of terrorism can engage international humanitarian law involves detailed consideration of a number of legal terms,
thresholds, and organizational responses, including the following under
the United Nations Charter – the meaning of use or the threat of force,
armed attack, and an act of aggression.[66] In examining the general question, there is a danger, as Watkin notes, that:

> A very low threshold of what constitutes an armed attack has the potential to
> blur the lines between armed conflict and criminal law enforcement. At the
> other end of the spectrum, too high a threshold may leave a state at risk, espe-
> cially if there is a credible threat involving the use of weapons of mass destruc-
> tion by a non-state actor.[67]

This indicates that a general response is inappropriate. Rather each particular situation where the applicability of international humanitarian
law is relevant should be assessed on its own merits (we have canvassed
some of the relevant factors in the previous chapter), and the appropriate thresholds must be independently assessed. However, in principle
we do not believe the applicability of international humanitarian law
to be excluded, and take the view that it may be applicable, and that
there may be a hybrid application in which significant parts of counter-
terrorism law would continue to operate from a crime control model
while in parallel contexts an armed conflict model would apply.[68]

Application of an armed conflict model to acts of terror is dependent
significantly on reaching particular thresholds of violence and intensity.

---

[65] Kenneth Watkin, "Controlling the Use of Force: A Role for Human Rights Norms in
Contemporary Armed Conflict" (2004) 98 *American Journal of International Law* 1; Sean D.
Murphy, "Terrorism and the Concept of 'Armed Attack' in Article 51 of the UN
Charter" (2002) 43 *Harvard International Law Journal* 41; Richard A. Falk, *The Great Terror
War* (Moreton-in-Marsh, UK: Arris, 2003); Antonio Cassese, "Terrorism is also
Disrupting Some Crucial Legal Categories of International Law" (2001) 12 *European
Journal of International Law* 993.

[66] Note also the problems engendered by the ICJ's decision in the case of *Military and
Paramilitary Activities in and against Nicaragua* (Nicaragua v. United States of America),
Merits (1986) *International Court of Justice Reports* 14, and its distinction between "most
grave" use of force and "less grave" use of force.

[67] Watkin, "Controlling the Use of Force," 4.

[68] For an interesting exploration of this see David Kretzmer, "Targeted Killing of
Suspected Terrorists: Extra-Judicial Executions or Legitimate Means of Defence?" (2005)
16 *European Journal of International Law* 171.

As we have explored in chapter 6, this terminology is not straightforward, and may be outdated in terms of the lived experiences of violence on the ground. We have suggested some rethinking that might be useful in terms of examining thresholds of violence sufficient to activate international humanitarian law, and different ways to recalibrate the tests of intensity (horizontal as well as vertical) as well as the interrelationship between time and violence in judging the relevance of international humanitarian law. Clearly too, such factors as the nature and ideology of the non-state actors require calibration in this equation,[69] as does their organizational capacity. None of these qualifiers can provide a "one size fits all" answer to a generic question about whether international humanitarian law applies to acts or situations involving terrorist violence. We strongly suggest that the clarity sought on answering the specific question would be augmented significantly if the threshold questions were more fully identified and given greater flexibility and nuance.

On the second question, concerning the legal regime which should apply to actions taken against al Qaeda on and since the events of September 11, we take the position that the relevant body of norms activated is Common Article 3 to the Geneva Conventions of 1949. We now set out the basis for that assessment. The relevant starting point is identifying why the law of internal armed conflict would be applicable over that of international armed conflict. A relevant history of the law of armed conflict tells us that the thrust of its provisions has been aimed at regulating "armed conflicts" between sovereign states.[70] Thus, article 2 of the Geneva Conventions of 1949 sets out that the laws of war apply to armed conflicts taking place between states, regardless of whether either state (or more) has formally declared war. A logical corollary of this activation threshold is that the full protections of the Geneva Conventions will only apply to armed conflicts which arise between High Contracting Parties. In the context of legally categorizing the nature of the hostilities between al Qaeda and the coalition of Western states led by the United States, Derek Jinks succinctly points out that, "Absent proof that al Qaeda acted on behalf of a state or that a state has recognized al Qaeda as a 'belligerent,' the only potentially applicable body of law is the law of war governing internal armed conflicts."[71] This lack

---

[69] See Jan Klabbers, "Rebel with a Cause? Terrorists and Humanitarian Law" (2003) 14 *European Journal of International Law* 299.

[70] Ingrid Detter, *The Law of War* (2nd edn, Cambridge: Cambridge University Press, 2000), pp. 1–61.

[71] Jinks, "September 11 and the Laws of War," 12.

of state nexus means that the conflict that was activated between al Qaeda and the United States on September 11 should not be defined as an international armed conflict. However, in claiming that an "armed conflict" was activated by the attacks, we accept that the combined elements of the nature and ferocity of the attacks (and the subsequent scale of destruction) – an intensity of violence threshold – in tandem with the legal responses by international organizations and other states – a recognition threshold (supported by the domestic legal responses of the USA) – join to don this stature.[72] We note, however, that separate issues arise as to the categorization of the conflict that was actualized with the bombing and invasion of Afghanistan in October 2001 and the conflict that was activated by the USA and its allies by the bombing and subsequent invasion of Iraq on March 20, 2003.

Only relatively recently has international humanitarian law focused its regulatory attention on internal conflicts, despite the proliferation and effects of such conflicts since World War II onwards.[73] This lag in regulation tells a deeper narrative about a consistent gap which has existed within the law of armed conflict, between the conflict(s) actually being experienced on the ground and the law's capacity to keep regulatory pace. Following the grievous harms inflicted and experienced during World War II, the Geneva Conventions of 1949 sought to put in place a system of law that would prevent such violations from occurring again in situations of war. However, the conceptualization which dominated the Diplomatic Conference was one of inter-state conflict, and Common Article 3 is the sole article of the conventions which addresses the problems of non-international armed conflicts. The opening paragraph to the article states: "In the case of armed conflict not of an international character occurring in the territory of one of the High Contracting Parties, each Party to the conflict shall be bound to apply, as a minimum, the following provisions..."

There are many policy-based and humanitarian reasons why the application of international humanitarian law may be desirable to the contemporary "war on terrorism."[74] However, we think it important to quantify the rationale for formal legal applicability, under specific legal

---

[72] See UN Security Council Resolution 1368, UN SCOR, 56th Sess., 4370 mtg., at 1, UN Doc. S/RES/1368 (Sept. 12, 2001).

[73] Lindsay Moir, *The Law of Internal Armed Conflict* (Cambridge: Cambridge University Press, 2002).

[74] Jinks, "September 11 and the Laws of War," 5–7. See also Kretzmer, "Targeted Killing of Suspected Terrorists," 186–88.

requirements of appropriate thresholds of violence, intensity, organization, and state acknowledgment of a situation of belligerency.

First, while the events of September 11 constituted a one-off series of
violent actions against the United States, a number of legal consequences
followed. First, immediately following the attacks the United Nations Security Council condemned the acts and recognized the inherent right
of the United States to self-defense against unambiguous external aggression.[75] The North Atlantic Treaty Organization (NATO) for the first
time in its history invoked article 5 of the Washington Treaty, demonstrating "NATO's overall approach to security can include the possibility
of collective action in response to a terrorist attack from abroad."[76] Second, the United States Congress authorized its president to use military
force against those responsible for the attacks against the territorial
integrity of the state.[77] Following from this, President Bush's executive
order, providing for trial of suspected terrorists by military commissions,
characterized the events of September 11 as an attack "on a scale that
has created a state of armed conflict that requires the use of the United
State's Armed Forces."[78] The scale and ferocity of the attacks also serve
a threshold function, excluding the argument that the scale of violence
falls below the Common Article 3 violence threshold. Recent jurisprudence concerning the contours of the term "armed conflict" from the
International Criminal Tribunal for the Former Yugoslavia also supports
this reading of Common Article 3.[79] Finally, we note that though not
required to activate the applicability of Common Article 3, the organizational structure of al Qaeda is such as to make them capable (though
clearly not willing) to reach the command and control prerequisites of

[75] Security Council Resolution 1368. See also Security Council Resolution 1373, UN SCOR,
56th Sess., 4385th mtg., UN Doc. S/RES/1373 (Sept. 28, 2001). See Thomas M. Franck,
"Terrorism and the Right of Self-Defense" (2001) 95 *American Journal of International Law*
839; Robert K. Goldman, "Certain Legal Questions and Issues Raised by the September
11th Attacks" (2001) 9(1) *Human Rights Brief* 2.

[76] See Statement to the Press, NATO Secretary General Lord Robertson, on the North
Atlantic Council Decision on Implementation of Article 5 of the Washington Treaty
following the 11 September Attacks against the United States, Oct. 4, 2001, available
online at http://www.nato.int/docu/speech/2001/s011004b.htm (last visited Aug. 8, 2005);
NATO Statement on Combating Terrorism: Adapting the Alliance's Defence
Capabilities, Press release (2001) 173 (Dec. 18, 2001), available online at
http://www.nato.int/docu/pr/2001/p01-173e.htm (last visited Aug. 8, 2005).

[77] Authorization for the Use of Military Force, Pub. L. No. 107–40, 115 Stat. 224, 224 (2001).

[78] Executive Order of November 13, 2001: Detention, Treatment, and Trial of Certain
Non-Citizens in the War against Terrorism, 66 Fed. Reg. 57, 833 (Nov. 13, 2001),
para. 1(A).

[79] Prosecutor v. Tadic (Appeal on Jurisdiction).

international humanitarian law. All of these factors combined with the value system underpinning the international humanitarian law regime justify classifying the hostilities between the United States (and other states) and al Qaeda as an "armed conflict" within the meaning of the Geneva Conventions.

The utilitarian question then arises as to what benefits accrue from such categorization. First, as a technical matter, by its explicit terms Common Article 3 imposes its obligation on *all parties to the conflict* but its application in no way affects the legal status of parties to the conflict. Affirming this is by no means of small symbolic or practical significance. As a definitional matter, the acts of terror perpetrated on September 11 and since by al Qaeda clearly violate the provisions of Common Article 3. Ensuring that conflicts that fall within article 3's mandate are formally recognized is important to protect (both for states and non-state actors) the core humanitarian values that Common Article 3 was designed to defend.[80] Applying Common Article 3 vacates the argument that there is a legal gap evident, exposed by recent acts of terrorism, which can only be filled by state domestic dictate. It also confirms the capacity of an armed conflict involving acts of terrorism to be contained within a model of accommodation provided by international law.

We would also point out that the application of Common Article 3 does not negate the derogation privilege of states, which specifically affirms armed conflict to be a basis for limiting the full application of the human rights regime. It does not, as we have outlined in detail in chapter 6, wipe out the application of the human rights system. Finally we acknowledge that movement between legal regimes is to be expected, and that the application of the Geneva Conventions does not mean that at some other stage counter-terrorism actions may not slip back fully into a crime control model from an armed conflict model, or that both models may not operate in tandem with one another.

In conclusion we highlight a couple of important procedural matters as regards the application of specific legal regimes. First, we acknowledge that a "formal" legal application issue arises when applying Common Article 3, namely that the provision only applies to armed conflicts occurring *in the territory of* a state party.[81] This raises the obvious question

---

[80] Gerald L. Neuman, "Humanitarian Law and Counterterrorist Force" (2003) 14 *European Journal of International Law* 283.

[81] Our thanks to David Kretzmer for pointing this out and encouraging clarity on the matter.

as to whether it can be applied in transnational contexts. A formalistic response would suggest that a conflict must be either an inter-state conflict (international) or an internal conflict (thereby taking place in the territory of a specific state). In response it might be argued that this clear-cut distinction exposes a lacuna in international humanitarian law in urgent need of attention. Our response is more nuanced. We suggest that to start with it would be helpful to probe the term "transnational" a little more critically. Namely, while the transnational identity of certain non-state groupings is an identifying feature, many such groups still continue to operate and identify locally, with the explicit or tacit consent of states. Furthermore, the terrorist actions post-September 11, 2001 (e.g., the terrorist attacks in London in July 2005) indicate that home-grown terrorists with a clear national and territorial link, though undoubtedly with international associations, might foster, in the long run, circumstances in which the material conditions for the application of international humanitarian law would apply within the traditional definitions, despite their transnational linkages. Third, we stress that it would be helpful to think less in either/or categories when applying international humanitarian law, namely solely in terms of international armed conflict or internal armed conflict. It is equally possible that a state will be in conflict on both levels – and that such conflict may be primarily aimed at non-state groupings and their state supporters where relevant. To some extent this duality may soak up some of the pertinent transnational elements of non-state groupings operating across and within state borders.

Second, as regards the application of international humanitarian law, when a situation of conflict is considered to fall within the parameters of an international armed conflict, such that the armed forces satisfy the prisoner of war conditions set out in article 4 of the Third Geneva Convention or articles 43–45 of Protocol I, then the fact that individual combatants may have engaged in acts of terrorism does not alter the continued application of international humanitarian law to the conflict. It also means that those combatants are still entitled to the protections of the Third Geneva Convention but, significantly, can be prosecuted for terrorist acts which constitute war crimes or other serious violations of international humanitarian law.[82]

Third, while we accept that there is no international consensus on a comprehensive definition of terrorism, and that as a result there is a

---

[82] Specifically they may be responsible for grave breaches of the Geneva Conventions and the Additional Protocols. See Gross, "The Grave Breaches System."

tendency to use loose labels (e.g., war on terrorism) to describe a particular sequence of actions by a state against terrorist actors or groups, this does not per se serve as a basis for defining the international legal obligations of states. We acknowledge that there are new elements to the terrorist phenomenon, specifically the reality of transnational groups unaffiliated substantially with states and prepared to make self-sacrifice for their cause on a scale hitherto unseen,[83] but this trend does not of itself vacate the applicability of international legal norms. We accept that an assessment of contemporary crisis experiences may require specific negotiation of some new legal norms that fall logically into the realm of international humanitarian law. Such norms might regulate the permissible range of responses by states to the actions of non-state groupings, which are entirely unaffiliated with a sovereign territory and whose political aims are not territorially premised. Such an instrument could address the new forms of "terrorist war" being waged against non-state actors.[84] We contend that some of the efforts currently being expended by states in augmenting suppression conventions would in fact be better spent pursuing this specific lacuna. This might alleviate the need to expand the suppression conventions, a process that does not necessarily address the current regulatory gap in international law and may endanger the protection of liberties more generally in democratic societies.

In the current context, with an eye to procedure as well as to the outcomes generated by faulty legal process, we think it is particularly important to stress the significance of the form of language used to describe and proscribe terrorist acts. Given both the stigma and the generally augmented punishments that follow at the domestic level from prosecution and punishment of terrorist crimes, it is critical that precise and unambiguous language be used to define the unlawful acts in question. International law has a direct relationship with clarity at the national level in this context, given that states have on a significant scale either adopted international treaty obligations directly into national law, or used the legal terms as set out in the international standards to frame the prohibition in question at the domestic level. The legal purpose of

---

[83] There is a substantial debate as to whether the view that contemporary terrorists show greater willingness to sacrifice their lives than those of previous generations is empirically correct. See Walter Laqueur, *No End to War: Terrorism in the Twenty-First Century* (New York: Continuum, 2003), pp. 71–97.

[84] In parallel vein Michael Reisman has urged that a flexible approach be taken to the regulation of terrorism. See W. Michael Reisman, "International Legal Responses to Terrorism" (1999) 22 *Houston Journal of International Law* 3 at 12–13.

strict definitional boundaries is to preserve the principle of legality at both the domestic and international level.

International legal responses post-September 11

Suppression conventions

Failing agreement on a singular definition of terrorism, states have successfully managed to plough ahead with legal agreements to suppress particular kinds of acts by terrorist actors. In addition they have sought to adapt and to synchronize the integration of national and regional measures to combat terrorism.[85] Specifically, states have enhanced extradition cooperation and streamlined associated procedures.[86] Notably here many states have concluded in a number of international anti-terrorism instruments that terrorist crimes are not to be regarded as political or related common offenses for the purposes of extradition or mutual legal cooperation.[87] They have given one another mutual legal assistance and shared intelligence and law enforcement sources of information across national boundaries. They have augmented inter-state cooperation on ordinary criminal matters, which often operates to hamper indirectly the financial and other resources which facilitate terrorist actors and networks. This inter-state cooperation is not without its critics. Many civil libertarians voice concerns about the lack of civil and human rights protections in these joint actions, and the danger that states with lower levels of privacy and due process protections may inadvertently affect the quality of rights protection experienced by individuals in states with higher protective standards.

Other mutually reinforcing action includes rigorous and sometimes controversial enforcement of measures to exclude, remove, or extradite

---

[85] An important means to achieve this is by implementing international norms against terrorism in municipal law. For example, the United Kingdom has domestic statutes relating to hijacking aircraft, ships, and other installations (the Aviation Security Act 1982, the Aviation and Maritime Security Act 1990), diplomats (the Internationally Protected Persons Act 1978), hostages (the Taking of Hostages Act 1982), nuclear installations and materials (the Nuclear Material [Offences] Act 1983), and other specific treaties dealing with such matters as extradition (the Suppression of Terrorism Act 1978).

[86] See, e.g., Framework Decision on the European Arrest Warrant; OAS Permanent Council Resolution 1293 (2001); see also notes 134–36 below.

[87] See the European Convention on the Suppression of Terrorism (1979) 1137 UNTS 93, 90 *European Treaty Series* 3, concluded on Jan. 27, 1977, article 1; Inter-American Convention against Terrorism, OAS AG Res. 1840, 32nd Sess., OAS Doc. XXXII-O/02 (June 3, 2002), entered into force July 10, 2003, article 11.

aliens suspected of participation in terrorist activities. One extreme response on this spectrum was the decision by the United Kingdom under Part IV of its Anti-Terrorism, Crime and Security Act (2001) to permit indefinite detention without trial of a certain category of detainee, specifically non-British citizens who cannot be deported because of a legal impediment derived from an international obligation or because of practical considerations (e.g., a non-functional home state such as Somalia). The United Kingdom has recently been found in violation of the European Convention on Human Rights by the House of Lords, in holding such persons indefinitely without the prospect of judicial review or trial.[88] Freezing and seizing financial and other assets has been an important component of many state responses to terrorism in general and the events of September 11 in particular. Increasingly we are also witnessing police and military actions against terrorist groups, either within a state's territory or within the territory of another state affiliated with such groups. Such actions are notable because they not merely constitute singular actions by specific states, but rather are founded on agreements with partner states in a formal legal pact.[89]

The major suppression treaties are multilateral treaties ranging from agreements that are sweeping in scope to those with much more specific aims. These suppression treaties illustrate the capacity of international law to adopt a quasi-legislative model in response to a particular form of crisis, namely terrorism. Hesitant beginnings on this form of regulation have been replaced by a rush to legislate in recent years. Some of the earliest agreements include the Convention on Offenses and Certain Other Acts Committed on Board Aircraft (Tokyo Convention),[90] The

---

[88] A v. Secretary of State (2004) HRLR 38 (CA Civ. Div.); A and others v. Secretary of State for the Home Department (No. 2) (2005) 1 WLR 414 (CA Civ. Div.). A UK Immigration Appeals Tribunal found in July 2002 that the powers under Part 4 of the act were "not only discriminatory and so unlawful under Article 14 to target non-British citizens but also…disproportionate in that there is no reasonable relationship between the means employed and the aims sought to be pursued." See Elena Katselli and Sangeeta Shah, "September 11 and the UK Response" (2003) 52 *International and Comparative Law Quarterly* 245; Human Rights Watch, "Neither Just nor Effective: Indefinite Detention without Trial in the United Kingdom under Part 4 of the Anti-Terrorism, Crime and Security Act 2001" (June 24, 2004), available online at http://hrw.org/backgrounder/eca/uk/anti-terrorism.pdf (last visited Aug. 8, 2005).

[89] "North Atlantic Council Decision on Implementation of Article 5 of the Washington Treaty"; NATO Statement, "Combating Terrorism: Adapting the Alliance's Defence Capabilities."

[90] Convention on Offenses and Certain Other Acts Committed on Board Aircraft, Sept. 14, 1963, entered into force Dec. 4, 1969, 20 UST 2941, 704 UNTS 219.

Convention for the Suppression of Unlawful Seizure of Aircraft (Hague Convention),[91] the International Convention on the Taking of Hostages (Hostages Convention),[92] the Convention for the Suppression of Unlawful Acts against the Safety of Civil Aviation,[93] and the Convention on the Prevention and Punishment of Crimes against Internationally Protected Persons.[94] These early agreements demonstrate the lack of consensus on more general prohibitions by states on terrorist acts, and substantial dispute over the definitional boundaries of such acts. Instead, states focused on agreements that were possible in specific arenas. State responsibilities emanating from such treaties generally required the defined acts to be criminalized under domestic law, affecting the range of crimes that were subject to extradition proceedings, and creating obligations of mutual legal assistance between states. The range and specificity of suppression instruments reinforces the more general definition failing.[95] It also highlights the danger of proliferating treaty obligations in an area where there is an enormous divergence of views (and real differences of opinion) on what in fact states understand the term terrorism to mean. More recent treaties include the United Nations Convention for

---

[91] Hague Convention for the Suppression of Unlawful Seizure of Aircraft, Dec. 16, 1970, entered into force Oct. 14, 1971, 22 UST 1641, 860 UNTS 105.

[92] International Convention against the Taking of Hostages, GA Res. 34/146, UN GAOR, 34th Sess., Supp. No. 46 at 245, UN Doc. A/34/146 (1979) (signed Dec. 17, 1979; entered into force June 3, 1983), reprinted in (1979) 18 *International Legal Materials* 1456.

[93] Convention for the Suppression of Unlawful Acts against the Safety of Civil Aviation, 24 UST 565, TIAS No. 7570, 974 UNTS 178 (signed Sept. 23, 1971; entered into force Jan. 26, 1973).

[94] Convention on the Prevention and Punishment of Crimes against Internationally Protected Persons, including Diplomatic Agents, 28 UST 1975, TIAS No. 8532, 1035 UNTS 167 (signed Dec. 14, 1973; entered into force Feb. 20, 1977).

[95] Others include the Convention on the Suppression of Unlawful Acts against the Safety of Maritime Navigation, Mar. 10, 1988, 1678 UNTS 221, reprinted in (1988) 27 *International Legal Materials* 668; Protocol Concerning the Suppression of Unlawful Acts against the Safety of Fixed Platforms Located on the Continental Shelf, Mar. 10, 1988, reprinted in (1988) 27 *International Legal Materials* 685; Protocol for the Suppression of Unlawful Acts of Violence at Airports Serving International Aviation, supplementary to the Convention for the Suppression of Unlawful Acts against the Safety of Civil Aviation, Senate Treaty Doc. No. 101-1 (1989); Convention on the Physical Protection of Nuclear Material, adopted Oct. 26, 1979, 1456 UNTS 1987, reprinted in (1980) 18 *International Legal Materials* 1419; Convention on the Marking of Plastic Explosives for the Purpose of Detection, Mar. 1, 1991, 2122 UNTS 359, reprinted in (1991) 30 *International Legal Materials* 721. For discussion of the conventions see M. Cherif Bassiouni, *International Terrorism: Multilateral Conventions, 1937–2001* (Ardsley, NY: Transnational Publishers, 2001).

the Suppression of Terrorist Bombings[96] and the United Nations Convention for the Suppression of the Financing of Terrorism.[97] Regionally, the Inter-American system has recently opened for signature the Inter-American Convention against Terrorism. The convention states the need for states in the region to "adopt effective steps in the Inter-American system to prevent, punish and eliminate terrorism through the broadest co-operation." What is unique about this document is that it firmly requires states to be fully cognizant of their international law obligations, and specifically their international human rights law obligations when creating or extending anti-terrorist measures. The regional approach has in general been marked – at least at the OAS level – by the notion that the initiatives against terrorism and the protection of democracy and human rights are complementary responsibilities.

In the Council of Europe context there have been significant developments since both September 11 and the events at Madrid. In 2003 states agreed a Protocol Additional to the 1977 European Convention on the Suppression of Terrorism. There are now concentrated attempts under the auspices of the Committee of Experts of Terrorism (CODEXTER) to agree a new Convention on the Suppression of Terrorism, specifically regulating such matters as apologists for and incitement to terrorism.[98] The council has also issued draft guidelines on providing compensation for the victims of terrorism.[99]

Despite the augmentation of suppression conventions over the past few decades and the spate of ratifications following the events of September 11, self-evidently the narrowness and limitations of these instruments have forced states to think about other legal means to confront terrorism. We argue that the emergence of new forms of "super-laws" at the United Nations and regional political level since September 11 illustrates where states have moved to gain maximum international legitimacy for actions against terrorist individuals and organizations, as

---

[96] International Convention for the Suppression of Terrorist Bombings, Jan. 9, 1998, GA Res. 164, UN GAOR, 52nd Sess., Supp. No. 49, at 389, UN Doc. A/52/164 (1998), reprinted in (1998) 37 *International Legal Materials* 249.

[97] International Convention for the Suppression of the Financing of Terrorism, Dec. 9, 1999, entered into force Apr. 10, 2002, UN GAOR, 54th Sess., 76th mtg. at art. 6, UN Doc. A/RES/54/109 (1999), reprinted in (2000) 39 *International Legal Materials* 270.

[98] See http://www.coe.int/T/E/Legal_affairs/Legal_co-operation/Fight_against_terrorism/3_CODEXTER/Default.asp (last visited Aug. 8, 2005).

[99] Council of Europe, Steering Committee for Human Rights (CDDH), Draft Guidelines on the Protection of Victims of Terrorist Acts, CDDH (2004) 030 Addendum, Nov. 29, 2004, available online at http://www.icj.org/IMG/pdf/GLCDDH.pdf (last visited Aug. 8, 2005).

well as increased legal standing for law-making at the domestic level.[100] These new super-laws are hybrid in nature: they specify mandatory compliance dictated at an international level but require actual enforcement through domestic law. Kim Lane Scheppele argues forcefully that the result of this nexus is the subversion of domestic constitutional norms to the dictates of external pressure around combating terrorism.[101] The point usefully highlights the extent to which a recalibrated international preoccupation with terrorism has served to cloak nefarious regimes using the international legal language of anti-terrorism to accomplish anti-democratic domestic goals.[102]

The events of September 11 were a graphic illustration, with global consequences, of the modern face of transnational terrorism. As the 9/11 Commission report makes clear, the "success" of the attacks from the terrorists' point of view was neither assured nor inevitable.[103] The commission has catalogued expertly both the "failures of imagination" by law enforcers, policy-makers, and politicians and the practical failures of systems that might have prevented or at least mitigated the effects of the attack. The political and legal effects of the attacks have stretched well beyond the shores of the United States. This chapter does not set out the effects of September 11 on state practice across regions and jurisdictions. Instead, we explore the effects of these events on international legal norms and institutions, and more generally comment on the extent to which anti-terrorism policy has come to dominate legal and political conversation in both national and international fora. This has a direct relationship with the widening of legal provisions for crisis in many states. We also contend that the permissibility to legislate and act against terrorism has been used and exploited by states to expand their capacities to regulate by crisis, and frequently used to quell legitimate

---

[100] Kim Lane Scheppele describes this phenomenon as an "international state of emergency." Kim Lane Scheppele, "The Migration of Anti-Constitutional Ideas: The Post 9/11 Globalization of Public Law and the International State of Emergency" in Sujit Choudhry (ed.), *The Migration of Constitutional Ideas* (Cambridge: Cambridge University Press, forthcoming).

[101] Ibid.

[102] Human Rights Watch, "In the Name of Counter-Terrorism: Human Rights Abuses Worldwide" (Mar. 25, 2003), available online at http://www.hrw.org/un/chr59/counter-terrorism-bck.pdf (last visited Aug. 8, 2005); US State Department, "Country Reports of Terrorism 2004" (April 2005), available online at http://www.state.gov/documents/organization/45313.pdf (last visited Aug. 8, 2005).

[103] "Final Report of the National Commission on Terrorist Attacks upon the United States (The 9/11 Commission Report)" (Washington, DC: US GPO, 2004), available at http://www.gpoaccess.gov/911/index.html (last visited Aug. 8, 2005).

dissent within both democratic and non-democratic states. In this way the insecurity bred by international terrorism has broadly facilitated a more general movement toward crisis regulation by many states. Thus, post-September 11 international regulation, a form of hyper-legislative accommodation, is breeding substantial challenges to the capacity of the models of accommodation to operate as effective constraints on the actions of states both domestically and internationally.

The most practical legal demonstration of the effect of September 11 was the articulation of a supra-national requirement to adopt anti-terrorism measures as set out by Resolution 1373 and the European Union Framework Decision on Combating Terrorism.[104] We are particularly interested in the extent to which these legal requirements have affected the domestic practices of states, and in the effects on human rights norms of the anti-terrorism "crusade." The relationship between human rights protections and the needs of the state in times of crisis has always involved delicate balancing. There is little doubt that this balance has been substantially recalibrated (for now) in the wake of September 11. We argued in chapter 5 that international law, through the human rights treaty system, has the inherent legal capacity to re-spond to the periodic crises of states through the mechanism of dero-gation. Post-September 11 that capacity has been significantly ignored by key international institutions and states.[105] We identify some prob-lems with this approach, namely that with such a high emphasis on state compliance with agreed measures against terrorism, the possibility exists to exploit a chilled environment to human rights norms by ap-plying anti-terrorism measures against legitimate protest and dissident groups. In this context, international legal and political requirements become a legitimate basis for illiberal states to act repressively, without the counter-balance of international attention to the full protection for human rights norms. An odd axis emerges as international norms based on principles of accommodation operate as a legitimizing vehicle for a

---

[104] Council Framework Decision 2002/475/JHA of June 13, 2002 on combating terrorism (2002) Official Journal L 164 (June 22, 2002). See also http://europa.eu.int/comm/justice_home/news/laecken_council/en/terroris m_en.htm (last visited Aug. 8, 2005). Support for UN instruments forms a key element of the Plan of Action adopted by the Extraordinary European Council meeting of Sept. 21, 2001, see http://europa.eu.int/comm/justice_home/news/terrorism/documents/ concl_council_21sep_en.pdf (last visited Aug. 8, 2005).

[105] See, however, Kalliopi K. Koufa, "Specific Human Rights Issues: New Priorities, in Particular Terrorism," Additional progress report prepared by the Special Rapporteur on Terrorism and Human Rights (Aug. 8, 2003), E/CN.4/Sub. 2/2003/WP. 1/Add. 1.

plethora of domestic measures that may serve ultimately to undermine the long-term goal of states to create a secure national and international environment. These, among other issues, are explored with reference to the impact of Resolution 1373 and the European Framework Directive on Terrorism. It is also important to register that the events of March 11, 2004 in Madrid and in London on July 7, 2005 have augmented the scale of European regional responses to terrorism.

The UN response to September 11

On September 12, 2001, the Security Council adopted Resolution 1368, which called upon the international community to "redouble its efforts" to prevent and suppress terrorist acts. The resolution also explicitly recognized the right of self-defense, and expressed the unanimous Security Council view that the United States would be justified in taking "all necessary steps" to respond to the attacks. Close on its heels came Resolution 1373 which was adopted by the Security Council on September 28, 2001 under Chapter 7 of the UN Charter. It requires states, among other things, to criminalize terrorist activities, to freeze the funds and financial assets of terrorists and their supporters, to ban others from making funds available to terrorists, and to deny safe haven to terrorists. In some ways Resolution 1373 can be described as a "super resolution" whereby its mandatory requirements added to its perceived political weight for states, making compliance with it a high priority. The impact of this resolution has been to augment substantially domestic legislative measures against terrorism.

The status of the resolution is pointedly illustrated by the speed with which states have fulfilled their reporting requirements as compared with the long delays of their human rights reporting obligations. Resolution 1373 has also generated high visibility as the international vehicle by which states can prove their commitment to combating terrorism. In this way, its lack of integration with the human rights mandate of the United Nations is not just a symbolic matter, but of enormous significance for the enforcement of such rights in a counter-terrorism context. It can be described as one of the most wide-ranging Security Council resolutions, placing mandatory obligations upon states, and with an enormous weight of international political consensus behind it. As Paul Szasz has noted, Resolution 1373 also manifests unusual legislative character in that it mandates compulsory action of a general nature for states with binding intent, and is unrelated to a specific situation of conflict affecting international peace and security.[106] He identifies this legislative mode as both unusual and momentous for the Security Council, effectively creating a new form of legally binding international obligation. We contend that this extended regulation moves terrorism into a heightened accommodation category. It suggests that international terrorism in general, though likely any form of terrorism,[107] creates exigency beyond the normal and requires extraordinary legal responses (i.e., beyond the usual emergency responses). We are not convinced that an incontrovertible case has been made for this implicit conclusion. In this context we identify the dangers that follow from the potential expansion of United Nations and European measures to strengthen the mechanisms requiring states to prosecute or extradite persons suspected of terrorist activity that followed Russian diplomatic pressure in the aftermath of the Beslan tragedy.[108] In short, there is a danger that the creation of a special hyper-regulatory category for some groups will inevitably involve slippage and the net will be cast more widely than is necessary to respond to the threat posed by those targeted.

The resolution is framed by its affirmation that terrorist acts and acts of international terrorism constitute a threat to international peace and security, while no definition of these key terms is offered. As demonstrated above this lack of definition reflects an ongoing tension at the UN around definitional clarity on the term "terrorism."[109] Resolution 1373 offers the familiar suppression convention solution to this problem,

---

[106] See Paul C. Szasz, "The Security Council Starts Legislating" (2002) 96 *American Journal of International Law* 901. Szasz identifies the unusual legislative character of Resolution 1373. He notes specifically that many conventions languishing for want of state ratification suddenly have the force of international law. See also Stefan Talmon, "The Security Council as World Legislature" (2005) 99 *American Journal of International Law* 175; Eric Rosand, "The Security Council as 'Global Legislator': Ultra Vires or Ultra Innovative?" (2005) 28 *Fordham International Law Journal* 542.

[107] See further, UN Security Council Resolution 1566 (2004), S/RES/1566 (Oct. 8, 2004). This resolution creates a working group consisting of all members of the Security Council to consider measures to be imposed on groups involved in terrorist activities, other than those designated by the al Qaeda/Taliban Sanctions Committee.

[108] J. Brian Gross, "Russia's War on Political and Religious Extremism: An Appraisal of the Law 'on Counteracting Extremist Activity'" (2003) *Brigham Young University Law Review* 717.

[109] Until then the Sixth Committee had been working on several conventions related to terrorism. See Eric Rosand, "Security Council Resolution 1373, The Counter-Terrorism Committee, and the Fight against Terrorism" (2003) 97 *American Journal of International Law* 333. Conventions drafted by the Sixth Committee include the International Convention for the Suppression of Terrorist Bombings, and the International Convention for the Suppression of the Financing of Terrorism.

namely, to place greater emphasis on certain positive acts by states such as suppressing the sources of finance and support for terrorism. However, as we explore below, Resolution 1373 goes beyond mere suppression and creates a set of positive and specific obligations upon state behavior.

Of particular concern to us (and others) is that measures contemplated by Resolution 1373 have far-reaching implications for the protection of human rights, but the resolution makes no comprehensive or even specific reference to the need for states to comply with human rights standards in the suppression of terrorism.[110] Instead, the preamble to the resolution affirms the need to combat terrorist acts "by all means, in accordance with the Charter of the United Nations." As the UN Charter makes substantial references to human rights protection, such a reference could constitute an implicit reference to the need to promote and respect human rights norms. However, the obliqueness of this positive interpretation only serves to highlight the lack of an explicit statement in the resolution, and "leaves the impression that human rights protection is a secondary consideration in the campaign against terrorism, instead of an essential component of any counter-terrorism strategy."[111] Further, the only explicit reference to human rights norms in the operative paragraphs of the resolution arises in the context of refugee and asylum seekers, where states are required to take appropriate measures to ensure that such persons have not been involved in the commission of terrorist acts.[112]

Implementing Resolution 1373

Under paragraph 6 of the resolution, a committee of the Security Council (Counter-Terrorism Committee) was established to monitor its implementation. States were required to report to the Counter-Terrorism Committee within ninety days, outlining what measures they had taken to conform with the resolution's requirements. This ninety-day

---

[110] See International Helsinki Federation for Human Rights, "Anti-Terrorism Measures, Security and Human Rights: Developments in Europe, Central Asia and North America in the Aftermath of September 11" (Apr. 2003) at 41–42, available online at 2003Apr18en_report_anti-terrorism_pdf.pdf (last visited Aug. 8, 2005).

[111] Ibid., at 42.

[112] UN Security Council Resolution 1373, para. 3(f) calls upon all states to "Take appropriate measures in conformity with the relevant provisions of national and international law, including international standards of human rights, before granting refugee status, for the purpose of ensuring that the asylum seeker has not planned, facilitated or participated in the commission of terrorist acts."

turn-around created many difficulties for states, as some struggled to enact sufficiently broad anti-terrorism laws that would meet their Resolution 1373 obligations. Two observations are relevant here. First, both states with and states without any nexus to, or experience of, terrorism were required to suppress and legislate. This suggests that states were being told implicitly that a threat existed of proportions outside the normal or even the "normal emergency," sufficient to give sweeping powers transnationally. The capacity of both normal law and the traditional models of accommodation of emergency law were not activated or explored as a means to respond to the perceived threat. Second, the short turn-around meant that many states rushed to legislate domestically. As we have noted in chapter 1, a haste to legislate in such contexts results frequently in ill-judged legislation that has a negative impact on constitutional rights' protections.

The requirements of Resolution 1373 should not be underestimated. States were required to legislate domestically against terrorism, essentially presenting mandatory legislative accommodation by international fiat. This legislative requirement potentially creates an entirely new dynamic in the nature and form of international law-making.[113] It comes without oversight and with little substantive discussion between states. Paradoxically, while circumventing the ordinary processes of international law-making, it failed to address why this law-making was unable to agree a definition of terrorism. The matter is not solved at either a domestic or international level by the operation of Resolution 1373. Effectively, states are left free to adopt their own definitions (or not) when legislating as required by the terms of Resolution 1373. Since the passing of the resolution, the Security Council has, with constant intercession by the United States, remained active on anti-terrorism. Under Resolution 1526 it established a Sanctions Compliance Monitoring Team to ensure that states were actually freezing assets and preventing weapons proliferation.[114] Resolution 1540 exhibits a legislative character in prohibiting states from assisting named organizations and individuals from acquiring nuclear, chemical, or biological weapons.

The Counter-Terrorism Committee (CTC) is made up of representatives of the fifteen countries currently sitting on the Security Council: the five permanent members of China, France, Great Britain, Russia, and the

---

[113] While the nature of law-making in the European Union has similar mandatory effect, in the EU context this has been reached by protracted and specific negotiation by states, and decades-long interpretation of impact by the European Court of Justice.

[114] Extended further by Security Council Resolution 1566, at para 9.

United States, plus the ten non-permanent members. In January 2003, the chair of the CTC, Ambassador Greenstock, reported to the Security Council that the committee had received reports from 178 states.[115] He noted that the vast majority of governments had started to respond to the requirements laid down in Resolution 1373. In almost every case he indicated that parliaments had begun to consider or had adopted new laws. Moreover, state reporting to that date indicated that governments had reviewed the ability of their institutions to suppress terrorism and in many cases had strengthened them. He also made clear that states that failed to report would be viewed as being in non-compliance with the resolution. He set out in general terms what the CTC viewed as necessary to improve the implementation of Resolution 1373. In this context, the first priority lay with legislation and addressing the matter of terrorist finance. States were expected to take prompt action, which included having a process in hand for becoming a party to the twelve relevant anti-terrorism conventions and protocols.

It should be recognized that the creation of the CTC in tandem with its specific mandate has significant institutional consequences within the UN. The CTC now sits at the apex of the UN's institutional hierarchy. It could be said to function as a mini-Security Council, with a powerful direct line to the Security Council itself. This recalibration of the internal institutional hierarchy at the UN is exacerbated by the single-issue focus of the committee, which is not balanced by any other committee or body of similar stature specifically mandated to oversee human rights protections. This structural effect tells us something about the nature of the crisis experienced (whether actual or perceived). It sends a strong message that a commitment to meaningful protection for human rights extends only "so far." This organizational recalibration, with power shifting to the executive branch, has been well documented in domestic contexts, where we know that the effect of emergencies is to centralize decision-making and to empower the executive. Interestingly the current exigency of transnational terrorism is causing the same effect upon international institutional structures. Of concern is that, unlike states which may have a populist or democratic counter-weight, to pull back the concentration of power, such forces are far more dispersed and frequently absent in international organizations which by their nature contain a de facto democratic deficit.

---

[115] See http://www.un.org/Docs/sc/committees/1373/submitted_reports.html (last visited Aug. 8, 2005).

Human rights and other lacunae in operating Resolution 1373

From an early point when the Security Council was considering measures required to respond to the events of September 11, concerns were raised that it failed to adopt a human rights framework that would have required any measures taken to comply with human rights standards.[116] This concern was further heightened when the Security Council also declined to appoint human rights experts to the Counter-Terrorism Committee. This has now been belatedly rectified. The lack of a human rights dimension in the substantive work of the committee has been confirmed by the lack of reference in the guidance given to states on their human rights obligations when reporting on their anti-terrorist measures.[117] The CTC has consistently declined to adopt proposals put forward by the UN High Commissioner for Human Rights to integrate a human rights dimension into the state reporting requirement.[118] The High Commissioner's Office has expressed its concerns that measures taken to eliminate terrorism may be activated in such a way as to infringe on fundamental freedoms.[119] Specific concerns articulated included the danger that non-derogable rights (e.g., freedom from torture, slavery, and ex-post facto laws as well as protection for the right to life) may be infringed as well as a lack of full implementation by states of their obligations to prevent discrimination. The United Nations Committee on the Elimination of All Forms of Racial Discrimination has recently issued a General Comment in which it specifically identified the

---

[116] See Amnesty International, "A Human Rights Framework for Responding to Terrorism" (Mar. 22, 2002), AI Index IOR 41/007/2002, available online at http://web.amnesty.org/library/Index/ENGIOR410072002?open&of=ENG-325 (last visited Aug. 8, 2005).

[117] See UN Commission on Human Rights, Resolution 2004/87, "Protection of Human Rights and Fundamental Freedoms while Countering Terrorism" (Apr. 21, 2004), 58th Meeting, UN Doc. A/59/428.

[118] UN High Commissioner for Human Rights, "Proposals for 'Further Guidance' for the Submission of Reports Pursuant to Paragraph 6 of Security Council Resolution 1373 (2001)" annexed to the UN High Commissioner's Report and Follow-Up to the World Conference on Human Rights (Feb. 27, 2002), UN Doc. E/CN.4/2002/18, pp. 17–21.

[119] See Office of the UN High Commissioner for Human Rights, "Terrorism and Human Rights," available online at http://www.unhchr.ch/terrorism/ (last visited Aug. 8, 2005) and Office of the UN High Commissioner for Human Rights, "Digest of Jurisprudence of the UN and Regional Organizations on the Protection of Human Rights while Countering Terrorism," available online at http://www.unhchr.ch/html/menu6/2/digest.doc (last visited Aug. 8, 2005).

problems that arise from racial profiling in an anti-terrorism context.[120]
Concern has been expressed about the danger that full procedural protections will be lacking in the area of pre-trial and fair trial processes.
The High Commissioner's Office has also carried out a preliminary review of state reports under Resolution 1373 and notes a number of issues.
Significant numbers of reports focus mainly on the legal framework to
counter terrorism, but do not address how these measures operate in
practice. Some measures may appear benign but could have a negative
impact on the enjoyment of human rights. For instance, some states
include in their domestic definition of terrorism certain non-violent activities. Several states have granted law enforcement agents additional
search, arrest, and detention powers and added limitations on legal rep-
resentation. The distinction between minors and adults is not always
clear. Some laws place severe and unwarranted restrictions on the right
to seek asylum, which may violate the non-refoulement right of refugees
(i.e., the right of those fleeing not to be returned to a state where they
may be persecuted on the grounds set out in the Refugee Convention).[121]
The High Commissioner's Office has also prepared guidance to states on
the preparation of CTC reports; at the time of writing this had not been
proactively circulated by the CTC.

As well as an activist role for the Office of the High Commissioner for
Human Rights, the roles of other United Nations bodies may shift and
change as a result of the recalibration of institutional competences. For
example, the Commission on Human Rights has the primary responsibility for safeguarding human rights standards, and it is not inconceivable
that it could establish a mechanism to monitor states' implementation of
Resolution 1373 from a human rights perspective. This suggestion was directly made to the commission by the former UN High Commissioner for
Human Rights, but failed to gain the requisite political support within
the commission, and has not been pursued.[122] Briefings by the CTC to
the Human Rights Committee took place in March 2003 and June 2003,
which demonstrate the start of an interface between the human rights

---

[120] UN Committee on the Elimination of Racial Discrimination, "Concluding
Observations of the Committee on the Elimination of Racial Discrimination: Canada,"
61 sess., CERD/C/61/CO/3 (Aug. 23, 2002), para. 24.

[121] UN High Commissioner, "Report and Follow-Up to the World Conference on Human
Rights," at 7–8.

[122] See Statement by Mary Robinson to the 58th Session of the Commission on Human
Rights, Mar. 18, 2002. Available online at http://www.nhri.net/pdf/58CHR-HCStatement
18%20March.pdf (last visited Aug. 8, 2005).

mechanisms and the CTC. Under some pressure from international human rights organizations and others, the United Nations Human Rights Commission has established the office of Independent Expert on the Prosecution of Human Rights and Fundamental Freedoms while Countering Terrorism. An American law professor, Robert Goldman, was the first holder of the post but he resigned early in 2005 without producing a major review.[123] External bodies such as the International Commission of Jurists and the coordinating body of National Human Rights Institutions have also started to express their views on the need to uphold human rights and the rule of law in combating terrorism.[124] However, the overall picture tells us that specialist UN human rights institutions have just started to flex some consistent institutional muscle in the post-September 11 context. Increased visibility by these bodies is an imperative so that some institutional balance can be regained. Moreover, pressure exerted by them may assist in teaching states that there is ultimate benefit in imbuing anti-terrorism measures with respect for human rights and humanitarian law. Only through such a holistic approach can long-term security be guaranteed for states. More particularly, human rights bodies within the UN are equipped to articulate the substantial experience of the international human rights system in confronting terrorism and situations of emergency. This experience is laid down within the human rights treaty system, both national and international, as outlined in chapter 5. We suggest that it is vital to draw on this reservoir of norms and that it be clearly understood that safeguarding human rights in the context of terrorism is not a new phenomenon. Rather, this experience has a long pedigree informed by an agreed system of norms created by states themselves.

Contextualizing the UN response

The concerns about overreach by the United Nations require a reflection on the body's overall approach to the regulation and suppression of

---

[123] Professor Goldman was named Independent Expert on the Protection of Human Rights and Fundamental Freedoms while countering Terrorism in July 2004.

[124] See The International Commission of Jurists, "The ICJ Declaration on Upholding Human Rights and the Rule of Law in Combating Terrorism" (The Berlin Declaration), adopted Aug. 28, 2004, available online at http://www.icj.org/IMG/pdf/Berlin_Declaration.pdf (last visited Aug. 8, 2005); and "The Seoul Declaration" at the conclusion of the Seventh International Conference for National Institutions for the Promotion and Protection of Human Rights (Sept. 17, 2004), available online at http://www.nhri.net/pdf/Seoul_Declaration_En.pdf (last visited Aug. 8, 2005).

terrorism. In addressing the institutional relationship between human rights and anti-terrorism discourses some attention should be paid to the *Report of the Policy Working Group of the United Nations and Terrorism*.[125] The Policy Working Group Report makes clear that the core strategies of the United Nations in opposing terrorism are, first, to dissuade those who are (or might be) involved in terrorism, second, to deny support (material, financial, political, and legal) to those involved in terrorism, and third, to sustain cooperation between states to thwart the actions and aims of those engaged in terrorism. Specifically, a link is made between the UN's role in addressing human rights violations and the resort to terrorist acts by disaffected individuals, groups, and minorities, because such violations can create the conditions in which terrorism thrives. Concerning denial, key aspects of the UN's work here include the technical legal assistance that UN agencies can provide to facilitate law-based responses, as well as the activities of the UN in the field of disarmament. Post-conflict peace-building is also identified as an important preventive action, which discourages the bedding down of hospitable environments for terrorism. The report makes clear that in its response to terrorism the "United Nations must ensure that the protection of human rights is conceived as an essential concern."[126] Specifically, the report states that "the fight against terrorism must be respectful of international human rights obligations."

Echoing this, the European Council of Minister's Guidelines state that "it is not only possible, but also absolutely necessary, to fight terrorism while respecting human rights." Criticism has been leveled at the Policy Working Group's recommendations for being "too vague and narrow in scope."[127] In particular, the document lays almost exclusive emphasis on the protection of non-derogable rights, which, while extremely important, should not operate to undercut emphasis on the general obligation of states to respect all international human rights obligations in the anti-terrorism context. The report specifically fails to pinpoint which UN

---

[125] "Report of the Policy Working Group on the United Nations and Terrorism," UN GA/SCOR, 57th Sess., Annex 1 at 8, UN Doc. A/57/273-S/2002/875 (2002), available at http://www.un.org/terrorism/a57273.htm (last visited Aug. 8, 2005). See also Recommendation 1550 (2002) of the Council of Europe's Guidelines on Human Rights and the Fight against Terrorism, as adopted by the Council of Ministers in July 2002; Parliamentary Assembly on Combating Terrorism and Respect for Human Rights Assembly Debate on Jan. 24, 2002; Rep. of the Committee on Legal Affairs and Human Rights.
[126] "Report of the Policy Working Group on the United Nations and Terrorism," 1.
[127] International Helsinki Federation, "Anti-Terrorism Measures," 44–45.

bodies should have the responsibility for monitoring the human rights dimension of counter-terrorism measures, as well as to identify mechanisms to ensure that effective remedies are available to those whose rights have been violated in that context.

The picture at the United Nations is not entirely doom and gloom with regard to the protection of human rights in the contemporary context. There has been some mainstream claw-back, as key actors and institutions have reaffirmed the centrality of human rights protections while countering terrorism. Thus, for example, General Assembly Resolution 57/219 affirms that states must ensure that any measures taken to combat terrorism comply with their obligations under international law, in particular, international human rights, refugee, and humanitarian law.[128]

As outlined above, a number of states have already legislated in response to Resolution 1373 and the European Union Framework Decision on Combating Terrorism, supplementing these international mechanisms with domestic legislative accommodation. Striking similarities in many of these legislative responses can already be identified. Most worrying they include a persistent tendency to go beyond the specified requirements of the Framework Decision and Resolution 1373.[129] When definitions of terrorism and terrorist acts are domesticated we can, almost without exception, find substantial reshaping of legal process as well as a fundamental disregard for applicable international human rights norms. Moreover, there is strong evidence that these international requirements are manipulated to effect extraordinary legal change in domestic systems on a variety of agendas, many tangentially linked to terrorism.

The European Framework Decision on Terrorism

The European Union's interest in regulating terrorism is not a product of the post-September 11 world. For some time the EU has sought to

---

[128] General Assembly Resolution 57/219, "Protection of Human Rights and Fundamental Freedoms while Countering Terrorism," 57th Sess., A/RES/57/219 (Feb. 27, 2003); see also Statement of the Committee against Torture: 22/11/2001, adopted at the 501st Session, Nov. 22, 2001.

[129] See Criminal Justice (Terrorist Offences) Bill 2002 (Ireland), and the Anti-Terrorism, Crime and Security Act 2001 (UK). On the latter see, for example, Virginia Helen Henning, "Anti-Terrorism, Crime and Security Act 2001: Has the United Kingdom Made a Valid Derogation from the European Convention on Human Rights?" (2002) 17 *American University International Law Review* 1263.

standardize broadly in matters affecting crossborder policing and criminal law. This has largely been an ordinary law approach that sought to standardize state responses across jurisdictional boundaries. At the European Council's 1999 Tampere meeting states agreed to adopt a list of measures to develop the EU's "Area of Freedom, Security and Justice." Specifically, states sought movement on creating mutual recognition in criminal matters and to put in place a European organization facilitating crossborder prosecutions within two years (Eurojust).[130] Prior to the catastrophic events of September 11 work was also underway to harmonize substantive criminal law in a variety of fields with implications for terrorism, including such areas as money laundering, and illegal entry and residence. These general discussions were dramatically reprioritized after the World Trade Center attacks. The two matters which were deemed urgent were the European Arrest Warrant, replacing existing extradition proceedings between states, and the Framework Decision, defining and punishing terrorism.

The Framework Decision is another clear example of international legislative accommodation. The Decision is derived from EU competence under Title VI of the Treaty on European Union (TEU). This is provided for in articles 31 and 34 of the TEU, which allows states to work cooperatively to enforce *minimum* rules in the arena of justice and home affairs. It is worth noting at the outset a more general concern that democratic control and accountability over EU actions in the area of criminal law lag behind developments of EU competence in this arena. Notably, Title VI does not offer a precise definition of Community competence in the judicial and home affairs context. Moreover, at the negotiation of the Maastricht Treaty the emphasis lay on the promotion of cooperation in defined areas.[131] There was no suggestion that this would entail the harmonization of aspects of domestic criminal law and procedure, or the reform of such law. The Treaty of Amsterdam raised EU competencies in matters of criminal law to a higher level, and while there were improvements from an accountability perspective, there was also an enormous growth in EU competence. The emphasis in the TEU lay in "developing

---

[130] See Steve Peers, "EU Reponses to Terrorism" (2003) 52 *International and Comparative Law Quarterly* 227. Convention established by the council in accordance with article 34 of the Treaty on European Union, on Mutual Assistance in Criminal Matters between the Member States of the European Union (July 12, 2000), *Official Journal* C 197/3.

[131] The areas included asylum policy, rules governing the crossing of member states' borders, judicial cooperation in civil matters, judicial cooperation in criminal matters, customs cooperation, and police cooperation in the areas of terrorism, unlawful drug trafficking, and other serious forms of international crime.

common action among the Member States," with a stated emphasis on cooperative ventures.[132] There is, arguably, a limited treaty basis for allowing the EU a competence which would shape basic principles and procedures underpinning domestic criminal law and criminal justice. As other commentators have noted: "In the European Union, the risk to fundamental rights posed by the adoption of measures to fight terrorism are [sic] all the greater since democratic and juridical controls are still very inadequate in the current institutional balance, particularly in the context of headings V and VI of the Treaty on European Union."[133]

The Framework Decision follows a number of prior political and legal measures taken by the European Union following the events of September 11, 2001. In response to Security Council Resolution 1373, the EU's member states adopted a number of implementing measures including Common Position 2001/930/CESP on combating terrorism,[134] Common Position 2001/931/CESP on the application of specific measures to combat terrorism,[135] and in respect of freezing assets, Council Regulation 2580/2001 of December 27, 2001.[136] Notably these two Common Positions evaded parliamentary scrutiny entirely as there is no requirement to consult or inform the European Parliament on any foreign policy matter or any third-pillar common position.[137] There is also no judicial scrutiny of foreign policy jurisdiction by the European Court of Justice. In addition to the Common Positions other legislative requirements for states include the EU Framework Decision on Money Laundering (notably terrorism is only one of a number of crimes to which this provision

---

[132] Treaty on European Union, (1997) *Official Journal* C 340/02 (Nov. 10, 1997), art. 29.

[133] EU Network of Independent Experts in Fundamental Rights, "The Balance between Freedom and Security in the Response by the European Union and its Member States to the Terrorist Threats" (Mar. 31, 2003) at 9, available online at http://www.statewatch.org/news/2003/apr/CFR-CDF.ThemComment1.pdf (last visited Aug. 8, 2005).

[134] Common Position 2001/930/CESP on combating terrorism (2001) *Official Journal* L 344/90 (Dec. 28, 2001).

[135] Common Position 2001/931/CESP on the application of specific measures to combat terrorism (2001) *Official Journal* L 344/93 (Dec. 28, 2001).

[136] Council Regulation (EC) No. 2580/2001 of Dec. 27, 2001 on specific restrictive measures directed against certain persons and entities with a view to combating terrorism (2001) *Official Journal* L 344/70 (Dec. 28, 2001). Other measures include Council Decision of May 2, 2002 implementing Article 2(3) of Regulation (EC) No. 2580/2001 on specific restrictive measures directed against certain persons and entities with a view to combating terrorism and repealing Decision 2001/927/EC (2002/334/EC) (2002) *Official Journal* L 116/33 (May 3, 2002).

[137] See Treaty on European Union, articles 21–39.

applies);[138] the Framework Decision on the European Arrest Warrant; the Framework Decision on Joint Investigation Teams; the Decision establishing Eurojust; and the Decision on implementing specific measures for police and judicial cooperation to combat terrorism. Notably all these measures were taken at the inter-governmental level, with the stated aim of implementing international commitments. Their mode of creation and enforcement acted to reduce the possibility of any domestic parliamentary control over their content, as well as forgoing any opportunity for open public debate about the measures and their impact. This lack of democratic dialogue has been the motif of European Union action in the anti-terrorism context. It also points to a fundamental difference between domestic and international models of accommodation by virtue of the latter's lack of any robust accountability mechanisms or democratic accountability through the ordinary parliamentary process.

Following from the Framework Decision's passage and influenced by the railroad bombings at Madrid, a number of new initiatives are pending. They include an EU Declaration on combating terrorism adopted by the EU summit of March 2004,[139] which was updated on March 31, 2005, and a set of proposals from the European Commission on combating terrorism.[140] The monitoring body Statewatch has identified a total of fifty-seven proposals ranging from the immediate declaration of solidarity by European states following the terrorist atrocities, to strengthening enforcement institutions such as Europol, Eurojust, and the Task Force of EU Police Chiefs, and placing wide-ranging EU controls on the retention of all communications by states. Other specific measures include the appointment of an EU "security coordinator," whose job would mirror that of the homeland security tsar in the United States. The rationale for this position is that it would enhance cooperation between the EU bodies and third countries, thereby streamlining activities in the fight against terrorism. The motivation for this appointment is logical but there is some genuine anxiety that any such office might function outside the EU's constitutional and legislative framework, or fail to respect it. The concern maps on to earlier discussions about the tendency of emergency

---

[138] Council Framework Decision of June 26, 2001 on money laundering, the identification, tracing, freezing, seizing and confiscation of instrumentalities and the proceeds of crime (2001/500/JHA) (2001) *Official Journal* L 182/1 (July 5, 2001).

[139] 7468/4/04 REV 4, Mar. 22, 2004. See Statewatch March 2004 EU Anti-Terrorist Declaration http://www.statewatch.org/news/2005/mar/jhaagenda-mar2005.pdf (last visited Aug. 8, 2005).

[140] MEMO/04/66, Mar. 18, 2004.

laws both nationally and internationally to concentrate executive powers to the detriment of democratic accountability and transparency. Another proposal by the Commission is the creation of a European Registry for issued travel documents, which would include biometric data. The proposal has prompted significant concerns about privacy and abuse of what amounts to a European population database. Other database developments include the creation of a database of persons, groups, and entities covered by restrictive measures in the fight against terrorism.[141] Concerted information collection is also at issue with the proposal to activate the lists of terrorist organizations (and those placed on them) so that they can become active in "real time." Concerns have already been raised about the manner in which individuals and groups are placed on national and international lists, thereby criminalizing persons on ideological and political grounds rather than on the basis of an objective security threat to the EU.

In conclusion, general disquiet has been raised by the Commission proposal that Commission and member states should monitor all legislative machinery and subject it to "ex ante" terrorism proofing. What this implies is that a whole range of legislative areas, including but not limited to asylum policy, justice, and home affairs, development, and even defense policy, become subject to a terrorist threat scrutiny. The enforcement of this policy reflects a further theme of this book, namely the difficulty of keeping emergency law contained in a separate sphere, and the unintended consequences that emergency regulation can have across a range of substantive areas.[142] The scale of potential EU policy-making in the anti-terrorism context is immense and cuts across what might be seen as traditional "anti-terrorism"/emergency measures into

---

[141] This is a Commission proposal and the major concern would be that the database should actually be limited to combating terrorism, and not used by states for wider crime-fighting purposes.

[142] Other substantive proposals include: legislation on cross-border pursuit; a coordination effort by the Directorates General JAI and RELEX on a range of issues including terrorism; creating a European Programme for the Protection of Witnesses; exchanging personal information including DNA and fingerprints but in spheres only linked to terrorism; creating a Europe-wide database on forensic material; enhancing the efficiency and effectiveness of the EU's mechanisms for freezing terrorist assets; improving cooperation on terrorist financing; exchanging information on convictions related to terrorism; agreeing and enforcing mandatory systems for identifying and investigating bank accounts; strengthening the role of Europol; strengthening the role of the Task Force of EU Police Chiefs; putting a European arrest warrant in place across all EU member states.

the realm of ordinary legal regulation.[143] In this lie some of the most pertinent concerns for the stability and neutrality of law in a time of considerable national and international flux.

Definitional issues arising from the Framework Decision

The Framework Decision itself is a generally worded and short document. It lays out a series of actions which, if committed, would constitute the definitional requirements for terrorist activity. This is in contrast to the UN measures which have focused, owing to a lack of state consensus, on banning specific acts without trying to define "terrorism." Commentators have noted that the EU measure is far wider than the UN conventions, particularly as regards the personal scope of injury and death, the scope of the prohibited damage to property and the means by which that damage would be caused, the consequences which flow from the threat of such action, as well as the scope of action in the arenas of biological and chemical weapons.[144] Its drafting history was contentious, as it was speedily rushed through the European Council and European Parliament in late December 2001.[145] As a result the final text was considerably amended from the initial text drawn up by the European Commission in September 2001. These amendments, while addressing some of the deficiencies in human rights protections, cannot be said to ameliorate the major defects of the Framework Decision.

Many of the specific concerns about the Framework Decision are located around its definitional limitations. Arguably, it follows a predictable pattern in failing to overcome the difficulties traditionally encountered when attempting to give a definition of terrorism which describes its specificity as compared with other forms of organized crime.[146] Article 1(1) sets out a three-part definition of terrorism "consisting of the context of an action, the *aim* of the action and the *specific acts* being committed."[147] The Framework Decision refers to the *degree of seriousness* which certain offenses exhibit: "given their nature or context, [these offenses] may seriously damage a country or an international

---

[143] Statewatch, "'Scoreboard' on Post-Madrid Counterterrorism Plans" (Mar. 23, 2004), available online at http://www.statewatch.org/news/2004/mar/swscoreboard.pdf (last visited Aug. 8, 2005).

[144] See Peers, "EU Reponses to Terrorism," 232.

[145] Formal adoption was delayed by national parliamentary scrutiny reserves.

[146] EU Network of Independent Experts in Fundamental Rights, "The Balance between Freedom and Security," at 7.

[147] See Peers, "EU Reponses to Terrorism," 228.

organization," *or their object*, that being to "seriously intimidate the population, unduly compelling a Government or international organization to perform or abstain from performing any act, seriously destabilizing or destroying the fundamental political, constitutional, economic or social structures or an international organization."[148] A particular concern in this context is the lack of a sufficiently precise definition of the offense of terrorism which raises the possibility of a lack of clear legal basis for specific indictments, as well as the application of specific procedural rules.[149] The Framework Decision also sets out offenses relating to terrorist groups in article 2, including the requirement that states punish the crime of "directing a terrorist group." Article 4 requires that states criminalize inchoate offenses of incitement, aiding, or abetting terrorist groups. Detailed penalties for the various acts defined as "terrorism" are left to the discretion of member states.[150]

There is a genuine danger that the Framework Decision has the capacity to suppress legitimate public expression or dissent, as well as to act as a means to target unpopular or marginal political views. Notably, the Explanatory Memorandum to the Decision referred to the potential use of the Framework Decision against "urban violence" and the Commission's website said measures were intended to counter "radicals committing violence." In the view of many observers the events in Gothenberg and Genoa were as fresh in the minds of the drafters as were those of September 11. While abhorrence of the violence which took place in those cities is entirely correct, it was entirely inappropriate for measures aimed at curbing terrorist action to function as a catching device for radical protest groups. It is important to stress here that no matter how unacceptable public and group violence may be, legal and political distinctions can and should be drawn between different forms of violence. This is particularly important as regards violence which is

---

[148] Art. 1 of the Framework Decision.
[149] In this context it is important to note the Directorate General of Human Rights, *Guidelines on Human Rights and the Fight against Terrorism Adopted by the Committee of Ministers on 11 July 2002 at the 804th meeting of the Ministers' Deputies* (Council of Europe Publishing, 2002), p. 8, Article III (Lawfulness of Anti-Terrorist Measures), available online at http://www.coe.int/T/E/Human_rights/h-inf(2002)8eng.pdf (last visited Aug. 8, 2005).
[150] Article 5 requires that all the offenses named in the Decision must be subject to extradition; that custodial sentences for terrorist offenses and related inchoate offenses must be heavier than would be the case for these offenses lacking the *mens rea* of terrorism, except where the penalties are already at a maximum of fifteen years.

politically motivated and that which is not. Sophisticated political systems are capable of drawing these distinctions, and applying nuanced legal sanction as appropriate. The failure to distinguish can result in a legal system operating as a very blunt instrument, which can exacerbate rather than address the causes of violence in a state setting. Ultimately, a statement (without legal status or effect) was attached to the Framework Decision seeking to distinguish between "terrorists" and the right to demonstrate in democracies.[151]

What should also be pointed out is that the European Union has already passed a plethora of measures aimed at curbing public protest. These include (1) the Justice and Home Affairs Conclusions of July 13, 2001 which puts in place a sophisticated surveillance system on protest groups; (2) the plan to create a new database on the Schengen Information System (SIS) on protestors; and (3) the plan to bring together paramilitary police units for EU summits and international meetings.[152] The net effect of all these measures is to create a supra-national set of legal and policy measures whose overall effect is to curb multiple forms of political protest within the European Union, unmatched by any formal mechanisms by which to challenge or even debate the legitimacy and necessity of the measures taken. Another point of definitional concern lies with definition (III) of the Framework Decision: "seriously destabilising or destroying the fundamental political, constitutional, economic or social structures of a country or an international organisation." The offenses which relate to this definition include "causing extensive destruction of a Government building or public facility, a transport system, an infrastructure facility, including an information system, a fixed platform located on a continental shelf, a public place or private property likely to endanger human life or result in major economic loss."

It is not inconceivable that individuals engaged in demonstrations which – for whatever reason – result in or are likely to result in, for example, extensive damage to private property may be legally processed as "terrorists" through the effect of their actions. While such actions may be socially undesirable and criminal, they do not necessarily fall

---

[151] Unfortunately some states that legislated on the basis of the Framework Decision have failed to incorporate even this additional distinction. The Irish Criminal Justice Bill (2002) made no attempt to distinguish between a legitimate right to demonstrate and the application of these measures to groups whose protest actions may bring them within the ambit of "terrorist" action.

[152] The Schengen Information System (SIS) went online in March 1995. See http://europa.eu.int/scadplus/leg/en/lvb/l33020.htm (last visited Aug. 8, 2005).

into the realm of terrorist violence, and the applicable legal definitions should exclude such a possibility. Once again the Framework Decision manifests the capacity to be used in ways which are both politically and legally undesirable.

The Framework Decision does not mandate the means whereby these definitions are incorporated into law; rather it only sets out the requirement that they be incorporated domestically. Unfortunately, as two surveys of state incorporation of the Framework Decision reveal, state practice has generally been to use the Decision as a means to augment and further legislate and not as a minimal base-line.[153] For example, in the Netherlands the Crimes of Terror Bill was submitted to the country's parliament in June 2002, and amended by the second chapter in August 2003. It came into force in mid-2004. The legislation criminalizes membership of, or participation in, a criminal organization with terrorist purposes by imprisonment of up to eight years. The imprisonment term can be increased up to fifteen years in cases where the person convicted is discovered to be a founder, leader, or administrator. Additionally a person who provides financial or other material support to a terrorist organization will be regarded as "participating" in the activities of the organization, and will be criminally liable. Finally, the legislation provides that the maximum sentences for serious crimes may be increased by 50 percent if these crimes are committed with a terrorist aim. The Netherlands provides an example of a broader phenomenon in the domestic context that, instead of palliating the uncertainties and limitations of the Framework Decision in national legislation, has tended to exploit and extend these loopholes.

State responses to Resolution 1373 and the European Framework Decision

It is not possible to outline all the specific measures taken by states by virtue of the obligations imposed by Resolution 1373 and the European Framework Directive. However, we want to outline some general trends which are evident in the form and substance of state responses to date. The EU Network of Experts has usefully identified eight key areas of rights protections that have been negatively affected by state responses to terrorism since the events of September 11.[154] The trends identified here have a particular resonance in the Western and Eastern European

---

[153] EU Network of Independent Experts in Fundamental Rights, "The Balance between Freedom and Security," 12–16.
[154] Ibid., at 17–19.

contexts, but can also be seen to apply to the global post-September 11 experience. First, the adoption of vaguely worded and overly broad laws that prohibit "terrorist acts" and "terrorist groups." The latitude of definition means that such legislation can be used against legitimate democratic expression and protection, particularly by marginal or unpopular political groupings or minorities. Second, the practice of setting up processes of detention, trial, and legal evaluation which seek to place persons accused of terrorist offenses outside the boundaries of normal legal protection.[155] Third, the activation of practices which involve racial or community profiling disproportionately affecting Muslims and other minorities including arrests, registration, and fingerprinting. The increased publicity for these communities as a result of their heightened public regulation has a link with racist attacks against visible members of these same communities. Fourth, the articulation and enforcement of necessary international, regional, and local efforts to halt the financing of terrorist groupings, containing no balancing procedural safeguards to ensure that fairness, appeal, and adverse public effects of inappropriate categorization are regulated by law. Fifth, the limitation of fundamental rights in relation to asylum and immigration processes.[156] Allied to this is genuine concern about the undermining of the non-refoulement

[155] The case *par excellence* of this is the status of prisoners held at Guantánamo Bay and inside Afghanistan by the United States. See, for example, Jules Lobel, "Preventive Detention: Prisoners, Suspected Terrorists and Permanent Emergency" (2003) 25 *Thomas Jefferson Law Review* 389; Stephen I. Vladeck, "The Detention Power" (2004) 22 *Yale Law and Policy Review* 153 at 181–95; Fleur Johns, "Guantánamo Bay and the Annihilation of the Exception" (2005) 16 *European Journal of International Law* 613; Mark A. Drumbl, "Guantánamo, Rasul, and the Twilight of Law" (2005) 53 *Drake Law Review* 897; Johan Steyn, "Guantánamo Bay: The Legal Black Hole" (2004) 53 *International and Comparative Law Quarterly* 1; Diane Marie Amann, "Guantánamo" (2004) 42 *Columbia Journal of Transnational Law* 263.

On October 13, 2004, the government of Nepal announced that it was repromulgating the Terrorist and Disruptive Activities (Control and Punishment) Ordinance (TADO) which allows the state to keep persons in preventive detention for up to one year. See International Commission of Jurists Press Release Oct. 21, 2004. See also the application of Malaysia's Internal Security Act provisions post-September 11. The Joseph R. Crowley Program in International Human Rights, "Unjust Order: Malaysia's Internal Security Act" (2003), pp.1–34; C. Raj Kumar, "Human Rights Implications of National Security Laws in India: Combating Terrorism while Preserving Civil Liberties" (2005) 33 *Denver Journal of International Law and Policy* 195; Australian Security Intelligence Organization Amendment (Terrorism) Act 2003; "Australia's Long Path in the US Antiterrorism Maze," *NY Times*, Jan. 29, 2005.

[156] See the statement of the High Commissioner for Refugees, R. Lubbers (Oct. 2001) to the 58th UN Human Rights Commission reiterating that refugees and asylum seekers should not be discriminated against because their ethnicity, religion, national origin, or political affiliation are perceived by some to be linked to terrorism; and

principle. Sixth, the undermining of the right to privacy in multiple jurisdictions, evidenced by the augmentation of search and seizure powers, surveillance powers, and transnational export of private and public data without appropriate safety or due process provisions. Seventh, restriction on freedom of expression in general and freedom of the media in particular. Eighth, the use of the post-September 11 political environment to target and repress non-violent domestic opposition in many states.

The human rights regimes of refugee and asylum protection are coming under particular stress. For example, there has been significant pressure on the European Union to "explore alternatives to extradition and deportation, where legally available and more efficient."[157] While this proposal is clearly in breach of the European Convention on Human Rights, it demonstrates the pressure that existing norms are experiencing in the current climate. This is also manifested by the calls to share immigration procedures for individuals alleged to have associations with terrorist organizations. The Schengen Information System is not open to non-Schengen states, and is subject to robust data protection safeguards. To open up these systems to non-European states with lower standards of procedural protection, and without the underpinning of commitment to international human rights treaty standards, is to introduce a back-door limitation on precariously balanced rights protections which already function outside the traditional state structure.

The same kind of dynamic described in relation to refugee and asylum standards is also evidenced in the area of data protection. Consistent political pressure has been applied to the European Union by the United States for retention of and access to telecommunications data. Moreover, greater emphasis on inter-agency access to telecommunications data in the anti-terrorist context has opened the floodgates on broader access by these agencies to more general information. Thus, in the aftermath of September 11, the EU Justice and Home Affairs Ministers Council adopted a series of measures. These included access to telecommunications data by law enforcement agencies for the purposes of "criminal investigations." These developments have substantially undermined the

---

Concluding Remarks of the Committee on the Elimination of Racial Discrimination in relation to Denmark (21/05/02), at para. 16.

[157] Letter from President George W. Bush to the President of the European Commission, Romano Prodi (Oct. 16, 2001), available online at http://www.statewatch.org/news/2001/nov/06Ausalet.htm (last visited Aug. 8, 2005). The letter contained more than forty proposals for US–EU counter-terrorism cooperation.

privacy rights long defended in the telecommunications access debates, and have widened the ambit of information held by both states and supra-national entities concerning individuals and organizations. The effects of coordinated efforts by the United States and Europe in the arena of information sharing are evident. Despite substantial public differences between the United States and Europe on the appropriate ways and means to conduct the "war against terrorism," cooperative measures being operationalized on the ground present a much more harmonious approach.[158] What can be seen in practice is an entirely new level of EU–US cooperation on internal security. As one observer has noted, "this represents a partial shift from informal transgovernmentalism . . . to the formalization of co-operation between the EU and the USA."[159]

Conclusion

This chapter has sought to engage with some of the contemporary debates about the interface between terrorism and emergencies. There is no easy tie-up on this discussion. As we have discussed in the post-World War II context, by and large state responses to terrorism were channeled through the emergency law prism domestically, and internationally through the derogation mechanism of international human rights law treaties. Despite the flaws of these mechanisms, they offered the potential for oversight with an eye to the primacy of certain human rights law norms. They also sent a normative signal to states, reinforced by states' own behavior, that responses to terrorism should be contained within a pre-agreed legal framework. For now, the events of September 11 challenge that supposition. The challenge is not an abstract one as this chapter demonstrates. Fundamental legal changes are taking place, and there is evident reordering of international legal institutions, as well as a challenge to the primacy of law-making capacity within the same bodies. We maintain that the case has not been persuasively made that terrorism per se constitutes an exception to the general rule of legality. The continued lack of definitional agreement on the meaning of terrorism also tells us that fundamental state understandings about these phenomena are in flux. What should be remembered is that existing international human rights law treaties through the derogation

---

[158] Ibid.

[159] See Tony Bunyan, "'The War on Freedom and Democracy' – An Analysis of the Effects on Civil Liberties and Democratic Culture in the EU" (Sept. 6, 2002), available online at http://www.statewatch.org/news/2002/sep/analysis13.htm (last visited Aug. 8, 2005).

regime reflect part of that debate, and the capacity to derogate was the means for states to respond to crisis and to contain the disagreement about such matters within an acceptable framework for all states. The derogation regime contains a general basis for dealing with the problem of terrorism and for states' needs to respond to it domestically. We also contend that where acts of terrorism meet the threshold for the application of international humanitarian law norms, these norms contain sufficient regulatory force (as well as clear prohibition on acts of terror) to serve as an appropriate general regulatory model in the "war against terror." We have also set out that in special cases of particularly exceptional circumstances the Extra-Legal Measures model may be utilized to respond to the particular exigencies posed by terrorist threats. We have also maintained throughout that the interaction of legal systems in times of crisis is a fluid one, where state legal responses can move between the various legal models set out in this work. That fluidity is essential both to retain the applicability of law to crisis and to acknowledge that the law applied in times of crisis may vary in substance and content, a quality dependent on the nature and intensity of the crisis itself at any particular point.

Bibliography

Acheson, Dean, "The Cuban Quarantine: Remarks" (1963) 57 *American Society of International Law Proceedings* 13
"Foreign Policy of the United States" (1964) 18 *Arkansas Law Review* 225
Morning and Noon (Boston: Houghton Mifflin, 1965)
Ackerman, Bruce, "Don't Panic" (2002) 24 *London Review of Books* 3, February 7, 2002
"The Emergency Constitution" (2004) 113 *Yale Law Journal* 1029
We the People: Foundations (Cambridge, MA: Belknap Press, 1991)
Adler, David Gray, "The Steel Seizure Case and Inherent Presidential Power" (2002) 19 *Constitutional Commentary* 155
Agamben, Giorgio, *State of Exception*, trans. Kevin Attell (Chicago: University of Chicago Press, 2005)
Ago, Robert, "Addendum to the Eighth Report on State Responsibility to the International Law Commission" (1979) 2 *Yearbook of the International Law Commission* 13, UN Doc. A/CN.4/Ser.A/1980/Add.1
Akehurst, Michael, *A Modern Introduction to International Law* (6th edn, London: Allen & Unwin, 1987)
Alexander, George J., "The Illusory Protection of Human Rights by National Courts during Periods of Emergency" (1984) 5 *Human Rights Law Journal* 1
Alexander, Larry and Frederick Schauer, "On Extrajudicial Constitutional Interpretation" (1997) 110 *Harvard Law Review* 1359
Alleg, Henri, *The Question* (New York: Braziller, 1958)
Allen, Mike and Bill Miller, "Bush Seeks Security Department; Cabinet Level Agency would Coordinate Antiterrorism Effort," *Washington Post*, June 7, 2002, at A1
Amar, Akhil Reed, *The Constitution and Criminal Procedure: First Principles* (New Haven: Yale University Press, 1997)
American Law Institute, *Restatement of the Law (Third), The Foreign Relations Law of the United States* (St. Paul, MN: American Law Institute Pub., 1987)
Anastaplo, George, "The Constitution at Two Hundred: Explorations" (1991) 22 *Texas Tech Law Review* 967

Andrews, Edmund L., "German Greens Patch Rift and Support Use of Military,"
     NY Times, November 25, 2001, at A6
Arnold, Vladimir I., *Catastrophe Theory* (3rd edn. Berlin: Springer-Verlag, 1992)
Aron, Raymond, *France, the New Republic* (New York: Oceana Publications, 1960)
Ashworth, Andrew and Peter Creighton, "The Right of Silence in Northern
     Ireland" in Jon Hayes and Paul O'Higgins (eds.), *Lessons from Northern Ireland*
     (Belfast: SLS, 1990)
Association of the Bar of the City of New York and Center for Human Rights
     and Global Justice, New York University School of Law, *Torture by Proxy:
     International and Domestic Law Applicable to "Extraordinary Renditions"* (Oct. 29,
     2004)
Atkin, Nicholas, *The Fifth French Republic* (New York: Palgrave Macmillan, 2005)
Aussaresses, Paul, *The Battle of the Casbah: Terrorism and Counter-terrorism in
     Algeria, 1955-1957* (New York: Enigma, 2005)
Bagnall, Nigel, *The Punic Wars, 264-146 BC* (New York: Routledge, 2003)
Bainbridge, Stephen M. and G. Mitu Gulati, "How Do Judges Maximize? (The
     Same Way Everybody Else Does – Boundedly): Rules of Thumb in Securities
     Fraud Opinions" (2002) 51 *Emory Law Journal* 83
Balkin, Jack M., "The Most Dangerous Person on Earth," *Hartford Courant*,
     September 22, 2002, at C1
Bank, Roland, "International Efforts to Combat Torture and Inhuman
     Treatment: Have the New Mechanisms Improved Protection?" (1997) 8
     European Journal of International Law 613
Banks, R. Richard, "Racial Profiling and Antiterrorism Efforts" (2004) 89 *Cornell
     Law Review* 1201
Banks, William C. and Alejandro D. Carrio, "Presidential Systems in Stress:
     Emergency Powers in Argentina and the United States" (1993) 15 *Michigan
     Journal of International Law* 1
Barak, Aharon, "The Role of a Supreme Court in a Democracy, and the Fight
     against Terrorism" (2003) 58 *University of Miami Law Review* 125
     Shofet be-hevrah demokratit (The Judge in a Democracy) (Jerusalem: Nevo, 2004)
     "The Supreme Court 2001 Term – Foreword: A Judge on Judging: The Role of
     a Supreme Court in a Democracy" (2002) 116 *Harvard Law Review* 16
Barber, Sotirios A., *On What the Constitution Means* (Baltimore: The Johns Hopkins
     University Press, 1984)
Barboza, Julio, "Necessity (Revisited) in International Law" in Jerzy Makarczyk
     (ed.), *Essays in International Law in Honour of Judge Manfred Lachs* (Boston:
     Nijhoff, 1984) 27
Barnett, Hilaire, *Constitutional and Administrative Law* (London: Cavendish, 1995)
Baron, Hans, *In Search of Florentine Civic Humanism* (Princeton: Princeton
     University Press, 1988)
Barth, Alan, *The Price of Liberty* (New York: Viking, 1961)
Barzilai, Gad, *Demokratyah be-milhamot: mahloket ve-konsenzus be-Israel (A Democracy
     in Wartime: Conflict and Consensus in Israel)* (Tel Aviv: Sifriyat Poalim, 1992)

Basler, Roy Prentice (ed.), *The Collected Works of Abraham Lincoln* (New Brunswick, NJ: Rutgers University Press, 1953)

Bassiouni, M. Cherif, "International Terrorism" in M. Cherif Bassiouni (ed.), *International Criminal Law* (2nd edn, Ardsley, NY: Transnational Publishers, 1999)

International Terrorism: Multilateral Conventions, 1937–2001 (Ardsley, NY: Transnational Publishers, 2001)

Basu, Durga Das, *Introduction to the Constitution of India* (9th edn, New Delhi: Prentice-Hall of India, 1982)

Battenfeld, Joe, "A Nation Rebuilds," *Boston Herald*, September 3, 2002

Baudón, Héctor R., *Estado de sitio* (Buenos Aires: M. Gleizer, 1939)

Beck, Ulrich, *Risk Society: Towards a New Modernity* (London: Sage, 1992).

Becker, Christine Noelle, "Clemency for Killers? Pardoning Battered Women who Strike Back" (1995) 29 *Loyola of Los Angeles Law Review* 297

Beckett, James, "The *Greek Case* before the European Human Rights Commission" (1970–71) 1 *Human Rights* 91

Beer, L.W., "Peace in Theory and Practice under Article 9 of Japan's Constitution" (1998) 81 *Marquette Law Review* 815

Belknap, Michael R., "The New Deal and the Emergency Powers Doctrine" (1983) 62 *Texas Law Review* 67

"A Putrid Pedigree: The Bush Administration's Military Tribunals in Historical Perspective" (2002) 38 *California Western Law Review* 433

"The Supreme Court Goes to War: The Meaning and Implications of the Nazi Saboteur Case" (1980) 89 *Military Law Review* 59

"The Warren Court and the Vietnam War: The Limits of Legal Liberalism" (1998) 33 *Georgia Law Review* 65

Bell, Christine, Colm Campbell, and Fionnuala Ní Aoláin, "Justice Discourses in Transition" (2004) 13 *Social & Legal Studies* 305

Bell, John, *French Constitutional Law* (New York: Oxford University Press, 1992)

ben Aderet, Shlomo ben Avraham *She'elot u-teshuvot ha-Rashba* (*Responsa*) (Jerusalem: Makhon Masoret Israel, 2000)

Bendavid, Naftali, "FBI's Mueller Reshapes Agency's Top Ranks," *Chicago Tribune*, December 4, 2001

Bendersky, Joseph W., *Carl Schmitt: Theorist for the Reich* (Princeton: Princeton University Press, 1983)

Bendor, Ariel, "The Right of Parties to Participate in Elections to the Knesset" (1988) 18 *Mishpatim* 269

Benjamin, Walter, "On the Concept of History" in Howard Eiland and Michael W. Jennings (eds.), *Selected Writings* (4 vols., Cambridge, MA: Harvard University Press, 2003)

Benneto, Jason, "Suspects Face Fast-Track Removal in Overhaul of Extradition Laws," *Independent* (London), June 21, 2002, at P6

Bennett, Geoffrey, "Legislative Responses to Terrorism: A View from Britain" (2005) 109 *Penn State Law Review* 947

Beres, Louis Rene, "The Meaning of Terrorism – Jurisprudential and Definitional Clarifications" (1995) 28 *Vanderbilt Journal of Transnational Law* 239

Berki, R.N., *Security and Society: Reflections on Law, Order and Politics* (New York: St. Martin's Press, 1986)

Berkovits, Eliezer, *Not in Heaven: The Nature and Function of Halakha* (New York: Ktav Publishing House, 1983)

Berlant, Lauren, "The Epistemology of State Emotion" in Austin Sarat (ed.), *Dissent in Dangerous Times* (Ann Arbor, MI: University of Michigan Press, 2005), p. 46

Berlin, Isaiah, "The Originality of Machiavelli" in Myron P. Gilmore (ed.), *Studies on Machiavelli* (Florence: G.C. Sansoni, 1972)

Bessette, Joseph M. and Jeffrey Tulis, "The Constitution, Politics and the Presidency" in Joseph M. Bessette and Jeffrey Tulis (eds.), *The Presidency in the Constitutional Order* (Baton Rouge, LA: Louisiana State University Press, 1981)

Best, Geoffrey, *War and Law since 1945* (Oxford: Clarendon Press, 1994)

BeVier, Lillian R., "The First Amendment and Political Speech: An Inquiry into the Substance and Limits of Principle" (1978) 30 *Stanford Law Review* 299

Biddle, Francis, *In Brief Authority* (Garden City, NY: Doubleday, 1962)

Bigel, Alan I., *The Supreme Court on Emergency Powers, Foreign Affairs, and Protection of Civil Liberties 1935–1975* (Lanham, MD: University Press of America, 1986)

Bird, J.C., *Control of Enemy Alien Civilians in Great Britain, 1914–1918* (London: Garland Publishing, 1986)

Bitel, David, *The Failed Promise: Human Rights in the Philippines since the Revolution of 1986* (Geneva: International Commission of Jurists, 1991)

Black, Charles L., Jr., "Mr. Justice Black, the Supreme Court, and the Bill of Rights," *Harper's Magazine*, February 1961
  The People and the Court: Judicial Review in a Democracy (New York: Macmillan, 1960)

Blackshield, Tony and George Williams, *Australian Constitutional Law and Theory: Commentary and Materials* (2nd edn, Annadale, NSW: Federation Press, 1998)

Blackstone, *Commentaries on the Laws of England* (1765) (Chicago: University of Chicago Press, 1979)

Blair, Chris, "Miranda and the Right to Silence in England" (2003) 11 *Tulsa Journal of Comparative and International Law* 1

Blasi, Vincent, "The Pathological Perspective and the First Amendment" (1985) 85 *Columbia Law Review* 449

Bobbitt, Philip, *Constitutional Interpretation* (Oxford: Basil Blackwell, 1991)

Bok, Sissela, *Common Values* (Columbia, MO: University of Missouri Press, 1995)

Bonner, David, *Emergency Powers in Peacetime* (London: Sweet & Maxwell, 1985)

Booth, William, "Alert Issued on Four Big California Bridges," *Washington Post*, November 2, 2001, at A1

Borger, Julian, "Blunders Prompt US Security Shake-Up: Bush Moves to Force CIA and FBI Cooperation," *Guardian* (London), June 7, 2002, at 1

Bosniak, Linda, "Citizenship Denationalized" (2000) 7 *Indiana Journal of Global Legal Studies* 447

Bowett, D.W., *Self-Defence in International Law* (Manchester: Manchester University Press, 1958)

"The Use of Force for the Protection of Nationals Abroad" in Antonio Cassese (ed.), *The Current Legal Regulation of the Use of Force* (Boston: Nijhoff, 1986)

Bowman, Harold M., "Martial Law and the English Constitution" (1916) 15 *Michigan Law Review* 93

Bowring, Bill, "The Degrading of International Law?" in John Strawson (ed.), *Law after Ground Zero* (Sydney: Glasshouse Press, 2002)

Boyle, Kevin, "Human Rights and Political Resolution in Northern Ireland" (1982) 9 *Yale Journal of World and Public Order* 156

Bracha, Baruch, "Checks and Balances in a Protracted State of Emergency – The Case of Israel" (2003) 33 *Israel Yearbook on Human Rights* 123

Bradford, Ernle D.S., *Julius Caesar: The Pursuit of Power* (New York: Morrow, 1984)

Bradley, A.W. and K.D. Ewing, *Constitutional and Administrative Law* (13th edn, New York: Longman, 2003)

Bradley, Curtis A. and Jack Goldsmith, "Congressional Authorization and the War on Terrorism" (2005) 118 *Harvard Law Review* 2047

Bravin, Jess and Ted Bridis, "Political Role Reversals Shape Antiterrorism Legislation," *Wall St. Journal*, October 8, 2001, at A8

Brennan, William J., "The Quest to Develop a Jurisprudence of Civil Liberties in Times of Security Crises" (1988) 18 *Israel Yearbook on Human Rights* 11

Brest, Paul et al., *Processes of Constitutional Decision-making* (4th edn, Gaithersburg, MD: Aspen Publishing, 2000)

Breyer, Stephen, "Keynote Address" (2003) 97 *American Society of International Law Proceedings* 265

Brierly, J.L., *The Law of Nations: An Introduction to the International Law of Peace*, ed. Humphrey Waldock (6th edn, Oxford: Clarendon Press, 1963)

Brown, Bartram S., "Primacy or Complementarity: Reconciling the Jurisdiction of National Courts and International Criminal Tribunals" (1998) 23 *Yale Journal of International Law* 383

Brown, C.G., *Chile since the Coup: Ten Years of Repression* (New York: Americas Watch, 1983)

Brown, Colin and Patricia Wynn Davies, "Ministers Want Silent Suspects to Be Filmed," *Independent* (London), February 18, 1992, at 2

Brown, Everett Somerville, *The Constitutional History of the Louisiana Purchase, 1803–1812* (Berkeley: University of California Press, 1920)

Brown, Judith Olans, "The Mythogenesis of Gender: Judicial Images of Women in Paid and Unpaid Labour" (1996) 6 *UCLA Women's Law Journal* 457

Brown, Patricia Leigh, "Preparing for a Potential Emergency," *NY Times*, October 4, 2001, at F12

Browne, Kingsley R., "Title VII as Censorship: Hostile-Environment Harassment and the First Amendment" (1991) 52 *Ohio State Law Journal* 481

Browning, E.S., "A 2% Fall Puts Index on Verge of Bear Level; Dow Falls 102 Points," *Wall St. Journal*, July 3, 2002, at C1

Brownlie, Ian, *International Law and the Use of Force by States* (Oxford: Clarendon Press, 1963)

"Interrogation in Depth: The Compton and Parker Reports" (1972) 35 *Modern Law Review* 501

Bühler, Jacques, *Le droit d'exception de l'etat: étude des droits publics allemand et suisse de 1871 à nos jours* (Geneva: Droz, 1995)

Bumiller, Elisabeth and Steven Lee Myers, "Senior Administration Officials Defend Military Tribunals for Terrorist Suspects," *NY Times*, November 15, 2001

Bunyan, T., "The 'War on Freedom and Democracy' – An Analysis of the Effects on Civil Liberties and Democratic Culture," *EU Statewatch*, September 6, 2002

Burgenthal, Thomas, "To Respect and Ensure: State Obligations and Permissible Derogations" in Louis Henkin (ed.), *The International Bill of Rights: The Covenant on Civil and Political Rights* (New York: Columbia University Press, 1981)

Burgers, J. Herman and Hans Danelius, *The United Nations Convention against Torture: A Handbook on the Convention against Torture and Other Cruel, Inhuman or Degrading Treatment or Punishment* (Boston: Nijhoff, 1988)

Burkeman, Olver, "FBI Says Dirty Bomb Suspect is No Big Fish" *Guardian* (London), August 15, 2002, at 12

Burns, James MacGregor, *The Vineyard of Liberty* (New York: Knopf, 1982)

Byrd, Janell M., "Rejecting Absolute Immunity for Federal Officials" (1983) 71 *California Law Review* 1707

Byers, Michael, "Preemptive Self-Defence: Hegemony, Equality and Strategies of Legal Change" (2003) 11 *Journal of Political Philosophy* 171

Calabresi, Guido, *A Common Law for the Age of Statutes* (Cambridge, MA: Harvard University Press, 1982)

Caldwell, Peter C., *Popular Sovereignty and the Crisis of German Constitutional Law: The Theory and Practice of Weimar Constitutionalism* (Durham, NC: Duke University Press, 1997)

Calmes, Jackie, "Washington Wire," *Wall St. Journal,* October 12, 2001, at A1

Campbell, Colm, *Emergency Law in Ireland, 1918–1925* (Oxford: Clarendon Press, 1994)

Campbell, Colm and Ita Connolly, "A Model for the War against Terrorism? Military Intervention in Northern Ireland and the 1970 Falls Curfew" (2003) 30 *Journal of Law and Society* 341

Campbell, Duncan, "September 11: Six Months on: US Sends Suspects to Face Torture," *Guardian* (London), March 12, 2002, at 4

Camus, Geneviève, *L'état de nécessité en démocratie* (Paris: Librairie Générale de Droit et de Jurisprudence, 1965)

Capua, J.V., "Early History of Martial Law in England from the 14th Century to the Petition of Right" (1977) 36 *Cambridge Law Journal* 152

Carr, Cecil T., "Crisis Legislation in Britain" (1940) *Columbia Law Review* 1309

Carr, Edward H., *Twenty Years' Crisis, 1919–1939: An Introduction to the Study of International Relations* (New York: Palgrave, 2001)

Carroll, Lewis, *Through the Looking Glass and What Alice Found There*, in *The Annotated Alice: Alice's Adventures in Wonderland and Through the Looking Glass* (New York: Bramhall House, 1960)

Carter, Bill and Felicity Barringer, "In Patriotic Time, Dissent is Muted," *NY Times*, September 28, 2001, at A1

Carty, Anthony, "Interwar German Theories of International Law: The Psychoanalytical and Phenomenological Perspectives of Hans Kelsen and Carl Schmitt" (1995) 16 *Cardozo Law Review* 1235

Cary, Max and Howard H. Scullard, *A History of Rome down to the Reign of Constantine* (3rd edn, New York: St. Martin's Press, 1975)

Casey, James P., *Constitutional Law in Ireland* (3rd edn, Dublin: Round Hall Sweet & Maxwell, 2000)

Cassese, Antonio, *The Current Legal Regulation of the Use of Force* (Dordrecht: Nijhoff, 1986

"A Tentative Appraisal of the Old and New Humanitarian Law of Armed Conflict" in Antonio Cassese (ed.), *The New Humanitarian Law of Armed Conflict* (Naples: Editoriale Scientifica, 1979), p. 461

"Terrorism is also Disrupting Some Crucial Legal Categories of International Law" (2001) 12 *European Journal of International Law* 993

Cavanaugh, K.A., "Emergency Rule, Normalcy Exception: The Erosion of the Right to Silence in the United Kingdom" (2003) 35 *Cornell International Law Journal* 491

Chafee Zechariah, Jr., *Free Speech in the United States* (Cambridge, MA: Harvard University Press, 1941)

Champion, Mark, "Europe Tour by Ashcroft Starts Sourly," *Wall St. Journal*, December 13, 2001, at A18

Chandrasekaran, Rajiv and Peter Finn, "US Behind Secret Transfer of Terror Suspects," *Washington Post*, March 11, 2002

Charters, David A., "Introduction" in David A. Charters (ed.), *The Deadly Sin of Terrorism* (Westport, CN: Greenwood Press, 1994)

Chayes, Abram and Antonia Handler Chayes, *The New Sovereignty: Compliance with International Regulatory Agreements* (Cambridge, MA: Harvard University Press, 1995)

Chemerinsky, Erwin, "Losing Liberties: Applying a Foreign Intelligence Model to Domestic Law Enforcement" (2004) 51 *UCLA Law Review* 1619

Chen, David W. and Somini Sengupta, "Not Yet Citizens but Eager to Fight for the US," *NY Times*, October 26, 2001

Cheng, Bin, *General Principles of Law as Applied by International Courts and Tribunals* (London: Stevens, 1953)

Chowdhury, Subrata Roy, *Rule of Law in a State of Emergency: The Paris Minimum Standards of Human Rights Norms in a State of Emergency* (London: Pinter, 1989)

Cicero, Marcus Tullius, *The Orations of Marcus Tullius Cicero*, trans. C.D. Yonge (London: H.G. Bohn, 1856)

Cinquegrana, Americo R., "The Walls (and Wires) Have Ears: The Background and First Ten Years of the Foreign Intelligence Surveillance Act of 1978" (1989) 137 *University of Pennsylvania Law Review* 793

Clark, D.M., "Emergency Legislation, Fundamental Rights, and Article 28.3.3 of the Irish Constitution" (1977) 12 *The Irish Jurist* 283

Clift, Ben, "Dyarchic Presidentialization in a Presidentialized Polity: The French Fifth Republic" in Thomas Poguntke and Paul Webb (eds.), *The Presidentialization of Politics: A Comparative Study of Modern Democracies* (Oxford: Oxford University Press, 2005)

Cloud, David S., "Cold War Echo: Soviet Germ Program is a Worry Once Again amid Anthrax Scare," *Wall St. Journal*, October 15, 2001

Clusellas, Eduardo L. Gregorini, *Estado de sitio y la armonía en la relación individuo-Estado* (Buenos Aires: Depalma, 1987)

Coffey, John P., "The Navy's Role in Interdicting Narcotics Traffic: War on Drugs or Ambush on the Constitution?" (1987) 75 *Georgetown Law Journal* 1947

Cohen, Marshall, Thomas Nagel, and Thomas Scanlon (eds.), *War and Moral Responsibility* (Princeton: Princeton University Press, 1974)

Cole, David, "Enemy Aliens" (2002) 54 *Stanford Law Review* 953

  Enemy Aliens: Double Standards and Constitutional Freedoms in the War on Terrorism (New York: New Press, 2003)

  "Judging the Next Emergency: Judicial Review and Individual Rights in Times of Crisis" (2003) 101 *Michigan Law Review* 2565

  "The Price of Morality: The Emergency Constitution's Blind Spot" (2004) 113 *Yale Law Journal* 1753

Collins, Liat, "GSS Agent Involved in Death of Harizat Transferred from Post," *Jerusalem Post*, May 1, 1995

Committee on the Administration of Justice, *No Emergency, No Emergency Law: Emergency Legislation Related to Northern Ireland: The Case for Repeal* (Belfast: CAJ, 1993)

Committee on Government Operations, 85th Cong., *Executive Orders and Proclamations: A Study of a Use of Presidential Powers* (Comm. Print, 1957)

Congressional Research Service, "Intelligence and Law Enforcement: Countering Transnational Threats to the US" (2001)

Constant, Benjamin, "The Spirit of Conquest and Usurpation and their Relation to European Civilization" (1814) in *Political Writings*, ed. Biancamaria Fontana (New York: Cambridge University Press, 1988)

Cooter, Robert, "Prices and Sanctions" (1984) 84 *Columbia Law Review* 1523

Cornish, Francis, "Keeping Terrorism's Advocates off British Air," *NY Times*, November 13, 1988

Corwin, Edward S., *The "Higher Law" Background of American Constitutional Law* (Ithaca, NY: Cornell University Press, 1955)

  "Martial Law, Yesterday and Today" (1932) 47 *Political Science Quarterly* 95

"Moratorium over Minnesota" (1934) 82 *University of Pennsylvania Law Review* 311

Total War and the Constitution (New York: A.A. Knopf, 1947)

Cotler, Irwin, "Thinking Outside the Box: Foundational Principles for a Counter-Terrorism Law and Policy" in Daniels, et al. (eds.), *The Security of Freedom*

Cotter, Cornelius P., "Constitutional Democracy and Emergency: Emergency Powers Legislation in Great Britain since 1914" (PhD dissertation, Harvard University, 1953)

Cover, Avidan Y., "A Rule Unfit for All Seasons: Monitoring Attorney–Client Communications Violates Privilege and the Sixth Amendment" (2002) 87 *Cornell Law Review* 1233

Cover, Robert M., "Obligation: A Jewish Jurisprudence of the Social Order" (1987) 5 *Journal of Law and Religion* 65

"Violence and the Word" (1985) 95 *Yale Law Journal* 1601

Cowell, Alan, "Seeking Moderate Support, Blair Meets Muslim Leaders," *NY Times*, July 20, 2005, at A10

Crawford, James, (ed.), *International Law Association, Report of the 64th Biennial Conference Queensland, August 19–25, 1990* (London: ILA, 1991)

The International Law Commission's Articles on State Responsibility: Introduction, Text and Commentaries (Cambridge, UK: Cambridge University Press, 2002)

Crawford, Michael H., *The Roman Republic* (Cambridge, MA: Harvard University Press, 1993)

Creighton, Donald G., *Dominion of the North: A History of Canada* (Boston: Houghton Mifflin, 1944)

Crelinsten, R.D., "Terrorism as Political Communication: The Relationship between the Controller and the Controlled" in Paul Wilkinson and Alasdair M. Stewart (eds.), *Contemporary Research on Terrorism* (Aberdeen: Aberdeen University Press, 1987)

Cruz Villalón, Pedro, *El estado de sitio y la constitución: la constitucionalización de la protección extraordinaria del Estado (1789–1878)* (Madrid: Centro de Estudios Constitucionales, 1980)

Estados excepcionales y suspensión de garantías (Madrid: Tecnos, 1984)

Cullen, Anthony, "The Parameters of Internal Armed Conflict in International Humanitarian Law" (2004) 12 *University of Miami International and Comparative Law Review* 189

Currie, David P., *The Constitution of the Federal Republic of Germany* (Chicago: University of Chicago Press, 1994)

Damrosch, Lori F., Louis Henkin, Richard C. Pugh, Oscar Schachter, and Hans Smit, *International Law: Cases and Materials* (4th edn, St. Paul, MN: West, 2001)

Dan-Cohen, Meir, "Decision Rules and Conduct Rules: On Acoustic Separation in Criminal Law" (1984) 97 *Harvard Law Review* 625

Daniels, Ronald J., Patrick Macklem, and Kent Roach (eds.), *The Security of Freedom: Essays on Canada's Antiterrorism Bill* (Toronto: University of Toronto Press, 2001)

Dao, James, "Defence Secretary Warns of Unconventional Attacks," *NY Times*, October 1, 2001, at B5

Davis, Kevin E., "Cutting off the Flow of Funds to Terrorists: Whose Funds? Which Funds? Who Decides?" in Daniels et al. (eds.), *The Security of Freedom*

Dempsey, James X. and David Cole, *Terrorism and the Constitution: Sacrificing Civil Liberties in the Name of National Security* (2nd edn, New York: New Press, 2002)

Dennison, George M., "Martial Law: The Development of a Theory of Emergency Powers, 1776–1861" (1974) 18 *American Journal of Legal History* 52

Dershowitz, Alan, "Is it Necessary to Apply 'Physical Pressure' to Terrorists – and to Lie about It?" (1989) 23 *Israeli Law Review* 192

"The Role of Law during Times of Crisis: Would Liberty be Suspended?" in Harry M. Clor (ed.), *Civil Disorder and Violence* (Chicago: Rand McNally, 1972)

"Torture without Visibility and Accountability is Worse than with it" (2003) 6 *University of Pennsylvania Journal of Constitutional Law* 326

Why Terrorism Works: Understanding the Threat, Responding to the Challenge (New Haven, CT: Yale University Press, 2002)

Detter, Ingrid, *The Law of War* (2nd edn, Cambridge: Cambridge University Press, 2000)

Dicey, Albert Venn, *Introduction to the Study of the Law of the Constitution* (8th edn, Indianapolis, IN: Liberty Classics, 1982)

Dickinson, John, *Death of a Republic: Politics and Political Thought at Rome 59–44 BC* (New York: Macmillan, 1963)

Dickson, Brice, "Northern Ireland's Emergency Legislation – The Wrong Medicine?" (1992) *Public Law* 592

Dillon, Sam and Donald G. McNeil, Jr., "Spain Sets Hurdle for Extraditions," *NY Times,* November 24, 2001, at A1

Dinh, Viet D., "Nationalism in an Age of Terror" (2004) 56 *Florida Law Review* 867

Dinstein, Yoram, *War, Aggression, and Self-Defence* (4th edn, Cambridge, UK: Cambridge University Press, 2005)

Djurisic, Paul I., "The Exon–Florio Amendment: National Security Legislation Hampered by Political and Economic Forces" (1990) 3 *DePaul Business Law Journal* 179

Dodd, C., "The Case of Marais" (1902) 70 *Law Quarterly Review* 143

Dodge, Guy Howard, *Benjamin Constant's Philosophy of Liberalism: A Study in Politics and Religion* (Chapel Hill, NC: North Carolina University Press, 1980)

Dodge, Kirstin S., "Countenancing Corruption: A Civic Republican Case against Judicial Deference to the Military" (1992) 5 *Yale Journal of Law and Feminism* 1

Donnelly, Jack, *Realism and International Relations* (Cambridge, UK: Cambridge University Press, 2000)

Doolan, Brian, *Constitutional Law and Constitutional Rights in Ireland* (3rd edn, Dublin: Gill & Macmillan, 1994)

Downey, William G., Jr., "The Law of War and Military Necessity" (1953) 47 *American Journal of International Law* 252

Dowty, Alan, "The Use of Emergency Powers in Israel" (1988) 21 *Middle East Review* 34

Draper, G.I.A.D., "The Geneva Conventions of 1949" (1965-I) 114 *Recueil des Cours* 59

"Humanitarian Law and Internal Armed Conflicts" (1983) 13 *Georgia Journal of International and Comparative Law* 253

Dressler, Joshua, "New Thoughts about the Concept of Justification in the Criminal Law: A Critique of Fletcher's Thinking and Rethinking" (1984) 32 *UCLA Law Review* 61

Dror, Yehezkel, "Terrorism as a Challenge to the Democratic Capacity to Govern" in Martha Crenshaw (ed.), *Terrorism, Legitimacy and Power* (Middletown, CT: Wesleyan University Press, 1983)

Dugger, Celia W., "India, Too, Weighs Anti-terror Measure against Liberties," *NY Times*, November 22, 2001, at A10

Dunbar, N.C.H., "Military Necessity in War Crimes Trials" (1952) 29 *British Yearbook of International Law* 442

Dutton, Geoffrey, *Edward John Eyre: The Hero as Murderer* (New York: Penguin, 1977)

Dutton, J.R., "The Military Aspects of National Security" in Michael H.H. Louw (ed.), *National Security: A Modern Approach* (Pretoria, South Africa: Institute for Strategic Studies, 1978)

Dworkin, Ronald, "The Rights of Myron Farber," *NY Review of Books*, October 26, 1978, at 34

"The Threat to Patriotism," *NY Review of Books*, February 28, 2002, at 44

Dyer, Clare, "UK Finally Complies with Rights Convention" *Guardian* (London), February 20, 2001, at 8

Dyzenhaus, David, "Holmes and Carl Schmitt: An Unlikely Pair?" (1997) 63 *Brooklyn Law Review* 165

"'Now the Machine Runs Itself': Carl Schmitt on Hobbes and Kelsen" (1994) 16 *Cardozo Law Review* 1

"The State of Emergency in Legal Theory" in Victor V. Ramraj, Michael Hor, and Kent Roach (eds.), *Global Anti-Terrorism Law and Policy* (New York: Cambridge University Press, 2005)

Easton, Susan, *The Case for the Right to Silence* (2nd edn, Aldershot: Ashgate, 1998)

Eaves, John, Jr., *Emergency Powers and the Parliamentary Watchdog: Parliament and the Executive in Great Britain 1939–1951* (London: Hansard Society, 1957)

Edgar, Harold and Benno C. Schmidt, Jr., "*Curtiss-Wright* Comes Home: Executive Power and National Security Secrecy" (1986) 21 *Harvard Civil Rights–Civil Liberties Law Review* 349

Edwards, Ward and Detlof von Winterfeldt, "Cognitive Illusions and their Implications for the Law" (1986) 59 *Southern California Law Review* 225

Eisenbuerg, Melvin A., "The Limits of Cognition and the Limits of Contract" (1995) 47 *Stanford Law Review* 211

Eisgruber, Christopher L., "The Most Competent Branches: A Response to Professor Paulsen" (1994) 83 *Georgetown Law Journal* 347

Eisgruber, Christopher L. and Lawrence G. Sager, "Civil Liberties in the Dragons' Domain: Negotiating the Blurred Boundary between Domestic

Law and Foreign Affairs after 9/11" in Mary L. Dudziak (ed.), *September 11 in History: A Watershed Moment?* (Durham, NC: Duke University Press, 2003)

"Military Courts and Constitutional Justice" (2002) (unpublished manuscript on file with author)

Elliott, W.A., *Us and Them: A Study of Group Consciousness* (Aberdeen: Aberdeen University Press, 1986)

Elon, Menachem, *Jewish Law: History, Sources, Principles*, trans. Bernard Auerbach and Melvin J. Sykes (Philadelphia: Jewish Publication Society, 1994)

Elshtain, Jean Bethke, "Reflections on the Problem of 'Dirty Hands'" in Sanford Levinson (ed.), *Torture: A Collection* (New York: Oxford University Press, 2004)

Ely, John Hart, *Democracy and Distrust: A Theory of Judicial Review* (Cambridge, MA: Harvard University Press, 1980)

War and Responsibility: Constitutional Lessons of Vietnam and its Aftermath (Princeton: Princeton University Press, 1993)

Emerson, Thomas I., "National Security and Civil Liberties" (1982) 9 *Yale Journal World Public Order* 78

England, Itzhak, "Majority Decision vs. Individual Truth: The Interpretations of the 'Oven of Achnai' Aggadah" (1975) 15 *Tradition* 137

"Nazi Criticism against the Normativist Theory of Hans Kelsen – Its Intellectual Basis and Post-Modern Tendencies" in Dan Diner and Michael Stolleis (eds.), *Hans Kelsen and Carl Schmitt: A Juxtaposition* (Gerlingen: Bleicher, 1999)

Epstein, Lee, Daniel E. Ho, Gary King, and Jeffrey A. Segal, "The Supreme Court during Crisis: How War Affects only Non-War Cases" (2005) 80 *New York University Law Review* 1

EU Network of Independent Experts in Fundamental Rights, *The Balance between Freedom and Security in the Response by the European Union and its Member States to the Terrorist Threats* (2003)

European Commission for Democracy through Law, *Emergency Powers* (Strasburg: Council of Europe Pub., 1995)

Evans, Christopher M., "Terrorism on Trial: The President's Constitutional Authority to Order the Prosecution of Suspected Terrorists by Military Commission" (2002) 51 *Duke Law Journal* 1831

Evans, Jennifer C., "Hijacking Civil Liberties: The USA PATRIOT Act of 2001" (2002) 33 *Loyola University of Chicago Law Journal* 933

Evans, Malcolm D. and Rod Morgan, *Preventing Torture: A Study of the European Convention for the Prevention of Torture and Inhuman or Degrading Treatment or Punishment* (Oxford: Clarendon Press, 1998)

Evans, Malcolm D. and Rachel Murray, *The African Charter on Human and Peoples' Rights: The System in Practice, 1986–2000* (New York: Cambridge University Press, 2002)

Fairman, Charles, *History of the Supreme Court of the United States: Reconstruction and Reunion, 1864–88* (New York: Macmillan, 1971)

The Law of Martial Rule (2nd edn, Chicago: Callaghan, 1943)

"The Law of Martial Rule and the National Emergency" (1942) 55 *Harvard Law Review* 1253

"Martial Rule, in the Light of Sterling v. Constantin" (1934) 19 *Cornell Law Quarterly* 29

Falk, Richard A., *The Great Terror War* (Moreton-in-Marsh, UK: Arris, 2003)

Fallon, Richard H., Jr., "Individual Rights and the Powers of Government" (1993) 27 *Georgia Law Review* 343

Fallon, Richard H. Jr., and Daniel J. Meltzer, "New Law, Non-Retroactivity, and Constitutional Remedies" (1991) 104 *Harvard Law Review* 1733

Farber, Daniel, *Lincoln's Constitution: The Nation, the President, and the Courts in a Time of Crisis* (Chicago: University of Chicago Press, 2003)

Farber, Daniel and Phillip P. Frickey, *Law and Public Choice* (Chicago: University of Chicago Press, 1991)

Farnsworth, Wald, "To Do a Great Right, Do a Little Wrong: A User's Guide to Judicial Lawlessness" (2001) 86 *Minnesota Law Review* 227

Farrell, Michael, *Arming the Protestants: The Formation of the Ulster Special Constabulary and the Royal Ulster Constabulary* (London: Pluto Press, 1983)

Fatovic, Clement, "Constitutionalism and Contingency: Locke's Theory of Prerogative" (2004) 25 *History of Political Thought* 276

Feingold, Cora S., "The Doctrine of Margin of Appreciation and the European Convention on Human Rights" (1977) 53 *Notre Dame Law Review* 90

Fenoglio, Gia, "Jumping the Gun on Terrorism?" (2001) 33 *National Journal* 3450

Ferejohn, John and Pasquale Pasquino, "The Law of the Exception: A Typology of Emergency Powers" (2004) 2 *International Journal of Constitutional Law* 210

Final Report of the National Commission on Terrorist Attacks upon the United States (Washington, DC: US GPO, 2004)

Finn, John E., *Constitutions in Crisis: Political Violence and the Rule of Law* (New York: Oxford University Press, 1991)

Firestone, David, "Senate Votes, 90–9, to Set Up a Homeland Security Dept. Geared to Fight Terrorism," *NY Times*, November 2, 2002, at A1

Fisher, H.A.L., *A History of Europe* (London: Arnold, 1936)

Fitzpatrick, Joan, *Human Rights in Crisis: The International System for Protecting Rights during States of Emergency* (Philadelphia: University of Pennsylvania Press, 1994)

"Jurisdiction of Military Commissions and the Ambiguous War on Terrorism" (2002) 96 *American Journal of International Law* 345

"Speaking Law to Power: The War against Terrorism and Human Rights" (2003) 14 *European Journal of International Law* 241

Flaherty, Martin S., "The Most Dangerous Branch" (1996) 105 *Yale Law Journal* 1725

Fletcher, George P., *Rethinking Criminal Law* (Boston: Little, Brown, 1978)

Fontana, David, "Refined Comparativism in Constitutional Law" (1999) 1 *University of Pennsylvania Journal of Constitutional Law* 640

Ford, Paul Leicester (ed.), *The Writings of Thomas Jefferson* (New York: G.P. Putnam's Sons, 1986)

Fox, Gregory H. and Georg Nolte, "Fox and Nolte Response" (1996) 37 *Harvard International Law Journal* 238

"Intolerant Democracies" (1995) 36 *Harvard International Law Journal* 1

Franck, Thomas M., "Criminals, Combatants or What? An Examination of the Role of Law in Responding to the Threat of Terror" (2004) 98 *American Journal of International Law* 686

"The Emerging Right to Democratic Governance" (1992) 86 *American Journal of International Law* 46

"Legitimacy in the International System" (1988) 82 *American Journal of International Law* 705

Political Questions/Judicial Answers: Does the Rule of Law Apply to Foreign Affairs? (Princeton: Princeton University Press, 1992)

The Power of Legitimacy among Nations (New York: Oxford University Press, 1990)

Recourse to Force: State Action against Threats and Armed Attacks (Cambridge, UK: Cambridge University Press, 2002)

"Terrorism and the Right of Self-Defense" (2001) 95 *American Journal of International Law* 839

"What Happens Now? The United Nations after Iraq" (2003) 97 *American Journal of International Law* 607

Franklin, Daniel P., *Extraordinary Measures: The Exercise of Prerogative Powers in the United States* (Pittsburgh: University of Pittsburgh Press, 1991)

Fridlington, Robert, *The Supreme Court in American Life: The Reconstruction Court, 1864–1888* (Millwood, NY: Associated Faculty Press, 1987)

Fried, Charles, *Right and Wrong* (Cambridge, MA: Harvard University Press, 1978)

Friedman, Lawrence M. and George Fisher, *The Crime Conundrum: Essays on Criminal Justice* (Boulder, CO: Westview Press, 1997)

Friedman, Thomas L., "Cool It!," *NY Times*, May 22, 2002, at A27

Friedrich, Carl J., *Constitutional Government and Democracy: Theory and Practice in Europe and America* (4th edn, Waltham, MA: Blaisdell, 1968)

Constitutional Reason of State: The Survival of the Constitutional Order (Providence, RI: Brown University Press, 1957)

Froomkin, A. Michael, "The Metaphor is the Key: Cryptography, the Clipper Chip, and the Constitution" (1995) 143 *University of Pennsylvania Law Review* 709

Fuller, Glenn E., "The National Emergency Dilemma: Balancing the Executive's Crisis Powers with the Need for Accountability" (1979) 52 *Southern California Law Review* 1453

Fuller, John F.C., *Julius Caesar: Man, Soldier, and Tyrant* (New York: Da Capo Press, 1991)

Gaeta, Paola, "The Armed Conflict in Chechnya before the Russian Constitutional Court" (1996) 7 *European Journal of International Law* 563

Galli, Carlo, "Carl Schmitt's Antiliberalism: Its Theoretical and Historical Sources and its Philosophical and Political Meaning" (2000) 21 *Cardozo Law Review* 1597

Ganev, Venelin I., "Emergency Powers and the New East European Constitutions" (1997) 45 *American Journal of Comparative Law* 585

Garcia Amador, Francisco V., "Report on Responsibility of the State for Injuries Caused in its Territory to the Person or Property of Aliens" (1959) 2 *Yearbook of the International Law Commission* 53

Garro, Alejandro M., "The Role of the Argentine Judiciary in Controlling Governmental Action under a State of Siege" (1983) 4 *Human Rights Law Journal* 311

Garro, Alejandro M. and Henry Dahl, "Legal Accountability for Human Rights Violations in Argentina: One Step Forward and Two Steps Backward" (1987) 8 *Human Rights Law Journal* 284

Gasser, Hans-Peter, "Acts of Terror, 'Terrorism' and International Humanitarian Law" (2002) 84 *International Review of the Red Cross* 547

"A Measure of Humanity in Internal Disturbances and Tensions: Proposal for a Code of Conduct" (January/Febuary 1988) 28 *International Review of the Red Cross* 38

Gavison, Ruth, "Twenty Years to the Yeredor Ruling – The Right to be Elected and the Lessons of History" in Ruth Gavison and Mordechai Kremnitzer (eds.), *Essays in Honour of Shimon Agranat* (Jerusalem: Graf Press, 1986)

Gearty, Conor A., "Airy Fairy," *London Review of Books*, November 29, 2001, at 9

"Terrorism and Human Rights" (2005) *European Human Rights Law Review* 1

Gelzer, Matthias, *Caesar: Politician and Statesman*, trans. Peter Needham (Cambridge, MA: Harvard University Press, 1968)

Giddens, Anthony, *Runaway World: How Globalization is Reshaping our Lives* (2nd edn, New York: Routledge, 2003)

Gilbert, Christopher D., "'There Will Be Wars and Rumours of Wars': A Comparison of the Treatment of Defence and Emergency Powers in the Federal Constitutions of Australia and Canada" (1980) 18 *Osgoode Hall Law Journal* 307

Goldman, Robert K., "Certain Legal Questions and Issues Raised by the September 11th Attacks" (2001) 9(1) *Human Rights Brief* 2

Goldsmith, Jack L., "Federal Courts, Foreign Affairs, and Federalism" (1997) 83 *Virginia Law Review* 1617

Goldsmith, Jack and Cass R. Sunstein, "Military Tribunals and Legal Culture: What a Difference Sixty Years Makes" (2002) 19 *Constitutional Commentary* 261

Gordon, Dan, "Limits on Extremist Political Parties: A Comparison of Israeli Jurisprudence with that of the United States and West Germany" (1987) 10 *Hastings International and Comparative Law Review* 347

Gorenstein, Gabriel W., "Judicial Review of Constitutional Claims against the Military" (1984) 84 *Columbia Law Review* 387

Gray, Christine, *International Law and the Use of Force* (2nd edn, Oxford: Oxford University Press, 2004)

Gray, J. Glenn, *The Warriors: Reflections on Men in Battle* (New York: Harper & Row, 1973)

Green, L.C., "Derogation of Human Rights in Emergency Situations" (1978) 16
    Canadian Yearbook of International Law 92
    "Low-Intensity Conflict and the Law" (1997) 3 *ILSA Journal of International and
    Comparative Law* 493
Greenawalt, Kent, "Distinguishing Justifications from Excuses" (1986) 49 *Law
    and Contemporary Problems* 89
    "The Perplexing Borders of Justification and Excuse" (1984) 84 *Columbia Law
    Review* 1091
Greenberg, Karen J. and Joshua L. Dratel (eds.), *The Torture Papers* (Cambridge,
    UK: Cambridge University Press, 2005)
Greenhouse, Steven, "As Tide of Haitian Refugees Rises, US Uses Cuban Base,"
    NY Times, June 30, 1994, at A3
Greenwood, Christopher, "International Law and the Pre-emptive Use of Force:
    Afghanistan, Al Qaida and Iraq" (2004) 4 *San Diego International Law
    Journal* 7
    "War, Terrorism and International Law" (2003) 56 *Current Legal Problems* 505
Greer, Steven, "The Right to Silence: A Review of the Current Debate" (1990) 53
    Modern Law Review 709
Greig, D.W., *International Law* (2nd edn, London: Butterworths, 1976)
Grey, Stephen, "America's Gulag," *New Statesman*, May 17, 2004, at 22
Groom, Brian, "Detaining Suspects not Abuse of Human Rights, Says Blunkett,"
    Financial Times (London), November 12, 2001, at 3
Gross, J. Brian, "Russia's War on Political and Religious Extremism: An
    Appraisal of the Law 'on Counteracting Extremist Activity'" (2003) *Brigham
    Young University Law Review* 717
Gross, Oren, "Chaos and Rules: Should Responses to Violent Crisis Always Be
    Constitutional?" (2003) 112 *Yale Law Journal* 1011
    "The Concept of 'Crisis': What Can we Learn from the Two Dictatorships of L.
    Quinctius Cincinnatus?" in *Diritti Civili ed Economici in Tempi di Crisi*
    (forthcoming)
    "'Control Systems' and the Migration of Anomalies" in Sujit Choudhry (ed.),
    The Migration of Constitutional Ideas (Cambridge: Cambridge University Press,
    forthcoming)
    "Cutting Down Trees: Law Making under the Shadow of Great Calamities" in
    Ronald J. Daniels, Patrick Macklem, and Kent Roach (eds.), *The Security of
    Freedom: Essays on Canada's Antiterrorism Bill* (Toronto: University of Toronto
    Press, 2001)
    "The Grave Breaches System and the Armed Conflict in the Former
    Yugoslavia" (1995) 16 *Michigan Journal of International Law* 783
    "The Normless and Exceptionless Exception: Carl Schmitt's Theory of
    Emergency Powers and the 'Norm–Exception' Dichotomy" (2000) 21 *Cardozo
    Law Review* 1825
    "'Once More unto the Breach': The Systematic Failure of Applying the
    European Convention on Human Rights to Entrenched Emergencies"
    (1998) 23 *Yale Journal of International Law* 437

"The Prohibition on Torture and the Limits of the Law" in Sanford
Levinson (ed.), *Torture: A Collection* (Oxford: Oxford University Press, 2004), p.
229

"Providing for the Unexpected: Constitutional Emergency Provisions" (2003)
33 *Israel Yearbook on Human Rights* 13

"On Terrorists and Other Criminals: States of Emergency and the Criminal
Legal System" in Eli Lederman (ed.), *Directions in Criminal Law: Inquiries in the
Theory of Criminal Law* (Tel Aviv: Tel Aviv University, 2001), p. 409

"Are Torture Warrants Warranted? Pragmatic Absolutism and Official
Disobedience" (2004) 88 *Minnesota Law Review* 1481

Gross, Oren and Fionnuala Ní Aoláin, "From Discretion to Scrutiny: Revisiting
the Application of the Margin of Appreciation Doctrine in the Context of
Article 15 of the European Convention on Human Rights" (2001) 23 *Human
Rights Quarterly* 625

"Emergency, War and International Law – Another Perspective" (2001) 70
Nordic Journal of International Law 29

"To Know Where We Are Going, We Need To Know Where We Are: Revisiting
States of Emergency" in Angela Hegarty and Siobhan Leonard (eds.), *Human
Rights: An Agenda for the 21st Century* (London: Cavendish, 1999)

Gross, Raphael, "Jewish Law and Christian Grace: Carl Schmitt's Critique of
Hans Kelsen" in Dan Diner and Michael Stolleis (eds.), *Hans Kelsen and Carl
Schmitt: A Juxtaposition* (Gerlingen: Bleicher, 1999)

Gross, Samuel R. and Debra Livingston, "Racial Profiling under Attack" (2002)
102 *Columbia Law Review* 1413

Gross Stein, Janice, "Network Wars" in Daniels et al. (eds.) *The Security of Freedom*

Grotius, Hugo, *De Jure Belli ac Pacis* (1646) (Washington, DC: Carnegie Institution
of Washington, 1925)

Groves, Edward E., "A Brief History of the 1988 National Security Amendments"
(1989) 20 *Law and Policy in International Business* 589

Guberman, Shlomo, "Israel's Supra-Constitution" (1967) 2 *Israel Law Review* 455

Gunther, Gerald, *Constitutional Law* (12th edn, Westbury, NY: Foundation Press,
1991)

Learned Hand: The Man and the Judge (New York: Knopf, 1994)

Gutfeld, Arnon, "'Stark, Staring, Raving Mad': An Analysis of a World War I
Impeachment Trial" (1995) 30 *Yearbook of German-American Studies* 57

Guthrie, Jonathan and Chris Tighe, "The Chilling Challenge of Home-Grown
Jihadis: We Need to Confront the Message, not just the Bombers," *Financial
Times* (London), July 14, 2005, p. 18.

"The Eerily Ordinary Extremists," *Financial Times* (London), July 16, 2005,
at 13

Gutman, Yechiel, *Taltelah ba-Shabak: ha-yoets ha-mishpati neged ha-memshalah
mi-parashat Tovyanski ad parashat Kav 300 (A Storm in the GSS)* (Tel Aviv: Yediot
Aharonot, 1995)

Haas, Ernst B., "The Balance of Power: Prescription, Concept, or Propaganda"
(1953) 5 *World Politics* 442

Haase, Paul J., "'Oh My Darling Clemency': Existing or Possible Limitations on the Use of the Presidential Pardon Power" (2002) 39 *American Criminal Law Review* 1287

Habermas, Jürgen, "Legitimation Problems in the Modern State" in trans. Thomas McCarthy, *Communication and the Evolution of Society* (Boston: Beacon Press, 1979)

Hadden, Tom and Colin Harvey, "The Law of Internal Crisis and Conflict" (1999) 81 *International Review of the Red Cross* 119

Haddock, Vicki, "The Unspeakable: To Get at the Truth, is Torture or Coercion Ever Justified?" *San Francisco Chronicle*, November 18, 2001

Hahn, Michael J., "Vital Interests and the Law of GATT: An Analysis of GATT's Security Exception" (1991) 12 *Michigan Journal of International Law* 558

Hakim, Danny, "States are Told to Keep Detainee Information Secret," *NY Times*, April 19, 2002

Hale, Matthew, *The History of the Common Law of England* (1713) (Littleton, CO: F.B. Rothman, 1987)

Hall, William E., *A Treatise on International Law* (8th edn, Oxford: Clarendon Press, 1924)

Hamon, Francis, *L'article 16 de la constitution de 1958: documents réunis et commentés* (Paris: La Documentation Française, 1994)

Hand, Learned, *The Spirit of Liberty: Papers and Addresses of Learned Hand*, ed., Irving Dillard (New York: Legal Classics Library, 1989)

Hanks, Peter, "National Security – A Political Concept" (1988) 14 *Monash University Law Review* 114

Harcourt, Bernard E., "Rethinking Racial Profiling: A Critique of the Economics, Civil Liberties, and Constitutional Literature, and of Criminal Profiling More Generally" (2004) 71 *University of Chicago Law Review* 1275

Hardy, Ernest George, *The Catilinarian Conspiracy in its Context: A Re-Study of the Evidence* (Oxford: Basil Blackwell, 1924)

Harris, David A., "New Risks, New Tactics: An Assessment of the Re-Assessment of Racial Profiling in the Wake of September 11, 2001" (2004) *Utah Law Review* 913

Harris, David J. and Stephen Livingstone (eds.), *The Inter-American System of Human Rights* (New York: Oxford University Press, 1998)

Harris, Grant T., "The CIA Mandate and the War on Terror" (2005) 23 *Yale Law and Policy Review* 529

Harrison, Alexander, *Challenging de Gaulle: The OAS and the Counterrevolution in Algeria, 1954–1962* (New York: Praeger, 1989)

Hart, H.L.A., *The Concept of Law* (Oxford: Clarendon Press, 1961)

Hartman, Joan F., "Derogation from Human Rights Treaties in Public Emergencies" (1981) 22 *Harvard International Law Journal* 1
"Working Paper for the Committee of Experts on the Article 4 Derogation Provision" (1985) 7 *Human Rights Quarterly* 89

Harvey, David, *The Condition of Postmodernity: An Enquiry into the Origins of Cultural Change* (Cambridge, MA: Blackwell, 1990)

Harvey, Paul, "Militant Democracy and the European Convention on Human Rights" (2004) 29 *European Law Review* 407

Harwood, John, "By Big Margin, Americans Support Bush on Fight against Terrorism," *Wall St. Journal*, September 17, 2001, at A24

Harzenski, Sharon, "Terrorism, a History: Stage One" (2003) 12 *Journal of Transnational Law and Policy* 137

Hasen, Richard L., "Efficiency under Informational Asymmentry: The Effect of Framing on Legal Rules" (1990) 38 *UCLA Law Review* 391

Hatchard, John, *Individual Freedoms and State Security in the African Context: The Case of Zimbabwe* (Athens, OH: Ohio University Press, 1993)

Hay, Alexandre, "The ICRC and International Humanitarian Law" (January/Febuary 1983) 23 *International Review of the Red Cross* 3

Hayward, Jack, "The President and the Constitution: Its Spirit, Articles and Practice" in Jack Hayward (ed.), *De Gaulle to Mitterrand: Presidential Power in France* (New York: New York University Press, 1993)

Hecht, Neil S. and Emanuel B. Quint, "Exigency Jurisdiction under Jewish Law" (1978–80) 9 *Dine Israel* 27

Heitland, William E., *The Roman Republic* (3 vols., Holmes Beach, FL: Gaunt, 1969)

Hekman, Susan J., *Weber, the Ideal Type, and Contemporary Social Theory* (South Bend, IN: University of Notre Dame Press, 1983)

Henkin, Louis, "Constitutionalism and Human Rights" in Louis Henkin and Albert J. Rosenthal (eds.), *Constitutionalism and Rights: The Influence of the United States Constitution Abroad* (New York: Columbia University Press, 1990)

Foreign Affairs and the United States Constitution (2nd edn, Oxford: Clarendon Press, 1996)

"NATO's Kosovo Intervention: Kosovo and the Law of 'Humanitarian Intervention'" (1999) 93 *American Journal of International Law* 824

"The United States Constitution in its Third Century: Foreign Affairs" (1989) 83 *American Journal of International Law* 713

Henning, Virginia Helen, "Anti-Terrorism, Crime and Security Act 2001: Has the United Kingdom Made a Valid Derogation from the European Convention on Human Rights?" (2002) 17 *American University International Law Review* 1263

Hershey, Amos S., *The Essentials of Public International Law* (New York: Macmillan, 1912)

Herz, John H., "Idealist Internationalism and the Security Dilemma" (1950) 2 *World Policy* 157

International Politics in the Atomic Age (New York: Columbia University Press, 1959)

Heymann, Philip B., "Civil Liberties and Human Rights in the Aftermath of September 11" (2002) 25 *Harvard Journal of Law and Public Policy* 441

Terrorism and America: A Commonsense Strategy for a Democratic Society (Cambridge, MA: MIT Press, 1998)

Hickman, Tom R., "Between Human Rights and the Rule of Law: Indefinite Detention and the Derogation Model of Constitutionalism" (2005) 68 *Modern Law Review* 655

Higgins, Rosalyn, "Derogations under Human Rights Treaties" (1976–77) 48 *British Yearbook of International Law* 281

Higgs, Robert, *Crisis and Leviathan: Critical Episodes in the Growth of American Government* (New York: Oxford University Press, 1987)

Higham, John, *Strangers in the Land: Patterns of American Nativism, 1860–1925* (New York: Atheneum, 1983)

Hillyard, Paddy, *Suspect Community: People's Experience of Prevention of Terrorism Acts Britain* (London: Pluto Press, 1993)

Hilvitz, Alter, "More on the Actions of Yehudah ben Tavai and Shimon ben Shetah because the Hour Required it" (1983) 92 *Sinai* 193

"Yehudah ben Tavai and Shimon ben Shetah and Their Actions" (1980) 89 *Sinai* 266

Hirschhorn, James M, "The Separate Community: Military Uniqueness and Servicemen's Constitutional Rights" (1984) 62 *North Carolina Law Review* 177

Hobbes, Thomas, *Leviathan* (1651), ed. C.B. Macpherson (Harmondsworth: Penguin, 1968)

Hodgson, Charles, "Plan to Curb Right to Silence Approved," *Financial Times* (London), November 9, 1988, at 15

Hodgson, Charles and Raymond Hughes, "King Curbs Right to Remain Silent," *Financial Times* (London), October 21, 1988

Hofnung, Menachem, *Democracy, Law and National Security in Israel* (Brookfield, VT: Dartmouth, 1996)

Hogan, Gerard and Clive Walker, *Political Violence and the Law in Ireland* (Manchester: Manchester University Press, 1989)

Hogg, Peter, *Constitutional Law of Canada* (2 vols., 4th edn, Scarborough, Ontario: Carswell, 1997)

Holdsworth, W.S., "Martial Law Historically Considered" (1902) 70 *Law Quarterly Review* 117

Holland, Denys C., "Emergency Legislation in the Commonwealth" (1960) *Current Legal Problems* 148

Holland, Thomas Erskine, *The Laws of War on Land* (Oxford: Clarendon Press, 1908)

Holland, Tom, *Rubicon: The Triumph and Tragedy of the Roman Republic* (London: Abacus, 2003)

Holmes, T. Rice, *The Roman Republic and the Founder of the Empire* (New York: Russell & Russell, 1967)

Holsti, Kalevi J., *Peace and War: Armed Conflicts and International Order 1648–1989* (New York: Cambridge University Press, 1991)

Horne, Alistair, *A Savage War of Peace: Algeria 1954–1962* (New York: Viking, 1977)

Horowitz, Dan, "The Israeli Concept of National Security" in Avner Yaniv (ed.), *National Security and Democracy in Israel* (Boulder, CO: Lynne Reinner, 1993), p. 11

Howard, Michael, "Protection for the Silent Majority," *Independent* (London), October 19, 1994, p. 19

Howell, Beryl A., "Seven Weeks: The Making of the USA PATRIOT Act" (2004) 72 *George Washington Law Review* 1145

Hulsebosch, Daniel J., "The New Deal Court: Emergence of a New Reason" (1990) 90 *Columbia Law Review* 1973

Huntington, Samuel P., *The Soldier and the State* (Cambridge, MA: Belknap, 1957)

Hurd, Heidi M., "Challenging Authority" (1991) 100 *Yale Law Journal* 1611

Hussain, Nasser, *The Jurisprudence of Emergency: Colonialism and the Rule of Law* (Ann Arbor, MI: University of Michigan Press, 2003)

Inis, Claude L., *Power and International Relations* (New York: Random House, 1962)

Irons, Peter H., *The New Deal Lawyers* (Princeton: Princeton University Press, 1982)

Israeli Government Press Office, *Commission of Inquiry into the Methods of Investigation of the General Security Service Regarding Hostile Terrorist Activity* (1987), reprinted in (1989) 23 *Israel Law Review* 146

Issacharoff, Samuel and Richard H. Pildes, "Between Civil Libertarianism and Executive Unilateralism: An Institutional Process Approach to Rights during Wartime" in Mark Tushnet (ed.), *The Constitution in Wartime: Beyond Alarmism and Complacency* (Durham, NC: Duke University Press, 2005)

Ivins, Molly, "Trampling all over the Constitution," *Chicago Tribune,* November 22, 2001, at N19

Jackson, John D., "Curtailing the Right of Silence: Lessons from Northern Ireland" (1991) *Criminal Law Review* 404

  "Inferences from Silence: From Common Law to Common Sense" (1993) 44 *Northern Ireland Legal Quarterly* 103

  "Recent Developments in Criminal Evidence" (1989) 40 *Northern Ireland Legal Quarterly* 105

Jackson, John and Sean Doran, *Judge without Jury: Diplock Trials in the Adversary System* (Oxford: Clarendon Press, 1995)

Jackson, John H., *The World Trading System: Law and Policy of International Economic Relations* (2nd edn, Cambridge, MA: MIT Press, 1997)

Jackson, John H., William J. Davey and Alan O. Sykes, Jr., *Legal Problems of International Economic Relations: Cases, Materials, and Text on the National and International Regulation of Transnational Economic Relations* (4th edn, St. Paul, MN: West Group, 2002)

Jackson, Robert H., "Wartime Security and Liberty Under Law" (1951) 1 *Buffalo Law Review* 103

Jacobs, Francis G. and Robin C.A. White, *The European Convention on Human Rights*, eds. Clare Ovey and Robin White (3rd edn, Oxford: Oxford University Press, 2002)

Jacobson, Arthur J. and Bernhard Schlink (eds.), *Weimar: A Jurisprudence of Crisis* (Berkeley: University of California Press, 2000)

Jamieson, Ruth and Kieran McEvoy, "State Crime by Proxy and Juridical Othering" (2005) 45 *British Journal of Criminology* 504

Jayasuriya, Kanishka, "The Exception Becomes the Norm: Law and Regimes of Exception in East Asia" (2001) 2 *Asian-Pacific Law and Policy Journal* 108

Jeffries, John C., Jr., "In Praise of the Eleventh Amendment and Section 1983" (1998) 84 *Virginia Law Review* 47

Jehl, Douglas, "Rule Change Lets CIA Freely Send Suspects Abroad," *NY Times*, March 6, 2005, at A1

Jenkins, Russell, Dominic Kennedy, David Lister, and Carol Midgley, "The London Bombers," *The Times* (London), July 15, 2005

Jennings, Robert Y., "The Caroline and McLeod Cases" (1938) 32 *American Journal of International Law* 82

Jervis, Robert, "Security Regimes" in Stephen D. Krasner (ed.), *International Regimes* (Ithaca, NY: Cornell University Press, 1983), p. 173

Jessup, Philip C., *A Modern Law of Nations: An Introduction* (Hamden, CT: Archon Books, 1968)

Jinks, Derek, "September 11 and the Laws of War" (2003) 28 *Yale Journal of International Law* 1

Johnson, Glen, "House Votes to Extend Patriot Act, Democrats Voice Civil Liberties Concerns," *AP DataStream*, July 22, 2005

Johnson, Loch K., *The Making of International Agreements: Congress Confronts the Executive* (New York: New York University Press, 1984)

Jolls, Christine, "A Behavioural Approach to Law and Economics" (1998) 50 *Stanford Law Review* 1471

Jolowicz, Herbert F., and Barry Nicholas, *Historical Introduction to the Study of Roman Law* (3rd edn, New York: Cambridge University Press, 1972)

Jonakait, Randolph N., "Rasul v. Bush: Unanswered Questions" (2005) 13 *William and Mary Bill of Rights Journal* 1103

Joseph, Bernard, *British Rule in Palestine* (Washington, DC: Public Affairs Press, 1948)

Joseph, Sarah, "Human Rights Committee: General Comment 29" (2002) 2 *Human Rights Law Review* 81

Junod, Sylvie, "Additional Protocol II: History and Scope" (1983) 33 *American University Law Review* 29

Justice, *Right of Silence Debate: The Northern Ireland Experience* (London: Justice, 1994)

Juviler, Peter and Bertram Gross, *Human Rights for the 21st Century: Foundations for Responsible Hope* (Armonk, NY: M.E. Sharpe, 1993)

Kadish, Mortimer R., and Sanford H. Kadish, *Discretion to Disobey: A Study of Lawful Departures from Legal Rules* (Stanford: Stanford University Press, 1973)

Kadish, Sanford H., "Torture, the State and the Individual" (1989) 23 *Israel Law Review* 345

Kagan, Robert, *Paradise and Power: America and Europe in the New World Order* (rev. edn, London: Atlantic Books, 2004)

Kahan, Rebecca M., "Constitutional Stretch, Snap-Back, and Sag: Why Blaisdell was a Harsher Blow to Liberty than Korematsu" (2005) 99 *Northwestern University Law Review* 1279

Kahn, Joseph, "The World's Economies Slide Together into Recession," *NY Times*, November 25, 2001, at A6

Kahn, Joseph and Judith Miller, "Getting Tough on Gangsters, High Tech and Global," *NY Times*, December 15, 2000, at A9

Kahneman, Daniel and Amos Tversky (eds.), *Choices, Values, and Frames* (New York: Cambridge University Press, 2001)

Kahneman, Daniel, Paul Slovic, and Amos Tversky (eds.), *Judgment under Uncertainty: Heuristics and Biases* (New York: Cambridge University Press, 1982)

Kalshoven, Frits, *Constraints on the Waging of War* (Geneva: International Committee of the Red Cross, 1987)

Kamisar, Yale, "Physician Assisted Suicide: The Problems Presented by the Compelling, Heartwrenching Case" (1998) 88 *Journal of Criminal Law and Criminology* 1121

Kant, Immanuel, "On the Common Saying: 'This May Be True in Theory, but it Does not Apply in Practice'" in *Political Writings*, ed. Hans Reiss (2nd edn, Cambridge, UK: Cambridge University Press, 1991)

Kaplow, Louis, "Rules Versus Standards: An Economic Analysis" (1992) 42 *Duke Law Journal* 557

Katselli, Elena and Sangeeta Shah, "September 11th and the UK Response" (2003) 52 *International and Comparative Law Quarterly* 245

Katyal, Neal K., and Laurence H. Tribe, "Waging War, Deciding Guilt: Trying the Military Tribunals" (2002) 111 *Yale Law Journal* 1259

Kaufman, Daniel J., "How to Analyze National Security: A Conceptual Framework" in Daniel J. Kaufman, Jeffrey S. McKitrick, and Thomas J. Leney (eds.), *US National Security: A Framework for Analysis* (Lexington, MA: Lexington Books, 1985)

Kavka, Gregory S., *Hobbesian Moral and Political Theory* (Princeton: Princeton University Press, 1986)

Keaveney, Arthur, *Sulla, the Last Republican* (London: Croom Helm, 1982)

Keir, David L. and Frederick H. Lawson, *Cases in Constitutional Law* (6th edn, Oxford: Clarendon Press, 1979)

Kellman, Barry, "Judicial Abdication of Military Tort Accountability: But Who is to Guard the Guards Themselves?" (1989) *Duke Law Journal* 1597

Kelly, John M., *The Irish Constitution*, ed. Gerard Hogan and Gerry Whyte (4th edn, Dublin: Butterworths, 2003)

Kelly, Joseph B. and George A. Pelletier, Jr., "Theories of Emergency Government" (1966) 11 *South Dakota Law Review* 42

Kelman, Mark, *A Guide to Critical Legal Studies* (Cambridge, MA: Harvard University Press, 1987)

Kelsen, Hans, *The Law of the United Nations: A Critical Analysis of its Fundamental Problems* (New York: Praeger, 1951)

Kennan, George F., *American Diplomacy, 1900–1950* (London: Secker & Walburg, 1951)

  Realities of American Foreign Policy (expanded edn, Chicago: Chicago University Press, 1984)

Kennedy, Duncan, "Form and Substance in Private Law Adjudication" (1976) 89 *Harvard Law Review* 1685

Kifner, John, "Flight from Cuba: The Refugees," *NY Times*, August 23, 1994, at A17

Kimmerling, Baruch, "Boundaries and Frontiers of the Israeli Control System: Analytical Conclusions" in Baruch Kimmerling (ed.), *The Israeli State and Society* (Albany, NY: State University of New York Press, 1989)

Kiss, Alexandre, "Commentary by the Rapporteur on the Limitation Provisions" (1985) 7 *Human Rights Quarterly* 16

Kittrie, Nicholas N., "Patriots and Terrorists: Reconciling Human Rights with World Order" (1981) 13 *Case Western Reserve Journal of International Law* 291

Klabbers, Jan, "Rebel with a Cause? Terrorists and Humanitarian Law" (2003) 14 *European Journal of International Law* 299

Klein, Claude, "The Defence of the State and the Democratic Regime in the Supreme Court" (1985) 20 *Israel Law Review* 397

Klieman, Aaron S., "Emergency Politics: The Growth of Crisis Government" (1976) 70 *Conflict Studies* 5

Klinghoffer, Itzhak Hans, "On Emergency Regulations in Israel" in Haim Cohen (ed.), *Sefer yovel le-Pinhas Rozen (Jubilee to Pinchas Rosen)* (Jerusalem: Hebrew University, 1962)

Knight, Sam and Simon Freeman, "New Terror Laws by December after Cross-Party Deal," *Times Online*, July 18, 2005

Knowles, Robert, "Starbucks and the New Federalism: The Court's Answer to Globalization" (2001) 95 *Northwestern University Law Review* 735

Koestler, Arthur, *Promise and Fulfilment, Palestine 1917–1949* (London: Macmillan, 1949)

Koh, Harold H., "On American Exceptionalism" (2003) 55 *Stanford Law Review* 1479

"The Coase Theorem and the War Power: A Response" (1991) 41 *Duke Law Journal* 122

The National Security Constitution: Sharing Power after the Iran–Contra Affair (New Haven, CT: Yale University Press, 1990)

"The Spirit of the Laws" (2002) 43 *Harvard International Law Journal* 23

"Why the President (Almost) Always Wins in Foreign Affairs: Lessons of the Iran–Contra Affair" (1988) 97 *Yale Law Journal* 1255

"A World without Torture" (2005) 43 *Columbia Journal of Transnational Law* 641

Koh, Harold H., and John C. Yoo, "Dollar Diplomacy/Dollar Defense: The Fabric of Economics and National Security Law" (1992) 26 *International Lawyer* 715

Kommers, Donald P., *The Constitutional Jurisprudence of the Federal Republic of Germany* (2nd edn, Durham, NC: Duke University Press, 1997)

Konig, D.T, "'Dale's Laws' and the Non-Common Law Origins of Criminal Justice in Virginia" (1982) 26 *American Journal of Legal History* 354

Kooijmans, Peter H., "In the Shadowlands between Civil War and Civil Strife: Some Reflections on the Standard-Setting Process" in Astrid J.M. Delissen and Gerard J. Tanja (eds.), *Humanitarian Law of Armed Conflict: Challenges Ahead: Essays in Honour of Frits Kalshoven* (Boston: Nijhoff, 1991)

Korobokin, Russell B. and Thomas S. Ulen, "Law and Behavioral Science: Removing the Rationality Assumption from Law and Economics" (2000) 88 *California Law Review* 1051

Koskenniemi, Martti, *From Apology to Utopia: The Structure of International Legal Argument* (Helsinki: Finnish Lawyers Publishing Co., 1989)

"'Intolerant Democracies': A Reaction" (1996) 37 *Harvard International Law Journal* 231

"The Politics of International Law" (1990) 1 *European Journal of International Law* 4

Kreimer, Seth F., "Commentaries, Invidious Comparisons: Some Cautionary Remarks on the Process of Constitutional Borrowing" (1999) 1 *University of Pennsylvania Journal of Constitutional Law* 640

"Exploring the Dark Matter of Judicial Review: A Constitutional Census of the 1990s" (1997) 5 *William and Mary Bill of Rights Journal* 427

"Watching the Watchers: Surveillance, Transparency, and Political Freedom in the War on Terror" (2004) 7 *University of Pennsylvania Journal of Constitutional Law* 133

Kremnitzer, Mordechai, "The Case of the Security Services Pardon" (1987) 12 *Iyunei Mishpat* 595

"National Security and the Rule of Law: A Critique of the Landau Commission's Report" in A. Yaniv (ed.), *National Security and Democracy in Israel* (Boulder, CO: Lynne Reinner, 1993), p. 153

Kretzmer, David, "Judicial Review over Demolition and Sealing of Houses in the Occupied Territories" in I. Zamir (ed.), *Klinghoffer Book on Public Law* (Jerusalem, 1993), p. 305

"Targeted Killing of Suspected Terrorists: Extra-Judicial Executions or Legitimate Means of Defence" (2005) 16 *European Journal of International Law* 171

Krishnan, Jayanth K., "'India's Patriot Act': POTA and the Impact on Civil Liberties in the World's Largest Democracy" (2004) *Journal of Law and Inequality* 265

Krotoszynski, Ronald J., Jr., "A Comparative Perspective on the First Amendment: Free Speech, Militant Democracy, and the Primacy of Dignity as a Preferred Constitutional Value in Germany" (2004) 78 *Tulane Law Review* 1549

Kumar, C. Raj, "Human Rights Implications of National Security Laws in India: Combatting Terrorism while Preserving Civil Liberties" (2005) 33 *Denver Journal of International Law and Policy* 195

Kuran, Timur and Cass R. Sunstein, "Availability Cascades and Risk Regulation" (1999) 51 *Stanford Law Review* 683

LaFave, Wayne, *Criminal Procedure* (3rd edn, St. Paul, MN: West Group, 2000)

Lahav, Pnina, "A Barrel without Hoops: The Impact of Counter-terrorism on Israel's Legal Culture" (1988) 10 *Cardozo Law Review* 529

Landy, Marc Karnis and Sidney M. Milkis, *Presidential Greatness* (Lawrence, KS: University Press of Kansas, 2000)

Laqueur, Walter, *Europe in our Time: A History, 1945–1992* (New York: Viking, 1992)

No End to War: Terrorism in the Twenty-First Century (New York: Continuum, 2003)

"Reflections on Terrorism" (1996) 65 *Foreign Affairs* 86

Lasswell, Harold D., *National Security and Individual Freedom* (New York: McGraw-Hill, 1950)

Lauterpacht, Hersch, *The Function of Law in the International Community* (Oxford: Clarendon Press, 1933)

"The Grotian Tradition in International Law" (1946) 23 *British Yearbook of International Law* 1

Lavender, Nicholas, "The Problem of the Margin of Appreciation" (1997) *European Human Rights Law Review* 380

Lawyers Committee for Human Rights, *Assessing the New Normal: Liberty and Security for the Post-September 11 United States* (New York: Lawyers Committee for Human Rights, 2003)

Uruguay: The End of a Nightmare? (New York: Lawyers Committee for Human Rights, 1984)

Lee, H.P., *Emergency Powers* (Sydney: Law Book Co. 1984)

Lerner, Max, "Constitution and Court as Symbols" (1937) 46 *Yale Law Journal* 1290

Leroy, Paul, *L'organisation constitutionnelle et les crises* (Paris: Librairie Générale de Droit et de Jurisprudence, 1966)

Leuchtenburg, William E., "The New Deal and the Analogue of War" in John Braeman, Robert H. Bremner, and Everett Walters (eds.), *Change and Continuity in Twentieth-Century America* (Columbus, OH: Ohio State University Press, 1964)

Levin, Stephanie A., "The Deference that is Due: Rethinking the Jurisprudence of Judicial Deference to the Military" (1990) 35 *Villanova Law Review* 1009

Levine, Stanley, "The Doctrine of Military Necessity in the Federal Courts" (1980) 89 *Military Law Review* 3

Levinson, Sanford, "'The Constitution' in American Civil Religion" (1979) *Supreme Court Review* 123

Constitutional Faith (Princeton: Princeton University Press, 1988)

"The David C. Baum Memorial Lecture: Was the Emancipation Proclamation Constitutional? Do We/Should We Care What the Answer Is?" (2001) *University of Illinois Law Review* 1135

"'Precommitment' and 'Post-Commitment': The Ban on Torture in the Wake of September 11" (2003) 81 *Texas Law Review* 2013

"'Veneration' and Constitutional Change: James Madison Confronts the Possibility of Constitutional Amendment" (1990) 21 *Texas Tech Law Review* 2443

(ed.), *Responding to Imperfection: The Theory and Practice of Constitutional Amendment* (Princeton: Princeton University Press, 1995)

(ed.), *Torture: A Collection* (New York: Oxford University Press, 2004)

Levinson, Sanford and Bartholomew Sparrow (eds.), *The Louisiana Purchase and American Expansion, 1803–1898* (Lanham, MD: Rowman & Littlefield, 2005)

Levitan, David M., "The Foreign Relations Power: An Analysis of Mr. Justice Sutherland's Theory" (1946) 55 *Yale Law Journal* 467

Levy, Daniel W., "A Legal History of Irrational Exuberance" (1998) 48 *Case Western Reserve Law Review* 799

Levy, Jack S., "The Diversionary Theory of War: A Critique" in Manus I. Midlarsky (ed.), *Handbook of War Studies* (Boston: Unwin Hyman, 1989)

Levy, Leonard W., *Origins of the Fifth Amendment: The Right Against Self-Incrimination* (2nd edn, New York: Macmillan, 1986)

Lewin, Tamar, "Rights Groups Press for Names of Muslims Held in New Jersey," *NY Times*, January 23, 2002, at A9

Lewis, Anthony, "A Different World," *NY Times*, September 12, 2001, at A27

Lewis, Neil A., "Judge Extends Legal Rights for Guantánamo Detainees," *NY Times*, Febuary 1, 2005, at A12

Lewis, Neil A., and Robert Pear, "Terror Laws Near Votes in House and Senate," *NY Times*, October 5, 2001, at B8

Lichtblau, Eric, "Senate Makes Permanent Nearly All Provisions of Patriot Act, with a Few Restrictions," *NY Times*, July 29, 2005, at A11

"US Uses Terror Law to Pursue Crimes from Drugs to Swindling," *NY Times*, September 28, 2003, at A1

Lillich, Richard B., "Paris Minimum Standards of Human Rights Norms in a State of Emergency" (1985) 79 *American Journal of International Law* 1072

Lindseth, Peter L., "The Paradox of Parliamentary Supremacy: Delegation, Democracy, and Dictatorship in Germany and France, 1920s–1950s" (2004) 113 *Yale Law Journal* 1341

Linfield, Michael, *Freedom under Fire: US Civil Liberties in Times of War* (Boston: South End Press, 1990)

Lintott, Andrew, *The Constitution of the Roman Republic* (Oxford: Clarendon Press, 1999)

Lipton, Lauren, "Preparing for the Worst," *Wall St. Journal*, October 5, 2001, at W14

Lissak, Moshe, "Civilian Components in the National Security Doctrine" in Avner Yaniv (ed.), *National Security and Democracy in Israel* (Boulder, CO: Lynne Reinner, 1993), p. 55

Livy, *The Early History of Rome*, trans. Aubrey de Sélincourt (Harmondsworth: Penguin Books, 1971)

Llewellyn, Karl N., *The Bramble Bush: On our Law and its Study* (New York: Oceana, 1951)

Cases and Materials on the Law of Sales (Chicago: Callaghan, 1930)

"A Realistic Jurisprudence: The Next Step" (1930) 30 *Columbia Law Review* 431

Lobel, Jules, "Emergency Power and the Decline of Liberalism" (1989) 98 *Yale Law Journal* 1385

"Foreign Affairs and the Constitution: The Transformation of the Original Understanding" in David Kairys (ed.), *The Politics of Law: A Progressive Critique* (rev. edn, New York: Pantheon Books, 1990)

Locke, John, *Two Treatises of Government*, ed. Mark Goldie (London: Tuttle, 1994)

Lockwood, Bert B., Jr., Janet Finn, and Grace Jubinsky, "Working Paper for the Committee of Experts on Limitation Provisions" (1985) 7 *Human Rights Quarterly* 35

Loewenstein, Karl, "Legislative Control of Political Extremism in European Democracies" (1938) 38 *Columbia Law Review* 591 and 725

  "Militant Democracy and Fundamental Rights" (1937) 31 *American Political Science Review* 417 and 638

Lofgren, Charles A., "*United States v. Curtiss-Wright Export Corporation*: An Historical Reassessment" (1973) 83 *Yale Law Journal* 1

Logan, Garrett, "The Use of Martial Law to Regulate the Economic Welfare of the State and its Citizens: A Recent Instance" (1931) 17 *Iowa Law Review* 40

Lohr, Steve, "IRA Claims Killing of 8 Soldiers as it Steps up Attacks on British," *NY Times*, August 21, 1988, at A1

Loveman, Brian, *The Constitution of Tyranny: Regimes of Exception in Spanish America* (Pittsburgh, PA: University of Pittsburgh Press, 1993)

Lowry, Lord, "National Security and the Rule of Law" (1992) 26 *Israel Law Review* 117

Luban, David, "The Coiled Serpent of Argument: Reason, Authority, and Law in a Talmudic Tale" (2004) 79 *Chicago-Kent Law Review* 1253

Luckham, A.R., "A Comparative Typology of Civil–Military Relations" (Winter 1971) 6 *Government and Opposition* 5

Lugones, Narciso J., *Leyes de emergencia: decretos de necesidad y urgencia* (Buenos Aires: La Ley, 1992)

Lurie, Jonathan, "Andrew Jackson, Martial Law, Civilian Control of the Military, and American Politics: An Intriguing Anagram" (1989) 126 *Military Law Review* 133

Lustgarten, Laurence and Ian Leigh, *In from the Cold: National Security and Parliamentary Democracy* (Oxford: Clarendon Press, 1994)

Lustick, Ian S., *Unsettled States, Disputed Lands: Britain and Ireland, France and Algeria, Israel and the West Bank-Gaza* (Ithaca, NY: Cornell University Press, 1993)

Lysaght, Charles, "The Scope of Protocol II and its Relation to Common Article 3 of the Geneva Conventions of 1949 and other Human Rights Instruments" (1983) 33 *American University Law Review* 9

McCarthy, Michael T., "Recent Developments, USA Patriot Act" (2002) 39 *Harvard Journal on Legislation* 435

McCormick, John P., *Carl Schmitt's Critique of Liberalism: Against Politics as Technology* (New York: Cambridge University Press, 1997)

  "From Constitutional Technique to Caesarist Ploy: Carl Schmitt on Dictatorship, Liberalism, and Emergency Powers" in Peter R. Baehr and Melvin Richter (eds.), *Dictatorship in History and Theory: Bonapartism, Caesarism, and Totalitarianism* (Washington, DC: German Historical Institute, 2004)

  "Schmittian Positions on Law and Politics?: CLS and Derrida" (2000) 21 *Cardozo Law Review* 1693

McDaniel, John B., "The Availability and Scope of Judicial Review of Discretionary Military Administrative Decisions" (1985) 108 *Military Law Review* 89

MacDermott, Lord, "Law and Order in Times of Emergency" (1972) 17 *Juridical Review* 1

Macdonald, Ronald St. J., "Derogations under Article 15 of the European Convention on Human Rights" (1997) 36 *Columbia Journal of Transnational Law* 225

McElree, Fiona and Keir Starmer, "The Right to Silence" in Clive Walker and Keir Starmer (eds.), *Justice in Error* (London: Blackstone Press, 1993), p. 58

MacFarquhar, Neil, "Saudis to Sign Agreement on Assets of Terror Groups," *NY Times*, November 6, 2001, at B4

McGoldrick, Dominic, *From "9/11" to the "Iraq War 2003": International Law in an Age of Complexity* (Oxford: Hart, 2004)
   The Human Rights Committee: Its Role in the Development of the International Covenant on Civil and Political Rights (Oxford: Clarendon Press, 1991)

Machiavelli, Niccolò, *Discourses on Livy*, trans. Harvey C. Mansfield and Nathan Tarcov (Chicago: University of Chicago Press, 1996)

Macnair, M.R.T., "The Early Development of the Privilege against Self-Incrimination" (1990) 10 *Oxford Journal of Legal Studies* 66

Majthay, Antal, *Foundations of Catastrophe Theory* (Boston: Pitman Advanced, 1985)

Malanczuk, Peter, *Akehurst's Modern Introduction to International Law* (7th edn, London: Routledge, 1997)

Malloy, Peter S., "Controls on the Export of Militarily Sensitive Technology: National Security Imperative or US Industry Impediment?" (1992) 18 *Rutgers Computer and Technology Journal* 841

Malone, Dumas, *Jefferson and his Time* (Boston: Little, Brown, 1978)

Maloney, Ed, "Britain Seeks to Abolish Key Civil Liberty in Ulster: London's Move Aimed at Thwarting IRA," *Washington Post*, October 21, 1988, at A1

Maloney, Richard, "The Criminal Evidence (NI) 1988: A Radical Departure from the Common Law Right to Silence in the UK?" (1993) 16 *Boston College International and Comparative Law Review* 425

Mandel, Robert, *The Changing Face of National Security: A Conceptual Analysis* (Westport, CT: Greenwood Press, 1994)

Mangan, Brendan, "Protecting Human Rights in National Emergencies: Shortcomings in the European System and a Proposal for Reform" (1988) 10 *Human Rights Quarterly* 372

Manning, Bayless, "The Congress, the Executive and Intermestic Affairs: Three Proposals" (1977) 55 *Foreign Affairs* 306

Mansfield, Michael, "Reform that Pays Lip Service to Justice," *Guardian* (London), October 6, 1993, at 22

Maran, Rita, *Torture: The Role of Ideology in the French Algerian War* (New York: Praeger, 1989)

Marcus, Maeva, *Truman and the Steel Seizure Case: The Limits of Presidential Power*
    (New York: Columbia University Press, 1977)
Margolis, Lawrence, *Executive Agreements and Presidential Power in Foreign Policy*
    (New York: Praeger, 1986)
Margulies, Peter, "Judging Terror in the 'Zone of Twilight': Exigency,
    Institutional Equity, and Procedure after September 11" (2004) 84 *Boston
    University Law Review* 383
Marx, Herbert, "The Emergency Power and Civil Liberties in Canada" (1970) 16
    McGill Law Journal 39
Massu, Jacques, *La vraie bataille d'Alger* (Paris: Plon, 1971)
Matthews, Mark and Julie Hirschfeld Davis, "Bush Warns UN not to be Fooled
    by Iraq," *Baltimore Sun*, September 18, 2002, at 1A
May, Christopher N., *In the Name of War: Judicial Review and the War Powers since
    1918* (Cambridge, MA: Harvard University Press, 1989)
May, Elaine Tyler, "Echoes of the Cold War: The Aftermath of September 11 at
    Home" in Mary L. Dudziak (ed.), *September 11 in History: A Watershed Moment?*
    (Durham, NC: Duke University Press, 2003)
Mayer, Jane, "Outsourcing Torture: The Secret History of America's Secret
    'Rendition' Program," *New Yorker*, February 14, 2005, p. 106
Meier, Heinrich, *Four Chapters on the Distinction between Schmitt, Political Theology
    and Political Philosophy*, trans. Marcus Brainard (Chicago: University of
    Chicago Press, 1998)
Mendez, Juan E., "Human Rights Policy in the Age of Terrorism" (2002) 46 *St.
    Louis University Law Journal* 377
    Truth and Partial Justice in Argentina (New York: Americas Watch, 1987)
Meron, Theodor, "The Geneva Conventions as Customary Law" (1987) 81
    American Journal of International Law 348
    "The Humanization of Humanitarian Law" (2000) 94 *American Journal of
    International Law* 239
    "International Criminalization of Internal Atrocities" (1995) 89 *American
    Journal of International Law* 554
    "Towards a Humanitarian Declaration on Internal Strife" (1984) 78 *American
    Journal of International Law* 859
Merrills, J.G., *The Development of International Law by the European Court of Human
    Rights* (2nd edn, Manchester: Manchester University Press, 1993)
Meyer, Josh, "FBI Expects Suicide Bomb Attack in US," *LA Times*, May 21, 2002,
    at A1
Michor, Peter W., *Elementary Catastrophe Theory* (Timişoara, Romania: Tip.
    Universitātii din Timişoara, 1985)
Mill, John Stuart, *Three Essays – On Liberty, Representative Government, the Subjection
    of Women* (1861) (Oxford: Oxford University Press, 1975)
Miller, Arthur S., "Constitutional Law: Crisis Government Becomes the Norm"
    (1978) 39 *Ohio State Law Journal* 736
    Democratic Dictatorship: The Emergent Constitution of Control (Westport, CT:
    Greenwood Press, 1981)

Milligan, Susan, "Critics Aid Terrorists, AG Argues," *Boston Globe*, December 7, 2001, at A34

Mills, Heather, "Tougher Policies Aimed at Helping Victims of Crime," *Independent* (London), November 19, 1993, at 6

Mirfield, Peter, *Silence, Confessions and Improperly Obtained Evidence* (Oxford: Clarendon Press, 1997)

Mironi, Mordechai, "Back-to-Work Emergency Orders: Government Intervention in Labor Disputes in Essential Services" (1986) 15 *Mishpatim* 350

Moir, Lindsay, *The Law of Internal Armed Conflict* (Cambridge: Cambridge University Press, 2002)

Mommsen, Hans, *The Rise and Fall of Weimar Democracy* (Chapel Hill, NC: University of North Carolina Press, 1996)

Mommsen, Theodor E., *The History of Rome* (1864) (5 vols., London: Macmillan, 1908)

Monaghan, Henry P., "The Protective Power of the Presidency" (1993) 93 *Columbia Law Review* 1

Montesquieu, Charles de Secondat, *The Spirit of Laws* (1748) (Berkeley: University of California Press, 1977)

Moore, Michael S., "Causation and the Excuses" (1985) 73 *California Law Review* 1091

Morgenthau, Hans J., *In Defence of the National Interest* (London: Methuen, 1951)
Dilemmas of Politics (Chicago: University of Chicago Press, 1958)
"Diplomacy" (1946) 55 *Yale Law Journal* 1067
Politics among Nations: The Struggle for Power and Peace (6th edn, New York: Knopf, 1985)

Mullerson, Rein, "The Efficiency of the Individual Complaint Procedures: The Experience of the CCPR, CERD, CAT, and ECHR" in Arie Bloed, Liselotte Leicht, Manfred Nowak and Allan Rosas (eds.), *Monitoring Human Rights in Europe: Comparing International Procedures and Mechanisms* (Boston, MA: Nijhoff, 1993), p. 25

Munday, Roderick, "Inferences from Silence and European Human Rights Law" (1996) *Criminal Law Review* 370

Munim, F.K.M.A., *Legal Aspects of Martial Law* (Dhaka: Bangladesh Institute of Law and International Affairs, 1989)

Murphy, Paul L., *The Constitution in Crisis Times* (New York: Harper Row, 1972)

Murphy, Sean D., "Assessing the Legality of Invading Iraq" (2004) 92 *Georgetown Law Journal* 173
"The Doctrine of Preemptive Self-Defense" (2005) 50 *Villanova Law Review* 699
"Terrorism and the Concept of 'Armed Attack' in Article 51 of the UN Charter" (2002) 43 *Harvard International Law Journal* 41

Murray, Robert K., *The Politics of Normalcy: Governmental Theory and Practice in the Harding–Coolidge Era* (New York: Norton, 1973)

Nagan, Winston P. and Lucie Atkins, "The International Law of Torture: From Universal Proscription to Effective Application and Enforcement" (2001) 14 *Harvard Human Rights Journal* 87

Nagel, Thomas, *Mortal Questions* (New York: Cambridge University Press, 1979)

Nagourney, Adam and Marjorie Connelly, "Poll Finds New York Fearful, but Upbeat over Future Too," *NY Times*, June 11, 2002, at A1

Neely, Mark E., Jr., *The Fate of Liberty: Abraham Lincoln and Civil Liberties* (New York: Oxford University Press, 1991)

Negretto, Gabriel L. and José Antonio Aguilar Rivera, "Liberalism and Emergency Powers in Latin America: Reflections on Carl Schmitt and the Theory of Constitutional Dictatorship" (2000) 21 *Cardozo Law Review* 1797

Neillands, Robin, *The Bomber War: The Allied Air Offensive against Germany* (Woodstock, NY: Overlook Press, 2001)

Neuman, Abraham A., *The Jews in Spain: Their Social, Political and Cultural Life in the Middle Ages* (2 vols., New York: Octagon, 1980)

Neuman, Gerald L., "Anomalous Zones" (1996) 48 *Stanford Law Review* 1197

"Humanitarian Law and Counterterrorist Force" (2003) 14 *European Journal of International Law* 283

Neumann, Franz, *The Rule of Law: Political Theory and the Legal System in Modern Society* (Dover, NH: Berg, 1986)

Ní Aoláin, Fionnuala,

"The Emergence of Diversity: Differences in Human Rights Jurisprudence" (1995) 19 *Fordham International Law Journal* 101

"The European Convention on Human Rights and its Prohibition on Torture" in Sanford Levinson (ed.), *Torture: A Collection* (Oxford: Oxford University Press, 2004), p. 213

"The Fortification of an Emergency Regime" (1996) 59 *Albany Law Review* 1353

The Politics of Force: Conflict Management and State Violence in Northern Ireland (Belfast: Blackstaff Press, 2000)

Niebuhr, Barthold G., *The History of Rome*, trans. Julius C. Hare and Connop Thirlwall (London: Taylor, Walton and Maberly, 1851)

Nippel, Wilfried, "Emergency Powers in the Roman Republic" in Pasquale Pasquino and Bernard Manin (eds.), *La théorie politico-constitutionelle du gouvernment d'exception* (Paris: Les Cahiers du CREA, 2000), p. 5

Nisbett, Richard and Lee Ross, *Human Inference: Strategies and Shortcomings of Social Judgment* (Englewood Cliffs, NJ: Prentice-Hall, 1980)

Nolte, Georg and Gregory Fox, "Intolerant Democracies" (1995) 36 *Harvard International Law Journal* 1

"Note: Blown Away? The Bill of Rights after Oklahoma City" (1996) 109 *Harvard Law Review* 2074

"Note: Developments in the Law: The National Security Interest and Civil Liberties" (1972) 85 *Harvard Law Review* 1130

"Note: Recent Emergency Legislation in West Germany" (1969) 82 *Harvard Law Review* 1704

Nozick, Robert, *Anarchy, State and Utopia* (Oxford: Blackwell, 1974)

"Moral Complications and Moral Structures" (1968) 13 *Natural Law Forum* 1

Nussbaum, Martha C., "The Costs of Tragedy: Some Moral Limits of Cost–Benefit Analysis" (2000) 29 *Legal Studies* 1005

Nye, Joseph S., Jr., *The Paradox of American Power: Why the World's Only Superpower Can't go it Alone* (Oxford: Oxford University Press, 2002)

O'Ballance, Edgar, *The Algerian Insurrection, 1954–62* (London: Faber, 1967)

O'Boyle, Michael, "Emergency Situations and the Protection of Human Rights: A Model Derogation Provision for a Northern Ireland Bill of Rights" (1977) 28 *Northern Ireland Legal Quarterly* 160

  "Torture and Emergency Powers under the European Convention on Human Rights: Ireland v. United Kingdom" (1977) 71 *American Journal of International Law* 674

O'Donnell, Daniel, "Commentary by the Rapporteur on Derogation" (1985) 7 *Human Rights Quarterly* 23

  "States of Exception" (1978) 21 *International Commission of Jurists Review* 52

O'Harrow, Robert, Jr., "Six Weeks in Autumn," *Washington Post*, October 27, 2002, at W06

O'Reilly, Gregory W., "England Limits the Right to Silence and Moves towards an Inquisitorial System of Justice" (1994) 85 *Journal of Criminal Law and Criminology* 402

Oake, Roger B., "Montesquieu's Analysis of Roman History" (1955) 16 *Journal of Historical Ideas* 44

Oakes, James L., "The Proper Role of the Federal Courts in Enforcing the Bill of Rights" (1979) 54 *NYU Law Review* 911

Ohana, David, "The Leviathan Opens Wide its Jaws: Karl Schmidt [sic] and the Origins of Legal Fascism" in Daniel Gutwein and Menachem Mautner (eds.), *Mishpat ve-Historya (Law and History)* (Jerusalem: Merkaz Zalman Shazar le-toldot Israel, 1999)

Oppenheim, Lassa, *International Law*, ed. Hersch Lauterpacht (7th edn, 2 vols., London: Longman, 1952)

Oraá, Jaime, *Human Rights in States of Emergency in International Law* (Oxford: Clarendon Press, 1992)

Organski, A.F.K., *World Politics* (2nd rev. edn, New York: Knopf, 1968)

Ortiz, Daniel R., "Pursuing a Perfect Politics: The Allure and Failure of Process Theory" (1991) 77 *Virginia Law Review* 721

Otty, Tim and Ben Olbourne, "The US Supreme Court and the 'War on Terror': *Rasul* and *Hamdi*" (2004) *European Human Rights Law Review* 558

Padover, Saul K. (ed.), *The Complete Madison: His Basic Writings* (New York: Harper & Row, 1953)

Palacios, Victoria J., "Faith in Fantasy: The Supreme Court's Reliance on Commutation to Ensure Justice in Death Penalty Cases" (1996) 49 *Vanderbilt Law Review* 311

Palley, Claire, "The Evolution, Disintegration and Possible Reconstruction of the Northern Ireland Constitution" (1972) 1 *Anglo-American Law Review* 368

Parry, John T., and Welsh S. White, "Interrogating Suspected Terrorists: Should Torture Be an Option?" (2002) 63 *University of Pittsburgh Law Review* 743

Paul, Joel R., "The Geopolitical Constitution: Executive Expediency and Executive Agreements" (1998) 86 *California Law Review* 671

Paulsen, Michael Stokes, "The Civil War as Constitutional Interpretation" (2004) 71 *University of Chicago Law Review* 691

"The Constitution of Necessity" (2004) 79 *Notre Dame Law Review* 1257

"The Most Dangerous Branch: Executive Power to Say What the Law Is" (1994) 83 *Georgetown Law Journal* 217

Paust, Jordan J., "Antiterrorism Military Commissions: The Ad Hoc DOD Rules of Procedure" (2002) 23 *Michigan Journal of International Law* 677

"Antiterrorism Military Commissions: Courting Illegality" (2001) 23 *Michigan Journal of International Law* 1

Peabody, Bruce G., "Nonjudicial Constitutional Interpretation, Authoritative Settlement, and a New Agenda for Research" (1999) 16 *Constitutional Commentary* 63

Peck, Darrell L., "The Justices and the Generals: The Supreme Court and Judicial Review of Military Activities" (1975) 70 *Military Law Review* 1

Peers, Steve, "EU Responses to Terrorism" (2003) 52 *International and Comparative Law Quarterly* 227

Peirce, Gareth, "Now for Some Civil Rights," *Guardian* (London), October 19, 1994, at 22

Peppin, Patricia, "Emergency Legislation and Rights in Canada: The War Measures Act and Civil Liberties" (1993) 18 *Queen's Law Journal* 129

Perrine, Aaron, "The First Amendment Versus the World Trade Organization: Emergency Powers and the Battle in Seattle" (2001) 76 *Washington Law Review* 635

Phillips, Andrew, "Gagging the IRA: Thatcher Imposes a Controversial Crackdown," *Maclean's,* October 31, 1988, at 34

Phillips, Michael M. and David S. Cloud, "US to Seize Assets in Antiterrorism Drive," *Wall St. Journal*, September 25, 2001, at A3

Pickles, Dorothy, *The Fifth French Republic: Institutions and Politics* (3rd edn, London: Methuen, 1965)

Pillard, Cornelia T.L., "Taking Fiction Seriously: The Strange Results of Public Officials' Individual Liability under *Bivens*" (1999) 88 *Georgetown Law Journal* 65

Pincus, Walter, "Silence of 4 Terror Probe Suspects Poses Dilemma for FBI," *Washington Post*, October 21, 2001

Plato, *The Laws*, trans. Trevor J. Saunders (London: Penguin Books, 1970)

Plous, Scott, *The Psychology of Judgment and Decision Making* (New York: McGraw-Hill, 1993)

Pollock, Frederick, "What is Martial Law?" (1902) 70 *Law Quarterly Review* 152

Popper, Karl R., *The Open Society and its Enemies* (2 vols., 5th edn, Princeton: Princeton University Press, 1971)

Porges, Amelia, Friedl Weiss, and Petros C. Mavroidis, *Guide to GATT Law and Practice* (Geneva: World Trade Organization, 1995)

Porras, Ileana M., "On Terrorism: Reflections on Violence and the Outlaw" (1994) *Utah Law Review* 119

Posner, Eric A. and Adrian Vermeule, "Accommodating Emergencies" (2003) 56
    Stanford Law Review 605
Posner, Richard A., *Catastrophe: Risk and Response* (New York: Oxford University
    Press, 2004)
    Law, Pragmatism, and Democracy (Cambridge, MA: Harvard University Press,
    2003)
    Overcoming Law (Cambridge, MA: Harvard University Press, 1995)
Powe, L.A., Jr., "Situating Schauer" (1997) 72 *Notre Dame Law Review* 1519
Priest, Dana and Barton Gellman, "US Decries Abuse but Defends
    Interrogations," *Washington Post,* December 26, 2002, at A1
Primus, Richard, "A Brooding Omnipresence: Totalitarianism in Postwar
    Constitutional Thought" (1996) 106 *Yale Law Journal* 423
Provost, René, *International Human Rights and Humanitarian Law* (Cambridge:
    Cambridge University Press, 2002)
Purdy, Matthew, "Bush's New Rules to Fight Terror Transform the Legal
    Landscape," *NY Times,* November 25, 2001, at A1
Putnam, Robert D., "Diplomacy and Domestic Politics: The Logic of Two-Level
    Games" (1988) 42 *International Organization* 427
Pye, A. Kenneth and Cym H. Lowell, "The Criminal Process during Civil
    Disorders" (1975) *Duke Law Journal* 581
Quarantelli, E.L. and Russell R. Dynes, "Community Conflict: its Absence and
    its Presence in Natural Disasters" (1976) 1 *Mass Emergencies* 139
Rabban, David M., *Free Speech in its Forgotten Years* (Cambridge, UK: Cambridge
    University Press, 1997)
Radin, Max, "Martial Law and the State of Siege" (1942) 30 *California Law Review*
    634
Raimo, Tyler, "Winning at the Expense of Law: The Ramifications of Expanding
    Counter-Terrorism Law Enforcement Jurisdiction Overseas" (1999) 14
    American University International Law Review 1473
Rakover, Nahum, *Shilton ha-hok be-Israel (The Rule of Law in Israel)* (Jerusalem:
    Sifriyat ha-mishpat ha-Ivri, 1989)
Randall, J.G., *Constitutional Problems under Lincoln* (rev. edn, Urbana, IL: University
    of Illinois Press, 1951)
Randall, J.G. and David Herbert Donald, *The Civil War and Reconstruction*
    (Lexington, MA: Heath, 1969)
Rankin, Robert S. and Winifried Dallmayr, *Freedom and Emergency Powers in the
    Cold War* (New York: Appleton-Century-Crofts, 1964)
Raskin, Marcus G., "Democracy Versus the National Security State" (Summer
    1976) 40(3) *Law and Contemporary Problems* 189
Rawls, John, *A Theory of Justice* (Cambridge, MA: Belknap, 1999)
Rees, Edward, "Guilty by Inference," *Guardian* (London), April 11, 1995, at 11
Rehnquist, William H., *All the Laws but One: Civil Liberties in Wartime* (New York:
    Knopf, 1998)
Reich, Charles A., "Mr. Justice Black and the Living Constitution" (1963) 76
    Harvard Law Review 673

Reichman, Amnon, "'When We Sit to Judge We are Being Judged': The Israeli GSS Case, Ex Parte Pinochet and Domestic/Global Deliberation" (2001) 9 *Cardozo Journal of International and Comparative Law* 41

Reidy, Aisling, Françoise Hampson, and Kevin Boyle, "Gross Violations of Human Rights: Invoking the European Convention on Human Rights in the Case of Turkey" (1997) 15 *Netherlands Quarterly of Human Rights* 161

Reisman, Michael W., "In Defense of World Public Order" (2001) 95 *American Journal of International Law* 833

"International Legal Responses to Terrorism" (1999) 22 *Houston Journal of International Law* 3

Relyea, Harold, *A Brief History of Emergency Powers in the United States* (Special US Senate Committee on National Emergencies and Delegated Emergency Powers, Working Paper No. 36–612, 1974) (Washington, DC: Government Printing Office, 1974)

Resolutions accepted by the Assembly of Jewish Lawyers in Palestine (February 7, 1946) (1946) 3 *Hapraklit* 62

Rich, Frank, "Wait until Dark," *NY Times*, November 24, 2001

Richards, H. Erle, "Martial Law" (1902) 70 *Law Quarterly Review* 133

Richardson, James D. (ed.), *A Compilation of the Messages and Papers of the Presidents* (New York: Bureau of National Literature, 1897)

Riley, Jason L., "'Racial Profiling' and Terrorism," *Wall St. Journal*, October 24, 2001, at A22

Roach, Kent, "The Dangers of a Charter-Proof and Crime-Based Response to Terrorism" in Daniels et al. (eds.), *The Security of Freedom September 11: Consequences for Canada* (Montreal: McGill-Queen's University Press, 2003)

Roberts, Hugh, *Northern Ireland and the Algerian Analogy* (London: Athol Books, 1986)

Robinson, Mary, *The Special Criminal Court* (Dublin: Dublin University Press, 1974)

Robinson, Paul H., "Should the Victims' Rights Movement have Influence over Criminal Law Formulation and Adjudication?" (2002) 33 *McGeorge Law Review* 749

Roche, John P., "Executive Power and Domestic Emergency: The Quest for Prerogative" (1952) 5 *Western Political Quarterly* 592

Rodick, Burleigh C., *The Doctrine of Necessity in International Law* (New York: Columbia University Press, 1928)

Rodley, Nigel S., *The Treatment of Prisoners under International Law* (2nd edn, Oxford: Clarendon Press, 1999)

Rohr, John A., *Founding Republics in France and America: A Study in Constitutional Governance* (Lawrence, KS: University Press of Kansas, 1995)

Roosevelt, Franklin D., *The Public Papers and Addresses of Franklin D. Roosevelt*, ed. Samuel I. Rosenman (13 vols., New York: Random House, 1938)

Roots, Roger I., "Government by Permanent Emergency: The Forgotten History of the New Deal Constitution" (2000) 33 *Suffolk University Law Review* 259

Rosand, Eric, "The Security Council as 'Global Legislator': Ultra Vires or Ultra Innovative?" (2005) 28 *Fordham International Law Journal* 542

"Security Council Resolution 1373, The Counter-Terrorism Committee, and the Fight against Terrorism" (2003) 97 *American Journal of International Law* 333

Rosenkranz, Nicholas Quinn, "Executing the Treaty Power" (2005) 118 *Harvard Law Review* 1867

Rosenthal, Peter, "The New Emergencies Act: Four Times the War Measures Act" (1991) 20 *Manitoba Law Journal* 563

Rossiter, Clinton L., *Constitutional Dictatorship: Crisis Government in the Modern Democracies* (Princeton: Princeton University Press, 1948)

(ed.), *The Federalist Papers* (New York: New American Library, 1961)

Rossiter, Clinton and Richard P. Longaker, *The Supreme Court and the Commander in Chief* (expanded edn, Ithaca, NY: Cornell University Press, 1976)

Rostow, Eugene V., "The Japanese American Cases – a Disaster" (1945) 54 *Yale Law Journal* 489

Roth, Brad R., "Democratic Intolerance: Observations on Fox and Nolte" (1996) 37 *Harvard International Law Journal* 235

Rousseau, Jean-Jacques, *The Social Contract and Discourses*, trans. G.D.H. Cole (New York: Everyman, 1993)

Rubinstein, Amnon, *Ha-Mishpat Ha Konstitutsyoni Shel Medinat Israel* (5th rev. edn, 2 vols., Jerusalem: Shoken, 1996)

Russell, C.A., C.A. Banker, and B.H. Miller, "Out-Inventing the Terrorist" in Yonah Alexander, David Carlton, and Paul Wilkinson (eds.), *Terrorism: Theory and Practice* (Boulder, CO: Westview Press, 1979), p. 3

Russett, Bruce, *Controlling the Sword: The Democratic Governance of National Security* (Cambridge, MA: Harvard University Press, 1990)

Rutenberg, Jim, "Talk of Chemical War Grows Louder on TV," *NY Times*, September 27, 2001, at C6

Rutten, Tim and Lynn Smith, "When the Ayes Have it, is There Room for Naysayers?" *LA Times*, September 28, 2001

Ryder, Chris, *The RUC: A Force under Fire* (rev. edn, London: Mandarin, 1997)

Saint-Bonnet, François, *L'état d'exception* (Paris: Presses Universitaires de France, 2001)

Saito, Taylor Natsu, "Crossing the Border: The Interdependence of Foreign Policy and Racial Justice in the United States" (1998) 1 *Yale Human Rights and Development Law Journal* 53

Sallust, *The Jugurthine War and the Conspiracy of Catiline,* trans. S.A. Handford (Baltimore: Penguin, 1963)

Sanchez, Peter M., "The 'Drug War': The US Military and National Security" (1991) 34 *Air Force Law Review* 109

Saunders, P.T., *An Introduction to Catastrophe Theory* (Cambridge, UK: Cambridge University Press, 1980)

Scalia, Antonin, "The Rule of Law as a Law of Rules" (1989) 56 *University of Chicago Law Review* 1175

Schachter, Oscar, "The Decline of the Nation-State and its Implications for International Law" (1997) 36 *Columbia Journal of Transnational Law* 7

International Law in Theory and Practice (Boston: Nijhoff, 1991)

"Self-Defense and the Rule of Law" (1989) 83 *American Journal of International Law* 259

"Towards a Theory of International Obligation" (1968) 8 *Virginia Journal of International Law* 300

Schauer, Frederick, "A Comment on the Structure of Rights" (1993) 27 *Georgia Law Review* 415

"Commercial Speech and the Architecture of the First Amendment" (1988) 56 *University of Cincinnati Law Review* 1181

"Community, Citizenship, and the Search for National Identity" (1986) 84 *Michigan Law Review* 1504

Decision-Making in Law and in Life (New York: Oxford University Press, 1991)

"Easy Cases" (1985) 58 *Southern California Law Review* 399

"Exceptions" (1991) 58 *University of Chicago Law Review* 871

Free Speech: A Philosophical Enquiry (New York: Cambridge University Press, 1982)

"Giving Reasons" (1995) 47 *Stanford Law Review* 633

"May Officials Think Religiously?" (1986) 27 *William and Mary Law Review* 1075

Playing by the Rules: A Philosophical Examination of Rule-Based Decision-making in Law and in Life (New York: Oxford University Press, 1991)

"The Questions of Authority" (1992) 81 *Georgetown Law Journal* 95

"Rules and the Rule of Law" (1991) 14 *Harvard Journal of Law and Public Policy* 645

"Slippery Slopes" (1985) 99 *Harvard Law Review* 361

Schell, Orville, "Rounding Up Americans," *NY Times*, January 1, 1984, Section 7, p. 22

Scheppele, Kim Lane, "The Migration of Anti-Constitutional Ideas: The Post 9/11 Globalization of Public Law and the International State of Emergency" in Sujit Choudhry (ed.), *The Migration of Constitutional Ideas* (Cambridge, UK: Cambridge University Press, forthcoming)

Scheuerman, William E., *Between the Norm and the Exception: The Frankfurt School and the Rule of Law* (Cambridge, MA: MIT Press, 1994)

"The Economic State of Emergency" (2000) 21 *Cardozo Law Review* 1869

"After Legal Indeterminacy: Carl Schmitt and the National Socialist Legal Order, 1933–1936" (1998) 19 *Cardozo Law Review* 1743

Liberal Democracy and the Social Acceleration of Time (Baltimore: The Johns Hopkins University Press, 2004)

Schlag, Pierre, "Rules and Standards" (1985) 33 *UCLA Law Review* 379

Schlesinger, Arthur M., Jr., *The Imperial Presidency* (Boston: Houghton Mifflin, 1989)

Schloemann, Hannes L. and Stefan Ohlhoff, "Constitutionalization and Dispute Settlement in the WTO: National Security as an Issue of Competence" (1999) 93 *American Journal of International Law* 424

Schmid, Alex P. and Albert J. Jongman, *Political Terrorism: A New Guide to Actors, Authors, Concepts, Data Bases, Theories and Literature* (Amsterdam: North-Holland, 1988)

Schmidt, Robert J., "International Negotiations Paralyzed by Domestic Politics: Two-Level Game Theory and the Problem of the Pacific Salmon Commission" (1996) 26 *Environmental Law* 95

Schmitt, Carl, *The Concept of the Political*, trans. George Schwab (New Brunswick: Rutgers University Press, 1976)

The Leviathan in the State Theory of Thomas Hobbes: Meaning and Failure of a Political Symbol (1938), trans. George Schwab and Erna Hilfstein (Westport, CT: Greenwood Press, 1996)

Political Theology: Four Chapters on the Concept of Sovereignty, trans. George Schwab (Cambridge, MA: MIT Press, 1985)

Schmitt, Eric, "There are Ways to Make Them Talk," *NY Times*, June 16, 2002, at D1

Schneiderman, David, "Terrorism and the Risk Society" in Daniels et al. (eds.) *The Security of Freedom*

Schreiber, Aaron M., *Jewish Law and Decision-Making: A Study Through Time* (Philadelphia: Temple University Press, 1979)

"The Jurisprudence of Dealing with Unsatisfactory Fundamental Law: A Comparative Glance at the Different Approaches in Medieval Criminal Law, Jewish Law and the United States Supreme Court" (1991) 11 *Pace Law Review* 535

Schreuer, Cristoph, "Derogation of Human Rights in Situations of Public Emergency: The Experience of the European Convention on Human Rights" (1982) 9 *Yale Journal of World Public Order* 113

Schwab, George, *The Challenge of the Exception: An Introduction to the Political Ideas of Carl Schmitt between 1921 and 1936* (2nd edn, New York: Greenwood Press, 1989)

Schwartz, Bernard, *A History of the Supreme Court* (New York: Oxford University Press, 1993)

Schwarzenberger, Georg, "The Fundamental Principles of International Law" (1955–I) 87 *Receuil de Cours* 191

Schwoerer, Lois G., *"No Standing Armies!": The Anti-Army Ideology in Seventeenth-Century England* (Baltimore: The John Hopkins University Press, 1974)

Seamon, Richard H. and William D. Gardner, "The Patriot Act and the Wall between Foreign Intelligence and Law Enforcement" (2005) 28 *Harvard Journal of Law and Public Policy* 319

Seelye, Katharine Q., "Moscow, Seeking Extradition, Says 3 Detainees are Russian," *NY Times*, April 3, 2002, at 19

Seidman, Louis Michael, "Torture's Truth" (2005) 72 *University of Chicago Law Review* 881

Semmel, Bernard, *Jamaican Blood and the Victorian Conscience: The Governor Eyre Controversy* (Boston: Houghton Mifflin, 1962)

Shamir, Ronen, "'Landmark Cases' and the Reproduction of Legitimacy: The Case of Israel's High Court of Justice" (1990) 24 *Law and Society Review* 781

Shapira, Amos, "Judicial Review without a Constitution: The Israeli Paradox" (1983) 56 *Temple Law Quarterly* 405

Shapiro, David L., "In Defense of Judicial Candor" (1987) 100 *Harvard Law Review* 731

Shapiro, Miriam, "Iraq: The Shifting Sands of Preemptive Self-Defense" (2003) 97 *American Journal of International Law* 599

Sheleff, Leon, "On Criminal Homicide and Legal Self Defense" (1997) 6 *Plilim* 89
"The Green Line is the Border of Judicial Activism: Queries about Supreme Court Judgments in the Territories" (1993) 17 *Iyunei Mishpat* 757

Shenon, Philip, "Threats and Responses: The Reorganization Plan," *NY Times*, November 20, 2002, at A14

Shenon, Philip and James Risen, "Terrorist Yields Clues to Plots, Officials Assert," *NY Times*, June 21, 2002, at A1

Sherwin, Emily, "Ducking Dred Scott: A Response to Alexander and Schauer" (1998) 15 *Constitutional Commentary* 65

Shestack, Jerome J., "Book Review" (1996) 90 *American Journal of International Law* 171

Shivakumar, Dhananjai, "The Pure Theory as Ideal Type: Defending Kelsen on the Basis of Weberian Methodology" (1996) 105 *Yale Law Journal* 1383

Shklar, Judith N., *Legalism: Law, Morals and Political Trials* (Cambridge, MA: Harvard University Press, 1986)

Sidak, J. Gregory, "To Declare War" (1991) 41 *Duke Law Journal* 27
"The Inverse Coase Theorem and Declarations of War" (1991) 41 *Duke Law Journal* 325
"War, Liberty, and Enemy Aliens" (1992) 67 *New York University Law Review* 1402

Sieghart, Marguerite A., *Government by Decree* (London: Stevens, 1950)

Sim, Joe and Philip A. Thomas, "The Prevention of Terrorism Act: Normalizing the Politics of Repression" (1983) 10 *Journal of Law and Society* 71

Simmons, A. John, *Moral Principles and Political Obligations* (Princeton: Princeton University Press, 1979)

Simon, Herbert A., *Models of Man: Social and Rational* (New York: John Wiley, 1957)

Simon, James F., *The Antagonists* (New York: Simon & Schuster, 1989)

Simpson, A.W. Brian, "The Devlin Commission (1959): Colonialism, Emergencies, and the Rule of Law" (2002) 22 *Oxford Journal of Legal Studies* 17
In the Highest Degree Odious: Detention without Trial in Wartime Britain (New York: Clarendon Press, 1992)
Human Rights and the End of Empire: Britain and the Genesis of the European Convention (Oxford: Oxford University Press, 2001)
"Round up the Usual Suspects: The Legacy of British Colonialism and the European Convention on Human Rights" (1996) 41 *Loyola Law Review* 629

Siracusa Principles on the Limitation and Derogation Provisions in the
    International Covenant on Civil and Political Rights (1984), reprinted in
    (1985) 7 *Human Rights Quarterly* 3
Slaughter Burley, Anne-Marie, "Are Foreign Affairs Different?" (1993) 106
    Harvard Law Review 1980
Slovic, Paul, *The Perception of Risk* (London: Earthscan, 2000)
Smith, Tony, *The French Stake in Algeria, 1945–1962* (Ithaca, NY: Cornell University
    Press, 1978)
Smolla, Rodney A., "Terrorism and the Bill of Rights" (2002) 10 *William and
    Mary Bill of Rights Journal* 551
Sofaer, Abraham D., "Emergency Power and the Hero of New Orleans" (1981) 2
    Cardozo Law Review 233
    War, Foreign Affairs and Constitutional Power: The Origins (Cambridge, MA:
    Ballinger, 1976)
Solf, Waldemar A. and W. George Grandison, "International Humanitarian Law
    Applicable in Armed Conflict" (1975) 10 *Journal of International Law and
    Economics* 567
Sorokin, Pitirim A., *Man and Society in Calamity: The Effects of War, Revolution,
    Famine, Pestilence upon Human Mind, Behavior, Social Organization and Cultural
    Life* (New York: E.P. Dutton, 1942)
Spiro, Peter J., "Foreign Relations Federalism" (1999) 70 *University of Colorado Law
    Review* 1223
    "Globalization and the (Foreign Affairs) Constitution" (2002) 63 *Ohio State Law
    Journal* 649
Statman, Daniel, "The Absoluteness of the Prohibition against Torture" (1997) 4
    Mishpat Unimshal 161
Steiner, Henry J. and Philip Alston, *International Human Rights in Context: Law,
    Politics, Morals* (2nd edn, New York: Oxford University Press, 2000)
Stephen, James F.-J., *History of the Criminal Law in England* (3 vols., London:
    Macmillan, 1883)
Steyn, John, "Guantanamo Bay: The Legal Black Hole" (2004) 53 *International and
    Comparative Law Quarterly* 1
Stohl, Michael, *War and Domestic Political Violence: The American Capacity for
    Repression and Reaction* (Beverly Hills, CA: Sage, 1976)
Stolleis, Michael, *The Law Under the Swastika: Studies on Legal History in Nazi
    Germany*, trans. Thomas Dunlap (Chicago: University of Chicago Press,
    1998)
Stone, Geoffrey, *Constitutional Law* (3rd edn, New York: Aspen, 2000 and Supp.
    2002)
    *Perilous Times: Free Speech in Wartime from the Sedition Act of 1798 to the War on
    Terrorism* (New York: W.W. Norton, 2004)
Strauss, Leo, "Comments on Carl Schmitt's *Der Begriff des Politischen*," reprinted
    and translated in Schmitt, *The Concept of the Political* (New Brunswick:
    Rutgers University Press, 1976)
Strauss, Marcy, "Torture" (2004) 48 *New York Law School Law Review* 201

Stuntz, William J., "Local Policing after the Terror," (2002) 111 *Yale Law Journal* 2137

Sullivan, Kathleen M., "The Justices of Rules and Standards" (1992) 106 *Harvard Law Review* 22

Sunstein, Cass R., "The Laws of Fear" (2002) 115 *Harvard Law Review* 1119
  Laws of Fear: Beyond the Precautionary Principle (New York: Cambridge University Press, 2005)
  "Probability Neglect: Emotions, Worst Cases, and Law" (2002) 112 *Yale Law Journal* 61
  "Problems with Rules" (1995) 83 *California Law Review* 953
  Why Societies Need Dissent (Cambridge, MA: Harvard University Press, 2003)

Swire, Peter P., "The System of Foreign Intelligence Surveillance Law" (2004) 72 *George Washington Law Review* 1306

Szasz, P.C., "The Security Council Starts Legislating" (2002) 96 *American Journal of International Law* 901

Taft, William Howard, *Our Chief Magistrate and his Powers* (New York: Columbia University Press, 1916)

Taft, William H., IV, and Todd F. Buchwald, "Preemption, Iraq, and International Law" (2003) 97 *American Journal of International Law* 557

Tain, Paul, *Criminal Justice and Public Order Act 1994: A Practical Guide* (London: Longman, 1994)

Talbott, John, *The War without a Name: France in Algeria, 1954–1962* (New York: Knopf, 1980)

Talmon, Stefan, "The Security Council as World Legislature" (2005) 99 *American Journal of International Law* 175

Tapia-Valdés, J.A., "A Typology of National Security Policies" (1982) 9 *Yale Journal World Public Order* 10

Tellegen-Couperus, Olga E., *A Short History of Roman Law* (London: Routledge, 1993)

Tenofsky, Eliot, "The War Measures and Emergency Acts" (1989) 19 *American Review of Canadian Studies* 293

Thomas, Joseph A.C., *Textbook of Roman Law* (New York: North Holland, 1976)

Thomas, Philip A., "September 11th and Good Governance" (2002) 53 *Northern Ireland Legal Quarterly* 366

Thucydides, *History of the Peloponnesian War*, trans. Richard Crawley (Vermont: Everyman, 1993)

Tolley, H., *The UN Commission on Human Rights* (Boulder, CO: Westview Press, 1987)

Tomuschat, Christian, "Quo Vadis, Argentoratum? The Success Story of the European Convention on Human Rights and a Few Dark Stains" (1992) 13 *Human Rights Law Journal* 401

Toner, Robin, "Now, Government is the Solution, not the Problem," *NY Times*, September 30, 2001

Townshend, Charles, "Martial Law: Legal and Administrative Problems of Civil Emergency in Britain and the Empire, 1800–1940" (1982) 25 *History Journal* 167

Political Violence in Ireland: Government and Resistance since 1848 (Oxford: Clarendon Press, 1983)

Trager, Frank N. and Philip S. Kronenberg (eds.), *National Security and American Society: Theory, Process and Policy* (Lawrence, KS: University Press of Kansas, 1973)

Travis, Alan, "Labour Attacks Justice Bill over End of Right to Silence," *Guardian* (London), January 12, 1994, at 6

"Right to Silence Abolished in Crackdown on Crime," *Guardian* (London), October 7, 1993, at 6

Trebilcock, Michael J. and Robert Howse, *The Regulation of International Trade* (2nd edn, New York: Routledge, 1999)

Tribe, Laurence H., "The American Constitutional Experience with Emergency Powers," Memorandum to the authors of the Constitution for the Czech and Slovak Federated Republic (January 8, 1991) (on file with the authors)

American Constitutional Law (3rd edn, New York: Foundation Press, 2000)

"The Puzzling Persistence of Process-Based Constitutional Theories" (1980) 89 *Yale Law Journal* 1063

Truman, Harry S., *Memoirs: Years of Trial and Hope* (2 vols., New York: Da Capo Press, 1956)

Tushnet, Mark, "Controlling Executive Power in the War on Terrorism" (2005) 118 *Harvard Law Review* 2673

"Defending *Korematsu*?: Reflections on Civil Liberties in Wartime" (2003) *Wisconsin Law Review* 273

(ed.), *The Constitution in Wartime: Beyond Alarmism and Complacency* (Durham, NC: Duke University Press, 2005)

Tversky, Amos and Daniel Kahneman, "Availability: A Heuristic for Judging Frequency and Probability" (1973) 5 *Cognitive Psychology* 207

"Framing of Decisions and the Psychology of Choice" (1974) 211 *Science* 453

Ulen, Thomas S., "Cognitive Imperfections and the Economic Analysis of Law" (1989) 12 *Hamline Law Review* 385

Valadés, Diego, *La dictadura constitucional en América Latina* (Mexico: UNAM, Instituto de Investigaciones Jurídicas, 1974)

Valbrun, Marjorie, "INS Handling of Visas Criticized," *Wall St. Journal,* May 21, 2002

Van Dijk, Pieter and Godefridus J.H. Van Hoof, *Theory and Practice of the European Convention on Human Rights* (3rd edn, Boston: Kluwer Law International, 1998)

Van Natta, Don Jr., and David Johnston, "New FBI Alert Warns of Threat Tied to July 4th," *NY Times,* June 30, 2002, at 1

Vercher, Antonio, *Terrorism in Europe: An International Comparative Legal Analysis* (Oxford: Clarendon Press, 1992)

Viljoen, Frans and Evarist Baimu, "Courts for Africa: Considering the Co-existence of the African Court on Human and Peoples' Rights and the African Court of Justice" (2004) 22 *Netherlands Quarterly of Human Rights* 241

Viroli, Maurizio, *From Politics to Reason of State: The Acquisition and Transformation of the Language of Politics, 1250–1600* (Cambridge, UK: Cambridge University Press, 1992)

Viscount Colville of Culross, *Review of the Operation of the Prevention of Terrorism (Temporary Provisions) Act 1984* (London: HMSO, 1987), Cmnd. 264

Viscusi, W. Kip and Richard J. Zeckhauser, "Sacrificing Civil Liberties to Reduce Terrorism Risks" (2003) 26(2–3) *Journal of Risk and Uncertainty* 99

Voisset, Michèle, *L'article 16 de la constitution du 4 Octobre 1958* (Paris: Librairie Générale de Droit et de Jurisprudence, 1969)

Volpp, Leti, "The Citizen and the Terrorist" (2002) 49 *UCLA Law Review* 1575

von Glahn, Gerhard, *The Occupation of Enemy Territory: A Commentary on the Law and Practice of Belligerent Occupation* (Minneapolis: University of Minnesota Press, 1957)

von Heinegg, Wolff Heintschel, "Factors in War to Peace Transitions" (2004) 27 *Harvard Journal of Law and Public Policy* 843

Vu, Huong, "Us against Them: The Path to National Security is Paved by Racism" (2002) 50 *Drake Law Review* 661

Wald, Matthew L., "US Begins Taking over Screening at Airports," *NY Times,* May 1, 2002, at A18

Waldron, Jeremy, "How To Argue for a Universal Claim" (1999) 30 *Columbia Human Rights Law Review* 305

  "Torture and Positive Law: Jurisprudence for the White House" (2005) 105 *Columbia Law Review* 1681

Walkatee, Jaap A., "The Human Rights Committee and Public Emergencies" (1982) 9 *Yale Journal of World Public Order* 134

Walker, Clive, *Blackstone's Guide to the Anti-Terrorism Legislation* (Oxford: Oxford University Press, 2002)

  "Irish Republican Prisoners: Political Detainees, Prisoners of War or Common Criminals?" (1984) 19 *Irish Jurist* 189

  The Prevention of Terrorism in British Law (2nd edn, Manchester: Manchester University Press, 1992)

  "Terrorism and Criminal Justice: Past, Present and Future" (2004) *Criminal Law Review* 311

Walker, Geoffrey de Q., *The Rule of Law* (Melbourne: Melbourne University Press, 1988)

Walsh, Dermot P.J., "The Impact of the Antisubversive Laws on Police Powers and Practices in Ireland: The Silent Erosion of Individual Freedom" (1989) 62 *Temple Law Review* 1099

  The Use and Abuse of Emergency Legislation in Northern Ireland (London: Cobden Trust, 1983)

Waltz, Kenneth N., "Realist Thought and Neorealist Theory" (1990) 44 *Journal of International Affairs* 21

Theory of International Politics (New York: McGraw-Hill, 1979)

Walzer, Michael, *Just and Unjust Wars: A Moral Argument with Historical Illustrations* (3rd edn, New York: Basic Books, 2000)

"Political Action: The Problem of Dirty Hands" in Marshall Cohen, Thomas Nagel, and Thomas Scanlon (eds.), *War and Moral Responsibility* (Princeton: Princeton University Press, 1974)

Warbrick, Colin, "The Principles of the European Convention on Human Rights and the Response of States to Terrorism" (2002) 3 *European Human Rights Law Review* 287

Wardlaw, Grant, *Political Terrorism: Theories, Tactics, and Counter-Measures* (2nd edn, Cambridge, UK: Cambridge University Press, 1989)

Watkin, Kenneth, "Controlling the Use of Force: A Role for Human Rights Norms in Contemporary Armed Conflict" (2004) 98 *American Journal of International Law* 1

Watkins, Frederick M., *The Failure of Constitutional Emergency Powers under the German Republic* (Cambridge, MA: Harvard University Press, 1939)

"The Problem of Constitutional Dictatorship" (1940) 1 *Public Policy* 324

Weber, Max, "'Objectivity' in Social Science and Social Policy" in Edward A. Shils and Henry A. Finch (eds.), *Max Weber on the Methodology of the Social Sciences* (Glencoe, IL: Free Press, 1949)

"Politics as a Vocation" in H.H. Gerth and C. Wright Mills (eds. and trans.), *From Max Weber: Essays in Sociology* (New York: Oxford University Press, 1946)

Wedgwood, Ruth, "Al Qaeda, Terrorism, and Military Commissions" (2002) 96 *American Journal of International Law* 328

"The Fall of Saddam Hussein: Security Council Mandates and Preemptive Self-Defense" (2003) 97 *American Journal of International Law*

Weida, Jason Collins, "A Republic of Emergencies: Martial Law in American Jurisprudence" (2004) 36 *Connecticut Law Review* 1397

Weiler, Gershon, *From Absolutism to Totalitarianism: Carl Schmitt on Thomas Hobbes* (Durango, CO: Hollowbrook, 1994)

Wells, Christina E., "Questioning Deference" (2004) 69 *Missouri Law Review* 903

Westin, Alan F., *The Anatomy of a Constitutional Law Case: Youngstown Sheet and Tube Co. v. Sawyer; The Steel Seizure Decision* (New York: Macmillan, 1958)

Westlake, John, *The Collected Papers of John Westlake on Public International Law*, ed. Lassa Oppenheim (Cambridge, UK: Cambridge University Press, 1914)

Wheen, Francis, "Bill that Costs Too Much," *Guardian* (London), September 2, 2002, at 5

White House, The, *The National Security Strategy of the United States of America* (September 17, 2002)

Whitney, Craig R., "Civil Liberties in Britain: Are They under Siege?" *NY Times*, November 1, 1988, at A18

Whittington, Keith E., "Extrajudicial Constitutional Interpretation: Three Objections and Responses" (2002) 80 *North Carolina Law Review* 773

"Yet Another Constitutional Crisis?" (2002) 43 *William and Mary Law Review* 2093

Wiecek, William M., "The Legal Foundations of Domestic AntiCommunism: The Background of Dennis v. United States" (2001) *Supreme Court Review* 375

Wiegandt, Manfred H., "The Alleged Unaccountability of the Academic: A Biographical Sketch of Carl Schmitt" (1995) 16 *Cardozo Law Review* 1569

Wilkinson, Paul, *Terrorism and the Liberal State* (2nd edn, New York: New York University Press, 1986)

Williams, Bernard, "Politics and Moral Character" in Williams, *Moral Luck: Philosophical Papers* (New York: Cambridge University Press, 1981)

Williams, Glanville, *The Proof of Guilt: A Study of the English Criminal Trial* (3rd edn, London: Stevens & Sons, 1963)

Willoughby, Westel W. and Lindsay Rogers, *An Introduction to the Problem of Government* (Garden City, NY: Doubleday, 1921)

Wills, Garry, *Cincinnatus: George Washington and the Enlightenment* (Garden City, NY: Doubleday, 1984)

Wilmerding, Lucius, Jr., "The President and the Law" (1952) 67 *Political Science Quarterly* 321

Winterton, George, "The Concept of Extra-Constitutional Executive Power in Domestic Affairs" (1979) 7 *Hastings Constitutional Law Quarterly* 1

Wise, David, "Spy-Game: Changing the Rules so the Good Guys Win," *NY Times,* June 2, 2002, at D3

Wolfers, Arnold, *Discord and Collaboration: Essays on International Politics* (Baltimore: The Johns Hopkins University Press, 1962)

Wood, James and Adam Crawford, *Right of Silence: The Case for Retention* (London: Civil Liberties Trust, 1989)

Woodcock, Alexander and Monte Davis, *Catastrophe Theory* (New York: Dutton, 1978)

Woodward, Bob, "CIA Told to Do 'Whatever Necessary' to Kill Bin Laden; Agency and Military Collaborating at 'Unprecedented' Level; Cheney Says War against Terror 'May Never End,'" *Washington Post,* October 21, 2001, at A01

Woodward, Calvin, "FBI, CIA Struggle to Put History of Animosity behind them in the Anti-terror Age," *Associated Press,* June 1, 2002, *LEXIS, Nexis Library, AP File*

Wormuth, Francis D. and Edwin B. Firmage, *To Chain the Dog of War: The War Power of Congress in History and Law* (2nd edn, Urbana, IL: University of Illinois Press, 1989)

Wright, Quincy, *The Control of American Foreign Relations* (New York: Macmillan, 1922)

"The Outlawry of War and the Law of War" (1953) 47 *American Journal of International Law* 365

Yergin, Daniel, *Shattered Peace: The Origins of the Cold War and the National Security State* (Boston: Houghton Mifflin, 1977)

Yoo, John, "International Law and the War in Iraq" (2003) 97 *American Journal of International Law* 563

"Judicial Review and the War on Terrorism" (2003) 72 *George Washington Law Review* 427

"Laws as Treaties?: The Constitutionality of Congressional–Executive Agreements" (2001) 99 *Michigan Law Review* 757

Young, Ernest A., "Dual Federalism, Concurrent Jurisdiction, and the Foreign Affairs Exception" (2001) 69 *George Washington Law Review* 139

"The Rehnquist Court's Two Federalisms" (2004) 83 *Texas Law Review* 1

Young, Mark G., "What Big Eyes and Ears You Have!: A New Regime for Covert Governmental Surveillance" (2001) 70 *Fordham Law Review* 1017

Zamir, Itzhak, "Human Rights and National Security" (1989) 23 *Israel Law Review* 375

Zellick, Graham, "Official Information, National Security and the Law in Britain" (1986) 98 *Studi Senesi* 303

"Spies, Subversives, Terrorists and the British Government: Free Speech and Other Casualties" (1990) 31 *William and Mary Law Review* 773

Zelman, Joshua D., "Recent Developments in International Law: Anti-Terrorism Legislation – Part One: An Overview" (2001) 11 *Journal of Transnational Law and Policy* 183

"Recent Developments in International Law: Anti-Terrorism Legislation – Part Two: The Impact and Consequences" (2002) 11 *Journal of Transnational Law and Policy* 421

Žižek, Slavoj, *Welcome to the Desert of the Real!: Five Essays on September 11 and Related Dates* (London: Verso, 2002)

Zoglin, Kathryn J., "The National Security Doctrine and the State of Siege in Argentina: Human Rights Denied" (1989) 12 *Suffolk Transnational Law Journal* 265

Zuckerman, Adrian A.S., "Coercion and the Judicial Ascertainment of Truth" (1989) 23 *Israel Law Review* 357

Index